# Shakespeare, Harsnett,
# and the Devils of Denham

# Shakespeare, Harsnett, and the Devils of Denham

### F. W. Brownlow

**DELAWARE**

Newark: University of Delaware Press
London and Toronto: Associated University Presses

Associated University Presses
440 Forsgate Drive
Cranbury. NJ 08512

Associated University Presses
25 Sicilian Avenue
London WC1A 2QH, England

Associated University Presses
P.O. Box 338, Clarkson Pstl. Stn.
Mississauga, Ontario
Canada L5G 4L8

The paper used in this publication meets the requirements of the American National Standard for Permanence of Paper for Printed Library Materials Z39.48–1984.

**Library of Congress Cataloging-in-Publication Data**

Brownlow, F. W. (Frank Walsh), 1934–
  Shakespeare, Harsnett, and the devils of Denham / F. W. Brownlow.
    p.  cm.
  Includes bibliographical references and index.
  ISBN 0–87413–436–6 (alk. paper)
    1. Shakespeare, William, 1564–1616. King Lear—Sources. 2. Shakespeare, William, 1564–1616—Knowledge—Occultism. 3. Harsnett, Samuel, 1561–1631. Declaration of egregious popish impostures. 4. Christianity and literature—England—History—17th century.   5. Demonology—England—History—16th century. 6. Catholics—England—History—16th century. 7. Exorcism—England—History—16th century. 8. Demonology in literature. 9. Exorcism in literature. I. Harsnett, Samuel, 1561-1631. Declaration of egregious popish impostures. 1992. II. Title.
  PR2819.B77 1992
  822.3'3—dc20
                                                              90–51010
                                                                  CIP

PRINTED IN THE UNITED STATES OF AMERICA

*To Kenneth Muir*

# Contents

# Preface

It has been well known since Lewis Theobald first published the fact in his edition of Shakespeare that Harsnett's *Declaration of Egregious Popish Impostures* influenced *King Lear*. Successive editors have added to Theobald's modest list of parallels between the two works, yet the extent of Harsnett's influence on *King Lear* was not known until the 1950s, when Kenneth Muir published the results of his research. Since then, several scholars, taking Muir's findings as their basis, have drawn upon Harsnett in the course of work on Shakespeare, among them William Elton in *King Lear and the Gods* (1966), Peter Milward in *Shakespeare's Religious Background* (1973), and Muriel Bradbrook in *Shakespeare: The Poet in His World* (1978). There have also been articles by Milward and Leo Salingar. John L. Murphy's *Darkness and Devils* (1984) is the first monograph to be devoted solely to Shakespeare's interest in the Denham possessions of 1585–86. In the meantime, scholars with other interests have turned to Harsnett and his books on exorcism and the dispossession of devils. Keith Thomas, in *Religion and the Decline of Magic* (1971), discusses Harsnett in the context of the Church of England's attack on belief in miracles and prophecy, and D. P. Walker, writing from a similar point of view in *Unclean Spirits: Possession and Exorcism in France and England in the Late Sixteenth and Early Seventeenth Centuries* (1981), gives some account of the cases of possession that Harsnett and his bishop, Richard Bancroft, dealt with. Most recently Stephen Greenblatt, in work based closely upon Walker's and Thomas's books, has attempted to explain the significance of Shakespeare's borrowings from Harsnett in sociohistorical terms. Greenblatt first ventured upon the subject in a short article published in *Genre* in 1982; this piece has undergone several mutations since then, growing considerably in the process and appearing most recently in *Shakespearean Negotiations* (1988).

Although everyone agrees that Shakespeare read and used Harsnett, there are differences as to the significance of the fact. Elton, following an earlier book, H. N. Paul's *The Royal Play of*

*Macbeth* (1950), takes the traditional view that Shakespeare used Harsnett to supply a racy topical allusion that would flatter King James I's intellectual vanity. For Peter Milward in *Shakespeare's Religious Background*, in this respect following the lead of Catholic scholars before him, Shakespeare's use of Harsnett to characterize Edgar as Poor Tom reflects his sympathy with the plight of recusants in general and of their hunted priests in particular. Without taking quite that view, Muriel Bradbrook in *Shakespeare: The Poet in His World* sees in Shakespeare's use of Harsnett the response of a sensitive imagination to a violent and devious text. In *Darkness and Devils*, John Murphy, like Milward, attributes to Shakespeare a fundamentally Catholic point of view. In his book, however, Harsnett is less important than the events he records, for Murphy believes, following Walker, that the Catholic exorcisms of 1586 were an episode in the development of the Babington Plot; hence Harsnett's book is part of a larger complex of history, reference, and allusion, to all of which *King Lear* is a response. In some respects Stephen Greenblatt's contribution to this literature returns to tradition, for he attributes to Shakespeare a wholly secular interest in Harsnett's subject and infers from his treatment of the book that on the whole he agreed with it. Greenblatt suggests that Harsnett's skepticism exposes the bases of belief itself to question and turns sacred institutions into fraud and dramatic illusion. *King Lear* is a "post-Christian" play, "haunted by a sense of rituals and beliefs that are no longer efficacious, that have been *emptied out.*" As an historian, Greenblatt is best on the Protestant cases of possession, where the printed pamphlets supply him with abundant material. He knows less about the Catholic exorcists, their patients and spectators, and has no sympathy with the religious view of life.

The present study originated as a dissertation, prepared under the auspices of the Shakespeare Institute, submitted in 1963, and consisting of an edition of Harsnett's text, a biography of Harsnett, and an inquiry into the exorcisms and Shakespeare's use of them. Over the years the dissertation has been used and cited, and Professor John Murphy especially, in his *Darkness and Devils,* urged its publication. So many years had passed, however, that I decided to rework the subject completely. The revised version incorporates much of the original but is essentially new in form and content. It focuses all the materials upon Harsnett's book, placing it in the context of his career and of the events and personalities that led to its being written. By presenting the text in this way, I hope to give a view of the power in the kingdom—intellectual, ecclesiastical, and political—that the book and its author once represented for everyone, including William Shakespeare, who read it. Archbishop

Harsnett, no lover of the theater or of actors, would be surprised, and probably disappointed, to know that it was an actor-dramatist's encounter with his book that had preserved the memory of his name among twentieth-century academics.

Like virtually all of his contemporary bishops in the Church of England, Samuel Harsnett has been dropped from the Whig tradition of English history. Yet he was a remarkable man who had a distinguished career. Born to a family of bakers in Colchester, he rose to become scholar, fellow, and Master of his college, Pembroke, Cambridge, and twice vice-chancellor of the university. In the church he was vicar, rector, canon, archdeacon, bishop, and archbishop. In the state, as one of the Lords Spiritual he sat in Parliament for twenty-one years, and for the last two years of his life he was a privy counselor. The two great friendships of his life seem to have been Richard Bancroft, archbishop of Canterbury, and Thomas Howard, earl of Arundel—and there were undoubtedly others: some affectionate, personal letters to Sir Henry Vane the elder survive in the State Papers.

Harsnett was a learned, eloquent man of taste and imagination. As an academic he enriched his college by wise investment, maintained the tradition of humane letters established there in the time of Spenser, Harvey, and Fulke, and worked hard to maintain the civility, orderliness, and independence of the university. As a churchman he was a leader in the generation that established the style and tone of religion that we now associate with the word *Anglican.* In the parliaments of Charles I, he spoke consistently for the liberties of the subject, and it was he who put the motion that sent the Petition of Right back to the king for a satisfactory answer. He deserves a biography.

In this monograph, Harsnett's career is treated as the context for his book on the Denham exorcisms, and for Shakespeare's encounter with it. The first part explains, partly by narrative, partly by analysis, how Harsnett's book came to be written, and what kind of document it was that Shakespeare read. The second part consists of an edition of the *Declaration of Egregious Popish Impostures,* with a commentary and glossary.

The story of Harsnett's text is a complex one, centered upon the state of ecclesiastical parties and policies, c. 1598–1602. My account of it begins by introducing the 1586 exorcisms. Then follow three chapters, on Bancroft and Harsnett, on their campaign against the puritan practice of devil-dispossessing, and on their investigation into the old Catholic case of 1585–86. Two related chapters conclude this inquiry, one on Harsnett's writing of his book, one on Shakespeare's reading of it. For completeness' sake there are two brief chapters outlining Harsnett's later career, and there are four appendixes: a biographical listing of the exorcizing priests; a glossary of some of the devils'names, a description of Harsnett's activity as licenser for the press, and a list of his surviving letters.

One way and another I have spent a long time with Samuel Harsnett. In taking leave of him once again, I am conscious of allusions still untraced, of puzzles still unsolved. I also realize that there are doubtless other ways of presenting Harsnett and his material, for inevitably, try as we might to transcend it, we see things from a point of view which is mostly that of our time, place, and métier. Harsnett, who has been studied mostly by literary scholars and topographical historicans, is really a subject for church and academic history. Literary scholarship, for instance, has overemphasized some aspects of his book (its theatrical imagery, for instance, which was commonplace for the subject and the period) and ignored others, such as his similes from games and hunting, which are equally vivid, authentic, and frequent but based on recreations not much pursued by modern academics. More significantly, with few exceptions modern scholarship has avoided the religious theme of Harsnett's books.

It has also been tempting to judge Harsnett anachronistically, to condemn him for harshness and bullying, and to attribute to him a wholly ecclesiastical, administrative interest in the exorcists' patients. Yet as an interrogator he elicited from at least one of the possessed, Sara Williams, a vivid, sometimes touching statement of her experiences. Sara knew about bullies, and sketches some of them unforgettably: Fr. Stamp, for instance, who looked her full in the face "with a flearing countenance," and talked to her as if she were a devil, not a sixteen-year-old girl; and another, unnamed priest, who answered her complaint of ill-treatment by "looking fullie upon her face under her hat," and asking "Is this Sara or the devil that speaketh these words?" There is no sign in Sara's statement that Harsnett bullied her; when she broke down and cried, it was because the accumulation of sordid, ridiculous detail defeated her little stratagems of poise and self-confidence.

Harsnett the rhetorician exploited Sara as he exploited every other detail of the story turned up by his bishop's inquiry, but Harsnett the investigator treated her kindly and humanely. To understand the case it is necessary to do justice to Harsnett in this respect without playing down the less savory aspects of his work on the possessions.

Literary scholarship has also tended to assume that in reading Harsnett, Shakespeare simply agreed with him. I have found unavoidable the conclusion, however, that there is an animus in Shakespeare's appropriation of Harsnett's language. Vituperative pamphlets were common enough, and nothing in the biographical record suggests that Shakespeare was a hypersensitive or contentious man. Yet Harsnett's book got under his skin, and the inference is natural that it troubled him, not only because of its subject, but because it savagely attacked people he knew, one of them almost certainly, another very possibly, his kinsman. Also, to judge by the way he adopts Harsnett's words, he recognized an inventiveness akin to his own in energy, but alien in spirit. Of course, it was not possible for Shakespeare openly to mock, refute, or qualify Harsnett's book; but in an unfree society imitation, in a different mode, and for a different purpose, can be a most effective means of comment or reply.

Finally, a word about the remaining term in the title of the first part, "the devils of Denham."

A literary historian who has neither medical nor pastoral training must be cautious about commenting upon such things as devils and possessions; the unwary can draw freakish conclusions about Elizabethan society on the basis of them. When I consulted Dr. Charles Cleland of the Ontario Hospital some years ago about the subject matter of the *Declaration*, including the disease called "the mother," he told me that he had never encountered such cases, but that there are fashions in mental illness as in other forms of behavior. The distinguished Jesuit historian John Hungerford Pollen, writing in the early years of this century, was probably right to say that the fashion for exorcism in early modern England was related to a European obsession with evil, also manifest in the witch-findings of the period. To this one might add that intersectarian rivalries fueled the obsession. Such "historical" explanations, however, do not really explain anything in particular, for every age has its evil as well as its history, and the great difficulty in dealing with particular cases is that the records are so unreliable. Meanwhile, one of the more bizarre developments since this edition was first prepared is that something calling itself diabolic possession has reappeared in Europe and America, in books, films, and actual cases reported in the newspapers and broadcast on television. This makes me skeptical of any generalizing explanation more committed to an hypothesis than Dr. Cleland's.

This is not, however, a subject to be lightly studied with any kind of particularity away from the printed page. Stephen Greenblatt writes of phenomena that "fascinate and charm the ethnographer," but there is nothing charming about any sixteenth-century English case that I know about. There is grotesque com-

edy. The impostures can be ridiculous, and the mistakenly diagnosed patients can be pathetic: all this is material for Jonsonian
farce, but it is not what interests either Harsnett or Shakespeare,
who both took the Denham exorcisms seriously, presumably
because each heard through the noise and tumult of the phenomena
an authentic note of agony and malignity. In response, Harsnett,
who had a political and ecclesiastical agenda to fill, wrote a savage
book; Shakespeare, who as writer enjoyed a freedom of thought
denied to Harsnett the ecclesiastical official, wrote a tragedy that
is—among all the other things that it is—a profound and humane
comment upon those strange events. For, to quote Fluellen, "There
is figures in all things," and as Shakespeare handles it in *King
Lear,* possession enacts the estrangement of humanity in a place
turned alien and hostile:

> Frateretto calls me, and tells me Nero is an angler in the Lake
> of Darkness. Pray, innocent, and beware the foul fiend.

# Acknowledgments

I would like to thank Professor Kenneth Muir, who first suggested to me that Archbishop Harsnett would prove an interesting subject for study; David Lockie, who guided me into the intricacies of recusant history; and Bernard Harris, who is my creditor for many things, but particularly for his companionship and help on an expedition to the Harsnett Library in Colchester.

I must also declare my gratitude for the use of their collections, and for the hospitality and assistance rendered by their librarians and curators, to the British Library, the Public Record Office, the Bodleian Library, Cambridge University Library, Pembroke College Library, Liverpool University Library, Birmingham University Library, the Marsh Library (Dublin), the Lambeth Palace Library, Michigan University Library, the Beinecke Library, the Folger Shakespeare Library, the Chapin Library, the New York Public Library, and the libraries of Mount Holyoke College, Smith College, Amherst College, and the University of Massachusetts, Amherst. I am also indebted to the archivists of the Essex Record Office, of the Norfolk and Norwich Record Office, the County Record Office, Chichester, and the Borthwick Institute, York.

A grant from the Rackham Graduate School of the University of Michigan enabled me to track Harsnett in the archives of his former dioceses in Sussex, Norfolk, and York. More recently a senior summer stipend from the National Endowment for the Humanities encouraged me to start putting this Harsnettian material in order. At the time Harsnett was to have been one among several related topics. That he became a topic in himself was partly owing to the bulk and complexity of the material, and partly to the encouragement received from several quarters, in particular from John L. Murphy, Calvin Thayer, Peter Milward, Brian Parker, Richard Streier, Jay Halio, Arthur Kinney, and Kenneth Muir. George Hunter alerted me to the existence of Leo Salingar's article. Dr. Malachi Martin kindly answered my technical queries about Fr. Weston's account of his curing of Nicholas Marwood. Although Stephen Greenblatt's later versions of his essay on Harsnett came too late to be incorporated into the structure of this work, I found them a valuable stimulus in the final revision of my own rather different version of the material. Here at Mount Holyoke College, Phillipa Goold untied some Greek and Latin knots for me; I owe the notes on Harsnett's letter to Bacon to her. During the final stages of checking and crosschecking, Katie Yao of the interlibrary order department of the college library was a great help in tracking down titles inaccessible in this rustic valley.

I must also thank my research assistant, Mrs. Beatrice Pugh, who secured for me photocopies of Harsnettian material in the Public Record Office, and who also supplied me with material I would not have otherwise have found, including the record of young Harsnett's appearance before the Ecclesiastical Commission as a Puritan.

Finally I owe a debt of acknowledgment to my wife, Jeanne P. Brownlow. Academic writers traditionally thank their wives for long-suffering, patience, and in some cases, criticism. I want to thank my wife for her help. Her hand is in this edition in the form of suggestions, notes, and transcripts of documents, made in the early days of the project and of our married life when, free of the cares of family, property, and joint careers, we did this sort of thing together, helped along as we traveled by an MGB in British racing green. Her latest contribution is the epigraph from Quevedo.

It should go without saying that, much as I owe to other people in preparing the book, I owe its mistakes solely to myself.

# Abbreviations

| | |
|---|---|
| *APC* | *Acts of the Privy Council* |
| Arber | Edward Arber, ed., *A Transcript of the Registers of the Company of Stationers of London, 1554–1640 A.D.* |
| BL | The British Library |
| *CRS* | *Publications of the Catholic Record Society* |
| *CSP Dom.* | *Calendar of State Papers, Domestic Series* |
| *DEP* | *A Declaration of Popish Impostures* |
| *DFP* | *A Discovery of the Fraudulent Practises of One John Darrel* |
| *DNB* | *Dictionary of National Biography* |
| HMC | The Royal Commission on Historical Manuscripts |
| PCC | Prerogative Court of Canterbury |
| *RES* | *Review of English Studies* |
| *PQ* | *Philological Quarterly* |
| *SEL* | *Studies in English Literature* |
| SP | State Papers |
| Tilley | Morris Palmer Tilley, ed., *A Dictionary of the Proverbs in England* |
| *VCH* | *Victoria History of the Counties of England* |

Shakespearean quotations and references follow the text of *The Riverside Shakespeare,* edited by G. Blakemore Evans (Boston: Houghton Mifflin, 1974). Citations from the *Calendar of State Papers (CSP Dom.)* give the volume and item number of each document calendared. This method of reference is interchangeable with references to the documents themselves (SP).

Unless otherwise indicated, texts are quoted as they appear in the source, except that abbreviations are expanded, and i/j, u/v, and long s are modernized.

# Part I
# Shakespeare, Harsnett, and the Devils of Denham

But leaving that aside, I want to tell you that we devils are offended by the travesties you make of us. You paint us with claws, when we're not little eagles; with tails, when we have none; with horns, when we're not married; and always ill-shaven, when there are devils among us who could pass for contemplatives and magistrates. You must correct this, because not long since Jerome Bosch arrived down there, and when we asked him why he had made such muddles of us in his imaginings, he replied, "Because to tell you the truth I had never believed that devils were real."

Francisco Quevedo, *Sueños y discursos.*

# 1

# Devils at Denham

In 1594, the Elizabethan government finally caught up with an intrepid Catholic gentleman called Robert Barnes and imprisoned him, charging him with fourteen articles of treasons and felonies. Because of the commonness of his name and the number of his aliases (Winkfield, Strange, Hynde, Mapledurham), Barnes is an elusive character; but he seems to have been one of an elite circle of Catholic gentlemen who served as couriers and guides for the missionary priests as they slipped in and out of England. Anne Bellamy, the Catholic woman who turned informer after being seduced—perhaps raped—in prison, accused him of traveling abroad with a priest called Birkett. He may also have been the Mr. Barnes who was said to have been present at the landing of another priest, George Douglas, at Dover, and he may be the Barnes who was with Fr. Robert Parsons at a house in Tuttlefields when the justices came to search, and Parsons escaped them by running to the haymow. In 1594, however, Barnes fell into the hands of the government's agent and torturer Richard Topcliffe, whom Geoffrey Hill has described without exaggeration as "an atrocious psychopath." Barnes suffered four years of harassment from Topcliffe, who wanted his property. Finally, Topcliffe and another official, Henry Lok, framed Barnes and another Catholic prisoner, Mrs. Wiseman, on a charge of assisting a priest. For this he was sentenced to death, although the sentence was not carried out. In the end he was one of a group of priests and laymen who went into banishment in 1603.[1]

While Barnes was in prison, he wrote a letter to Sir Robert Cecil, dated 23 July 1598. From this it appears that among the arti-

[1]On Barnes's imprisonment and trial, see J. H. Pollen, "Unpublished Documents Relating to the English Martyrs," *CRS* 5 (1908): 287, 362ff. On the landing of Fr. Douglas, see ibid., 5:89, and for the escape from Tuttlefields, see Fr. Parson's *Memoirs, CRS* 2 (1906): 29. Barnes's banishment is in Richard Challoner, *Memoirs of Missionary Priests*, ed. J. H. Pollen (London: Burns, Oates, and Co., 1923), 268. Geoffrey Hill's description of Topcliffe is in his essay "The Absolute Reasonableness of Robert Southwell," in his *The Lords of Limit* (London: André Deutsch, 1984), 22–74.

cles found at his capture there was a "book of exorcisms" that Topcliffe had been showing to other people:

> And as concerning the book of exorcisms which he showeth, the truth is this, I being newly a Catholic, wrote a copy thereof at the request of a friend, and utterly disliking thereof, never kept any copy for myself, neither was I at the exorcism, nor party or privy thereunto.[1]

This is the "English treatise in a written hand" that Harsnett, writing in 1602–1603, says had been found some three or four years earlier, in the hands of "one Ma: *Barnes,* a Popish Recusant" (*DEP,* 201). Harsnett calls it, contemptuously, the *Miracle Book* or *Book of Miracles,* and it must have come into his and his master Bishop Bancroft's hands about 1598. No doubt Robert Cecil passed it on to them. This fits with the date, 2 March 1598/99, when Bancroft examined Friswood Williams, his first witness to the events described in the book. Moreover, Bancroft's interest in the case at that time is explained by his involvement in the affair of John Darrell, the Puritan devil-dispossessor of Nottingham, which ended in May 1599 with the Ecclesiastical Court of High Commission's condemnation of Darrell.[2]

The *Miracle Book,* along with the witnesses' depositions, became part of the archives of the Ecclesiastical Court of High Commission. These were destroyed during the civil wars. Harsnett, however, quotes so much from the *Miracle Book* that we can form a fairly good idea of its contents.

First, it appears from Harsnett's quotations and references as well as from Barnes's letter to Cecil that the *Miracle Book* was a compilation, not a single entity, and that there must have been several copies of its different parts in circulation, one of which may yet turn up, perhaps in some European archive. Barnes's version consisted largely of a diary of Sara Williams's experiences (partly written by the ex-exorcist and apostate Anthony Tyrrell, according to his deposition) and a narrative of Richard Mainy's possessions and visions. Harsnett also quotes from Fr. William Weston's own Latin account of the possession of Nicholas Marwood; whether this was part of the *Miracle Book* or a separate work is not clear. In a marginal note to chapter 3, Harsnett describes it as "[Weston's] owne tract. upon record." There was certainly an essay on possession and exorcism "prefixed" to the *Miracle Book,* and this was Fr. Weston's work (*DEP,* 203).

---

[1] HMC, *Salisbury MSS.,* 8:273.

[2] *DFP,* sig. C1. The well-informed anonymous author of *The Triall of Maist. Dorrell,* sigs. A5v, A7, says "the last hearing of the matter" was "at Lambeth on Whitsun Eve last" i.e., 26 May 1599.

In addition to these documents, there were originally at least three more narratives in existence. There was one describing Friswood Williams's possession (*DEP*, 364), another about Anne Smith (373), and, according to Tyrrell, Weston wrote an account of Mainy's visions: "For he thought . . . to have wrought some great matter by him, but was disappointed very ridiculously, so as I thinke the said visions will hardly come to light" (390). This is a considerable body of material, and one important aspect of it needs to be emphasized: Harsnett's quotations from Weston's writings and Tyrrell's confession both reveal that these priestly narratives of supposedly miraculous events are not simply factual, eyewitness accounts. They were written, in a tradition of writings about miracles, for the edification of the faithful. Even when the account is firsthand, like Weston's account of Marwood, improvement upon fact is detectable. Tyrrell also admits that much of his own account was based upon hearsay, and that he arranged his materials "with the best skill I had to make them seeme strange and wonderfull" (*DEP*, 394). The element of falsehood in the narratives leads directly to the question of fraud in the exorcisms themselves, since Tyrrell, who confessed to falsifying his narrative, also took part in the exorcisms. He claimed to have been present at some of the "miracles," and, after the exorcisms had ended, had some of the supposedly preternaturally produced objects in his keeping.[1]

A tendency to improve appearances certainly influenced the exorcists' behavior. If Friswood Williams is to be believed at all, Fathers Stamp and Sherwood both practiced fraud, Stamp in the trick of the needles in her leg, Sherwood in the trick played upon Mr. Bridges, who had got his mother's maid with child (*DEP*, 365, 366). Yet apart from the problem of Friswood's veracity, which is very dubious, at the time of the inquiry she presented herself as a complete skeptic. During the exorcisms the mentality of priests and demoniacs alike was quite different. Given a belief in the reality and the commonness of possession, it followed in the minds of all concerned that a tendency to improve upon appearances was only a heightening of that reality. During the exorcisms it is likely that neither demoniacs nor priests could tell the difference between truth and falsehood.

Improved or not, the *Miracle Book* told an extraordinary story. In and around London, between autumn 1585 and late spring or

[1]Tyrrell's narrative of his role in the miracles, as well as his account of the objects (a hooked pin, a piece of lead, a shirt string, two needles, and a piece of rusty knife) is in John Morris, *Troubles of our Catholic Forefathers*, 3 vols. (1872–77, reprint, Farnborough, U.K.: Gregg International, 1970), 2:327–30, 412–14. Tyrrell claims to have played the role in the miracle of the needles that Friswood Williams attributes to Fr. Stamp.

early summer 1586, a group of priests, all except the Jesuit William Weston trained in the Douay-Rheims seminary for refugee English Catholics, had exorcised seven young people supposed to be possessed with devils. This series of exorcisms began when William Weston successfully treated Nicholas Marwood, a servant to Anthony Babington, sometime in late summer or early fall of 1585. This event became the talk of Catholic circles in and around London, and soon the practice began to spread. Robert Dibdale, a seminary priest living in the household of Edmund Peckham at Denham in Buckinghamshire, became convinced that a servant in the house, a Protestant girl called Sara Williams, was possessed. In the course of her exorcising, she announced that another servant, a young man called William Trayford, was also possessed. When her sister, Frideswide Williams, generally known as Friswood or Fid, came to look after her and help in the house, it was not long before she too caught the diabolic contagion. By then other priests had joined in, no doubt because the notoriety of the events brought audiences of the curious, but also because the sheer complexity of the exorcisms required a team of exorcists. The chief assistants were Fathers Stamp (another Peckham chaplain), Weston himself, Cornelius and Sherwood (both chaplains in the family of Sir John Arundell), Dryland, Thomson, Thulys, and Tyrrell.[1]

Another addition to the corps of demoniacs came about because Edmund Peckham, visiting Lady Stafford at Ivy Bridge in London, met there a woman called Alice Plater. She was fascinated by the stories of the Williams sisters because her own sister, Anne Smith, had been sent to live with her suffering from the hysterical condition then called "the mother." Alice Plater thereupon paid a visit to the Peckham's household, inspected the demoniacs, and decided that her sister was possessed. On Christmas Eve, 1585, Anne Smith (who remained skeptical of the diagnosis) found herself at Denham as a demoniac.

The fourth possessed girl, Elizabeth Calthrope, remains a mystery. She was exorcised at the earl of Lincoln's house in London in mid-February 1585/86 and died soon after, apparently because she broke her neck falling down a flight of stairs (*DEP*, 390).

The most inventive and mischievous demoniac was a relation of the Peckhams called Richard Mainy, a younger son of a well-known Kentish family. This young gentleman had been sent by his mother, a pious widow who hoped he would become a priest, to be educated at the seminary at Rheims. He arrived there in May 1580,

---

[1]For information on the exorcising priests, see Appendix A. They are often described as Jesuits, but this is a mistake. Only Weston was a Jesuit.

about twelve or thirteen years old, a rather sickly boy, according to his own account. By September 1583 his education had proceeded as far as his admission into minor orders (in a group that included Richard Yaxley, later to be Sara Williams's confessor); a year later, in September 1584, he was vested as a novice in the order of the Fratres Minimi or Bonhommes. Neither the life nor the diet was to his liking, so on Good Friday 1585, apparently to the intense disappointment of his pious relations, he returned to England, conformed to the Church of England, and proceeded to enjoy himself "as other young Gentlemen did." But he ran out of money and found himself obliged to board with his married brother John, a keen Catholic, who was living at the earl of Lincoln's house in Cannon Row, London.[1]

John Mainy had married Sir George Peckham's daughter and received as her dowry the furniture of Denham House. Richard Mainy, therefore, took to riding out to Denham with his brother. In the account he wrote for the ecclesiastical commissioners in 1602, his main concern was to exculpate himself from complicity in treasonable wrongdoings, and at the same time to explain away his ungentlemanly performance as a demoniac. Nonetheless, reading between the lines of his self-serving confession one can see that the bizarre events at Denham fascinated him. Sara Williams, a very attractive girl, also fascinated this seminary-bred adolescent. Meanwhile the priests sized him up quickly. His abandoning the Bonhommes, his conformity to the heretical Church of England, his high spirits, all spelled devils to them. He soon found himself trapped, like the other demoniacs, by the peculiar, circular logic of the diagnosis, according to which everything he said or did (which included denying that he was possessed) was the deed of the devil. Caught in the ethos of belief, he gave as good as he got and put on spectacular performances as a visionary and energumen. The climax of his possession was a grand charade of the seven deadly sins, which proved intensely enjoyable for everyone present.

The exorcisms took place chiefly at Denham, although some were held at other local houses, and there were important sessions in London in Cannon Row. Marwood and Sara were both exorcised at Lord Vaux's house in Hackney, then a village outside London. One needs, however, to keep Marwood's case separate from the succeeding imitative six, which form a set by themselves.

The chief lay support for the exorcisms came from the two young married men, John Mainy and Edmund Peckham. Accord-

---

[1]Mainy told part of this story to the High Commission. His career at Rheims is recorded in T. F. Knox, ed., *The First and Second Douay Diaries*, 2 vols. (London, 1878), 1:166, 169, 196, 198, 202.

ing to Harsnett, Peckham was a sort of quartermaster for the priests
and their patients, arranging their movements, their lodgings, and
their upkeep. Indeed, the former demoniacs' depositions reveal
how complex and effective the Catholics' underground organization was. Movements from house to house that Harsnett treats as
the journeys of a troupe of actors on tour were probably necessi-
tated by the need for safety. After the end of the exorcisms with the
raid on Denham House in early summer 1586, the transfer of the
former demoniac girls from safe house to safe house was ingenious, although, like most of the exorcising circle, they were
arrested later in the aftermath of the Babington Plot.[1] Had Fid
Williams not turned informer, Bishop Bancroft might never have
found her sister, Sara.[2]

Because writers on the subject have usually accepted Harsnett's
version of the exorcisms with little question or modification, it is
worth stressing the point that while the former demoniacs may
have told the ecclesiastical commissioners what they wanted to
hear, they did not necessarily tell them all they knew. For instance,
the *Miracle Book* claimed that very large audiences saw the exorcisms, of whom many were reconciled to Catholicism. Tyrrell also
claims five hundred conversions (*DEP,* 390). Harsnett, otherwise a
skeptic in all things concerning the exorcisms, accepts this figure
because it validates his own treatment of exorcism as a serious
threat to the established religion. Yet this is a self-serving, propagandist statement, not to be taken at face value.[3] The actual
audiences consisted of local Catholics and their trusted friends and
relations. Not all of the latter approved of what they saw. Mr.
Hampden of Hampden, who had Catholic kinsfolk, was taken to an
exorcism by his "cousin," Mr. Ashfield. As he entered the room,
the supposedly possessed Mainy, recognizing him as a Protestant,

---

[1]Although it does not appear in their statements (an indication they did not tell the
commissioners everything), Anne Smith and Fid Williams, after escaping from Bridewell
Prison (*DEP,* 384), were hidden with the French ambassador (Morris, *Troubles* 2:421).
Anne's version of this is that her mother placed her as a servant with the ambassador's
wife.

[2]The dispersal of the exorcising priests in early summer 1586 did not entirely stop
exorcising at Denham House. In December 1586, according to a report from Justice
Young to Walsingham, Lady Peckham herself died under exorcism (*CSP Dom., Elizabeth,* vol. 195, no. 58).

[3]Tyrrell's higher figure, three or four thousand, is not his own and is ridiculously
high, yet some modern writers have taken it seriously, e.g., Keith Thomas, *Religion and
the Decline of Magic* (London: Weidenfeld and Nicolson, 1971), 492, and D. P. Walker,
*Unclean Spirits: Possession and Exorcism in France and England in the Late Sixteenth
and Early Seventeenth Centuries* (London: Scolar Press, 1981), 44, whose language ("the
lowest estimate of the conversions . . . is five hundred") confers a dignity on these figures
they simply don't have.

saluted him—with characteristic high spirits and inventiveness—as his fellow-justice. Mr. Hampden, outraged, made an angry speech and left the room. This dismayed the exorcists, for an angry Protestant meant danger. The priests usually maintained better control over their audiences, a policy illustrated by their attitude to the Williams sisters. They tolerated no communication between the girls, who had been reconciled, and their Protestant parents. Had the priests really seen the exorcisms as a nearly infallible tool of conversion (as the *Miracle Book* and Harsnett both imply), then the parents of two star demoniacs would have been prime targets. They were not.[1]

As the attentive reader of Anthony Tyrrell's contradictory statements learns, the exorcisms did not validate faith; faith, on the contrary, validated the exorcisms. The phenomena did not explain the faith; the faith explained the phenomena. Consequently, although one will never know exactly what happened at the exorcisms (for even Mainy's performance of the seven deadly sins would be hard to reconstruct) we *can* say that they were entirely an event within the besieged world of Elizabethan Catholicism, and one that gave expression to its fears, hatreds, yearnings, and admirations. This probably explains the peculiar attitude of the civil authorities at the time. They knew that exorcisms were happening but seem not to have paid much attention to them, even after most of the exorcists had been arrested. Of the priests taken in the great Catholic roundup that followed the arrest of Anthony Babington and his associates in August 1586, only Dibdale seems to have had exorcising held against him at his trial. Anne Smith was in prison at the time: Justice Young remembered her and produced her in evidence against him. Of the other captured priests, Dryland, Green, Stamp, Thulys, and Weston all ended up in Wisbech Castle, but not for exorcising.

Nor did the authorities show any greater interest in the former demoniacs. Sara Williams was in prison in Oxford for fourteen weeks shortly after Dibdale's execution, but there is no hint in her statement that she was questioned about her possession. In 1592 or 1593 she was examined about the exorcisms by Sir Anthony Cope and Dr. Thomas D'Oyly, the famous physician; she told them nothing. Friswood was imprisoned for recusancy at Aylesbury around 1590, and by then, if we are to believe her, she was pre-

---

[1]Fid tells the Hampden story (*DEP*, 370). On 26 January 1583/84, a raid on the house of Mrs. Hampden of Stoke, Buckinghamshire, produced various Catholic articles such as books, pictures, beads, and "a picture made upon yowloe sarcenet called by Mr. Fytten Veronyca" (SP/12/167, no. 47). Both Williams sisters say that they were in effect prisoners and separated from their kinsfolk and friends (*DEP*, 346, 374).

pared to answer any question. Yet when the Privy Council examined her, they asked for information about the movements and whereabouts of priests, not, it seems, about the exorcisms. Anne Smith seems not to have been questioned apart from her appearance at Dibdale's trial; yet it was to her that the most spectacular phenomenon was attributed, the production of a piece of knife from her insides. Mainy was summoned before the council and questioned by Lord Strange, but it was his own fault because he had been boasting about his fits and visions. He denied everything and blamed the priests.[1]

Marwood was the only demoniac imprisoned for more than mere recusancy, but it was not for being exorcised, even though Walsingham had a report of some of his sayings during his fits. (When asked what had become of Zwinglius, Jerome of Prague, Luther, and Calvin, he had answered in a loud voice that they were all damned; but of Campion, Sherwyn, and Throgmorton, he had answered "ragingly and repyningly" that they were saints in heaven.) He was still in prison in September 1588, described as a dangerous person who refused to take the loyalty oath.[2]

Nor is there much other evidence of official interest in the exorcisms. Weston tells of a young man who told Lord Burghley, "You could actually see the devils gliding and moving under the skin . . . they looked just like fishes swimming here there and everywhere." This conversation seriously irritated Burghley, who ordered the young man out of his sight, but there is no hint in Weston's anecdote that he took the matter very seriously.[3]

All this amounts to very little and leads one to conclude that the authorities did not think the exorcisms very important. Throughout the period exorcism was a great deal commoner than we realize, and though, like all priestly activity in England, it was offensive to authority, it was probably not nearly as offensive as saying mass. To understand this we need to bear in mind the peculiarly legalistic approach of Elizabethan authority to these matters. Under the laws against the practice of Catholicism, it was illegal for a priest to exercise his office in England; consequently, saying mass was a

[1] All this information is based on their own statements and so is not altogether trustworthy. They may have played down the seriousness of the questioning (*DEP*, 358, 376, 384, 398).

[2] The report of Marwood's behavior is in SP/12/192, no. 57, a faded document, difficult to read. For his imprisonment, see *CRS* 2(1906): 283.

[3] Philip Caraman, ed. and trans., *An Autobiography from the Jesuit Underground* (New York: Farrar, Strauss and Cudahy, 1955), 25. John Hungerford Pollen, "Supposed Cases of Diabolical Possession in 1585–6," *The Month* 117 (May 1911): 449–64, interprets Burghley's reaction to mean that he saw "no political significance in the movement" (460).

serious felony because it was something that only a priest could do. In fact, short of personal confession, saying mass was the only certain proof that a man *was* a priest. Casting out devils, on the other hand, though a nuisance, was something a layman or a Protestant could claim to do; and though, depending upon the circumstances of the case, it might fall within the scope of the laws against witchcraft and conjuring, there was no specific civil enactment against it.[1]

The authorities' attitude, combined with the priests' mastery of underground tactics, enabled the exorcisms to go on for over eight months, drawing Catholic audiences from London and its neighborhood. Those audiences were treated to a remarkable show. Unlike other rites of the Church, exorcism was (and is) an improvisatory affair, proceeding by well-defined stages and not ending until the exorcist has mastered the entity that he believes to be occupying the patient's body and expelled it. The Catholic Church did not regularize the rite until the seventeenth century; consequently there was considerable room for invention by the exorcist. Exorcism in the Catholic Church is based on the belief that a priest, canonically ordained in the apostolic succession, may cast out demons in the name of Jesus; but that authority, which is the authority of Jesus himself, is mediated by more than the person and voice of the exorcising priest. The intercession of saints, for instance, has always been a feature of Christian exorcism, and the Elizabethan missionary priests used an Italian manual that allowed them to mobilize against their devils the full spiritual panoply of the Church: they used every kind of sacred object, including relics of recently martyred English priests, and they also contributed some bizarre features of their own to the procedure. They strapped the demoniacs into a chair, for instance, and forced them to drink a "holy potion" of wine, salad oil, and herbs. They also fumigated them with a smoking mixture of noxious herbs. As Harsnett says, the treatment would have possessed a horse with a devil. The results, considered as theater of the violent and grotesque, must have rivaled in excitement anything on the public stages of the period.[2]

[1]In the period there was nothing intrinsically peculiar about exorcism. It had been part of the pre-Reformation baptism service, and an echo of it survives in the "renunciation of Satan" in the baptismal rite of The Book of Common Prayer and all later Anglican rites. Exorcism of salt and water was a regular part of the Sarum and Tridentine rites. Private exorcism as a kind of healing service was also common. The Denham exorcisms were unusual for England in being a series, in the number of priests involved, in being public, and in the propagandist use made of them.

[2]Harsnett's description of the exorcists' manual (*DEP,* 286) indicates that it must have been the *Flagellum daemonum* of Girolamo Menghi, first published at Bologna, 1578, and still very up to date in 1586. Menghi also published exorcisms under the titles

It has recently been argued that the reason the authorities allowed these strange events to continue was that, as D. P. Walker writes,

> They were regarded by the government as part of the Babington plot, which proposed the assassination of Elizabeth, the invasion of England by the Spanish, and the installation of Mary as Queen of Britain. Walsingham knew all about this plot from the beginning, and held his hand as long as possible. . . .[1]

This opinion goes back to Harsnett, whose whole view of the exorcisms is that they were a calculatedly fraudulent performance timed to coincide with the maneuvers of Catholic conspirators. Francis Hutchinson, an eighteenth-century cleric writing in the context of Jacobite intrigue, repeated Harsnett's case. Most recently John L. Murphy has argued that the government actually knew that the exorcisms were part of the plot. Murphy even speculates that the treasonable mouthings of the supposed demons were a cause of Babington's behavior.[2]

Insofar as the exorcisms took place in and around London in 1585–86, they occurred among the same people at approximately the same time and in the same atmosphere that produced the tangled, controverted, and mysterious affair called the Babington plot. It may even be true, although there is no evidence for it at all, that the exorcisms influenced Babington.[3] Similarly, someone today might see a spy movie or read a political thriller and then go out and shoot an American president. Proving the causal connection in a law court would be difficult; and even if it were proved, it would

---

*Fuga daemonum* and *Fustis daemonum*. He gives a recipe for the fumigation of the possessed, a technique also used on the French demoniac Marthe Brossier (See Abraham Hartwell, trans., *A True Discourse upon the Matter of Martha Brossier of Romorantin* [London, 1599], sig. E4v). The revolting "holy potion" is "unprecedented" (Walker, *Unclean Spirits,* 46); Walker finds it difficult to believe that it "was quite innocently used," a judgment most people would agree with. The fumigations were doubtless warranted by the episode of Tobias, the angel Raphael, and the devil Asmodeus in the apocryphal book of Tobit, 3–8.

[1]Walker, *Unclean Spirits,* 44.

[2]John L. Murphy, *Darkness and Devils: Exorcism and 'King Lear'* (Athens: Ohio University Press, 1984), 35, quotes the relevant passage from Hutchinson but without pointing out that it is entirely based on Harsnett. Murphy's speculations on the devils' treason are on p.51. He also argues, 30–31, 48, that Tyrrell's 1602 deposition to the ecclesiastical commissioners proves that he could make no explicit connection between the plot and the exorcisms. Nonetheless, Murphy maintains that there was one, and, 60–61, criticizes me severely for doubting it.

[3]Influence could not have gone the other way. When Babington, according to Conyers Read (*Sir Francis Walsingham* [Oxford: Clarendon Press, 1925], 3:20–21) met Ballard in May 1586 and the plot began in earnest, the exorcisms were all but over.

hardly make the writer or the director a party to treason. Walker's argument is also vulnerable because Walsingham did not "hold his hand" in the matter of the exorcisms. The Babington arrests were made in August 1586, but the first arrest in the exorcising circle was made on Ascension Day (12 May 1586), when Richard Davies, like Mainy a layman in minor orders, was picked up after being at Denham.[1] The house itself was raided in mid-June. There was delay in arresting Weston and the rest of his associates in exorcism, not because Walsingham considered them part of the unfolding plot but because any major arrest would put the conspirators on their guard. As it happens, Weston was accidentally arrested a little early, on 4 August, and Walsingham's secretary wrote, "That [which] I mislike and doubt in Edmond's [Weston's] apprehension is that being missed now peradventure by Bal[lard] and his company (for he no doubt was going to them), it will disperse them." This does not prove that Weston was part of the plot, but that the government fervently hoped that he was, and were doing their best to play him into the net. For whatever else the Babington Plot was, it was an opportunity for Sir Francis Walsingham to strike a major blow against the whole Catholic organization in and around London. One has only to read the prison lists for late summer 1586 to see that. One can even observe Walsingham, earlier in the year, preparing the jails to accommodate his catch.[2]

   The strongest evidence against a connection between the exorcisms and the plot, however, is Harsnett's own book. To judge from the depositions, each of the witnesses at Bishop Bancroft's inquiry was asked whether Babington and his associates were at the exorcisms. Mainy, the gentleman, was allowed to write his own statement, and he makes no mention of Babington; but Sara, Fid, and Anne, whose depositions are the record of answers to questions, all said that Babington and his friends were present, Fid as usual giving the most detail. Tyrrell, whose treachery had already contributed to the hanging of the Babington conspirators, in particular of his friend John Ballard, seems to have been asked Professor Murphy's question: did the exorcisms influence Babington? He gave the answer he was expected to give (as the witnesses always did), but in words that indicate a tenable opinion, not a conviction:

[1]On Davies, see Appendix A.

[2]For the Denham arrests, see *CRS* 2(1906): 250, 253, 255; Challoner, *Memoirs,* 117, and *DEP,* 383. For the comment on Weston's arrest, see Morris, *Troubles* 2:151. The 1586 prison lists and Walsingham's preparations are documented in *CRS* 2(1906): 253–87.

> Wee had out of question procured unto our selves very great favour, credit, and reputation, so as it was no mervaile if some young Gentlemen, as Ma: *Babington* and the rest, were allured to those strange attempts which they tooke in hand by maister *Ballard,* who was an Agent amongst us. . . . (*DEP*, 391)

It would not be surprising if Babington was at the exorcisms. Everyone in Catholic London seems to have been there at one time or another, and his own servant was the first patient. The commissioners' only reason for asking the question was to associate Babington with the exorcisms and therefore to sustain their hypothesis or accusation of fraud practiced for a political purpose, which was to be the basis of Harsnett's book.

Harsnett knew as well as the modern historian that no link between conspiracy and exorcism was ever proved in the courts. Weston, one of the bigger fish Walsingham would have liked to catch, was not implicated in the plot and never brought to trial. Harsnett, therefore, despite the former demoniacs' answers to the commissioners' question, has to make his case by smear and innuendo, on the principle of guilt by association:

> And this new tragedie of devils had his time of rising and his fatall time of fall with the true tragedie performed upon *Babington* and his complices. . . .(208)

Or:

> It may suffice that it is said, [Marwood] was *Anthony Babington* his man. (218)

Even so, the Babington Plot is a very minor motif indeed in Harsnett's book. He imputes to the priests a larger, more general intention, "to with-draw the harts of her Majesties Subjects from their allegeance," and this, not the Babington Plot, is the theme of his last chapter, "Of the ayme, end, and marke of all this pestilent tragaedy."

Finally, the possession of Marwood, Babington's servant, is the weakest part of Harsnett's case for fraud. No serious historian has ever accused William Weston of fraud. He may have been a holy fool, perhaps a credulous fanatic, but he was honest and courageous according to his lights, and he was certainly not stupid. Marwood was his first patient, and because the ecclesiastical commissioners never traced him, he is the most interesting offstage character in the whole drama. The passages quoted from Weston's account of his case, allowing for rhetorical flourish, describe genuine symptoms as well as the moment of release from them; there was certainly something wrong with Marwood that Weston seems to have cured, and Harsnett's own book, by quoting Weston's material, makes the point.

It remains possible, nonetheless, that the exorcisms influenced Babington; but if they did, he was fairly unhinged himself. We should not be too surprised by the constant flow of treasonable talk kept up by the supposed demons. In the first place, this was the sort of thing Elizabethan Catholics must have thought to themselves all the time. Second, it is obvious from Harsnett's quotations from the *Miracle Book* that in addition to much that was grotesque and violent in the exorcisms, there was a great deal of broad comedy. When Sara's devil was asked whether Mainy really had the "mother" or not, and replied, "That is a *Mother* indeed" (*DEP,* 404), the audience must have gone into fits of laughter. Similarly, when the devil called Puff said on St. Hugh's Day (Accession Day) that he was going to ring for the Queen (344), that too must have got a laugh. Comedy has a hard time surviving miracle books and ecclesiastical courts, but that does not mean it was never there. After all, there was a long and vigorous tradition of comic devils in English drama and art; even Sara's devils' names are funny. I suspect that the exorcisms had much in common with a modern political cabaret, and that to the extent that they made people laugh and cry, mourn and rejoice, and brought into the open thoughts and feelings normally kept secret, they would discourage treason while they encouraged belief. In this respect the Denham exorcisms seem to have been quite different from the Protestant dispossessings of John Darrell, which frightened people out of their wits with no leavening of comedy. One cannot imagine one of Darrell's patients scaring away a pursuivant by telling him that his buttons were covered with devils, but this apparently happened in the Weston exorcisms.[1]

Did Harsnett understand this dimension of the exorcisms? He was a very intelligent man with a strong sense of the comic and some knowledge of the way drama works. A reader must understand that Harsnett's book is as much a performance in its own way as the exorcisms were in theirs. To anticipate the argument a little, Harsnett constructed for himself a very elaborate persona as the author of his *Declaration,* and its least attractive feature is what Christopher Devlin, with justice, called "pious bombast." Harsnett certainly knew that the exorcisms had no connection worth talking about with the Babington Plot. He probably knew equally well

---

[1]Caraman, *Autobiography,* 26.

that, considered as a threat to national security, they were harmless. After all, they had happened some sixteen years before he began to write, Elizabeth was still securely on her throne, a Cecil was Master Secretary, and Catholicism was decidedly a lesser threat in 1602 than it had been in 1586. It is even doubtful whether Harsnett's ferocious anti-Catholic rhetoric was genuinely felt. As his later career would show, he was not at all the sort of Protestant that harbors fantasies of disguised priests who "defile your chast houses, pollute your tender virgins, deprave and inveigle your owne wives lying in your bosoms" (*DEP,* 198). There were such people in Elizabethan England, but Samuel Harsnett, whose closest friend and patron in later years was the earl of Arundel, was not one of them. As Bishop Harsnett he was accused more than once, with some justice, of pro-Catholic opinions. Why then did he write as he did? Why did he write the book at all, since the exorcisms were sixteen years in the past? And for whom, exactly, did he write it?[1]

[1]Christopher Devlin criticizes Harsnett, not altogether fairly, in "The Case of Anthony Tyrrell," *The Month* 192 (1951): 357. As bishop of Chichester, Harsnett was rebuked by the Privy Council for lenience to recusants (*APC* 34:34–35), and much of the quarrel between Harsnett, as Master, and the fellows of Pembroke College, 1612–16, turned upon the pro-Catholic views of his deputy, Ralph Poclynton, who among other things spoke slightingly of Lancelot Andrewes's reply to Bellarmine, objected to a sermon of execration in memory of Guy Fawkes, and apparently believed in the Real Presence in the sacrament (Pembroke College MSS, "College Box," M11).

# 2

# Bancroft and Harsnett

Questions about Harsnett's motives in writing his *Declaration* are inseparable from the character and abilities of his friend and patron Richard Bancroft, bishop of London and, later, archbishop of Canterbury. Probably the ablest politician-administrator of all the Protestant archbishops of Canterbury, Bancroft was a striking character with an intimidating presence, a powerful speaker and preacher with a sardonic sense of humor, and an administrator with a passion for research and detail. He is also surely the only archbishop of Canterbury whose hobby was wrestling; it is reported that visitors to his palace at Fulham when he was bishop of London might be asked to try a fall with him.

Bancroft was born, the son of a gentleman, in Farnworth, Lancashire, in September 1544.[1] His education began at the grammar school in Farnworth. Then a maternal great-uncle, Hugh Curwen, bishop of Oxford, provided for further education at Christ's College, Cambridge. There Bancroft was elected scholar, and proceeded B.A. in 1566–67. The grant of an Irish prebend with leave of absence from the performance of its duties eased his financial circumstances, but he was required to leave Christ's for Jesus College. At Jesus he was a successful teacher, but he was never elected fellow, and there is a presumption that at this stage of his life there was a Puritan streak in his makeup.

Serious preferment came in March 1575/76 with the grant of a rectory and his election as one of twelve university preachers. His real career began a few years later at Bury assizes. The sheriff of the county, not knowing of a suitable local preacher for the assizes, applied to the university, who sent Bancroft. While he was in Bury he went browsing among the local churches, which was the sort of thing Bancroft liked to do. In one of them he found a libel hung up, comparing the Queen to Jezebel. With the efficiency in detection

---

[1]This sketch of Bancroft's career is based on *DNB*, R. G. Usher, *The Reconstruction of the English Church*, 2 vols. (New York and London: Appleton & Co., 1910), virtually a biography, and Stuart Babbage, *Puritanism and Richard Bancroft* (London: S.P.C.K. Press for the Church Historical Society, 1962).

for which he later became famous he followed up the case, and two Brownists were arrested, tried, and convicted.

For a while advancement followed quickly. In 1585 he proceeded D.D. The next year he became treasurer of St. Paul's, and Sir Christopher Hatton, a supporter of anti-Puritans, gave him another benefice. After Bishop Cox of Ely died, Bancroft was appointed a commissioner for the diocese, which (one of the ecclesiastical scandals of Elizabeth I's reign) remained vacant. Then he became a member of the Ecclesiastical Court of High Commission itself, and, in 1587, a canon of Westminster Abbey.

This is the career of a vigorous and efficient manager, not of a contemplative. Bancroft's career, in fact, was based on the detection, exposure, and removal of threats to the English religious establishment, an avocation in which he had no rival. Some of his findings and opinions were made public in three publications, a Paul's Cross sermon preached in February 1588/89, and two books that came out in 1593: *Daungerous Positions and Proceedings, Published and Practised within this Iland of Brytaine,* and *A Survay of the Pretended Holy Discipline.* These exposures of the aims and organization of the Puritan element in the Church of England (defined by Robert Parsons as "the hotter sort of Protestants"[1]) probably did more serious damage to their cause than any merely theological controversy, for Bancroft very shrewdly exposed them not so much as bad theologians but as unreliable subjects and Englishmen. Nor was his exposure made of rhetorical hot air; it was based on police-work and facts.

In 1592 he had become a chaplain to Archbishop Whitgift, but otherwise the stream of preferment seemed to have dried up. This is not surprising, because a cleric of Bancroft's views would have found fewer friends than enemies in Elizabethan London. In 1597, therefore, Whitgift wrote a remarkable letter to Elizabeth advancing the claims of his chaplain on her attention and describing his achievements. His abilities first appeared, said Whitgift, when as commissioner for Ely diocese he had carried out a visitation "about twelve years since," that is, about 1585. By his diligent search he had found out the Marprelate press and books, and by his advice "that course was taken which did principally stop Martin and his fellows' mouths, viz. to have them answered after their own vein in writing." It was Bancroft, therefore, who brought professional

---

[1]In the dedication of his *A Brief Discours* (1580); quoted by Thomas H. Clancy, *Papist Pamphleteers: The Allen-Persons Party and the Political Thought of the Counter-Reformation in England, 1572–1615* (Chicago: Loyola University Press, 1964), 205, and by Patrick Collinson, *The Elizabethan Puritan Movement* (Berkeley and Los Angeles, CA.: University of California Press, 1967), but without attribution.

writers, including Lyly and Nashe, into the Marprelate controversy. He was also, said Whitgift, the man who gave the instructions to the Crown counsel when Martin's agents were brought into
Star Chamber. Finally, he had unearthed Cartwright's and his
agents' "discipline" in many shires, "their *Classes,* decrees, and
book of discipline." A formidable character emerges from
Whitgift's letter. Yet, said Whitgift, others had been promoted
while Bancroft worked, and he urged the Queen very strongly to
prefer him according to his abilities and service.[1]

There had been talk of Bancroft as successor to Aylmer as
bishop of London. Aylmer's tenure of the see, however, had been
predatory and ineffective, and he put conditions on the succession
that were unacceptable to Bancroft. A more complaisant candidate,
Richard Fletcher, "a comly and courtly prelate," John Harrington
calls him, succeeded Aylmer, not without rumors of corruption.
His tenure only lasted eighteen months. On 9 May 1597 Bancroft
was confirmed and consecrated bishop of London, and the most
vigorous and effective administration in the Protestant Church of
England's history began. Whitgift, an able archbishop, was in failing health, and soon Bancroft was archbishop in all but name.[2]

One of the new bishop's first acts was to appoint his friend Samuel Harsnett as one of his chaplains and to secure suitable preferment for him. And so, with Bancroft's promotion, Harsnett's
career, which hitherto had had its ups and downs, began in earnest.

Like many of the Jacobean and Caroline episcopate, Harsnett
came from very modest beginnings.[3] He was born in a family of
Colchester bakers, a younger child of William and Agnes

[1]Whitgift's letter is in Usher, *Reconstruction* 2:366–69, also in John Strype, *The Life and Acts of John Whitgift,* 3 vols. (Oxford, 1822), 2:387. Bancroft's exposure of the Presbyterian movement's secret organisation into "classes," for which he was long the only authority, was confirmed by the discovery of the minute book of the Dedham "classis." See R.G. Usher, ed., *The Presbyterian Movement in the Reign of Queen Eliza-beth as Illustrated by the Minute Book of the Dedham Classis,* Royal Historical Society Publications, Camden Series, 3d ser., vol. 8 (London, 1905).

[2]Aylmer left the episcopal palaces needing £2,500 in repairs. As Bancroft said, "They were ready to fall down when I came." He also cut timber to the value of £6,000. He had a large family to provide for and so tied up his estate that although Bancroft was awarded over £4,000 in dilapidations, he never seems to have received any of it (Usher, *Reconstruction* 1:114). On Bishop Fletcher see *DNB,* also John Harington, *Nugae Antiquae,* 3 vols. (London, 1779), 3:25–32. Fletcher's first promotion, to Bristol, involved simoniacal alienations of property to courtiers. Bancroft's confirmation and consecration are in Archbishop Whitgift's register, vol. 3, fol. 83 (Lambeth Palace MSS).

[3]Archbishop Neile's father was a candlemaker, Archbishop Abbot's a clothworker, and Archbishop Montaigne's a gardener. Bishop Andrewes's father was a seaman. In Parliament in 1641 Lord Brooke, a proto-Whig peer, said that the bishops "in respect of their parentage" were *"de faece populi,"* i.e., from the dregs of the population (Thomas Fuller, *The Church History of Britain* [London, 1655], sig. 5A2).

Halsnoth, who had him baptized in the parish church of St. Botolph on 21 June 1561. The Halsnoths (Harsnett himself changed the spelling of the name) had been bakers for some generations. Harsnett's grandmother Margaret bequeathed her "bolting vessells" to two of her grandchildren, Samuel's elder brother Isaac being one of them. After William Halsnoth died in 1574, his widow Agnes carried on the business, and Isaac in turn succeeded her. They were by no means the only Halsnoths in Colchester. The name was fairly common in and around the city, its bearers mostly tradespeople.[1]

The Halsnoths were not well to do (they were not as well off as Shakespeare's parents, for instance), but they had property enough to maintain their independence. Harsnett's grandmother had a house to bequeath; she kept three servants and left ten shillings for the parish poor. When Harsnett's mother made her will in 1595, she left instructions for a local preacher to deliver a funeral sermon. A kinsman, Adam Halsnoth the elder, a joiner, was a servant-at-the-mace in the city and left £160.

Everything about Harsnett's early life suggests that he was brought up in strongly Protestant surroundings. His father's will has a Calvinist tone; the testator hopes and believes that by the merits of Christ's passion and death once offered for him, he will have remission of his sins and be in the company of the elect. After his father's death, Harsnett, then a twelve-year-old schoolboy, presumably at Colchester Grammar School, found a patron in Richard Bridgewater, a wealthy ecclesiastical lawyer, an Etonian and Kingsman, who lived in the neighboring town of Dedham. Dedham was a center of Calvinism; there was a secret Presbyterian classis there in the 1580s, and Bridgewater, as a fellow of King's, was one of those who accused Provost Baker of popery. Under Bridgewater's patronage, young Harsnett matriculated at King's College as a sizar on 8 September 1576, probably as companion and servitor to Bridgewater's own son, who entered the college at the same time. The provost of King's was Roger Goad, another strong Calvinist.[2]

---

[1] The facts of Harsnett's early life are available in a number of books and articles: *DNB;* Gordon Goodwin, *A Catalogue of the Harsnett Library* (London, 1888); Philip Morant, *The History and Antiquities of . . . Colchester,* 2 vols. (Chelmsford, 1815), 1:121; W. G. Benham, *Archbishop Samuel Harsnett* (Colchester: Benham, 1932); "Pedigree of Archbishop Samuel Harsnett," *Essex Review* 40 (1931): 105. Harsnett family wills are at the Essex Record Office: D/ACR 5 (Margaret); D/ACR 6 (William); D/ACW 3/80 (Agnes); ACW 6/100 (Isaac); D/ACW 6/194 (Adam, the elder).

[2] Colchester School failed with the dissolution of religious foundations under Henry VIII, who reestablished it in 1539 out of chantry monies. By 1583 it had failed again, and Elizabeth refounded it in 1584 (Morant, *Colchester* 1:171; *VCH, Essex* 2:502. Richard Bridgewater was elected to King's from Eton, 1555, proceeded B.A. in 1559 and M.A. in 1563; he was proctor, public orator (1573), and received his LL.D. in 1579. In July 1579

Harsnett did not remain at King's. When he proceeded B.A. in 1580–81, it was from Pembroke Hall, where he had recently migrated, having been at King's as late as the Easter term of 1579. At Pembroke he held a scholarship. Then, 27 November 1583, he was elected to a fellowship, and in 1584 proceeded M.A. He thus became a member of the society that had Gabriel Harvey for a fellow, Lancelot Andrewes as catechist, and William Fulke, one of the most popular teachers in the university, for master. Fulke was a famous Puritan, a veteran of the vestiarian controversy at St. John's in the sixties. Andrewes, a much younger man, was already developing, in the catechistical lectures for which he became famous in the university and its environs, the anti-Calvinist theology that made him a leader of the emerging High-Church party, but which he, characteristically, always refused to define.[1]

The next stage of Harsnett's career is mysterious. He buried it so effectively in later life that no account of it appears in any of the many epitomes of his career that exist, manuscript or printed. Sometime in 1583–85 he must have been ordained, although diligent search has failed to turn up any record of the ceremony. This may simply be because records for the diocese of Ely, vacant at the time, are missing,[2] or because the episcopal registers for Lincoln, another possible place of ordination, are also defective for the period. Nonetheless, it is surprising that an archbishop of York should have left no record of his ordination behind him at all. He could have been ordained deacon after June 1583, when he was twenty-two (the canonical age), and priest's orders could have followed after he reached twenty-four in June 1585. He was certainly a priest by April 1586, for in that month he had a cure of souls and was being examined by the Ecclesiastical Court of High Commis-

---

he was appointed chancellor and vicar-general in the diocese of Ely. He died 15 February 1587/88 (C. H. Cooper and Thompson Cooper, eds., *Athenae Cantabrigienses,* 3 vols. [Cambridge: 1858–1913], 2:19). For Bridgewater's patronage of Harsnett, see Goodwin's Introduction to his *Catalogue.* Harsnett's matriculation date is from *DNB* and *Biographia Britannica,* 6 vols. (London, 1746–66), 4:2543. John Venn and J. A. Venn, eds., *University of Cambridge: Matriculations and Degrees . . . from 1544 to 1659* (Cambridge: Cambridge University Press, 1913), 326, and *Alumni Cantabrigienses, Part 1: From the Earliest Times to 1751,* 4 vols. (Cambridge: Cambridge University Press, 1922–27), 2:319, give the date as Easter term, 1579, but this is evidently wrong since he graduated in 1580–81. He must have still been in residence at King's in 1579. On the Dedham classis, see Usher, *Presbyterian Movement.*

[1]For Harsnett's degrees, see John Venn, ed., *Grace Book Δ* (Cambridge: Cambridge University Press, 1910), 336, 376. His scholarship and fellowship are recorded in Pembroke College MS. C.θ, fol. 3. For Fulke, see *DNB.* H. C. Porter, *Reformation and Reaction in Tudor Cambridge* (Cambridge: Cambridge University Press, 1958), 119ff., 391ff. gives excellent accounts of Fulke and Andrewes.

[2]There are no *sede vacante* ordinations in Whitgift's register at Lambeth.

sion for refusing to wear a surplice. The account, a transcript of Harsnett's own words, is so interesting that I quote it in full:

> The B[ishop] asked me if I would wear the surplice. I said I was not resolved. *Bishop.* Why so? *Answer.* Because it would bring my ministry into contempt and I should do no good among the people, seeing I have not joined with it a long time. How is that? said the bishop. Why thus: I should be accused of great lightness and inconstancy now to admit it, having so long refused it. Then the bishop said that to obey the Queen's law was to bring my ministry into contempt. Not so, said I, but to wear the surplice, because of the people. Then I reason thus, said the bishop: to wear the surplice is to bring your ministry into contempt, but to wear the surplice is to obey the Queen's law. *Ergo,* to obey the law is to bring your ministry into contempt. Answer! said the bishop. I said I came not to reason. Repeat the syllogism! said he. I would not. He repeated it, not weighing that his reason was captious. Mark what he saith, said he to [name missing], the law of the prince is to bring his ministry into contempt. Take me not so, said I. I spake of the surplice, and not of the law. Yes, said he. And so committed me.[1]

Harsnett will have been prosecuted under Whitgift's "Articles touching preachers and other orders for the Church," drawn up between 4–25 June 1584, in particular Article 4: all preachers and others in ecclesiastical orders are "to wear and use such kindes of apparel" as are prescribed by "the booke of advertisments and her Majesties Injunctions, anno primo."[2] Evidently, the twenty-five-year-old Harsnett was an antivestiarian minister after the pattern of William Fulke, and not only prepared to stand up to the High Commission for his opinion, but so committed to the principle that he contributed an account of his experience to a "party" compilation. Moreover, since the document's "committed" is ambiguous, he may even have gone to prison.

This episode put an end to Harsnett's ecclesiastical career for the time being. His Pembroke brethren, however, continued to support

---

[1]"The Seconde Part of a Register" 2:104, no.22, The Morrice MSS, Dr. Williams' Library, London. These MSS belonged in the seventeenth century to Roger Morrice, one of the deprived clergy of 1662, who says that the collection was made "by a most faithful understanding and observing gentleman who died about the end of it." Mrs. Beatrice Pugh, to whom I owe the transcript and description, suggests that this was James Morice, attorney of the Court of Wards, who died in 1597. A. Peel, who printed a summary of the MSS in 1915, suggests that Lady Anne Bacon might have helped Morice. The collection, made about 1593 and intended for publication, contains originals and copies. The item preceding the Harsnett entry is dated April 1586, the succeeding one 7 April 1586. The bishop will have been Archbishop Whitgift. The item is headed "Mr Harsnet of Pembrook Hall." I have modernized punctuation and spelling to bring out the drama of the scene for the modern reader.

[2]Archbishop Whitgift's register, vol. 1, fols. 97–98.

him, and with great promptness they wrote a letter to the bailiffs, burgesses, and commonalty of Colchester, 3 May 1586, recommending Samuel Harsnett for the post of schoolmaster in the recently refounded grammar school there. Following this letter, and no doubt in recognition of his status as a native son and a sufferer in the cause of true Protestantism, Harsnett was chosen schoolmaster, March 1586/87.[1]

He planned to stay some time in Colchester, for he spent money on the school building and its orchard. Yet only eighteen months later he resigned, and once again there is some mystery in the circumstances. "It hath pleased God," he wrote to the bailiffs, 28 October 1588,

> whose pleasure is good, to chaung the thoughts of my harte, and to dispose of my purposes, besides my purpose, unto the studye of divinitye: pardonne me, right worshippful, if I crave your pardonne, and your prayer bothe, that it may be to his glorie, and the good of his Churche.[2]

Perhaps he found schoolmastering intolerable, although this seems unlikely in view of his long career as a college teacher and his founding of a grammar school in old age. Whatever changed the thoughts of his heart, he did his best to secure the vacant post, including the twelve-month period of notice required by his contract, for a university contemporary, Mark Sadlington of Peterhouse. The bailiffs, however, had other ideas. They wished to appoint William Bentley, a fellow of Clare College, Cambridge, and schoolmaster in the neighboring town of Dedham. Bentley had a splendid set of testimonials. His academic referees were Lawrence Chaderton, master of Emmanuel; Roger Goad, provost of King's; William Whitaker, master of St. John's and Regius Professor of divinity; and Andrew Downes, professor of Greek and fellow of St. John's.[3] What is striking about this contest for the schoolmastership of Colchester is that in advancing Sadlington's candidacy, Harsnett the Protestant rebel and surplice-refuser was opposing the whole Cambridge Calvinist establishment. For Bentley was a party candidate and his list of referees reads like an ad hoc committee of the Calvinist leadership. A schoolmastership,

---

[1]For a copy of the fellows' letter see BL MS. Add. 5860, fol. 153v. It is published in Morant, *Colchester* 1:176, Note C, and *European Magazine* 35 (1799): 224. For Harsnett's election, see Morant 1:171.

[2]*Biographia Britannica* 4:2543, Note C. Also printed with Harsnett's other letters to the bailiffs in Goodwin, *Catalogue*, vi–viii. I have not traced the originals.

[3]Morant, *Colchester* 1:176.

after all, was an important post. What was taught in the school largely determined what was later thought in the minds of townspeople, and the contest over the Colchester schoolmastership foreshadows the great Cambridge debates of the 1590s that defined and divided Calvinist and anti-Calvinist in the Church of England.

In 1581 Chaderton had opposed Peter Baro, the anti-Calvinist Lady Margaret Professor, and was to do so again in 1595. Goad opposed Baro in 1596 and Baro's pupil Barrett in 1595. In 1599 he opposed John Overall. In 1596 Harsnett joined with Lancelot Andrewes and Overall in their support of Baro in his last clash with the university Calvinists, which ended with his retirement from Cambridge.[1] The Calvinists won the Colchester skirmish, too, although one notices that they brought out their biggest guns for the engagement. The bailiffs appointed Bentley. It seems that Harsnett's change of heart in 1588 was a change of theological principle and of churchmanship.

With his return to Cambridge, Harsnett's career again becomes obscure, although he began to advance academically, serving in 1592 as junior proctor with Thomas Grimston, ". . . which office," says Anthony à Wood (on what evidence we do not know), "he went through with great Credit to himself." He was junior treasurer of Pembroke, 1590, and senior treasurer, 1591.[2] In 1594 he emerged publicly as a leader among the anti-Calvinists when he preached a famous sermon at Paul's Cross in London, "Tuchynge Universall Grace."

This sermon, which exists in three manuscripts and a text printed in 1656, is usually dated 27 October 1584 by the date given in the printed text; but this date can hardly be right. Harsnett was only twenty-three years old in 1584; there was no theological context for so powerful an attack on the doctrine of predestination, and that particular day was a Wednesday, when there would have been no call for a sermon at Paul's Cross. The simplest explanation of the erroneous date is that the printer of 1656 or his manuscript copy misrepresented a digit in the Queen's regnal year, producing "26" instead of "36," and so 1584 instead of 1594. In 1594 the doctrinal battles were being joined in earnest; Harsnett had the maturity of person and style to write and deliver such a sermon, and 27 October was a Sunday. It is also inconceivable that the man who was before the archbishop and the High Commission for not wearing the surplice in 1586 at twenty-four, had eighteen months ear-

<hr>

[1]On these theological quarrels see Porter, *Reformation and Reaction,* 344–63, 378–90. For Harsnett's role, see Strype, *Whitgift* 2:343.

[2]Anthony à Wood, *Athenae Oxonienses,* ed. Philip Bliss, 2 vols. (London, 1813–20), 2:874–75; Pembroke College, MS. C.θ, fol. 3.

lier, and at most a deacon, delivered the most trenchant denuncia-
tion of Calvinist doctrine so far publicly heard under Elizabeth.
Precocity has its limits. The more likely date for the sermon is
therefore 27 October 1594.[1]

H. C. Porter, in his *Reformation and Reaction in Tudor Cambridge* gives an excellent account of the personalities and
principles—theological, intellectual, and pastoral—engaged in the
Cambridge debates that were the context of Harsnett's sermon.
Suffice it here to say that Harsnett speaks in agreement with
Hooker, Baro, Andrewes, and Overall in finding a place for free
will by observing a distinction in the will of God between his absolute and his conditional will:

> [God's] absolute will saith, lett there bee light and there was light, lett
> there bee a firmament and there was soe. This will cannott be resisted,
> for it speaketh but the word and the thinge is done. But God useth not
> this will in the matter of our salvacon, els should wee bee saved as the
> heavens are made: but in the case of our salvacon God useth his condi-
> tional will: And he hath sett us three Condicons accordinge to our
> three estates, which if wee breake wee justly forfeit our estate. The
> first condicon was in Paradize, eate not and thou shalt live, and that
> wee would not keepe: The second was under the Lawe, doe this and
> thow shalt live; and that wee could not keepe. The third under Christ,
> beleive and thou shalt live: and that wee may all keepe, and if wee
> keepe it not, wee forfeite our estate in Christ, and are willfully guilty
> of our damnacon, the reason is sweete out of St. Augustine: *qui creat
> te sine te, non salvat te sine te,* but seeke and thou shalt find, aske and
> thou shalt receive, knocke and it shalbee opened unto you. (fol. 126v)

The delivery of this theology from such a pulpit at that time will
not have been accidental; Harsnett and his friends must have
intended it as a public attack on what they judged to be the anti-
intellectualism and obscurantism of the Calvinist position, which
denied to the will and the reason any effective role in human salvation. What a modern reader notices most is the exuberant power of
the language; see Harsnett, for instance, as he turns back upon his
opponents their own punctiliousness towards the transcendent
glory of God:

[1]The MSS are BL MS. Royal 17C xxv; Cambridge University Library, MS. Ff.5.25,
fols. 116–30; Bodleian Library, MS. Rawlinson D 1349, fols. 156ff. The printed text is in
Dr. Richard Stuart, *Three Sermons* (London, 1656), 121–65: "A / Sermon / preached at S.
Paul's Cross in / London, the 27. day of *October,* Anno Reginae Elizabethae 26, by /
*Samuel Harsnet* then Fellow of *Pembroke-Hall* in *Cambridge,* but / afterwards Lord
Arch-bishop of *Yorke*." The text quoted here is based upon the Cambridge MS. On the
Paul's Cross Sermons, see Millar Maclure, *The Paul's Cross Sermons, 1543–1642*
(Toronto: University of Toronto Press, 1958). As Maclure says (11), the preachers were
often young men up from the universities to make their mark; nonetheless, Harsnett
seems excessively youthful in 1584.

Nowe concerninge Godes glory which to us all is more deare then our life, this opinion hath told a very inglorious and shamefull tale: For it saith that Allmighty God would have many soules to goe to hell, and that they may come thither hee must have them to synne, that soe hee might have just occasion to condemne them. Allmighty Godes glory ariseth of his justice and revenginge of synne, and for that it tells us a very unpleasant tale as I have sayd; For who taketh pleasure to heare a Prince say after this fashion, I will begett mee a sonne that I may kill him, & I will have him to get mee a name, and that I may have some colour to kill him, I will begett him without both his feete, and when he is growne, I will commaund him upon paine of death to walke, and when he breaketh my commaund, I will put him to death. (fols. 122–22v)

Only a very bold, independent mind would have carried an attack on Calvinism in London in 1594 as far as to represent the implications of the doctrine of predestination by a savage parody of the Incarnation.

A temperamental skepticism toward the grounds of human presumption underlies Harsnett's attack on Calvinism. His mind is strong, not subtle; what he sees as absurdity irritates him. It offends his common sense. Yet there is another strain in the sermon, different from his skepticism and satire. As is so often the case with satirists, Harsnett's passion issues from a conviction of the mystery of things and the fallibility of human nature. He makes a virtue of the intellectual simplicity that will not juggle with texts, and when he comes to speak of the mysteries of the divine will, "God is love" is all he really has to say. His one certainty in the controversy is that in a universe filled with grace, mankind is unworthy: "Noe odds in the grace, but in the men," he says (fol. 128v), a phrase that has the ring of a motto. His prose is equal to its implications:

Wee are by nature poore miserable Cripples and have neither hands to lifte up, nor feete to goe, nor joints to move, unto our gracious God. Our Saviour Christ passinge by hath fastned his eyes upon us, and saith unto us, Come unto mee all you that are halt and blind and lame, I will receave you to everlastinge rest: And if he give us nether hand to lift up, foote to goe, nor joynte to move unto him, alasse poore miserable Creatures that we are, what ment our Saviour to say soe unto us? (fols. 127v–28)

This passage, not unique in the sermon, reveals an emotional strain that will surprise those who only know Harsnett in the *Declaration*. Personal records of Elizabethan lives are rare, but at moments in this sermon one hears the tones of an individual voice, and it is an attractive one:

> I thinke on Peter, I consider the Theefe, I behold Zacheas, I looke up on Marye saith *Gregory:* and what doe I see? *An Apostata,* a Theefe, an usurer, an harlott, and these are Godes favorites, and such darlings unto him that some of them must needes suppe with him att his installment in Paradise. (fol. 124)

Preaching on these doctrines was rash, and in 1596 Lancelot Andrewes boasted that in sixteen years of priesthood he had never disputed publicly or privately upon points of free will and predestination: "I have followed Augustine's advice: mysteries I cannot open I have wondered at shut."[1] Years later, accused by some Norwich Puritans of popery, Harsnett told the Lords "he thought it might be long of his disputations and his sermon at Paules Crosse of Predestination negativé, unadvisedly preached by him, for which he was checkt by the Lord Archbishopp Whitguifte, and commanded to preach no more of it, and he never did; though nowe Doctor Abbotts late Bishop of Sarum hath since declared in print that which he then preached, to be no popery."[2] Whitgift must have been surprised to see the former surplice rebel before him again as a mature college dignitary accused of popery.

This time Harsnett's career was not affected. By now his circle of friends and his reputation were growing. On 4 December 1595 he writes from Pembroke Hall with jocular familiarity to Mr. Francis Bacon as his patron, to thank him for an attempt to do a favor for a friend and pupil called Buckenham, also a fellow of Pembroke:

> Righte Worshippfull my dutie in all humble wise remembered:

> Your Worship hathe deserved of one Mr. Buckname a gentleman, that knowes neither howe to thanke you, nor howe to holde his peace. For thoughe his happe was so harde as that he fayled of his suyte, your Brother Syr Nicholas being devote to Faren his belles, yeat he accounted him selfe as highlie bounden unto you, as if he had by your favour ben invested Highe Priest. When I will him thanke you, he sweares he dares not; And when I aske him whye, he saies that verilie you are more then a man: and if you wear a god yeat might you be thanked, and he aunsweres: *Maius quiddam, debetur vis.* And that your Worship may see howe his greate deale of modestie does verye

---

[1]"Judgement of the Lambeth Articles," *Works,* edited by J. P. Wilson and James Bliss, 11 vols. (Oxford, 1841–54), 6:290).

[2]Bodleian MS. Tanner 114, fol. 20.

well beseeme his little witte, he willethe me to tell you that he hath sent you to London a baskett full of pearmaynes; with his owne Suppose that if everie apple were Jupiter his apple, and had εχετο καλλιστος[1] written uppon it, and he the Umpier, Your Worship sholde have them all before eny gentlemen livinge in the worlde; And this is I see your Worship his fortune, to be admired of all, and ταλ.[2] to the rest. I may end this wittie dialogue when I will with your good leave, consistinge of *inquam, inquit,* and a baskett of apples. I singe still one songe: Dii si qua est ca'lis pietas quae taleis curat, persolvant grates dignas.[3]

The letter is addressed to Bacon as "my singuler good Patron," and fulsome though it is, suggests a degree of friendship as well as of dependence. Harsnett, whom we have so far seen in the roles of rebel, schoolmaster, and sardonic and contemplative preacher, here appears as an academic humanist, man of the world, and friend and flatterer of the important. The contrast with the world of his origins is immense, the repertoire of playable roles impressive.[4]

The next year, 1596, Harsnett joined Andrewes and Overall in refusing to condemn Peter Baro's opinion of the Lambeth Articles.[5] Then, on 9 May 1597 Bancroft became bishop of London and on 14 June Harsnett was instituted to the vicarage of Chigwell, Essex, the first of a series of preferments. On 5 August 1598 he became a prebendary of St. Paul's when he received the prebend of Mapesbury. On 11 October 1599 he became rector of St. Margaret's, Fish Street, London, and this series of preferments ended with his collation to the archdeaconry of Essex on 17 January 1602/3.[6] All these livings, except Chigwell, were directly in

---

[1]"Let the best man have it," an adaptation of the words on the golden apple thrown by Discord among the guests at the wedding of Peleus and Thetis, "Let the fairest have it."

[2]Harsnett's abbreviation of και τα λοιπα, "and the rest," equivalent to "et cetera."

[3]Harsnett's adaptation of *Aeneid* 2.536–7: "If there is in heaven any justice to care for such men, may the gods pay fitting thanks." The autograph of this letter is at Lambeth Palace, MS. 660, fol. 153. There is a copy in BL MS. Sloane 4122 (an eighteenth-century copy of Anthony Bacon's letterbook, in a poor hand), fol. 87v.

[4]Earlier in the same year, on 10 March, at home with his family in Colchester, he wrote out his mother's will, presumably to her dictation. Although she describes herself as "of good and perfit memorie (thankes be unto Almightie God)," it was probably a deathbed will, for the copy is marked by water smears, as if someone had wept over it. She asks to be buried as near to her father as possible, and appoints her sons Isaac and Samuel executors (Essex Record Office, D/ACW 3/80).

[5]Strype, *Whitgift* 3:340–42.

[6]During this first period of preferment, Harsnett married. His wife was a widow, Thomasine Kemp, née Waldgrave, daughter of William Waldgrave of Hitcham, Suffolk, and his wife, Elizabeth, daughter of Richard Poley of Boxsted (W. C. Metcalfe, ed., *Visitations of Norfolk* [London, 1875], 1:121). Her first husband was William Kemp, third son of Robert Kemp of Gissing, Norfolk (Metcalfe, *Visitations* 1:176), who died c. 1594 (C. Harold Ridge, ed., *Prerogative Court of Canterbury, Administrations, 1581–1595*

Bancroft's gift as bishop of London. Chigwell was in the gift of its rector. In the fifteenth century the rectory had been appropriated to the office of confessor and penitentiary of St. Paul's, which was held with the prebend of St. Pancras. In Harsnett's time the prebendary of St. Pancras was Lancelot Andrewes, who was also master of Pembroke. He, therefore, nominated Harsnett, probably at Bancroft's prompting.[1]

The friendship between Bancroft and Harsnett was evidently not new, but there is no evidence of its origin. In the little world of ecclesiastical and academic society the two men could have met through some intermediary. Harsnett's first patron, Bridgewater, who was chancellor and vicar-general of Ely when Bancroft was a commissioner for the diocese, or Francis Bacon, with whom Bancroft had dealings, could have made the introduction. The two men could also have met through Bancroft's investigation of the Marprelate case, which had Cambridge connections, or through his enquiries into the classis movement. There was a classis at Dedham, outside Colchester. As a Puritan schoolmaster in Colchester, Harsnett would have had knowledge of the comings and goings of the "preciser sort." However it began, the friendship was close, and when Bancroft made his will, he appointed Harsnett executor.[2]

[London: British Record Society, 1954], 91). When Harsnett wrote to Attorney-General Coke at the time of the Hayward affair (See Appendix C, "Harsnett as Examiner for the Press"), 20 July 1600, his wife was in childbed. She gave birth to a girl, also named Thomasine. The child died the same year, and on 3 February 1600/01, the mother died (Benham, "Pedigree of Harsnett," 109). Both were buried in Chigwell church.

[1]For these preferments see George Hennessy, *Novum repertorium ecclesiasticum parochiale Londinense* (London, 1898), 36, 276; Richard Newcourt, *Repertorium ecclesiasticum parochiale Londinense,* 2 vols. (London, 1778), 1:73, 173, 2:143. Bancroft's register provides details of patrons and also credits Harsnett with a B.D. Two copies of his disputations survive, in the Harsnett Library at Colchester, and in BL MS. Harleian 3142, fol. 54. His theses were "Nemo necessario damnatur" and "Certitudo uniuscuiusque salutis non est certitudo fidei." Harsnett's prebend of Mapesbury was in the parish of Willesden. The area remained rural until the end of the nineteenth century but is now built over, and only a Mapesbury Road preserves the name of the prebend.

[2]Jeremy Collier, *An Ecclesiastical History of Great Britain, Chiefly of England,* 9 vols. (London, 1840), 7:190ff., followed by P. M. Dawley, *John Whitgift and the Reformation* (London: A. & C. Black, 1955), 214, says that Harsnett was a chaplain to Whitgift. There seems to be no basis for this. Bancroft's will is *PCC,* 96 Wingfield.

# 3

# Bancroft, Harsnett,
# and the Campaign against Exorcism

Throughout the reign of Elizabeth I, the reformed Church of England found itself engaged in a war of words and sometimes of deeds on two fronts at once, against Protestants eager for further reformation and against Catholics hoping for an end to the schism with Rome. Compromise with either side was difficult, if not impossible, because the reformed church was a nationalized institution with the monarch as its head; and even though the royal headship did not extend to matters of faith and doctrine, both the more extreme Protestants and the Catholics made claims to authority in church government as well as in doctrine that Elizabeth I and her council could not tolerate. They took for granted the incompatibility of such claims with a peaceful, stable social order under the Crown. Bishop Bancroft's campaign against exorcists, which might strike modern students as a peculiar, even eccentric use of episcopal time, was the first major counterattack of his episcopate against just such an assertion of authority; and he and Harsnett are unusual among Anglicans because their campaign engaged both enemies at once.

The usual pattern for Church of England controversialists under attack by Catholics was to reply from a fundamentally Calvinist position but to reply from a more or less Catholic one if attacked by Protestants. Richard Field's *Of the Church* (1605) exemplifies the first tactic, Hooker's *Laws of Ecclesiastical Polity* the second. Hooker, in controversy with extreme Protestants, defines the Church as a supernatural society, a visible, law-making body that offers to its faithful the means of salvation in the sacraments; whereas Field, arguing with Catholics, defines the Church as an invisible body comprising God's elect, and "known only to them that are spiritual."[1]

[1] See Richard Hooker, *The Folger Library Edition of the Works of Richard Hooker*, gen. ed. W. Speed Hill, 4 vols. (Cambridge: Belknap Press of Harvard University Press, 1977–82), 1:130–31, 194ff., 235ff.; Richard Field, *Of the Church, Five Books. Vol. I: Containing the First Three Books* (Cambridge, 1847), 31–32:

Hooker, however, is soon in a quandary because although his church is a law-making body, he cannot grant it authority in faith and morals because to do so would imply acceptance of the full Catholic position. Hooker's church, therefore, only legislates matters of ceremony and order that, although important for all kinds of civil, social, moral, and aesthetic reasons, are in the long run *adiaphora,* "things indifferent," and not very important at all. Moreover, by the church as a law-making body he actually means the local church, or local churches in communication with each other, like nations. The Church as transmitter, definer, and interpreter of dogma means for Hooker local churches in continuity with the church of the apostles and early fathers, a position that neatly evades the problem of authority. For who is to define doctrine among these churches and keep them orthodox? Hooker's church does not claim that kind of defining authority.[1]

Field fares no better with the problem of authority:

The Church is the multitude and number of those whom Almighty God severeth from the rest of the world by the work of his grace, and calleth to the participation of eternal happiness, by the knowledge of such supernatural verities as concerning their everlasting good he hath revealed in Christ, and such other precious and happy means as he hath appointed to further and set forward the work of their salvation.[2]

This church of the elect, visible only to the spiritual, has only one source of authority for its certainties, the revealed word of God in Holy Scripture; membership in this church (of which the member himself might be ignorant) is an effect, not a cause of salvation. In Field's scheme, the visible church militant is a kind of social club

---

Though it be visible in respect of the profession of supernatural verities revealed in Christ, use of holy sacraments, order of ministry, and due obedience yielded thereunto, and they discernible that do communicate therein; yet in respect of those most precious effects, and happy benefits of saving grace, wherein only the elect do communicate, it is invisible; and they that in so happy, gracious and desirable things have communion among themselves, are not discernible from others to whom this fellowship is denied, but are known only to God. . . . The persons, then, of them of whom the Church consisteth are visible; their profession known even to the profane and wicked of the world, and in this sort the Church cannot be invisible, neither did any of our men teach that it is or may be. . . . *Notwithstanding, because the truth and excellence of the faith and profession of Christians, is not discerned by the light of nature, but by faith alone; the excellency of this society of Christians above other profane companies in the world, and their happiness that are of it, is invisible, hidden and unknown to natural men, and is known only to them that are spiritual.* (My italics)

[1]For example: "The Catholike Church is in like sort devided into a number of distinct societies, every of which is termed a Church within it selfe" (*Works* 1:205). The principle that the jurisdiction of a church, so defined, extends only to ceremonies and order, and not to the substance of the faith, is basic to Hooker's whole enterprise.

[2]*Of the Church,* 25.

for the saved, where they get to know each other and "make confession unto salvation" (32). As dean of Gloucester Cathedral, Field had every reason to preserve the idea of the Church among his people; but if his congregation had told him one morning that they were going home to read their Bibles and speak as the spirit moved them, there is little in his own book that would have dissuaded them.

Field and Hooker, of course, are writing controversy. It is not enough for either of them to assert the orthodoxy, practicality, or attractiveness of his position; he must assert its authority, too. So Field takes his heavy weaponry from Geneva, Hooker from the fathers and the scholastics. In this way each draws upon a source of authoritative statement he cannot fully acknowledge, Field the inspired, prophetic reading of Scripture, Hooker the visible, teaching Church of the apostles and the sacraments: on the one side Protestant prophecy, on the other the Catholic miracle. This peculiarly Anglican dilemma also leads to a peculiarly Anglican doctrine, the renunciation of authority: God has revealed his will once and for all in the Scriptures and the ministry of Jesus:

> His surceasing to speake to the world since the publishing of the Gospell of Jesus Christ, and the deliverie of the same in writing, is unto us a manifest token that the way of salvation is now sufficiently opened, and that wee neede no other meanes for our full instruction, then God hath alreadye furnished us withall.[1]

That is to say, there are no more miracles and no more prophecies because there is no more need of them. If someone claims to work miracles, he must be a fraud because that which cannot happen does not happen; and if someone claims to be a prophet, he must either be a lunatic or a fanatic. Doctrine, therefore, does not develop: the work of revelation is finished. Everything needful is already there, in the early church, and all the conscientious Christian has to do is find it. The Church of England, then, has a past but, strictly speaking, it seems not to have a future. Its peace is the peace of the museum, and any drama will be provided by misguided Catholicizing or Protestantizing movements.[2]

[1]Hooker, *Works* 1:127–28.

[2]The difficulty persists in the Anglican churches. Evelyn Waugh expressed it pungently in a letter to his friend John Betjeman, a keen Anglo-Catholic. See *The Letters of Evelyn Waugh*, ed. Mark Amory (New Haven and New York: Ticknor and Fields, 1980), 242. The problem of authority in the Church of England led some of the Jacobean and Caroline clergy towards a kind of Gallicanism or Cisalpinism. Lancelot Andrewes' reply to Cardinal Perron (*Works* 11:13–36), suggests that his mind was moving in that direction and that reunion with Rome was a negotiable possibility for him.

Some recent writers on Elizabethan possession and exorcism have commented upon the Anglican disbelief in miracles and prophecies,[1] but have not noticed the very interesting abdication of doctrinal authority that accompanies it. Philip Hughes makes the striking observation that the reformed Church of England was a scholar's church:

> Nowhere is the claim made, by any of these reformers, that this new knowledge of the truth comes from some new divine revelation, nor that any of the pioneers is inspired as were the prophets of the Old Testament or the evangelists of the New. It is really in the name of honest scholarship that the missionaries stand forth, with no other credentials than the books they have read and their *apparatus criticus*.[2]

He quotes an equally striking passage from Usher's study of Bancroft's episcopate:

> This scholarship is anti-religious at bottom: it curtails the specifically religious spirit, substituting the critical. The authority of religion as a way of life embodied in the Church, is at an end. No more *experiences,* no more *miracles,* no more *daily mystery* in the mass, no cults, nothing, in a word, that transcends the *spirit of the age.*[3]

All this makes it sound to a modern student like a sane, level-headed enterprise. Yet as Dickens's Mr. Sleary says, "People mutht be amuthed, Thquire, thomehow," and as Keith Thomas has drily observed "the Anglican Church's confessed impotence in this [miracle-working] sphere was a frequent source of irritation to its defenders."[4] D. P. Walker, though, is probably truer to the peculiar tone of the institution Bancroft and Harsnett were defending as well as defining in their attack on miracle-workers when he says that the Anglican doctrine of the cessation of miracles "makes it possible for a pious Christian to live in a world entirely devoid of any supernatural occurrences."[5]

When Bancroft became bishop in 1597, there was no longer a serious Catholic threat to English security, although this was not obvious at the time. The Jesuit missionaries' assertion of Rome's

---

[1]See especially Walker, *Unclean Spirits,* 66–73, and Thomas, *Religion and the Decline of Magic,* 479; also Peter Milward, "Shakespeare and Elizabethan Exorcism," in his *Shakespeare's Other Dimension,* Renaissance Monographs, No. 15 (Tokyo: The Renaissance Institute, Sophia University, 1987), 46–57.

[2]*The Reformation in England,* 3 vols. (New York: Macmillan Co., 1954), 3:69.

[3]*Reconstruction* 1:85–86, quoted by Hughes, *Reformation in England* 3:69.

[4]*Religion and the Decline of Magic,* 492.

[5]*Unclean Spirits,* 73.

claim on Catholic loyalties had failed to weaken the stronger claims of English nationalism. The success of their mission was more modest and no threat at all to the safety of England: at terrible risk to themselves, the missionaries brought the sacraments to individual Catholics, and—most surprisingly—by introducing their countrymen to the meditative and personal devotion of the Counter-Reformation they contributed greatly to the religious and cultural life of the reformed Church of England.[1]Puritanism, too, seemed to be weakened. Its chief defenders at court had mostly died, and the able administration of Archbishop Whitgift, backed up by Bancroft's police work and Hooker's writing, had begun to give the Church of England a recognizable identity of its own. Yet a Puritan threat was developing in the Midlands that Bancroft (a specialist, it must be remembered, in Puritan tactics) took very seriously.

The rallying point for the new Puritan enthusiasm was provided by the activities of John Darrell, a Nottinghamshire man, born probably at Mansfield about 1562, who matriculated at Queen's College, Cambridge, in 1575 as a sizar, and proceeded B.A. in 1579. After studying law for a while in London, he returned to Nottinghamshire, first to Mansfield, then to Bulwell, where he had a farm. In both places he preached, presumably as a free lance, since Harsnett says he was "no minister."[2] By 1596 he was settled at Ashby-de-la-Zouche, where he attended Puritan meetings and became friendly with Arthur Hildersham, an organizer of the Millenary Petition of 1604. In the 1580s he had become interested in the detection and dispossession of devils, and by 1598 these activities had brought him a measure of fame as well as election to a lectureship in St. Mary's Church, Nottingham, his first regular ministerial job.[3]

[1]St. Robert Southwell's *St. Peter's Complaint* and *Marie Magdalen's Funeral Tears*, first published in 1595 and 1591, went through ten and seven editions, respectively, before 1616. Robert Persons's *A Christian Directory*, plagiarized and adapted for Protestant use by an Anglican clergyman, Edmund Bunny, was immensely popular before 1640. The standard work on the influence of Catholic devotional literature on English poetry is Louis L. Martz, *Poetry of Meditation* (New Haven: Yale University Press, 1954, rev. ed. 1962); see also Helen C. White, *Tudor Books of Private Devotion* (Madison: University of Wisconsin Press, 1951).

[2]*DFP*, sig. B1. Several modern writers call him a clergyman, but he seems not to have been ordained. In *A Breife Narration*, sig. B1, he is called "a Minister of Gods worde," and I[ohn] D[enison], the editor of Jesse Bee's *The Most Wonderfull and True Storie*, calls him "a faithfull Preacher of the Gospel." He was apparently a self-appointed preacher.

[3]For modern accounts of Darrell, see *DNB*; R. A. Marchant, *The Puritans and the Church Courts in the Diocese of York, 1560–1642* (London: Longmans, 1960), 300–301; C. H. Rickert, *The Case of John Darrell, Minister and Exorcist* (Gainsville: University of Florida Press, 1962), which contains many inaccuracies; Thomas, *Religion and the Decline of Magic*, 483–85, and Walker, *Unclean Spirits*, 52–73.

Darrell's exorcising career began in 1586 when, aged about twenty-three or twenty-four, he treated a girl of sixteen, Katherine Wright, of Derbyshire. He was not entirely successful, for her fits continued. Nonetheless, he wrote up a narrative of the case and gave a copy to Lady Bowes, a prominent local supporter of the Puritans.[1] This tract, along with his own willingness to talk about his gifts, brought him some attention although, as he later said, "Some thought that I did glorie somewhat too much in the action of casting forth Divels" (*DFP*, sig. B1v). In March 1596 his exorcising career began again when he became involved in the case of Thomas Darling, the thirteen-year old Boy of Burton, as he came to be called.

Like all these cases, this one is fraught with grotesque and pathetic comedy. According to the boy, his possession began when a local woman, Alse (Alice) Goodridge, commanded her familiar spirit to enter him. The familiar's name was Minnie. Here is Harsnett's account:

> Hee meeting *Alice Goodridge* in a Coppice, did let an escape (as the booke termeth it,) which shee taking to bee done in her contempt, used these words: *Gip with a mischiefe, and fart with a bell, I will goe to Heaven, and thou shalt goe to Hell.* And thereupon her *Minnie* entred into him. (*DFP*, sig. G1)[2]

As a result old Alice was convicted of witchcraft, and died in prison.

The book that Harsnett mentions is a narrative of Darling's fits written by a workingman called Jesse Bee, "a private Christian and man of trade."[3] One of the more bizarre elements in this strange case is this man's association with the boy during most of his illness; his amateur interest in witchcraft and devils can have done neither him nor the boy much good. There is also religious fanaticism in the air. This child of thirteen believes that he has the spirit

[1] Marchant, *Puritans and the Church Courts,* 151.

[2] It was agreed that possession could only occur by divine permission, but the bases of that permission were controversial. King James I, *Daemonologie* (Edinburgh, 1597), sigs. I3v–I4, asserts that the devil possesses two sorts of people, "Such as being guiltie of greevous offences, God punishes by that horrible kinde of scourdge, or else being persones of the beste nature . . . GOD permittes them to be troubled in that sort for the tryall of their patience, and wakening up of their zeale." That covers everyone. Harsnett, making mocking reference to the writing of the Jesuit expert Peter Thyraeus, says that all agree that mortal sin can cause possession; the hard question is whether venial sin will cause it. After giving examples he concludes that Darling's possession was caused by a venial sin, although "*Thomas Darlinges* veniall sin exceeded the rest" (DFP, sig. G1).

[3] Jesse Bee, *The Most Wonderfull and True Storie of a Certain Witch named Alse Gooderige of Stapen Hill . . .* (London, 1597), sig. A2v.

of God within him. He lives in daily expectation of death (as he tells the "good Christians" he most enjoys talking with), and longs to be with Christ; nonetheless, when he grows up, he would like to be a preacher and "thunder out the threatenings of Gods word against sinne and all abhominations, where with these days doo abound" (A3v). The well-known Puritan minister Arthur Hildersham was the boy's hero, even though he had failed to cure him by his prayers.[1] "Oh Maister *Hildersham*," he called out on one occasion, "I thought he would have torne me in peeces, preach judgement against all sinners, flames of fire, flames of fire: See Maister *Hildersham,* preach and teach, Oh fast and pray night and day" (sig. E1v). Rhyming speech was a feature of Darling's performance.

Having heard of the case, Darrell visited the boy, diagnosed devils, and advised fasting and prayer as the best treatment. Following this advice, the boy's family and friends cured him the next day in a scene that comes straight from the world of folk drama and the mumming plays. *"Brother Glossop,"* said one little devil (always speaking through the boy, of course), *"wee cannot prevaile, his faith is so strong, and they fast and pray, and a preacher prayeth as fast as they."* Another, more powerful demon cried out, *"Radulphus, Belzebub can doe no good, his head is stricken off with a word"* (*DFP,* sig. G4v).

After this success at Burton, Darrell was called to Lancashire, where he and another minister, George More, dispossessed seven children in the family of a Lancashire gentleman called Starkey. This time the possession was supposed to have happened because a "cunning man" called Edward Hartley, who had been hired to cure the children, "breathed *wicked spirites into them,* (as it was supposed) *by kissing them"* (*DFP,* sig. F3). Hartley had already been hanged as a witch when Darrell and More appeared. They were successful in treating the children, although one of the girls, Jane Ashton, relapsed and fell into the hands of Catholic exorcists.[2]

Cases like this were common in Tudor England, and none of them by itself would have engaged Bishop Bancroft's attention. The Nottingham case of William Somers, however, was different.[3]

[1]Walker, *Unclean Spirits,* 52–56, has a good account of this case.

[2]*DFP,* sig. B1v; *The Triall of Maist. Dorrell,* sig. A8v: *"Jane Ashton . . .* is repossessed, & by Popish Priestes made a spectacle to Papistes."

[3]The following brief account of Somers's case is based on Harsnett's *Discovery* and Darrell's *A Briefe Narration of the Possession, Dispossession, and, Repossession of William Somers* (1598).

In October 1597 in Nottingham, a musician's apprentice called William Somers began to be "strangely tormented," and on 5 November Darrell, now famous in the district, was called in to examine him. He diagnosed possession, and on 7 November the dispossession began with a general fast. Somers was dispossessed by the prayers of Darrell and 150 people. This did not end matters. The boy was soon possessed again and, in fact, "stucke in [Darrell's] fingers almost five monethes" (*DFP,* sig. B2). The result was an intensity of preaching, fasting, and praying that had the town in an uproar. The pro-Darrell party included the vicar, Aldridge, and with his approval Darrell became lecturer in the parish. This admitted him to the pulpit, from which he was able to attack skeptics and encourage supporters. He seems to have preached about nothing but devils, and he caused a state of near-panic in many townspeople with his explanations of the strange doings amongst them:

> The partes taking on both sides beganne to be more violent, and the town became to be extraordinarily devided, one rayling upon an other, at their meeting in the streets. . . . The pulpets also rang of nothing but Divels, and witches. (*DFP,* sig. B4v)

Somers soon began to name witches as the cause of his trouble, and according to Harsnett, Darrell began to say that he could discover all the witches in England—which, as D. P. Walker says, "opens up alarming prospects." In March 1598, Matthew Hutton, archbishop of York, sent an ecclesiastical commission of the northern province to inquire into Darrell's activities. It was not a success. The vicar and his friends were strong in Darrell's support. Somers retracted the confession of fraud that the skeptics had earlier persuaded him to make and said it was a slander against Darrell's godliness. Then Somers threw a fit that so frightened the commissioners that they found no fault with Darrell although, for the sake of quiet, they revoked his license to preach.

This did not satisfy the skeptics. Mr. Freeman, a justice of the peace and an alderman, had a kinswoman among the accused women. He had extracted a confession of fraud from Somers, who "therefore . . . forbare his fittes whilest he was present. But he was no sooner out of the dores almost, when [Somers] fell to his prankes" (*DFP,* sig. 2H1v). As Freeman left the room, the vicar's wife was heard to say, *"The Devill woulde not shew anything to them that did not believe."* There were other skeptics besides Freeman. George Richardson became suspicious of the knockings that were supposed to be the work of spirits. As he later told the High Commission:

*Again, to the tapping and rapping, I have heard the same, and did upon the hearing of it, imagine that it was the fillipping of one toe with an other upon the bed, and sometimes with his fingers as he found occasion, which I suspecting, did at my going to bed secretly practise it. And it fell out to be so agreeable with that which the boy did, as my wife being in bed with mee, was on the sodaine in greate feare, that* Somers *spirite had followed me* (*DFP*, sig. 2H4v).

In April the case came before the Nottingham assizes, where Alice Freeman was to be tried for witchcraft on the evidence of Somers's allegations. Once more, questioned by Sir Edmund Anderson (a great believer in witches), Somers confessed fraud and conspiracy between him and Darrell. Alice Freeman was acquitted. Anderson, appalled by the fraud and the disorders, wrote to Archbishop Whitgift, and so the case came to Bishop Bancroft's attention. On advice from Lord Chief Justice Popham, Darrell was summoned to Lambeth for examination by the Ecclesiastical Court of High Commission. Whitgift presided over the court, but Bancroft was the directing spirit of the prosecution. With his usual thoroughness, he found out witnesses. He sent Harsnett into Derbyshire to interview Katherine Wright and he installed Thomas Darling in Harsnett's vicarage under his tutelage. Somers and the people from Nottingham came up from Nottingham to give evidence before the High Commission. Bancroft's own copies of Bee's account of Darling and of George More's account of the Lancashire case survive in the Lambeth Palace Library.[1] Harsnett, as his chief assistant in the case or, as it became, campaign, provided himself with a working library on witchcraft and the demonic, most of which survives in the Harsnett Library at Colchester.[2] Between them Bancroft and Harsnett conducted the questioning ("our two English inquisiters," Darrell calls them), and they later saw to the publication of the court's view of the case.[3]

[1] On this volume, see H. N. Paul, *The Royal Play of Macbeth* (New York: Macmillan Co., 1950), 101.

[2] Harsnett owned two copies of Menghi, *Flagellum daemonum*, in the editions published at Venice in 1597 and 1599, as well as his *Fuga daemonum* (Venice, 1596); also Johann Nider, *Myrmecia bonorum, sive formicarius Joannis Nyder* (Douay, 1602); Valerio Polidoro, *Practica exorcistarum* (Venice, 1606); two copies of Jacob Sprenger and Heinrich Kramer, *Malleus maleficarum* (Frankfurt, 1582); Johann Tritheim, *Antipalus maleficiorum* (Mainz, 1605). There must have been more at one time. The text of his *Declaration* shows that he owned Petrus Thyraeus, *De daemoniacis* (Cologne, 1594), and Reginald Scot, *The Discoverie of Witchcraft* (London, 1584). The only works from the Darrell campaign in the library are John Deacon and John Walker's *Dialogicall Discourses of Spirits and Divels* (London, 1601) and *A Summarie Answere to al the Material Points in Any of Master Daral his Bookes* (London, 1601). There are no copies of Harsnett's own books.

[3] John Darrell, *A Detection of that Sinnful Shamful, Lying, and Ridiculous Discours of Samuel Harshnet* (1600), sigs. A1, A4.

Bancroft's object was to discredit and silence Darrell, and to do this he had to prove fraud. It also had to be Darrell's fraud. Fraud by Somers was not enough to silence Darrell, and this meant that the efforts of the Nottingham skeptics, useful though they were, were insufficient. Bancroft had to prove that Darrell had caused Somers to fake possession, that there had been conspiracy between them. Only then could he put Darrell out of business.

The case came to rest on Somers's claim that he had met Darrell at Ashby-de-la-Zouche. He said he had gone into an alehouse with some other boys and found Darrell there. "Playing the wag, and shrewd boy with my companions," he took no notice of Darrell. Darrell, however, waited, then engaged his attention, and told him about Katherine Wright and her tricks. If Somers is to be believed, Darrell frightened him, telling him how she "foamed at mouth, gnashed with her teeth, cried and scritched, catched & snatched at those stood by her." In Somers's version, Darrell even performed the motions, told him to practice them and, when he was perfect, to fall into apparent illness and ask for Darrell. The benefit to Somers in all this was that Darrell promised to arrange for his release from his master. Somers even claimed that Darrell had written his instructions down for him. Questioned on the point, he said that he had learned them by heart, and then torn the paper:

> Hee writ them in one of his bookes, called *Sententiae pueriles:* which booke, together with three others, one *Mary Holding,* then servant with *M. Gray* . . . kept from him . . . in lieu of eight pence, which he did owe unto her. (*DFP,* sig. M1v)

Whether this book was ever traced is not revealed.[1]

Such was Bancroft's case. Darrell denied having ever met Somers before he came to Nottingham, and he wrote seven pamphlets in self-vindication. As proof of fraud, the case is not convincing. It rests on the word of an unstable boy who had already been caught in lies. Nor did the court allow him to perform his fits, which would have been interesting, to say the least. One feature of them, it seems, was a lump the size of a mouse that was supposed to run about his body (*DFP,* sig. E4); unfortunately, the credulous witnesses from whom such testimony comes had been so frightened by Somers that their evidence is not reliable, and another witness claimed that the lump was nothing but Somers's hand. The case ended May 1599 with the court condemning Darrell, deposing him from the ministry, and committing him to prison for sentencing (*DFP,* sig. C1). In the event, neither he nor his companion

[1] *DFP,* sigs. L4ff.

More, "who tooke upon him to justifie the said *Darrell,* and had otherwise greatlie misbehaved himselfe" (*DFP,* sig. C1), was sentenced, and Darrell was out of prison two years later.[1]

Convincing or not, the case was as good as Bancroft and Harsnett could make it, and most people (if they can resist the temptation to invoke modern standards of legal procedure and tolerance) would agree that with a man like Darrell some kind of case had to be made. It was, and presumably is, impossible to prove to a believer that a case of possession is fraudulent, illusionary, or even natural. The vicar's wife's attitude to Freeman has already been quoted. Darrell made similar answers all the time. When Somers confessed fraud, Darrell "said to those that hearde me, that they might not in any sort believe me, because it was not William Somers, but the Devill that so saide. . . . So as I was at my wits end what I should doe" (*DFP,* sig. P1). If someone believes that discarnate spirits can possess people, and that the signs of possession are to be recognized from scriptural precedent and church tradition, no argument is going to prove the contrary. *Ad hominem* argument alone might work. Bancroft's episcopal power was one kind of *ad hominem* argument, Harsnett's ridicule another.

Harsnett wrote his *Discovery of the Fraudulent Practises of One John Darrel* after the case closed, and the book was entered in the Stationers' Register on 15 November 1599. It produces the evidence of many witnesses interspersed with Harsnett's and, presumably, Bancroft's interpretations of it. Harsnett argues that the possessions were fraudulent, and he attacks Darrell and all such "illuminate dotrels" for "making religion a pageant of Puppites" or a "pure play" for no other reason than "to crosse God his governors in the Church, who profess not this prettie feate" (*DFP,* sig. A3)—a particularly offensive way of attacking Puritans, who thought, as Stephen Greenblatt has pointed out, that theaters really were the devil's playhouses.[2] Harsnett also shows considerable sympathy for the people who were won over by Darrell's performances:

And to say the truth, those grounds presupposed to be true, (which M. *Darrell* had taught them,) vz. that whatsoever he did or spake in his fittes, it was not *Somers,* but the devill that did it and spake it: it may rather be marvayled, that they deposed no more, then blamed that they

---

[1]Walker, *Unclean Spirits,* 64.

[2]Stephen Greenblatt, *Shakespearean Negotiations* (Berkeley and Los Angeles: University of California Press, 1988), 110. Although Greenblatt does not mention it, the story that the conjurations of Dr. Faustus in Marlowe's play brought a real devil on to the stage was spread by Puritans. See John Bakeless, *The Tragical History of Christopher Marlowe,* 2 vols. (Cambridge: Harvard University Press, 1942), 1:298–300.

deposed so much. For who seeing a man lye, in his conceite, as senselesse as a blocke, would not admire the very shaking of his toe: especially being perswaded, that the Devill made the motion. But when he should see him leape and friske, move the calves of his legges, the flesh of his thighes, thrust out his belly, and make sondry strange motions with his jawes, eyes and tounge: it could not bee chosen, but it must seeme terrible. Adde hereunto the weakenes of mens nature, which is subject to be terrifyed with Devilles, and wicked spirites, especially when they suppose the saide spirites to be present, and in action before their eyes. (*DFP,* sigs. 2E1–1v)

There can be no doubt, either, that Harsnett and Bancroft were convinced that the possessions were fake, and that Darrell, as well as his patients, was guilty of fraud. Modern writers on the subject are reluctant to believe this of Darrell, yet pious fraud is very common, and its perpetrators are usually persistent in self-defense.

How many were persuaded by Harsnett's book and its version of the case is doubtful. The sophisticated were, however, among them William Shakespeare. For an audience in 1601, Feste's words in *Twelfth Night* as he puts on the black Geneva gown to minister to the allegedly possessed Malvolio, "I would I were the first that ever dissembled in such a gown" (4.2.5), can only have referred to Darrell.[1] Ben Jonson's references to fake possession in *Volpone* (5.12) and to the Darrell case in particular in *The Devil is an Ass* (5.8) show complete agreement with Harsnett, also that the affair stayed in people's minds. Yet Darrell put up a hard fight in print, bringing out seven surreptitiously published pamphlets. Bancroft brought in a pair of ministers to supplement Harsnett's book with weightier theological argument, but they failed to silence Darrell, who answered both their books and seemed to have the last word in the controversy.[2] Yet no matter how pertinaciously Darrell defended himself, his career as a preacher and dispossessor of devils was finished. It is hard to be very sympathetic with him. Alse

[1]Kenneth Muir, *Shakespeare's Sources* (London: Methuen, 1957), 70, thinks that Feste's word "bibble-babble" (4.2.97) indicates Shakespeare's familiarity with Harsnett's *Discovery,* but Shakespeare had already used the expression in *Henry V,* 4.1.71, probably written in the summer of 1599, after the case was over, but before the book had come out. He could have picked up the word from the court proceedings. This was not Shakespeare's first reference to exorcism; see *The Comedy of Errors,* 4.4.40–130, 5.1.237–46 for the exorcist Dr. Pinch. Peter Milward, *Shakespeare's Religious Background* (Bloomington: Indiana University Press, 1973), 52–53, thinks his name is a joking allusion to R. Phinch, who attacked Catholic exorcism in *The Knowledge and Appearance of the Church,* 1590.

[2]The two ministers, Deacon and Walker, began in 1601 with *Dialogicall Discourses.* Darrell replied with a *A Survey of Certaine Dialogical Discourses.* Deacon and Walker answered this in *A Summarie Answere.* Darrell had the last word in *The Replie of John Darrell to the Answer of John Deacon, and John Walker* (1602).

Goodridge died in prison condemned as a witch, and Darrell did his best to get Alice Freeman similarly convicted. Nor did he show much sympathy with Somers when the boy's condition showed itself to be a subtler sickness than demonic possession. "If Som[ers] did counterfeit, he is to be burnt as a blasphemer," he said.[1] When the boy exposed the frauds, Darrell said, *"Thou art a lying boy, and wert possessed, dispossessed, and art now repossessed with many Devilles: and art in a desperate case"* (DFP, sig. 2B1). Darrell's happiest moments came when Somers lay quiet, and he could expound upon the works of the devil without interruption (for example, DFP, sig. R1). And of course, he had the town of Nottingham in an uproar for six months.

He has lately found defenders in D. P. Walker and John L. Murphy. Walker finds the trial unjust because the court preferred the word of an unreliable boy over that of "a clergyman of unblemished character," and Murphy expresses a "sense of outrage" at the proceedings.[2] This is strange. From Bancroft's and Harsnett's point of view, Darrell was hardly a clergyman. Until he took to dispossessing devils, he was an ex-law student and small farmer whose hobby was prayer meetings. Walker's description of him begs all the questions and makes him sound like a Victorian vicar. Bancroft's assessment of him as a dangerous religious maniac was more realistic. Professor Murphy certainly knows that Elizabethan jurisprudence and medicine are not to be judged by contemporary American standards, and that by Elizabethan standards the Court of High Commission did not treat Darrell so very harshly. After all, the civil authorities hanged, drew, and quartered three of the Catholic exorcists, and the rest whom they captured they kept in prison seventeen years and then banished. Bancroft and Harsnett used, in accordance with the law of their times, the means they had to stop behavior they judged intolerable, and in doing so they were performing the function expected of them. Indignation about their methods obscures the more interesting question for the student of Harsnett's writings and their significance: Why did he and Bancroft take Darrell so seriously?

By the time Sir Edmund Anderson, the assize judge, wrote to Whitgift (which was how the whole ecclesiastical process began), Darrell had recently conducted dispossessions in three counties. He had succeeded with Thomas Darling, whom the famous Mr. Hildersham had failed to cure, and his handling of the Somers case had enabled him, in effect, to take control of the town of

[1] Darrell, *A Breife Narration* (1598), sig. B2v.

[2] Walker, *Unclean Spirits*, 65; Murphy, *Darkness and Devils*, 85.

Nottingham. His method of dispossession by prayer and fasting involved large numbers of people in extemporaneous prayer meetings indistinguishable from the "prophesyings" earlier prohibited by the Queen. Furthermore, although the Puritans joined with the Anglicans in declaring the age of miracles to have ceased, they believed passionately in the prophetic function of the ministry as proclaimers and witnesses of the power of the word of God in Scripture. Although it confused the theory of his cases, Darrell's claim to be able to control the preternatural (the devil) by invoking the supernatural (divine grace) through extempore prayer proved thrilling to his strongly Protestant followers.

Walker argues that the Puritans' disbelief in miracles "severely crippled the propaganda that could be made out of their dispossessions,"[1] but this is not borne out by their own statements. Darrell may not have been very interested in the human sufferer before him, but he was very interested indeed in the devil's testimony to the value of Puritan practices like prayer and fasting, preaching and testifying. He and More were delighted to find that the "stinted prayers" of The Book of Common Prayer were not nearly as effective as the extemporized prayers "as for the present occasion they conceived" (DFP, sig. F2). As More wrote:

> If the Church of Englande have this power to cast out devills, then the Church of Rome is a false Church, for there can be but one true Church, the principall marke whereof (as they say) is to worke miracles, and of them this is the greatest, namely to cast out Devills.[2]

Even Puritans who were more clear-headed on the subject of miracles believed that a diabolic possession could be "sanctified to the beholders, and the possessed himselfe" by a dispossessing ministry of prayer.[3] This was the kind of propaganda the Puritans wanted.

[1] Unclean Spirits, 68.

[2] More, A True Discourse, sig. A3, also quoted by Thomas, Religion, 484.

[3] The quoted phrase is from Hildersham's opinion, given in Jesse Bee's narrative of Thomas Darling, The Most Wonderfull and True Storie, sigs. D3v–D4:

> Howsoever the Papists boasted much of the power their priests had to cast out divells, and the simple everie where noted it as a great discredit to the Ministers of the Gospel, that they do want this power, yet did he professe there was no such gift in them, that thogh the Lord oft in these daies, by the praiers of the faithful casts out divils, yet could he not assure them to cure him [i.e. Darling]. To hold this faith of myracles to remaine still in the Church, is an opinion dangerous. That seeing to be possessed is but a temporall correction, & such as whereby both the glorie of God and the salvation of the partie may be furthered, it can not without sinne be absolutely prayed against: al which notwithstanding, that there is a good use of praier in such a case, and of fasting also, to procure that the judgement may be sanctified to the beholders, and the possessed himselfe; yea so obtain that he may be delivered also from it, if the Lord see it be best for his owne glorie.

It interested them more than miracle-propaganda, although Darrell and others were tempted by the latter; the author of *The Most Wonderfull and True Storie* calls the dispossession of Thomas Darling "a miraculous worke" (sig. F4).

It was no wonder, therefore, that Darrell's fame spread, and that well-known Puritan ministers took part in his ministry, among them Arthur Hildersham, John Brinsley the elder, Richard Bernard, John Ireton, and Robert Ervington.[1] To judge by his response, Bancroft thought that Darrell's movement was the most dangerous threat to the establishment since the classis movement of the eighties. So easy, successful, and dramatic a practice was bound to spread. It was popular and exciting, and the devil gave more effective testimony than a shopful of books—or a roomful of Puritans, for that matter. Harsnett saw what the future held had Darrell not been silenced:

> We should have had many other pretended signes of possession: one Devill would have beene mad at the name of the *Presbyter:* an other at the sight of a minister that will not subscribe: an other to have seene men sit or stand at the Communion. And that this conjecture may not be thought to be a vaine collection, you shall see how stinted (as they tearme them) and read prayers, are notably foyled. (*DFP*, sig. F2)

Despite Bancroft's energetic campaign, the movement showed signs of spreading in 1602 when a girl of fourteen, Mary Glover, had fits and accused a woman of bewitching her.[2] A dispossession by fasting and prayer took place at which no fewer than six ministers were present, a dramatic confirmation of Bancroft's fears of the practice as a rallying point for the Puritans. He therefore mobilized every weapon he had: the press, the medical profession, the resources of his and Archbishop Whitgift's ecclesiastical establishments, the Paul's Cross pulpit, the University of Cambridge, the Court of High Commission, and finally, the new King himself, James I.[3] For the Church of England, the upshot of the campaign

[1] Thomas, *Religion,* 483 and n. 3.

[2] Walker, *Unclean Spirits,* 79–80, gives some account of Mary Glover, based on *A True and Breife Report, of Mary Glovers Vexation* (1603), written by John Swan, one of the dispossessing ministers, in response to Harsnett. See also Paul, *The Royal Play,* 103–12. For this case Bancroft called in the College of Physicians, following French precedent in the affair of Martha Brossier. Of the four doctors who examined Mary, two diagnosed hysteria, and one of them, Edward Jordan, published a pamphlet, *A Briefe Discourse of a Disease Called the Suffocation of the Mother* (London, 1603), which Bancroft personally licensed for printing and which was exactly contemporary with Harsnett's *Declaration.*

[3] In addition to the publications by Harsnett, Deacon and Walker, and Jordan, one of Whitgift's chaplains, Abraham Hartwell, published a translation of the French physician Marescot's exposure of Marthe Brossier, *A True Discourse, upon the Matter of Martha*

was a change in church law. In the new canons and constitutions that Bancroft promulgated in 1604, canon 72 forbade any minister, unless licensed by his bishop, to take part in or conduct "prophesyings" (that is, meetings for prayer and fasting) under pain of suspension for the first offense, excommunication for the second, and deposition from the ministry for the third. Nor was any minister, under pretext of an alleged possession or obsession, to use prayer and fasting for the casting out of devils (unless similarly licensed by his bishop) under pain of censure as an impostor and deposition from his ministry.[1] The assumption behind the new canon was that no Anglican bishop would license a priest to cast out devils. To my knowledge, none ever has.

Skepticism towards prophecy and miracles thus became legally and institutionally a part of the Church of England, and Bancroft, Harsnett, and their associates deserve the credit for the humane consequences. They seldom receive it. G. L. Kittredge, for instance, in his influential study of witchcraft, insisted that Bancroft's campaign was "ecclesiastical, not humanitarian," its aim "not to save witches, but to crush exorcists,"[2] and he has been followed in this emphasis by other writers. He supports his opinion with evidence from the Mary Glover case, showing that although Bancroft dealt smartly with the ministers who treated her (apparently with some success), and although he was convinced that the girl was suffering from natural illness, he did nothing to protect the alleged witch when she was arraigned and convicted. Kittredge fails to notice, however, that the ministers were in Bancroft's jurisdiction; the witch was not. She was in the hands of the secular courts. Anderson, the judge, threw out the evidence for

---

*Brossier of Romorantin, Pretended to be Possessed by a Devill* (London, 1599). He dedicated it to Bancroft, saying in the epistle dedicatory (17 October 1599) that having been concerned in the Darrell investigation, he wished the proofs might be published, "so as every man thereby may see, what notable practises have been undertaken" (sig. A2v). Since Harsnett's book was entered in November, this was really a prepublication advertisement. The Paul's Cross sermon attacked the "judge, jurie, and witnesses" and argued for the "clearinge or acquittinge the Witch" accused in Mary Glover's case (Swan, *True and Breife Report,* sig. A4). Thomas, *Religion,* 484, briefly describes the university's activities. The vice-chancellor forbade the sale of Darrell's works, and dissenting views were silenced. At commencement, William Barlow, later bishop of Lincoln, maintained the thesis that possession was no longer possible. An incident probably related to all this activity was the sentencing in February 1603 of Thomas Darling of Merton College, Oxford, to have his ears cropped for libeling the vice-chancellor (John Chamberlain, *Letters,* ed. N. E. McClure, 2 vols. [Philadelphia: American Philosophical Society, 1939], 1:186–87). On Bancroft's approach to King James, see Paul, *The Royal Play,* 100.

[1]*Constitutiones sive Canones Ecclesiastici* (London, 1604), canon 72. The phrasing of the prohibition suggests that Bancroft was more concerned to stop the prophesying than the dispossessions that were its occasion.

[2]*Witchcraft in Old and New England* (New York: Athenaeum, 1957), 300.

hysteria, and there was nothing Bancroft could do about it. At a witch trial at the London sessions in 1599 Bancroft had smiled at some of the evidence, and he attempted to explain to the judge (Anderson again) the kinds of fraud he had recently investigated. Anderson rebuked him for smiling and lectured him on his evidence, quoting Scripture at him in proof of the truth of witchcraft. Even a bishop of Bancroft's authority could not cross a judge in his own court.[1] He could, however, influence public opinion, and he must have arranged for the Paul's Cross sermon attacking judge, jury, witnesses, and verdict in the trial of the accused witch, Elizabeth Jackson. Bancroft and Harsnett certainly had no belief in witches. The most famous passage of Harsnett's *Declaration*, the description of a witch in Chapter 21, is proof of that. Their Puritan opponents accused them of favoring atheists and even hinted that they might be attacked by the devil themselves.[2]

It required intellectual and moral courage for the bishop and his chaplain to publish and act upon their skepticism, and no attentive reader of Harsnett's books can doubt that his skepticism was sincere or that his sympathy for the victims and the gulled spectators was genuine, even if he had none for the perpetrators. The last case he is known to have been concerned in illustrates his interest in the human side of the campaign. In 1605 a Windsor girl called Anne Gunter came down with such strange symptoms that people were convinced that she was bewitched. James I, by now deeply interested in such cases, had her brought before him. Dr. Jordan, who had diagnosed Mary Glover's hysteria, was called in, and he said that Anne was an impostor. She confessed that she had acted under instruction from her father, who wished by this means to injure a local woman. The King absolved her from blame, encouraged her in a courtship, and even provided a marriage portion for her. James usually receives the credit for the outcome of this case, and he deserves it for acting humanely and generously upon humane advice. But who were his advisers? There was Dr. Jordan, who was certainly brought in on the advice of the Bancroft group, and there were two clerics, Richard Neile, dean of Westminster, and Samuel Harsnett. Letters from Neile to his patron, Cecil, reveal that Harsnett was in charge of the investigation. Neile wrote the outgoing letters, Harsnett received the incoming ones, and Anne Gunter

---

[1]This story, cited by Walker, *Unclean Spirits*, 72, is from the anonymous and surreptitiously published defense of Darrell, *The Triall of Maist. Dorrell*, sig. F4–4v, whose author strongly approves of Anderson's attitude.

[2]Swan, *True and Breife Report*, sig. I3v.

was in his care at his rectory. James gave the marriage portion; Harsnett did most of the work and gave the advice.[1]

This, then, was the context in which Bancroft and Harsnett decided to investigate, for their own purposes, the thirteen-year-old affair of the Denham exorcisms.

[1]On Anne Gunter, see Kittredge, *Witchcraft,* 321, and Paul, *The Royal Play,* 119–27. Neile's letters are in HMC, *Salisbury Papers* 18:423 (wrongly dated 1606), and 17:471. Harsnett's rectory was Shenfield, Essex, where Sir Thomas Lucas had presented him to the living, 16 April 1604 (Newcourt, *Repertorium* 2:526).

# 4

# The Inquiry into the Denham Exorcisms

In July 1598 Robert Barnes tried to explain to Sir Robert Cecil how he came to own a copy of *The Miracle Book* in his own handwriting, and in early March 1598/99, the Court of High Commission questioned Fid Williams and Anne Smith about their part in the exorcisms. Sometime between these dates the *Miracle Book* came into Bancroft's and Harsnett's hands. At precisely this time, bishop and chaplain were making preparations for the trial of John Darrell. He was brought to Lambeth sometime after Alice Freeman's acquittal in April 1598, and in late May 1599, the High Commission condemned him.[1]

The ex-exorcist Anthony Tyrrell's own copy of the *Miracle Book* had fallen into the authorities' hands years earlier. The exorcisms were ancient history, and since the activities of Catholic priests in England came under the jurisdiction of the secular courts, the Court of High Commission would not have spent time on the *Miracle Book* unless Bancroft wished to use it in his campaign against Darrell and his supporters. Even so they did not spend much time on it. To judge by Anne Smith's deposition, the first inquiry was brief and formal. On the basis of her short, factual statement, T. G. Law, forgetting that by 1598 she was a woman in her early thirties, decided that Anne, compared to Sara and Fid, was a "timid, and apparently modest and truthful girl." It is just as likely that she said no more because she was asked no more, and that had she been recalled to augment her statement later, as Fid was, the second version would have been more detailed. The second inquiry, conducted between April and June 1602, was more thorough, as the length of the depositions shows. The simplest explanation is that at the first inquiry in 1599 Bancroft was assembling a dossier on exorcism in his usual thorough way, whereas at the second inquiry in 1602 he and Harsnett were gathering materials for a book. Their decision to make a book out of the old

[1]*DFP,* sig. C1. According to the author of *The Triall of Maist. Dorrell,* sigs. A5v, A7, the final hearing of Darrell's case took place on Whitsun Eve, 1599, i.e., 26 May.

Denham case was almost certainly based on developments in the Darrell case and, simultaneously, among the Catholics.[1]

When Bancroft resumed his inquiry into the Denham exorcisms in 1602, the quarrel known as the archpriest controversy, raging between rival parties of the Catholic clergy in England, was at its height. On the one side were the secular clergy (although by no means all or even a majority of the secular clergy in England held the views of the party), and on the other were the Jesuits and their supporters. It was a quarrel that grew out of the peculiar situation of the English Catholics, who found themselves isolated from Catholic Europe, cut off from their own English past, and with no local system of ecclesiastical government. It had begun as a disagreement between factions of Welsh and English at the English Hospice in Rome in 1578, and it widened into a controversy over the whole question of the government of priests in England. The Jesuits were a carefully selected group of men, and because of their intelligence, discipline, and efficient organization, they had tended to take control of the mission to England. Even to call the ministry a mission was to give it a Jesuit name. On the other hand, although many, perhaps the majority, of the seculars were brave and saintly men, they were a more haphazardly assembled body, not all of them suited to the priesthood, let alone to the lonely and strenuous life of an underground missionary. Without a hierarchy to whom they were answerable, they were vulnerable to scandal and failure, and for examples one can cite the Denham exorcisms themselves and the various betrayals of Anthony Tyrrell.[2] Nonetheless, much as the seculars needed hierarchical supervision, they would not accept control of their affairs by the Jesuits as a substitute, and extrapolated their refusal into a difference of policy.

Where the militant Jesuits insisted that there could be no compromise between Catholics and Elizabeth I's heretical state, the seculars grudged at the strain that policy put upon Catholic loyalties and blamed the Jesuits for the government's severity after the landing of Edmund Campion and Robert Parsons in 1580. Whereas the Jesuits, insofar as they interested themselves in politics at all, looked for support to Spain and the papacy and favored a policy of militant intervention in English affairs, the seculars looked more to France and hoped for a compromise that would allow Catholics to

---

[1]On the taking of Tyrrell's *Miracle Book,* see Morris, *Troubles* 2:330. T. G. Law's statement is from his article "Devil-Hunting in Elizabethan England," *The Nineteenth Century* 35 (1894): 403.

[2]Interestingly enough, at one point Tyrrell thought he might like to be a Jesuit, but he received no encouragement to apply (Christopher Devlin, *Hamlet's Divinity and Other Essays,* [London: Rupert Hart-Davis, 1963], 130).

practice their religion and remain loyal subjects. There was also jealousy over the distribution of funds. The seculars charged the Jesuits with living luxuriously on funds intended for all.[1]

When Cardinal Allen, founder of the Douay seminary, died in 1594, no generally accepted leader of his authority emerged to preserve unity between the parties. The quarrel flared up in England at Wisbech Castle and centered upon William Weston. There were thirty-three priests held in long-term captivity at the castle, living in circumstances that made any kind of disciplined priestly life very difficult. In the winter of 1594–95, Weston proposed that to bring order into their communal life they should band themselves into an organization with rules and a head. Some readily agreed and elected Weston head of the new community. Henry Garnet, vice-prefect of the English Jesuits, confirmed his election. Some prisoners, however, opposed the idea. They refused the new regulations and they would not even eat or pray with those who did not. These "Wisbech Stirs," as the affair came to be known, were a prelude to the archpriest controversy itself. They were a scandal to the Catholics and intensely interesting to the Protestants.

In 1598 Rome attempted to bring ecclesiastical order to England. The Cardinal Protector of England appointed a secular priest, George Blackwell, to the position of "archpriest," with jurisdiction in England and Scotland. His authority, however, did not extend to the Jesuits, whom he was instructed to consult on important matters. This exception, joined to Blackwell's own dictatorial behavior, infuriated the secular party. The writing of recriminatory pamphlets began in 1601, and in eighteen months' time the seculars had produced eighteen of them.[2]

This was because the quarrel had long been known to the state. Bancroft, working in close collaboration with the Privy Council, saw in it a chance of aggravating the disunity of the Catholics, even of ending Jesuit influence in England and, with it, the meddling of Rome and Spain in English affairs. Anything that weakened the influence of Rome and Spain would also tend, in the long run, to weaken English Catholicism itself: Bancroft, always a realist, agreed with the Jesuits' assessment of the principles at stake. In

[1]On the archpriest controversy and the "Wisbech Stirs," see T. G. Law, *A Historical Sketch of the Conflicts between Jesuits and Seculars in the Reign of Queen Elizabeth* (London: D. Nutt, 1889); idem, *The Archpriest Controversy. Documents Relating to the Dissensions of the Roman Catholic Clergy, 1597–1602*. 2 vols. (London: The Camden Society, n.s., 56 [1896], 58 [1898]; Usher, *Reconstruction* 1:143–90, 2:89–112; P. Renold, ed., *The Wisbech Stirs, 1595–1598*, CRS 51 (1958); Clancy, *Papist Pamphleteers*, 81–87; David Kaula, *Shakespeare and the Archpriest Controversy* (The Hague: Mouton, 1975); 1–17.

[2]Kaula, *Shakespeare and the Archpriest Controversy*, 7; 9, n. 11.

the short run, the scandal of the quarrel was benefit enough. There-fore, always with the backing of the Privy Council—for this was a very dangerous game—Bancroft gave the seculars' pamphleteers access to the press. He even gave two of them, Watson and Bluet, the hospitality of his palace at Fulham.[1] If the seculars thought he meant them well, they were deluded. His only purpose was to divide and discredit the Catholic clergy.[2]

Insofar, therefore, as Harsnett's *Declaration* attacks William Weston personally and as an instrument of Jesuit arrogance and subversion, it is part of the archpriest literature. By portraying Weston as the leader of the exorcising secular priests, Harsnett hopes to show the dangers of Jesuit domination as well as the ill effects of the seculars' disorganization. To that extent his book shares the seculars' point of view.

The connection between the *Declaration* and Darrell's case is equally important but more complex. By 1602 Darrell, condemned in 1599, was convinced that although he had lost the court case he had won the pamphlet war. He had replied immediately to Harsnett's *Discovery* with *A Detection of that Sinnful Shamful, Lying, and Ridiculous Discours of Samuel Harshnet,* and the title of his reply alone, with its use of Harsnett's name, reveals his con-fidence. He published his own accounts of the Starkey and Somers cases, as well as separate defenses of Somers's possession. There was also an anonymous book protesting the conduct of his trial. When Deacon and Walker brought out their ponderous *Dialogicall Discourses of Spirits and Divels* in 1601, Darrell again replied immediately with his *Survey of Certaine Dialogical Discourses,* and in his preliminary address to the reader leaves no doubt that in his own mind he has defeated the bishop and his assistants.

As most people who have read it agree, *Dialogicall Discourses* is a dull book. Yet this does not mean that it has no interest as part of Bancroft's campaign; on the contrary, it played a very interest-ing part indeed. It should always have been obvious (though no one, I think, mentions it) that Darrell could neither have published so many pamphlets nor been so confident had he been acting alone. There was an effective, well-funded, and powerful organization behind him. That being so, the first interesting thing about the *Dis-courses* is that the book is dedicated to the Lord Chancellor, the Lord Chief Justice, the Lord Chief Justice of the Common Pleas,

---

[1]Ibid., 11, n. 14.

[2]As Anthony Rivers, S.J., wrote to Robert Parsons, June 1602: "He termed both sides knaves, but the appellants [i.e., the seculars] good instruments to serve the state" (Henry Foley, *Records of the English Province of the Society of Jesus,* 7 vols. [London, 1877–84], 1:43, cited by Kaula, *Shakespeare and the Archpriest Controversy,* 11).

and the Lord Chief Baron of the Exchequer. There could be no clearer message that the campaign against Darrell was more than ecclesiastical and that it was very serious. Then, in the dedication itself, the authors say that Darrell is a group rather than an individual. They speak of "the *principall parties* with other their *under-hand favorites*" (sig. A2v), as well as the "secret support of their *under-hand Favorites,*" and they believe that this party organization is the cause of the continuing controversy. One can only assume that this accusation, made in a dedication to the chief legal officers of the kingdom, is based on accurate knowledge.[1] They also say that they wrote their book three years earlier, but suppressed it; and if this is true (there is no reason to disbelieve it), then the *Discourses* must have been finished very soon after Darrell's trial, perhaps before Harsnett's own book.

Who were Deacon and Walker? Neither of them was on Whitgift's or Bancroft's staff, and it appears from their books that they were a pair of sober, well-educated, intensely loyal, conforming ministers with Puritan tendencies who did not agree with Bancroft about everything. For instance, they did not think that Darrell conspired with Somers,[2] and they originally seem to have written because they were midlanders from Darrell's own part of the country who knew him and judged him deluded. John Deacon, who graduated B.A. from Magdalen College, Cambridge, in 1575–76, had even been minister of Nottingham in 1586. Walker is not so easily identified, but he was also a midlander, born in Staffordshire, who graduated from Merton College, Oxford, in 1583–84.[3] It seems probable that they had their own motives for writing and began independently of Bancroft.

The crux of their case against Darrell is the doctrine that miracles have ceased, and that consequently diabolic possession as we know it from the Gospels no longer occurs. As their spokesman, *Orthodoxus,* says to *Exorcistes:*

All true *Christian Churches,* and the soundest *Divines* in our daies, doe generallie conclude a *finall discontinuance* of the *miraculous*

---

[1]It is interesting that the author of *The Triall of Maist. Dorrell* dedicates his book to Popham, the Lord Chief Justice, and claims to be an impartial witness won over to Darrell's side by the conduct of the trial. This is a pose. He rails against "lordly bishops," "Romish hierarchy," and "ceremonies enforced" in his dedication, and very early on slips into the plural "we": "we doubt that [the bishop] will . . . curtall the Depositions," thus proving the point he aims to conceal, that there is a party behind Darrell.

[2]*Dialogicall Discourses,* sig. Z8v. Walker, *Unclean Spirits,* 66, and Murphy, *Darkness and Devils,* 84, notice this.

[3]Venn and Venn, *Alumni Cantabrigienses,* pt. 1, 2:25; Joseph Foster, ed., *Alumni Oxonienses, 1500–1714,* 4 vols. (Oxford, 1891–92), 3:1557.

*faith,* in these daies of the *Gospell;* and therefore (by *consequence*) the undoubted *determination* of the *divell* his extraordinarie *power of actuall possession.* (*Dialogicall Discourses,* sig. Q1v)

In reply Exorcistes asks, "Do you then, verie confidently denie *all power* to the *divell:* in these daies of the *Gospell*?" To this Orthodoxus replies, rather surprisingly, "I onely impugne his supposed *extraordinarie power,* for the *perpetuitie of actuall possession:* I denie not his *power* of *obsession* at all." It then appears that by "obsession" Orthodoxus means inward or outward temptation, the former including "ungodly motions, affections, lustes, and desires," and the latter such things as "fleshly affections . . . and carnall practises" (sig. Q2). He has turned "obsession" as Exorcistes would use it, meaning an external attack or manifestation by an evil spirit, into a figure of speech.

The debaters' definition of miracles, offered by a character named Physiologus, is equally significant:

It is by the extraordinary working power of the Lord, some such unaccustomed action, as verie highly surmounteth the whole faculty of ·everie created nature: and is therefore thus admirablie effected to the end it might rather affect the beholders with an admiration thereof, & might the more certeinly confirme their faith in the truth of the worde. (sig. X1v)

Physiologus is also certain that the final cause, or purpose, of a miracle is to confirm faith. A miracle is a kind of divine rhetoric, meant to persuade. There is no hint in the *Discourses* of the Catholic understanding that the whole work of Christian redemption is in its essence miraculous.

Darrell, replying in *A Survey of Certaine Dialogical Discourses,* agrees with all this. A true miracle, he says, "is an hard and unusuall worke, surpassing all faculty of created nature, done by the devine power to that ende, it may move the behoulders with admiration, and confirme their faith in the word of God" (sig. K2v).

To this he adds that miracles are of two kinds, those wrought by God and those wrought by human ministry. Only the latter have ceased. The former continue, and as examples he mentions, among others, the burning bush and the new star of 1572. He disagrees, however, about the devil. He pounces on Deacon's and Walker's definition of "obsession" because it leaves so little power to Satan, and turns him into little more than a figure of speech for humanity's own weaknesses (sig. I1v). Their argument makes the part greater than the whole, and "doth open a dore to Athiesme." For, as he says, everyone can see that the Lord's Prayer's "Lead us not into temptation, but deliver us from evil" is a petition against possession; and if prayer is a defense against the devil, it must also offer deliverance from him (sig. I2).

Nonetheless, even though Darrell insists on the reality of possession, he argues equally firmly that it is not miraculous either in itself or in its cure. Just as people still fall sick in a world where miraculous cures no longer happen, so are they possessed by devils; and just as prayer will end a drought, so will it dispossess a devil. Yet even though "a faithfull congregation making suite to the Lord in the mediation of his Sonne" may "obtaine the deliverance of their brethren from the vexation of divels" (sigs. L1, L1v), this act and its result are not to be confused with exorcism. There is no such thing as an exorcist who dispossesses people of devils by command, thereby claiming to perform a miracle.[1]

This, therefore, is a controversy between parties who agree on the main point, that miracles have ceased. They also agree on the definition of miracles. Yet they disagree over the reality of possession, and this is an important disagreement, because at this point in the argument both sides argue from experience, not from authority. Deacon and Walker look at the cases and see illness, fraud, or even—as in Somers's case—a mixture of both. Darrell sees devils, and in answering his opponents produces so many bizarre modern examples that he begins to sound like a credulous fanatic; and the more he does this, the more he presents himself as a target for Harsnett's final contribution, ostensibly not aimed at him at all, the *Declaration.*

Unlikely as it seems at first, I suggest that this was the strategic reason for Deacon's and Walker's inclusion in the controversy. Harsnett's *Discovery* was a large, thorough, skeptical, jocular, but not uproarious exposure that Darrell answered at once as an outraged believer, going on to defend himself in a whole series of secretly printed pamphlets. For bishop and chaplain to have engaged themselves in a pamphlet war on Darrell's terms would have been futile, as Bancroft, veteran of the Marprelate episode, certainly knew. Then Deacon and Walker appeared, midlanders of Puritan sympathies, one of them a former minister of Nottingham and both with their own reasons for writing against Darrell.[2]

[1]Not all Protestants shared the views of Darrell and his party. In the cases of Rachel Pynder and Agnes Briggs, two litle London girls who confessed to fraud in 1574, the apparent dispossessions were accomplished as much by the traditional exorcising formulae used by the two leaders, Turner and Long, as by the prayers of the little congregation. There was no fasting at all. See *The Disclosing of a Late Counterfeyted Possession by the Devyl in Two Maydens within the Citie of London* (1574).

[2]They could have met Harsnett in the midlands. According to the author of *The Triall of maist. Dorrell,* sig. B3, Harsnett went into the midlands to gather evidence for the Darrell trial.

They disapproved of the disorders he caused and they were embarrassed by his success as a devil-finder. Bancroft encouraged them because, writing from much the same standpoint as Darrell's, they would expose his eccentricities. Deacon and Walker, for instance, would have had no objection, provided authority permitted it, to the use of prayer and fasting against assaults of the devil as they defined them.

Meanwhile, Bancroft and Harsnett were preparing a book about the old Catholic exorcisms, designed to accompany Bancroft's manipulation of the archpriest controversy. Its form was not to be that of the *Discovery;* rather it was to be a *Declaration,* an elaborately organized rhetorical presentation of two principal themes announced on the title page, egregious imposture and Jesuitical subversion. The weight of attack falls heavily on the first topic and includes in its sweep anyone, Catholic or Protestant, who is taken in by or who practices any kind of devil-dispossession. The generality of the attack is implicit throughout because Harsnett derides the phenomena themselves, not just the priests, their methods, and their patients. One is not surprised, therefore, that toward the end of the book Harsnett also attacks the Protestant dispossessors by name:

> And if they want devils in Italy to exorcise and aske Oracles of, let them come but over into London in England, and wee have ready for them *Darrells wife, Moores Minion, Sharpe, Skelton, Evans, Swan,* and *Lewis,* the devil-finders and devil-puffers, or devil-prayers; and they shal start them a devil in a lane as soone as an Hare in *Waltham* forrest, that shal nick it with aunswers as dead as *Westons* and *Dibdales* devils did. (*DEP,* 331)

Thus the Protestant dispossessors find themselves tarred with the same brush that has disfigured their Catholic enemies and opposites.

This strategy may seem overelaborate, but no one who has followed Bancroft's career will underestimate his gift for counterinsurgency. The man who so completely entangled the secular priests in his manipulation of the archpriest controversy by playing on their vanity and lust for power understood John Darrell well enough. All Bancroft had to do was provide a context in which Darrell's vanity and fanaticism would isolate him from the more sober elements in his party. Few people have read Darrell's replies to Deacon and Walker, but to read them knowing that Harsnett's *Declaration* was in preparation as he wrote casts an ironic light on page after page. The cleverness of the strategy was that Darrell, who had answered everything written against him, and who had conducted himself throughout his trial with ostentatious dignity, could not answer the *Declaration* without first wearing the shoes Bancroft and Harsnett had made for him. After its publication he was not heard from again.

Darrell's presence as an implicit object of attack in the *Declaration* explains a peculiarity of its rhetoric. Harsnett addressed it to the Catholics, but in it he continually speaks to the Protestants who are its real audience. Insofar as Harsnett speaks to Catholics at all, it is only to embarrass and disgust them. On the other hand, he addresses the Protestants as friends, playing on their fears and prejudices, enlisting them on his side. Read thus, by a Protestant audience, the *Declaration* is as much the last word in the Darrell campaign as it is an attack on the Catholic mission to England. In fact Harsnett's approach, presenting Jesuitry and Puritanism as two varieties of the same fanatical threat to sound religion, became the common strategy of Anglican argument until the resurgence of evangelicalism in the later eighteenth century. Swift, in *A Tale of a Tub,* is its most brilliant exponent.

To sum up the reasons for Bancroft's inquiry into the old Denham exorcisms and for Harsnett's writing of the *Declaration:*

1. It was meant to discredit the claims made for the exorcisms in the *Miracle Book,* and to undo, if possible, any effect the exorcisms might have had.

2. It was meant to discredit William Weston and to injure the Jesuits in their quarrel with the seculars.

3. It was meant to discredit the practice of exorcism in general and to publicize further the position Bancroft had taken in the Darrell case.

4. It was meant to associate Darrell and his supporters with the Catholic exorcists as men driven by a lust to exploit and domineer.

5. It was meant to constitute an attack on belief in demonic possession that John Darrell could not reply to.

This was a formidable agenda for one book, but Bancroft and Harsnett were a formidable pair.

The second inquiry into the Denham exorcisms lasted from 24 April 1602, when Sara Williams was examined, until 15 June, when Anthony Tyrrell swore to his written statement. The proceedings were well known. Fid Williams says that she was abused and threatened for revealing her sister's whereabouts (*DEP,* 380), and the same Anthony Rivers who wrote to Robert Parsons about Bancroft's role in the archpriest controversy also told him that "Mr. Bancroft" had plans for a book on the exorcisms, but was having difficulty with his clerical witness, the ex-priest and exorcist Anthony Tyrrell:

> Tyrrell hath refused to swear to the truth of such things as he hath confessed, which hath not a little troubled Mr. Bancroft, for that he meaneth nothing shall be said in his book but that which is avouched by the oath of others.[1]

Thorough and careful preparation had always been Bancroft's method of exposure, and in 1602, in the atmosphere of publicity surrounding the whole subject of possession, he would have been foolish to take any other approach. Hence it is not surprising that Harsnett makes a strong avowal of scrupulousness with evidence in his dedicatory epistle, "To the seduced Catholiques of England":

> And that this declaration might be free from the carpe and cavill of ill-affected or discomposed spirits, I have alledged nothing for materiall or authenticall heerein but the expresse words, eyther of some part of the *Miracle booke* penned by the priests and filed upon Record where it is publique to be seene, or els a clause of theyr confession who were fellow actors in this impious dissimulation. Whose severall confessions and contestations (the parties beeing yet living) are heere published in print that the world may be a witnesse of our integrity herein. . . . If I have wittingly falsified or feigned any thing out of that booke of wonders, God doe so to me, and more, for dooing them so much wrong. (*DEP,* 198)

That is a strong statement, and in general there is no reason not to accept it. No doubt Harsnett prints and quotes his materials accurately, and no doubt they were on record "publique to be seene"—although inquirers may not have been effusively welcomed. Nonetheless, quite apart from the effect of Harsnett's rhetorical and stylistic treatment of the evidence, at least three kinds of falsification seem to have operated in his and Bancroft's collection and use of it: (1) a knowing use of falsehoods, possibly allied to tampering with the witnesses' statements; (2) suppression or avoidance of undesirable evidence; and (3) a persistent use of leading questions and suggestions in the inquiry itself. For the High Commission's task was not to establish the facts as they actually happened, but to establish a case for fraud and subversion. Bancroft and Harsnett had no interest in evidence that might have pointed in other directions.

The suspicion of falsehood attaches to all the witnesses' statements, except perhaps Anne Smith's, because they were all eager

---

[1]Morris, *Troubles* 2:103; also quoted by Usher, *Reconstruction* 1:178.

to exonerate themselves. Richard Mainy, for instance, was certainly a fraudulent demoniac; he may even have been the chief author of the more glamorous frauds in the girls' exorcisms as well as his own. The mischievous, teenaged Mainy who appears in the Williams sisters' statements must have thought it a great lark to see Weston and the rest of the spectators on their knees praying to the divine personages he told them were in the corners of the room (*DEP*, 407). His disclaimers of responsibility for this and other pranks carry no conviction at all:

> I doe faithfully avow it that I never saw any such sights, but did therein *frame my selfe* to doe as I had heard by the priests and others that *Sara Williams* and the rest had done before mee. And I doe believe that Ma: *Edmunds* himselfe knew as much, and that hee did but seeme to worship (as is before expressed), thereby to induce the rest of the company so to doe. (408)

That is simply incredible, and it is directly contradicted by Anthony Tyrrell, who tells us that Weston "writ a quire of paper of Ma: *Mainyes* pretended visions. For he thought . . . to have wrought some great matter by him, but was disappointed very ridiculously, so as I thinke the said visions will hardly come to light" (390). Weston was obviously Mainy's dupe, and for Harsnett to present Weston as a knowing fraud on Mainy's evidence was dishonest.

A different kind of dishonesty attaches to Fid Williams's statement. The priests diagnosed her as stupid and possessed with "a malicious lying spirit" (*DEP*, 369), and wrong as they were in so many things, they were right in this one. Fid Williams was one of nature's fablers.[1] Moreover, unlike her sister, Sara, who was still Catholic at the time of the inquiry and professed great surprise at what she heard written about her in the *Miracle Book*, Fid had become Protestant again, and she claims to have been willing to help the authorities as far back as about 1590–91 (377). (Fid's claim to have been skeptical of the exorcisms during and immediately after them, however, is proved false by a report of her prophesies supposedly uttered under possession by a good spirit while she was staying with Mrs. White after her removal from Denham.[2]) It was through her information that Bancroft found out where Sara was living, and her only regret at the end of her statement was that she could not tell more. After her first question-

---

[1] An interesting, internal sign of Fid's fabling is that she consistently casts herself as the heroine of her stories.

[2] SP 12/192, n. 57. See Pollen, "Supposed Cases," 463, n. 2.

ing in March 1598/99, some priests, she said, asked her not to reveal anything. When she refused, they threatened her with a heretic's fire "if ever the world changed." Not only did she tell the commission all this, but she went on to name the five priests, of whom one (Sherwood) was either banished or dead, another (Green) was in Wisbech Castle, another (Bruerton) was not a priest at all, and another (Blackman) never existed.

This is a good example of Fid's veracity. She was a government informer who must always be suspected of lying. She tells an amazing tale, full of circumstantial detail, of having married the martyr priest William Harrington in the Marshalsea Prison in the days before he was a priest (*DEP*, 376ff.), and she says that a priest called Lister "used certaine Latine words" at the ceremony. There actually was a priest called Lister in the Marshalsea in 1586 who had been committed in 1585,[1] and Fid's account of Harrington's movements, moreover, tallies with the record: his second trip to the Continent, his capture within a year of his return, and his execution.[2] Nonetheless, the story is unbelievable. Harrington was not in or around London at the time, and, all question apart of his later being a priest, why would a young man in his circumstances marry Fid Williams, and in the Marshalsea of all places? The Catholics had their revenge for this story by spreading the rumor that Fid was Bancroft's mistress and had a child by him![3]

Fid's statement ends with a tacked-on paragraph accusing the priests of sexual relations with their patients and others:

> The priests at theyr departure from *Denham* tooke every one thence his woman with him: Ma: *Edmunds* the Jesuit had for his darling mistris *Cressy,* then a widdow, who was a daily guest there, and one that did contribute very much both to him and the rest of the priests; *Anne Smith* was at the disposition of Ma: *Driland; Sara Williams* of maister *Dibdale;* mistris *Altham* of *Cornelius,* and this examinate of Ma: *Leigh,* a priest likewise. (380)

[1] *CRS* 2 (1906): 273.

[2] In 1586 William Harrington, returning in ill health from a visit to Douay, Rheims, and Tournai, was arrested upon entering England and sent to his father in Yorkshire. He went overseas again in 1591 and was ordained in France, 1592. He returned to England and was captured, May 1593, in the rooms of Henry Donne. He was very cruelly executed, 18 February 1593/94, being cut down alive; he struggled with the hangman before being disembowelled and quartered (Challoner, *Memoirs,* 197; *CSP Dom., Elizabeth,* vol. 245, no. 14; *DNB,* s.v. "John Donne."

[3] Richard Davis sent the story over to Douay in 1626 in his account of Robert Dibdale: "The other was called *Fid,* who, after the apprehension of Mr. *Dibdale,* became concubine to Bancroft, called Archbishop of Canterbury, and had a child by him, as I have heard" (Challoner, *Memoirs,* 117).

There is no point in a lie unless it has some relationship to the truth, and as with all Fid's fables, there is a tiny grain of truth in this one. We know from Anne Smith's statement that the greater part of the Denham household dispersed, priests and demoniacs, shortly before the pursuivants arrived, and that she, two other women, Fr. Dryland, Alexander the apothecary, Mr. Swithin Wells, and some manservants were left behind. On a Sunday in the middle of June, the men were arrested, and on the Monday, Dryland's servant took Anne to safety in London.[1] Fid is right to the extent that Dryland seems to have been responsible for Anne. Similarly, Dibdale was Sara's chief exorcist and confessor, and at one time entertained ideas of her being a nun, even collecting £40 for her dowry (358). Yet Fid's accusation is not only ridiculous; it may not have been entirely hers.

First, it is tagged on at the end, out of sequence with the rest of her statement, and the style is different. "Ma: *Edmunds* the Jesuit had for his darling mistris *Cressy*" does not sound like her at all. That kind of sarcasm does not appear elsewhere in her statement, where, moreover, her sister is usually referred to as "this examinates sister" or simply "her sister." To call her "Sara Williams" looks peculiar. It is possible that we have here an addition to Fid's statement by someone in the court. Even if it is her own, it is another example of her wild fabling, for Fr. Leigh, the priest she claims to have gone off with herself, was either not a priest in 1586, or not in England in time for the exorcisms. This paragraph, and Harsnett's unscrupulous use of it (*DEP,* 318), is evidence of collusion between Fid Williams and the court.

There may be other interpolations, too. All the witnesses were asked whether Babington and his friends were at the exorcisms (Mainy, writing his own statement, does not mention the subject), and the name of John Ballard, the priest who was executed with the conspirators, appears in all three lists of exorcists, Harsnett's, Fid's, and Anne Smith's. Yet there is no mention of him as an exorcist in the statements or in the quotations from the *Miracle Book,* and it is most unlikely that he was even a regular visitor at the exorcisms. Tyrrell calls him, ambiguously, "an Agent amongst us" (*DEP,* 391), but this does not prove that he was an exorcist.

Of the three lists of exorcists, Anne Smith's is the most reliable. Ballard's name comes last and could easily have been inter-

---

[1]Anne dates the arrests a fortnight after Whitsun, i.e., Sunday, 5 June. Dryland, however, was committed 20 June, and James Stanborough, a servant who was also arrested, was committed on Sunday, 19 June (*CRS* 2 [1906]:269, 270). A prison list endorsed 18 June has Dryland's name in an added note with the comment "newly taken" (*CRS* 2 [1906]:253).

polated.[1] Harsnett's list seems to have been padded,[2] and one can have very little confidence in Fid's. One cannot rule out tampering with the statements. A curious feature of the *Declaration* is that despite the court's efforts to implicate the exorcists in the Babington Plot, Harsnett makes little use of the idea and no use of Ballard as an exorcist at all.[3]

There was also suppression of available evidence. At the time of the inquiry, several of the exorcists, including Weston himself, were prisoners at Wisbech. If they were questioned at all, which seems unlikely, no use was made of the results. In addition to the priests, there must have been a number of lay people available for questioning, and Harsnett himself mentions "the getting of foure chiefe Daemoniacks together, besides many more assistants." Yet only one hint surfaces in the *Declaration* that more evidence was garnered than Harsnett prints. The court apparently questioned Sir George Peckham, owner of the manor of Denham at the time of the exorcisms:

> Touching *Denham*, the Gentleman, chiefe owner of the Manor, testifieth that the four *seers* or impostors had borne him in hand that there was great store of *Treasure Trouvé* hidden in his said Manor, and appointed him a night certaine when to digge for the same, which time they kept; and that himselfe with divers of his servants being present, there was nothing found but olde empty earthen pots. And concerning *Fulmer,* the same Gentleman tells us also. . . . (214)

We naturally wonder what else Sir George had to say.[4]

The printed evidence also makes it obvious that the commissioners put leading questions to their witnesses. The first witness was Sara Williams, who seems to have been a very likable, attractive woman. "One of a very good personage, favour, and wit" (*DEP*, 219) is Harsnett's assessment of her. She was thirty-two or three at the time of the inquiry. She was not illiterate, and one's first impression of her evidence is that it was spontaneous and intelligent. At first she was nervous under the questioning, but she soon

---

[1]It may be significant, in connection with possible interpolations in the evidence, that the author of *The Triall of Maist. Dorrell* accused Harsnett of adding to Darling's confession "that which he never spake" (sig. B3).

[2]See Appendix A.

[3]As has been already pointed out, the exorcisms were all but over when Babington met Ballard in May 1586, and throughout the period of the exorcisms, from fall 1585 to May 1586, Ballard was traveling up and down England (Read, *Walsingham* 3.17).

[4]The Peckham estates at Denham were seized by the Crown for debt and granted to William Bowyer in 1596 until settlement of the debt. Sir George died in 1608, and the Peckhams never redeemed the estates (*VCH, Buckinghamshire* 3:257).

settled down and began to say sensible things. In denying that she had seen the head of a child in the chalice, for instance, she added that if she ever had seen such a thing, she would never have forgotten it (355). Nowhere, however, does Sara accuse the priests of fraud. The portrait of the exorcists that emerges from her evidence is of men in a state of fanatical, even crazy credulity, and therefore capable of extraordinary cruelty and harshness. Yet she never accuses them of intentional fraud. Her own confessor, Dibdale, seems to have been a kindly man when he was not obsessed with devils. She speaks affectionately of him and reproduces a touching conversation in which she tried to warn him of Mainy's hypocrisy and randiness (349).

She does, however, repeatedly accuse the author of the *Miracle Book* of lying, and she also says that she sometimes heard the priests exaggerating her experiences: "They would tel many things of her which she knew to be false, but durst not say any thing against them, for offending of them" (343). Her explanation of the element of fraud in the exorcisms is that she made things up to please the priests. They had diagnosed devils in her and she believed them. They attributed everything she said or did to diabolic agency, and so the only way she could enjoy a measure of peace was to produce diabolic phenomena. Her reward was to escape some of the demeaning cruelty and nastiness of the exorcisms. Yet we must also remember that even Sara, despite the liveliness and candor of her testimony, wishes to portray herself in as attractive a light as possible, and it is probable that at fifteen she, like Mainy, had a touch of exhibitionism she preferred not to dwell on at thirty-two. As the long process of interrogation from the narrative of her fits goes on, Sara's tone changes; her surprised candor turns, first to cheekiness—"The most mornings shee would tell them one tale or other, or els (as she saith) how should they have had writing worke" (355)—then to distress, for as the sordid tale of her performance unfolds, she finally breaks down and cries (356).

None of this was what the High Commission wished to hear, and at two places in her statement language appears, obviously not of her own invention, that puts her testimony as the commissioners wished to hear it. The first occurs in the paragraph on the casting out of "Captaine *Frateretto*":

She saith that it was the ordinary custome of the priests to be talking of such as had beene possessed beyond the seas, and to tell the manner of theyr fits, and what they spake in them: also what ugly sights they saw somtimes, and at other times what joyfull sights, and how when reliques were applied unto them the parties would roare: how they could not abide holy water nor the sight of the sacrament. . . . *These things* (she saith) *she now remembreth* by hearing those things which are written in the booke of her selfe, and *confesseth* that by the said tales shee well perceived *how shee might please them, and did frame herselfe accordingly* at such times as she wel perceived it was their intent she should so doe. (346, my italics)

Similar language and the same periodic sentence structure appear later in the statement when the commissioners, after allowing her considerable freedom of reminiscence, bring her back to the *Miracle Book* and the specific rebuttals they require:

Whereas in the afore-said booke there are a number of things reported of this examinate, what she should doe, see, and speake in her fits: she verily thinketh that (some foolish things of her owne devise excepted) she neither did speake nor pretended to see any thing but in such sort as she had heard the priests report that other women beyond the Seas had done, seene, and spoken: According to which reports, she this examinate being in the priests hands *did frame her selfe* to doe and speake and report she saw this and that, as she had heard of them, that those parties did, that thereby *shee might please them.* (353, my italics)

Evidently Sara was twice asked a carefully prepared question or set of questions, to which she more or less answered yes. By this means she was brought to implicate the priests in conscious fraud, but her answers to both sets of questions contradict the rest of her testimony, in which she says that the *Miracle Book* lied about what she said and did, and that she made up her own fictions once she realized what would please the priests. She flatly denies having visions of the sacrament (which would indeed be evidence of prompting, and thus support the commission's hypothesis), and attributes them to Mainy (353).

Since the words "frame my selfe" as well as the phrases "leading questions" and "instructing questions" appear italicized in Mainy's written statement, I think we can conclude that they are quotations from the commissioners' questioning. If this is so, then the commissioners did what they accuse the priests of doing; they put ideas into the witnesses' heads. Mainy and Tyrrell, the sophisticated witnesses, seem to have realized this and to have understood that their answers to the questions by no means disposed of all aspects of the exorcisms. Mainy's last paragraph communicates a real fear that he might be diagnosed as possessed again, and Tyrrell ends by saying that should he become Catholic again, he would revoke his confession—a statement that tends to support the rumor that he was unwilling to vouch for his confession by oath. For both of them, the commissioners' questions established something short of absolute truth, and their attitude gives us, as Harsnett's bluff skepticism can not, a glimpse into the real world of the possessions. In that world belief in the phenomena of possession follows upon faith in the religion. How could Richard Mainy know, despite the reassuring skepticism of the bishop and his chaplain, that he had really faked the seven deadly sins? And when Weston was "ridiculously disappointed" in Mainy's visions, who did he think had disappointed him? Mainy or the devil?

Harsnett, writing in 1602, could no more answer that kind of question than anyone else. We do not know whether he and Bancroft ran the risk of questioning Weston, and of thus encountering that absolute faith in the miraculous world. Someone did question Weston, about a year after his capture, and he describes the encounter in a fascinating passage of his autobiography:

> One day a secret examiner was sent to me in prison to get information. He was an inquisitive man and questioned me in great detail [about a possessed girl and a pursuivant]. Then, making fun of it, he said he had seen simple people taken in by that same kind of thing done by mere juggling. To end his insolence, I told him of other occurrences of that period, and went on to say that I wished the Queen had been present or one of her Council to witness the sights, or that they could have taken place in public, for I was certain that there were many people who, given an opportunity of observing the majestic power of the Church over evil spirits and monsters, would see and acknowledge at once the difference between the two religions, and award the victory to the Catholic faith. At this he swore a great oath, and said that on no account would he like to have witnessed such horrific scenes. He showed, in fact, what little support is to be had from a bad conscience when it is brought face to face with instruments of God's power.[1]

One would like to know who this examiner was. He could have been someone like Bancroft or Harsnett. This story reveals something that a modern reader might not suspect at all, that Bancroft's and Harsnett's skepticism was as much a psychological necessity for them as credulity was for the priests. It was their only defense, as ecclesiastics and individuals, against otherwise dangerous and inexplicable phenomena. Consequently they, like the exorcists, tolerate inconsistencies in their position that their own strong intelligence would otherwise reject. Harsnett's case for simple, intentional fraud is continually breaking down because, like the exor-

---

[1]Caraman, ed., *Autobiography*, 26–27. There is also a translation, in some respects preferable, in Morris, *Troubles* 2:102–3.

cisms themselves, it strains credulity. Quite apart from the failure of Sara's testimony to support such a hypothesis, Harsnett has no evidence at all that Marwood was a fraud. He can argue a probability on the basis of his convictions, but he has no evidence. In Mainy's case, it is obvious that there was fraud, and that Mainy, not the priests, was its chief agent. Nor does the second part of Harsnett's argument, that the fraud was a part of a larger, political conspiracy, succeed any better. For if there was no intentional, conscious fraud, then there was no conspiracy; but even if we consider the conspiracy as something separate from the particular events of the exorcisms and allow the government's position that all Catholic activity was conspiratorial, Harsnett's only evidence for conspiracy is Anthony Tyrrell's statement about Weston's political interests—and as Professor Murphy has very acutely pointed out, the one thing Tyrrell's words prove is that he had no knowledge of any such interests at all.[1]

In the *Declaration,* two kinds of passion meet in conflict: the passionate belief of the *Miracle Book* and the passionate disbelief of Harsnett and his bishop. The minds of the ex-demoniacs and the ex-priest Tyrrell provide the battlefield, and because of the way the commission conducted its inquiry, we have no real check on the claims of either side. Whatever criticisms one makes of the handling of Darrell's case, the fact that it was a live issue, and that Darrell himself was present and ready to answer back, forced a certain sobriety and discipline into the proceedings. The Denham exorcists were either dead or in prison, and the Catholics among whom and for whom they performed the exorcisms were people deprived by statute of the right to any opinion of their own at all. As lapsed Catholics or as Protestants, the witnesses were free to agree with the commissioners; as Catholics they could say nothing. The *Declaration,* therefore, represents in literary form the exercise of absolute power in the state. It is surely strange that the highest ecclesiastical court in England, empowered by royal commission and presided over by a powerful bishop, should have transcribed, printed, and quoted Fid Williams's wild allegations against men who were either dead or held in prison, in some cases without trial. The only explanation is that already offered: Bancroft and Harsnett were fighting what they judged to be a deadly enemy, and in the passion of the fight used any available weapon.

---

[1]*Darkness and Devils,* 30–31. Tyrrell says, "Hereof I doubt not but that sundry Catholiques in England had sufficient notice from beyond the seas [of the plot], and especially Ma: *Edmunds,* alias *Weston,* the Jesuit, who was then the chiefe, as maister *Garnet* (as I take it) is at this present, and therefore could not be ignorant of such important matters wherein principall men of his owne societie were engaged" (*DEP,* 389).

Yet one has only to step out of the company of these two passionately skeptical clerics into the world of passionate belief they opposed for the sympathies they have alienated to be rekindled. The commissioners' evidence may not establish their case, but it establishes the inhumane consequences of careless belief. In all four ex-demoniacs' statements, even Fid's, one hears the voice of bewildered, apparently pointless suffering.

Modern apologists for the priests sometimes argue that the exorcisms, however violent, were only a standard form of treatment for various conditions—hysteria and epilepsy, for instance—that we nowadays leave to the medical profession.[1] The exorcists would have indignantly rejected that defense. Anne Smith knew that she suffered from "the mother," that formerly common hysterical condition that no longer occurs. The priests insisted that she was possessed, and they so strapped her into a chair to exorcise her "as they almost lamed her armes, and so brused all the parts of her body with holding, tying, and turmoyling of her, that she was so sore, she was compelled afterwards by the space of three yeeres to swathe her body" (DEP, 386). Poor Mainy had some kind of nervous affliction, a male equivalent of "the mother," that a Scotch doctor in Paris diagnosed as "vertigo of the head" (401).[2] The priests took him to a doctor to prove him wrong and set about removing a devil from him. Like the girls he was bound, forced to drink the disgusting holy potion, and suffumigated with stinking herbs: "No man (I suppose) is able to endure such a perfume without extreame torment" (405). William Trayford's only ailment was an inflamed toe, caused by "a spice of the gowt" (224).

Sara Williams had nothing wrong with her at all as far as one can tell until the exorcisms gave her fainting spells and "the mother." Yet this fifteen-year-old was not only bound, dosed, and fumigated; she was also told that her first menstruation was diabolical, a diagnosis that licensed her tormenters to squirt various holy liquids into her. They even applied their relics to her vulva (DEP,

---

[1] See Caraman, ed., *Autobiography,* xiv, xix; Devlin, "Anthony Tyrrell," 346ff.

[2] In his forthcoming *Medicine and Shakespeare in the English Renaissance* (University of Delaware Press, 1991), F. D. Hoeniger explains the condition in the terms of sixteenth-century medicine. He argues that since "the mother" was, strictly speaking, a female complaint, Harsnett was mistaken to use the term of Mainy, and passed his mistake on to Shakespeare. I would suggest something rather more complex. Harsnett applies the term with some contempt to Mainy, but shows off his own medical knowledge by also using the correct term "hysterica passio" (DEP, 223); Mainy is not sure whether "the mother" is the correct name for his disease or not; nonetheless he consistently uses it, and the priests use it too. From this I would conclude that "the mother" was in colloquial use to describe a male condition, but that "hysterica passio" would normally only be used of women. Hence Lear's use of both the common and the learned names (2.4.55–56) is not so much a mistake as an intentionally grotesque expression.

350, 357). Fid, too, seems to have been quite healthy until she slipped in the kitchen. She also went through the binding, dosing, and fumigation, and in addition says that she was whipped with a long, knotted girdle made of whipcord (369).[1]

Of all the supposed demoniacs, only Marwood seems to have been genuinely disturbed. Anne Smith had a chronic nervous condition, yet she was the most disappointing demoniac of them all. She entered upon the exorcisms as a last hope of curing her condition, and she puzzled the exorcists when she produced no more than the symptoms from which her possession was first diagnosed. Mainy was highly strung, possibly neurotic, but his mischief was intelligent, ingenious, and thoroughly explicable. All of them were young. Sara, at fifteen, was the youngest, Anne, at eighteen, perhaps the oldest. Only Mainy could be described as educated, even though Sara, and probably Fid, could read. All except Mainy were servants, ready without question to admit the priests as their social as well as spiritual superiors. None of them except Mainy (if he is telling the truth) questioned the priests' judgment. They had no defense against the diagnosis, and in this lies the true explanation of the frauds.

Provided that they all believed in their devils, which at first they did, they could not understand the nature of their impostures because, according to the theory, everything they did or said was done by the possessing devil or devils. As Fid said, probably quoting Bancroft, the potion and the fumes would have made a horse sick; but they were intended to make devils sick, and as far as the priests and spectators understood the results, they did. The substitution of a preternatural, unverifiable cause for the natural causes of all the demoniacs' functions was so thoroughgoing that only a very strong mind and will could have challenged it. When the girls expressed disgust at having relics put into their mouths, their natural reaction was diabolic, not human (*DEP,* 366). When Anne Smith laughed at the ridiculous notion that her devil had thrown Alexander the apothecary off his horse, it was the devil that laughed, not her own common sense (387). This treatment, allied to physical cruelty, brought all of them, except Anne, who did not suffer long enough, to the verge of desperation. Sara's attempt to escape and Mainy's last frauds were the acts of children at their

[1]Weston later wrote that the shrieks and other noises made by the possessed made it very difficult to treat them (Caraman, ed., *Autobiography,* 24). This leads Pollen to comment upon the dangers of the exorcisms ("Such sounds pierced the whole house, and alarmed the neighbours") and to argue that "the exorcisms were applied from a charitable motive, and with risk to the exorcist" ("Supposed Cases of Possession," 454). While this is true, it is also true that the exorcisms caused most, if not all, of the noise, and that from Harsnett's point of view the noise was part of the performance.

wits' end; indeed, read as Mainy's revenge on Weston, the grand finale of his exorcism is very funny (410).

In a passage of his autobiography written many years later, Weston said that the purpose of the exorcisms was to relieve the sufferers and bring peace to the houses where they lived. This is obviously not entirely true, though Weston probably thought it was. Events may have begun that way with Marwood, but one need only read a few fragments of the *Miracle Book* or of Weston's own account of Marwood to see that it was not the comfort brought to the sufferers that caught the priests' imagination, but the drama, religious and psychological, of the rite. In this they were following Continental, in particular French, precedents familiar to them all.[1] Marwood's devil, Pippin, testified to Edmund Campion's martyrdom by going into agonies at a touch from the dead priest's cincture, and he revealed the power of the Catholic priesthood over hell when a touch of Weston's hand made him sweat so much that it was one man's job to mop up the streams that flowed from his face (*DEP*, 266, 260). The other priests seemed to have equal success. The devils (instructed chiefly by Mainy, it seems) testified to the real presence in the sacrament, proclaimed saints, and claimed great friendship with Protestants and loathing of Catholics. The chief dramatic purpose of the exorcisms was to endorse Catholic belief and vilify heresy, and in this respect they were successful, as Catholic enthusiasm for them shows.

Yet not everyone approved. According to Tyrrell, the older priests disapproved, and the "graver sort . . . imprisoned at *Wisbich* were greatly offended there-with . . . and said that howsoever for a time wee might be admired, yet in the end wee would thereby marre all, and utterly discredit both our selves and our calling" (*DEP*, 393). Fid says that "divers auncient Catholiques" disliked the exorcisms—but she may have taken this from Tyrrell's confession. Tyrrell says that there were even skeptics among the exorcising priests (392). If this is true, then the exorcisms were not performed in a completely uncritical atmosphere, and one would be justified in accusing the skeptics of conscious fraud. Even if we discount Fid's accusations of overt fraud, the remaining "miracles" (identifying relics, understanding Latin and French, reacting to holy objects, producing objects from the mouth, and so forth) have all the appearance of crude imposture.

[1]On the French exorcisms at Laon and Soissons, see Walker, *Unclean Spirits,* 19-33. Except for Weston, the English exorcists were all young priests trained at the Douay-Rheims seminary who would have known all about these cases. See also the fine article of H. Weber, "L'exorcisme à la fin du XVIe siècle, instrument de la Contre Réforme et spectacle baroque," *Nouvelle Revue du Seizième Siècle* 1 (1983): 79–101.

Nonetheless, the same explanation applies to the priests' behavior as to the demoniacs'. Whatever Tyrrell told the commissioners in 1602, his description of his state of mind in 1586, shortly after the exorcisms, reveals something quite different:

> Truly I do not lie. I would sometimes when my candle was put out imagine my chamber to be full of devils, especially of those that I had tormented in my former exorcisms. I imagined them how they environed me round about, triumphing of their possession of me, and watching when they should carry my soul as their perpetual prey unto eternal damnation. Ah, good Lord! how I was affrighted in my mind when I thought what torments I had inflicted upon those accursed spirits by power of the Catholic Church. . . .[1]

As long as even a wavering, weak-willed priest like Tyrrell believed that the devil, a real spiritual being, and not a figure of speech or an allegory, was omnipresent, he believed enough to make it impossible for him to know whether the devil was there or not, but to make it very probable that he was.

Such an idea made rational thought impossible. If the priests noticed that the demoniacs often repeated in exorcism what they had been told about other demoniacs, that did not prove that the devil was absent or that the demoniacs were faking; it meant that the devil, whose behavior is the same in all circumstances, might be trying to make them think he was absent. Even a fraudulent priest who believed that the possessions were fundamentally genuine could not alter either the hypothesized fact or his own belief by a trick. The lies of the *Miracle Book* will have seemed to Tyrrell to be comparable to the arts of a rhetorician. No matter how much he improved on fact, at the core of his narrative truth nestled inviolate, like a pip in an apple. A little fraud improved the spectacle and encouraged "godlie credulitie" (*DEP,* 392) in the faithful. It did not touch the fundamental truth. The devil was there, and if on a certain day he was reluctant to appear, the exorcist who played his part for him was only imitating reality.

The inquiry did not reveal that the frauds were part of a subversive Jesuit plot, but that they were the direct consequence of monstrous credulity flourishing among eager young priests working in circumstances of great danger and without proper ecclesiastical supervision. Both the traditional accounts and the ex-demoniacs' statements reveal the leaders among the exorcising priests to have been Weston, Dibdale, and Cornelius. One would reject as wellnigh unbelievable the portrait of the three presented in the wit-

[1]Morris, *Troubles* 2:434.

nesses' statements except that their credulity provides the only explanation for the events.[1] They acted with unquestioning belief upon the idea that discarnate spirits could, and often did, infest human bodies, especially the bodies of people who disagreed with priests. As a result they denied the young victims of their fanaticism a right fundamental to law in the kingdom of England, namely the right to "a fundamental liberty of their persons."[2] On the unverifiable hypothesis that they were possessed, and their bodies no longer theirs, they were subjected to virtual kidnapping and imprisonment, and to a series of violent assaults, physical and mental, upon the dignity and integrity of their persons, which none of them, whether by age, education, or rank, was fitted to withstand.

This was a serious breach of the Queen's peace, and Bancroft understood very well the danger that such beliefs, translated into action, presented to the body politic. What no one seems to have grasped was that the best way to protect the body politic and to combat dangerous belief was to protect the individual subject. It never occurred to anyone to prosecute exorcists for breach of the Queen's peace by depriving her subjects of their juridical rights. Tudor government, after all, itself ignored those rights. Yet the potentiality of such an approach was present in English law, and by a curious historical irony, when it began to emerge in the Petition of Right debates in the Parliament of 1628, Bishop Harsnett—almost alone among the spiritual lords—argued persistently for the rights of the subject against the assertion of absolute, divinely sanctioned authority, this time in the form of the royal prerogative, the wellhead of absolute power in early modern England.[3]

When in 1598 the Lord Justice Anderson discovered fraud in the Somers case, he saw to it that the accused witch was acquitted. Yet although the frauds had caused civic turmoil in Nottingham, he turned the prosecution of Darrell over to the ecclesiastical court. This was proper enough, since Darrell came under their jurisdiction as a lecturer in the parish. Exorcising Catholics came under

[1]See especially the stories of Cornelius and the rat (352) and of Dibdale and the ring and the "ragged colt" (351), told by Sara. For Weston's credulity, see Mainy's trick visions of Christ and the Blessed Virgin (407).

[2]The phrase is Harsnett's, from his draft of the Lords' Resolutions of 25 April 1628: "2. That his Maiestie would be pleasd graciously to declare, that according to Magna Charta, and the statutes beefore named, as allso accordinge to the most ancient Customs and Lawes of this Land, every free Subiect of this Realm *hath a fundamentall propriety* in his Goods, and a *fundamentall liberty of his Person*" (SP 16/102, no. 14).

[3]He was joined by Abbot, archbishop of Canterbury, and Williams, bishop of Lincoln.

the jurisdiction of the secular courts, yet only Robert Dibdale seems to have had an ex-demoniac produced in evidence against him, and that was certainly not in protection of the witness, herself in prison for religion.

Giving advice to our predecessors gratifies vanity but leaves history unchanged. At the time, responsibility devolved upon the bishop and his chaplain. Their diagnosis of the civil dangers of the miraculous and the prophetic was proved true in the experience of the civil wars and the interregnum, a sobering episode that brought a majority of the English people round to their way of thinking. In 1602, however, the only defense against the believing mentality was robust and passionate skepticism, backed by the power of the Crown. As we have seen, Deacon's and Walker's attempt to tame belief in the preternatural by psychologizing the devil met with contempt from Darrell, who called it a door opened to atheism. Harsnett's attempts to argue conscious fraud for politico-religious reasons fared no better with either Darrell or, presumably, the Catholics, who certainly did not stop exorcising. In that context, Harsnett's satirical laughter is the voice of reason and sanity. Unfortunately he did not leave it at that, but marshalled a countermyth of his own against the illusions of the exorcists.

# 5

# The Writing of the *Declaration*

When Harsnett joined Bancroft as his chaplain in 1597, for nine years he had been living a wholly academic life as a teacher and administrator. As a fellow of Pembroke Hall, he had taken his share of university and college duty, and he had taught regularly in the course of study leading to the B.A. and M.A. degrees. He must have enjoyed the work and been good at it, for the mutual affection and loyalty between him and his pupils lasted well beyond the college years.[1] Nor did clerical preferment end his academic life. He was twice vice-chancellor of the university, in 1605 and 1614, and in 1605 he succeeded Lancelot Andrewes as master of Pembroke.[2] As a young man he had been a brilliant scholar, and he was remembered for his learning after his death. "A man of great learning, strong parts, and stout spirit," Fuller calls him, and Anthony à Wood (who also spoke of his leaving "four or more MSS. fit for the press, of which one is, *De Necessitate Baptismi*") called him "a learned and judicious prelate."[3]

[1]As bishop of Chichester. Harsnett found preferment for a group of former Pembroke pupils. Prebends went to Richard Buckenham, Theophilus Kent, John Nutt, Owen Stockton, and Thomas Tallcott (of Colchester, probably a relative). Thomas Muriell, a former pupil, his chaplain and deputy at Pembroke, became cathedral precentor in 1613. Buckenham also became archdeacon of Lewes (W. D. Peckham, ed., *Acts of the Dean and Chapter of the Cathedral Church of Chichester, 1545–1642*, Sussex Record Society 58 [1959]: 199, 212, 215, 219). These and other preferments are also entered in Harsnett's register, Sussex Record Office, Ep 1/1/18. Of these men, Muriell, Stockton, and Nutt were fellows of Pembroke at the time of the quarrel between the Harsnett and Andrewes factions that ended with Harsnett's resignation as master. They remained loyal to Harsnett (BL MS. Harleian 7031, fol. 99v). Another Harsnett pupil was Randolph Barlow, who received preferment in the Irish church, becoming archbishop of Tuam in 1629 and afterwards archdeacon of Winchester. He seems to have kept in touch with Harsnett (William Laud, *Works*, 7 vols. [Oxford: Library of Anglo-Catholic Theology, 1847–60], 6:258).

[2]Thomas Fuller. *The History of the University of Cambridge*, ed. J. Nichols (London, 1840), 221; Aubrey Attwater. *Pembroke College* (Cambridge: Cambridge University Press, 1936), 59. According to custom he proceeded D.D. upon election as vice-chancellor. His theses were *Scriptura non armat subditos in principem* and *Ultima resolutio fidei est in scripturam* (BL MS. Harleian 7038, p. 86, col. 2).

[3]Fuller, *Worthies*, 181; Wood, *Athenae Oxonienses* 2:874–75.

He approached the writing of the *Declaration* as a teacher and an academic humanist rather than as a cleric. The book is arranged in academic fashion in a rhetorical, not an analytic or narrative style, and its contents are organized according to the time the events occurred, the places where they occurred, the people to whom and by whom they occurred, and the manner in which they occurred. The whole then ends with a long declaration of the purpose "of all this pestilent tragaedy." The book abounds in characteristically academic references to plays (some of them probably university plays), to poems, and to prose works. Harsnett was obviously an enthusiastic reader of contemporary as well as ancient literature who had a humanist's delight in experiment with tone, syntax, and vocabulary. The book's most striking quality is a gift for pungent satire and comedy that will stop at very little. Harsnett will even quote Scripture for comic purposes; it is no wonder he shocked John Darrell.

All this marks Harsnett in the society of Pembroke Hall more as a man in the mold of William Fulke and Gabriel Harvey than of Lancelot Andrewes and his neoclericalist followers. Harsnett's skepticism may owe much to Fulke, who was presumably one of his teachers;[1] and although Harsnett is a better writer than Harvey, he certainly read Harvey's books. The very title of the *Declaration* comes from Harvey.[2] In his time, then, Harsnett was a modernist, a progressive who brusquely dismissed from serious consideration any kind of belief in the preternatural world of devils, witches, and the like:

They that have their braines baited and their fancies distempered with the imaginations and apprehensions of Witches, Conjurers, and Fayries, and all that Lymphatical *Chimaera*, I finde to be marshalled in one of these five rankes: children, fooles, women, cowards, sick or blacke, melancholicke, discomposed wits. The Scythians being a warlike Nation (as *Plutarch* reports) never saw any visions.

The frightful fancies and fond gastful opinions of all the other dotrels arise out of one of these two rootes: weakenes of wit or unstayednes in religion. (*DEP*, 309)

[1]Fulke wrote *Antiprognosticon that is to saye an Invective agaynst . . . the Astrologians.* His *Goodly Gallery*, a fairly popular book that went into four editions between 1563 and 1639, gives an entirely natural explanation of "meteors." For Fulke's skepticism in a case of alleged possession, see Thomas, *Religion*, 490.

[2]The phrase "egregious imposerures" is from *Pierces Supererogation* (*Works*, ed. A. B. Grosart, 3 vols. [London and Aylesbury: Privately printed for the Huth Library, 1884–85], 2:291). It occurs in a passage on Scot's *Discoverie of Witchcraft*, one of Harsnett's favorite authorities on his subject. "Egregious" was a favorite word with Harvey: see *Works* 1:175; 2:39, 91, 129.

In Harsnett's mind, Catholicism, medieval romance, and rustic folklore form a trinity of ignorance and unreason:

> . . . what a world of hel-worke, devil-worke, and Elve-worke had we walking amongst us heere in England, what time that popish mist had befogged the eyes of our poore people? How were our children, old women, and maides afraid to crosse a Churchyeard or a three-way leet, or to goe for spoones into the Kitchin without a candle? (306)

The four books he singles out for censure as causes of superstition and because they "puffe up our young gallants with bigge lookes and bombast phrases" (307) are *Lancelot du Lake, The Mirrour of Knighthoode, Guy of Warwicke,* and *Amadis de Gaule*—a list in which we no doubt hear the voice of the teacher who disapproves of his students' reading matter. The only medieval author he quotes approvingly is Chaucer, whom he read as an anticlerical, anti-Catholic satirist, and his favorite contemporary author on his subject is the equally skeptical Reginald Scot, on whose *Discoverie of Witchcraft* he draws heavily for his twenty-first chapter.

Like all effective satirists, Harsnett knows intimately the rustic world of superstition that he exposes. Country usages and allusions tell us that he grew up in this world of mummers, masquers, Christmas games, merry tales, proverbs, fairies, wood-demons, elves, witches, pucks, and bogies. This material contributes as much to his prose as his Cambridge education and the witty talk at the college table; the mingling of the two elements makes his style very distinctive:

> The great skar-buggs of old time, as *Hercules* and the rest, had a great humour (as the Poets faigne) to goe downe to *Styx* and to visit hell to see *Pluto* and his uglie ghosts, and to behold the holes and dennes where hee lodged his blacke guard. (248)

Such a passage depends for its effect on techniques, common to all comic satire, that flatter the reader into accepting the author's implied standards of decorum. The vocabulary is everywhere inventive and ebullient, ranging from Harsnett's own classically inspired neologisms to the dialect usages of the countryside. The syntax at its best has a firmness and symmetry derived from Harsnett's classical education. The result is a contrast running through the book between clownishness of the subject matter and the witty commonsense of its treatment: only a bumpkin, the style implies, could believe the exorcists' nonsense.

Given Harsnett's extreme skepticism and his conviction that the exorcisms were a total imposture, it is not surprising that his whole attack should depend for effect upon comparison of the exorcisms to a theatrical performance. There is nothing original in the simile itself, which appears in all such literature of the period, because exorcisms often were a theatrical spectacle in the later sixteenth century[1] and because theatricality was a standard topos of anti-Catholic rhetoric. Harsnett brings the simile to life by the detail, variety, and intellectual consistency of his use of it.

Kenneth Muir has counted some 230 words derived from the theater in Harsnett's book, and he has remarked on the "detailed and unclerical knowledge" of the theater that they reveal. Other writers have followed Muir, and it has also been suggested that Harsnett's knowledge of the stage might be partly based on his work as an examiner of books for the press, a task deputed to the archbishop of Canterbury and the bishop of London, which they in turn delegated to their chaplains.[2] This, however, gives a misleading emphasis to Harsnett's theatrical imagery. It is no more unclerical than the *Declaration* as a whole, in which Harsnett writes as an intellectual, a humanist, and a man of letters, not as a cleric.

The allusions to the stage are systematic and detailed. The Roman priesthood is a company of actors whose chief director is the pope. From his "tyring house" at Rome, he sends out touring companies "masked with the vizard of holy burning zeale" who "do play Almighty God, his sonne, and Saints upon a stage, and do make a pageant of the church" (196, 197). The exorcisms are a "play of sacred miracles," a "devil-Comedy" written by William Weston, "alone the Author, Actor, and penner of this play" (202, 280, 270). Its genre is "*Tragico-comaedia,*" but it is also an episode in a larger "tragedie of devils" that "had his time of rising and his fatall time of fall with the true tragedie performed upon *Babington* and his complices" (319, 208). The costumes and props came "out of the holy wardrop at Rome" (203).

Although "a devil-Comedy may be plaid in a chimnies end with an halfe peny worth of cost" (280), Weston's company chose the places for their performances carefully, says Harsnett. To be suit-

[1]On the theatricality of exorcism, see Weber. "L'exorcisme à la fin du XVIe siècle." In France an exorcism might be performed before a very large audience upon a stage erected in the church. As theater the Denham exorcisms were a small-scale, amateurish affair, no match for the private theaters with their audiences of about four hundred, let alone the public theaters with audiences as large as three thousand.

[2]Muir, *Shakespeare's Sources,* 148; M. C. Bradbrook, *Shakespeare: The poet in His World* (London: Weidenfeld and Nicolson, 1978), 194. On the arrangements for the licensing of books, see W. W. Greg, *Some Aspects and Problems of London Publishing Between 1550 and 1650* (Oxford: Clarendon Press, 1956), 9, 52–62. On Harsnett as licenser, see Appendix C.

able a house needed capacity, security, and remoteness: "The holy troupe . . . removed bagge and baggage as your wandring Players use to doe," but "theyr principall Theatre" was Sir George Peckham's house at Denham. Here "the hangings were tricked up, the houses made ready, and the greatest part of the wonders of this comedie was performed" (210ff.).

Harsnett fits himself into this scheme as the discriminating spectator who, having missed the performance, is anxious to know how good it was:

> whether the partes have beene handled handsomlie and cunningly, or no, what the scope of the Author *Edmunds* and his associates was in this wonderful pageant, and whether good *decorum* have beene kept in acting the same. (202)

His standards of judgment are academic, modern, and sophisticated, as his use of "decorum" tells us. So he finds the play's great success to be owing to the gullibility and simplicity of the audience, not to its own merits. Even by the standards of the old morality plays, it was crude, old-fashioned, and carelessly performed:

> It was a prety part in the old Church-playes when the nimble Vice would skip up nimbly like a Jacke an Apes into the devils necke, and ride the devil a course, and belabour him with his woodden dagger til he made him roare, wherat the people would laugh to see the devil so vice-haunted.

The Denham devils, however, had no fight in them; the mere picture of a vice made them roar:

> [These] devils be surely some of those old vice-haunted cassiered woodden-beaten devils that were wont to frequent the stages, and have had theyr hornes beaten off with *Mengus* his clubbe, and theyr tayles cut off with a smart lash of his stinging whip: who are so skared with the *Idaea* of a vice and a dagger, as they durst never since looke a paper-vice in the face. (291)

Sara "acted . . . commendably well" (249), and Marwood "played his part *extempore* there on the stage with a verie good grace;" but the vizards were "bare and made all of browne paper," and "all was a *Stygian* comedy to make silly people afraid:" (218, 226, 257)

> you have never a child of tenne yeeres that is a looker on, but will see and discerne their grosse packing, rude bungling, and palpable jugling so apparantlie, as hee wil dare to take the devil by the visard, and play with the fooles nose, and cry, away with the priest and the devil, they have marred a good play. (272)

Notice that the comparison implied in these quotations is with the professional theater of tiring-houses, fools, vices, vizards, hangings, houses, even of actor-dramatists who perform in their own plays. Harsnett presents the exorcists and their patients as if they were a second- or third-string touring company sent out into the provinces. Their play is bad and the acting is worse. The implication is that Harsnett has no very high opinion of the professional theater.

Harsnett licensed Ben Jonson's *Every Man Out of His Humour* for printing, and he entered into his copy of Maunsell's catalogue a list of attacks on the stage.[1] Neither is evidence of interest in, or even of dislike for, the stage. He certainly enjoyed classical drama, as his quotations show. He will have taught some classical comedy to his pupils at Colchester, and he probably took an interest in university drama. During his second vice-chancellorship, when James I visited Cambridge, a play, *Ignoramus,* was planned, and a student of Puritan convictions, Samuel Fairclough, was at first chosen for the part of Surda, an old woman. He judged it improper for a man to wear female clothing under any circumstances, and asked the vice-chancellor to excuse him. Harsnett tried to laugh the boy out of his scruples, but when he realized that he was serious, he gave the part to another student. If Corbett's poem on the occasion can be taken as evidence, Harsnett enjoyed the performance very much, even though the courtiers grew impatient, for it lasted six hours:

> His Lordshipp then was in a rage,
> His Lordship lay upon the stage,
> His Lordshipp cry'd all would be marr'd. . . .[2]

To have a liking for classical comedy and academic drama based on classical models is by no means the same thing as approving of the public theaters. Two of Harsnett's references to professional actors are utterly contemptuous. The second, more detailed one calls them "vagabonds" and accuses them of the same immoralities that the Puritans made much of:

[1] Arber 3:159. Harsnett's copy of Andrew Maunsell, *Catalogue of English Printed Books* (1595) contains several additions in a Roman hand that is probably Harsnett's. On sig. G5, Maunsell has a subdivision headed "Of the Plague, or Pestilence," and on the facing leaf, Harsnett has set out a new category, "Against Playes," where he lists Rankins, *A Mirrour of Monsters* (1587), Gosson, *The Schoole of Abuse* (1579), *The Ephemerides* (1579), *Plays Confuted in Five Actions* (1582), and *A Second and Third Blast of Retrait from Plaies and Theaters* (1580).

[2] Richard Corbet, *Poems,* ed. J. A. W. Bennett and H. R. Trevor-Roper (Oxford: Clarendon Press, 1956), 12.

> It is the fashion of vagabond players that coast from Towne to Towne with a trusse and a cast of fiddles to carry in theyr consort broken queanes and *Ganimedes,* as well for their night pleasance as their dayes pastime. (318)

Therefore, although Harsnett compares the exorcisms in general to a professional troupe's touring repertoire, his actual allusions to specific plays are either to classical drama, academic drama, or to "old plays"—the interludes, miracles, and moralities. He seems not to have frequented the public theaters. His terminology is noticeably academic: *plaudite, suspendite* (203), *ad ornandam scenam* (281), "such agents, patients, and assistants as have furnished the stage" (202). In his references to English drama, he seems to have thought especially of "church-plaies" or of private Christmas performances, the sort of event he knew from his own boyhood or that was familiar to him from the social life of his academic and ecclesiastical world.[1] The exorcisms at Denham and at Lord Vaux's house at Hackney during the Christmas season of 1585 very naturally brought Christmas plays to mind:

> The devil looked into *Denham* house as *Prestons* dogge looked into his neighbours doore, of no malicious intent to eate any *Christmas-pie,* but to see how *Christmas* went: and seeing a play towards, and that they wanted a devil, was content to make one in the play, and to curvet, foame, and tumble with a very good devils grace. (292)

At Hackney, Sara "happily . . . dreamed of [motly vizards] in a Christmasse night, having seene Maskers in the day", and the dispossession of her devils was the conclusion to the devil's "motly mummerie" (311).

There is a description of a "hell mouth" (258), which could apply either to a public or a private performance, and some of Harsnett's other theatrical terms are applicable to either kind of theater: "cue-fellowes," "prompters," "directers," "teachers." (218) Nonetheless, it seems prudent to conclude that Harsnett's theatrical knowledge was not drawn primarily, if at all, from the public theaters. His word "*Devill-mastix*" (243) may indicate knowledge of the "war of the theatres," but not certainly so, and even if it did, it would not make him into a theater-goer. He compares exorcising

---

[1]In this connection it is interesting that he licensed Nashe's *Summers Last Will and Testament* (Arber 3:175), written for performance in Archbishop Whitgift's household at Croydon in 1592, and that Bishop Bancroft had earlier suggested the employment of professional writers and dramatists to answer Martin Marprelate (For the date of Nashe's play, see *Works,* ed. Ronald B. McKerrow, 5 vols. [Oxford: Basil Blackwell, 1958], 5:416–18).

to play-acting because both activities strike him as tricks depen-
dent upon a spectator's willingness to be duped—not a line of
thought one would expect from an habitual theater-goer. There is a
kind of contemptuous nostalgia in his references to the old drama,
and he is prepared to enjoy theater as recreation or festivity. Yet
even here, the famous description of the vice, as Professor Edmund
Creeth pointed out to me, corresponds to no surviving example of
the vice's part. Harsnett's theater images may not be based entirely
on experience; they are a calculated part of his rhetoric, drawn
from a mixture of reading, hearsay, and experience, and meant to
belittle the exorcisms from an antitheatrical point of view.[1]

The irony is that despite Harsnett's suspicion of the stage and its
illusions, his book is itself a bravura performance, a long oration
put into the mouth of a witty don with an exuberant classroom
manner. Even the clever openings of his chapters, which contain
some of the book's best writing, have a touch of the lecture room.
Harsnett seems to have realized that this aspect of his book would
puzzle some readers, and that what was suitable for a small audience of the well-educated might alienate the less sophisticated.
Therefore he slips in a word of explanation:

> If the forme and phrase be distasting to some clowdy spirits, as too
> light and ironicall for one of my profession, let the matter be my
> Advocat that draweth me thereunto, and the manner my Apologie a
> little too: trusting I may be excused to jest at their jesting that have
> made a jest of God and of his blessed Saints in heaven.(199)

The appeal to decorum reflects the conscious, rhetorical manner of
his book.

Harsnett the classically trained, satirical humanist is an attractive, amusing person who writes some of the best prose of his time:

> The Philosophers old *aphorisme* is, *cerebrum Melancholicum est
> sedes daemonum,* a melancholicke braine is the chaire of estate for the
> devil. And an other *aphorisme* they have, founded on experience,
> *nullum magnum ingenium sine dementia,* there is no great wit without
> some mixture of madnesse. *John Bodin* the Frenchman is a perfect
> *Idaea* of both these, who beeing in his younger yeeres of a most pierc-
> ing, quicke, speculative wit, which grew of a light, stirring, and dis-
> cursive melancholie in him, fell (as *Hermogenes* the mirror of wit did)
> in the midle of his age to be a pure sot. (304)

[1]Greenblatt, *Shakespearean Negotiations,* 106–114, proposes an interesting sce-
nario for the way Harsnett's theatrical imagery translates the phenomena of the exorcisms
into "a powerful, if sleazy, tragicomedy." It would only work, however, for readers pre-
disposed against the theater, and already convinced, on other grounds, of the fraudulence
of the exorcisms.

In the rhythm and inventiveness of that prose Harsnett is a pure artist. As I have already argued, however, mixed motives underlay the writing of the *Declaration,* resulting in the book's being written not so much to persuade Catholics or to amuse ironic B.A.s as to enlist the keener Protestants in the campaign against possession and exorcism. The antitheatrical rhetoric has an obvious role to play in flattering those same Protestants. By chapter 7 Harsnett is associating himself with his audience as "us Protestants" (226), and the "gentle reader" (230) he apostrophizes following the description of Fid's baptism is also a Protestant. While John Murphy is right to associate Harsnett the satirist with a Church-of-England tradition that includes Hall, Swift, Sidney Smith, and the pre-Catholic Newman,[1] Harsnett the anti-Catholic bigot belongs to an entirely different tradition stemming chiefly from Foxe's *Book of Martyrs* and similar Protestant works. The mingling of the two strains gives the book its peculiar, acrid tone.

Most of Harsnett's scholarly readers have not noticed this aspect of his book or have ignored it or thought it insignificant. Walker, for instance, quotes Harsnett's description of the relics of Edmund Campion, "fresh greene new reliques" (296), as an example of his "typical bad taste;"[2] but this does not prevent him from accepting Harsnett's version of the exorcisms. Murphy regrets that "Harsnett allows his fine railing to desert him for a space and falls into that nauseous cant that disfigures so much of the polemical divinity of these times,"[3] but he does not examine the nature of the disfigurement in Harsnett's case. M. C. Bradbrook is alone in feeling how powerfully the "gloating taunts . . . brutal jeers and savage obscenities of this most unchristian work" dominate the tone of Harsnett's book.[4] William Elton's description of the book as "a work of polemical divinity" is wide of the mark.[5] Judged as divinity, and neglecting for a moment the strain of purely imaginative satire that redeems it, Harsnett's book belongs to the same category of subliterature as a nineteenth-century tract about walled-up nuns. Unless we understand that, we shall not do justice to Shakespeare's encounter with the book.

When Harsnett treats subjects like the mission and execution of Edmund Campion or the nature of Catholic ceremonial and belief, he falls into repetitive abuse made up of adjectives that grow

[1] *Darkness and Devils,* 72

[2] *Unclean Spirits,* 47.

[3] *Darkness and Devils,* 44.

[4] *Shakespeare,* 194–95.

[5] *King Lear and the Gods* (San Marino, Calif.: Huntington Library, 1966), 89.

increasingly less effective, such as "hellish," "impure," "impious," "blasphemous," and "detestable." Harsnett's surviving letters, papers, and books show him to be a writer whose effectiveness depended upon his ease in the role required by the occasion: preacher, teacher, counselor, bishop, patron, client, friend. In the *Declaration,* his efforts at sectarian vituperation are so labored that one has to conclude that the role did not come easily and made no appeal to his imagination.

There was one kind of anti-Catholicism, however, that kindled his imagination. Although the institution of the Catholic church itself, its policies, its structures of belief and practice, remained abstract to him, its priesthood aroused in him strong emotions of fear and loathing. In Harsnett's mind (and in this he is typical of the long tradition of British anti-Catholicism) the Catholic priest is a figure of mystery, his world and his work a secret, and his mere presence a challenge to the safety of the kingdom. Because his claims to sanctity and spiritual authority are denied by the premises of the national argument against his church, he can only be an agent of destructive forces and he must therefore be a conscious fraud or hypocrite. This was to be the accusation that Charles Kingsley made in 1864 against the entire body of the Catholic clergy in the person of John Henry Newman, and in 1602 Harsnett argues it in all sobriety against William Weston:

> The difference betweene a Pagan and a Popish priest, as I take it, is this, that the one doth seriously and in good sadnesse perswade himselfe that his halowed person, charmes, and consecrate attire, as his scepter, his crowne, and Albe, doth awe, terrifie, and depel the devil indeed; the other doth not in earnest so thinke or dreame, but doth know the cleane contrary, that there is neither vertue, ability, nor proportion in any of these gewgawes to move or stil the devil, no more then there is in a white sheet to scare a sober man. . . . (271)

The presence of this belief in Harsnett's book defines its tone; there is a world of difference between, say, the genial comedy of Erasmus' use of a story of play-acting to expose superstition in his colloquy *Exorcism and the Spectre,* and Harsnett's use of the same figure.[1] Harsnett's priests put on a performance meant to deceive; nonetheless, according to him, the performance conceals a terrible reality. He has exposed the devils of Denham as fakes, but the images of the performance have left an indelible impression of violence and obscenity on his mind, and that manifest evil requires an

---

[1]*Colloquies,* trans. by Craig R. Thompson (Chicago: University of Chicago Press, 1965), 231–37. Murphy, *Darkness and Devils,* 72–78, compares Harsnett and Erasmus. He attributes the difference in Harsnett's tone to the influence of Reginald Scot.

explanation. To provide one he substitutes the agency of the priests for that of the devil, a maneuver that, in the tradition of Lucianic or Erasmian satire in which he claims to be writing, he is free to perform. The decorum of the mode, however, should lead him to expose the priests as fools and knaves and their performance as farce. Instead, he treats the devils as the fools and turns the priests into the devils. Thus Harsnett as humanist critic exposes a bad comedy of ludicrous, comic, and bogus devils; as dramatist or fictioneer he reveals the plot of a sinister, Gothic tragedy, so far unwritten, in which the exorcisms are only a grotesque, farcical episode.[1]

The motif of the demon-priest runs through the book from the introductory epistle to the last chapter. Its most fully worked-out version appears in chapter 17 in the horrific emblem or allegory of the priest-exorcist as a walking hell on earth. In this piece of Elizabethan Gothick, Harsnett's sense of decorum deserts him, as it always does in these passages, and so one is not entirely sure of the intended effect. He may have may meant it to be funny but, especially towards the end, as he sets his demon-priest walking the streets of London, he develops an atmosphere of real horror:

> And ere you stirre your imagination, doe but imagine him a little further, walking in our London streets a little before day light, what time the Chimny-sweepers use to make theyr walke, and crying in his hellish hollow voyce, *hay ye ere a devil to drive? hay yee ere a wench to fire? hay yee ere a boy to dispossesse?* (276)

One should not underestimate the calculation of this vividly imagined passage. Not only has Harsnett given the priest the "hollow" demonic voice that seems always to be a feature of possessions;[2] he has also not forgotten John Darrell. The call for a "boy" and the use of "dispossess" rather than "exorcise" is meant to recall Darrell

---

[1]Greenblatt, otherwise uninterested in Harsnett's bigotry, describes this maneuver as "the reinscription of evil onto the professed enemies of evil" and compares it to the modern trying of revolutionaries as counterrevolutionaries (*Shakespearean Negotiations,* 1988, 98). While I am not sure what "reinscription" means, the comparison that follows is surely wrong, for Harsnett never concedes that he and the exorcists might once have been on the same side. Religious bigotry is a different nastiness from the kind that put on the show trials of this century; it would be less persistent, more easily dealt with, if it were not.

[2]There are many descriptions of the demonic voice in the literature of possession. See for instance Malachi Martin, *Hostage to the Devil* (1976, reprint, Bantam Books, 1977), 22–23. According to Murphy, *Darkness and Devils,* 207, the BBC recorded such a voice in the case of the "Enfield Poltergeist." It is by all accounts a distressing, inhuman sound. Unlike Professor Murphy, I doubt whether such a voice was heard at Denham. It seems to be inimitable; certainly no actor playing Edgar could imitate it, as Murphy suggests.

and his two most famous patients, the Boy of Burton and William
Somers. Moreover, Harsnett means to frighten his reader; and to do
this the same man who mocks superstitious Catholics, women, and
girls for fearing to walk into a kitchen in the dark or to venture
down a lane at night sets a monster of his own devising in the London streets at break of day.

This is the quality in the *Declaration* that leads Muriel
Bradbrook to say that "he is seduced by his own 'game', and his
deviousness and violence give a mirror image of all he
denounced."[1] There is even more to it than this. In his last chapter Harsnett finally rewrites the priests' play for them, arranging
their dialogues with the devils to illustrate his own interpretation,
that their play was an act of calculated treason. His comments
include a good deal of what Murphy calls "nauseous cant," an eloquent phrase that for the modern reader has an antiseptic effect,
dissipating the power some of these passages might have for a
reader who shared Harsnett's preoccupations:

> The loathsome abhominations and Ethnike Impostures of the Church
> of Rome where-with they have gulled and made drunken the Kings of
> the Nations, being by the piercing glorious light of the Gospel dis-
> played and uncovered to the open view of the world: and that church
> for her whoredome being deprived of the holy spirit of Almighty God,
> and given over to the spirit of darknes, giddines, and jugling deceite,
> having now neyther testimonie from Gods divine Oracles, nor
> breathings from that heavenly cleare fountaine, nor presence of holy
> Fathers to countenance their monstrous deformations: doe in a desper-
> ate fury and hellish resolution resort unto the Oracles of the devil. . . .
> (333)

That is "nauseous cant" because Harsnett certainly did not, in any
ordinary, straightforward sense of the word, believe it.[2] By
adopting the Hebrew prophetic manner and expressing it in
Ciceronian syntax, Harsnett has assumed the authority associated
with those religious and literary modes. Instead of speaking in his

---

[1] *Shakespeare*, 195.

[2] Hooker gives a summary of the extreme Protestant position that the Church of
Rome is antichrist in *Laws of Ecclesiastical Polity*, bk. 4, chap. 3 (*Works* 1:280–83). His
strongest, most succinct statement of the Church of England position, with which
Harsnett would have agreed, is to be found in bk. 5, chap. 28 (*Works* 2:121):

> Some thinges they doe in that they are men, in that they are wise men and Christian
> men some thinges, some thinges in that they are men misled and blinded with error.
> As farre as they followe reason and truth, we feare not to tread the selfe same steppes
> wherein they have gon, and to be theire followers. Where Rome keepeth that which is
> ancienter and better; others whome we much more affect leavinge it for newer, and
> changinge it for worse, we had rather followe the perfections of them whome we like
> not, then in defectes resemble them whome we love.

own, merely private voice, he has put on a performance. Yet although the passage is insincere and pretentious, it has power because in manipulating his readers' fears Harsnett draws, once again, upon fears of his own, as the very next paragraph reveals:

> Heare their lamentable voyce, fraught with despaire, *quid dicis?* Prince of darknes, what sayest thou for our Masse? What sayest thou for our Sacrament of the Altar? And now (good Reader) observe the top of hellish resolution and the gulf of dispaire wherein the Romish church is plunged, when neither God, Angel, nor devil can be gotten to speake for them. For heere was neither Angel, S. *Mary,* S. *Barbara,* nor devil, nor spirit, in all this faigned tragedie, as we have let you to see thorough the whole course of the same. O lamentable desolation! *Weston* and his twelve Priests doe play the devils themselves. . . . (333)

This passage is a microcosm of the book. First Harsnett tells us that the exorcist goes to the devil (who is not a fool or vice in this context, but the Prince of Darkness) to have his beliefs validated. This devil, however, is a play-devil, performed by the exorcist, who therefore addresses his questions to an emptiness in which there is neither angel nor devil, and from which he receives for answer only the echo of his own voice. The darkness, therefore, is real, William Weston the demon-priest is its prince, and the *frisson* of fear or horror is focused in the phrase *quid dicis,* a variant or parody of the plangent question, *quem dicunt* that Christ puts to his disciples in the synoptic gospels: "Quem me dicunt esse homines esse?" (Mark 8:27; Whom do men say that I am?). That question, in the context of the bogus exorcisms, opens up the possibility of an alternate reality. For a Protestant who believed, like many of the English of Harsnett's time, that the prophecy of the antichrist was fulfilled in the Church of Rome, Harsnett's insistence in this passage on "*Weston* and his twelve priests" would emphasize the parodic blasphemy of the priests' performance, and define that alternative. For Harsnett himself, who probably believed no such thing, his identification of Weston and his companions as a parody of Christ and the Apostles is a detail in a conscious rhetoric deployed to express his own fiction. Nonetheless, that fiction in turn expresses an emotion of real fear and horror, not aroused by the literal, necessarily tawdry blasphemy of an antichristian church and priesthood, but by Harsnett's own vivid imagination of a real darkness empty of all belief and authority. Harsnett seems to have succeeded in frightening himself.

Stephen Greenblatt's description of the *Declaration* as "a massive document of disenchantment" is, besides its hyperbole, too

simple and cheery an assessment.[1] Harsnett may have intended
to demystify the exorcisms; intentionally or not, he remystified the
events by presenting them as performances by a demonic priesthood whose purpose is the subversion of English social order.
This, to quote Bradbrook again, is "a mirror image of all he
denounced." He may be a humanist, a skeptical cleric in a church
that has abdicated dogmatic authority, and a disbeliever in miracle
and prophecy, yet those positions bring with them their own anxie-
ties for a man who takes belief seriously. None of them relieves
him of the need, or of the weight, of authority; and none of them
satisfactorily explains the presence of evil and good in a world of
cause and effect.

For Harsnett authority at its simplest was vested in the state, specifically in his friend, master, and patron, Richard Bancroft. The
personal effects of that authority and of the tribute it demands
appear in the dissonances of his text and its persona, in what
Bradbrook calls its "deviousness and violence." Harsnett was a
superbly gifted writer, but he never wrote as his own man, and in
the *Declaration* he finds himself caught in the same processes as
the priests, themselves the servants of absolute authority. In such a
context, even his humanism and skepticism have untoward consequences. For while the world of magical evil was dying out of the
English people's consciousness even as Harsnett attacked and ridi-
culed it, another world of historical and secular evil incarnate in
people and events was coming into being; and this is the world that
Harsnett's humanism substitutes for the magical one. Nor was it a
less malignant and mysterious world. Harsnett's demon-exorcist
has his place in the development of the dark anti-Catholic fantasies
of the British and, by extension, the American Protestant and
agnostic imagination.

Harsnett, of course, did not invent the fantasy, nor should he be
indicted for its consequences, still at work in the world. He drew
upon it, however, to accomplish a particular literary and political
purpose. It is a part of his text, to be included in the account. It is
certainly ironic that so humane and enlightened a man should have
written so prophetically violent a text.

It is impossible to assess the book's effect. Among its more
important readers were the future Archbishop Abbot, who quoted
from it in 1604; Thomas Fuller, who quoted it in his *Church History,* and Robert Burton, who calls it a "just volume" and remarks
that the exorcisms were "ordinary tricks only to get opinion and

---

[1]*"King Lear* and Harsnett's 'Devil-Fiction,'" *Genre* 15 (1982): 240. (To judge from
the much expanded and developed versions of this piece published while I was writing
this account of Harsnett, Professor Greenblatt might agree with this sentence.)

money, mere impostures"[1]—a view more benign but even less accurate than Harsnett's. The book also had a more malign kind of influence, being plagiarized by less respectable authors. John Gee, author of the peculiar anti-Catholic tract, *The Foot out of the Snare* (1624), plagiarizes it heavily. He also names its author, "*Harsenet, now Bishop of Norwich,*" which could have been embarrassing to Harsnett in 1624, and goes on to say:

> If the Booke cannot easily be gotten, I wish it might bee imprinted againe, for that the Priests exorcising power is there fully discovered: and I have heard, that the most of these bookes which were formerly printed, were bought up by Papists, who (no question) tooke so much delight in reading them, that they burned as many as they could possibly get of them. (sig. H2v)[2]

The printing history of the book makes this story unlikely. Another Grub Street plagiarist, the author of *Balaam the Devil* (1636), an account of the notorious possession of the Ursulines of Loudun, borrows his imagery, references, and tricks of speech from Harsnett, and the author, like Gee, praises Harsnett for having "learnedly and wittily set downe all the circumstances of their villany" (sig. C2).

The *Declaration* seems to have had no great effect on the behavior of Catholic exorcists.[3] It did, however, silence John Darrell.

---

[1]George Abbot, *The Reasons which Doctor Hill hath Brought* (1604), sig. K4v; Fuller, *Church History*, bk. 10, sect. 4, par. 55; Burton, *Anatomy of Melancholy*, pt. 2, sect. 1, mem. 3.

[2]On Gee and his book, see Theodore H. B. M. Harmsen (ed.), *John Gee's Foot out of the Snare (1624)* (Nijmegen: The Cicero Press, 1992).

[3]Thomas, *Religion*, 489: "Every year the reports of the Jesuit Mission in England recorded successful exorcisms of bewitched persons and dispossessions of those attacked by evil spirits."

# 6

# Shakespeare and Harsnett

Sometime between its publication in the early summer of 1603 and the writing of *King Lear,* probably in late 1604–5, Shakespeare read Harsnett's *Declaration.* An echo of the book appears in *Othello,* datable 1603–4, and this would push Shakespeare's reading of it back almost to the date of publication. Unfortunately the echo in *Othello* occurs at 3.2.383–90, a passage found in the Folio text but not in the Quarto, and it might be an addition.[1]

Shakespeare's interest in the book is not surprising. Both the controversies to which it contributed, the Darrell case and the archpriest scandals, were subjects of keen public interest, engendering between them over thirty books, and David Kaula has argued that some of the archpriest pamphlets influenced Shakespeare's work from *Hamlet* to *Macbeth.*[2] By its nature, this is a hard proposition to prove, but many of Kaula's verbal parallels are curious and striking, involving the kind of idiosyncratic phrase and word that Shakespeare also picked up from Harsnett. We can assume that Shakespeare will have read some of the pamphlets. They were lively, scandalous reading. He was certainly interested in the Darrell affair; the anti-Puritan gibes in *Twelfth Night,* including Feste's lampooning of a Puritan minister as exorcist, show him taking the anti-Darrell side. It seems safe to infer that he read Harsnett's *Discovery* and that he found it a funny book as well as an interesting one. Having enjoyed the *Discovery,* he would naturally be interested in the *Declaration.*

We should also credit Shakespeare with an interest in the larger principles at debate in both controversies. Is authority a principle found in nature, to be elicited and defined by reason, and is nature,

[1]Othello's phrase "begrimed and black" is influenced by Harsnett's passages describing the blackening of Sara Williams's face with the fumigations (*DEP,* 235). His "cords . . . suffocating streams" and "I'll not endure it" reflect a speech by Marwood (*DEP,* 259) as well as a phrase in Harsnett's portrait of a demon-exorcist, "streamers of scorching smoke" (*DEP,* 276). For a detailed discussion of the passage from *Othello* and the parallels in Harsnett, see Brownlow, "Samuel Harsnett and the meaning of Othello's 'Suffocating Streams,'" *PQ* 58 (1979): 107–115.

[2]*Shakespeare and the Archpriest Controversy.*

and therefore humanity, self-sufficient? Or is authority an attribute of the divine, its exercise an aspect of the supernatural? Specifically, are there miracles and are there prophecies? The fascination of the Darrell case and the archpriest controversy is that they raised these questions in the form of human character and action, not in the abstract terms of the schools. In both controversies the reader's judgment must follow the establishment of fact: What happened? That being so, Darrell, his patients, and the people of Nottingham; William Weston, his fellow-exorcists, their patients, and his later friends and opponents at Wisbech Castle—all become sharply delineated characters in rival versions of their stories. Even Harsnett assumes a role and becomes a character.

Shakespeare also had personal reasons for his interest in the *Declaration*. One of the exorcists, Robert Dibdale, the Peckham's chaplain at Denham, was born in the parish of Stratford-upon-Avon about 1556. He was the elder son of a husbandman of Shottery, John Dibdale, who was a determined recusant. At one time the family owned property in Stratford itself, in Rother Street. Besides Robert, there were three other children: Richard (indicted as a recusant in 1592), Agnes, who married John Pace on 20 October 1578, and Joan. In 1581, Agnes's husband witnessed Richard Hathaway's will, in which Shakespeare's wife, Anne Hathaway, received £6/13s/4d.[1] Robert Dibdale, therefore, was exactly contemporary with Anne Hathaway, and probably a schoolfellow with Richard Quiney and John Field at Stratford Grammar School. So although it is incorrect to say that Dibdale was Shakespeare's schoolfellow, and unfounded to say that he was his friend (for which there is no evidence), Shakespeare's wife must have known him and his family and would have had an interest in knowing of his fate. Shakespeare himself would have had little opportunity to know Dibdale, a boy seven or eight years older, who left Stratford in 1575 to go overseas. Nonetheless, Shakespeare would surely have been interested in the activities of a fellow-Stratfordian, and especially if, as Fripp speculates, he were related to him. Young Dibdale and Simon Hunt, the Stratford schoolmaster, crossed over to the Continent at about the same time, and when Hunt was admitted to the Society of Jesus in Rome in 1578, Robert Dibdale was also in the city. They probably traveled together.[2]

[1]Edgar Fripp, *Shakespeare's Haunts Near Stratford* (Oxford: Oxford University Press, 1929), 30–31. Fripp also wonders whether Dibdale and Shakespeare might have been kinsmen through their mothers: "Palmer," Dibdale's alias, will have been his mother's name, and it may also have been the maiden name of Shakespeare's maternal grandmother, Mrs. Robert Arden (33, 53, and n.).

[2]Bradbrook, *Shakespeare,* 194, and Milward, *Shakespeare's Religious Background,* 52, mistakenly call Shakespeare and Dibdale schoolfellows. The best account of the scholarship identifying Simon Hunt the schoolmaster with the Hunt who became a Jesuit

In late 1579, Robert Dibdale left Rome for the Douay-Rheims seminary, arriving there on 29 December 1579. There he found another Stratford connection, the future Jesuit martyr Thomas Cottam, executed with Edmund Campion in 1582. This Cottam was the younger brother of John Cottam, schoolmaster at Stratford from 1579 to 1581 or 1582;[1] and when Thomas Cottam left the Continent for England in 1580, he carried with him an affectionate letter from Robert Dibdale to his parents in Stratford. Harsnett's attacks on the memory of Thomas Cottam (*DEP,* 294) would have been another source of Shakespeare's personal interest in the *Declaration.*[2] Finally, Harsnett attacks the memory of Edward Arden of Park Hall, executed as a Catholic on charges of treason, 20 December 1584 (268). In 1599, only about four years before he read Harsnett's book, Shakespeare had applied in his father's name to the heralds for authority to quarter his arms with those of Arden of Park Hall. The obvious inference is that he considered himself related to them; in fact he and Edward Arden were probably cousins by common descent from Walter Arden of Park Hall, who would have been Shakespeare's great-great-grandfather.[3] In any case, Shakespeare would not have read the name Arden in

---

in Rome in 1578 is John Henry De Groot, *The Shakespeares and 'The Old Faith'* (New York: Columbia University Press, 1946), 135–39. Mark Eccles, *Shakespeare in Warwickshire* (Madison: University of Wisconsin Press, 1961), 55–56, followed by S. Schoenbaum, *Shakespeare: A Documentary Life* (Oxford: Clarendon Press, 1975), 53, is not reliable. Although both he and Schoenbaum depend heavily on Fripp's work, neither mentions Dibdale's connection with the Hathaways or with Simon Hunt. Oddly enough, Eccles (154, n. 6) has a reference to Robert Stevenson, *Shakespeare's Religious Frontier* (The Hague: Martinus Nijhoff, 1958), in which Dibdale figures prominently.

[1]The most recent survey of information about John Cottam, giving much new material, is Ernst Honigmann's in *Shakespeare: The 'Lost Years'* (Totowa, N.J.: Barnes & Noble, 1985), Chap. 4, "John Cottom of Tarnacre." Honigmann has revived the possibility that Shakespeare spent time in a Lancashire recusant household as a teacher and as an actor in the household company of actors. He argues that Cottam the schoolmaster was Shakespeare's link with Lancashire.

[2]*CRS* 5 (1908): 18–19. Eccles (154, n. 6) gives this reference, and knows that Cottam brought a letter for John Dibdale of Shottery; but he gives no account of its contents or its author.

[3]For an account of the application, see Schoenbaum, *Shakespeare,* 166–73. Shakespeare's recent biographers have been reluctant to explore his relationship, through his mother, with the Ardens, perhaps because lower-class origins are a necessary part of the contemporary Shakespeare mythos, and perhaps because of the Ardens' Catholicism. Eccles, *Shakespeare in Warwickshire,* 14, says "No connection has so far been found between the Ardens or Arderns of Park Hall and Thomas Arden of Wilmcote [Shakespeare's great-grandfather]." John Semple Smart, *Shakespeare: Truth and Tradition* (London: Edward Arnold, 1928), 64, demonstrates just such a connection: Walter Arden of Park Hall and Thomas Arden of Wilmcote (whom Smart believes to be Walter's younger son) had a common friend in Sir Robert Throckmorton of Coughton, just outside Stratford, who acted as a trustee for each of them in property transactions. Eccles prints this information on the next page of his book, but without observing its significance, and gives the reference to Smart.

Harsnett's book without a twinge. It is possible, even likely, that the Shakespeares, because of the family connection and their own recusancy, found themselves embroiled to some extent in the Ardens' distresses.[1]

Whatever the specific motivation that drew Shakespeare to a bookstall to buy a copy of Harsnett's *Declaration,* he found in his hands a complex document with at least three layers of text. The first two layers consist of the materials from which it was made: the priestly accounts of the exorcisms, quoted at length throughout, and the statements of the witnesses. Each layer, too, has its own strata. There are two priestly accounts: Weston's Latin tale of Marwood, the first demoniac, and the seminary priests' *Miracle Book* in English describing some of the later cases. There are five witnesses' statements, each of them very different in tone from the others. The third layer is Harsnett's "declaration" of the meaning of the other two, and it also has its complexities. It seems to be addressed to Catholics but is really meant for Protestants, to whose fears, prejudices, and sympathies it constantly appeals. The author's voice modulates from ironic, witty satire to savage mockery, to what Bradbrook calls "gloating taunts" and "brutal jeers." There is also a vein of what Devlin describes, justly, as "pious bombast," a humorless Ciceronian rant on sectarian themes.[2] A writer as accomplished as Shakespeare in manipulating sources and voices will have noticed all this; he will also have recognized the calculated intent of the whole performance.

To trace the effect of the book on Shakespeare's imagination and feelings, one must first examine his use of it. Lewis Theobald was the first to observe that the unique devils' names that occur in *King Lear* (Flibbertigibbet, Smulkin, Modo, Mahu, Frateretto, Purr, Hobbididence, Obidicut) can have no other source:[3]

[1]There is an abundant scholarly literature on the evidence that Shakespeare's family was Catholic, its most important recent exemplars including De Groot, *The Shakespeares and 'The Old Faith';* H. Mutschmann and K. Wentersdorf, *Shakespeare and Catholicism* (New York: Sheed and Ward, 1952); Peter Milward, *Shakespeare's Religious Background;* and Ernst Honigmann, *Shakespeare: The 'Lost Years'.* The classic works are H. S. Bowden, *The Religion of Shakespeare* (London: Burns & Oates, 1899), a book based on the papers of Richard Simpson, the biographer of Edmund Campion, and John Semple Smart, *Shakespeare: Truth and Tradition.* The argument focuses on the eighteenth-century finding of John Shakespeare's "spiritual testament" in the roof of his former house, on the anomalies of Shakespeare's marriage, and on the Stratford recusancy return of 1592. On the latter see F. W. Brownlow, "John Shakespeare's Recusancy: New Light on an Old Document," *Shakespeare Quarterly* 40 (1989):186–91.

[2]Bradbrook, *Shakespeare,* 194–95; Devlin, "Anthony Tyrrell," 357.

[3]3.4.115, 140, 144; 3.6.6, 30, 45; 4.1.59–60. I. B. Cauthen, Jr., "The Foul Flibbertigibbet," (*Notes and Queries,* n.s., 5 [1958]: 98) points out that "Flibbertigibbet" is peculiar neither to Shakespeare nor Harsnett. Nonetheless this set of names occurs only in Harsnett and Shakespeare.

The greatest Part of [Edgar's] dissembled Lunacy, the Names of his Devils, and the descriptive Circumstances he alludes to in his own Case, are all drawn from this Pamphlet, and the Confessions of the poor deluded Wretches.[1]

Theobald also suggested that the origin of Edgar's complaint that the fiend "hath laid knives under his pillow, and halters in his pew" (3.4.54) was Fid's account of the episode of the knives and the halter (*DEP*, 368). Following Theobald, Edmond Malone found a parallel for "A servingman, proud in heart and mind; that curl'd my hair, wore gloves in my cap" (3.4.85) in the priests' account of Mainy's enactment of the seven deadly sins: "*Ma:* Mainy . . . *curled his haire, and used such gestures as Ma:* Edmunds *presently affirmed that that spirit was* Pride" (410). Steevens, Wright, and Percy noticed other parallels missed by their predecessors.[2]

The full extent of Harsnett's influence on *Lear* was not known until Kenneth Muir published the results of a detailed comparison of the two texts. Muir traced over eighty passages in Harsnett for which a parallel could be found in the play. Since over fifty of the parallels appear in the third act, he concluded that the storm scenes owe more to Harsnett than to any other source.[3]

Muir's case is based on the appearance in *Lear* of a number of words, all in Harsnett's book, that Shakespeare had not previously used. Harsnett, for instance, says that "an old corkie woman" (221) is an unfit subject for exorcism; Cornwall orders his servants to "bind fast" Gloucester's "corky arms" (3.7.29), and (although Muir does not notice this) Harsnett also affects the detail of the binding. For Anne Smith tells us three times in her short statement how she was "bound" in a chair, the third time with injury to her arms: "They did bind her so fast . . . in a chayre, as they almost lamed her armes" (386).

Another of Muir's words is "bo-peep," used by the Fool in one of his songs, "That such a king should play bo-peep" (1.4.177). Harsnett uses the word of a devil lying in a girl's toenail, "Where hee must lye for a skout like the Sentinel in a watch, and suffer every boy to play bo-peepe with his devilship" (251). Once again, as John Murphy has noticed, the field of influence from this pas-

[1]*The Works of Shakespeare*, ed. Lewis Theobald, 7 vols. (London, 1733), 5:164.

[2]H. H. Furness, ed., *The Variorum King Lear* (Philadelphia: Lippincott [1880]), 190, 194, 209, 219, 236, 242.

[3]Kenneth Muir, "Samuel Harsnett and *King Lear,*" *RES,* n.s. 2 (1951): 11–21; *Shakespeare's Sources* (1957), 147–61, rev. ed., *The Sources of Shakespeare's Plays* (New Haven: Yale University Press, 1977), 202–206. Muir prints a list of the parallels in Appendix 7 of his New Arden *King Lear.*

sage radiates from more than the one word "bo-peepe."[1] Harsnett wonders "that never an unhappy fellow in the company shewed so much unhappie wit as to offer to take a knife and pare away the devil lying in the dead of the nayle" (251), and this speculation connects with the Fool's "unhappy" joke uttered a few lines after his song: "Thou hast par'd thy wit o' both sides. . . . Here comes one o' the parings." Harsnett then ends his paragraph with a funny, clever pun on "babble" / "bauble" that turns the name of Darrell's notorious patient Will Sommer (as Harsnett prints it in his *Declaration*) into the name of Will Somers, Henry VIII's famous fool, also the presenter of Nashes's play *Summers Last Will and Testament,* licensed for printing by Harsnett on 28 October 1600:[2]

> O that *Will Sommer* had come to this pleasant bargaine betweene the Exorcist and the devil; how handsomly would he have belaboured them both with his bable for playing theyr parts so handsomlie?"

As a fool, Will Sommer would beat the exorcist and the devil about the head with his bauble; as a demoniac, he would belabor them both with his hysterical babble. If Murphy is right, then in this peculiar fusion of demoniac and fool we find not only a parallel to Lear's pathetic, suffering, half-crazy boy-fool, but a possible source for his role as well.

Nor does this exhaust Shakespeare's transformation of the passage. "Would not this have spighted any devil," asks Harsnett,

> to be thus hardly handled by a priest, to be turned out of his warme nest where hee cabined in the wench, and to be lodged at little ease in the edge of her nayle next to wind and weather, where he must lye for a skout like the Sentinel in a watch, and suffer every boy to play bo-peepe with his devilship?

"Little ease," another of Harsnett's puns, implies a reference to the notorious torture cell in the Tower of London, known by that name. The phrase thus links up with other ambivalent images of suffering whose potential sadism registered upon Shakespeare's imagination. Also, as Muir observes (although he does not list the parallel in his appendix to his New Arden *King Lear*)[3], Harsnett's exposed sentinel may have suggested Cordelia's "poor perdu!" (4.7.34); and the whole sequence of words in Harsnett, "turned out . . . lodged at little ease . . . next to wind and weather" is one of several passages that prefigure Lear's hovel in the storm.

[1]*Darkness and Devils,* 172–77.

[2]Arber 3:175.

[3]*Shakespeare's Sources,* 161.

Often the mere outlandishness of one of Harsnett's words seems to have caught Shakespeare's attention, and the word alone will appear, apparently free of its Harsnettian context, for example "conspirants" (218), "auricular" (209), "apish" (229), "gaster" (307), and "asquint" (277). More often, some of the context follows a striking word into the text of the play, as in the case of "pendulous": ". . . all these sensible accidents should be made pendulous in the ayre like *Archimedes* Dome" (326). This influences Lear's lines: "Now all the plagues that in the pendulous air / Hang fated o'er men's faults light on thy daughters!" (3.4.67).

Muir also shows that many details of Lear's madness and Edgar's simulated possession derive from Harsnett's idioms and the experiences of the demoniacs. Fid's experiences with the needles, knives, and halter, Mainy's randiness, the priests' confusion of feminine sexuality with evil in their treatment of Sara, Marwood's storm-caused, melancholic possession all appear transformed into imagery and action in *King Lear*. Shakespeare, therefore, did not merely read Harsnett to gather arcane details for Edgar's part or to make a topical allusion, as older critics thought. The book entered deeply into his imagination, its contents to be transmuted into the iterative image of human suffering that Caroline Spurgeon was the first to detect: the image "of a human body in anguished movement, tugged, wrenched, beaten, pierced, stung, scourged, dislocated, flayed, gashed, scalded, tortured, and finally broken on the rack."[1] Most of these words, or the actions they represent, appear in the *Declaration:* for example, beaten (283), scourged (289); stung (292); flayed (274); tortured (244); scalded (256); pierced (287); on the rack (296). This but is a small sample of Harsnett's lexicon of pain.[2]

One of the most interesting of Muir's conclusions is that "it may even be suggested that the thunderstorm itself was partly derived from Harsnett."[3] In the old play of *King Leir* the murderer is frightened into repentance by a clap of thunder, but there is no storm; and in the other major source of *King Lear,* Sidney's story of the Paphlagonian king, there is a storm, but without thunder and lightning. In Harsnett's text, however, there are some striking examples of imagery based on the language of storms and tempest. For instance, he describes the exorcists' adjurations as storms:

[1] *Shakespeare's Imagery and What It Tells Us* (Cambridge: Cambridge University Press, 1935), 339.

[2] Leo Salingar, "*King Lear,* Montaigne and Harsnett," *Aligarh Journal of English Studies* 8 (1983): 124–66: "Harsnett set Shakespeare thinking about episodes of Satanism and moral perversion" (160).

[3] *Shakespeare's Sources,* 152.

it served . . . in steede of thunder and lightning to bring *Jupiter* upon the stage, by these dreadful frightful Exorcismes, thundring, clapping, and flashing out the astonishing of Gods names, *Jehovah, Tetragrammaton, Adonai,* and the rest, to amaze and terrifie the poore people, and to possesse them with an expectation of some huge monster-devil to appeare. Who standing at gaze with trembling and feare, hearing the huge thunder-cracke of adjuration flie abroad, and no devils to roare; and then seeing the Exorcist in a rage to throw away his thunder booke behind him, and hunt the devil with his owne holy hands; and instantly hearing the devil rouze out of his cabin as a Lyon out of his denn, and bellow out with his roaring voyce, *Oh, oh, oh, I burne, I burne, I scald, I broyle, I am tormented:* this must needes make the poore Madge Owlets cry out in admiration of the power of the potent priesthood. . . . (287)

Here Harsnett presents the exorcism as a terrifying storm, associated with the gods. It is also a storm of words addressed, like Lear's, as an adjuration to a concealed evil. Shakespeare, on the other hand, presents his storm as an exorcism, with King Lear as its interpreter:

> Let the great gods,
> That keep this dreadful pudder o'er our heads,
> Find out their enemies now. Tremble, thou wretch
> That hast within thee undivulged crimes
> Unwhipt of justice!
>
> (3.2.46–53)

The trembling that Lear envisages, as well as his thought of whipping, are both Harsnettian motifs, as in "Instantly began the possessed to tremble, to have horrour, and rage thorough out his whole body" (255), and ". . . and how was the poore devil then rent, battered and torne, may we deeme, when for not telling his name he was enjoyned untrusse, and to take quietly five lashes with the *Stole*." (273). Moreover, as the exorcist's metaphorical storm of adjuration makes the devil "rouze out of his cabin," so Lear's apostrophe to "poor naked wretches," followed by his adjuration, "Take physic, pomp," draws Edgar's demoniac voice from the hut, followed shortly by Edgar himself, who then (3.4.28–62) narrates his sufferings in words closely based on Harsnett.

The similarity between Harsnett's storm imagery and the storm speeches of *King Lear* is very noticeable. Harsnett describes a conjurer's spirit,

so violent, boystrous, and bigge as that he will ruffle, rage, and hurle in the ayre worse then angry God *Aeolus* ever did, and blow downe steeples, trees, may-poles, and keepe a fell coyle in the world. (217)

As Muir observes,[1] Shakespeare uses "ruffle" twice in the play, "rage" three times (once about the foul fiend, twice about the storm), and makes Lear command the storm to rage until it has "drench'd our steeples."[2] Harsnett speaks of "a shelter against what wind or weather so ever" (244) and "lightning from heaven" (259), and another of his words, "vaunt-courrier" (213) appears in Lear's apostrophe to the storm (3.2.5). A further parallel, unnoticed by Muir, based on a passage in which Harsnett mocks the power of the priests' breath to terrify the devils, strengthens his case because the verbal correspondences are particularly striking:

> Now what a monstrous coyle would sixe or seaven *ignivomous* priests keepe in hell if they should let loose the full fury of their blasts as *Aeolus* did upon the Sea, and distend their holy bellowes in consort amongst the poore ghosts? (258)

This passage is reflected in the speech of the gentleman who describes Lear in the storm to Kent. The words "blasts," "fury," "sea," and "rage" recur:

> Bids the wind blow the earth into the sea,
> Or swell the curled waters 'bove the main,
> That things might change or cease; tears his white hair,
> Which the impetuous blasts, with eyeless rage,
> Catch in their fury. . . .
>
> (3.1.5–9)

We have seen that in Harsnett's passage on the devil in the woman's toenail there is a complex of associations with the fool, the hovel, and the storm; similarly, in his description of the demoniac Nicholas Marwood there is another set of associations with Edgar, his disguise, and the storm: "*Marwood* . . . beeing pinched with penurie and hunger, did lie but a night or two abroad in the fieldes, and beeing a melancholicke person, was scared with lightning and thunder that happened in the night, and loe, an evident signe that the man was possessed"(222). This passage seems to have influenced the conception of Edgar's performance as Poor Tom, and particularly his soliloquy:

> Whiles I may scape
> I will preserve myself, and am bethought
> To take the basest and most poorest shape

[1]Ibid., 153.
[2]3.2.3; 2.4.301; 3.7.41; 3.1.8; 3.2.1.

> That ever penury, in contempt of man,
> Brought near to beast . . .
> . . . . . . . . . . . . . . . . . .
> And with presented nakedness outface
> The winds and persecutions of the sky.

(2.3.5–12)

The phrase "pinched with penurie and hunger" also affects the gentleman's speech with its "belly-pinched wolf" (3.1.13).

The influence of Harsnett on the part of Lear himself extends beyond the storm scenes to the mad scene (4.6). Here, as Muir observed, Lear's misogynistic sexual nausea is related to the exorcists' treatment of Sara Williams, who was told that she had a devil in her vagina and that her first menstruation was diabolic (297, 350, 357). Harsnett, moreover, harps on the priests' hunting of the devil through the women's bodies, especially Sara's (261), and in an exceptionally obscene passage seems to imply that the devil's fear of a priest's glove was owing to the feminine scent it acquired from contact with the priest's hand. He goes on to suggest that this is why English Catholic gentlewomen are such strong supporters of the clergy (264). Muir's collocation of this background with such specific phrases from the *Declaration* as "filthy fumes" (239), "the bottomlesse pit of hell" (250), "scalded" (256), "thicke smoake and vapour of hell" (276), "brimstone . . . burning" (276), and "Brimstone . . . ugly blacknes, smoake, scorching, broyling, and heate" (287) casts a dark light on Lear's words:

> Beneath is all the fiends': there's hell, there's darkness,
> There is the sulphurous pit, burning, scalding,
> Stench, consumption.

(4.6.127–29)

John Murphy thinks that in this scene Lear is actually possessed, and that his mouse, the brown bills, and the "troop of horse" are devils.[1] This is an interesting suggestion. There is a mouse-devil in the *Declaration* (255), and Mainy says that "it was given forth . . that the horse I rid upon was a devil, and that I had devils attending upon me in liverie coates" (400). Nonetheless, although Mainy's demon horse probably appears in the text of *King Lear* as Edgar's "Bay trotting-horse" that rides over "four-inch'd bridges" (3.4.56–57), it is surely essential for the structure of the play's action that Lear be sick of a natural madness, and not possessed.

---

[1] *Darkness and Devils,* 212–13.

Muir would certainly agree that some of his parallels might be coincidental. On the other hand, assiduous reading could lengthen his list considerably because although Harsnett's influence must be proved through specifics, it becomes increasingly clear as one works with the text that the whole book affected Shakespeare's imagination. If, however, one takes Muir's list of parallels to be a representative sampling of the Harsnettian echoes in *King Lear,* then some important conclusions about them emerge.

First, the echoes are concentrated in, but by no means restricted to, the third act, and they focus upon the storm, the hovel, and Edgar's false possession. They appear almost entirely in the speeches of the male characters, with the exception of Cordelia's "poor perdu!" (4.7.34), spoken when she is imagining her father's sufferings. Edgar and Lear have more Harsnettian echoes than anyone else, and they divide them about equally. Others appear in the words of the fool, Kent, Albany, Cornwall, and the gentleman.

As I have already suggested, some of the parallels represent simply the adoption of a striking word, which one would expect from one writer's reading of another's exuberant and idiosyncratic style. In the most interesting cases, however, Shakespeare seems to have transmuted Harsnett's text into the imagery of his own work, sometimes in contexts that prepare for the enunciation of the play's strongest ideas. In Albany's scene with Goneril, for instance (4.2), his "head-lugg'd bear" has its parallel in Harsnett's "as men leade Beares by the nose" (285); and his "Thou changed and self-cover'd thing, for shame / Bemonster not thy feature" is sharply paralleled by Harsnett's "To disguise, difforme, and monster-like to mishape the nature of this thrice blessed communion . . . and to blaze this their hellish impiety before the eyes of all the world" (301). When Albany calls Goneril "a fiend," her reply to him, ending in the animal noise "mew!" would have hinted at diabolic possession for many in the audience. All this provides a suitable frame for the famous lines:

> If that the heavens do not their visible spirits
> Send quickly down to tame [these] vild offenses,
> It will come,
> Humanity must perforce prey upon itself,
> Like monsters of the deep.
>
> (4.2.46–50)

In this case, too, we see Shakespeare reading Harsnett metaphorically and figuratively, taking him even more seriously than he took himself, and thus transforming sectarian rant into a dark epiphany of an evil that is real and not performed, either by a troupe of exorcists or by the Church of England's spokesman.

It also appears from the nature of Harsnett's influence upon *King Lear* that Shakespeare did not read Harsnett while he was writing the play. The Harsnettian echoes did not leak, so to speak, into a sensitive and receptive mind already engaged upon a task for which the *Declaration* suddenly acquired an accidental and fortunate relevance. Shakespeare read Harsnett *before* he wrote *Lear,* and the reading so affected his conception of the central themes, scenes, and characters of the play that it may have been the determining influence upon his decision to write the play at all. In writing *King Lear* Shakespeare did not, as we say, "use" the *Declaration;* Harsnett's book is not in the ordinary sense a source at all. Rather the play is the result of an encounter with another text: a kind of dialogue has taken place between the cleric and the poet, and the play is a massive reply to the cleric's argument, rhetoric, and purpose. Shakespeare has appropriated his book and returned it, transformed in the medium of his play, to the state and the society for which Harsnett wrote it.

To have a proper sense of the power of Shakespeare's response to Harsnett and of the magisterial assumption of poetic authority in his making it, one must remember that Harsnett's book was not a fly-by-night pamphlet. It was the climax to two major political and religious campaigns waged by a powerful bishop; the power of the Court of High Commission, the voice of the Crown itself in ecclesiastical affairs, validated its findings. Its publication was an act of state. When the King's own troupe of actors performed *King Lear* at court on St. Stephen's day, 1606, that in its way was also an act of state. For everyone in that court audience familiar with the *Declaration* and the controversies of which it formed part, the implied dialogue of poet and cleric, play and book, must have been a part of their experience of the tragedy.

Before some of the themes of that dialogue can be briefly suggested, it is necessary to consider how topical reference or allusion works in a play like *King Lear.* Theobald, in addition to discovering Harsnett's presence in the play, also inaugurated a long and, in my opinion, pernicious tradition of criticism when he said that Edgar's asssumed possession "is Satire levell'd at a modern Fact, which made no little Noise at the Period of Time, and consequently, must have been a rapturous Entertainment to the Spectators, when it was first presented."[1] The idea that the material

[1] *Works of Shakespeare* 5:164.

from Harsnett is a topicality inserted to please the audience has
proved durable. H. N. Paul has even turned it into a theory of composition. He imagines that Shakespeare began *Lear* in late 1605,
when he "set up" the main plot.[1] Then, after the discovery of the
Gunpowder Plot, the *Lear* subplot, "which has been woven into
[the main plot]," began to take shape as Shakespeare read
Harsnett's attack on the priests "to learn the tricks of this kind of
fraud."[2] Shakespeare spliced this "Jacobean furniture" into his
play to please James Stuart with "a timely satirical picture."[3] William Elton also wonders why, since Edgar's role strikes him as dis-
proportionate, Shakespeare should have risked "such apparently
unfunctional distraction . . . in this mature achievement of his
art."[4] His answer is the same as Theobald's and Paul's: to please
James I by showing that possession and miracles are frauds.

As it happens, Muir's researches and the complexity of
Harsnett's text in itself and as an historical event refute these sim-
plicities. Even without them, the idea that an integral part of the
third act of *Lear* was an afterthought should never have survived
serious reading or production of the play.[5] Nonetheless, an allusion is being made, as Theobald understood, but to what? Harsnett
claimed that his book presented facts and told the truth; but a play
is a fiction made of words and gestures. What was the "modern
fact" that Theobald assumed to exist outside the play? Two modern
Catholic scholars have seen in Edgar's performance an allusion to
the plight of hunted missionary priests. A recusant spectator in the
court audience of 1606 might have had a similar thought.[6] As
Murphy has noticed,[7] Harsnett wonders whether "our vagrant
devils . . . did take theyr fashion of new names from our wandring
Jesuits, who . . . have alwaies three or foure odde conceited names
in their budget" (239); and since it is Harsnett's whole thesis to say
that the priests were in effect the devils, then to make a wandering,
possessed beggar into a figure of the hunted priest would be a neat

[1]*The Royal Play*, 139n.

[2]Ibid., 139n, 31, 127.

[3]Ibid., 398, 97n.

[4]*King Lear and the Gods*, 88.

[5]Muir develops his analysis of the sources of *Lear* and especially of Shakespeare's
use of Harsnett, into a strong argument for the integrity of the play's composition and
design, for example, "The main plot and the sub-plot are not merely parallel: they are
closely linked" (*Sources* [rev. ed., 206–208).

[6]Devlin, "Anthony Tyrrell," 357; Milward, *Shakespeare's Religious Background*,
54, 72. The latter quotes interesting parallels to Edgar's speech, 2.3.1–5, from a letter by
Edmund Campion and from Robert Southwell's *Humble Supplication*.

[7]*Darkness and Devils*, 180.

reversal of Harsnett's attack. We may doubt the interpretation because Jesuits traveled disguised as gentlemen and soldiers, not as bedlam beggars. Yet that might be too literal-minded a response; Edgar and the fugitive priests share, besides the experience of being hunted for their lives, the sense of alienation and exile from their own people within their own country.[1]

The reason such an interpretation (which no imaginative reader or spectator will dismiss) arises is that in appropriating Harsnett, Shakespeare does not allude primarily to a fact, but to a far-reaching, important debate about the appearances that lead people to wonder about the nature of a fact and its significance. The Harsnettian influence affects more than the role of Edgar and reflects more than Shakespeare's passing interest in a fraud. When Lear calls out "Darkness and devils!" (1.4.252) or

> O how this mother swells up toward my heart!
> *Hysterica passio,* down, thou climbing sorrow,
> Thy element's below.
>
> (2.4.56–58)[2]

neither of these exclamatory echoes of Harsnett leads us to smile in memory of clerical trickery; on the contrary, each figuratively names and diagnoses an experience of present mental agony and proposes a relationship between psychic disintegration and a principle of evil located "below," both in human nature and the cosmos. As Edgar in the role of Poor Tom later says, "Nero is an angler in the lake of darkness. Pray, innocent, and beware the foul fiend" (3.6.6–8). He also reminds us in a famous sentence that in the world of experience expressed by *King Lear* normal expectations of moral direction are reversed: "The prince of darkness is a gentleman" (3.4.143)—a remark complimentary neither to gentlemen nor the devil. Insofar as *King Lear* is a mirror held up to nature, it shows humanity in the state of alienation from reality and truth named by St. Augustine the "land of unlikeness," the *regio dissimilitudinis.* At the heart of the play, possession and madness are the supreme figures for this state of being, so that when Lear

---

[1]It has long been known that *King Lear* was acted by recusant actors in Yorkshire, 1609–10. This by no means proves it a Catholic play, but it does seem to prove that it was not an anti-Catholic one. For a lucid account of the company, the Simpsons of Egton Bridge, see C. J. Sisson, "Shakespeare's Quartos as Prompt-Copies (*RES* 18 (1942): 134–40. John Murphy gives the most recent and detailed account of these players in *Darkness and Devils,* 93–118.

[2]Cf. "Resort unto the Oracles of the devil . . . and . . . conjure up from hel the Prince and power of darknes" (*DEP,* 333), and "Ma: *Maynie* had a spice of the *Hysterica passio,* as seems, from his youth; he himselfe termes it the Moother"(223).

sees himself in Mad Tom, he sees the figure of an entire life lived in denial of its true nature and now at a crisis of identity, human and personal: hence the scriptural echo to the Psalms and the Book of Job in Lear's question, "Is man no more than this?" (3.4.102–3): "What is man, that thou art mindful of him?" (Psalm 8:4) and "What is man that thou shouldest magnify him?" (Job 7:17).[1]

Thus through his use of Harsnett Shakespeare registers "the form and pressure," in Hamlet's words on the nature of drama, of the "age and body of the time," its whole drift and tendency. The older critics were right to this extent, that the role of Edgar as Poor Tom in its relationship to the *Declaration* is the most obtrusive example of the process in Shakespeare's plays. Utterly disregarding decorum as Harsnett understood it, Shakespeare has set down at the heart of his play among his ancient British characters the figure of a contemporary demoniac beggar. Nor is this the act of an opportunistic or king-pleasing playwright, but of an entirely conscious artist. With extraordinary boldness, in Edgar's last words as a demoniac, Shakespeare opens a window onto the appearances of the contemporary world that the play reflects: "Five fiends have been in poor Tom at once: of lust, as Obidicut; Hobbididence, prince of dumbness; Mahu, of stealing; Modo, of murder; Flibbertigibbet, of mopping and mowing, who since possesses chambermaids and waiting-women" (4.1.58–63). And so Sara, Fid, and Anne Smith enter *King Lear,* bringing one of their devils with them, as well as a reference to Harsnett's comment on their performance in the words "mopping and mowing" (*DEP,* 308).

The audience's task is to apprehend the significance of the appearance glimpsed through the dramatic window. In this example the word to notice is "since." There is no simple relationship of time between the events of a play and those of the historical world. It makes no sense to say that "since" Flibertigibbet left Tom (whom he never possessed in the first place) he has possessed chambermaids and waitingwomen. What does make sense is, first, a rough translation, "lately" or "recently," made in the moment of hearing. A more reflective understanding of the word, however, leads one to give Tom's experience priority over the Denham girls'; he becomes their type or prefiguring symbol. What he is they have been, and the implication for those who know about the

[1] Augustine, *Confessions* 7.10. On the concept of the "land of unlikeness" see Charles Dahlberg, *The Literature of Unlikeness* (Hanover, N.H.: University Press of New England, 1988), also Edgar Schell, *Strangers and Pilgrims: From* The Castle of Perseverance *to* King Lear (Chicago: University of Chicago Press, 1983), 17–19, who cites an important use of the term from St. Bernard. On the scriptural echoes in *Lear,* see Peter Milward, *Biblical Influences in Shakespeare's Great Tragedies* (Bloomington: University of Indiana Press, 1987), 156-204.

events at Denham is surely that if the girls' possession was mistaken or assumed, their suffering was not. Moreover, because their suffering is now seen through the theater and as theater, like Tom's it has its figural dimension. Thus translating the girls' possessions out of the metaphorical theater of Harsnett's diatribe into the real tragic theater, restores to them the potentiality of generating significance, which Harsnett had tried to negate.[1]

Such windows as this continually open as the play unfolds, and what they reveal will depend, although within certain limits, upon the audience's predisposing beliefs, knowledge, and memory. Harsnett's readership has always been smaller than Shakespeare's enormous audience, of whom a majority has always been ignorant of the running allusion to Harsnett's book: after all, the entire printing of the *Declaration* would not supply a copy each for the Globe audience. In Shakespeare's own time, however, the publicity of the controversies and the importance of the questions at debate would alert any intelligent spectator to the themes of the allusion. As the play worked upon the spectator's mind, it would thus acquire a kind of mute chorus of offstage characters: the possessed girls and servingmen and their exorcists, also John Darrell and William Somers; the bishop of London and his chaplains and, behind them, the whole apparatus of monarchical authority—even, eventually, the entire divided society of readers and participants in the controversies, which becomes in effect the play's audience, the world for which, about which, and from which it is written. This is the context in which Shakespeare undoes Harsnett's book, unravels his text, reopens matters that Harsnett had meant finally to close.

To see how the book thus enters the play, we should attend closely to the way Harsnett presents his account of Nicholas Marwood, the first demoniac, the onset of whose possession is

---

[1]Stephen Greenblatt also comments upon the transference of the possessions from Harsnett's text to the theater, but interprets it differently: "But if false religion is theater, and if the difference between true and false religion is the presence of theater, what happens when this difference is enacted in the theater?" (*Shakespearean Negotiations,* 126). His answer is that the "official position" (i.e., Harsnett's) is "*emptied out,* even as it is loyally confirmed," and adds, "This 'emptying out' resembles Brecht's 'alienation effect' and, even more, Althusser and Macheray's 'internal distantiation.'" This interpretation attributes to Shakespeare and his audience a capacity for radical skepticism that seems to me anachronistic, and is based upon an oddly positivistic understanding of religious faith and phenomena. Greenblatt says, for instance, that medieval resurrection plays "offered the spectators ocular proof that Christ had risen" and that "Lear's craving for just such proof . . . would seem to evoke precisely this theatrical and religious tradition, but only to reveal itself, in C. L. Barber's acute phrase, as 'post-Christian'" (125). Mystery plays, however, prove nothing ocularly. They enact beliefs. The ending of *Lear* resembles a crucifixion play rather than a resurrection play. Like a crucifixion play, it leaves its spectators with a sign that no more interprets itself than did the corpse of a priest newly executed on that other kind of Elizabethan scaffold, the place of execution.

most closely related to Edgar's performance as Poor Tom.[1]
Bancroft and Harsnett never interrogated Marwood, and they could
not therefore enlist his voice in their revised version of "this play
of sacred miracles" (202). Yet this does not prevent Harsnett from
using Marwood and supplying him with a voice of his own invention. To do this, he first presents the text of Weston's own Latin
description of Marwood's exorcism, which he then translates, not
always quite accurately. Then, by interpretation and commentary,
he rewrites Weston, so that his reader has both declarations simultaneously before him, Weston's as well as his own.

Marwood's possession began when, homeless, hungry, cold, and
depressed, he slept out in the fields and was frightened by thunder-
storms (222). Later we hear that his devil "affects *Marwood* to lie
in the fields and to gape at the Moone" (240). He was first exorcised, without success, by Stamp and other priests (255, 266).
Weston then took over and in one session at Lord Vaux's house
performed a successful exorcism. This was the first "grand miracle" (211), and the rest of the exorcisms seem to have followed in
imitation. (Incidentally, although Harsnett says that Marwood was
Anthony Babington's servant, it is not clear whether this was
before or only after his dispossession.)

Harsnett quotes at length from three incidents in the exorcism of
Marwood: first, the imposition of Weston's hand and its effects;
second, the use of a vestment that had belonged to Edmund
Campion; and finally the application of relics of Campion's body,
which seems to have cured him.

In the first incident, when Weston put his hand on Marwood's
head, he immediately fell "into a furie," not only stretching out his
body, beating with his feet and hands and snatching at the priest,
but crying out in a sort of Senecan rant (as Weston reports it)
which Harsnett the humanist finds very funny (259ff.). The most
interesting detail, which Harsnett supplies without directly quoting
Weston, is that "the sweat that flowed from *Marwoods* face was in
such current streames as it was the office of one man to stand and
dry them up" (260). This is one of the passages that seems to have
influenced a speech in *Othello.*

The second incident involved the use of what seems to have
been Edmund Campion's cincture or girdle, a vestment that he
wore when celebrating mass. Here is part of Harsnett's translation
of Weston's Latin:

[1]Greenblatt, *Shakespearean Negotiations,* 117, says of Sara's devils' names that
they "carry with them a faint but ineradicable odor of spuriousness." This is nicely said.
Marwood's devil's name, however, "Captain Pippin," sounds genuine to me—whatever it
might mean to say so.

Taking in his hand a certaine silken twist which Fa: *Campion* did alwayes cary about with him, and used it at the celebration of the Masse, and which he often said had beene at Jerusalem, and girded our Saviours tombe: applied the same gently to *Marwoods* side, at the touch whereof he presently began to tremble and turmoile, and the paine of his side shifted into a new place; whereby *Edmunds* discerned that *Marwood* was a Demoniack in deede. (267)

After this, when one of the bystanders applied the cincture to Marwood's mouth, he reacted violently and begged them to remove "that ill-favored thing that troubled him so much" (268). Weston then constrained the devil to tell him why he was so troubled; Marwood identified the cincture as Campion's, whereupon Weston called to the spectators: "Beare witnes my maisters of Fa: *Campians* most glorious martyrdom, whose smallest cord, which before that time they had never seene with their eyes, hath cast the devil into such an heate" (268). (The absurd "had never seene with their eyes" and the bathetic "such an heate" are Harsnett's translations of "nunquam viderant" and "tantas illi faces miserat.")

The third incident was what Harsnett calls the "grand" or "monster" miracle, the curing of Marwood:

Heere certaine peeces of father *Campians* body did wonderfully burne the devill, all the organs of all his sences seeming to be broken and rent asunder, crying out one while his eyes, one while his eares, one while his tongue was rent out and rent in peeces; and besides other excruciations, hee was tormented with such a strange vomite as though he would have spued out his very entralls and guts. . . . Last of all (thanks be to God), all of us pittying and weeping for remorse, *Marwood* crying out *Edmunds, Edmunds,* he was quit of the devill. (296)[1]

Harsnett treats each of these incidents as if it were a scene in a play. Of the first, immediately after the detail of the extraordinary perspiration, he says, "This was the finger of *Ignatius* devil indeede, to teach a yong Popish Rakehell so cunningly to act and

---

[1]English Catholics treasured the relics of their executed priests and fellow-Catholics, and it will come as a surprise to the modern reader to learn that some of the relics used in Marwood's dispossession still survive. Stonyhurst College has Campion's cincture, nearly twelve feet long, and a piece of his blood-stained linen. St. John's, Roehampton, has a portion of his thumb, a relic mentioned by Harsnett, and probably the one involved in Marwood's cure (Bede Camm, *Forgotten Shrines* [London: MacDonald and Evans, 1910], 363, 377–78, and passim.). It was later used on Friswood Williams (*DEP,* 366). Technically speaking, Father Weston will have believed that Marwood was cured by the intercession of Edmund Campion, a miracle to be taken as evidence of the dead man's sanctity. Less technically, and from the standpoint of the onlookers, Marwood was cured by the touch of Campion's hand, a priest's thumb in particular, as Harsnett jeeringly remarks elsewhere (277), being anointed during ordination.

feigne the passions and agonies of the devil. . ." (260). He interprets the second incident as a dialogue between "*Edmunds* the
devil *senior*" and "*Edmunds* devil *Junior,* or *Marwood, Edmunds*
ghost" (268). The third is a "monster-miracle acted upon
*Marwood,*" and Weston is its presenter, "like *Julius Caesar* the
commenter of his owne worthy exploites" (296). By presenting the
incidents in this way, of course, Harsnett himself becomes a
presenter—a role to which he draws attention by his theatrical
imagery—but a presenter intent upon sabotaging the play. In the
first two incidents his technique is to treat the events straightfor-
wardly, in a style of jocular indignation and bluff contempt. His
approach to the third, however, is more devious and less assured.
First, he mistranslates Weston's report of Marwood's cry
"*Edmunde, Edmunde*" as "Edmunds, Edmunds," thus making it
appear to the unLatined reader that Marwood was calling upon his
exorcist, whereas he was actually calling upon Edmund Campion;
and although he gives the correct translation, "Edmund," in the
next paragraph, he does not correct the false impression already
given. This does not merely sabotage the play, it falsifies it. Second, he mocks the relics themselves rather than the use made of
them, or, to use his own metaphor, he mocks the matter of the play,
not its art or its performance:

> And heerein I commend their wisedome in choyse of their reliques
> very much. First, in that they took fresh greene new reliques that were
> not antiquated and out of date. For reliques (for oft wee see) worke
> like an Apothecaries potion or new Ale: they have best strength and
> verd at the first, and therefore *Campians* girdle, now like old Rubarb,
> begins to allay. (296)

In all three incidents, therefore, the reader has the phenomena
themselves as described by Weston—which is all that Harsnett
had—and Harsnett's presentation and interpretation of them. All
open-minded readers would agree that his presentation, judged as
art, can be amusing and effective, if not always honest or charitable; they would also agree that his interpretation, judged as argument, is unconvincing. To present the exorcisms as a bad play is an
excellent way of making them appear ridiculous, but to interpret
them as a bad play is a very weak argument.  It requires us to
believe that William Weston was a liar, an hypothesis for which
Harsnett offers no evidence at all, and which his extracts do not
support. Nor does the interpretation explain the phenomena, neither the perspiration nor the vomit of the first and third incidents
(for it appears that Marwood was not treated with the potion and

the fumes), nor the apparent cure. Harsnett's reading of the events is actually an attempt to prevent us from reading them for ourselves by sealing off Weston's text from contact with our imaginations. Should we defeat his attempt to control our reading by taking him at his word and reading him as part of the play he presents, and therefore no less fallible than its other actors, then other readings besides his become possible. Two hypotheses suggest their range:

1) If Weston was telling the truth and diagnosed appearances correctly, then Nicholas Marwood was possessed. He was cured by the intercession of Saint Edmund Campion and a miracle took place.

2) If Weston was trying to tell the truth but failed, then Nicholas Marwood was sick of a disease that neither Weston nor Harsnett understood. He was cured by a resource of the spirit we call fiction, and to all intents and purposes a miracle took place.

Shakespeare as dramatist responds to Harsnett as presenter-critic by admitting his audience to a sight of the phenomena. Edgar performing as Poor Tom imitates some of the signs of possession. The audience in the theater knows he is performing and can therefore concentrate on enjoying and understanding the performance, but the characters on stage do not; he terrifies the Fool, and to Lear he is unbearably figurative of the human condition in general and of his own in particular. The effect is surely not a satire on fake possession, but—because in the theater everything is fiction and figure—an initiation of the audience into some realities that the signs of possession might portend. Similarly, when Edgar takes his father through the strange ritual of the false suicide, the effect should not be to turn the audience against miracles but to make them wonder what the definition of a miracle might be. Edgar's fiction, after all, saves the old man from suicidal despair by proving more real than his suffering; and Shakespeare, like the conjuror who reveals the cards in his hand, works his wonder the more powerfully by exposing, even dramatizing, his character's deceits.

In the case of Lear, on the other hand, the audience knows that he is naturally mad, and neither possessed nor a performer of possession. They only know this, however, because it is what they are told and shown. It is not a diagnosis they make for themselves on the basis of his symptoms. The less imaginative might think that because Lear's disease is natural, his cure must be natural too. After all, there is a physician present who gives sound advice.[1] In

---

[1] In the Folio text, the physician is a gentleman, although it seems likely enough, on the basis of 4.7.18–19, found in both texts ("Be govern'd by your knowledge, and proceed / I'th'sway of your own will. Is he array'd?"), that he is indeed a doctor.

the design of the play, however, Lear's cure is complementary to Gloucester's. The stories of these two old men and their families do not merely reflect each other; they emanate from a common moral center, a psychic place where first the usurpation, then the exercise of absolute power occurs, reckless of secular or religious constraint—in a phrase, a place of power without prudence or grace, Nero's lake of darkness, equally accessible from the public or the private realm, where king and beggar, master and servant are kin. For both old men, the only way out of this place is through purgatorial experience, and both are delivered to the world again by the love of a child. In both cases the miracle, if there is one, is in the workings of love itself, not in the means or signs, ritualistic or naturalistic, through which it works.

This reading of Shakespeare's encounter with Harsnett will not support the view, perennial in one version or another, that Shakespeare subordinated his art to the myths and claims of the Tudor-Stuart monarchy or that, in particular, he adopted Harsnett's presentation of his materials. *King Lear,* like *Richard II,* is about the consequences of the claim to absolute authority. Through an unlawful, disorderly stretch of his power, through, in short, not knowing himself, a monarch has delegitimized his kingship and state, bringing dreadful suffering to himself and to others. The play, moreover, gives us the crisis of a long development.[1] Harsnett's book gave Shakespeare a microcosm of the claim to authority and its results.[2] The paradox of Harsnett's book, however, is that it issues from, and gives expression to, an authoritarianism as offensive as anything that its author attacks in the name of skeptical enlightenment; the insincerity and violence that Harsnett attributes to the fanatically sincere and simple William Weston recoil upon himself and the state he serves. Although Shakespeare seems to have found Harsnett's first book on Darrell amusing, he found the *Declaration* disturbing, even horrifying. He certainly did not find it funny.

According to Harsnett, two kinds of people, Catholics and actors, are trash, and two institutions, the Roman church and the theater, are the sources of lies and illusions. His device for regulating both is decorum, the exclusionary principle of the fitting and

[1] I have developed this argument in relation to *Richard II* in *Two Shakespearean Sequences* (London: Macmillan Press, 1977), 95–111. See also Calvin G. Thayer's essay on absolutism and *Richard II* in his *Shakespearean Politics* (Athens: Ohio University Press, 1983), 1–61.

[2] Kaula, *Shakespeare and the Archpriest Controversy*, 18–29, argues that parallels between *Lear* and one of the pamphlets, *A True Relation,* point to an association in Shakespeare's mind between the actions of Lear in ruining his kingdom and the effects of Weston's demeanor at Wisbech on the English Catholics.

proper, which applies not only to plays and the subjects and styles suitable for them, but to the world of which plays are the mirror. The only kind of drama he approved was classical or academic comedy. On the evidence of the *Declaration,* he did not think that the theater should treat themes from religion or politics, and he had no liking for tragedy of any kind. This does not mean that he did not enjoy the theater, rather that like generations of British theater-goers after 1642, he expected nothing from it but harmless enter-tainment. A name for Harsnett's attitude would be "genial Puritan-ism," and as a way of taming the theater it proved more effective in the long run than the ungenial kind.

The same rule of decorum, applied to the real world of history and nature, provided Harsnett with his only real argument against miracle and prophecy. They are inconsistent with history and nature; they are in bad taste, and they render the world ungovern-able.

*King Lear* is Shakespeare's reply to Harsnett, an immense pro-phetic miracle play on religious and political subject matter, com-posed as a romantic tragedy of outrageous indecorum, appropriat-ing or engulfing Harsnett's own book, and situating its contents in a landscape of violence and alienation that, whether we read it as pre- or post-Christian, offers a devastating commentary on the spir-itual condition of contemporary England. Thus the poet, the pro-fessed fictionalist, answers the cleric who claims authority over fact. He answers him, moreover, from within his own literary tradi-tion of scriptural humanism, replying to the insolence of office with paradoxes: the wisdom of the world is made foolish; the mighty are put down from their seats, and the humble and meek are exalted; it profits us nothing to gain the world and lose our souls; service is freedom; unless we die we shall not live; and love is as strong as death.

There is a pointedness about some of the play's moments, too, which had Harsnett by some chance ever seen the play, he must have felt. "It is to be hartily wished," he writes of "the holy Traytorly rout" that watched the exorcisms, that "they were sent to the Creator of the Romish Saints, *Tiburne* their *Coronator,* by him to be convayed where Gods mercy shal designe" (269). This is a cruel, even savage sentence, but for Harsnett's purposes it passes for a great joke to say that Tyburn and hell are makers of saints: "*Campians* Saintship had been in a faire taking but for the gallows and the devil; and would it not doe any man good to be thus Sainted from hel" (268). A reader of Harsnett and *King Lear* can-not help noticing that in the figural dramaturgy of *Lear,* Edgar and Cordelia are both "sainted from hell," purified and ennobled by cruelties meant to destroy them. This is a theme most clearly stated in Lear's speech as he and Cordelia are led to prison:

> Come let's away to prison:
> We two alone will sing like birds i' th' cage;
> When thou dost ask me blessing, I'll kneel down
> And ask of thee forgiveness. So we'll live,
> And pray, and sing, and tell old tales, and laugh
> At gilded butterflies, and hear poor rogues
> Talk of court news; and we'll talk with them too—
> Who loses and who wins; who's in, who's out—
> And take upon 's the mystery of things
> As if we were God's spies; and we'll wear out,
> In a wall'd prison, packs and sects of great ones,
> That ebb and flow by th' moon.
> . . . . . . . . . . . . . .
> Upon such sacrifices, my Cordelia,
> The gods themselves throw incense. Have I caught thee?
> He that parts us shall bring a brand from heaven,
> And fire us hence like foxes.
>
> (5.3.8–23)

There is an echo of Harsnett in this speech in the imagery of "fire us hence like foxes": "to fire [the devil] out of his hold, as men smoke a Foxe out of his burrow" (*DEP*, 278). As I have suggested elsewhere, however, some of the thought and imagery of this counter-statement to Harsnett's cruelty was suggested by the work of the Jesuit poet and martyr St. Robert Southwell.[1] His *Epistle of Comfort*, "the eighth chapter," expatiates upon the paradoxical freedom found in "imprisonment in a good cause," and in particular Southwell provides a close parallel to Lear's lines upon singing and devotion:

Honorable it is in Gods quarrell, to be abridged of bodilye libertye, for mainteyning the true libertye and freedome of our soule. The birdes beinge used and naturallye delighted with the full scope of the ayre, though they be never so well fedd in the Cage, yett are they all wayes pooringe at every cranie to see whether they maye escape. For why, they understand not, that in the Cage they are both surer from the kyte hauke, and fouler then abroade. . . . But for a reasonable creature, and withall a Christian Catholicke so much to affecte a daungerous libertye, as not to accounte of the benefitt of his prison in so good a

---

[1] "Shakespeare and Southwell" in *KM 80: A Birthday Album for Kenneth Muir* (Liverpool: printed for private circulation by Liverpool University Press, 1987), 27.

cause, it can not but be thought an imperfection, especiallye consideringe how manye perils of our soule are cutt off, and how highlye our spirituall welfare is advaunced. *Lett us not in this be lyke the senselesse byrdes, but rather imitate them in an other propertye, which is that in the cage they not onlye singe their naturall note, both sweetlyer and oftener, then abroade, but learne also diverse other, farre more pleasant, and delightsome. So we both keepe, and oftener practise our wonted devotions, and besydes, learne new exercises of vertue.*[1] (My italics)

In the same chapter the thought expressed in Lear's enigmatic words, "And take upon's the mystery of things," finds a strikingly close parallel in "So that we see the prison is a schoole of divine and hidden misteries, to Gods frendes" (O3v). The thought of the gods as witnesses, audience, and (in the ecclesiastical sense of the word) celebrants of human suffering, who throw incense "on such sacrifices," appears in Southwell's chapter 10, "that the violent death and foregoing torments are tolerable in a good cause":

We are allotted to a glorious combat, in which the onlye comforte of so honorable lookers on, were enough to harten us againste all affrontes. *Preliantes nos* sayeth S. Cyprian, *et fidei congressione pugnantes spectat Deus, spectant Angeli eius, spectat et Christus. . .* When we skirmish or fight in the quarrell of our fayth, God beholdeth us, hys Angels beholde us, and Christ looketh on." (sig. R3)

Southwell, exhorting his fellow-Catholics to martyrdom, quotes Cyprian's words evoked by the sufferings of martyrs in the Roman arena; Shakespeare's words in these speeches carry the motif of martyrdom into the secular context of the play.[2]

Southwell is one of the greatest Elizabethan prose writers. "In the Elizabethan 'hinterland,'" asks Geoffrey Hill in his superb essay on Southwell, "where spectacular 'closet' horror can at any time become the routine hideousness of public spectacle, how can one say where metaphor ends and reality begins?" And he answers his own question: "This weak rhetorical question . . . is out of keeping with Southwell's power to distinguish and affirm."[3] Robert Southwell, born in 1561, was Harsnett's and Shakespeare's contemporary; Shakespeare would certainly have known people

---

[1] *An Epistle of Comfort*, sig. N5–N5v. The *Epistle* was first published in 1587; I have used the edition of 1605.

[2] Cf. Kent's image at 5.3.314–16 ("He hates him / That would upon the rack of this tough world / Stretch him out longer") that carries associations with the contemporary racking of priests such as Edmund Campion into the moment of Lear's death.

[3] *Lords of Limit*, 34.

Southwell knew, and indeed, if Christopher Devlin's genealogy is correct, the two men were remotely related to each other.[1] If Southwell's voice as well as Harsnett's is indeed present in Lear's prison speech, as I believe it is, then it is a sign of the personal element in Shakespeare's engagement with Harsnett as well as its seriousness that he should allow the dead poet-priest to speak through the mouth of his player king at this moment of the tragedy. That the play should have been performed at court, on St. Stephen's of all nights, in the year after the Gunpowder Plot, is a sign of Shakespeare's cool and cunning authority in the face of his times.[2]

The Harsnett influence continued to surface in Shakespeare's work to the end of his career. Muir cites *Pericles,* 4.6.118–19 and *The Tempest,* 2.2.5–12 as instances, and to these can be added *Cymbeline,* 5.5.210–14.

[1]Christopher Devlin, *The Life of Robert Southwell* (London: Longmans, Green and Co., 1956), 263.

[2]The feast of St. Stephen the proto-martyr is one of the few non-apostolic saint's days observed in the Church of England. On that day, virtually every spectator of the play at court would have heard the collect, epistle (Acts 7:55–60), and gospel (Matthew 23:34–39) of the day recited at least once, all three texts plangent with implied significance in juxtaposition with the play-world of *Lear.*

# 7

# Harsnett: 1603–1620

Harsnett probably never thought of himself as a writer, and he would be surprised as well as disappointed to know that he is now remembered because a book he did not bother to preserve in his own library had influenced a play. He would have liked to be remembered as a restorer of the Church, a founder of schools, and a conscientious bishop of some courage, independence, and integrity. His distinguished later career sheds an interesting, somewhat ironic retrospective light on his *Declaration.*

When Harsnett wrote the *Declaration,* he was archdeacon of Essex, a canon of St. Paul's, rector of St. Margaret's, Fish Street, and vicar of Chigwell, Essex. On 16 April 1604 he added another benefice to his collection when Mr. Thomas Lucas, of Colchester and Shenfield Hall, presented him to the living of Shenfield.[1] In September 1604 he resigned St. Margaret's, and in late 1605 he also resigned Chigwell; then, May 1606, he accepted the living of Hutton, near Shenfield. In 1609 he shed all these preferments, including his prebend (Hutton went to a kinsman, Adam Harsnett, a cleric of Puritan leanings, who kept it until his death[2]), and on 28 September 1609 Bancroft presented him to the rich living of Stisted, Essex, with a glebe of 133 acres.[3]

These changes were made in preparation for Harsnett's elevation to the episcopate. On 3 November 1609, Bancroft wrote to Cecil that the king had given the bishopric of Chichester to Dr. Harsnett

[1]Newcourt, *Repertorium,* 2:526. In a letter to Archbishop Abbot, 6 October 1625, Harsnett described Lucas as "the dearest freind that ever I did enjoye in this world" (SP 16/7, no. 27). Exactly a year later, on 20 April 1605 Harsnett did Lucas a favor in return when he leased the mansion house and land belonging to his prebend of Mapesbury to Lucas's son Thomas for £20 per annum (Bancroft's register). The transaction has a slight whiff of simony about it. (Thomas was born to his parents before they married, and so was illegitimate in English law. Hence his younger brother was his father's heir.)

[2]Newcourt, *Repertorium,* 2:344. He was the son of Adam Harsnett, servant at the mace in Colchester. A letter of thanks and spiritual counsel to Lady Barrington, written in Puritan style, survives (BL MS. Egerton 2650, fol. 274).

[3]Hennessy, *Novum repertorium,* 276, 36; Newcourt, *Repertorium,* 2:143, 344, 562; Philip Morant, *The History and Antiquities of the County of Essex* (Chelmsford, 1816), 2:389.

as successor to Lancelot Andrewes, who had been translated to Ely. Down in Chichester, on 10 November, the dean of the cathedral presented the royal letters patent directed to the dean and chapter granting license to elect a bishop; they were read, and on Monday, 13 November, after sung matins in the choir, the seven canons who were present elected Harsnett bishop. Twenty-one absent canons were declared contumacious. In London on the same day, Bancroft consecrated Harsnett, who was installed in his cathedral, but by proxy, 30 January 1610. Such was the process of electing a Jacobean bishop.[1] On becoming a bishop, Harsnett was allowed to keep Stisted rectory, although he resigned all his other benefices.

His pluralism was typical of clergy marked out for preferment either because of their ability or their connections. Bancroft resigned some eight rectories on becoming bishop of London.[2] Because of the shortage of educated clergy, and because many livings could not support a full-time priest, pluralism was unavoidable. In fact, Harsnett's preferments reflect Bancroft's attempt to mitigate the evils of pluralism. He arranged for smaller livings within a mile or two of each other to be united, and he encouraged pluralists to exchange livings to enable them to care for more than one at a time.[3] Of course, the policy assumed that men wished to be conscientious, and many clergy had no wish of the kind. All the evidence of Harsnett's career, however, shows that he was a hardworking priest who shared his bishop's opinions about pluralism. He will have taken on Hutton because it was a small parish near Shenfield; he must have resigned Chigwell and St. Margaret's because he could not look after them properly. In 1624, as bishop of Norwich, answering accusations brought by Norwich Puritans, he said:

> As touching preaching and non-Residentes he hath been reckned more then halfe a Puritan. His Lordshipp remembred his manner of leaving his service with the late Lord Archbishop of Cant. that he might go to his cure.[4]

As bishop, too, he resided in his diocese. There is little sign of his being much in London or at court, and one would not expect a non-

[1]*CSP Dom., James I,* vol. 49, no. 14; Peckham, *Acts of the Dean and Chapter,* 179–80, 181–82. Bishops Neile and Andrewes assisted at the consecration.

[2]Usher, *Reconstruction* 1:114.

[3]Ibid. 2:263.

[4]Bodleian MS. Tanner 114.

resident careerist to show the affection Harsnett retained for Chigwell, his first parish.

As Bancroft's chaplain, Harsnett learned a great deal about the state of the church. Even so, he could have had no better—or worse—introduction to the financial and administrative problems of the Church of England than the small, impoverished see of Chichester. Among the causes of the fall in the value of church endowments in the sixteenth century—inflation, rapacious laymen, greedy clerics (especially bishops), and the Tudors (who nationalized the church)—none had injured Chichester as much as the last. Elizabeth I had taken eight out of thirteen manors from the diocese. According to Bishop Montagu (1628), she gave in return for £2,500 thus acquired, £229/2s/6d in the form of four "impropriated" parsonages and "dead rents in tithes." The tithes were hard to collect, and in giving them and the parsonages to Chichester Elizabeth was only reapportioning part of the church's own income, and no doubt depriving four parishes of clergy as well. Among the results for Chichester were dilapidation of the cathedral and the episcopal properties, and the impossibility of maintaining a proper number of residentiaries. Even the bishops had to have other livings *in commendam* if they were not to live in poverty. That is why Harsnett was allowed to keep Stisted. Under Bishop Curteys (1570–83), the residentiaries were reduced to four besides the dean. Consequently the relationship of the cathedral with the diocesan parishes was broken, and it became impossible to keep up a proper schedule of services. Moreover, since "residence" came to mean absence for nine months out of twelve, the cathedral buildings fell into decay. There was no continuity of administration, and because the prebendaries could no longer afford to live in their prebendal houses in the close, they leased them out to laymen. The disgraceful state of the cathedral precincts can be imagined.[1]

A bishop's authority over the dean and chapter of his cathedral was limited to the period of his triennial visitation. He could also bring pressure to bear, if necessary, through the church courts, but bishops naturally preferred to have friendly relations with their cathedral clergy. In Chichester, Harsnett set to work immediately. His predecessor, Lancelot Andrewes, spent little time in the diocese and did little for the cathedral,[2] but the result of Harsnett's

[1]W. R. W. Stephens, *The South Saxon Diocese, Selsey-Chichester* (London: SPCK Press, 1881), 196, 213–14.

[2]J. G. Bishop, *Lancelot Andrewes, Bishop of Chichester, 1605–1609* (Chichester: Chichester City Council, 1963), 1. Andrewes' treasurer, Henry Isaacson, in his life of Andrewes, *An Exact Narration* (1650, reprint, Newcastle-upon-Tyne, 1817), claims that Andrewes spent £420 in repairs to the bishop's palace, but records at Chichester show

first visitation in 1610 was a new set of statutes meant to bring order and decency into the running of the cathedral, imposing more strict residential requirements on the prebendaries and trying to discipline the behavior of the cathedral staff. Many of the statutes were aimed at improving the cathedral's music, then under the direction of the alcoholic genius Thomas Weelkes.[1]

Reforming an English cathedral in 1611 was not easy. The questions put to the staff five years later at Harsnett's third visitation in 1616 show how little effect the 1611 statutes had. Since the answer to all the questions was obviously yes, one gathers that the copes, "monuments," and other vestments were missing, that the choirboys were not being instructed, that the singing men had been "all or most of them" absent at the beginning of services, that the clergy were living outside the close, laymen inside it, that laymen held the keys, that there were ale houses in the close, and that boys and hogs "did beastly defile" the walls and yards of the cathedral. No wonder the bishop asked why there had been no improvement after his complaints and instructions in the past! Once again, he persuaded the dean and chapter to accept a new set of statutes.[2]

There are two rewards for the reader of Harsnett's visitation articles and statutes. First, they reflect his irrepressibly lively style. Second, they reveal him to be one of the first real Anglicans. He may not have believed in miracles and prophecies or experienced the emotional religious life that accompanies them; but he took intense pleasure in thinking of a cathedral church where the fabric was impeccably maintained, the daily ceremonial correct, impressive, and neat. Above all, he wanted a properly trained choir, in place, on time, well-behaved, in clean surplices and ready to sing beautifully to the glory of God. His 1616 statutes give a clear picture of his ideal. The Chichester choir was small—twelve men and eight boys, a "half" choir, not a "double"—and it seems never to have been at full strength. Nonetheless, Harsnett wished it to be a good one. He required the master of the choristers to conduct proper auditions and to rehearse the boys morning and afternoon. The boys were to walk to and from church "orderly by two and by two," each boy to have his own Book of Common Prayer, and his

---

him spending £63/12s from 1606–9, a more realistic sum (Chichester Diocesan Record Office, Ep I/75/1).

[1] Statue Book B (Chichester Diocesan Record Office, CAP I/1/2, fols. 6b–7). The cathedral statutes were edited by Bennet et al. (Chichester, 1904), and excerpted in HMC, *Various Collections* 1:201. For Weelkes at Chichester, see C. E. Welch, *Two Cathedral Organists: Thomas Weelkes (1601–1623) and Thomas Kelway (1720–1744)* (Chichester: Chichester City Council, 1957).

[2] CAP I/1/2, fol. 27b (Visitation articles, 1616); fol. 7 (Statutes, 1616).

surplice "white and cleane." One has only to add to this procession of surpliced choirboys the verger, "solemnly" leading the chapter in procession into the chancel, as required by statute, and one has a characteristic part of the ceremonial of a modern English cathedral.

It is sometimes said of Harsnett that he was a court bishop, a vaguely defamatory term that in his case is unjustified.[1] As Bancroft's favorite chaplain he experienced every aspect of church life, having been a working vicar, canon, archdeacon, and chaplain. It might have been expected that as a bishop Harsnett would rise rapidly to the highest preferments. Yet this did not happen. He became one of a group of able men who devoted themselves to their dioceses, avoiding or being avoided by the court. Even his ten-year occupancy of Chichester is revealing. Like Rochester, Bath and Wells, Coventry, St. David's, and Carlisle, Chichester was an anteroom to greater things. Because of its comparative closeness to London, the men who were sent there were often, like Andrewes and Montagu (and Harsnett himself at his appointment), rising stars marked for further promotion. Yet Harsnett, whose administration of both Chichester and Norwich shows him to have been conscientious and able, stayed in both places nearly ten years. When his elevation to York came, he had only two years to live, and the men who promoted him knew that the archbishopric would soon be empty again.[2]

After Bancroft's death in 1610, Harsnett showed little sign of eagerness to ingratiate himself in court circles. On the contrary, the only real difficulties he encountered at this time of his life were caused by his opposition to more courtly ecclesiastics' policies and proceedings.

On 9 November 1605 Harsnett had become master of Pembroke in succession to Lancelot Andrewes, and when he also succeeded Andrewes at Chichester, he imitated him in retaining the mastership. Unlike Andrewes, however, he was not a nonresident bishop. Instead he became an absentee master, and Pembroke was soon divided by severe quarrels centering upon his deputy, Thomas

[1]See Paul Welsby, *George Abbot: The Unwanted Archbishop, 1562–1633* (London: SPCK Press, 1962), 154; Marchant, *Puritans and the Church Courts,* 50.

[2]Andrewes was at Chichester four years. Barlow, Neile, and Walter Curle had Rochester three, two, and one years respectively. Laud and Curle were at Bath and Wells two and three years respectively. Because there was no suitable move available, Laud had to stay six years in the insignificant see of St. David's. He was seldom in the diocese. Neile, Overall, and Abbot held Coventry for four, five, and one years. On the other hand, Arthur Lake and James Montague were at Bath and Wells for ten and eight years, Lake dying there. George Carleton died in Chichester after nine years. Thomas Morton, one of the best and least-known Jacobean bishops, was thirteen years at Coventry.

Muriell, an ex-pupil of whom he evidently thought highly.[1] The leader of the anti-Harsnett group among the fellows was Matthew Wren, a protégé of Andrewes, and a future Laudian bishop. When Muriell stepped down in 1612, Harsnett's appointment of John Pocklington, an outsider from Sidney Sussex College, did not improve matters. The upshot of the affair, which dragged on for four or five years, was that the rebellious fellows presented a petition to the king in May 1616. The king referred the case to a committee consisting of Archbishop Abbot, Lord Treasurer Suffolk, and the bishops of Ely (Andrewes) and Lincoln (Neile). Harsnett was forced to resign.[2]

The complainants' case is well documented because the drafts of their petition survive at Pembroke. The papers of the committee of enquiry are lost, and so Harsnett's replies are unknown. One cannot judge the truth of the complaints on the basis of the petition alone. Much of it concerned financial management. Andrewes had accumulated a surplus, which Harsnett invested in property; in fact, on becoming a bishop he had asked to be kept on as master to complete his purchase. As the college records show, Harsnett had been an extremely thorough senior treasurer and his investment proved immensely valuable to Pembroke.[3] At the time, when the less far-sighted Andrewes party opposed the investment because it seemed risky and unthrifty, Harsnett responded with obstinacy and high-handedness. In the earlier stages of the petition there were

[1]Through Harsnett he became precentor of Chichester (10 April 1613) and archdeacon of Norfolk (28 December 1621). He was university proctor in 1611 (John Le Neve, *Fasti ecclesiae anglicanae,* corrected and continued by T. Duffus Hardy, 3 vols. [Oxford: Oxford University Press, 1854], 1:266, 2:485, 3:621). He was one of Harsnett's chaplains and rector of Hildersham. A letter survives from Harsnett to Mr. Paris, patron of the living, thanking him for presenting it to Muriell (Pembroke College MS. LC.II.230, fol. 86). Muriell was an excellent appointment as precentor of Chichester. In 1616 he made an important anthology of contemporary verse anthems (BL MSS. Add. 29372–7); it includes, for instance, Gibbons's "See, see the word incarnate" (Thurston Dart, "Music and Musicians at Chichester Cathedral, 1545–1642," *Music and Letters* 42 [1961]: 221–26; *The New Oxford History of Music* [London: Oxford University Press, 1968], 4:505–6). It has been argued, however, on the basis of a signature in an italic hand, that the Myriell who made the anthology was rector of St. Stephen's, Walbrook, not Harsnett's precentor (Pamela J. Willett, "Musical Connections of Thomas Myriell," *Music and Letters* 49 [1968]: 36–42, and "The Identity of Thomas Myriell," *Music and Letters* 53 [1972]: 431–33). I would hesitate to base an argument on an italic signature; the Chichester precentor is still a more likely anthologist than the London rector.

[2]The file of the affair is at Pembroke College, MSS. M1–M23, C.θ, A.γ. Much of this material is copied in BL MSS. Harleian 7029, 7031, 7034. Attwater, *Pembroke College,* 58–70, gives an account of the college from 1606 to 1629 that adopts more or less uncritically the Andrewes-Wren point of view.

[3]Pembroke College MSS, Treasury accounts, 1550–1641; Attwater, *Pembroke College,* 62–63.

accusations of bribery, but they were frivolous, like many of the original complaints, and were dropped.[1]

The real reason for the quarrel's getting out of hand was Harsnett's absenteeism. Even Muriell and another Harsnett pupil, Barlow, had refused his initial request for leave. Academic quarrels are seldom simple, however, and in this case passions arose from a clash of personalities and principles between Harsnett and Andrewes.

Andrewes enjoys a high reputation for learning, piety, and sanctity. In High-Church circles he is revered as the founding father of Anglo-Catholicism. Yet as his most recent biographer has shown, as a bishop he was a courtier, even a time-server;[2] and intellectually, seen against the background of his time, he appears cautious and conventional, despite the subtlety of his mind and the complexity of his style. Harsnett was a different character, rougher and more independent. His policy as master seems to have been the reverse of Andrewes' in every way. Hints of the difference emerge from the complaints. His deputy Muriell, the rebels said, did not take part in disputations. He neglected his "commonplaces" or private sermons. Under him, an ancient custom of "philosophical and theological discourse and disputations" at table fell into disuse because he would never initiate it. Presumably Muriell disliked these customs and saw little point in them. At the height of the quarrel, Harsnett is said to have told the bishop of Bath and Wells that the fellows' predecessors were "dunces and drunckards"—a party phrase that stigmatizes the fellows as reactionaries and associates the speaker with antischolasticism and modernism.

The first evidence of Andrewes' personal involvement in the quarrel is a letter, based on information supplied him by the Pembroke rebels, that he wrote to Sir Thomas Lake in 1612, accusing Harsnett of corruption, protesting his disinterestedness, and pushing his own candidate for the mastership.[3] This candidate was a former pupil called Felton, an exact contemporary of Harsnett. The real purpose of the letter was to gain the king's ear, and in that respect it was part of a campaign. Later, the fellows themselves wrote to the courtiers Haddington and Villiers, as well

---

[1]Harsnett had advised a fellow "to get mony in his purse, as being the only and ready way now, to procure himselfe any promotion or living by paying for it" (MS. M7). This satirical remark was taken without irony and made the basis of gossip. Harsnett said the stories about him were "all naught save this [i.e., the money-in-purse remark], and this to no purpose" (MS. M8).

[2]Paul Welsby, *Lancelot Andrewes, 1555–1626* (London: SPCK Press, 1958). This is a good, nonhagiographical life.

[3]SP 14/70, no. 15.

as to the members of the royal committee.[1] A letter from Andrewes to the rebels, not meant for anyone else to see, proves the truth of this analysis. It shows Andrewes in an unpleasant light:

> ... Your Master will not be persuaded but that he shall hold his mastership still I wish he may but if I be not deceived he will be deceived in that when and from whence he thynketh least. Yow shall do well emong your selves to provide yow be not over raught. For he wilbe, (as I much doubt). Have one that is or that hath ben of your selves: a suit so honest so agreable to nature as if yow can be *unanimes* and sta[. . .] for it will not I suppose be denied yow. It will much furder or assist my mind from some good I entend if he be such a one as I shall have cause to lyke of. . . .[2]

Harsnett thought that he had a friend at court. Andrewes is telling the fellows that he knows better and that the ground for their petition is well laid. All they have to do is ask for a new master from inside the college, and if they wish to enjoy Andrewes' continued favor, they will choose Felton. Naturally, they did. His mastership proved a short one, and it is clear from the college documents and Attwater's history that Harsnett's enemies (in particular Wren, a future Laudian bishop) continued to have the dominant voice within the college, Andrewes outside it.

It is easy to see that Harsnett should have resigned, equally easy to see that once Andrewes had intervened he could not resign without confirming unpleasant rumors. Nor is it surprising that he grew angry, calling one fellow "a stiff, saucy clown," and bidding another to go schoolmastering in the country. His second deputy, Pocklington, made no secret of his low estimate of Andrewes' abilities. He said that *Tortura Torti* and *Responsio ad Apologiam Bellarmini* (controversial works that Andrewes wrote against Cardinal Bellarmine at the behest of James I) "were works of small worth," and in the heated arguments that followed went as far as to say that "Bellarmine and Baronius in all worth far excelled all Protestant Divines." He offended the fellows by criticizing a scholar's oration against Guy Fawkes on Gunpowder Day: "It was a great offence of our Church to speak evil of any that are dead." When these unacceptable views were reported to Harsnett, "he slightly put it off as an idle matter."[3]

---

[1]Matthew Wren wrote Sir Francis Nethersole that Harsnett was "so potent, crafty, and violent an adversary . . . he is afraid to be ript up in the court but here at home, he presumes any daubing would serve him" (BL MS. Harleian 7034, p. 153). Wren was Harsnett's match in vituperation. It is curious that so violent and caustic a speaker should have been, like Harsnett himself in earlier years, the meek Andrewes' protégé.

[2]Pembroke College MS A.γ, fol. 1 (14 February 1616).

This affair had an ironic coda. When Felton resigned three years later, the division between the fellows reappeared over the choice of a successor. After intense politicking, they chose the court candidate, Jerome Beale (Andrewes' informant in his letter to Lake). In 1626, Andrewes' death ended his influence over Pembroke, and when Harsnett became archbishop of York in 1628 and privy councilor in 1629, the fellows wrote congratulating him on both occasions. In particular they requested his good offices with the council, a request he fulfilled when he was put on a commission to inquire into a petition presented by the fellows against their master, Beale. They accused him of pre-election of fellows against the statutes. Harsnett and his fellow commissioners declared the charges proved and recommended that Dr. Beale not remain in office. The sentence was not confirmed. The university complained that the fellows' direct petition to the Crown breached university privilege, and the commission was canceled.[2]

The Pembroke affair was not Harsnett's only encounter with court meddling in university affairs. In 1615 James I visited Cambridge University. Harsnett was vice-chancellor again that year, with responsibility for entertaining the king and a great "concourse of gallants and great men." "He did his part every way," wrote John Chamberlain, "as well in moderating the divinitie act, as in taking the great paines in all other things, and keping exceding great cheere."[3]

The visit had its trials. Harsnett's Pembroke opponents, Wren, Reade, and Brownrigg, despite his opposition, had been chosen to take part in the philosophy act before the king, and Lancelot Andrewes ostentatiously rewarded them with tips and praise. The Latin comedy *Ignoramus* proved to be six hours long, and the courtiers became very impatient. Worst of all, all the courtiers expected to have honorary degrees conferred upon them. Up to a

---

[3]Attwater, *Pembroke College,* 139; Pembroke College MS C.θ, fol. 9v; BL MS. Harleian 7034, p. 146.

[2]Attwater, *Pembroke College,* 69–70. The university also wrote congratulatory letters (Cambridge University MS. Addit. 4021, fols. 11, 16, with further copies in MS. Add. 3126, pp. 12, 31, 47, and MS. Mm.1.44, pp. 216–17. There are also copies in BL MS. Add. 5873 (Cole MSS), p. 37, with a note: "The University had woful Experience some 10 years after that Learning, Truth, and the University had bitterer and more envenomed Enemies than the Filth of the Roman Lerna, and they were all Soused in a Presbyterian and Independent Lake into which it is likely they may have another washing. Wm. cole, Jan. 14. 1778. . . ." The original documents of the Beale case are SP 16/159, nos. 16, 29; 160, nos. 3, 14–44, 55–63; 161, no. 8.

[3]For the royal visit to Cambridge, see John Nichols, *The Progresses, Processions, and Magnificent Festivities of King James I,* 4 vols. (London, 1828), 3:39ff. Chamberlain's comment is in *Letters* 1:586–89. Harsnett's statutes for the occasion are copied in BL MS. Add. 5485 and printed in Nichols, *Progresses* 3:43–45.

point the university was prepared to humor them, and "Almost all the courtiers went foorth masters of art," as John Chamberlain wrote to Dudley Carleton. Doctors, however, the university would not make, and refused all demands, even the king's: "Few or no Doctors [went forth] saveng Younge," Chamberlain reported,

> which was don by a mandat beeing sonne to Sir Peter the Kings schoolemaster. The vice chauncellor and universitie were exceeding strict in that point, and refused many importunities of great men among whom was Master Secretarie that made great meanes for Master Westfeild, but yt wold not be, neither the Kings intreatie for John Dun wold prevayle, yet they are threatned with a mandat which yf yt come yt is like they will obey but they are resolved to geve him such a blow withall that he were better without yt. Indeed the bishop of Chichester vice chauncellor hath ben very stiffe, and caried himself very peremptory that way, wherein he is not much to be blamed, beeing a matter of more consequence then at first was ymagined.[1]

The royal mandate came, and the university complied with it, not without angry words. As Chamberlain wrote again:

> John Dun and one Cheeke went out Doctors at Cambrige with much ado after our comming away, by the Kinges expresse mandat, though the vicechauncellor and some other of the heades called them openly *filios noctis et tenebriones* [sons of night and darkness] that sought thus to come in at the windowe, when there was a fayre gate open.[2]

Harsnett, in the midst of his Pembroke troubles, had every reason to please the court. Instead, he asserted the university's independence.[3]

The period 1615–1616 was the low point of Harsnett's public life. Yet soon after these events, and possibly because of them, he acquired a friend and patron, Thomas Howard, earl of Arundel. Five letters survive from Harsnett to Arundel. The earliest of them is dated 12 September 1617, and it shows that their friendship was not new.[4] The most interesting of these letters is that dated 29

[1]Attwater, *Pembroke College*, 61; Nichols, *Progresses* 3:68; Corbet, *Poems*, 12ff.; Chamberlain, *Letters* 1:587–89.

[2]Chamberlain, *Letters* 1:591.

[3]Donne, of course, having originally been Catholic, did not have a degree of any kind, but needed one if he was to rise in the national Protestant church.

[4]Mark Aloysius Tierney, *The History and Antiquities of the Castle and the Town of Arundel* (London, 1834), 433. Tierney prints two of Harsnett's letters to Arundel. He made transcripts of three more (BL MS. Add. 39948, fols. 184–87v). Whether there are more Harsnett letters at Arundel I do not know. I was unable to consult the originals of Tierney's transcripts.

December 1617 from Harsnett's house at Ardham, refusing an offer of promotion:

> . . . My good lord, I have a great witnesse in heven, my great and dread judge, that I never affected the place I am in, nor eny bishoprick in the kingdom. I saw them shadowes without bodye, and myselfe lesse then a shadowe. Sithence I was Bishop, I never had eny seute of the place, nor never affected to bee higher. My good lord, the true ground is this. I am not for these tymes, nor these tymes for mee. A true touch hereof your lordship had plainely in viewe,—my late requitall for my poor true service to his majestie and my moother. I praye God I may never remember it, nor eny true subject feel the like: It may happilye shake him at the root. My phantasme of these tymes is this. All the witt, lerninge, wisdom, gravitye, government, that is to bee founde in all our ranke (quae scio quam sint exigua) putt into one man, cannot make him a Bishop: nor all-assistinge nobilitye stirre him one ace higher. Then, my good lord engage not that gemme which hath made your name illustriouse (that is, true auncient honor) at the stake of base corruption, for a man more weary and full of the tymes, then the tymes are of him; one that doth as much loathe the nowe stepp of climbinge ambition, as hee doth the stepps to hell.
>
> My Lord, I am now off the stage, sine dedecore [without disgrace], thoughe not sine vulnere [without injury]. Bringe not your servant on againe: lett mee dye a silenced, obscured, deaded man.[1]

This letter shows how much the Pembroke affair, to which the phrase "service . . . to my moother" refers, hurt Harsnett; it also shows that Arundel knew about it and had it in mind in offering his support. A few months earlier, 22 September, Harsnett had brought up the subject of Pembroke in soliciting Arundel's support for his former deputy Pocklington:

> . . . Mr. Poclinton, my chaplaine, and late president of Pembroke Hall, one whoe for nothing, but because hee is an honest, just, and Religiouse man, and a strict governor, hath lately suffered (as your Lordship maye well remember) moste unworthie things at the hands of the societye of Pembroke Hall; now by his lerned and godlie Sermons, preached unto that Hospitall, God hath so wrought in the hearts of all the house, that they have, under all their hands, petitioned that hee maye succeed in the place of their Governor lately dead . . . but, because the Lord Archbishop doth distaste him, and for no colour of reason but onely because hee was, in the furye of the fellowes of

---

[1]Ibid., 431. Ardham must be Hardham, a village about fifteen miles northeast of Chichester, six miles north of Arundel. There was a small Augustinian priory there, dissolved in 1535 by agreement with the patron, Sir William Goring, when it became a dwelling. Harsnett must have leased this property from the Gorings.

Pembroke Hall, traduced for a papist, he muste needs couche downe
under the burthen of his Grace his implacable disaffection.[1]

The offer Harsnett turned down was the bishopric of Norwich,
vacant in 1617 by the death of Bishop Jegon, a former fellow-
chaplain with Harsnett and a rather worldly bon vivant. Harsnett
having refused, John Overall was appointed. When Overall died
little more than a year later, Arundel renewed his offer of support
and Harsnett accepted. He became bishop of Norwich in June
1619, and the most successful period of his life began.[2]

Thomas Howard, second earl of Arundel (1585–1646) was the
only son of Blessed Philip Howard, who died in the Tower in 1595
when his son was ten. Thomas was brought up Catholic by his
mother, Anne, countess of Arundel, a saintly and heroic woman.
As a child, he was known as Lord Maltravers; then, with the accession of James I his titles of Arundel and Surrey were restored. He
married Alathea, heiress of Gilbert, earl of Shrewsbury, and with
her fortune bought back much of the sequestered family property.
On 25 December 1615 at court he took communion in the Church
of England, and thus became Protestant.[3]

Arundel was a  reserved, austere man, in his later years not a
popular figure at the Stuart court. He was the first English art collector of real knowledge and taste, and he patronized learned men
in general. He employed the mathematician Oughtred to teach his
children; he brought Wenceslaus Hollar from Prague, and he is
supposed to have discovered Inigo Jones's talent for architecture.
He patronized Rubens and Mytens. John Selden and Robert Cotton
were among his friends, and he obviously enjoyed Harsnett's company. "I have written to my noble Lord Byshoppe," he writes to his
agent in 1627, ". . . I would have you assure that worthy Lord that I
am sensible of his extraordinary love. . . ."[4]

In 1620 Arundel placed his little son, William, in Harsnett's
household as a page. His letter of instruction to the child (who

[1]BL MS. Add. 39948, fol. 184. Nicholas Felton became bishop of Bristol, as well
as Master of Pembroke Hall, in 1617. On Archbishop Abbot's role in the founding of
Sutton's Hospital (the Charterhouse), see Welsby, *George Abbot,* 54.

[2]The royal assent to Harsnett's election was given on 10 June 1619 (*CSP Dom.,
James I,* vol. 109, no. 126). The dean and chapter elected him on 27 June (J. F. Williams
and B. Cozens-Hardy, eds., *Extracts from the Two Earliest Minute Books of the Dean and
Chapter of Norwich Cathedral, 1566–1649,* Publications of the Norfolk Record Society,
vol. 24 [Norwich: Norfolk Record Society, 1953], 55).

[3]*DNB,* s.v "Howard, Thomas." On the countess of Arundel, see Christopher Devlin,
*The Life of Robert Southwell, Poet and Martyr* (London: Longmans, 1956).

[4]Mary F. S. Hervey, *The Life, Correspondence and Collections of Thomas Howard
Earl of Arundel* (Cambridge: Cambridge University Press, 1921), 258.

must have been all of six years old) survives. It is headed, "Instructions for you my son William how to behave yourself at Norwich."

> You shall in all things reverence, honour, and obey my Lord Bishop of Norwich as you would do any of your parents; esteeminge whatsoever he shall tell or command you, as if your grandmother of Arundel, your mother, or myself should say it: and in all things esteem yourself as my Lord's page,—a breeding which *youths of my House, far superior to you, were accustomed unto;* as my grandfather of Norfolk, and his brother my good uncle of Northampton, were both bredd as Pages with Bishops.[1]

In sending his son off as page to a bishop, Arundel was following family custom, as he says, but it can not have been an easy custom for a Howard to follow in 1620. One concludes that these unlikely friends, the scholar bishop and the collector earl, held similar views of the world and of man's place in it.

A letter from Inigo Jones to the earl survives, saying that "Mr. William was verry merry at his departure, and the bushop and he ar the greatest frends that may be." In Harsnett's household at Norwich, William Howard was taught by Henry Peacham, who dedicated to him *The Compleat Gentleman,* with a notice of Harsnett: ". . . since it was my good hap to enjoy your acquaintance, and to spend some hours with you at your Booke in Norwich; where at this present you have your education under the Reverent, Religious, and my Honorable Good Lord, the now Lord Bishop of Norwich."[2]

---

[1] Printed in *The Gentleman's Magazine* 103, pt. 2 (1833): 11, n. 2.

[2] Hervey, *Life of Arundel,* 168–71. Blessed William Howard, viscount Stafford, became Catholic. In the Popish Plot mania of 1680 he was condemned on false witness and beheaded. He was thus the last undoubted English martyr under the Elizabethan penal laws, a fate one does not imagine Bishop Harsnett would have rejoiced in, despite his savage remarks on the subject in his *Declaration.* The sentence was annulled by private act of Parliament in the early nineteenth century (*DNB,* s.v "Howard, William.").

# 8

# Harsnett: 1620–1631

With his translation to Norwich in 1619, Harsnett's life settled into a clear pattern. His academic career was over; he was a bishop and nothing else. He had income sufficient to live as he thought a bishop should, hospitably and charitably, and he had Arundel's friendship. His Norwich years were happy and successful.

The bishops of Norwich owned the lands formerly belonging to the Norfolk abbey of Saint Bennets, and the first Protestant bishops lived in the abbey. When the abbey itself fell into disrepair, Bishop Freake repaired an abbey property, a hall or grange called Ludham Hall. This pleasantly situated house became the country residence of his successors, "who," says Browne Willis, the eighteenth-century history of the abbies and cathedrals, "had here round about them about 300 or 400*l*. per annum. Demains, and all sorts of Meats, Venison, Wildfowl, Rabbits, Fish, in great plenty of their own, and thereby were enabled to live honourably and hospitably." Bishop Jegon enlarged and improved this house, but during his tenancy it burned down in a disastrous fire and Harsnett rebuilt it. He spent about £2000 on the house and a new chapel, where he held ordinations for the first time on 21 September 1628. At Ludham, says Willis, he "kept residence and hospitality . . . fitt for his place and degree." He was much loved in the diocese, says Francis Blomefield, the historian of Norfolk, "for his affability, eloquence, and hospitality, and particularly, for his repairing the Bishop's seat at Ludham." Besides looking after his own episcopal properties, at Norwich he began making donations to other churches. He repaired and ornamented Ludham parish church, and gave the parish a new bell to convert their peal of four bells into five. In 1627 in King's Lynn he granted and consecrated a font for the chapel of St. Nicholas, a medieval chapel of ease to the parish church of St. Margaret; the font cover (a modern replica of the original) is an elaborate piece of woodwork about fifteen feet high. He must have made many similar unrecorded benefactions. When he went to York as archbishop in 1629, he continued to make gifts. He was so pleased with the condition of All Saints, North Street,

York, that he gave the parish a fine silver communion cup. He left money in his will for the residentiaries of Southwell Minster to furnish their communion table. At Cawood outside York, where the archbishops had a residence, he began to build a poorhouse and a causeway.[1]

No bishop of Norwich, however, succeeded in conforming the East Anglian Puritans to the Church of England. Harsnett's predecessor Overall, for being "a discreet presser of conformity . . . got the ill-will of many disaffected thereunto,"[2] and Harsnett fared no better. In 1624, a group of Norwich Puritans accused him before Parliament of popery. Sir Edward Coke, an unpleasant character, himself a Norfolk man, and probably an influence on the complainants, reported the accusations to the Commons. The alleged offenses were suppression of lectures and sermons, exaction of undue fees, negligence in keeping registers, prosecuting parishioners for not facing east to pray and not standing for the Te Deum, setting up images in churches, and excommunicating several people for attending a private catechism.[3]

[1]Browne Willis, *An History of the Mitred Parliamentary Abbies, and Conventual Cathedral Churches,* 2 vols. (London, 1718–19), 2:148, describes Ludham. (The quotation continues: ". . . till Bishop *Montague* came, who leased it out upon lives to provide for his family; since which time the Bishops have been forced to live at *Norwich,* with nothing to supply their Tables but what they buy by the Penny at Market." Montague was a Laudian High Churchman.) Bodleian MS. Tanner 228, fol. 88, one of Anthony Harrison's miscellanies, gives an account of the Ludham fire. Information about Harsnett's expenditures at Ludham is from Bishop White's suit for delapidations against Harsnett's estate (SP 16/270, no. 67). The chapel ordinations are entered in Harsnett's register (Norwich Diocesan Registry, REG/16, fol. 31v). According to Francis Blomefield, *An Essay Towards a Topographical History of the County of Norfolk,* (London, 1805–10), 3:566, Harsnett consecrated the chapel on Christmas Day, 1627. No order for the consecration survives, although the Borthwick Institute, York (MS. R.Bp.8/4a–c), has a seventeenth-century order for the consecration of a bishop's chapel that in my tentative opinion may be similar to Harsnett's; it combines the two available seventeenth-century orders of Bishop Barlow (1607) and Bishop Andrewes (1620) in a way that suggests a date of 1625–30. I owe to Mrs. Beatrice Pugh a description of the King's Lynn font. The *Guide to St. Catherine's Church, Ludham,* describes Harsnett's bell and its inscription: "Hae Quinque Campana et Quatuor Facta Fuere 1619. Annoque Samuelis Harsenet, Episcopi Primo." The benefaction to All Saints' is related in *Yorkshire Archaeological and Topographical Journal* 8 (1883–84): 314–15: "Samuel Harsnet formerly Arch Bishop of York coming to view this Church in July, 1630, commended it for its beauty, was pleased to give . . . one *Silver Chalice and Cover,* with his Coat of Arms engraved upon it. . . ." The bequests to Southwell and Cawood are detailed in Harsnett's will (PCC 78 St. John).

[2]Fuller, *Worthies,* 536.

[3]The charges and Harsnett's responses to them are preserved in Bodleian MS. Tanner 114 and SP 14/165, no. 2. Tanner 114 is the more complete. It is a copy of the Lords' record of proceedings, endorsed 30 December 1640, when it was extracted by someone searching on behalf of Parliament for evidence against the bishops. Coke's report to the Commons is described in a letter from Sir Francis Nethersole to Carleton, 15 May 1624 (SP 14/164, no. 86).

When Harsnett first heard of the accusations, he was said to make light of them as a calumny and attributed them to a man called Stokes, a disappointed candidate for the archdeaconry of Norfolk. When the Commons formally sent the accusations up to the Lords, Harsnett asked permission of the Lords to reply in the Commons, but when the Lords found this unsuitable, he replied "in his place" to every point:

> He gave such satisfaction that the howse would have hard no more of it, if my Lord of Norwich himself had not desired that their witnesses might bee examined, for the satisfaction of the howse, and reparation of his creditt, whereupon the matter was referred to the examination of the Lord Archbishop of Canterbury, who is to certifie to the howse.[1]

No such report now exists. Harsnett also complained of Stokes to the Lords, accusing him of a clumsy attempt at blackmail. He seems to have been unbalanced. Stokes and the other complainants were bound over to appear before the council for slander, and Stokes was ultimately ordered "to make an humble submission and give satisfaction" to the bishop.[2] The case is particularly interesting because a complete reply to the accusations exists. Seventeenth-century Puritan literature is full of similar accusations against the bishops, and all too often historians print them as if they were proven truth. Prynne's accounts of Harsnett, for instance, are mostly fiction.[3]

[1]Locke to Carleton, 21 May 1624 (SP 14/165, no. 21). Nethersole, no friend to Harsnett, writing to Carleton, 6 May 1624, was the person who said Harsnett "maketh light of it" (SP 14/164, no. 46).

[2]Harsnett's complaint to the Lords about Stokes is in *The Lords' Journals* 3:390. See also *APC* 39:237.

[3]E.g., *The Antipathie of the English Lordly Prelacie* (1641), 221; *A Breviate of the Prelates Intollerable Usurpations* (Amsterdam, 1637), 161–62. Edmund Calamy, author of *The Nonconformist's Memorial*, tells a long story about Samuel Fairclough, a well-known East Anglian Puritan. Harsnett first encountered him in 1615 when, a student at Cambridge, he refused to take a woman's part in the comedy *Ignoramus,* to be performed before the King. Later, as a preacher at King's Lynn (according to Calamy), he ran into opposition from the alehouse keepers because his preaching hurt their business. He was in trouble with Harsnett because he refused the sign of the cross in baptism and was considered so popular that "he must be nipt in the bud." The upshot of the story is that proceedings against him in the Court of High Commission were dropped when "a good number of *Jacobusses* [King James guineas] engaged a certain lady of that city to gain such a certificate from the bishop as obtained a full discharge." It is not clear whether the lady or the bishop was bribed, nor does it occur to Calamy that the bribe discredits Fairclough and his friends as well as the lady and the bishop. Yet Christopher Hill has printed this undocumented, confused, and uncharacteristic story as evidence of corruption among the higher clergy (Calamy, *The Nonconformist's Memorial,* "The Second Edition," 3 vols. [London, 1802–3], 3:275; Christopher Hill, *Society and Puritanism* [New York: Schocken Books, 1964], 317).

When a case involving Harsnett with the people called Puritans is well documented, it invariably proves more complex than a simple case of lordly bishop versus godly preacher. No town, for instance, gave Harsnett more trouble than Yarmouth. In 1624, he had to put down a congregation of Anabaptists there. In 1628, when he submitted a list of Yarmouth separatists to the council, he commented that there were many more, that their numbers continually increased, and that people came to the town's conventicles from ten miles around. In 1627, as a result of his efforts to resolve a quarrel between the dean and chapter of Norwich cathedral over the right to appoint a minister, the town complained to the King that the bishop was harassing them with lawsuits, two in Chancery, one in the King's Bench, one in the Prerogative Court, three in the High Commission, and a complaint before the council, all instigated by him, they said, though some were in other men's names. Yet this was a complex case, involving not just the churchmanship of the rival parties but the patronage of the living. Before it was settled it involved the courts, the archbishop, and the King. The final result was a compromise: the town was to have two ministers, one appointed by the dean and chapter, one by themselves.[1]

Like many similar cases, the quarrels over the Yarmouth nomination involved property rights as well as religious opinions. The parish church of St. Nicholas, Yarmouth, originally belonged to the prior and monks of Norwich; then, after the dissolution, it passed to the dean and chapter of the new cathedral of Norwich, who, in Edward VI's time leased out the parsonage and priory of Great Yarmouth. In 1607 William Gostlynge was the farmer of the property, and the town complained to the bishop and to the dean and chapter that the clergyman serving the rectory was inadequate. In 1611 this complaint led to an agreement between the corporation and the farmer that the corporation should nominate its own minister. In 1624, Charles Gostlynge, brother and executor of William, confirmed the agreement. At the same time the minister resigned, whereupon the dean and chapter opposed the corporation's right of nomination. A vacancy ensued that Harsnett, as bishop, offered to fill by sending the bailiffs a letter appointing the bearer, Mr. Gammon, as officiant during the interim.

The town, however, while accepting Gammon for the interim, decided to contest its right to nominate, and in April 1625 the bailiffs gave a letter of attorney to some merchants to nominate John

[1]Henry Swinden, *The History and Antiquities of the Ancient Burgh of Great Yarmouth* (Norwich, 1772), 827–33, narrates the affair of the Anabaptists, including a letter from Harsnett. Harsnett's autograph list of separatists is SP 16/124, no. 81. Swinden, *History*, 833–44, gives the whole story of the nomination dispute.

Brinsley, a very young man, the son of John Brinsley the elder, a well-known Puritan minister in the midlands. The dean and chapter responded with a suit in Chancery, which included accusations that the town encouraged separatists. The Court of Chancery referred the case to the archbishop, who ruled that the original lease did not give any power of nomination to the farmer of the parsonage, and that although it was permissible for the dean and chapter to allow the farmer to nominate as long as no inconvenience arose, their doing so took away no part of their own right in law. The archbishop also found that because Yarmouth had connections with schismatics in Amsterdam, and because there were conventicles in the town, the King, by mandate, had enjoined the dean and chapter to resume their right. The archbishop ruled against Gammon because he had another living, and against Brinsley because he was unsuitable.

Brinsley, therefore, was dismissed in June 1627, but this did not end the litigation. When the town petitioned King Charles I for relief from the many suits they were engaged in with the bishop and others as a result of the dispute, the King appointed a commission and fixed 14 February 1628 for the hearing. Harsnett then wrote again, instructing the town to choose a second minister of its own. The bailiffs did not reply to this letter until 12 September, when they wrote choosing Brinsley once again, "a man not better known unto us than to your Lordship, being at first by your honour recommended unto us."[1] Harsnett's successor in the diocese, Francis White, wrote a cautious and guarded reply. Not suprisingly, Brinsley's nomination was not found "free from . . . just exception," and in 1632, the King in council forbade his officiating in Yarmouth entirely.

A clergyman of Harsnett's principles must have disapproved of the dean and chapter's lease of the parsonage, and even more strongly of their neglect of the responsibility to name the incumbent. He therefore used his authority to recover the dean and chapter's right at law, and to annul an irregular agreement between the farmer and the town. It was absurd that the corporation should be using the church's own revenues to undermine it. Nonetheless, he was prepared to allow the town a preaching minister of its own appointment. Therefore, following a well-established principle, he proposed a civically paid and appointed lecturer in addition to the vicar appointed by the dean and chapter. While such lecturers often held strongly Protestant opinions, there was no reason in principle

[1] A letter also survives from a member of the Yarmouth corporation describing Brinsley as "given to them by their present diocesan, who recommended him highly" (Bodleian MS. Tanner 137, fol. 170).

why they and the church authorities should not cooperate. What Harsnett and his fellow ecclesiastics found intolerable was the intransigeance of men like Brinsley and his supporters, which made it impossible for a bishop to carry out his pastoral responsibility. As Harsnett's letters reveal so interestingly, he took that responsibility seriously; it was his episcopal duty, upon "peril of souls," to "see that the church be not unprovided of an able and sufficient preacher to officiate the cure."[1]

Yet despite these quarrels, Harsnett was a good friend to Yarmouth. In November 1621 he led a commission of inquiry into the ruinous condition of the harbor. As a result of Harsnett's findings and recommendations, a general tax was laid on the county, to the great relief of the town. There was opposition to a tax on the county at large, and Harsnett therefore wrote a covering letter to the letters from the Privy Council. The letter is fascinating because Harsnett so easily bases his argument on the metaphor of the body and its members and so simply assumes that while people are free to do the right thing, they are not free not to do it. After Harsnett had left the diocese, and when he was on his deathbed, he still had Yarmouth's affairs on his mind when he wrote to Secretary Dorchester, asking that business relating to the town's charter be settled.[2]

As a bishop Harsnett sat in Parliament as one of the lords spiritual, and in the first two Parliaments of Charles's reign, in 1626 and 1628, he played an important part as a consistent opponent of the absolutist policies of Buckingham and his supporters, including most of the bishops. There were four major issues before the Lords in 1626: (1) proxies, by which, as Lord Say argued, "The whole house may be enclosed in two or three and their voices, with certain pieces of parchment"; (2) the imprisonment of Arundel because of his son's marriage, which the Lords took as a breach of their privilege; (3) the court's accusation of Lord Bristol and his counter-accusations of Buckingham, and (4) the movement to

---

[1]After dismissal from Yarmouth for the second time in 1632, Brinsley was presented to the living of Somerleyton by Sir John Wentworth. In 1642, with the fall of the royal government and the established church, Brinsley was recalled to Yarmouth to be one of the two town preachers. He served tne Presbyterians in the chancel of the divided parish church, while the Congregationalists worshiped in the nave. At the Restoration he was ejected once again when he refused to conform to the restored Church of England. He died in 1665 and is buried in St. Nicholas's church, Yarmouth (*DNB*, s.v. "Brinsley, John (1600–1665").

[2]Commission documents are SP 14/120, no. 2; 121, nos. 67, 133; 123, nos. 113, 114; 132, no. 51. Harsnett's letter to the deputy lieutenants and justices of the peace, accompanying the council's letters ordering a levy, is in Bodleian MS. Tanner 177, fol. 55. For Harsnett's last letter, see SP 16/189, no. 26.

impeach Buckingham. In all four matters Harsnett took an active part. On the impeachment question he was one of the committee of eight that reported to the Lords on a meeting with the Commons, and his autograph report of Eliot's speech against Buckingham survives in the State Papers. He was one of the lords who drew up the petition asking the King not to dissolve the Parliament, which Charles refused to hear. Harsnett's behavior in this Parliament won him considerable admiration. After the dissolution, a newsletter writer whose sympathies were with the opposition to Buckingham wrote that whereas the earls of Holland and Dorset, by "beplastering the Duke's sores," had lost more esteem "then 'tis thought theyr rich clothes, or refined Courtship will ever bee able to regayn them, while they live . . . The Earles of Essex, Lincolne, Warwick, the Lord Say, and the Bishop of Norwich, have purchas'd to themselves an eternall memory, by theyr well-temper'd boldnes, and more-upright behaviour." An example of the boldness admired by the letter writer is Harsnett's reply to Buckingham's insinuation that the Lords' committee had repeated treason in making their report of the words used in the Commons. Their commission, said Harsnett, was "to set down the words and what our conceits were," and as for treason, "No rational construction can be made of anything that can touch the King's honour."[1]

In the events of the Parliament of 1628 leading to the enactment of the Petition of Right, one of the fundamental guarantees of the liberties of the subject in English law, Harsnett's "well-temper'd boldnes" was equally marked. During the long debates on the royal prerogative, which began when the Commons submitted their four resolutions on taxation and imprisonment to the Lords on 7 April, and which ended with the royal assent to the petition on 7 June, Harsnett spoke consistently with Bristol, Say, Arundel, Archbishop Abbot, and Bishop Williams in support of the Commons' view of the law. It was due to the persistence of this small group that the Lords, at first disposed to take the side of the Crown, were finally brought to unanimity with the Commons, making it possible for Parliament to send the petition back to the King for a full and satisfactory answer.

Fairly early in the Lords' debates, their wish to provide a "saving" or accommodation of the royal prerogative led to a proposal

[1] S. R. Gardiner, ed., *Notes of Debates in the House of Lords, officially taken by Henry Elsing, Clerk of the Parliaments,* The Camden Society, n.s., no. 24 (London: Royal Historical Society, 1879), 112–15 (proxies), 126–28 (Arundel), 156ff. (Bristol), 190–98 (Buckingham). The newsletter is among the Newdigate MSS, Arberry Hall. Harsnett's report of Eliot's speech is SP 16/27, no. 2.

from the earls of Arundel and Pembroke suggesting that instead of rejecting the Commons' resolutions, the Lords should draw up counterresolutions of their own. Harsnett prepared them. His attempt at compromise did not satisfy the Commons because its terms inevitably begged the questions the Commons were most anxious about. For instance, in Harsnett's language every freeman had "a fundamental liberty in his goods and a fundamental liberty of his person," but as Coke pointed out in the Commons, "fundamental liberty" was the point at issue. What did the phrase mean? Although the Commons rejected the Lords' proposals, they had the great merit of clarifying the debate. On 10 May, when the Commons presented the Lords with the Petition of Right, the successor to their four resolutions, Harsnett was a member of the Lords' committee that, leaving the question of imprisonment to the Commons and making a few amendments to soften criticism of the government, accepted the petition.[1]

When the King gave an unsatisfactory answer to the petition, the Commons set about a remonstrance on the state of the kingdom, and the earl of Bristol proposed what was in effect a motion of no confidence. In this atmosphere, on 7 June, Harsnett rose, after some slight business had been attended to, to make a momentous speech:

> Now the House is full I shall crave pardon to utter unto your lordships the thoughts of a troubled heart. And, not to hold you long with expectation of any greate matter, it is that wee shall not rise at the end of this parlement with that comfort and joy as I thought wee should have done. When I returned and [saw] the Answere [to the petition] . . . though it bee full of grace it is not that [which] comes home and gives full satisfaction to the Peticion as was expected. My mocion [is] to send to the House of Commons that this may bee yssue of the Conference . . . that wee may all humbly and affectionately peticion the Kynge to give such an Answer as may flow fully to the Peticion.[2]

As a result of Harsnett's motion, which was accepted, a deputation led by Buckingham was sent to the King to ask for a clear and satisfactory answer to the petition. At four o'clock that afternoon, the King gave his answer. "Read your petition," he said, "and you shall have such an answer as I am sure will please you." The peti-

[1]Harsnett's draft of the lords' resolutions is in SP 16/102, nos. 9–15. S. R. Gardiner, *The History of England from the Accession of James I to the Outbreak of the Civil War, 1603–1642,* 10 vols. (London and New York, 1894–96), 6:260–62, 276. Gardiner's narrative of events in the parliament of 1628 (6:256ff.) is still the best.

[2]F. H. Relf, ed., *Notes of Debates in the House of Lords, 1621, 1625, 1628* (London: Offices of The Royal Historical Society, 1929), 216–17.

tion was read; the clerk pronounced the statutory words of approval, "Soit droit fait comme est desiré." Thus the petition became law.

In the simplification that passes for history in the popular mind and in the schools, the role of the House of Lords in the making of the Petition of Right is seldom thought of, and Bishop Harsnett, who put the motion that sent it back to the King, is forgotten entirely.[1] The Lords' debates are a fascinating example of how serious argument, conducted in an atmosphere free of party allegiance, can define a question and bring it to a resolution. That Harsnett acted out of independence of mind, not only as Arundel's friend, emerges from the details of his role, and also from his attitude to another dramatic case, the affair of the absolutist sermon preached by Roger Mainwaring in June 1627. When Pym brought charges against Mainwaring to the Lords, Harsnett and Williams, the only two bishops to speak, both recommended severe sentences. This kind of independence of the other bishops and of the court did not make him popular in those quarters. In a letter to Arundel of 20 June 1627, he mentions briefly Archbishop Abbot's troubles over his refusal to license for printing another sermon, Sibthorpe's *Of Apostolic Obedience*

> Touching the newes of Canterbury, I was much troubled at it: but it was no more then I foresawe, and forewarned my Lord and his followers of. His Grace grewe so passionate and discontent, it was not possible for him to subsist. . . . I knowe I am deepe in their black book.[2]

The passing of the Petition of Right had little effect on the relations of Crown and Commons, who proceeded with their remonstrance, which was rejected. They then prepared a bill for the granting of tunnage and poundage, thus putting a bold interpretation on the taxation clause of the petition. When Charles announced the prorogation of Parliament, the Commons produced another remonstrance, claiming that tunnage and poundage were

[1]Since this account was first written, Kevin Sharpe has published an important essay on the role of Arundel and his friends in opposing Buckingham. See Kevin Sharpe, "The Earl of Arundel, His Circle, and the Opposition to the Duke of Buckingham, 1618–1628" in *Faction and Parliament: Essays on Early Stuart History* (Oxford: Clarendon Press, 1978), 209–44. He concludes, "The political activities of Arundel and his circle during these years suggests rather the importance of personalities and personal connections—not connections based on constitutional principles or ideological committments nor connections founded on the mere pursuit of office, but connections strengthened by traditional beliefs about correct behaviour and modes of action, about methods not policies" (244). In Harsnett's case his friendship with Arundel seems to have been based on shared beliefs which had the force of constitutional principle.

[2]BL MS. Add. 39948, fol. 187. On Mainwaring, see Relf, *Notes,* 222; Gardiner, *History* 6:312–13.

subject to Parliamentary grant. Prorogation followed. The Commons' claim was illegal, and the lords who had supported the petition rejected it. As a result, during the summer Bristol and Arundel were both back in favor at court; Wentworth was made a peer and appointed Lord President of the North, and Bishop Williams was reconciled with Buckingham. Samuel Harsnett became archbishop of York, the first announcement of his elevation coming on 3 November 1628.[1] Without some knowledge of the changes at court during summer 1628, this is an inexplicable event. Prynne thought that Laud was responsible, but Prynne was wrong in virtually everything he wrote about Harsnett. Laud could undoubtedly think of several men he would rather have seen in York. Harsnett, however, was senior to all the bishops who had a claim to York except Neile, who less than a year earlier had moved to Winchester. He had held an important diocese for nearly ten years. He was a distinguished man and he had the backing of Arundel, which was probably decisive. He was consecrated 13 January 1629. At the ensuing feast he distributed £10 among his servants, expended eight bushels of flour on bread, nine bushels and a peck on pastry, one and a half loads, ten bavins, and ten sacks of coal, and three hogsheads of beer: he had been praised before for keeping "great cheer" and on this occasion can have disappointed no one's expectations. Between the announcement of his elevation and the consecration, he received the last of his honors, being sworn of the Privy Council on 10 November 1628. Thus the intransigeant element in the Commons drove the moderate men into office, and Charles I began his years of personal government with their support.[2]

As archbishop, Harsnett had authority over affairs outside his own diocese for the first time.[3] In 1629 he and Laud conferred and drew up articles, *Considerations for the better settling of church government,* distributed to the bishops in early 1630. Most concerned discipline, restricting lecturers and private chaplains, and enforcing solemn and careful ordination, as well as uniformity in ceremonial. The two articles most necessary for effective church government had no connection with nonconformity, but were

[1]Gardiner, *History* 6:334–38; *CSP Dom., Charles I,* vol. 120, no. 8.

[2]SP 16/132, nos. 13 (the consecration) and 14 (the feast); *Biographia Britannica* 4:2546. There was even a rumor in early November that Harsnett was to be Lord Keeper (HMC, *Seventh Report,* "Sackville MSS," 257a).

[3]Unfortunately, he had to go into Yorkshire, and like many a southerner before him, he did not much like the north. As he wrote to Lord President Conway, 6 October 1629, "Our Northern Coald Climates are barren of occurrences worthie your Lordships [eye] or eare . . . the church I finde infested with the men of Dan and Bethel, whose heartes are over seas, and I wishe their bodies and heartes were confined together" (PRO FO 16/150, no. 28).

directed at nonresident bishops, whom they commanded to reside
in their episcopal houses. Thus Harsnett tried to make his own
practice a principle of the church. Archbishop Abbot, who did not
approve of the measures to control lecturers, was pleased with
these orders.[1]

Harsnett continued active through 1629 and 1630, resident
partly in London on Privy Council business, and partly in York,
where his favorite place of residence was Southwell. Yet he must
have had a sense of the approaching end because in early 1629 he
set about the major charitable foundation of his life, the Chigwell
schools. He first built two schoolhouses and a house for a Latin
master, bought a house for another master, and provided a garden
for each house. Then by indenture dated 13 April he vested these
premises in twenty-one feoffees, together with the impropriated rectory of Tottington in Norfolk, assigned as an endowment. (The
advowson of the rectory also went to the feoffees; they were to
present suitable candidates who, if possible, should either be educated at Chigwell Latin School or be natives of Chigwell.) Choice
of a master lay with a board of governors consisting of the vicars
of Chigwell and Loughton and ten able and substantial parishioners of Chigwell.

The English School's master was to be able to write "fair secretary and Roman hands . . . to be skilful in cyphering and casting of
accounts." The Latin School's master was to be

> a Graduate of one of the Universities, not under Seven and Twenty
> Years of Age, a Man skilful in the Greek and Latin tongues, a good
> Poet, of a sound religion, neither *Papist* nor *Puritan,* of a grave
> Behaviour, of a sober and honest Conversation, no Tippler nor
> Haunter of Alehowses, no *Puffer of Tobacco;* and above all . . . apt to
> teach and severe in his Government.

The children are to be taught from "Lilly's Latin, and Cleonard's
Greek grammar." "For phrase and style" the master is to "infuse

---

[1]SP 16/153, nos. 100–102; Welsby, *George Abbot,* 137. At his trial Laud attributed
the *Considerations* to Harsnett (William Prynne, *A Breviate,* sig. 3B2v). Peter Heylyn,
Laud's chaplain, replied that "Some conference had passed betwixt [Laud] and Harsnet . .
. which being reduced into form, and by *Laud* presented to his Majesty, were . . . published in *December* following" (*Cyprianus Anglicus* [1668], 188). This evades a clear
statement. That Harsnett may have merely been consulted emerges from his letter to Secretary Dorchester, 13 December 1629: "According to his Majesties pleasure signifyed
unto mee by your Lordships lettars dated the 9th of this present december, I have
perused, and diligently weighed the severall pointes sett downe in this draught which I
received from you: and I returne them unto you without eny alteration, conceivinge them
to bee juste, piouse, and necessary for the publike wellfare of the church at this present:
humbly begginge of his Majestie: that they may bee putt in due and speedy execution."
(SP 16/153, no. 50).

into his scholars no other than Tully and Terence; for poets, to read the ancient Greek and Latin; no novelties, nor conceited modern writers." Harsnett also strictly forbade excessive corporal punishment:

> I constitute and ordain that the Schoolmasters do not exceed in their Corrections above the number of *Three Stripes* with the Rod at any one Time; that they strike not any Scholar upon the Head or the Cheek with their Fist or the Palms of their Hands, or with any other Thing upon Pain of Loss of Forty Shillings for every such Stripe or Stroke.

If these ordinances were properly enforced, Chigwell must have had two of the most humane schools in England at the time.

Humanity was the basis of the foundation. "I publish to all Men," Harsnett wrote, with the eloquence that came easily to him, "the true Intentions of my Heart":

> that I more affectionately desire that the poor Scholars of my Schools be *nurtured and disciplined in good Manners than instructed in good Arts;* and therefore I charge my Schoolmasters respectively, as they will answer it to God and good Men that they bring up their Scholars in the fear of God, and Reverence towards all Men; that they teach them Obedience to their Parents, Observance to their Betters, Gentleness and Ingenuity in all their Carriages; and, above all, that they chastise them severely for three Vices, *LYING, SWEARING,* and *FILTHY SPEAKING,* that Men seeing the Buds of Virtue in their Youth may be stirred up to bless them, and to praise God for their pious Education.

It is also best to let Harsnett speak for himself in explaining his reason for founding the schools. First, he charges his governors

> As they shall answer to God before his holy Angels, for their own Children, the Loss of their Time in their Golden Youth, the Corruption of their Manners, the Cheating them of their Learning . . . that they look duly, carefully, and conscionably, to the due keeping and observing of the Statutes and Ordnances following.

Then he lays the first "Bond and Obligation" upon himself:

> humbly upon my Knees, during my Life, to praise and magnify the Goodness of God, who, from a poor Vicar of this Parish, hath called me to so high a Dignity in his Church, and to enable me to offer this Mite of my Thankfulness unto Him for all the Blessings that in Mercy He hath bestowed upon me.[1]

---

[1]Harsnett's ordinances are printed in Nicholas Carlisle, *A Concise Description of the Endowed Grammar Schools in England and Wales,* 2 vols. (London, 1818), 1:416–22. They are also privately printed as *The Deeds and Ordinances of the Founda-*

His last act as a scholar bishop was to bequeath his library to his native town of Colchester, "Provided that they provide a decent Rowme to sett them up in that the Clergie of the Towne of Colchester and other Divines maye have free accesse for the readinge and studdyenge of them." The library consists mostly of classical authors, liturgies, and theological works—a severe collection, as one would expect. The problem with libraries, of course, is that as working collections they go out of date. The town welcomed its bequest and provided a chamber for it. They even appointed a librarian. Neglect came with the period of the civil wars. The collection was not developed and for a long time it became all but inaccessible. In 1888 a catalogue appeared, and for much of this century the books have been housed in a handsome room in the Colchester Public Library, well kept and useable. More recently they have become semi-inaccessible again.[1]

The first signs that Archbishop Harsnett's health was failing appear in early 1630, and the surviving letters from this period are burdened with a knowledge of his approaching end and the gathering troubles of the kingdom. "It is very true, that the gallant auncient composure of our glorious state," he wrote in the course of a long, chatty letter, 16 January 1630, in a shaky hand to his friend Sir Henry Vane the elder, "is much declined, and is like a bodye without blood and sinewes":

> Howe this vitall spirit of many shold bee quickened and restored to bringe the body unto the auncient lustre: *hic labor, hoc opus est: non Oedipo sed Hercules opus est* [Here is the task, this is the need: and not of Oedipus but of Hercules is the need], and not hee, if hee were livinge could effect it, for his clubb could quell monsters, but not Nestors consumptions. Wee are consumed wee doe consume, and wee have but our true Aesculapius (God blesse him) that taketh care of the common soares: yeat for our graciouse Josiah his sake; I hope almighty god will by his more then ordinary hand releive and support us.

In so writing of the kingdom at large, he was surely thinking of the state of the little kingdom of himself.[2] He continued active dur-

---

tion Schools at Chigwell *founded at Chigwell in the County of Essex, by deed of April 13th 1629* (1904). See also Daniel Lysons, *The Environs of London*, 4 vols. (London, 1796), 4:128–29.

[1]Harsnett's will, PCC 78 St. John; Morant, *Colchester* 1:168; *Notes and Queries*, 2d ser., 12:396; J.H. Round, "The Harsnett Library," *Athenaeum*, No. 2909 (28 July 1883), 113–14; Goodwin, *Catalogue*.

[2]SP 16/158, no. 55.

ing 1630, but in January 1631 he suffered a serious illness, and when he wrote to Secretary Dorchester, 30 January, to recommend Dean Hassall of Norwich to his patronage, he had to use an amanuensis:

> Nowe the clowde of my drowsinesse is a little lightened, I am able to call to minde your Lordships private Letters sent unto mee, the lively characters of your true Noblenesse and worth, by castinge the eye of your Favour, and Love upon a man old in yeares, worne with infirmities, farr distante from the Sunne, without precedinge Meritts, and unable, within the little Circle of his time, to expresse his due thankefullnesse . . . I beseech your Lordship at your best opportunitie to remember the honestest Mann in the world Called Doctor Hassall.[1]

On 13 February 1631, "weake in body, and myndefull of humane frailetie," he made his will. About this time he went to Bath to try the hot springs for his illness. His last surviving letter, 25 April, is another request to Dorchester, written from Bath, and recommending to him a Yarmouth petitioner (who presumably delivered the letter).[2] It was characteristic that Harsnett's last letter should beg a favor for people from his old diocese. Returning from Bath, he died in the village of Moreton-in-the Marsh, Gloucestershire, 25 May 1631.[3]

Seventeenth century people understood death to be the judgment passed by Almighty God on every human life, the only release from it to be found in God's mercy. In the presence of death, human judgment was irrelevant, and people who were accustomed to talk of life as a play and the world as its theater gave their lives playlike endings. As with plays, so with funerals and epitaphs; neither the last speech nor the last ceremonies were verdicts on the action completed so much as carefully fashioned endings to be judged by their fitness and congruency with what had passed before.

Archbishop Harsnett stage-managed his own end and wrote his own epitaph, declining the pomp of the one and the fulsomeness of the other so common in his time. The austere ceremony tells one what he thought a bishop should be. It is his last word on that subject.

As Thomas Fuller wrote, "There is a secret *loadstone* in every man's native soyle effectually attracting them home again to their

[1]SP 16/183, no. 42.

[2]SP 16/189, no. 26.

[3]SP 16/192, no. 78.

country, their centre."[1] So it was that on 7 June Harsnett's servants brought him, as his will instructed, to his first parish, Chigwell, in his native county of Essex, "to be buried within the Parrishe churche . . . withoute pompe or solempnitye at the feete of *Thomazine* late my beloved wief." Twelve poor widows in black gowns attended his hearse. The funeral was celebrated "with common Divine Service of the Churche only withoute any Sermon (or that which is unaptly termed an Exercise)." After the burial there was "a sober civill Banquett for as many of the Parrishoners" as accompanied his body to the grave.[2]

In due time there was laid down for him, as he had willed, a marble stone upon his grave:

> with a Plate of Brasse moulten into the Stone an ynche thicke haveinge the *effigies* of a Bysshoppe stamped uppon it with his Myter and Crosiers staffe, but the Brasse to be soe rivited and fastened cleane throughe the Stone as sacrilegious handes maye not rend of[f] the one withoute breakinge the other. And I will that this Inscripcion be ingraven rounde aboute the Brasse: *Hic iacet Samuel Harsnett quondam vicarius huius ecclesie Primo indignus Episcopus Cecistrensis Dein indignior Norwicensis Demum indignissimus Archiepiscopus Eboracensis* [Here lies Samuel Harsnett sometime vicar of this church, first the unworthy bishop of Chichester, then less worthy bishop of Norwich, at last most unworthy archbishop of York].

This fine brass with its life-sized portrait, one of the last of its kind to be made, was a conscious archaism, a statement of continuity with the kingdom's religious and artistic past, and a protest against iconoclasm past and to come. The effigy shows a thin, stooping man, weakened by age; he has the high-bridged English nose and long head, with a square chin beard. He is fully vested as a bishop. He holds what is presumably The Book of Common Prayer in his right hand; his crosier is in his left, and on his head is the first mitre worn in an Anglican portrait. In the bottom right-hand corner is his personal coat of arms: azure, *two bars dancetté ermine between six crosses crosslet, or, 3, 2, and 1*. In the other three corners this coat is impaled with the arms of his three dioceses. The epitaph is "ingraven rounde aboute," as he asked, and the designer of the brass has exceeded his instructions to the extent of including, besides the arms, a stone plinth under the figure with an inscription that reads: "Quod ipsissimum Epitaphum ex abundanti

[1]*Abel Redivivus* (1651), 21.

[2]A letter dated Chigwell, 4 June 1631, from Peter Mease to Sir John Coke says that "My Lord's corpse next Wednesday are brought to Chigwell to their more abiding place" (HMC: *Twelfth Report*, "Appendix 2," 432).

humilitate sibi poni Testamento curavit Reverendissimus Praesul"
[Which very epitaph this most reverend bishop of his abounding
humility caused to be placed by his will].

This, then, is Harsnett's image of a bishop: intentionally and
defiantly it is not a Canterbury-capped Protestant who looks out
from the brass, but the bishop of a Catholic and Apostolic church
of England. The image is the visual complement to the statement
of faith made in the will:

> I dye in the auncient faithe of the true Catholicke and Apostolicke
> Churche called the Primative Churche, that Faithe as it was professed
> by the auncient Holy Fathers next after the blessed Apostles the greate
> Renowned Pillars of the same, and signed and sealled with theire
> Bloude: Renowncinge from my harte all moderne Popishe Superstiti-
> tions and alsoe all novities of *Geneva* not concordant with the
> *maximes* of the Primative Renowned Churche, relyenge and restinge
> my sinfull Soule uppon the alone merrittes of Christe Jesus my only
> Saviour and most blessed Redeemer, To whome be all praise, honour,
> and glorie, worlde withoute ende, Amen.

In the generation after Harsnett's, there was a feeling that an
opportunity to establish the kingdom and the church on a secure
foundation had been lost when James I chose the inexperienced,
unsuitable George Abbot to succeed Richard Bancroft as archbishop of Canterbury. For more than twenty crucial years, the
Church of England was without effective leadership. "I read in a
modern author," says Fuller, "Had Bishop Laud succeeded
Bancroft, and the project of conformity been followed without
interruption, there is little question to be made but that our Jerusalem (by this time) might have been a city at unity with itself."[1]

This may have been wishful thinking. Nonetheless, Harsnett's
brass, his funeral, and his confession of faith; his schools, his other
charities, his care of his episcopal properties and churches; his
demeanor in Parliament and as a governor in the church, the modest estate he left to his heir: all form a strongly willed portrait of
what he, trained by Bancroft, thought an English bishop should
be.[2] At the same time, as his last letters and the riveted brass

---

[1]*Worthies,* 552. Clarendon wrote similarly: "[Bancroft] countenanced men of the
greatest parts in learning, disposed the clergy to a more solid course of study than they
had been accustomed to; and, if he had lived, would quickly have extinguished all that
fire in England which had been kindled at Geneva; or if he had been succeeded by Bishop
Andrewes, Bishop Overal, or any man who understood and loved the Church, that infec-
tion would easily have been kept out, which could not afterwards be so easily expelled"
(*History of the Rebellion,* 8 vols. (Oxford: Clarendon Press, 1826), 1:157).

[2]The bulk of his estate consisted of a house and land in Chigwell, called Stitmarsh,
a lease of the manor and parsonage of Oving, and a lease of a farm at Norton, Sussex.
The amounts his executor and heir, his nephew Samuel Harsnett, Jr., had to pay were

make clear, he was convinced of approaching disaster. One might argue, too, that he foresaw tragic disaster, originating not in some miscalculation of policy, but in the human material itself. That would explain why, concluding his life as a bishop, he should have thought it necessary to retrace his life, to take himself back, full circle, to the parish where he began, a primate of England returning to the center and origin of his priestly career, the work of a modest vicar in a country parish. The brass effigy has the last word, juxtaposing the honors it depicts to the epitaph that disclaims them. Nor can one doubt the sincerity of the image or the words.

This is why Harsnett's distinguished episcopal career (of which this narrative is a much-abbreviated sketch) casts an ironic retrospective light on his *Declaration* (for him a minor incident in a long, successful life) and its influence on Shakespeare. The assertion of power made in the *Declaration* for reasons of state, working in Shakespeare's imagination, was a cause of *King Lear*. Yet the persona that made that assertion was by no means identical with the man portrayed on the funeral brass. As a bishop Harsnett understood the hubris of absolutism, and he felt the demands placed by the burden of divinely sanctioned office on human weakness. A Jacobean bishop, like a Shakespearean king, was *persona mixta*, a bipersonate man, a human body and a consecrated body. To internalize the divine, as the Puritan did, neither lessened the burden of office nor removed the danger of hubris. Harsnett's monument, like all the great funeral brasses, of which it is a very late example, expresses with great candor the tragedy and the beauty of human dignity. In that respect it inhabits the same imaginative world as the drama of Shakespeare; and the mentality that ripped out the funeral brasses has always wanted to close down the tragic theater as well.

The archbishop who "put off this mortality" on 25 May 1631 was a better man than the brilliant, cocksure rhetorician fresh from

---

small, totalling £357. The modesty of this estate appeared when Neile, his successor at York, sued, incredibly, for £7,000 in delapidations. As Harsnett's nephew said, his uncle's whole estate did not come to £4,020, the amount Neile was claiming for two episcopal houses not lived in for fifty years. Neile, a time-serving careerist, notorious for his vulgarity and ignorance, expected a man who had been a bishop for over twenty years to leave a substantial estate. Andrewes left £12,000 and people had expected more, since he was known to have been tight with his money. It is hard to believe that Neile would sue the estate of a man who held the archbishopric little more than two years for about two or three times the annual income. Perhaps the suit reflects Neile's disgust at having to wait out the last two years of Harsnett's life before moving into the archbishopric himself. Either Harsnett's heir or his heir's son was a colonel on the parliamentary side in the civil wars, not an altogether surprising development. See Colonel Samuel Harsnett, *A Full Relation of the Defeate Given* (1645).

his classroom triumphs who wrote the *Declaration*. One of the minor curiosities of Shakespearean criticism is that, obedient to the Whig tradition of English historiography, Shakespeareans have forgotten the archbishop and assumed that Shakespeare agreed with the rhetorician—a proposition not easily believed in.

# Appendixes

## A. The Exorcists

There are three lists of exorcising priests in the *Declaration:* Harsnett's (201), presumably though not certainly based on the *Miracle Book;* Fid Williams's (361), and Anne Smith's (382). Anne's is the most reliable. She gives six names, all with one exception known as exorcists from the depositions, from Harsnett's quotations from the *Miracle Book,* or from an independent source. The exception is John Ballard, the priest executed with Babington and his coconspirators. He is named in all three lists but never mentioned in any account of the events themselves. Fid Williams says that he brought Marwood, the first demoniac, to Denham (218), in a party that included Anthony Babington and his friends. This, however, does not make him an exorcist, and it is suspicious testimony open to the charge that it was said in order to link Ballard and Babington with the exorcisms (it is also apparent that Fid herself was not at Denham when the exorcisms began there). Ballard's name comes last in Anne's list, possibly a sign of tampering with the evidence. In addition to the names on her list, Anne also mentions Weston (who seems not to have exorcised her), Dibdale, and Thomson (of whom she is uncertain).

Fid's list is as unreliable as the rest of her testimony. She gives fourteen names, excluding Weston, Dibdale, and three men named by Harsnett: Dakins, Mud, and Winkefield. Several of the men she names were not involved in the exorcisms at all. Richard Yaxley, Sara Williams's confessor after the exorcisms were over (350), worked in Oxford, where he was arrested and later executed. He did not arrive in England until the end of January 1586. Although Sara's evidence shows that he had dealings with Fr. Dibdale, it also shows that he was not an exorcist. Fid's Middleton is probably Anthony Middleton, sent on the English mission in July 1586, much too late for the Denham exorcisms.[1] Her "Blackman" is a mystery, possibly a mistake for George Blackwell, later appointed archpriest, and a center of controversy between Jesuits and secular priests. Though he does not appear as an exorcist, he has some connection with the Denham circle because he was reported to be

[1] Anstruther, *Seminary Priests,* 1:229, 389–90.

with "widow Mayney" in Lancashire in 1586; this is Richard Mainy's mother.[1] Nor is Fid's Bruerton traceable as either a priest or an exorcist. "Bruerton" was the alias of a layman, Roger Yardley, committed to prison 21 August 1586, still imprisoned in September, and listed as a dangerous person.[2] When first arrested in the roundup of Catholics following disclosure of the Babington Plot, he was said to have crossed into England "at the instant of this trobble."[3] It is very unlikely that he could have been present at any of the exorcisms.

Harsnett's list also seems to be padded. His Winkefield is Richard Davis alias Winkefield alias Foster, who was arrested on Ascension Eve (12 May) 1586, after leaving Denham. He was probably a layman, in minor orders only, although Challoner calls him "an ancient missioner" and Anstruther lists him as a priest.[4] "Ancient missioner" usually refers to a priest ordained before Elizabeth I's accession, but this can not be so in Davis's case, who was admitted to minor orders in September 1583 in a group that included Richard Mainy.[5] The authorities themselves seem to have been puzzled about him, although they knew all about his activities. He was present at the exorcisms and years later (1626) sent over to Douai an autobiographical statement, including an account of the exorcism of Anne Smith. He was not, however, an exorcist. Like Barnes, in whose possession the *Miracle Book* was found, he seems to have been an agent of the Catholic underground, one of the men whom earlier writers called "gentlemen volunteers." According to the spy generally known as Nicholas Berden, "This Companyon was shyfted oute for a laye man by the name of Davys, he was the principal person that Received Campion Persons and Edmondes, and conducted them throughe England and the Corrupter of William Fytton his mother in lawe and all there Famylle, with dyverse others."[6]

Harsnett also lists a priest called Mud, who has proved untraceable, although a John Mushe was reported "since Easter," 1586, with Weston and Cornelius "at Mitcham with Mr. Talbot."[7] Harsnett's Dakins is Edward Dakins, sent to England in 1582, and again on 20 January 1586. Like Mushe he was a northerner and

[1]Ibid., 1:40.

[2]*CRS* 2 (1906): 268, 283.

[3]Ibid., 2:260.

[4]Challoner, *Memoirs,* 118; Anstruther, *Seminary Priests* 1:97–98.

[5]Knox, *Douay Diaries* 2:198.

[6]*CRS* 2 (1906): 275.

[7]Morris, *Troubles* 2:159.

does not appear as an exorcist, although he too is named in a gathering of the exorcising group at Sir Thomas Tresham's. In 1593 he was reported to be in the north.[1]

The following list includes only priests whom the ex-demoniacs or an independent source name and describe as active in the exorcisms. There are ten of them, including Weston.

CORNELIUS, JOHN, alias Mohun. Born at Bodmin, Cornwall, of Irish parents, 1557. His patron, Sir John Arundel of Lanherne, enabled him to go to Oxford, but "misliking of the new religion," he went to Rheims, then to the English College, Rome, entering 1 April 1580. He was ordained priest and left for England in 1583. He survived over ten years, being seized 14 April 1594 at Chideock Castle, Dorset, where he was chaplain to Lady Arundel. He was taken to London for examination and remanded back to Dorchester for trial, where he was condemned to death. While he was in prison he was admitted to the Society of Jesus. He was executed at Dorchester, 4 July 1594, with James Bosgrave, S.J., John Carey, and Patrick Salmon, a servant from Chideock. The local people are said to have used his head as a football.[2] At the bar before Justice Anderson, he is said to have appealed to the law of God, to which Anderson is alleged to have replied, "We come not hither to do the law of God, but the law of the Queen."[3] Challoner's account of his exorcising attributes to him the "miracle" of Anne Smith's knife (*DEP*, 385), and his exorcising is also mentioned in an intercepted letter to Agazarri, General of the Jesuits: "Father Cornelius, called by the Protestants a conjuror and enchanter, is in safety, and doth much good by his singular gift in preaching."[4]

DIBDALE, ROBERT. Born c. 1556 in the parish of Stratford-upon-Avon, son of John Dibdale, a husbandman in Shottery. At one time the family owned property in Rother Street, Stratford. His sister Agnes's husband, John Pace, was a witness to Richard Hathaway's will in which Ann Hathaway received £6/13s/4d. Dibdale was probably educated at Stratford Grammar School, and when Simon Hunt, the schoolmaster, went to Rome, Dibdale probably went with him. He was in Rome when Hunt became a Jesuit, 20 April

---

[1] Anstruther, *Seminary Priests* 1:96; *CRS* 5 (1908): 222. John Gee, *The Foot out of the Snare* (London, 1624), 71, says that Dakins was martyred.

[2] Foley, ed., *Records* 7.1.70; Camm, *Forgotten Shrines*, 363.

[3] *CRS* 5 (1908): 293.

[4] Challoner, *Memoirs*, 198; Morris, *Troubles* 2:99.

1578. About a year later, Dibdale left Rome for Rheims, where he arrived 29 December 1579. There he found another Stratford connection, Thomas Cottam, younger brother of John Cottam, schoolmaster at Stratford. When Cottam left for England, 5 June 1580, he carried an affectionate and touching letter from Dibdale to his parents. He was arrested on arrival and the letter confiscated. Dibdale left for England 22 June and was also arrested on arrival. His name occurs among Gatehouse prisoners in 1581, and his father sent him food and money, delivered by Greenaway, the Stratford carrier. He was released 10 September 1582 by order of the Lord Treasurer and returned to Rheims to continue his studies. He was ordained by Cardinal Guise, 31 March 1584, and on 2 August 1584 left for England as a missioner. He seems to have become a chaplain to the Peckhams of Denham, Buckinghamshire, where, in 1585, he began exorcising after William Weston's success with Nicholas Marwood. He was captured in the aftermath of the Babington Plot, his name appearing in a list of priests lately committed, drawn up 25 September 1586. He was then in the Gatehouse with his fellow-exorcists Dryland, Stamp, and Thulys. He was tried before Justice Young, and Anne Smith was produced in evidence against him. On 8 October he was executed with John Lowe and John Adams.[1]

DRYLAND, CHRISTOPHER. A native of Canterbury, ordained at Rheims 31 March 1582, he was sent to England 27 June 1582. In June 1586 he was arrested at Denham House with Swithin Wells, Alexander the apothecary, and Edmund Peckham's servant James Stanborough. He was committed to prison 20 June. Berden, the spy, played some part in saving Dryland's life, since he wrote to Walsingham thanking him for having spared Dryland at the sessions and requesting his banishment. Instead he was transferred to Wisbech Castle with his companions Weston, Stamp, and Green, where he became Weston's spiritual father. After seventeen years of imprisonment he was banished in 1603, arriving at Douay 24 April. On 17 September he set out for Rome, where he was admitted to the Society of Jesus.[2]

GREEN, JOHN, alias Strawbridge. He was born in 1561, the son of William and Cassandra Green of Staffordshire. He entered the English College, Rome, in 1581, was sent to Rheims in 1582 and

[1]*CRS* 2 (1906): 258, 5 (1908): 18–19; Knox, *Douay Diaries* 1:200; Challoner, *Memoirs,* 117 (who mistakenly calls him Richard and describes his exorcising); Fripp, *Shakespeare's Haunts,* 30–33; Anstruther, *Seminary Priests* 1:101; *DEP,* 384.

[2]*DEP,* 383; *CRS* 2 (1906): 253, 270, 273, 279–80; Foley, *Records* 7.1.212; Challoner, *Memoirs,* 268; Anstruther, *Seminary Priests* 1:105–6.

ordained September 1585. He left for England in November 1585, and at Christmas 1585 he was reported to be in the house of John Gardiner, Grove Place, Buckinghamshire; according to Harsnett, this was one of the places where exorcising took place. Fid Williams describes his arrival "from beyond the Seas" with "graines, medals, and *Agnus dei.*" He was betrayed by Tyrrell while staying with Mrs. Dorothy White, and was in the Woodstreet Counter, 10 March 1587, described as "a Seminary prieste who hath for two yere laste paste frequented the houses of many Recusantes and hath done muche harme aboute London and is very obstinate." By March 1588 he was in Wisbech and remained in prison until he was banished in 1603. He returned to England, was again in prison at Wisbech, 1608, and is last heard of in 1626.[1]

SHERWOOD, JOHN. There were two Sherwood brothers. Richard, ordained June 1584, and sent into England in August, was committed to the Woodstreet Counter in October 1585. Berden the spy described him as "a man of no accompte meet to mak a stale to take byrds of his kynd." He was banished in 1586. John will have been the exorcist. He was ordained March 1584, sent into England from Rheims 4 May, and served as a chaplain to Sir John Arundel at Isleworth, where he was a companion of John Cornelius. He died at Chideock, Dorset, in Lent 1593.[2]

STAMP, THOMAS, alias Dighton. According to both Sara and Fid Williams, he took a major part in the exorcisms. He was apparently a chaplain to Sir George Peckham, at Holborn in 1579 and at Denham in 1586. He was arrested during the summer of 1586 and committed to the Gatehouse with Dibdale, Dryland, and Thulys, being singled out with Dryland and Weston as "specially to be dealt withall and touched for this last conspiracye." Like Dryland, he was not charged in the Babington conspiracy, but was moved to Wisbech Castle by warrant, 7 January 1586/87, with the comment that he had "done muche harme in the Lord Vaux his house and was one of them that did conjure and exorcise at Denham and other places. His companion Dipdale was executed." By 1594 he was released, and no more is heard of him, unless he is "Stamp a jesuit priest" reported in Herefordshire, 1605.[3]

[1]*DEP,* 368; Anstruther, *Seminary Priests* 1:136–37; *CRS* 2 (1906): 276–78.

[2]*CRS* 2 (1906): 256; Foley, *Records* 7.2.709; Anstruther, *Seminary Priests* 1:313–14.

[3]*CRS* 2 (1906): 258, 280; Anstruther, *Seminary Priests* 1:331.

THOMSON, WILLIAM, alias Blackburn. He was born in Blackburn, Lancashire. He arrived at Rheims in May 1583, was ordained 31 March 1584, and sent into England. He was chaplain to Blessed Anne Line. Captured in Robert Bellamy's house, Harrow-on-the-Hill, he was tried and condemned 18 April 1586 and executed at Tyburn, 20 April.[1]

THULES, CHRISTOPHER, alias Ashton. He was born 1560, the son of William and Anne Thules, Whalley, Lancashire, and was admitted to minor orders in Rome in 1579 at the age of nineteen while a student at the English College. He entered priest's orders in 1584 and left for England in 1585. He was arrested in Cheshire, August 1586, and committed to the Gatehouse. Although he was recommended for banishment, he was sent to Wisbech and remained a prisoner until banishment in 1603. He returned to England later, and was in the Clink in 1622.[2]

TYRRELL, ANTHONY, alias Browne. His experience of exile began early when he left England with his father, George Tyrrell, brother of Sir Henry Tyrrell. He returned to England in 1574, was arrested, released in 1576, and left England again for Rome. In 1580 he was ordained priest and sent to England, where he was caught again and imprisoned. He escaped with John Ballard in 1582. The pair then went to Rome, where according to the unreliable Tyrrell they inquired into the legality of assassinating the Queen. They returned to England in 1584. "I began to be in expenses," Tyrrell said later, "not considering that I lived upon the alms of other men. Then fell I to haunt taverns and ordinaries far unfit for my profession, to spend with the best, to ride up and down upon pleasure only, and to slack the spiritual harvest." By April 1585 Tyrrell had left Ballard and joined William Weston. He then became one of the exorcists. He was captured in the summer of 1586 at about the same time as Dryland. Justice Young removed him to the Clink in September, and he is listed as discharged in December. He was in the Clink again in July 1587 and in the Woodstreet Counter, March 1588. These imprisonments reflect the vicissitudes of his faith. When first released, he had apostasized and become an informer upon his old friends. Then after an arraignment before his fellow priests, he became reconciled in February 1587 and escaped into Germany. Then he returned and gave himself up, apostasizing

[1]Morris, *Troubles* 2:51; Anstruther, *Seminary Priests* 1:351.

[2]*CRS* 2 (1906): 258, 272, 279; 5 (1908): 154, 234; Anstruther, *Seminary Priests* 1:354.

again. The authorities arranged for him to preach a sermon at Paul's Cross, but instead of an apostate sermon, he preached a reaffirmation of his faith. Once again he was imprisoned and once again he turned, this time becoming a Church of England minister and marrying. In 1593 he again tried to become Catholic; he was caught, imprisoned, and sent back to his wife. In old age he slipped across to the Continent and died Catholic in Naples, 1615. Tyrrell was one of several seminary priests who were strikingly unsuited for the life of a missionary in Protestant England, or, perhaps, even for the priesthood. He affirmed or denied the truth of the possessions according to whether he was Catholic or Protestant. He gives a fascinating account of his state of mind during the exorcisms, and from this and the rest of his life's story it emerges that for those who either took part in or witnessed the exorcisms, faith validated the possessions: the possessions did not validate faith. Although he wrote a "confession" for the Court of High Commission in 1602, he was rumored to be reluctant to seal it with his oath. Tyrrell's story makes one sceptical of the claims made in the *Miracle Book* that the exorcisms caused large-scale conversions and reconciliations. That was a propagandist claim made by Tyrrell himself as author or part-author of the *Miracle Book*. Waverers may have been confirmed, but it is doubtful that any real Protestants were affected.[1]

WESTON, WILLIAM, alias Edmunds alias Hunt. He was born at Maidstone, 1549–50, educated at Oxford, where he proceeded B.A. in 1568–69 and was contemporary with Edmund Campion, from whom he later took his usual alias. From Oxford he went to Paris, to Douay (1572), and to Brussels where, in 1573, he took minor orders. In 1575 in Rome he became a Jesuit. He completed his novitiate in Spain, where he was ordained in 1579 and stationed as confessor at San Lucar and Cadiz. From 1582–84 he taught Greek at Seville. Then, on Parsons's recommendation, he was appointed to the English mission. He began the exorcisms with the treatment of Nicholas Marwood, a servant, sometime in 1585. He was arrested 4 August 1586, and first imprisoned in the Clink before being moved to Wisbech. There he became the central figure in the notorious "Wisbech Stirs" that divided Jesuits and seculars and gravely weakened English Catholicism. In 1598 he was moved to the Tower, where he continued until the accession of James I, when he was given the choice of taking the oath of alle-

[1]Devlin, "Anthony Tyrrell," 346ff.; Anstruther, *Seminary Priests* 1:361–63; *CRS* 2 (1906): 253, 270, 273, 277, 279; Morris, *Troubles* 2:103, 287ff.

giance or going into exile. He chose exile, leaving England in 1603, returning in 1604 to Seville where, in 1605, he was appointed spiritual father of the English College. In June 1614 he was made rector of the English College in the University of Valladolid, where he died, 9 June 1615.[1]

## B. The Devils' Names

Sara Williams said that the authors of the *Miracle Book* wrote down these names "in better order then she did utter them" *(DEP, 344)*. Except for Marwood's devil, Pippin, most were her invention, including the name of Mainy's devil, Modu. She said that some names came from "merry tales," other from names written on the walls under the hangings at Denham. By no means all are explicable, but if most were derived from folklore and folk idiom, then meanings can be suggested for some of them:

*Cliton.* Cf. "clit-clat," a gossip or tattle-tale. Wright places the word in Yorkshire, Lancashire, and Derbyshire; but a number of words Wright places in the north were used in the south in earlier times.

*Cornerd-cappe* ("Cornercap" in Sara's deposition, 344). A priest's or academic's hat, sometimes used by Protestants as slang for a priest.

*Frateretto.* Probably not "little brother," an unlikely invention for Sara, but "little flatterer," the substitution of *r* for *l* being easy.

*Fliberdigibbet.* A chatterer, especially female *(OED),* still common in American English.

*Helcmodion, Hilco.* The element *-modion* is probably analogous to "Modu," a "non-significant name" *(DEP, 240)* of Sara's invention. In Yorkshire and Lancashire a helc can be a heavy person, a pile of rocks, or a thunderstorm (Wright). Sara was first frightened by a cat and a thunderstorm.

*Hiaclito.* Probably another "non-significant name," made up of elements of other names, such as Hilco and Cliton.

*Hillio, Hilo.* A hellion is a devil or hell-dweller, and a hillocket is a giddy, light-headed person (Wright).

*Hob.* In common use for a rustic or a goblin, appearing in compounds like Hob Headless, Hobbedy's Lantern (the Will o' th' wisp), and Hobouchin, the owl (Wright).

*Hoberdidance, Haberdicut.* The latter is probably a variant of the former, the name of a Rumpelstiltskinlike hero in a tale told to Sara by her mistress (343).

[1] *CRS* 2 (1906): 268, 279; *DNB;* Caraman, *Autobiography.*

*Kellicocam.* Perhaps related to the name Killico, the suffix -*cocam* either arising by reduplication or else meaning "cock" in the sense of bully, chief, or penis. There is also a dialect word, "kelks," for testicles (Wright).

*Killico.* Either a variant of Kellicocam, or related to "kilcow," a braggart or bully.

*Lustie Huffe-cap.* A huff-cap was either a swaggerer or something good, or strong, to drink (Wright).

*Maho.* Sara attributed this name to a tale told by her uncle (344). This abbreviation of Mahomet was a standard name for the devil, appearing in Scots English as "auld Mahoun" *(OED).*

*Molkin.* A variant of "mawkin," a common word meaning many things, among them a maid for light housework, a slattern, a scarecrow, and a hare. The hare, because of its association with witches, provides a likely meaning here.

*Nurre.* OED defines nurre as a foster-child or nurseling, but in dialect speech an oakgall is a knurr, and the word can be used figuratively to mean a rough, hard man. A "knurrer" is a dwarfish man (Wright).

*Pudding of Thame.* Listed only in Sara's deposition. Not a name, but a refusal to give a name. Until quite recently the formula was common among American schoolchildren: "What's your name? / Puddin Tame. / Ask me again / And I'll tell you the same."[1]

*Puffe, Purre.* These are the "two fat devils that had beene conjurd up for mony, anno 84, and would not home to hell againe" (242). The names probably signify cats.

*Smolkin.* The suffix -*kin* is a diminutive suitable to this mouse-devil. The first element of his name may be related to "Smulk," meaning "a dirty beast" (Wright), or to a variously spelled Scottish word of Scandinavian origin with many derivatives, "smule" or "smool" meaning "little pieces" (Wright).

*Soforce.* Mainy's weak invention for Anne Smith's silent devil, perhaps analogous to "so-forth" as in *The Winter's Tale,* 1.2.218: "Sicilia is a so-forth."

*Wilkin.* Wright defines this as a rustic name for a particularly cunning person, but "quilkin," a west-country name for a frog or toad is a more likely source. Variant forms are "quilking," "wilkin," and "wilky." There is also proverb, "As cold as a quilkin" (Wright).

*Anonymos, Bonjour, Delicat, Lustie Dickie, Philpot, Pippin, Tocobatto* or *Cocobatto* and *Pour-dieu* need no explanation except

---

[1] Iona and Peter Opie, *The Lore and Language of Schoolchildren,* (Oxford: Clarendon Press, 1959), 156–57, give this verse and some analogues.

that Pippin is more likely suggested by the name king Pepin than by the word for an apple. "King Pepin" or "Pippen" seems to have been slang for a penis. See *All's Well That Ends Well,* 2.1.76. For *Bernon, Modu, Motubizanto,* and *Portirichio* I have no suggestion.

## C. Harsnett as Examiner for the Press

Under a Star Chamber decree of 1586, no book was to be printed before it had been passed free of seditious or libelous content by the archbishop of Canterbury or the bishop of London. Since neither dignitary could read all the books himself, they delegated the task to chaplains or to ministers in or around London. In 1588, Archbishop Whitgift drew up a list of such clerics. Eight were senior officials, any one of whom could "allow" a book alone; the remaining four had to act in pairs. The inclusion of Bishop Aylmer's chaplain, William Hutchinson, suggests that the list had the bishop of London's sanction. It included William Cotton, Harsnett's predecessor in the rectory of St. Margaret's, Fish Street, presumably another nominee of Aylmer's.[1] As Bancroft's chaplain, Harsnett was an examiner.

There is no record of the appointment of new examiners as members of the original group dropped out, but Harsnett's name first appears in the Stationers' Register as an examiner on 21 August 1598, when he allowed William Smythe's *Gemma Fabri.* From then until 26 November 1605, when he licensed his last book, he allowed sixty books. The subject matter is diverse and cannot be assumed to reflect his own literary tastes. Among the more famous books he allowed were Nashe's *Summers Last Will and Testament* and *Nashes Lenten Stuffe;* Jonson's *Every Man out of his Humour;* Marston's *The Scourge of Villanie,* and Will Kempe's *Kempes Nine Daies Wonder.*[2]

After he had been an examiner for some four months and had allowed ten books, Harsnett allowed, on 9 January 1598/99, Dr. John Hayward's *The First Part of the Life and Raigne of King Henrie the IIII. Extending to the End of the First Yeare of his Raigne.*[3] When the book was suspected of treasonable implications, Harsnett found himself in some trouble with the authorities.

A Latin dedication to the earl of Essex first drew suspicion to the book, and although Essex was at the time back in favor, his

[1]Greg, *London Publishing,* 9, 52–62; W. W. Greg and E. Boswell, eds., *Records of the Court of the Stationers' Company, 1576–1602, from Register B* (London: Bibliographical Society, 1930), 28–29; Hennessy, *Novum repertorium,* 276.

[2]Arber 3:124, 305, 175, 134, 159, 125, 160.

[3]Ibid. 3:134.

sensitivity to being associated in any way with the deeds of Henry Bolingbroke prompted him to write to Archbishop Whitgift, asking that the book be suppressed. Whitgift did not suppress the book but ordered that the offending dedication be removed from unsold copies. He evidently saw nothing treasonable in the book itself. This was also the opinion of Bacon, who told the queen that he saw no treason in it, only felony, since the author had stolen his sentences (i.e., "sententiae") out of Tacitus.[1] John Chamberlain reported the rumors to Sir Dudley Carleton at Ostend:

> The treatise of Henry the fourth is reasonablie well written. The author is a younge man of Cambridge toward the civill lawe. Here hath ben much descanting about yt, why such a storie shold come out at this time, and many exceptions taken, especially to the epistle which was a short thinge in Latin dedicated to the erle of Essex, and objected to him in goode earnest, whereupon there was commaundment yt shold be cut out of the booke, yet I have got you a transcript of yt that you may picke out the offence yf you can; for my part I can finde no such buggeswords, but that every thinge is as yt is taken.[2]

This was on 1 March 1598/99. Meanwhile the queen had grown suspicious and a second edition containing an epistle "apologetical" to the reader was seized and burnt by Bancroft's orders.[3] Things then became serious for all associated with the book. By June 1600 Essex was in disfavor, charged with neglect of duty. In July Hayward was summoned before Star Chamber and committed to the Tower. The printer, John Wolf, was also examined by Star Chamber. In January 1600/1 Essex was known to be plotting treason, and on 22 January Hayward was again interrogated, this time in the Tower.

In all this Harsnett was not ignored. At the time of Hayward's first interrogation, Harsnett was asked to explain his licensing of the book, and in reply he sent Coke, the attorney-general, a formal statement under four heads, with a covering letter pleading for understanding and lenience. Although the opening of his letter suggests that there was no immediate danger of proceedings against him, he was frightened:

> Right Worshipfull, I have not yet received eny bookes from my Lord of London[4] and so am not able to performe my taske in comparing

[1]*DNB,* s.v. "Hayward, John."

[2]Chamberlain, *Letters* 1:70.

[3]Margaret Dowling, "John Hayward's Troubles over His *Life of Henry IV*," *The Library,* 4th ser., 11 (1930): 212–24.

[4]Harsnett must be referring to copies of the two editions of Hayward's book, which he had been asked to compare with his memory of the manuscript. Greg, "Samuel

them according to my promise. this for griefe of hart and confusion of face I am skarce able to write, that I shold be behinde hand to your most graciouse divine kindnesse towards me. I have sent myne aunswer enclosed the onelie part of my dutye that I cold performe, most humblie beseeching your goodnes to accept it in good part, and to be a father unto me as you have begunne. the god of Heven sees and knowes I am innocent. At casus Leso Numine crimen habet. my poore estate, my credit, my selfe and more then my selfe doe hang uppon your graciouse countenance for I muste crave pardon to tell an unmannerlie secrett, I have a poor weake gentlewoman my wife in child bed who since your messanger his being at myne house did neither eat, nor drink nor sleape for feare, and yet I have twentie tymes reade over your most graciouse Lettars unto her. the Lord of Heven requite you for I and my poore frends shall never be able & so with teares I humblie take my Leave. from my poor house at Chigwell this xxti of July 1600.[1]

Harsnett's enclosure is interesting because of the information it gives about the workings of the censorship under Elizabeth I. His four grounds of excuse are as follows:

In moste humble wise complaininge sheweth unto your Worship your dailie Orator Samuel Harsnett, that where as the Author of a Pamphlet published in print in anno 99 Intituled the Raigne of Kinge Henry the fourth hath endeavored to excuse his publishinge the sayd pamphlett, as being allowed and approved by your sayd Orator, it may please your Worship in your grave wisdome to consider that this his allegation can be no colour of excuse unto him in regard of these reasons ensuynge.

Firste for that it hath been custome and use, for eny man that entended in good meaning to put a booke in print, the Author him selfe to present the booke unto the Examiner and to acquaynt him with his scope and purpose in the same: the Author of this pamphlet concealed him selfe and nether spake nor conferred with your orator concerning this pamphlett (notwithstanding we were both students togither in Pembrook hall in Cambrige and both of a tyme and standing in the Colledge[2]) but the author delivered his pamphlet unto a gentleman in

Harsnett and Hayward's *Henry IV," The Library,* 5th ser., 11 (1956): 1–10, thinks the reference is to books sent Harsnett in the ordinary way of business, although as he says there could be no reason why these should interest Coke.

[1]PRO SP 12/274, no. 61. The letter is printed by Greg, "Harsnett and Hayward's *Henry IV,*" 3–5.

[2]Hayward proceeded B.A. in 1581 from Pembroke and M.A. in 1584. He and Harsnett came together in the B.A. *ordo* of the college, Harsnett standing twelfth, Hayward thirteenth (Venn, *Grace Book* Δ, 337. In the M.A. standings, Harsnett was fourth, Hayward sixth. These standings are not simple academic rankings, and college and university standings do not necessarily correspond. In the 1581 B.A. *ordo,* a man called Capell stood third in the university, seventh in Pembroke. Felton, sixth in the college, was seventy-fifth in the university.

my Lord of London his house who begged your Orator his approbation unto the same in the name of a cantel of our Englishe chronicles phrased and flourished over onlie to shewe the Author his pretie Witt.

Secondlie that whereas your Orator his approbation of eny booke whatsoever is but a leading and inducement to my Lord of London my Master to passe his Lordship his further approbation to the same without which his Lordship his further approbation your Orator his allowance is no sufficient warrant for the Author to prynt his booke: the author of this pamphlett published his pamphlett without my Lord and master his approbation at all, contrarie to warrant in that behalfe.

Thirdlie the Author hath wronged your said Orator muche, and hath abused your Worship with false enformation in alledging for him selfe that your Orator allowed his pamphlet as it was and is published in prynt. for that the Author knoweth in his conscience this is true that when his pamphlett had mine approbation it was heddlesse without epistle, preface, or dedication at all which moved me to thinke it was a meer rhetorical exornation of a part of our English historie to shewe the foyle of the Author his witt: after myne approbation gotten thereuntoe the Author foysted in an Epistle dedicatorie to the Earle of Essex which I neither allowed nor sawe, and which if I had seen I protest I shold never have allowed the rest of the Pamphlett.

Fourthlie it may please your grave wisdome graciouslie to consider your Orator his mean condition and capacitie that your sayd Orator is a poore divine unacquainted with bookes and arguments of state, and with consequenceis of that nature: that your Orator for ten or twelve yeares past neither spake with nor saluted the Author of this pamphlett, and so is cleer from privitye with his entendementes and overtures in the same: that your Orator sett to his hand sodeinlie as mooved by his freind never reading (uppon his salvation) more then one page of the hedlesse pamphlett for which his unadvised negligence he humblie beggeth your moste graciouse milder Censure that it may be no imputation of bad meaninge unto him, who doth dailie in his poore calinge most hartilie and Zealouslie pray for the happinesse of her sacred Majestie and the state, and for the long continuance of her Highnes most graciouse, blessed, divine government over us, and doth from the bottom of his hart wishe shame and dreadfull confusion uppon all calumniators, and underminers of the same.

This is the letter of a man keen to extricate himself from an absurd and tricky situation. Much of it is disingenuous. In saying that his approval was "but a leading and inducement to my Lord of London" to give his approval, and that only the bishop's approval constituted authority to publish, Harsnett was probably stating the legal position correctly. Whitgift's delegation of authority was only an arrangement between archbishop and stationers that left responsibility under law with the bishops. Yet in practice everyone accepted the examiner's signature as sufficient authority. The point was a quibble. Nonetheless he probably made it at Bancroft's suggestion. If the bishops could not read the books, and if their deputies, being "poore divines," were inexperienced in matters of state, then a weakness in the censorship was revealed that would exonerate the bishops as well as their deputies should they be blamed for passing unsuitable matter. Already, in June 1599, and probably as a result of this case, Whitgift and Bancroft had charged the stationers that "no English Histories be printed except they be allowed by some of her Majesty's Privy Council."[1] If privy councillors could not detect treason, then no one could.

Harsnett's strongest point is his third, that as presented the book lacked its dedication. If Whitgift saw nothing wrong with the book except perhaps its dedication, then Harsnett could not be blamed for allowing it without it. (He presses the point too far when he says that, had he seen the dedication, he would have disallowed the whole book; this contradicts his protestation of ignorance in matters of state.) Even here an administrative deficiency in the censorship is revealed, because it was common practice for prefatory matter not to be added until late in the process of publication. In 1637 Star Chamber removed this bar to complete censorship when it decreed that incidental matter had to be licensed.[2]

Yet all protestations of humility and innocence aside, Harsnett was probably speaking truthfully when he said he would not have allowed the dedication. The reality of the matter was that he was neither innocent nor careless, and nor was he a poor, ignorant divine. He was a bright, able administrator who, in dealing with an important bully like Coke, had no alternative to eating large pieces of humble pie. The evidence for this is an alchemical manuscript by Sir Hugh Platt, licensed for printing by Harsnett, which survives in the British Library. His licensing signature, "Examinat & approbat Sa: Harsnett," appears on the title, fol.1, and at three more places, fols.17b, 47, and 56b, where a section of the manuscript ends. If Harsnett licensed this text after the Hayward affair, then perhaps this shows the effect of stricter procedures. It is equally likely that the text reflects Harsnett's practice from the first day he acted as an examiner.[3]

[1]Greg, *London Publishing,* 10.

[2]Ibid., 12.

[3]If there was reason for suspicion, Harsnett would not act alone without consultation. The entry of *Nashes Lenten Stuffe,* 11 January 1598/99, two days after Hayward's book, shows that in view of the watchfulness of the authorities towards Nashe's work, Harsnett would not accept sole responsibility for publication. The book was entered to Cuthbert Burby "upon Condicon that he gett yt lawfully Authorised," and the rest of the

The Hayward case reveals the sensitivity of the authorities, also the laxity of the censorship when there was no *a priori* cause for suspicion. Hayward may have been guilty of no more than dedicating a book to a generous patron and of using a friendly contact in the bishop's establishment to relieve himself of bother in having it approved. Equally likely, he may have had an ulterior motive in publishing the first part of his history when he did.[1] Harsnett's career was not affected.

He allowed ten books before passing Hayward's on 9 January 1598/99. Between then and 14 May he allowed six more, then none until 4 December 1599. Thereafter he was quite busy for a short time, allowing sixteen books between 4 December and 18 April 1600. Then he disappears again from the register until 14 July 1600, six days before he wrote to Coke. From this time on, until he stopped licensing altogether, his appearance in the register is sporadic. He allowed no books between 3 March 1600/1 and 28 May 1602. After another gap of six months between 31 December 1602 and 10 June 1603, he allowed only four books in two and a half years, ending with his last performance of this duty on 26 November 1605.

These gaps in his activities as an examiner have nothing to do with his difficulties over Hayward's book. The first, between 14 May and 4 December 1599, coincides with the period when he was writing his long *Discovery of the Fraudulent Practises of One John Darrel:* the High Commission ended its investigation in late May, and the book was entered in the stationers' register on 15 November.[2] Thereafter he must have found examining an increasingly unimportant part of his work for Bancroft. More High Commission work led to his second book, the *Declaration,* and again the six-month gap in examining between 31 December 1602 and 10 June 1603 coincides with the period of that book's writing. He also had the normal duties of his clerical profession to attend to, and after his collation to the archdeaconry of Essex, 17 January 1602/3, he stopped examining almost entirely. It was never his major employment as a chaplain, and he was never as active an examiner as Abraham Hartwell or Nicholas Pasfield, two other clerics whose names recur continually in the register during the same period as his.

---

entry reads, "To the whiche copie master Harsnettes hand is sett for th'allowance thereof with the wardens handes" (Arber 3:134). This certainly implies that higher authority than Harsnett's and the wardens was needed, and so it supports Harsnett's first argument to Coke, that his signature was only advisory.

[1]The manuscript of the unpublished second part survives at the Folger Shakespeare Library.

[2]*DNB,* s.v. "Darrell, John"; Arber 3:150.

## D. Harsnett's Letters

1. Autumn 1588. To the Bailiffs, Aldermen, and Council of Colchester (Goodwin, *A Catalogue of the Harsnett Library,* vi–vii).

2. 28 October 1588, Pembroke Hall. To the same (*Biographia Britannica* 4:2543, Note C; Goodwin, *A Catalogue of the Harsnett Library,* vii–viii).

3. 7 November 1588, Pembroke Hall. To the same (Goodwin, *A Catalogue,* viii).

4. 4 December 1595, Pembroke Hall. To Mr. Francis Bacon (Lambeth Palace MS. 660, fol. 153: holograph; BL MS. Add. 4122, fol. 87b: copy).

5. 20 July 1600, Chigwell. To Sir Edward Coke (PRO SP 12/274, no. 61; printed by Greg, "Samuel Harsnett and Hayward's *Henry IV,*" 1–10).

6. 21 November 1611. To Sir Walter Covent (BL MS. Harleian 703, fol. 146: holograph).

7. Undated, 1612. To Mr. Paris (Pembroke College MS. LC.II.230, fol.86: copy).

8. 12 September 1617, Ardham. To Thomas, earl of Arundel (Tierney, *History,* 433).

9. 22 September 1617, Ardham. To the same (BL MS. Add. 39948, fol. 184: copy).

10. 20 December 1617, Ardham. To the same (BL MS. Add. 39948, fol. 184b: copy).

11. 29 December 1617, Ardham. To the same (Tierney, *History,* 431).

12. 26 January 1619/20. To Sir Charles Cornwallis (Bodleian MS. Tanner 228, fol. 91: copy; Norwich Diocesan Registry MS. HAR/3, p. 165: copy).

13. 28 December 1621. To Mr. Jernegan Jenny (Bodleian MS. Tanner 138, fol.137b: copy).

14. 23 January 1621/22. To the Privy Council (PRO SP 14/127, no. 41: copy).

15. July 1622. To the Deputy Lieutenants and Justices of the Peace, Norfolk (Bodleian MS. Tanner 177, fol. 55: copy).

16. July 1624. To the Bailiffs of Yarmouth (Swinden, *History,* 830).

17. 22 December 1624, Norwich. To the same (Ibid., 834).

18. 25 September 1625, Colchester. To Lord Conway, Principal Secretary to his Majesty (PRO SP 16/6, no. 105: holograph)..

19. 6 October 1625, Colchester. To Archbishop Abbot (PRO SP 16/7, no. 27: holograph).

20. 20 July 1627, Norwich. To Thomas, earl of Arundel (BL MS. Addit 39948, fol. 186: copy).

21. 23 January 1627/28, Ludham. To the Bailiffs, Aldermen, and Common Assembly of Yarmouth (Swinden, *History,* 842).

22. Summer, 1629. To the Privy Council (SP 16/135, no. 66: copy).

23. 12 August 1629. To William, earl of Newcastle (PRO SP 16/149, no. 24: holograph).

24. 6 October, 1629, Bishopthorpe. To Lord President the Lord Conway (PRO SP 16/150, no. 28: holograph).

25. 6 November 1629, London. To Sir Henry Vane, Ambassador to the Hague (PRO SP 16/151, no. 24: holograph).

26. 16 November 1629, London. To the same (PRO SP 16/151, no. 80: holograph).

27. 12 December 1629. To Secretary Dorchester (PRO SP 16/153, no. 50: holograph).

28. 16 January 1629/30, London. To Sir Henry Vane (PRO SP 16/158, no. 55: holograph).

29. 30 January 1630/31, Southwell. To Secretary Dorchester (PRO SP 16/183, no. 42: amanuensis).

30. 25 April 1631, Bath. To Secretary Dorchester (PRO SP 16/189, no. 26: amanuensis).

# Part II
## A Declaration of
## Egregious Popish Impostures
by
## Samuel Harsnett

# Editorial Introduction

## Publication and Date

Harsnett's *Declaration* was entered in the Stationers' Register on 16 March 1602/3.[1] Publication followed, the first issue dated 1603. Two further issues followed, in 1604 and 1605, identical save for minor changes in the title page from [her Maiesties] to [his Maiesties].

One would normally assume that the date of entry in the register, 16 March 1602/3, came soon after the completion of the manuscript, and that publication followed in due course. H. N. Paul, in fact, dates the publication of the 1603 issue in April 1603 because John Swan, a Puritan dispossessor of devils harassed by the authorities, mentions the *Declaration* in the preface to his *True and Briefe Report, of Mary Glovers Vexation* (1603). According to Paul, Swan says that *A Declaration* was presented to James I upon his arrival in London. Swan, however, does not date the presentation, and Paul's dating of *A Declaration*, on the face of it reasonable, cannot be correct.[2]

Harsnett could have begun to write his book as soon as the High Commissioners finished interrogating their witnesses. This was sometime in June 1602, for the last evidence they took appears to be Anthony Tyrrell's statement of 15 June, intended to verify the exdemoniacs' depositions. This is the earliest date for Harsnett's beginning of the book. Two references in the last chapter complicate the dating of its completion. First, Harsnett mentions some Puritan dispossessors, including John Swan and three others who treated Mary Glover on 14 December 1602. This suggests that he was still at work in the last days of 1602. Earlier in the same chapter he refers cryptically to a new Catholic conspiracy "to set up a new Queene" (321); this, he says, is a desperate blasphemy against God and the King. His use of "King" moves the completion of the book well on into the new year, for it requires us to conclude that this conspiracy must be the strange affair known as the Bye and

---

[1] Arber 3:229.
[2] *The Royal Play of Macbeth* (New York: Macmillan Co., 1950), 100.

Main Plot, which focused upon the Lady Arbella Stuart and involved the appellant priest Watson and other Catholics, as well as Lord Cobham and Sir Walter Raleigh. The first reference to a conspiracy of this sort in the State Papers appears in an anonymous, undated letter of April 1603, but the plot was not common knowledge until June-July. The Privy Council issued warrants for the arrest of the chief plotters on 12 July.[1]

As Bishop Bancroft's friend, confidant, assistant, and chaplain, Harsnett would have had early knowledge of this conspiracy, but it is most unlikely that he would anticipate public disclosure by a reference in a printed book, a tactless if not dangerous act. This being so, one must conclude that Harsnett was still tinkering with the book as late as June or July, when it was still in the press. The reference to Lady Arbella and the Bye and Main plotters must be a last-minute addition meant to add a touch of topicality to a book written in the context of Elizabeth's reign.

A later dating is supported by the appearance of a six-month lull in Harsnett's activities as a licenser for the press, from 31 December 1602 until 10 June 1603. There was a similar break in his licensing activities when he wrote the book against John Darrell, from 14 May until 4 December 1599. The recurrence of the pattern suggests that Harsnett wrote the *Declaration* during the first six months of 1603. If this is so, then the book was not finished when it was entered in the Stationers' Register on 16 March 1602/3.

It seems that the printer was also worried about the timing and topicality of the book. The title page of the 1603 issue speaks of "her Majesties Subjects" and "her Majesties Commissioners," but a variant state of the issue exists in the Marsh Library, Dublin, whose title page reads "his Majesties." It is identical with the title page of the 1604 issue; it is not a cancel, and it shares its verso table of contents with the 1603 title page. The printer, Roberts, must have altered the title page during printing. Were it not for Harsnett's reference to the Bye and Main Plot, the natural conclusion would be that the final stages of printing, including as usual the title page and the prefatory matter, coincided with the Queen's death on 24 March and the ensuing proclamation of the new king.

Instead, the evidence suggests a more haphazard series of events. The *Declaration* is a long book, and an official, state-sponsored one. Not only may it have been unfinished when it was entered in the register; it may also be that the elaborately composed title page and epistle, important adjuncts of the book's purpose as propaganda, having been decided upon and composed very

---

[1] *CSP Dom. James I*, vol. 1, no. 63; vol. 2, no. 43; *APC* 32:500.

early in the process of writing, were printed first, while the Queen was still alive, instead of last, as was usual. Her death must have caused an interruption in the printing and finishing of the book. It seems to have been neither completely finished or printed until midsummer.

Since it was still 1603 when Roberts changed the date on his new title page to 1604, he either anticipated delayed publication or a slow sale. Then, having completed the outer forme of gathering A, he was sufficiently foresighted to run some extra copies of the new title, and these served as cancels for the second issue, 1604.

Even this did not exhaust the stock, and a third issue, the rarest of the three, was required in 1605. Some writers, confusing issues with editions, have thought the book was popular, but it seems to have had a slow sale. Writers who expose preternatural or super-natural events as fraud seldom attract a very large audience. Yet the book evidently had some effect, and probably the one intended: it discouraged the propagandist exploitation of supposed posses-sion by extreme Protestants.

There seems to be no evidence for H. N. Paul's assertion[1] that the book had "its greatest vogue just after the Gunpowder plot in 1605."

## Authorship

Although Harsnett's name does not appear on the title pages of either his *Discovery of the Fraudulent Practises of One John Darrel* or his *Declaration,* he undoubtedly wrote both works. Dar-rell immediately identified his tormentor by the initials "S. H." appended to the introductory epistle to *A Discovery,* and replied with *A Detection of that Sinnful Shamful, Lying, and Ridiculous Discours of Samuel Harshnet* (1600). "There is no doubt," says Darrell (sig. A4), "but that S. H. stands for Samuell Harsnet, chaplaine to the bishop of *London.*" He calls Harsnett Bancroft's "examiner," and attacks bishop and chaplain as "our two English Inquisiters" (sig. A1). The same S. H. signs the prefatory epistle to the *Declaration* and leaves no doubt that he alone is responsible for the manner and content of the book. In later life, when Harsnett was bishop of Norwich, he acknowledged his authorship of the book when he replied in Parliament to accusations made by some Norwich Puritans that he was pro-Catholic.

Harsnett's master Bancroft, nonetheless, was the chief cause of the book's being written, and people at the time thought it was his

---

[1]*The Royal Play,* 96.

book. An English Jesuit, Rivers, writing to Parsons about the bishop's researches into the exorcisms, said that he "meaneth nothing shall be said in his book but that which is avouched for by the oath of others."[1] Darrell also said that some people thought *A Discovery* was partly, perhaps wholly, the bishop's book:

> Whether [Harsnett] alone, or his lord and hee have discovered this counterfeyting and cosonage, there is the question. Some think the Booke to be the Bishops owne doing: and many thinke it to be the joynt worke of them both. (sig. A4)

Darrell said that *A Discovery* was "bedecked and adorned with my L. of Londons flowers" (sig. A2). The anonymous author of *The Triall of Maist. Dorell* also accused Bancroft of writing *A Discovery,* and accused him of fathering it "as a bastard upon another, viz. S. H" (sig. F1). More recently H. N. Paul has revived the idea that Bancroft was author or part-author of *A Discovery* and has attributed to him parts of the *Declaration* as well, including the most famous passage of all, the description of a witch (*DEP,* 308). The theory is given some color by another minister's account of a scolding by the bishop in language that is identical to a passage in the *Declaration.*[2]

Nonetheless it is obvious that the minister, writing years after the event he describes, is plagiarizing Harsnett, also that Darrell, a brave if misguided man, was attacking a powerful bishop by attributing to him the language of a book that Darrell and his supporters considered scurrilous. There is a sense in which the Jesuit letterwriter was correct to think of the book as Bancroft's because he commissioned it; but there is no reason to believe that he wrote any of it.

Bishop Bancroft and his chaplain, Samuel Harsnett, were close friends as well as professional associates. They shared jokes, witticisms, and turns of phrase. Together they conducted the inquiries into the events revealed in both books, and they must have discussed the books in detail at every stage of production. The responsibility of authorship, however, is solely Harsnett's.

## *This Edition*

Harsnett's *Declaration* is not an excessively rare book. The text is competently printed, and there are no significant press variants.

---

[1] Quoted by Ronald G. Usher, *Reconstruction of the English Church,* 2 vols. (New York: Appleton & Co., 1910), 1:178.

[2] *The Royal Play,* 92, 109, 106.

I have collated the Bodleian, British Library, and Marsh Library copies of the first issue with the Folger copy of the second issue. For the second issue I have also consulted the Cambridge University Library copy, and for the third issue, the Bodleian copy.

The edition is meant to provide a text that is pleasant and clear to read. Since those who quote Harsnett do so for preference in old-spelling, this is a modified old-spelling edition. Long [s] and the old use of [i], [j], [u], [v], and [vv] are modernized, as are [of] and [to] for [off] and [too], which can be misleading as well as irritating. Standard abbreviations such as [Ma:] and [Mrs:] are kept and standardized; all others are expanded, as are numerals, unless they signify a date or are a part of a king's or a pope's style. There is no alteration in the use of italics and capitals.

The original punctuation, which is the work of the compositors, is very heavy, and often makes nonsense of the grammar. To judge from his surviving papers, Harsnett was not a heavy punctuator. As Speed Hill writes of Hooker, "He seems to have expected the syntax itself to signal the rhetorical form of his sentences."[1] I have therefore repunctuated the text in the interest of sense and readability, hoping to avoid too rigid an application of modern principles (especially in the use of the parenthetical comma), and to mitigate the illogical fussiness of the quarto, which punctuates almost by the phrase.

Harsnett's sidenotes are included in the footnotes to the text, where they are indicated by [H]. I have incorporated the corrections listed in the publisher's errata list, and I have corrected the few obvious misprints.

[1]W. Speed Hill, ed., *The Works of Richard Hooker,* 4 vols. (Cambridge: Belknap Press of Harvard University Press, 1977–82), 2:xliv.

# *A*
# Declaration of Egregi-

ous Popish Impostures, to with-draw the
*harts of her Majesties Subjects from their*
allegeance, and from the truth of Christian Religion
*professed in England, under the pretence of*
casting out Devils.

PRACTISED BY EDMUNDS, ALIAS
*Weston,* a Jesuit, and divers Romish
Priests his wicked associates.

*Where-unto are annexed the Copies of the*
*Confessions, and Examinations of the parties*
themselves, which were pretended to be possessed,
*and dispossessed, taken upon oath before her Majesties*
*Commissioners, for Causes Eccle-*
*siasticall.*

AT LONDON
Printed by James Roberts, dwelling in
Barbican. 1603.

# The Argument of the seve-

## rall Chapters.

1. The occasion of publishing these wonders, by the comming into light of the penned booke of Miracles.
2. The fit time that the Popish Exorcists chose to act these miracles in.
3. The places wherein these Miracles were played.
4. More speciall considerations touching their choyse of places.
5. The persons, their Disciples pretended to be possessed, and dispossessed.
6. Their wayes of catching and inveigling their Disciples.
7. Their holy pretences to make their Disciples sure unto them.
8. Their meanes, and manner of instructing their Schollers.
9. Of the secrets, and strange operation of the holy chayre, and holy potion.
10. Touching the strange names of their devils.
11. The reasons why somtime one devil alone, somtimes an hundred, sometimes a thousand, are cast out at a clap.
12. Of the secret of lodging and couching the devill in any part of the body that the Exorcist please.
13. Of dislodging, rowsing, and hunting the devil by the dreadfull power of the presence, approach, and bodily touch of a priest.
14. Of the strange power of a Catholique Priests breath, and of the admirable fire that is in a Priests hands to burne the devill.
15. Of the admirable power in a Priests gloves, his hose, his girdle, his shirts, to scorch the devill.
16. Of the wonderfull power in a Priests albe, his amice, his maniple, his stole, to whip and plague the devil.
17. Certaine questions aunswered, concerning the Church of Rome her making and accumulating yet more dreadfull tooles and Engines for the devill.
18. Of the dreadfull power of holy water, hallowed candell, Frankincense, Brimstone, the booke of Exorcismes, and the holy potion, to scald, broyle, and to sizle the devill.
19. Of the astonishable power of Nicknames, Reliques, and Asses eares in afflicting and tormenting the devill.

# TO THE SEDUCED
## *Catholiques* of England.

*Seduced and disunited Brethren: there be two grand witches in the world that seduce the soules of the simple, and lead them to perdition:* Lying wonders *and* Counterfeit zeale. *The power of these two the spirit of God hath most lively expressed unto us, one in the person of* Simon Magus[1] *the Sorcerer who with his lying wonders had so bewitched the simple people as they followed him with this acclamation:* This man is the power of the great and mighty GOD; *the other in the person of some of the* Corinthians[2] *who by the feigned zeale of the counterfeite Apostles were bewitched and carried from S.* Paule, *the true and blessed Apostle of our Saviour Christ. These two witching powers have many yeeres since combined and united themselves in the Pope of Rome and his disciples, who take upon them the soveraigne power[3] of our saviour Christ, with authority to commaund uncleane spirits and to make them obey: and doe pretend such a burning holy zeale unto you as that they regard neither the pleasures, profits, nor preferments of this world, nay not theyr owne liberty and lives, but doe offer them up both, as a sacrifice for your soules consolation. These are mighty powers to sway your judgements and affections from us unto them. Now if it shall appeare unto you as cleere as the light of the sunne that these powers be feigned and counterfeite in them, and that they be in truth nothing els save the mists and illusions of Satan, to dimme the ey of your understanding, and bewitch your affections to doate uppon theyr impious superstition; what can you or any ingenuous[4] spirits*

[1] A sorcerer baptized by Philip the Deacon (Acts 8:5–24); the archetypal false teacher and miracle-worker, upon whom all false doctrine is based, as opposed to Simon Peter, upon whom the true Church and true doctrine are based.

[2] 2 Corinthians 11:3–4.

[3] "In my name they shall cast out devils" (Mark 16:17).

[4] *Ingenious* was often confused with *ingenuous. OED* gives an example from Hooker, "in requital of which ingenious moderation." Hooker, however, corrected this in MS; hence the Folger text reads "ingenuous" *(Works* 2:272). Assuming *ingenious* to be a compositor's error, I have emended it.

*doe lesse, then bewaile your seduced misaffection unto us, and to account them as the grand Impostors and enchaunters of your soules? And that this may be cleerly manifested unto you, I beseech you in the bowels*[1] *of our blessed Saviour to let open your eares and eyes to this short declaration, to peruse and read it with single ey and impartiall affection; and if it shall not most perspicuously appeare unto you that the Pope, and his spirits he sendeth in here amongst you, do play Almighty God, his sonne, and Saints upon a stage; do make a pageant of the Church, the blessed Sacraments, the rites and ceremonies of religion; do cog and coine devils, spirits, and soules departed this life to countenance and grace, or face out their desperate abhominations: then stand disunited and disaffected as you doe. It is not in any man (I confesse) to feele those divine beames of burning zeale that were in S.* Paule,[2] *who wished himselfe* Anathema *for his kinsmen according to the flesh; yet a man of* Jonas *spirit I can easily name, that would most gladly be cast into the sea to calme this tempest of opposition risen here amongst us; and of* Jeremies *devotion, that doth pray for a fountaine of teares to bewaile the lamentable blindnes of his owne nation: that men as you are, borne free of an understanding spirit and ingenuous disposition, should so basely degenerate*[3] *as to captivate your wits, wils, and spirits to a forraine Idol Gull composed of palpable fiction and diabolicall fascination; whose enchaunted chalice of heathenish drugs and Lamian*[4] *superstition hath the power of* Circes *and* Medaeas[5] *cup to metamorphose men into asses, bayards,*[6] *and swine. Is it not their owne brand*[7] *they have stamped on your forheads, that England hath beene always good asse to the Pope?*

*Who doth not bewaile the sely doating Indian Nation, that falls downe and performes divine adoration to a rag of red cloth:*[8] *and the besotted Aegyptians, that kissed with earnest devotion the Asse uppon which the Idol* Isis *sate: and the lymphaticall priests of* Baal, *that launced theyr owne flesh before an Idol of wood? Would*

[1]Cf. Philippians 1:8: "I beseech you all in the bowels of Christ."

[2]Romans 9:3.

[3]"Borne free of an understanding spirit" virtually translates *L ingenuus,* "freeborn" or "ingenuous," therefore "open and frank," the opposite of "basely degenerate."

[4]Not in *OED.* A "lamia" was a she-demon that sucked blood.

[5]Harsnett is wrong; Medea's potion renewed Aeson's youth.

[6]Bayard, the name of the horse that Charlemagne gave Renaud, became proverbial for recklessness. See Tilley, B110–12.

[7]Cf. Revelation 13:16, 20:4.

[8]In his Pembroke lectures as catechist, which Harsnett undoubtedly heard, Lancelot Andrewes mentions people who worship "a red clout hanging on a pole" *(Works* 6:24).

*God your bewitched dotage were not as palpable and more lamentable then theyrs, that fall downe and adore a morsell of bread, that kisse and clip with religious devotion the Popes toe for bearing the feigned counterfeit of our Saviour on earth (performed with the right Aegyptian glose,* non Pape sed Petro, non asinae sed deae, *this honour is not to the Pope but to S.* Peter, *not to the asse but to* Isis), *your Popes beeing proclaimed by your owne Oraclists to the world, one to be an Asse, another a Fox, another a Wolfe.*

*What people but you were ever so bewitched as to be borne in hand that a house was carried in the ayre from* Palestina *to* Loretto; *that a painted Image in a wall doth worke as high miracles as ever were performed by the eternall sonne of God; that the prints of S.* Frauncis *stripes, the tayle of our Saviours Asse, the milke of our blessed Lady are this day to be seene; and these gracelesse, saltlesse gulleries either to be believed or countenaunced by men of wit, understanding, and spirit, such as are this day many in the Romish Church? If you aske me the cause, what can it be but this, that God hath given them over to the spirit of illusion to believe unsavory lies for refusing in their pride to embrace the pure naked synceritie of the Gospell of Christ? He that sits in the heavens, Almighty God, with his Angels and Saints, do laugh these mishapen monsters to scorne.*

*And who can but bleede in hart to see you as farre bewitched on our imposturising renegadoes that come fresh from the Popes tyring house, masked with the vizard of holy burning zeale? First it may please you to observe that the wiser, graver sort of them do keepe themselves warme in theyr Cloysters at home, and doe feede themselves fat with the spoiles of your confusion. These lighter superfluities whom they disgorge amongst you, how they play the Bats and Moales! either trenching themselves in the mines of your labyrinths at home, or masking in your gold and silver abroade,[1] in the fashion of great Potentates; untill Gods revengefull arme doth uncase them to the view of the world, and then they suffer the mild stroke of justice with a glorious ostentation, as you in beguiled simplicitie doe imagine, for theyr conceited religion; but as the wiser see, the state did alwaies know, and is of late published in theyr own writings, for high and odious treasons, and professed by their owne Maisters that have made them after their own images, to be of a spirit of contradiction to our Governours and Prince; and it is wondred at by themselves, considering theyr treasonable machinations, that her Highnesse and the state have carried so milde and mercifull an hand over them,*

[1] I.e., Living secretly in great houses, or traveling in fine disguises.

*and that any one of them is left alive to libell against the admirable lenity of her Majesties gracious proceedings.*[1] *Wherein be ye well assured, that if the sword of justice were drawne, and inflicted according to the waight and measure of their detestable designes, that fewer of them would come over, and that this covey of night-birds would shrowde themselves warme under the gentle wings of theyr holy father at Rome.*[2] *But admit (as you conceive) that they died for the credit of their conceited superstition: what did* Lucians Peregrinus[3] *lesse, then offer himselfe in fire at* Olimpia *for the credit of his fascination? What did* Aesculapius[4] *uppon the hill* Aetna *to get himselfe a name, but cast himselfe headlong into the burning flames? What doe the Indian priests at this day, but sacrifice themselves for the countenauncing of theyr diabolicall incantation? It is no new nor strange thing for the authors and maintainers of sects and factions in all kindes to die with seeming shew of glorious resolution. Doe but seriously recount the quality of this fugitive generation, and see what pious resolution can lodge in theyr breasts. What are they afore they goe over but discontended, ruinate, stigmaticall, refuse people: of a factious, ambitious, exorbitant conversation abroad, exploded or cunningly discarded their owne Societies where they lived? And how ghostly and priestly they demeane themselves here amongst you at theyr returne, I referre you for demonstration to this short and perspicuous declaration. Wherein you may plainly see, if you doe not wilfully hoodwinke your owne eyes, that the holy pretended hote zeale of the fiery spirits from Rome is the meer Heathenish jugling of* Bells *priests to devour your goods, lands, and patrimonies, the rights of your posterity, and auncient monuments of your name; to defraude your children of theyr bread and cause you offer it to impure dogs; to enrich theyr owne Cloysters, Colledges, and Churches with the spoyles of your desolation; to defile your chast houses, pollute your tender virgins, deprave and inveigle your owne wives lying in your bosoms, especially by that poysonable engine of hypocriticall Confession; and finally to offer you up as a pray to that Monster of Rome, the head of all unnaturall and detestable rebellion.*

*And that this declaration might be free from the carpe and cavill*[5] *of ill-affected or discomposed spirits, I have alledged*

---

[1]A run-on sentence, not really correctible.

[2]Cf. Psalm 91:4.

[3]A cynic turned Christian who committed suicide by throwing himself on the flames at the Olympic Games, A.D. 165. See Lucian, *The Passing of Peregrinus.*

[4]An error for Empedocles, who according to late tradition threw himself into the volcano (Lucian, *The Runaways* 3).

[5]Proverbial. See Tilley, C95.

*nothing for materiall or authenticall heerein but the expresse words, eyther of some part of the* Miracle booke *penned by the priests and filed upon Record where it is publique to be seene, or els a clause of theyr confession who were fellow actors in this impious dissimulation. Whose severall confessions and contestations (the parties beeing yet living) are heere published in print that the world may be a witnesse of our integrity herein. All which had beene long ere this offered to your equall consideration, but that the* Miracle-booke *came but lately to hand, and the getting of foure chiefe Daemoniacks together, besides many more assistants, beeing persons of that quality and condition, was a matter of some paines and travell to effect.*

*If the forme and phrase be distasting to some clowdy spirits, as too light and ironicall for one of my profession, let the matter be my Advocat that draweth me thereunto, and the manner my Apologie a little too: trusting I may be excused to jest at their jesting that have made a jest of God and of his blessed Saints in heaven. If I have wittingly falsified or feigned any thing out of that booke of wonders, God doe so to me, and more, for dooing them so much wrong; but if all be truly and authentically set downe, give* GOD *his glorie, his Church her honor, your Soveraigne her allegeance, your Brethren theyr due affection, and the Pope and his jugling companions their deserved detestation. And so I leave you to the protector of all truth, and the revenger of all falshood and hypocriticall dissimulation.*

Yours in Christ

*S. H.*

# A declaration of Popish imposture in casting out of Devils.

## CHAP. 1.

*The occasion of publishing these wonders, by the comming to light of the penned booke of Miracles.*

About some three or foure yeeres since, there was found in the hands of one Ma. *Barnes,* a Popish Recusant, an English Treatise in a written hand, fronted with this Latine sentence taken out of the Psalmes, *Venite, et narrabo quanta fecit Dominus animae meae,*[1] come and I wil shew you what great things the Lord hath done for my soule. Which treatise when we had perused uppon this holy invitation, we found it a holie fardell of holy reliques, holy charmes, and holy consecrated things applied to the casting out of many thousands of devils out of six young persons, three young men and three proper young maides, accomplished by the meanes of Fa: *Edmunds,* alias *Weston,* a principall Jesuit of his order in those times, and twelve secular Priests, his reverend assistants.[2]

The names of the parties supposed to be possessed were these: *Marwood,* servaunt (as hath beene enformed) to Ma. *Anthony Babington; Will: Trayford,* attendant at that time uppon Ma: *Edmund Peckham; Richard Maynie,* Gentleman, lately before come out of Fraunce; *Sara Williams, Friswood Williams,* two sisters, and *Anne Smith,* all three meniall servaunts to Maister *Peckham* aforesaid.[3] The names of the Actors in this holy Comedie were these: *Edmunds* alias *Weston, rector chori,*[4] of whom you have heard afore, Ma: *Cornelius,* Ma: *Dibdale,* Ma: *Thomson,* Ma: *Stemp,* Ma: *Tyrrell,* Ma: *Dryland,* Ma: *Tulice,* Ma: *Sherwood,* Ma: *Winkefield,* Ma: *Mud,* Ma: *Dakins,* Ma: *Ballard,* and some other besides that were daily commers and goers.

---

[1]Psalms 66:16 (AV).

[2]For the priests, see Appendix A. There were not really twelve; Harsnett no doubt chose the number for propagandist and rhetorical reasons.

[3]Except for Marwood, imprisoned in 1586 *(CRS* 2 [1906]: 283), and Mainy, these persons are not known, apart from accounts of the possessions. Frideswide or Friswood Williams, however, known as Fid, and given the baptismal name Francis by the priests *(DEP,* 230), is probably the same person as the prophetic maiden who was living in London with Mrs. Dorothy White in August, 1586 (SP 12/192, n. 57). Mainy's career at the Rheims-Douay seminary is recorded in Knox, *Douay Diaries* 1:166, 169, 196, 198, 202.

[4]Head chorister, here used ironically to mean "the leader of the band."

This play of sacred miracles was performed in sundry houses accomodate for the feate, in the house of the *Lord Vaux*[1] at *Hackney,* of Ma: *Barnes* at *Fulmer,*[2] of Ma: *Hughes*[3] at *Uxbridge,* of Sir *George Peckham* at *Denham,*[4] and of the *Earle* of *Lincolne*[5] in *Chanon Row* in London. The time chosen to act and publish these wonders were the yeeres 85 and 86, ending with the apprehension and execution of *Ballard* and *Babington* and the rest of that impious consort.

And because the gentle Invitator of us to *come and see* his wonders, when wee come to see them, himselfe and his actors doe play least to be seene, it hath beene thought meet to send for him, and as many of his play-fellowes as *Tiburne* will give leave to come, to conferre further with them touching this mysticall play: whether the partes have beene handled handsomlie and cunningly, or no, what the scope of the Author *Edmunds* and his associates was in this wonderful pageant, and whether good *decorum* have beene kept in acting the same. Wherein (I must tell you) some paines have beene taken by some in authoritie for the finding out of such agents, patients, and assistants as have furnished the stage, and in bringing them to say their parts so perspicuously on the stage, as

[1]William, third baron Vaux of Harrowden, ?1542–95, a Catholic peer impoverished by his recusancy. See Anstruther, *Vaux of Harrowden.*

[2]Harsnett is not clear about these places. In chapter 3 he associates Fulmer with Mr. Gardiner, but neither he nor Barnes seems to have owned property there. Richard Branthwaite sold the manor of Fulmer, a village in Buckinghamshire, to Sir Marmaduke Darrell in 1595 *(VCH, Buckinghamshire* 3:276).

[3]Untraced. Uxbridge Manor belonged to the earls of Derby, but there was another property, Colham Garden, regularly leased after 1506 *(VCH, Middlesex* 4:74).

[4]At the dissolution of the monasteries this manor passed by grant of Henry VIII to Edmund Peckham, whose family already owned another estate in Denham, Southlands. Harsnett's Sir George Peckham inherited Denham from his brother, Robert, who died in Rome, 1569. (His heart, enclosed in lead, was sent home to Denham for burial.) Sir George was a merchant adventurer who hoped to recover family wealth lost by recusancy; in 1583 he financed an expedition by Sir Humphrey Gilbert and Sir Richard Grenville. Meanwhile in 1578, he had settled Southlands and part of Denham Manor on his son, Edmund, and his wife, Dorothy, daughter of Sir Thomas Gerrard. On 7 July 1586 Edmund died, and his son, George, then seven, became heir. In September, Sir George, his son-in-law John Mainy, and "Mr. Peckham thoughte to be his sonne" (perhaps his grandson) were imprisoned following the Babington Plot. In 1596 the Crown seized the Denham estates for debt, granting them to William Bowyer pending settlement. Sir George died in 1608. The Peckhams never recovered their property (Pollen, "Supposed Cases of Possession," 461; *VCH, Buckinghamshire* 3:257; *CRS* 2 [1906]: 257). In 1554, the Peckhams acquired the land on which James Burbage's Theatre later stood. Having sold it, in 1582 they began a complex and ultimately successful legal battle to recover it from Burbage's landlord, Giles Allen. In 1582 Edmund Peckham sent men "to harass the Theatre, and Burbage had to hire people to protect it" (Berry, *Shakespeare's Playhouses,* 10, 27–29).

[5]This was Henry Fiennes de Clinton, and not his father, Edward, 1512–85, Lord High Admiral and a strong Protestant.

that every young child may see who hee is, what hee meanes, and whether his part tends.

*Marwood* and *Trayford* cannot yet be found; it is thought they are conveyed beyond seas (as some other of theyr play-fellowes should have beene) for telling of tales. The other foure possessed have come to light, and uppon gentle conference have frankly and freely advowed, and have sealed it with their voluntary oathes taken uppon the holy Evangelists, that all in effect that passed between them and the Priestes in this wonderous possession and dispossession was naught else save close packing, cunning jugling, feate falshood, and cloked dissimulation. One of the reverend Priests who was himselfe a principall actor in this holy legerdemaine, being examined, hath contested with the confession of the other examinats touching the unfolding of this sacred packe. All whose severall examinations, confessions, and relations touching the beginning, proceeding, and finishing of this tragicall comedie, wee have thought meete *ad verbum* to publish in print, that all men may see wee have dealt truly and sincerely heerein, and that all may likewise see *quanta fecit Dominus* (according to the saying of that Latine sentence prefixed to the discourse), how great things the Lord in his mercie dooth by course of times reveale of that man of sinne, of the mysterie of iniquitie, and of those reverend jugling Priests his disguised comedians.

Wherein, that every person may appeare in his owne proper colours, the devill in his, and the devils charmers in theyrs: that every part may be considered, how well it hath been plaied and what actor hath best deserved the *plaudite* or *suspendite* for his good action and wit: *venite et narrabo,* come and see it set out in the sacred robes out of the holy wardrop from Rome, their holy attire, theyr holy reliques, their consecrated creatures, theyr own speech, action, and fashion: and thus it begins.

# CHAP. 2.

*The* time *when the Popish Exorcists chose to act these miracles.*

The Politikes maxime of using and plying of time hath beene so well practised and plyed by his *Holines* of Rome and his holy crue as that little time hath been lost wherein something hath not beene attempted against her Majestie and the kingdome, since her first comming to the crowne to this present time. I will onely point at those former times as I come along to our time of this tragedie of devils.

Her Highnesse was no sooner come to the Crowne but *Marie,* then wife to the King of Fraunce, was declared in Paris to be the lawfull Queen of England, and the armes of both her Majesties kingdoms, England and Ireland, were commaunded to be set *in vasis et tapetibus regiis, et reliquis utensilibus.*[1] The popish Bishops,[2] lately before deprived in the second yeere of her Majesties raigne, purposed to lose no time when presently after their said deposition: *plerique eorum excommunicationis censuram, adversus reginam aliosque nonullos adhibendam censuerunt.* It was no long time after this, when it should have been a Canon set down[3] in the Counsell of Trent by the instigation of his *Holines* Agents there present, *de Elizabetha haeretica declaranda,* if the Emperor had not interposed to stay that course. It was time well plyed when the same his *Holines* contriving her Majesties utter destruction (as appeares in the life of *Pius 5.* published in Italian[4]), and drawing the king of Spaine into the same, he sent over one *Robert Ridolphi,* a Florentine, under the colour of Merchandise, hether into England to excite a rebellion,[5] and furnished him with 15000. Crownes towards the same: by whose cunning perswasion the Noble men in the North parts beeing risen in Armes,[6] forth commeth the Popes *Bull,*[7] blanched with a

[1] "In the royal dishes and hangings, and other necessaries." Mary Stuart was daughter-in-law to the king of France, who proclaimed her Queen of England and had her arms quartered with those of England (Hughes, *Reformation in England* 3:8).

[2] 1559 [H].

[3] 1562 [H]. In the twenty-third session of the council in 1562, Pius V asked that Elizabeth be denounced as schismatic and heretic and her Protestant bishops declared unlawful. He withdrew when the Spanish ambassador said this would cause the murder of the remaining English Catholic bishops. The emperor Ferdinand II interposed the following year. See Waterworth, *Canons and Decrees,* ccxvii–viii; Hughes, *Reformation* 3:244, based on Bayne, *Anglo-Roman Relations,* 190–92.

[4] Giovanni Girolamo Catena, *Vita del Papa Pio Quinto* (Mantua, 1584). The author was the pope's secretary of state, "a bragging and inaccurate panegyrist" (Hughes, *Reformation* 3:279, n. 5).

[5] 1567 [H]. A Florentine banker who settled in England after Mary I married Philip II. He intrigued with France and Spain on behalf of the English Catholics, but although Pius V sent him money to be forwarded to the rebel earls, the pope did not send him into England, he did not foment the rising, and the rising did not coincide with the papal bull against Elizabeth, which came too late to help the rebels *(DNB;* Read, *Burghley,* 38–50).

[6] Thomas Percy, seventh earl of Northumberland, later beatified by Leo XIII, and Charles Neville, ninth earl of Westmoreland, led the Rising of the North in late 1569, the counterpart of the Pilgrimage of Grace in 1537, and ferociously suppressed by Elizabeth's government. The purpose was to free Mary, Queen of Scots, and restore Catholicism. Westmoreland escaped to the Continent. Northumberland found asylum with the Scots, who betrayed him to England for £2000. He was executed at York, 22 August 1570. Child, *Ballads* 3:401–23, prints three northern ballads on the Rising. See also Read, *Cecil,* 455–68.

[7] *Regnans in excelsis,* 25 February 1570.

fayre goodly face of pastorall zeale and love to the Catholique religion, excommunicating of pure devotion (God wot) the Queenes Majestie, and discharging her subjects from their allegeance unto her: beeing indeede naught els save a devilish Engine to strengthen the rebellion: which beeing dissolved, and the heads thereof dispersed,[1] the time was plied on still with consolatorie Letters written from the Pope, containing matter of new comfort and encouragement to the *Duke of Norfolk*,[2] the close designed head of that rebellion, by his intended mariage with the *Scottish Queene.* Forces were promised to be sent over with all speede from beyond seas to the ayde of the saide *Duke* under the leading of *Vitelli*,[3] appointed to that office by name from the king of Spaine: the comming of which forces the *Duke* him selfe did stay by losing his head.[4] And least the King of Spaine should quaile in his princely designements against this kingdome in regard of his infortunate successe, *Saunders* (the Popes darling[5]) eggs him on with a fresh assault to keepe the Spanish Engines in worke, alledging this as his maine battery to cause the King to be dooing: that the whole state of Christendome stoode upon the hote assayling of England.[6]

Neither was it long time ere this vigilant champion had gained time againe by obtaining of his *Holinesse* men, mony, and munition, with which hee came with open armes into Ireland like a Furie from Hell, and in his vaine hopes had devoured that

---

[1]1569 [H].

[2]Thomas Howard, fourth duke of Norfolk and first in precedence among English noblemen, was drawn into negotiations with Ridolphi and the bishop of Ross aimed at marrying him to Mary, Queen of Scots, and putting her on the throne with the aid of Spain. On 24 March 1571 Ridolphi left London carrying dispatches from Norfolk and Mary as well as assurances from forty peers, but the government had already intercepted enciphered letters from Ridolphi to Norfolk and Ross, and he never returned to England. Norfolk was tried for treason, 15 January 1572, and sentenced to death. He was executed 2 June 1572. See Read, *Burghley,* 38ff.

[3]Marquis of Catena, an officer in the duke of Alva's army. He came to England ostensibly as envoy in 1569, but really in preparation to command a Spanish force when it landed. He had fifty captains and civil engineers in his retinue. He came to support the northern earls, not Norfolk, and after Cecil heard from the Continent that Alva meant to aid the rebels and was assembling ships, Elizabeth dismissed Vitelli *(DNB,* s.v. "Percy, Thomas, seventh earl of Northumberland," and Read, *Cecil,* 464.

[4]1572 [H].

[5]Nicholas Sanders, 1530–81, controversialist, historian, and conspirator, had a pension of three hundred ducats from Philip II. He schemed to dethrone Elizabeth. Sent as papal nuncio to Ireland to incite the Irish clans to rebellion, he set up the papal standard at Smerwick, having landed at Dingle in the west; after many escapes, he died of cold and starvation in the Munster hills, 1581 *(DNB).*

[6]1577 [H]. This famous sentence is from a letter from Sanders to William Allen, 6 November 1577: "The state of Christendome dependethe upon the stowte assallynge of England." See Knox, *Letters,* 38.

kingdome for the use of his holy Father the Pope forsooth, and for his young Maister the Popes Nephew. Where he breathing out his furious Ghost as a pledge of his wicked attempt,[1] *Parsons* the Popes Minion[2] entertaines the time with a new-coyned plot,[3] comming into England[4] upon no meaner errand then to contrive the deposing of her Majestie and the setting up of another Prince.

The wise espying and circumspect implying of the advantage of these times, you see from what heads and fountaines of holinesse they came; yet none of these is the time that doth consort with our *casting out of devils* we have now in hand. Ours is the time when his *Holinesse,* the King of Spaine, and *Parsons* theyr *Entelechie*[5] were plotting beyond the seas for the delivery out of prison of the *Queen* of *Scots* by forcible attempt: which action after mature deliberation beeing cast upon the *Duke of Guise,* he the said *Duke* was then busily preparing his forces for England for the suddaine effecting of the said attempt.

I omit how *Charles Paget*[6] plyed his time in comming secretly into England to sollicite the *Earle* of *Northumberland* to divers trecherous attempts; how *Frauncis Throgmorton*[7] plyed his time at the instigation of *Mendoza* in busily sounding of

[1]1579 [H]. Sanders died in 1581.

[2]Robert Parsons or Persons (1546–1610), the famous Jesuit convert, controversialist, and man of affairs, an exile since 1574 from Oxford University, where he was dean of Balliol College.

[3]1580 [H]. This was the plot of 1580–82 between Henry of Guise, Philip II, and Gregory VIII to invade England through Scotland with the help of D'Aubigny, earl of Lennox. A letter from the papal nuncio to Allen, 8 May 1582, says that Parsons is just "come from England where he has been two years [in reality a little over one year] handling this business" (Read, *Walsingham* 2:366ff.; Knox, *Letters,* 405 ["è venuto d'Inghilterra, dove è stato dui anni trattando questo negotio"], cited by Meyer, *England and the Catholic Church,* 198).

[4]1580 [H]. On setting out for England in 1580, Parsons and his fellow missioner Edmund Campion were instructed not to deal in matters of state, "except perhaps with those whose fidelity has been long and steadfast," a qualification later removed when they were ordered unconditionally not to meddle in politics. See Meyer, *England and the Catholic Church,* 142, cited by Read, *Walsingham* 2:279.

[5]"Perfect instrument"? *OED* gives this use as an example of the misuse of Aristotle's *entelechia,* "the realization or complete expression of some function." Harsnett's usage, however, is probably intentional and meant to give a bizarre, satirical effect. The word seems to be one of his Harveyisms. Cf. Nashe, *Works* 3:50, mocking Harvey: "One that dieth all kinde of entelechy in fine Greece, and the finest Tuscanisme in graine that may bee, or any colour else ye cold desire." As McKerrow says, Harvey often used the word, apparently to mean "the divine spirit in man" (Nashe, *Works* 5:258).

[6]Secretary to Beaton, archbishop of Glasgow, came to England in September 1583, some think to arrange an invasion by the duke of Guise. See Read, *Walsingham* 2:384.

[7]Son of Sir John Throgmorton of Feckenham, Worcestershire. He met Paget and Morgan in Paris, c. 1580, and was drawn into conspiracy. At home he organized a secret correspondence for Morgan and Mendoza with Mary. He was arrested October 1583 and executed 10 July 1584 (Read, *Walsingham* 2:381–86).

Havens for the safe arrivall of the *Guisian* forces; how Doctor *Parry*[1] plyed his time in enforming his conscience for the suddaine and desperate murthering of the Queene (for there was no time spared, no meanes unassaied, no devise unthought upon, no person unattempted; every one of that holy hellish association striving to win the garland from other by having his hands soonest and deepest dyed in her Majesties blood); and I come to the time when the *Guisian* exploit grewe towards the prime, and was on foote for England.

Which stratageme beeing inspired by the Pope into *Parsons,* by *Parsons* into *Edmunds* alias *Weston,* a Provinciall of the order of Jesuits for that time residing heere in England (between *Parsons* and whom, as betweene two *Intelligences* in a superior and an inferior sphaere, there was a mutuall communication of all matters of import), and by the same *Edmunds* beeing breathed into the breastes of all theyr subordinates and dependants heere in the Land: it cannot be conceived what a spirit, life, and alacritie the whole Popish bodie of Traytors (halfe dead before) did suddainly conceive: how every limb, member, and joynt of that holy bodie did bestir it selfe to be serviceable to this holie designe: but Fa: *Weston* above all, whose head and hart were so bigge with the *Guisian* attempt as hee thought his time come to advaunce the banner of *Ignatius* for ever heere in England by making himselfe and his order famous by some notable exploit. And it beeing Gods permissive providence that this popish body, compiled of so many horrible and detestable treasons, should be wholy inspired from the spirit of his *Holinesse* and of hell, *Weston,* as a limb of the same body, mooved with the same spirit, chooses to eternize himselfe from the power of hell by casting out devils. Wherein hee bestirs himselfe so spritely, and playes such a devill-prize at the Lord *Vaux* his house in *Hackney,* with such a wonderfull applause, as *Array,*[2] *Parsons* Ape, a runnagate Priest, and a notable

[1]William Parry, son of Harry ap David of Northrop, Flintshire, squandered his and his wife's fortunes and took to spying on Catholic exiles. In 1579–80 he became a secret Catholic and was eventually arrested, March 1585, for plotting to assassinate Elizabeth. Parry was a rascal, but his case is peculiar, for besides being unbalanced, he was also one of the goverment's own agents (Read, *Walsingham* 2:399–405; Pollen, "Politics of English Catholics," 71–85).

[2]Martin Array. Educated at Louvain and ordained at Cambrai, 1577, he was an original member of the English college at Rome, where he took part in the squabbles of English and Welsh that led to Jesuit rule. A student list, 23 April 1579, gives his age as twenty-eight and says that he was sent on the English mission. He was in England in 1585, was captured and committed to the Woodstreet Counter, 13 June 1586. By December 1586, as a result of the intercession of friends, he was released upon bond to depart the realm, but was still lingering in the north, for which the spy Nicholas Berden said that he "deserveth well to be hanged" (*CRS* 2 [1906]: 132, 147, 252, 275). After leaving England he never returned, but went to Spain, Rome, and Naples. He became provost of the English residence at San Lucar. He died some time before 1621 (Anstruther, *Seminary*

*Polypragmon* heere in our state, meetes with Ma: *Tyrrell*[1] newly come from beyond seas, and vaunts with a bigge looke, that Fa: *Weston* had shewed such a soveraigne authority over hell, as the devils themselves should confesse theyr kingdom was neere at an end. And the same *Array* was so full fraught with hope and confidence in the *Spanish* and *Guisian* attempt then in hand, as his first congee was in Maister *Tirrels* eare at theyr entring into *Paules,* bidding him to be of good cheere for that all things now went very well forwards. *The King of Spaine*[2] (quoth he) *is now almost in readinesse with his forces for England; it standeth us now in hand that be Priests to further the Catholique cause as much as possibly in us lyeth.*

*Paget* and *Morgan,* two principall limbs of this popish body, being acquainted with the aforesaid plot, and fearing that the *Guises* attempt, by delivering the *Scottish* Queene by open Armes, would sparkle abroad before it were ripe, and so receive a check by our English forces before it came to the push, cast about in theyr braines for a shorter way at home: *Ballard* the bloodie Priest[3] is dealt withall to pricke on *Babington, Tilney,* and the rest of that aspiring popish band, to attempt a desperate truculent act by laying violent handes uppon her Majesties sacred person. Which whilst it was in hammering, the Catholique Priests, not caring by what meanes they effected theyr trecherous designes, set themselves on worke on all hands with working of wonders by dispossessing of devils: unto the acting of whose miracles *Babington* and his consorts doe divers times repaire to Sir *George Peckhams* house at *Denham* with foure or five Coaches full at once. And this new tragedie of devils had his time of rising and his fatall time of fall with the true tragedie performed upon *Babington* and his complices for theyr detestable treason. The pestilent drift and pernicious course of this devill-worke you shall heare of heereafter.

---

*Priests* 1:10–11.

[1] See Tyrrell's confession, *DEP*, "Examinations and Confessions," 389.

[2] A loyal generation of Priestes [H].

[3] As is lately confessed by Fa: P. in his Apolog. [H]. John Ballard, son of William Ballard of Wratting (probably West Wratting, Cambridgeshire), was educated at King's College, Cambridge, where he graduated B.A. in 1574/75. He then went to Rheims, where he arrived 29 November 1579. He was ordained 4 March 1580/81 and sent to England 29 March. He met Anthony Tyrrell in the Gatehouse (one of the London prisons) in 1582, "a friendship that was to cost him his life" (Anstruther). He and Tyrrell spent the next two years in various parts of England and went to Rome in 1584, returning to England the same year. In May 1586 he became embroiled in the Babington Plot, was arrested 4 August, condemned, chiefly on the evidence of Tyrrell, and executed 20 September "with appalling cruelty" (Anstruther, *Seminary Priests* 1:19–20; *DNB*, s.v. "Ballard, John"; Read, *Walsingham* 3:18–21, 44–45).

# CHAP. 3.

*The* places *wherein these miracles were plaid.*

It hath been alwaies the ill fortune of this holy order of *Exorcists* that the professors of it have been reputed errand Juglers and Impostors, yea sometimes by the greatest protectors of theyr owne religion. A great man told *Mengus* that if there were fiftie Exorcists at once standing before him, hee should deeme nine and fortie of them for no better then Impostors; and *Mengus* (as seemes) was afraid himselfe should have made up just tale. Wherefore the Maisters of the Art have so warily devised theyr rules and canons, as a man may see they labour to preoccupate mens minds for feare of suspition; which gives the greater occasion to suspect them the more.

*Mengus* his caveat[1] of declaring places not meete for exorcisme is this: *Praecavere debet Exorcista quantum potest, ne absque gravi necessitate exerceat hoc officium adjurandi daemones in domibus privatis, ne detur occasio scandali pusillis.* His positive rule for the place appointed is, *Sed debet exorcizare in Ecclesia, vel in alio loco Deo dicato vel alicui sancto.* His reasons against private houses and for Churches, or at least consecrated places, are: first, that beeing doone publiquely, the weaker sort may have no occasion to suspect the action of fraud. 2. *Tum quia in domibus privatis, ut in pluribus, adsunt mulieres quarum consortium debet summopere ab exorcistis vitari, ne incidant in laqueum diaboli:* that is, *because in private houses there are commonly some women, whose company the Exorcists ought to decline, least happilie they fall into the snares of the devill.* 3. *Tum quia ibi fiunt multa turpia, tacenda potius quam hic inserenda:* that is, *because in such houses turpitudes be committed meeter to be silenced then heere to be named.* 4. *Tum quia Ecclesia proprie est locus deputatus ubi Energumeni debent exorcizari:* that is, *because the Church is properly the place appointed to that action, wherein the possessed ought to be exorcised.* And what need these cautious rules to avoyde suspition of *jugling, turpitude,* and *women,* if nothing were amisse? Auricular confession is an holie action of more privacie, solitude, and familiarity with women, yet because no man (without reason) may suspect but that all is wel between a ghostly father and his ghostly child, there be no rules made of *jugling, tur-*

---

[1]Cap. 15. flag. daemon: [H]. Girolamo Menghi, *Flagellum daemonum* (Bologna, 1578), the manual used by the Denham exorcists, owned by Harsnett in the Venice editions of 1597, 1598.

*pitude,* or *women* in that mysticall function. Sure all is not well in this exorcising craft, that *jugling, turpitude,* and *women* must be so precisely avoided.

Indeed whereas in his 17. chapter[1] Fa: *Mengus* disputes that though exorcising ought to be done in the church, yet the doores of the Church may be close shut about them: his fatherhood gives us just cause to suspect that though he would seeme to have it publique touching the place, for a seeming shew of avoyding *jugling, turpitude,* and *women,* yet he can be content by shutting the doores to have it privately done: or such onely let in as the Exorcist best liketh.

See the practise heereof in the jugling Exorcists at *Paris,* anno 1599, who to make a shew of avoyding of that which they onely intended, jugling deceit, they must have theyr Minion *Martha Brossier*[2] exorcised in a Chappell forsooth: but yet with such a warie eye cast upon the spectators, as there comming in amongst the rest one *Marescot* a Physician, a man they did not affect, *Seraphin* the holy Exorcist cries out with a loude voice, *if there be any heere that is incredulous and will trouble* Martha Brossier, *the devill will carry him away in the ayre.* Wherefore yee see it was very wisely provided of *Mengus* to have an eye to the doore; the like ill-favoured accident fell out amongst our holy crew at theyr principall Theatre, Sir *George Peckhams* house at *Denham,* where for want of having a watch at the doore there comes in one Ma: *Hambden* of *Hambden:*[3] who being one of the *incredulous* per-

[1]Harsnett mistakes the reference, which should be to the eighteenth chapter, and misrepresents Menghi, who says that the position of exorcist is one of the seven orders of the Catholic Church, which do nothing secretly, and that exorcism ought to be public "propter bona spiritualia, quae inde fidelibus proveniunt."

[2]page .6. of that booke. [H]. "That booke" is *A True Discourse upon the Matter of Martha Brossier* (London, 1599), translated from the French by Whitgift's chaplain, Abraham Hartwell, and dedicated to Bancroft. The epistle dedicatory, dated Lambeth, 17 October 1599, reveals that Hartwell was involved in the Darrell case and that his book was meant to influence public opinion about Darrell. He asks for the evidence in the Darrell case to be published "so as every man thereby may see, what notable practises have been undertaken," and sounds very like Harsnett when he describes "the *stoicall* conversation and *Holy life* of the Chiefe *Choragus* [Darrell], that brought all those *Actors* upon the *Stage*" (sig. A2v). Like the Denham girls, Martha Brossier was "perfumed": "Another pretie tricke was, that my Masters of the *Clergie* in *Orleans,* would needes make experiment of the graund Remedie to drive away the *Devill,* and that is called the *Parfume.* They did set fire to this *Parfume,* and offered those villanous and stinking vapours to her Nose, she in the meane while being bound to a chayre, but her feete at libertie to play withall: and then began shee to crie out, *Pardon me, I am choaked, He is gone away*" (sig. E4v). Walker, *Unclean Spirits,* 33–42, gives some account of the case.

[3]See Friswoods Confess: [H]. Griffith Hampden, grandfather of the famous parliamentarian, whose wife was Catholic. In January 1584, books and other "popish relics" were found in her house at Stoke, Buckinghamshire *(CSP Dom., Elizabeth,* vol. 167, no. 47 [26 January 1583/84]).

sons that F. *Seraphin* complaines of afore, and espying theyr bungling, and using these wordes in detestation of theyr jugling, *I see this dealing is abhominable; and I marvaile that the house sinketh not for such wickednes committed in it,* and so departing utterly discontent: this *incredulous* spectator so skared our holy actors with feare, that they slunke out of the house every man his way, as a dogge that had been bitten by the tayle, and leaving theyr patients alone, gave the devils an *otium* or leave to play for that night.

Now let us looke in a little amongst our twelve holy Exorcistes, or rather twelve holy disciples, and Fa: *Weston* theyr holy head: who though they be not a working, yet by this time they are whetting theyr tooles: and let us see how warily they have put in ure theyr Maister *Mengus* his canon of choosing a Chappell or holy publique place to exorcise in for feare of suspition of *jugling, turpitude,* and *women.* First, it doth not appeare that they acted any of theyr wonderous dispossessions in any Church, Chappell, or consecrated place, as F. *Mengus* had appointed them: except happily they slipped into some Noble mans voide house in London: which houses, in regard of theyr owners callings being above reach of authority, are commonly now adayes the sanctuaries for Popish treason, consistories for plots of rebellion, and Chappels for all Romish loathsome abhomination: not that the Noble men themselves are privie to such meetings, but theyr corrupt house-keepers much in fault for entertayning such guests: and yet the owners themselves not altogether free from blame for making no better choise of those to whom they commit that charge.

But it appeares not (as I said) that they met in any chappel or holy place at all; but the chief places of their solemne meetings were the Lord *Vaux* his house at *Hackney* neere London, Maister *Gardiners* house at *Fulmer,*[1] Ma: *Hughes* his house at *Uxbridge,* and Sir *George Peckhams* house at *Denham,* places very fitly accomodating theyr holy intentions: first, for theyr capacitie, beeing able to receive the holy troupe and theyr traine (for they removed bagge and baggage as your wandring Players use to doe); next, for theyr security, the owners beeing trustie tried sure cardes, and commaunders of theyr neighbours adjoyning, if any suspition should arise; and then for their situation, beeing remote and secluse from ordinary accesse.

At the Lord *Vaux* his house at *Hackney* was the prime grand miracle performed by the grand Maister of the craft, Fa: *Weston*

---

[1]John Gardiner of Grove Place, Chalfont St. Giles, Buckinghamshire, and other properties, inherited in 1558, aged 11. A Catholic, he was imprisoned in the Gatehouse, 1587, for sheltering priests, and eventually lost most of his property. He died between 1595–1601. He was connected by marriage to the Tyrrells (*VCH, Buckinghamshire* 3:189).

himselfe, uppon one *Marwood,* servant to *Babington* the traytor: where a wonderful thing fell out. Fa: *Weston,* at the very first encounter with the devill, stunted the devils wits, and the devill being once put out, could never hit in againe, but untrusses and cries out, *O me stultum, insanum, et infaelicem:*[1] *O foolish, mad, and miserable devill that I am:* which put all the whole company of spectators into such astonishment, as there was a confused shout made of weeping and joy for this foyle of the devill. And the Epilogue was this, *O Catholicam fidem, ô insensatos haereticos: O the Catholick faith, ô sencelesse haereticks,* that could never learne the feate, to skare a devill from his wits.

At *Fulmer* house there were no great miracles done, onely the groundes of theyr Art layde sure, and a little trying of their tooles, whether their tew would holde or no.

At *Uxbridge* they lay but two or three nights at the most, and yet the place was graced with a punie miracle or two. *Dibdale* the Priest had his wench set so close unto him in the way thether (for avoyding *turpitude* and *women*) as she felt her selfe to burne,[2] and could hardly endure the heate of the holy man. *Trayford* cryes out by the way *water, water,* as the Frier did that by *Absolon* in *Chawcer* was scalded in the toote.[3] And thus were theyr Journalls towards *Denham,* where the Court stayed; the hangings were tricked up, the houses made ready, and the greatest part of the wonders of this comedie was performed. Their harbinger and host both, in all these journies (for the owners of houses and theyr families still left theyr owne houses, and made all cleere for these holy comedians, as is used to be done towards the comming of a Court), was one *Edmund Peckham,*[4] an excellent purveior for such a campe: one of a very ruinate estate, an intemperate disposition, an uncleane conversation, and a man so deeply engaged to this holy band as that himselfe, his wife, his concubine, and his whole familie lived wholy at their charge. This is the man that stil furnished the camp with all kind of luggage and pleasing provision, that scoures the coasts to see that all be cleere, that lookes to the trusses and fardels, that no jugling sticks be left out: the sacrist of

---

[1]In his owne tract. upon record. page 2. [H].

[2]Although Harsnett predictably associates this burning with sex, it may have had a different cause. Lady Catherine Milnes Gaskell ("Old Wenlock and Its Folklore," 264\ recalls that in her time there was a witch in Much Wenlock, Shropshire, called Nanny Morgan, who was described by a villager as having "two grey eyes as could strike through you like knives, and seemed to burn you inside like Devil's fire."

[3]An inaccurate memory of the ending of *The Miller's Tale.*

[4]Harsnett's contempt for Peckham, dead in 1586, must be based on something in the record, though nothing defamatory of him now survives.

these holy mysteries, playing himselfe five or six parts in this comedie, the harbinger, the host, the steward, the vauntcourrier, the sacrist, and the Pandar. And this shall suffice touching their places in generall; more speciall considerations of the same, you shall heare in the chapter ensuing.

# CHAP. 4.

*More speciall considerations, touching their choise of places.*

*Vino vendibili non opus est hedera.*[1] *Weston,* in regard of his owne fame, needed nothing more then ordinarie to commend him in this admirable science; but his twelve disciples being but punies and newly entred by him into the schoole of legerdemaine, stoode in neede of some grace and commendation to bring themselves into custome; therefore, like wise retaylers they chose unto themselves places of advantage to advaunce their profession. Where it is to be observed, that whilest the chiefe of the Popish holy body heere in England had their heads, harts, and hands full of practises of treason, some other Priests there were that bestirred themselves as fast in imploying all their wit and skill about getting into their hands huge mines and masses of gold, silver, and treasure (called by the Artisans in that mysterie *Treasure Trouvé*[2]), supposed to be hidden in divers houses, woods, and plots of ground heere in England: whether to furnish the heads and leaders of the conspirators for their holy service they had in hand against her Majestie and the state, or to enrich their owne cofers, I leave it to conjecture.

For compassing of this treasure, there was a consociation betweene three or four priests, *devill-conjurers,* and four *discoverers* or *seers* reputed to carry about with them their familiars in rings and glasses,[3] by whose suggestion they came to notice of those golden hoards. The names of the *discoverers* or *seers* were these: *Smith, Rickston, Goodgame,* and *James Phiswick* (The

---

[1]"A good wine needs no bush." Cf. Erasmus, *Adagia,* 589C: "Vino vendibili suspensa hedera nihil opus."

[2]On hunting for treasure by invocation and conjuring see Kittredge, *Witchcraft,* 204–13. It was a felony under the witchcraft laws of Henry VIII (1542) and Elizabeth I (1563), and therefore not within the jurisdiction of an ecclesiastical court like the High Commission. Harsnett's reticent account of this obscure episode, however, suggests that the commissioners took more evidence than he prints.

[3]Spirits in rings and glasses were necessary equipment for treasure-seekers. The glasses were for crystal gazing. William Stapleton, a secular priest who practiced between 1527 and 1530, used a glass and a ring, but he retired after six failures to find treasure. He also used a boy for scrying, magic books, a plate, a circle, a sword, and three demons named Oberion, Inchubus, and Andrew Malchus (Kittredge, *Witchcraft,* 210).

names of the *devill-conjuring* priests for some reasons I forbeare); and two of the places (amongst many) wherein they dealt were *Denham* and *Fulmer*.

Touching *Denham,* the Gentleman, chiefe owner of the Manor, testifieth that the four *seers* or impostors had borne him in hand that there was great store of *Treasure Trouvé* hidden in his said Manor, and appointed him a night certaine when to digge for the same, which time they kept; and that himselfe with divers of his servants being present, there was nothing found but olde empty earthen pots. And concerning *Fulmer,* the same Gentleman tells us also that the impostors aforesaid departed from his house to *Fulmer.* But the *penner of these miracles* remembers more distinctly both the yeere, moneth, and day when they went thither. The 22. of *October,* anno 84, there came three conjurers to *Fulmer* upon a Thursday (saith he) and there remained working in their Arte untill the Tuesday following.

Upon occasion of the practitioning of these coseners and devill conjuring priests for money, was phancied a conceite, and from phancie grew rumours and tales amongst the common sort (as upon any sleight occasion of such matters have used to be) of spirits, devils, and bug-beares, walking and haunting those places and houses where the conjuring had beene. *Sara Williams,* one of their patients, saith, *That shee had not beene long at* Fulmer, *but she heard say that the house was troubled with spirits.* The *penner of the miracles,* as if he meant to scare us with the very noyse, reports us the manner of the Hobgoblins in a very tragicall stile. *The whole house* (saith he) *was haunted in very terrible manner, molesting all that were in the same, by locking and unlocking of dores, tinckling amongst the fier-shovels and the tonges, ratling uppon the boards, scraping under their beds, and blowing out the candels, except they were halowed.* And further, that these ill mannered urchins did so swarme about the priests, in such troupes and thronges, *that they made them sometimes to sweat,* as seemes, with the very heate of the fume that came from the devils noses. Ma: *Maynie,* a pittifull possessed, doth affirme that within a day or two after his comming to *Denham,* the maid-cooke told him that there was great walking of spirits about the house, and that divers had beene greatly affrighted by them. And if you will not beleeve these, beleeve the devill himselfe in his Dialogue with *Dibdale,* crying in his devils roaring voyce that *he came thither for* Money, Money.

And if you happen to wonder why I called these houses of *Denham* and *Fulmer,* in the beginning of this chapter, advantagious unto our holy impostors, considering Fa: *Mengus* his rule of places for exorcising, cited before, that they must be consecrated, halowed, or holy places at least: you will wonder somewhat more when you heare Fa: *Thyraeus* prescribing that at any hand before the holy workes of exorcising the ill affected party be begun, first and above all to purifie and exorcise the place, that the house being cleansed from those troublesome haunting companions that doe *make men sweate,* the holy worke may proceede the more facile, and with better successe.

Where by the way you are to observe out of learned *Thyraeus* his 70. chapter *De locis infestis* the whole course heereof (that is, of exorcising the places), which must be performed by these five holy works: *Divini auxilii imploratione: psalmorum gradualium recitatione: lectione Evangelii: thurificatione: et conclusione. By calling upon God, the blessed virgin* Mary, *and the Saints: by saying over the fifteene graduall Psalmes: by reading over the Gospell of S.* John *concerning* Zacchaeus *climing up into a tree: by holy fumigations: and the Epilogue of the whole worke.* These be the five holy scare-devils which our Exorcists should have used to have driven the devils from the house. And heere I must needes shame my selfe, and lay open unto you the shallownesse of my wit that is not able to dive into the bottom of this sacred mysterie: why above all other Gospels, the Gospell of S. *John* touching *Zacchaeus* climbing into a tree should have such a potency to fright a devill out of a house. Whether there be any hidden antipathie between the nature of devils and a Sycamore tree, as was between *Scaliger* and a Cat: or that the devill bare a spight to the tree for helping low *Zacchaeus* to see our Saviour passe by: or that the devill had himselfe some mischance out of the tree: or that our Saviours dinner at *Zacchaeus* house was dressed with the wood of that tree: or els his crosse for hast made of that tree, *Oedipo opus est,*[1] I am at a full point. And if I send you to *Thyraeus* to unridle the ridle, I doubt you will laugh at him as you doe at me.

Howsoever it be, our holy Exorcists used neyther that nor any other of the five terrors to flight the devils from *Fulmer* nor *Denham,* but were content with theyr companie, and fell to theyr worke. And heerein they shewed a part of theyr greatest skill of legerdemaine. First, this fabulous rumor of the houses haunted with devils did blanch over and blaze theyr Art the more of *casting devills out,* and so brought them into credit. Secondly, if they had read the Gospell touching *Zacchaeus,* and skared them away, they had wanted devils to furnish out the pageant. Thirdly, it bred a reverend opinion and an admiration in all that came to see wonders, at the vertue and holinesse of the Priests, that durst walke up and

[1]Proverbial: "It would take an Oedipus."

downe amongst the thickest swarme of devils, and never a devill so hardy as to touch an haire of their beards. Fourthly, it served their purposes excellent well to cover their bungling, jugling, and legerdemaine, in that the servants of the houses having their phancies oppressed with the conceit of spirits and devils haunting in every corner of the house, they were so distracted with feare as they had use of neither wit nor will to doubt or looke into their packing.

And by this you see our punie Exorcists, as young as they be, shewed more wit and skill then either *Mengus* their Maister or *Thyraeus* their prompter in picking out these places of Hobgoblins to make the stages for their Comedy, and not offering first by holy fumigations to scare the urchins away. One doubt I have more, wherein I must crave your gentle assistance.

Some curious head, more nice then needes, may pick at a moate[1] and aske mee two or three questions out of this narration. First, whether a man may be a conjurer, sorcerer, or Enchaunter, that is, enter into league, friendship, and familiarity with the devill, as the priestes that conjured for mony at *Denham* did, and yet be accounted a ghostly Confessor, a reverend father, and an holy priest still? A simple doubt, God wote. *Sylvester, Bonifacius,* and some other Popes, have beene errand devill-conjurers, and yet theyr holinesse not an halfepeny the worse. This simple questionist must understand that God hath tied the spirit of holines with so sure a chaine to S. *Peters* chayre, as that let the Pope or any popeling be an Ethnick, a Turke, a Saracen, or a devill, hee cannot avoide it, but by sitting in that chaire he must weare out his holinesse, and be holy still.

Secondly, if he would know how it commeth to passe that the famous *Thyraeus* having laboured and sweat so much to set downe all the causes, waies, and meanes how wicked spirits doe come to haunt houses, and having by the dexteritie of his wit found out twelve waies, this way of haunting houses after conjuration is none of his twelve: we must tell him that our Exorcists are not of his old plodding fashion, but of the new cut, and such as you shall find (by that time you have them a little hote in theyr worke) will set *Mengus, Thyraeus,* and *Sprenger*[2] to schoole.

---

[1]Probably proverbial. Cf. Nashe, *Works* 1:304: "thou impotent moate-catching carper." Harsnett's meaning is not clear because a mote can be either a speck of dust or a blemish, and "pick at" implies the presence of a sore or scab; hence his "curious head" is either being fussy about a trifle or worrying at something that bothers him.

[2]James Sprenger, O.P., coauthor with Heinrich Kramer of *Malleus Maleficarum* (Nuremberg, 1494–96), a standard sixteenth-century text on witchcraft. Harsnett owned two copies of the Frankfurt edition of 1582.

Thirdly, if hee tell us, by the rules of that blacke Magicke Art concerning conjuring up of spirits, that the Conjurers great art and industrie is not so much in raising up a spirit as in commaunding him downe againe, and that if hee cannot lay him downe quiet, the Artist himselfe and all his companie are in danger to be torne in peeces by him; and that hee is so violent, boystrous, and bigge as that he will ruffle, rage, and hurle in the ayre worse then angry God *Aeolus* ever did, and blow downe steeples, trees, may-poles, and keepe a fell coyle in the world; and uppon this will be questioning how it happened heere, that our haunting spirits at *Denham* and *Fulmer,* raysed by the blacke Art, did not ruffle and rage in the world as those conjured spirits use to do, but did put theyr heads in a bench-hole for a twelve month together till these holy good men came to theyr work? I must tell him that our haunting spirits were of a more mild, calme, and kinde disposition, loving the companie of wenches and holy priestes; and for theyr staying so long about the house as Rats about a Barne, wee say they did that kindly, expecting the priests theyr holie Maisters to come to set them a work. And so these quiddities being satisfied, I hope I may proceed.

## CHAP. 5.

*The* persons *pretended to be possessed and dispossessed.*

After that our holy order were resolved of their holie wonders of casting out devils, and had both time and place fit for theyr purpose, a meane-witted man would aske the question that young *Isaac* did of his father in a much holier cause, *Loe heere are all things ready, but where is the sacrifice?*[1] The time is heere fitting, and the places prepared, but where are the possessed parties upon whom these miracles must be shewed? The young gallant in the comedy thought it an impossible matter that his Sycophant should be furnished at a daies warning both with money and a Merchant to cosen the Baude; and his Sycophant cheeres him up thus: *consilii, dolique, copiam structam gesto in pectore mecum.* And so was it with our cunning Comedians; they had a world of devises to get themselves patients, readie coyned in their budget. Trustie *Roger* the *Leno*[2] had his hookes so sweetly bayted, and his sprindges so artificially set in every haunt and glade, that he was alwaies sure of either a Gudgin or a Woodcocke to furnish out

[1]Genesis 22:7.

[2]Edm. Peckam [H]. A pimp or go-between in Latin comedy.

a service.[1] It is a common ground with them (as with all other conspirants[2] in any badde practise or science) not to deale with any that are not in some degree or other obliged unto them. *Marwood,* Ma: *Anthony Babingtons* man the traytor, the first subject, whereon the grand miracle at *Hackney* was playd, is not now forth comming, as I gesse, for feare of his telling tales out of schoole. And if one should kindly aske Fa: *Weston* in his eare, what is become of him that hee might be spoken withall, I suppose of his modestie hee would sooner blush then tell. This actor played his part *extempore* there on the stage with a verie good grace; and if hee had now the good hap to be conferred with-all, I doubt not but he could and would relate (as other his cue-fellowes have done) how hee came to that facility in his part, who were his prompters, his directers, his teachers, and who did help him put on the devils vizard on his face. It may suffice that it is said, he was *Anthony Babington* his man.

*Trayford* the young Gentleman, forsooth, was of Ma: *Peckhams* privities, or privie counsell if ye will, the *Leno* his owne *Hypodromos,*[3] sworne true to the Pantofle,[4] young maister of the Maydens, serving in the nature of a refresher to furbush over his maisters brayed wares: one that couth his actions and motions so readily, and expressed them so lively in the sceane of possession, as *Sara Williams* his play-fellow had almost forgotten her part, and marred the play; sure I am she confesseth that she loved the young devill too well.[5] Ma: *Mainie,* by birth a Gentleman, by education a Catholique, one that had suckt from his mother the taint of Romish contagion, was by her convayed beyond Seas ere he was fourteene yeeres old, and for his deeper grounding in Popish superstition being maintained two yeeres in the Seminarie at *Rhemes,* entred himselfe into the order of the *Bonhommes,* but shortly left his fraternity and came over into England: where his brother Ma: *John Mainie* having married Ma: *Peckhams* sister, and he accompanying his brother somtimes to Ma: *Peckhams* house at *Denham,* fell eft-soones in acquaintance with this holie league

---

[1]Cf. Tilley, S788, "A springe to catch a woodcock," i.e., a trick to catch a fool, and G473, "To gape for a gudgeon," i.e., believe any tale. Springes are snares for small game, especially birds; woodcocks were supposed to be very easy to catch, and a gudgeon is a bait fish.

[2]First use of this word in *OED,* followed by Shakespeare's in *King Lear* 5.3.136.

[3]In late Latin, a latrine; here one who looks after "privy" matters of all kinds.

[4]Ambiguous. To be true to the pantofle or slipper means either that one is a devoted valet, or, because of the Catholic practice of kissing the pope's slipper, an enthusiastic Catholic.

[5]In her examination. [H].

there: and seeing amongst their societie no *Bonhomes* at al, but wares of a much lighter and pleasanter glosse, was the more easily allured into the holy combination, and being once entangled could not get out againe, but of a metamorphozed *Bonhomme* became an excellent devill-comedian: though now ye may perceave the Gentleman doth rue that ever he did set his foote on the stage.[1] This man had bonds enow about him to make good his trust and fidelity to the holy association: education, religion, affiance, and, besides, to some kinde she-devils of that order, no unkind affection.

*Anne Smith,* attending at times upon Mistris *Peckham* (a maid when she came to the league), of eighteen yeeres of age, nusled up in the true rites and ceremonies of the Popish fascination, and so an affectionate proselyte to that Mimick superstition (it being the onely religion to catch fooles, children, and women, by reason it is naught else save a conceited pageant of Puppits and gaudes), shee was first seazed uppon by olde *Harpax* the *Leno,*[2] graund probationer[3] of the devils female in the play, by the meanes of her sister, one *Alice Plater,* his sweet Mistris forsooth: shee was directed downe to *Denham* for her better instruction in mysterie of possession, and thence, after an acte or two of probation, she returned to London: whence she became *Stamp* the Priests peculiar,[4] to be convayed againe to *Denham.*

*Sara Williams* (a mayd when she came to the league, borne at *Denham,* not above fifteen yeeres olde when shee entred these sacred mysteries), an appendant to the familie of Sir *George Peckham* of *Denham,* one of a very good personage, favour, and wit: shee was a long time managed to be brought to the lure,[5] and for her better advauncement in her maisters eye shee was made mistris *Peckhams* chamber-mayd pardie: the pleasing parts she brought with her to the campe were much envied and eyed by those naughty haunting devils, that would blow out her candel *except it were hallowed.* The poore wench was so Fayrie haunted as she durst not goe, especially to Ma: *Dibdale* his chamber, alone. But you shall heare her owne confession.[6]

---

[1] See his examin. [H].

[2] Ed: Peckham. [H]. A slave in Plautus, *Pseudolus,* but not a *Leno,* whose role is to complete the purchase of a girl for his master. The Latin adjective "harpax" means "rapacious."

[3] A candidate; here one who supervises candidates, an ironic use based on "probation," meaning the period of trial for novices in a religious order.

[4] Another ironic use with ecclesiastical overtones, since a peculiar is a benefice exempt from diocesan visitation.

[5] A falconer's expression, it being part of a bird's training to be taught to "come to the lure," hence to respond to teaching and come under control.

[6] See her examina: [H].

*Friswood Williams,* sister to *Sara* (a mayde when shee came to the league, about sixteen yeeres old), a plant of the same soyle, and a hanging to the same house, her father having beene Sir *George Peckhams* man: shee was sent downe to *Denham* under colour of visiting her sister *Sara,* whom she heard to be ill at ease, as also to be helpfull to mistris *Peckham* about the possessed, under whom shee was admitted to be attendant in a place of reversion: who had not been long within the compasse of that holy circle, but shee was discovered to have a tang of possession. Shee kept her scene at her cue with her fellow play-devils so long, as at the last she got such a pinch of *Tom Spanner* in the darke (one of the haunting crue), that the markes of it were many dayes after to be seene.

Here you may perceive in what termes the patients on both sides with their holy Maisters stood, how the devils of both kindes, hees and shees, became combined together by the cunning *Leno* his meanes, and were so farre engaged each to other and to the whole band that they had as good play their parts well, and have good cheere, good store of gold, much making of, and other gentle pleasing curtesies for their paines, as by stepping aside to spoyle the play, and to blot their owne reputations besides.

We might now proceede towards the presenting of some of our Actors upon the stage, but that old doating *Mengus,* uppon pure spight to hinder our sport, hath dropped out a dry thred-bare rule forged in his own braine, a caveat of avoyding suspition, forsooth: telling us that we have marred all in our holy play of devils at first dash for taking upon us to exorcise young wenches, beeing flatly against the Canon of that sacred Science, which is this in his booke: *Si mulier sit quae exorcizatur, sit valde senex: We must not exorcize a woman except she be old.*[1] To this Canon wee aunswer that *Mengus* speakes like an olde worne Exorcist whose marke is out of his mouth:[2] his rule hath many faults and infirmities in it. First, it is against the maxime of charitie that biddes us doe good unto all: and what greater good can be to a young maide, then to ease her of a devill? Secondlie, we finde by experience and the confession of our young demoniacks, as you heard, that our exorcising priests be of a very hote temper and fierie complexion, so as but touching the young wenches they cry out that they burne: this were verie dangerous for an olde dry woman, least shee should take fire. Thirdly, this would much abate the credit and custome of *Mengus* his own profession, for we find not an old woman in an

[1]Menghi, *Flagellum daemonum,* Chap. 18.

[2]One told a horse's age by the "mark of the mouth." Cf. Nashe, *Works* 2:241: "The mark is clean out of my Muses mouth."

age to be possessed by the devill: the devils of our time in this *Horizon* loving more tender daintie flesh. And indeed it would be a *Quaere,* handsomly interlarded with *Obs* and *sols,*[1] why all both Popish and other devils which begin to swarme prety well in these dayes, beare such a spite to young Lads, but especially to young girles and maides, that they ordinarily, or not at all, vexe any but such. But I leave that to the profound Maisters and professors of this holy hellish science. Fourthly, *Mengus* shewed no wit in teaching this rule: for there be certaine actions, motions, distorsions, dislocations, writhings, tumblings, and turbulent passions fitting a devils part (to make it kindly expressed) not to be performed but by supplenesse of sinewes, pliablenesse of joynts, and nimblenesse of all parts, which an old body is as unapt and unweldie unto, as an old dog to a daunce. It would (I feare mee) pose all the cunning Exorcists that are this day to be found, to teach an old corkie woman to writhe, tumble, curvet, and fetch her Morice gamboles as *Martha Brossier* did. These *anus decrepitae* be *asinae ad lyram*[2] to this geare: and therefore their Patron *Mengus* may weare the eares himselfe, and leave these stagers out.

## CHAP. 6.

*Theyr waies of catching and inveigling theyr disciples.*

The gift of discerning of spirits spoken of by S. *Paul*[3] being (as it is supposed) ceased in Gods Church, it becommeth a point of highest difficultie in the old and new exorcising craft, by what meanes a man shall come to be certaine whether the partie affected be possessed or no.

Learned *Thyraeus* discourseth touching the signes of possession in three large chapters *de doemoniacis.*[4] First he saith that nei-

[1] Academic debating jargon; abbreviations of "objections" and "solutions."

[2] *Anus decrepitae* are "worn-out old ladies." *Asinae ad lyram* is proverbial in English and Latin. Cf. Tilley, A366, "To see an ass play on a harp." "Asinae" are she-asses.

[3] 1 Corinthians 2:6–16.

[4] Chap. 22, 23, 24. [H]. The scriptural signs of possession include dumbness (Matthew 12:22, 9:32–33; Luke 11:14), nakedness, abiding in no house but among graves and in the wilderness, supernatural strength demonstrated by the breaking of fetters (Luke 8:27–39), foaming at the mouth, gnashing of teeth, falling violently, rolling about, casting oneself into water or fire (Matthew 9:14–28). These, with variants (such as fierceness, crying, the party's self-wounding), are the signs relied upon by Darrell *(DFP,* sigs. E3–E3v), who admits how easily they can be counterfeited and how unsatisfactory they are as signs of the supernatural: "Seeing that men in this matter are growne more incredulous then heretofore, it hath pleased God . . . to give other signes also more free from cavill, to make his glorious works most apparant and certaine" *(DFP,* sig. E4), and he gives as an example "the running in *Somers* flesh, of a lumpe as bigge as a Mouse." The more spectacular signs, derived either from folklore (such as the confession of a witch) or

ther the confession of the partie, nor his fierce behaviour, nor his brutish and barbarous voice, nor his terrible countenaunce, nor the privation almost of all his vitall functions, nor his diseases and pangs incurable in physick, nor the having the devill oft in ones mouth, nor for a man to consecrate himselfe to the devil to be presently snatcht away by him, nor the revealing of secret matters, nor the knowledge of strange languages, nor extraordinary strength, nor all the signes that appeared in such as were spoken of in the Gospell to be possessed, are sufficient and undoubted signes and rules that the partie in whom they appeare is indeed possessed. And then going along and naming other signes unto us, he puzzels himselfe pittifully and leaves his Reader in a wood.

Our late popish Exorcists have certaine new devised signes of their owne observation, more fitting the times and effectuall for the gracing their gracelesse profession. Theyr Empiricall signes be these. 1, If the partie affected cannot for burning abide the presence of a Catholique priest. 2, If shee will hardly be brought to blesse herselfe with the signe of the Crosse. 3, If a casket of reliques beeing brought her, shee turne away her face and cry that they stinke. 4, If S. *Johns* Gospel being put in a Casket and applied unto her, she rubbe or scratch any part of her body and cry it burnes, it is an evident demonstration that the enemie dooth lurke in that part. 5, If she can hardly be brought to pronounce these words, *Ave Maria, the mother of GOD*, and most hardly *the Catholique Church.* 6, If a Casket of reliques covered with red doe seeme white unto her. 7, If shee tumble and be vexed when any goe to confession. 8, If shee have a shivering at Masse. 9, If shee fleere and laugh in a mans face.

But our holy Tragaedians heere had hast of theyr sport, and therefore they would not stay the trying of any such curious signes, but tooke a shorter cut. *Marwood, Westons* patient, beeing pinched with penurie and hunger, did lie but a night or two abroad in the fieldes, and beeing a melancholicke person, was scared with lightning and thunder that happened in the night, and loe, an evident signe that the man was possessed. The priests must meet about this pittifull creature. *Edmunds* must come,[1] the *holie Chaire* must be fetcht out, the holy budget of sacred reliques must be opened, and all the enchaunting mysteries applied about the poore man.

---

from church traditions (such as those cited by Harsnett from the *Miracle Book)* were as easily counterfeited. Harsnett would allow the breaking of chains and fetters *(DFP,* sig. E3), but doubts that a possession would ever be vindicated by such a sign. James I allowed only three signs: strength, physical rigidity, and speaking in unknown languages *(Daemonologie,* sigs. K3v–K4).

[1] Weston Tractat. [H].

Ma: *Maynie* had a spice of the *Hysterica passio,*[1] as seems, from his youth; hee himselfe termes it the Moother (as you may see in his confession) and saith that hee was much troubled with it in Fraunce, and that it was one of the causes that mooved him to leave his holy order whereinto he was initiated, and to returne into England. For this, and for leaving the order of *Bonhommes,* see here an evident signe that *Maynie* had a devil: whatsoever hee did or spake, the devil did and spake in him: the horse that he rid upon to *Denham* was no horse, but the devil: *Maynie* had the devils in livery-coates attending upon him: and all this tragicall out-cry for leaving his order, and a poore passion of the Mother, which a thousand poore girles in England had worse then ever Ma: *Maynie* had.

Before I come to their women patients, I must tell you a tale that I have heard which happily hath but too authenticall records for the nature of a tale. There was an holy man who had more then a months minde to a daintie peece of flesh that was oft in his eye, and by gloses and gifts and Court-tricks had as much as hee desired. This holy man was a setter to an exorcising crue, and to make his game as sure to the holy association as he had done unto himselfe, he tels his sweet *Cressida* that himselfe was much troubled in minde in her behalfe, and should get no quiet to his conscience till they had both confessed themselves to an holy Catholique priest: which when she had done, the silly Conie was caught; she was seazed upon for brayed wares, and was enforced to become a *privada,* and to follow the holie Campe. Heere is no morrall (gentle Reader), and therefore let us have no application.

*Anne Smith* was somewhat more affected with that hystericall humor of the Mother, and came to London out of Lancashire to her sister for physick: where meeting with the common badger or kiddier for devils, Ma: *Peckham,* at the Lord *Staffords* house in London, she was marked out for the Court of possession, and by devise was sent downe to the holy hote-house at *Denham,* where after she had tasted a little of the discipline of the *holy chaire,* her heaving of the Mother proved a monstrous shee-devill; and she was chaire-haunted so long, till shee was faine for her better ease to use swathing bands for three yeeres after.

*Sara Williams* had a little paine in her side (and in an other place beside), but because that was not enough to discover a devill, she was Cat-bitten too. That is, once seeking for egges in a bush by a

---

[1] Strictly speaking, an affection of the womb, or mother, and exclusively a female affliction. It appears from Mainy's use of the term *mother* that while he suspects it is not the correct medical name for his condition, it was commonly used of men in certain cases; he uses it of himself, his brother, and Edmund Peckham, and the priests also use it (*DEP,* 401, 404).

Woods side, and a Cat leaping out of a bush where she had lyen a-
sleepe, *Sara* was scared with the sodaine leaping of the Cat, and
did a little tremble as persons sodainly moved with feare use to
doe: loe heere a plaine case, *Saraes* Cat was a devill, and she must
be Cat-hunted or Priest-hunted for this sight.

*Fidd: Williams* was devill-caught by a very strange meanes.[1]
Shee dwelling with Mistris *Peckham*, and being one day in the
Kitchin wringing out a bucke of cloathes, *Dibdale* the Priest came
into the Kitchin where she was a-washing, and tapping her on the
shoulder told her that her Mistres looked for her, to whom she
aunswered that she had almost done washing, and then she would
goe.

Presently after this, she lifting at a tub of water which stoode
there ready filled to be used in her washing, her feete slipped from
under her, the Kitchin being paved, and having a shrewd fall, did
hurt her hippe, with the griefe whereof she was constrained for two
or three dayes to keepe her bed. Here begins the devil from the
Kitchin. Into her chamber comes the loving crue of pittifull devill-
catching Priests; they bemoane the mishap of her hippe forsooth,
and after some other kinde ceremonies, they fish out of her at
length that she had beene sometime past troubled with a paine in
her side. Ah Sir, the case is plaine: these two put together, her hip
and her side, make up a just devill, and a monstrous one too, compounded of two such dissimilar partes I weene. But wil you see
how? It was the devill that tripped up *Fidds* heeles in the Kitchin
and gave her the shrewd fall. And why, would you guesse? The
wicked spirit could not endure her because she had washed
amongst her buck of cloathes a catholique priests shirt. *Jesu Maria.*
And a worse thing in it then so, but I will give the records leave to
speake it for me. I trust you will not looke for any other after this
dangerous fall on the hippe, but that this should prove a reall possession, as in deede it did.

Young *Trayford*, the sixth patient, being a boon-companion, as
seemes, and loving wine and women well (as appeares by the declaration), had enflamed his toe, and at some times felt a spice of
the gowt: a plaine case (as the nose on a mans face) the young man
had a devill and must be conjured all over for his wicked toe. Now,
what a wofull taking are all those poore creatures in that have
about them by birth, casualty, or mishap any close imper,[2] ache,

---

[1]Looke her Confess. [H].

[2]The term is glossed by its context, but what word the spelling represents is not
clear. It could be a noun, "impair," an unequalness or unevenness, from Latin *impar;*
*OED* gives two uses of the form *impar,* one an adjective, one a noun, dated 1697.
Harsnett may have invented his *imper* from vulgar Latin *impeiorare,* "to worsen," the
source of Modern English "to impair" (Partridge, *Origins,* s.v. "pair" and "pessimism").

or other more secret infirmity? when a paine in a maides belly, a stitch in her side, an ache in her head, a crampe in her legge, a tinckling in her toe (if the good Exorcist please), must needes hatch a devil and bring forth such chaire-worke, fier-worke, and devill-worke as you shall heare heereafter? and what a deliration is this in our grave, learned, and famous Colledge of auncient renowmed Physicians, to undertake a long, costly, and painfull course of study in those excellent worthies of learned times *Galen, Hippocrates*, and the rest, and to spend their money, strength, and spirits in searching the treasurie of Nature: let them cassier those olde monuments of Ethnick prophane learning, and turne Wisard, Seer, Exorcist, Jugler, or Witch: let them turne over but one new leafe in *Sprenger, Nider, Mengus*, or *Thyraeus,* and see how to discover a devill in the Epilepsie, Mother, Crampe, Convulsion, Sciatica, or Gowt, and then learne a spell, an amulet, a periapt of a priest, and they shall get them more fame and money in one week then they doe now by all their painfull travaile in a yeere. It is a very poore bayte, as you may see by *Trayfords* gowtie toe, whereout our hungry Exorcists will not, rather then faile, nibble a devill. And if I be not much deceaved, I have heard it credibly reported by some that have cause to know, that the Popes Holines himselfe may be devill-caught by this trick. For it is credibly avouched that this sweet natured *Clement* the 8, with using too much some sweet sawce, is molested with the gowt. Now what a *Quaere* would this prove, if a *Lynceus* Exorcist[1] should discover a devill in his *Holines* toe? How would the *Scotists* and *Thomists* belabour and trick the devill with questions in the Popes toe? First, whether his *Holines* being necessarily invested with the holy spirit of God can possibly admit of a devill, no. Then graunting, by way of admittance, that his *Holines* may be possessed, whether his resolutions be to be taken for the Canons of Gods holy spirit or the maximes of the devill: and lastly, if the devill may lurk in the Popes toe, whether his wise, holy sweet babes with beards that have kissed his toe have kissed the devill, yea or no, in his toe: but my wit is too shallow to sound these deepe profundities: I must goe on and tell you what farther newes from *Denham.*

[1]Lynceus, a Messenian, one of the Argonauts, was famous for sharp sight.

## CHAP. 7.

*Their holy pretences to make their Disciples sure unto them.*

You will wonder that these visards, being so bare and made all of browne paper, should ever serve the turne to make a maske for a devill, untill you heare how handsomly the glew of holy church doth make it hang together, and how it is stitched up with packthreed of holy devotion. If their patients be Catholiques whom they set their hooke for, a lime-twigge of a rush wil serve the turne to catch them, hold them, and fasten them to their tackling; but if their Conies be Protestants and such as goe to Church, then some holy ceremonies for good fashion sake must be solemnly used to combine them the neerer unto their holy Fathers, that the band and knot may be the surer betweene them for untying againe, and to bring them to lye betweene the sweete breasts of their holy Mother the Romish Church, that the mammaday which shall be given them, may doe them the more good.

Heere you are to understand that all or the most of us Protestants are, forsooth, in a most wofull case; for the most of us already, without the helpe of either passion of the Mother, Sciatica, Gowte, Cat-biting or hipping, according to the Romish Kalender are plainly and really possessed with devils. In so much as the reverend *Thyraeus* disputes it very profoundly *pro et con*, and soyles a whole chapter with this learned probleme: *Utrum heretici sint vere a daemonibus obsessi? Whether Protestants* (whom he termes Haeretiques) *be truly possessed with devills.*[1] Where first he sayes for us that wee have *magnam conjunctionem, vel communionem cum Daemonibus: Great fellowship, and neere friendship with the devil.* 2. *Quam plurimi cum diabolo egerunt, vel ab eodem tanquam magistro sua dogmata acceperunt. That very many of us have dealt with the devill and have receaved our principles of no other maister then the devill:* And these reasons, he sayth, will easily perswade some to thinke we have actually devils in deede. But he for his part, of pure good will unto us, will thinke that wee are not to be accounted properly possessed. *Propterea quod vera in ipsis signa, quae obsessos produnt, desiderantur.* His reasons that moove him to thinke so well of us are because wee doe not tumble, wallow, foame, howle, scricke, and make mouthes and mops as the popish possessed use to doe. Loe, doth not the good man deserve you should give him a bribe for so mildly concluding his aphorisme on your sides, that you are

[1]*De Daemo:* Cap. 18. [H].

not to be said to be really possessed: but onely to deale, talke, make league, friendship, and familiarity with the devill. But our twelve Apostolicall Exorcists and *Weston* their head, in their deeper in-sight and experience of us Protestants, have long since set olde *Thyraeus* to schoole and bidden him turne over his booke to an other leafe; for they plainly see, teach, and avouch that the greatest part of us Protestants are possessed in deed. *Sara Williams* saith in her deposition that *it was an usuall saying with the Priests that many Protestants were possessed.* But *Friswood* goes further, and sayes in plaine termes, That *the Priests in talking of the Protestants have affirmed of them in her hearing that the greatest share of them were possessed with devils.* I could wish that whilst our Exorcists are in this good mood to say and avouch that you have devils, and you in your good moode for hearing them so say, that you had some twelve of their holiest Exorcists amongst you, and *Weston* their champion, to trie whether they could conjure a devill out of you, or you conjure them for saying you have the devil. But I pray you in the meane while help them out of their muse, for they are sorely perplexed to think upon that day when England shall become Catholique againe, how the Catholiques shal be pestered with worke in casting out devils by reason of the infinite number of us protestants that, having devils in us, must come into theyr handling. *Our hands* (say they) *shall then be full of chaire-worke indeed.* And verily as many as be young women and maides, and marke in the course of this storie the kind handling of *Anne, Fid,* and *Sara* (three proper young maids) by the Doctors of the *Chayre,* and withall shall observe well the manner of the *Chayre,* theyr holy brimstone, holy potion, and the rest of that holy geere, wil (I doubt not) be much delighted with the contemplation of that day; and rather then faile, hartily both wish and pray that all theyr holy works may grace *Tiburne,* as they have worthily deserved, with new holy reliques before that day come.

Well, howsoever you like them or theyr *holy chaire,* this is theyr theoreme sure and sound, that the greatest part of Protestants be possessed; and so they proceeded with *Anne, Fid,* and *Sara.* Who before they became entangled in their holy ginnes, were protestant maydes and went orderly to Church. Mary, after that they and their *Leno* had caught them with cat-biting, hipping, and crosbiting (as you have heard), and that they had brought them with their Syrensongs to believe that some wicked spirit had lyen a long time lurking in theyr bellies and theyr sides, why then they enchaunt them a fresh with this lamentable dolefull dittie: *That theyr harts doe bleede for sorrow to see them in this pittifull wofull plight, being in Satans possession; that they burne with bowels of commiseration and compassion of theyr distressed estate; that they would spend theyr best spirits and lives to doe them any good: onely one little thing is a barre that hinders the influence of all divine grace and favour upon them, and that is theyr religion: which they must first abandon, and be reconciled to the Pope, or otherwise all theyr holy ceremonies are of no availe.* And heere beginnes their holy pageant to peepe into the stage. First, they tell *Friswood* and *Sara* (as you may see in their confessions) that theyr baptisme they had received in the Church of England must be amended in regard it wanted many rites, ceremonies, and ornaments belonging to the baptisme of the Church of Rome.

Heere *Allen* and *Parsons* will con you little thanke for so little setting by their resolution in cases for England.[1] Their words are these: *Ceremoniae omissae baptismi in pueris, cum possunt commodè suppleri, debent, non autem id faciendum consulimus in iis, qui sunt provectioris aetatis, ne inde nascatur scandalum aut opinio priorem baptismum non valuisse.*[2] Your Ceremonies (say your two Gods) may be fitly played upon the baptisme of children, but upon an *adultus* not so; least a conceit or scandale arise thereby that the former baptisme should not be of it selfe good. *Allen* and

---

[1]In their booke of Cases for England. [H]. This work is not mentioned in T. G. Law's list of Parson's writings *(DNB,* s.v. "Parsons, Robert"), nor in Thomas Cooper's list of Allen's works *(DNB,* s.v. "Allen, William"). Parsons wrote it in preparation for going to England: "I gathered out in Latyn the compendium of all the controversies, that served afterwards for myself and others that went thither, as also the particular cases for England to be discussed for that mission" (Pollen, *Memoirs of Father Robert Parsons,* 25). There are at least three MSS: Bodleian MS. Rawlinson C.588; Balliol College MS. E.14.9; MS. Douay 484. Pollen describes an addition to the Douay MS, *Quaestiones pertinentes ad Baptismum &c.,* and suggests that these eighty-five "questions" are Cardinal Allen's work. Harsnett evidently refers to a copy of the Douay text, and his note confirms Pollen's ascription.

[2]Cf. Fortescue and O'Connell, *Ceremonies,* 423ff.:

If the Convert is CERTAINLY ALREADY BAPTISED, there can be no question of baptising him again. It would be the gravest sacrilege to repeat baptism . . . the commonest case in England is that of converts doubtfully baptised. Such a convert makes his profession of faith and abjures heresy. He is then baptised conditionally (the condition to be expressed), and privately with lustral water (not baptism water). . . . Children (Boys under fourteen, girls under twelve, or probably fourteen in the matter of censures) who are received from heretical sects, and are either certainly or doubtfully baptised, do not make any abjurations, nor are they absolved from censures which they cannot have contracted. They make a simple profession of faith. . . . If necessary, they are then baptised conditionally.

Hooker, *Laws,* bk. 5, chap. 62 *(Works* 2:270–71), agrees: "Iteration of Baptisme once given hath bene allwaies though a manifest contempt of that anciente apostolique Aphorisme, *One Lord, one faith, one baptisme* . . . And because second baptisme was ever abhord in the Church of God as a kinde of incestuous birth, they that iterate baptisme are driven under some pretense or other to make the former baptisme voyde." Law, "Devil-Hunting," 403, assumes that the Denham girls were baptized conditionally, presumably because the priests doubted the validity of their Church of England baptism.

*Parsons* determine *Friswood* and *Saras* English baptisme good enough without your goodly ceremonies florished over their heads, and yet you must be dooing in spight of them both. Your implements were ready for the purpose, and it fitted your devill-worke better, and so you esteemed not *Allen* or *Parsons* a pinne. And in good sooth, you might aswell have kept these goodly Ceremonies in your budget, except you cleerly meant to mocke almighty God, and to make the sacrament naught els save a rattle for fooles, babes, and women to make sport withall. In my opinion, there was never *Christmas-game* performed with moe apish, indecent, slovenly gawdes then your baptising and super-baptising ceremonies are. Your puffe, your crosse-puffe, your expuffe, your inpuffe uppon the face of a tender infant, beeing the impure stinking breath of a foule impure belching swaine: your enchaunted salt, your charmed grease, your sorcerised chrisme, your lothsome drivell that you put uppon theyr eyes, eares, noses, and lyppes, are fitting complements for *hynch pynch and laugh not; coale under candlesticke; Frier Rush,* and *wo-penny hoe.*[1] Which are more civilly acted, and with lesse foule soyle and lothsome *indecorum,* then your spattring and greasing tricks upon the poore infant; and yet old doting *Bellarmine* blurres three whole leaves of paper in displaying the banner of this ridiculous trumpery, telling us a long tale that they came from tradition of the Church: when we can aswel tell, as hee can his *Ave Marie,* from what sniveling Pope, what drunken Frier, what Heathenish imitation they did all proceede.

But see these popish guegawes acted upon *Friswood* herselfe. First, out comes the *holy chaire,* and *Friswood* the new babe is

---

[1] In Harsnett's metaphor of the exorcisms as game or play, the content of these "Christmas games" is sex, fraud, and horror. "Hynch pynch and laugh not" is probably, and "coale under candlesticke" is certainly a proverbial phrase; "Frier Rush" and "Wo-penny hoe" are proper names. Cf. Tilley, C512, "Coll under canstick, he can play with both hands," who cites Heywood, *Proverbes,* "Colle under canstyk she can plaie on both hands; Dissimulacion well she understands." For "Wo-penny hoe" see Nashe, *Works* 3:63: "No vulgar respects have I, what *Hoppenny Hoe* & his fellow *Hankin Booby* thinke of mee." McKerrow here cites Melbancke, *Philotimus:* "Thy Argumentes are drawne from the disport called *Ho penni ho,* wherein all must say as one saith, & do as he doth." I have found no other reference to "Hynch pynch." Friar Rush was a Continental goblincleric: he is adescribed in *Gammer Gurton's Needle,* 3.2.18–20: "Saw ye never Fryer Rushe / Painted on a cloth, with a side-long cowes tayle, / And crooked cloven feete, and many a hoked nayle?" By 1584 Reginald Scot, in his *Discourse upon divels and spirits,* appended to his *Discoverie of Witchcraft,* is describing him as "Rush of England" and comparing him to "Hudgin of Germanie": *"Hudgin* is a verie familiar divell, which will do no bodie hurt, except he receive injurie: but he cannot abide that, nor yet be mocked. . . . There go as many tales upon this *Hudgin,* in some parts of *Germanie,* as there did in *England* of Robin good fellowe. . . . Frier *Rush* was for all the world such another fellow as this *Hudgin,* and brought up even in the same schoole, to wite, in a kitchen. . ." *(Discoverie* [ed. 1584], 522). See also Kittredge, *Witchcraft,* 216, and Hazlitt, *Tales and Legends,* 134–55.

placed very demurely in it with a cloth upon her head and a crosse upon it. Then in comes the priest attired in an Albe or a Cope with a candle in his hand (or else he is *Anathema* by the Counsell of *Trent*); and after the performance of a whole anticke-sute of Crosses, hee approches very reverently to *Friswood* in the chayre. Then, as herselfe in her confession describes it, he first charmes her in Latine, then he puts salt in her mouth, spittle uppon her eares and eyes, and annoints her lippes and her nose with oyle, and so God and Saint *Frauncis* save the young childe: in steade of *Friswood,* christening her by the name of *Frauncis,* because that Saint had such a soveraigne commaund over the birds of the ayre that *his name for it was made communicable both to hee and shee:* and *Sara* was christened by the name of *Mary.*

Suppose now (gentle Reader) that *Friswoods* Mother had come sodainly in and seene the Priest with his candell in his hand and his Cope upon his backe, busie in his enchaunting Latine charme, and with-all had espied her daughter *Friswood* musled in her chaire of estate, with a cloath and a Crosse and her other sacred geare: I wonder what she would sodainly have thought, whether she would not have beene much amazed at this infernall incantation, and have imagined that a ghost in steede of *Friswood* had beene conjured out of hell. But if shee had had the hart to have spoken unto *Friswood* and to have called her by her name, and she should sodainly have stepped out of her enchaunted chaire, and have said that her name had not beene *Friswood* but *Frauncis,* verily they would have taken her for a ghost in deede, or have feared that the Priest had enchaunted her out of her wits.

But stay, what hast? For after these new transformed creatures had their ceremonies and rites done uppon them, and were framed, fashioned, and attired for their parts, and were ready for the chaire and the stage, nò man abroad could be admitted to either sight or speech with them: *intus res agitur,*[1] they were now mysticall creatures, and must attend their sacred close mysteries within. *All must be mum:* Clum, *quoth the Carpenter,* Clum *quoth the Carpenters wife, and* Clum *quoth the Friar.*[2] You shall be more thoroughly confirmed by *Friswood* her selfe touching this poynt, who saith in her examination,[3] *That neither shee nor her sister* Sara *did see either father or mother, being in the same Towne, all the while that they were in theyr hands; neyther would they suffer their father or*

[1] "This affair is to be handled in private."

[2] A reminiscence of Chaucer, "The Miller's Tale," *(Canterbury Tales,* Fragment A, 3638–39).

[3] See her examina: [H].

*mother to speake with them, though they desired it many times;
and that her mother growing into some earnestnesse and hard
speech with the Exorcists because she could not be permitted to
see her daughters, the priests did shake her off with angry words,
saying that shee had as much neede to be exorcised as her daughters had.* A man would now verily perswade himselfe that their
game was sure set and needed no more watching; and yet yee shall
see a nayle or two driven in more to rivet the frame more sure.

After her new christendome, *Friswood* in her examination saith
that *before she should come to receive the sacrament, they told her
that shee must first vow and promise by the vertue of that holy sacrament that shee would ever afterwards hold the religion of the
Church of Rome, and never goe againe to any of the Protestants
Churches, nor never reade the English service or the English Bible
or any other English bookes written by the Protestants in matters
of religion.* And this vow (as shee saith) is ordinarily made by all
that are reconciled.

## CHAP. 8.

*Their meanes and manner of instructing theyr schollers.*

When they have brought in theyr Conies and made them as sure
as flesh and blood can make them, have enchaunted them with
their compassionate devotion, have engaged them unto their
ghostlie Fathers, have fascinated them with their solemne incantation, have initiated them into theyr Church by their new mock-
Christendome, have confirmed them with their sacraments, and
have bound them by vow never to forsake theyr ghostly communion: then begin they to reade them Lectures by rote in their
schoole of legerdemaine, and to acquaint them with their parts they
have in hand to play. Wherein the good conceit of their scholler to
apprehend her lesson well, to carry in minde what her Master hath
said over, to apply it to her owne case, and to put it handsomly in
ure, is a little required.

First, they omit no occasion at all times, in all places, when they
be together and their schollers by their sweet side, to talke of the
strangenesse of possession, of the wonders they have seene in possession, of the many marvelous possessions they have been at; and
the *Echo* in all meetings is still possession. Then they tell over and
over how wonderous strangely the parties possessed, whom they
have dealt withall, have been affected; and they say over very
treatably, particularly, and distinctly the whole Catalogue of the

actions, motions, passions, peturbations, agitations, gestures, tumblings, distortions, deformations, howlings, skrikings, visions, apparitions, changes, alterations, speeches and railings that the parties possessed have used and practised in theyr severall fits.

Heare *Sara Williams* theyr scholler report her owne lesson in these words. *It was the ordinary custome of the Priestes to be talking of such as had been possessed beyond the seas, and to tell the manner of theyr fits and what they spake in them; also what uglie sights they saw somtimes, and at other times what joyfull sights; and how, when reliques were applyed unto them, the parties would roare; how they could not abide holy water, nor the sight of the sacrament, nor the annointed Priests of the Catholique church, nor any good thing; how they would greatly commend hereticks; how the devills would complaine, when the Priests touched the parties, that they burnt them and put them into an extreame heate; how sometimes they could smell the Priests.* Heere is her lesson read over; and marke the scholler how well she conned it and made application thereof. *By the said tales* (said shee) *shee well perceived how shee might please them; and did frame herselfe accordingly, at such times as she well perceived it was theyr intent that she should so doe.*

Heare *Friswood, Saras* sister, repeate her lesson by hart that her good Maisters had said over to her when shee came first to schoole. Her words are thus:[1] *That the priests would be often talking in her hearing of certaine women that were possessed beyond the seas, how the devill in them could not abide the* holy potion *nor the burning of hallowed brimstone, nor the applying unto them of holy reliques, nor the presence or touching of Catholique priests, nor holy water, nor the holy candle, nor the blessed sacrament; but would start at it, and say they burned, rage and raile against the Priestes, and commend upon every occasion those that were the Protestants.* See how in time she could[2] her lesson by hart, and profited in this godly schoole. *By this meanes she learned* (as she saith) *what to say and doe when the priests had her in hand: that is, to start sometimes when they brought reliques unto her, to pretend that she could not endure the presence of the sacrament.* Marrie, *Friswood,* beeing a scholler not of the quickest apprehension, did not con her lesson by hart the first day (which cost her the setting on in the *holy chaire* for her dulnesse); but it was some six or seaven weekes ere she found their meaning, *and then* (quoth shee) *I began to find theyr jugling, and how that my selfe saying this or that spake nothing but what I had learned of the Priests.*

[1] See her examina: [H].

[2] "She learned," preterit of "to can," to know or learn.

Heare *Anne Smith* report how shee learned her cue to come into her fits. There are her words: *She had been told by divers* (as she confesseth) *how others had been troubled, viz: how in theyr fits they were greatly tormented; how they could not endure the priestes to come neere them; how when a Priest did lay his hand uppon any part of them, the said partie would be so hote as though it would burne them to the bone; how the devill in them would raile upon the Catholiques and greatly commend the Protestants; and many other such things.*

Heare Ma: *Maynie* theyr chiefe scholler relate how by degrees hee grew to his perfection in the jugling schoole. *First* (saith he) *beeing at my Lord* Vaux *his house at* Hackney *at dinner, in the dinner time there was much communication of the late possession and dispossession of one* Marwood *by certaine Priests, and chiefely (if I do not forget my selfe) by Ma:* Edmunds: *the tales which were told of that matter seemed strange unto mee, as what extraordinary strength he had in his fits, how he roared like a Bull,* and many other such things. *After this, beeing at* Denham,*the women of the house came unto me, and reported unto me the manner of the fits of the two possessed in the house, describing them in such sort as I was much amazed therewith. Then they permitted me to have accesse unto* Sara Williams *when she was in her fits, and enformed mee likewise of the manner how she and others had been troubled; and when I had learned theyr humour, and perceived as well by the rest as by mine owne experience what would content them, I framed my selfe accordingly.*

Loe, here the Captaine of this holy school of legerdemaine tells you what was the highest point to be learned in this schoole, and what was the perfection of a scholler of the highest forme: to wit, to *frame* themselves jump and fit unto the Priests humors, to mop, mow, jest, raile, rave, roare, commend, and discommend: and as the priests would have them, upon fitting occasions (according to the difference of times, places, and commers in) in all things to play the devils accordinglie, as Ma: *Maynie* heere saith, and his other play-devils afore. As every scholler in this schoole had the wit and good grace to *frame himselfe* betimes to the bent of his holy Maister, and to act his feates kindly, roundly, and artificially at a beck, so was theyr proceeding with him or her more gentle and mild. For if he could once read his lesson in his Maisters eyes and face, what needed any other hard horne-booke to beate about his head? But if he were dull and slow unto this *framing himselfe*, and must heere his lesson many times said over by hart by the Priest, and yet could not learne his cue, or else not perfectly remember his severall changes and keyes, why then hee must tast of the discipline of the schoole to rouze up his spirits better, and cause him entend his geare well; and that was the discipline of the *holy chaire* (wherof ye shall heare anon), such a discipline as by that time it had been tasted soundly but once or twice, I suppose the devill himselfe (if he could have had the sence of it that these poore schollers had) would rather have chosen to have roared, fomed, and wallowed, and have turned him into all shapes as the priests would have him, then ever to have endured the course of the same. But his chayre could not be spared for many good offices; and therefore of that more at large heereafter.

# CHAP. 9.
### *Of the secrets and strange operation of the* holy Chaire *and* holy Potion.

*Salve prisca fides tripodis,*[1] saith the Poet to the enchanted seate at *Delphos,* which was so famous for the holy inspiration of the God *Apollo* that his Prophetesse could give no Oracle except shee were placed over that sacred stoole. We have heere in hand a more sacred enchaunted seate, which was so potent and of so various uses and offices to our holy Impostors, as without it they could shew few or no wonders or miracles at all. And that is the blessed chayre which I eft-soones mentioned unto you, which served them to more good purposes for their holy legerdemaine then ever the chayre or sword at *Delphos* did *Apolloes* priests. I should doe you wrong if I should not first describe this blessed Engine barely and nakedly unto you, and there repeate you the manifold commodities and delights of the same.

You shal have *Fidd:* and *Sara* the reporters of it unto you, who by reason of their wofull experience have best skill to doe it.

*At the end of the first Masse*[2] (saith Fidd: Williams) *that ever she saw, which was said by Ma:* Dibdale, *hee told her that now they would make triall what was in her. And thereupon she being perfectly well, and telling Ma:* Dibdale *and the rest as much, yet they would needes have her sit downe in a chayre, which she did. Then they began to binde her with towells, whereat she greatly mervailed, and was there-with cast into a great feare, as not knowing what they meant to doe with her. Being in this case, Ma:* Dibdale *began to reade in his booke of Exorcising, and after a good while, seeing no other alteration in her then the tokens of feare, which encreased by reason of his words and dealings, then*

---

[1]"Hail to the old faith of the triple seat" (Statius, *Thebaid* 1.509).
[2]See her examin: [H].

*they urged her to drinke above a pinte of Sacke and Sallet-oyle,*
*being hallowed and mingled with some kinde of spices. When shee*
*tasted this drinke, which they termed an* holy potion,*it did so much*
*dislike her that shee could drinke but a little of it at once, her*
*stomacke greatly loathing it. And then the Priest said, all that*
*came from the devil, who hated nothing worse then that holy*
*drinke. So as she was held, and by very force caused to drinke it up*
*at divers draughts. Heere-upon shee grew to be very sicke and*
*giddy in her head, and began to fall into a cold sweat, verily then*
*beleeving that (as the Priest said) it was a wicked spirit that*
*caused her to be in such case. Whereas afterwards, when she bet-*
*ter had considered of their dealing with her, shee easily perceaved*
*that the drinke they gave her was such as might have made a horse*
*sicke.* This was the first part of the chayre-work, and the second
was sweeter then this. When her stomacke, head, and veines were
full of the holy drinke, then to take brimstone and burne it in a
chafing dish of coales, and by force to hold downe her face over
the fume. Which broyling with brimstone Ma: *Maynie* confesseth
he saw so butcherly practised upon *Sara Williams, as hee had*
*seene her face after it looke more blacker and swart with the fume*
*then any chimney-sweepers did.*

Now I present unto your imaginations *Sara Williams* sitting
bound in a chayre (as poore wench shee often did), with a pinte of
this *holy potion* in her stomacke, working up into her head and out
at her mouth, and her eyes, nose, mouth, and head stuffed full with
the smoake of holy perfume, her face being held down over the
fume till it was all over as blacke as a stocke; and think if you see
not in your minde the lively *Idaea* of a poore devill-distressed
woman in deede.

And heere, least good Father *Mengus* should take it in ill part
that we leave him out of this devillish worke, who had his greatest
part in prescribing the perfume for the chayre, you shall first heare
his *Dos* touching the bill for the holy perfume; and then I shall be
able to give you a perfect receite to make an horse possessed.

After his holy benediction, *Page 173, Flag. Daemon.,* this is his
perfume. *Accipiatur Sulphur, Galbanum & caet. Take Brimstone,*
Assa faetida, Galbanum, S. Johns Wort, *and* Rue.[1]   *All these*

---

[1]Harsnett misses out Aristolochia, and the rubric he quotes is actually for fuming the
devil's picture *(Flagellum daemonum,* 202). However, in the book's addendum,
"Remedia Efficacissima," the same recipe appears with the following rubric: " . . . velit,
nolit, vexatum . . . diu facias super dictum ignem suffumigari." All these plants were
commonly prescribed for various unpleasant conditions. In *The Greate Herball* (1561),
sig. A3v, assa foetida ("The more it stynketh the better it is") is prescribed for
"asmatyke," "fever quartayne," "mylte," "toth-ache," "[swollen] belly," and "palsey." Rue
is for "the falling evell" or epilepsy (sig. R1), Galbanum for "lytargy," "to breke a
postume," and "wormes in the wombe" (sig. K3). Ypericon or St. John's wort, was powerful against demons (Kittredge, *Witchcraft,* 119–22).

*things, being hallowed according to their owne proper and peculiar benediction, must be cast upon the fire, and the smoake thereof applied to the nosethrills of the possessed.* Now you have have your full number of simples, take your whole bill to possesse a horse with a devill. Take a lusty young stond horse and tye him with a big rope to a Smiths forge, take the *holy potion* compounded of Rue, Sacke, Drugges, and Sallet-oyle *Ana*[1] more then a pinte, put it with an horne downe into the horses throat, that done, take Brimstone, *Assa faetida, Galbanum, S. Johns Wort, and Rue,* burne them all together upon a chafing-dish of coales, apply the smoake so long to the nosethrils of the horse till you have made his face with the smoake looke as blacke as the Smith: and if the horse doe not snort, flyng, fome, curvet, and take on like a devill, you may pay the Smith for his holy drinke, and take the horse with you for your paines. There is neither Horse, nor Asse, nor Dogge, nor Ape, if he had beene used as these poore seely creatures were, but would have beene much more devillishly affected then they. Neither is any man living (as I suppose) of that mortified patience, who would not be much moved with indignation to heare the seely maides complaine of the usage of that holy infernall crue.

First, *Fidd: Williams* complaines, as ye have heard in her relation, That *it made her giddy, and cast her into a cold sweat.* 2. *That it cast her into a rage, and caused her to speake shee wist not what.* 3. It did so intoxicate and benum her sences, as *in one of her fits where-into they had cast her by their* holy potion *and brimstone, there were two needles thrust into her legge by one of the Priests* (whereof in an other place), *and she wist it not till after shee had recovered her sences.* 4. For her complaining to them of their incivill and inhumane usage of her by their potion and perfume, *They had her to the chayre,* and so plagued her with both, *as being there-with wonderfully sicke, she fell into a swound.* 5. It was so loathsome a thing to the beholders to see the holy potion given unto them, *that divers Gentlewomen present did weepe for pitty* to see them goe to their geare. 6. She was so haunted heerewith, and *grew so weary of her life by this meanes, as shee cried aloude unto her uncle, whom shee heard by chaunce on the other side of a garden wall: O good Uncle, helpe me from hence, for I am almost killed amongst them heere already, and shall not live if I continue heere long.* 7. Being grown to great weakenes, and almost desperate, shee told the priests plainly, at the end of one of her fits whereinto they had cast her by their drinks, slibber-sawces, and brimstone, that *if shee had a devill in her they had best to cast him out.*

[1]Medieval latin, from Greek *ana,* used in recipes for "of each."

*For* (quoth she) *if ever you torment me so againe, dispatch me if you list; otherwise I will certainly by one meanes or other get away from you, and will tell my friends of all your proceedings and dealings heere, both with me and others.* Thus farre *Fidd. Williams.* And was *Sara* her sister lesse beholding to their *holy potion,* holy brimstone, and the chayre? Let her selfe tell you, who hath best cause to remember.

First, she saith, *shee dooth not remember every severall time when they bound her in the chayre, but they troubled her very often* (praying God to forgive them); and affirmeth that *when she came to the chayre, she was so used as that every time, if she might have had her choyse, shee would rather have chosen to have ended her life then to have gone into it.* Secondly, that *if at any time shee was past the use of her sences, it was by reason of the* holy potion *they compelled her to take.* Thirdly, that *shee fell into the passion of the trembling of the hart onely upon griefe of their bad usage of her; and that thorough that passion she did divers times swound.* Fourthly, that *they used their holy brimstone so much as the stinke of it never went out of the chamber.* Fiftlie, that foule *holy potion* made such an impression in her phancie, and *the loathsomnes of it did so sticke in her mind, as yet to this day she cannot endure the tast nor savour of any thing that was in the same.* In so much as *about three yeeres since, she feeling a pangue of sicknes in the Market at* Oxford, *some of her neighbours at unawares gave her a little Sacke: which as soone as she perceaved, shee fell to be very sicke upon it, and was constrained to lye there all night, the offence of the Sacke being the onely griefe that she had after shee was recovered of her saide pangue.* Sixtly, *they would holde her nose and face perforce so neere over the smoake of brimstone, feathers, and such other stinking geare, that the very paine she felt caused her to crie and scritche very lowde, and to struggle as much as possibly she could till her strength failed her. At one time, she was so extreamely afflicted with the said drinke that her sences went from her, and she remained in a swound; and after that, her head was so giddie with the potion, and her sences so troubled with the brimstone smoake, as she spake and babled many idle foolish words.* Seaventhly, their chaire, potion, and brimstone perfume grew so hatefull to her sister *Fidd,* and so untolerable to her selfe, as upon her sisters suggestion *she attempted to runne from the house, and to wade through a brooke halfe a yard deepe of water.*

Thus much *Sara Williams.* And did Ma: *Maynie,* their prime professour, escape the chayre, the brimstone, and the blessed potion? That had beene great pitty, the devil alias *Weston* loved him much better then so. Of whom Ma: *Maynie* complaineth *That he was constrained by him to drinke most loathsome draughts of such confections as he had ready for him. And that sometimes they burnt such abhominable, stinking, and violent things, holding his nose by force over the smoake, as I think* (quoth he) *would have made an horse mad.* But in another place he tells us a shrewder tale of *Weston,* that holy devill, touching this devillish potion. *God knoweth* (saith he) *whether* Weston *supposed I would have taken some course to have shortned mine owne time, as constrained in some sort there-unto by the great weakenes and wearines of my life.* Is this an effect of your blessed loathsome potion, to drive *Fidd, Sara,* and Ma: *Maynie* into a loathing of their owne lives, and to enter into a desperate resolution touching shortning the same? Then holy gentle devils, the Maisters of this devil-tragedy, let me aske you a question (but it shall be in your eare, that the Catholiques who hold you for ghostly fathers may not heare): how many drammes of this *holy potion* had you given to the wench that you wote of, whom you exorcised so long, till shee fell from off a paire of stayres and brake her necke?[1] Whether for telling of tales or that you feared after-claps, it is very probable you had filled her head full of your holy perfume.

*Anne Smith* was yet in a farre better case then these; for she confesseth she was so gently tyed and hampered in the *holy chaire* that she was compelled for three yeeres space after she was released to swadle her body for the very sorenes she felt of their holy hands.

Gentle spectators, we have held you som-what long ere our play begin; but now you see the devils are come upon the stage in their proper colours, Belzebub, alias *Weston,* and his twelve gracious assistants. For if the devils themselves should have devised a devillish potion to have intoxicated poore creatures and cause them to play the devils, they could not have invented a more potent potion then this. *Lucian* tells a tale, that the passengers to hell are made to drinke a draught of a potion that makes them to forget all they have said or done in their life.[2] Our *Stygian* Impostors goe farre beyond that *stygian* lake, for they have composed a potion that brings not only a privation of wit, memory, and sences, but makes their patients to scritch, tumble, and roare like the devils in hell. And this (good man devill-whipper *Mengus*), as seemes, is the

---

[1]Eliza Calthrope, another supposedly possessed girl who, sometime after 19 April 1586 broke her neck falling down a flight of stairs at John Mainy's house in Green's Alley. It does not appear whether she was pushed or fell, or was in a drugged condition, but Tyrrell's statement suggests a hushed-up affair *(DEP,* 390).

[2]The potion was Lethe water; see *The Downward Journey* 1.28.

mysterie of your sweet compose, to fume a devill out at a mans nose like the smoake of Tobacco?

Whereas your prescript is compounded of these delicate simples, Brimstone, *Assa faetida, Galbanum, S. Johns Wort, and Rue: Porphyrie* and *Iamblichus,* men acquainted with the nature and disposition of devils afore your whip had ere a string to it, doe affirme that those forcible violent savours and stinking odours are the very delicacies for devils, and allectives to their noses, and that the devill would not vouchsafe to come give his Oracle at the *statua* at *Dodona* untill he were wooed by these delicious perfumes.[1] Those devils of that clime are belike of an other temper then these under your lash, or else let me tell your riddle; you never meant (good man) to scare out a devill by these filthy fumes, but to scare poore soules into the fashion of devils by these pestilent fumigations.

## CHAP. 10.

### *The strange names of their devils.*

Now that I have acquainted you with the names of the Maister and his twelve disciples, the names of the places wherein, and the names of the persons upon whom these wonders were shewed: it seemes not incongruent that I relate unto you the names of the devils whom in this glorious pageant they did dispossesse. Wherein we may call unto *Porphyrius, Proclus, Iamblicus,* and *Trismegistus,* the old Platonicall sect that conversed familiarly and kept company with devils, and desire their help to expound us these new devils names, and to tell us at what solemne feast and meeting in hell these devils were dubbed and halowed with these new strange names. It cannot be but our holy devill-crue had surely met with *Menippus* proclaiming himselfe new come out of hell: *adsum profundo Tartari emissus specu.*[2] Else they could never have beene so deeply sighted and acquainted with the Musterbooke of hell. Or else it may seeme that our vagrant devils heere did take theyr fashion of new names from our wandring Jesuits, who to dissemble themselves have alwaies three or foure odde conceited names in their budget. Or els they did so plague the poore devils with theyr holy charmes and enchaunted geare, and did so intoxicate them with their dreadful fumigations, as they made some

[1]Porphyry, *De Abstinentia* 2.42; Iamblichus, *De Mysteriis* 5.10–15.

[2]The cynic philosopher. His speech "Here I come forth from the deep caves of Tartarus" is a paraphrase of Lucian, *Menippus* 1.

so giddy-headed that they gave themselves giddy names, they wist not what. Or else there is a confederation between our wandring Exorcists and these walking devils, and they are agreed of certaine uncouth non-significant names which goe currant amongst themselves, as the Gipsies are of gibridge which none but themselves can spell without a paire of spectacles. Howsoever it is, it is not amisse that you be be acquainted with these extravagant names of devils, least meeting them otherwise by chance, you mistake them for the names of Tapsters or Juglers.

First then, to marshall them in as good order as such disorderly cattell will be brought into, you are to understand that there were in our possessed five Captaines or Commaunders above the rest: Captaine *Pippin, Marwoods* devill; Captaine *Philpot, Trayfords* devil; Captaine *Maho, Saras* devil; Captaine *Modu, Maynies* devill, and Captaine *Soforce, Anne Smiths* devil. These were not all of equall authoritie and place, but some had more, some fewer under theyr commaund. *Pippin, Marwoods* devill, was a Captaine (marry, either cassierd for some part of bad service hee had done, or else a malecontent standing upon his worth), like some of our high Puntilios scorned to sort himselfe with any of his ranke, and therefore like a melancholick *Privado* he affects *Marwood* to lie in the fields and to gape at the Moone, and so of a *Caesars* humor, he raignes in *Marwood* alone.

Captaine *Philpot, Trayfords* devill, was a Centurion (as himselfe tels you), and had an hundred under his charge. Mary, he was (as seemes) but a white-livered devill, for he was so hastie to be gone out of *Trayford* for feare of the Exorcist that hee would scarce give him leave, beeing a bed, to put on his breeches. The names of ther punie spirits cast out of *Trayford* were these: *Hilco, Smolkin, Hillio, Hiaclito,* and *Lustie Huffe-cap;* this last seemes some swaggering punie devill dropt out of a Tinkers budget. But *Hiaclito* may not be slipped over without your observation; for he scorning a great while (as the Author saith) to tell his name, at last hs aunswered most proudly, *my name is* Hiaclito, a *Prince and Monarch of the world.* And beeing asked by the Exorcist what fellowes he had with him, hee said that *hee had no fellowes but two men and an urchin boy.* It was little beseeming his state (I wis), beeing so mighty a Monarch, to come into our coasts so skurvily attended; except hee came to see fashions in England, and so made himselfe private till the Exorcist reveald him. Or els that he was of the new Court cut, affecting no other traine then two crasie fellowes and an urchin butter-flie boy.

*Soforce, Anne Smiths* possedent, was but a musty devill; there was neither mirth nor good fellowship with him, affecting so much sullennesse as he would hardlie speake. Yet as all melancholike creatures use to have, he had a restie tricke with him. For whether *Alexander* the Apothecarie had put too much *Assa Faetida* in the fumigation for the devill, or had done the devill some other shrewd turne with his drugges, sure it is that *Alexander* the Apothecarie riding one day towards London to fetch more Priests to *Denham,* his horse fell a plunging and *Alexander* came downe; and returning to *Denham,* hee constantly affirmed that it was *Anne Smiths* devill that playd the Jade with him.

*Modu, Ma: Maynies* devill, was a graund Commaunder, Mustermaister over the Captaines of the seaven deadly sinnes: *Cliton, Bernon, Hilo, Motubizanto* and the rest, himselfe a Generall of a kind and curteous disposition; so saith *Sara Williams* touching this devils acquaintance with Mistres *Plater* and her sister *Fid.*

*Sara Williams* had in her at a bare word *all the devils in hell.* The Exorcist askes *Maho, Saras* devil, what company he had with him, and the devil makes no bones, but tels him in flat termes, *all the devils in hell.* Heere was a goodly fat *otium* this meane while in hell! The poore soules there had good leave to play; such a day was never seene since hell was hell. Not a doore-keeper left, but all must goe a maying to poore *Saras* house. It was not kindly done of the devils to leave the poore soules behind, especially going to make merry amongst theyr friends. But what if the soules had fallen a madding or maying as fast as the devils and had gone a roming abroad amongst their good friends, had not this (trow we) made a pretie peece of worke in hell?

And if I misse not my markes, this *Dictator Maho* saith hee had beene in *Sara* by the space of two yeeres; then so long hell was cleere and had not a devill to cast at a mad dogge. And soothly I cannot much blame the devils for staying so long abroad. They had taken up an Inne much sweeter then hell, and an hostesse that wanted neither wit nor mirth to give them kinde welcome.

Heere, if you please, you make take a survay of the whole regiment of hell, at least the chiefe Leaders and officers, as we finde them enrolled by theyr names.

First *Killico, Hob,* and a third *anonymos* are booked downe for three graund Commaunders, every one having under him three hundred attendants.

Coronell *Portirichio* had with him two Captaines and an hundred assistants, and this he affirmes to be true uppon his oath taken upon the blessed sacrament, and then you must believe him: an admirable new way to make the devil true and cock-sure of his word, to offer him an oath upon the blessed sacrament, and then dog with a fiddle.[1] But the devill is like some other good fellowes in the world that will not sweare except he allow theyr Commission that tenders him his oath;[2] and Commissioners for the devill are onely holy Exorcists, and then it must be the sacrament of the Masse, too, else I wis it is not all worth a beane.

*Frateretto, Fliberdigibbet, Hoberdidance, Tocobatto* were foure devils of the round or Morrice whom *Sara* in her fits tuned together in measure and sweet cadence. And least you should conceive that the devils had no musicke in hell, especially that they would goe a maying without theyr musicke, the Fidler comes in with his Taber and Pipe, and a whole Morice after him with motly visards for theyr better grace. These foure had forty assistants under them, as themselves doe confesse.

*Lustie Jollie Jenkin* (an other of *Saras* Captaine devils names) by his name should seeme to be foreman of the motly morrice. Hee had under him, saith himselfe, forty assistants; or rather (if I misse not), he had beene by some old Exorcist allowed for the Master setter of Catches or roundes used to be sung by Tinkers as they sit by the fire with a pot of good Ale betweene theyr legges: *Hey jolly Jenkin, I see a knave a drinking, et caet.*[3]

*Delicat,* an other Captaine or vicenarie in *Sara,* having under him twenty assistants, seemes by his English name to be *yeoman* of the *Sprucery,*[4] to see the devils motly visards, after they were soiled with Brimstone and sweat, to be brusht up and kept sweet, neate, and cleane. These were the Officers or Commaunders names that had taken up theyr lodging in *Sara Williams.* Now the many, rascality, or black-guard of hell were God knows how many in her, for all were there, tag and ragge, cut and long-tayle; yet divers of them it pleaseth the holie Exorcist to commaund theyr names to doe them some grace. Others he lets goe out leaving no names but an ill savour behind them. The names of such as the Exorcist thought good to favour were these: *Puffe* and *Purre* (the two fat

---

[1]Proverbial, expressing the incongruity of the devil taking his oath on the sacrament. Cf. Tilley, S679: "A sow to a fiddle."

[2]A reference to the oath *ex officio mero* offered to persons being examined before the Court of High Commission, which constrained them to answer all interrogatories administered to them. See Marchant, *Puritans and the Church Courts,* 1–10, for an excellent discussion of this procedure.

[3]This drinking song and its refrain are printed in William Elderton, *New Merry News* (1606): "To whom drinke you, Sir knave to you, / with hey jolly Jenkin, I see a knave a drinking, / And trole the bole to me" (Nashe, *Works* 5: "Supplement," 45).

[4]Compare *Twelfth Night,* 2.5.39–40: "The Lady of the Strachy married the yeoman of the wardrobe." "Sprucery" seems to be Harsnett's invention. "Spruce" and "spruceness" existed, but were recently formed words *(OED).* The derivation is from "Prussia," called "Pruce" or "Spruceland" since the fourteenth century.

devils that had beene conjurd up for mony, anno 84, and would not home to hell againe till good company came for them), *Lustie Dickie, Cornerd-cappe, Nurre, Molkin, Wilkin, Helcmodion, Kellicocam.* These were like the *Sporades in via lactea,*[1] having neither office, order, nor ranke. All these were *Saras* devils.

*Maho* was generall *Dictator* of hell; and yet for good manners sake hee was contented of his good nature to make shew that himselfe was under the check of *Modu*, the graund devil in Ma: *Maynie.* These were all in poore *Sara* at a chop; with these the poore soule travailed up and downe full two yeeres together, so as during those two yeeres it had beene all one to say one is gone to hell or hee is gone to Sara Williams. For shee, poore wench, had all hell in her belly. And had had it still to this day for any thing we know, if it had not pleased Fa: *Weston* and his twelve holy disciples to have delivered her of that devil-childe. But of this you shall heare heereafter. Now I may proceed.


## CHAP. 11.

*The reasons why sometime one devill alone, sometimes an hundred, sometimes a thousand, are cast out at a clap.*

You have formerly heard of the names of the Priests, graund rectors of this Comedie, and lately of the names of the devils, their Cue-fellowes in the play. Good order seemes to require that I should marshall them together as birds of a feather; but I choose rather to violate good method, and put my selfe upon my Reader, then to offend our *devill-mastix* by such an unpleasing combination. Now because some may wonder how it commeth to passe that hell in this *Jubile* was broken up, and that such millions of devils, like Herrings in a barrell, were packed up in *Sara Williams* and the rest; and sometimes one alone, sometimes sixe, sometimes nine hundred were cast out together, and yet *Maho* with a million of assistants left still behind: this containes many mysteries as fit to be learned as the rest. We will consider these two heads a sunder, for the worthines of the matter: first, why these devils are said to be so manie; next, why sometimes one, sometimes many are said to be cast out at a time.

In the first, our holy devill-charmers have the vantage of Tinkers and Surgeons by much. For these, the one hath his certaine number of holes to mend, and the other his certaine number of sores to salve, and when he hath done, except by some prety knack in his

---

[1] Scattered stars in the Milky Way.

budget he can multiply one hole into foure, and the other draw one sore into sixe, he is in danger to be out of worke; but our holy budgetters having to deale with devils, in nature invisible, and in number innumerable, doe wisely provide so many to be packed up in one patient together, as except hell it selfe be drawne dry, they can never want worke.

*Sara Williams* was a patient that pleased their handling well, and therefore shee was furnished with all the devils in hell at a clap; so as if *Hercules* himselfe had beene in this hell, there had beene worke enough both for him and his club. The casting a devill out of *Sara* was like the drawing of a bucket of water out of a Well, it made the devill spring the quicker, and like to cutting off one of *Hydraes* heads, which made seaven more to arise in his place.

This ground must be well layd, and this principle wel conned by all the professours of this black Art, that they be sure of hell and devils enow in the party at the first: which being not well advised of by some simple witted men of ours,[1] late probationers in this science, they were enforced for enlarging their worke to bungle it out wofully, and to say that the devils they had cast did rebound backe againe, and so made them new worke to begin againe: which by this provision of thrumming in devils at the first might most easily have been avoyded.

Secondly, this device of an huge many of devils to be in one party served them as a shelter against what wind or weather so ever. If the parties they had in handling grew weary of their occupation, as loathing their drugs, fearing their tortures, and hating their cosenage, and so were like to breake from them and to tell tales out of Schoole, they had (by this devise) their evasion at hand. There were yet many devils in the party forsooth, and it was not he or she that so said, but the devill; so as if he saith any thing in opening their legerdemaine, hee shall be possessed as long as he lives; and then may he say and sweare what he will, for hee shall be no more credited then *Pippin* their devill. And that which would anger any poore soule at the hart, what so ever he doth or saith, it must not be he that so doth or saith, but the devill.

Let poore *Sara Williams* give you instances of this.[2] She grew so farre discontented with their *holy potion* and their chayre as she begins to speake bugs words and tell them, *she would complaine.* The priests had their *ward-word*[3] ready; *it was not* Sara *but the devill* that so spake, because he could abide no Catholique priests.

---

[1] A reference to Darrell, who claimed that his patient William Somers was repossessed.

[2] Reade her examin: [H].

[3] Italicization suggests an unusual word, probably suggested by the title of Parson's

She attempts to take her heeles, and runne away from them: the common voyce was *it was not* Sara *but the devill;* she did not runne, but was caried by the devill. She smiles, and it must not be she that smiles, *but the devill.* She weepes, and she was borne downe that it was not her selfe that wept, *but the devill;* so as she said *she was at her wits end,* fearing (as seemes) so much as to mutter, hum, or spit, for feare the priests should make it not of her owne spitting, but the devils. This devise is in steede of all the Orators in the world, to free them from imputation and to secure their jugling. For say anie thing distasting to them and to their holy crue, ye shall be sure to have the devill put upon you for your labour; and they have several spirits to command for their bayards, to beare their severall fardles of crimes. Tell them that they are Impostors and deserve to be branded on the foreheads with the Character noting their trade. Loe, say they, it is not you, but the spirit of malediction. Put them in minde of their devill daliance with *Fidd.* and *Sara Williams;* it is not you, but the spirit of lust. Note their factious ambition in seeking soveraigntie and commaund; it is not you that so speake of them, but the spirit of pride. And not onely words and speeches such as they liked not well, but even actions, motions, jestures, and cariage of the body, if it make any thing against their lewd jugling, shall be branded with no other stampe, then *the devill.*

You may see a pretie peece of this puppet-play (and so judge of the rest) acted betweene Ma: *Maynie* the dumbe Actor and *Weston* his Interpreter.[1]

Ma: *Maynie* the Actor comes mute upon the stage with his hands by his side, and his haire curled up. *Loe heere* (cries *Weston* the Interpreter) *comes up the spirit of* pride. Sodainly the mute Actor cries out, *Ten pounds in the hundred. That voyce* (cries *Weston) is the voyce of the spirit of* avarice. *Maynie* makes a scornfull face, and *that is the spirit of* Envie. He bends and knits his browes, and *that is the spirit of* Wrath. He yawnes and gapes, and *that is the spirit of* Sloth. Thus *Weston* in Ma: *Maynies* face reades you the devils that are the seaven Authors of the seaven deadly sinnes; and as many devils (if he list) can he shew in any Protestants face at any time he pleases, all or most of us, in his opinion, being really possessed with devils.

For the second point, why sometimes a devill alone, sometimes an hundred, sometimes a thousand, are blowne out at a clap, there

---

pamphlet *A Temperate Ward-word to the Turbulent and Seditious Watch-word of Sir Francis Hastings Knight* (1599).

[1]See Maynies confess. [H].

are two waighty reasons attending that devise. One is to advaunce heereby the reputation of some man of especiall note and credite amongst them, who must be their *Hercules,* to controle with his club the monster maister-devils of greatest potencie and commaund. Every plodding priest could cast out an urchin or boy devill, the rascall guard that attended Prince *Hiaclito;* but *Modu* the Generall of *Styx* with his seaven Colonels under him, the seaven maisters of the seaven deadly sinnes, must be a monster reserved for *Westons* owne club, and none but his. And whereas every fidling Exorcist in his holy conjuration did use the holy *amice, Weston,* for the solemnity of the action and his better grace, must come upon the stage more solemnly adorned with the holy Albe, or an holy Cope, and other consecrated geare.[1] And the devill many times of his owne good nature, or else upon some speciall acquaintance betweene him and the priest, expresly tells by whom and by no other he will be cast out; and then he alone must be gotten to come, and (to make the devill no lyer) he must gippe the Gudgin and hit the Woodcocke on the bill, and the other scurvie crue of Exorcists must hold him the candell.[2] Learned *Thyraeus* tells us, *page 67, de Daemon.,* that the foule devill that possessed one *Malachia* had vowed he would not out till Fa: *Bernadine* were gotten to come: who no sooner appeared, but the devil shewed himselfe a man of his word; for hee slinkes closely away like a dogge at the sight of a whip.

A second use they have of this huge difference of casting out sometime one alone, sometime a whole million of devils, farre more passing and precious then the former. And that is to grace by this drift, and to blaze the vertue of some new Saint, and new greene reliques, as yet not growne into credite in the world. Marie, it must be especially of such a Martyr or Saint, of whose vertue and sanctitie there is greatest cause of suspition abroad, whether the good man were a slye Jugler or a holy man in deede. And this suspitious Saint or his cast relique shall worke you a wonder beyond God his forbid cleane.

It was sufficient for the gracing of *Campion* amongst the Catholiques in England, with whom he was in especiall reputation, that his girdle, which came from *Jerusalem* and was worne at

---

[1] A cope is a vestment of silk or other material resembling a long cloak, made of a semicircular piece of cloth. In the Catholic Church it is not exclusively sacramental; in the Church of England it is worn by those who administer Communion *(Constitutions and Canons* [1604], No. 24).

[2] Conflates two proverbs: "To hold a candle before the devil" (Tilley, C42), meaning to help in a bad cause, and "He that worst may, must hold the candle" (Tilley, C40), which means the same as "The weakest goeth to the wall."

*Tyburne*, should at the first touch of the party possessed stunt the devils wits. Where-uppon *Westons* acclamation to the Spectators was this: *Testes estote clarissimi patris* Campiani *Martyrii, cuius hic vel minutissimus funiculus tantus illi faces miserat: Beare witnes, I charge you, of the most worthy Martyrdome of good Fa:* Campion, *whose simple girdle hath cast the devill into such a heate.* Marie, for that *Ignatius* their founder hath many enemies in the world, and is lately called into question for a graund cheater: to grace this *Monsignior* and to bring him into credite, he must doe transcendent miracles, strained upon such a key as our blessed Saviour and his holy Apostles never came neere. And for this purpose, to divulge this Founders deitie, there is composed a Diarie of all his diabolicall (I meane hyperbolicall) wonders, done by that worthy Mountebanke both alive and dead!

First, for his better credit, the devill himselfe proclaimes him to Fa: *Baptista Peruso* for a Saint in heaven; and I trust you will not doubt of it, since it comes from so holy an Oracle as the devils own mouth, and therefore I wonder the Pope doth so long stand out. At *Maurisca* hee lay eight dayes in a traunce without all signe of life, save the beating of his hart; in his prayer he saw Almighty God, and his sonne standing by him with his Crosse upon his shoulders, and hee heard Almighty God commend him and his company to the protection of his Sonne. Thus farre agree Fa: *Ignatius* and the devil.

At *Sena* the devils durst not looke uppon his picture, but hung theyr heads in theyr bosomes for very pure shame. His picture in *Malacia* scared away a devill. His picture in paper at *Madena*, pinned closely uppon a wall, skared away a whole troupe of devils out of foure women possessed. The bare pronouncing his name at *Rome* skared out two legions of devils. A peece of his coife that hee wore heales a woman of the phrensie. A peece of leather that he used at his stomack cures the plague. A peece of his hayre-cloth purges an holy Nunne, in the space of a yeere, of an hundred stones. A peece of a relique of his, close shut in a boxe, burnes a devill and makes him to roare the bredth of a chamber off. A peece of a relique cast into the sea calmes the waves and stills the windes. But the bare subscription of his name in a morsel of paper passeth all the rest. This written in a patch of paper and brought unto the partie, heales the tooth-ache, the crampe, the gowte, the Sciatica, the Leprosie, the skurvies; and beeing layd uppon the belly of a woman that hath endured her paine of travaile two, three, or foure dayes, and is past all hope of life, takes away her paine, facilitates the birth, and recovers her life. A sweet protecting Saint to that sweet sex, the syllables of whose name are of more potencie and saving health then the sacred syllables of the blessed name of our ever blessed Saviour was ever read to be of. *Spectatum admissi risum teneatis.*[1] Is it not a wonder above all wonders that any man should looke upon these Antick wonders without a wonderous laughter: *hic nebulo magnus est, ne metuas,*[2] this foule wonder-maister is too full of wonders ever to be good.

# CHAP. 12.
### *Of the secret of lodging and couching the devill in any part of the body that the Exorcist pleaseth.*

The great skar-buggs of old time, as *Hercules* and the rest, had a great humour (as the Poets faigne) to goe downe to *Styx* and to visit hell to see *Pluto* and his uglie ghosts, and to behold the holes and dennes where hee lodged his blacke guard. Our holy skar-devils, if they had lived with them, would have eased them of that paines, for they would have shewed them hell and devils heere above, and have carried them with a wet finger[3] to their cabines and lodges. And you shall find very deepe and waighty reasons of this.

*Mercurie* prince of Fairies had a rodde given him by *Jupiter* his Father, whereby he had power not onelie to raise up and drive afore him what ghosts hee pleased, but also to remaund and still, with the same rod, as many as hee list. The holy Romane Church hath as potently armed her twelve Worthies of hell and *Weston* their *Blacke prince* as ever *Jupiter* did arme his sweet sonne, giving them a power not onely to call up, drive, and puffe out with theyr breath as many devils as they pleased, but also to controll, cap, lodge, and couch them as stil as a curre at the sound of his Maisters whippe is couched under a table. By that time I have opened you the causes and secrets of this, and have shewed you their severall lodges and formes, I doubt not but you wil be able to tel me more newes from hell.

It is a poynt in the blacke art of deepest skill and power, not to raise a spirit, but to be able to rule and couch him safely and well; and in this holy infernal science of casting out devils *Thyraeus* tells us that *devils be not all of a nature, quality, and sise; some be watry, some ayrie, some fierie, and some savour of the earth. The watry and ayrie doe tast of theyr element and be easily mooved; the fierie are more fierce, and the earthy, like the melancholicke men, more sullen, not easily controld.* See this exemplified as cleerly in our patients as the nose on a mans chin.

---

[1]Horace, *Ars Poetica* 5.

[2]Terence, *Eunuchus* 4.7.

[3]Proverbial: "with the greatest of ease." Cf. Tilley, F234.

*Soforce, Anne Smiths* devill, was a sullen and silent spirit (so herselfe records him) and could hardly be gotten by all dreadful conjurations so much as to speake. Captaine *Maho* in *Sara* was of a fel and furious moode, and many times when he was hunted up into her body grew there so unruly and outragious that the Exorcists seemed to feare least her bowels would burst. Then was all hast made to get him downe againe, which somtime was done with good seeming toile, difficultie, and sweat, that when it fel out pat as the devil and the priest would have it, it bred in the poore sillie spectators a wonderful admiration of the dignitie of the priesthood and power of the Catholique Romish Church.

*Sara,* their apt scholler, acted this scene commendably well where, after a sore skirmish between the Exorcist and the devill, or *Sara* and the Priest, the devill was with much a-doe commaunded downe into her foote; but in another scene shee hit the needles eye, where after a hote and sore encounter, all the spirits with much adoe being commaunded to goe downe into her left foote, they did it with vehement trembling and shaking of her leg to the great admiration of many of the standers by, seeing the power of the Catholique Romish Church: the partie crying that *her shooe would not be able to hold them all.* Heere this act of lodging the devil had a *plaudite* in the midst of the play.

Secondly, who can but mate his wit with wonder, having no more wits then one, and stare out his eyes with amazement, having but two, to see the poore devil brought into such a taking, and to savour so rankly (lying at untrusse), that he would faine be gone out? and shal see the tyrannical dreadful power of an enchaunting Priest, by his remaunding might to keepe him in stil, in spight of his nose, and to commaund him for his more disgrace to take up his lodge in a homely place, of which you shal heare heereafter if it be not too foule. Would not some tender-harted body in pure pittie of the devils cry, take off the priest, and let the poore devil be gone! as I have heard of a good-natured gentleman at *Parish-garden* that cryed, take off the dog, for shame, and let the poore Beare alone! Pittiful *Hiaclito* would rather then his life, for pure feare of the priest, have slunke out of *Trayford* behinde; but it would not be, he must be stayed until hee had his payment. Yea, *Maho* himselfe was taken downe so low with the devil-squirting potion that he would have given all the poynts at his hose to be gone; and *Dibdale* would none, but commaunds him to his lodge until the Brimstone by some dreadful enchauntment were made hote enough to scald his breech soundly. Heere this lodging-power was more dreadful to the devil and astonishable to the people by ods then the dispossessing was.

Thirdly, this commaund to lodge would at no hand be spared, for by this they made sure to have a devil readie at a trice at all assaies to furnish out the stage: whom beeing safe lodged, they caried about with them from place to place as the Juglers use to carry a Bee in a box, or an ape in a string, or puppits in a pageant, to squeale, skip, and tumble wheresoever they pitch downe theyr trusse.

You shal heare an act of this puppet-play performed betweene a priest and a wench as it is deposed uppon oath, for a tast of the rest.[1] There was a priest not many yeeres since in *Lancashire* in the habit of a gentleman, who carried about with him (as Tynkers doe their bitches) a wench, pretended by the priest to be possessed. This wench at every safe station (where there was concourse of simple people, the founders of miracles) hee presents to play her pranks, and his fashion was this: when it was a full Court, out brings he his *Mattachina* and places her in a chayre, and then approching demurely to her, takes her by the toe, and then dialoguizes with the devil according to his pleasure. The end of the dialogue between the priest and the devil is a remaund of the devil to his lodge: which (to avoyde *inquam* and *inquit*) I have presented you in both theyr persons, speaking sweetly together.[2]

> Pri: *I commaund thee to goe to the place appointed, and that thou doe not hurt her in thy going downe, nor make her sicke in body nor minde.*
> Wo: *Fie upon thee, hee is in my knee.*
> Pri: *I commaund thee to thy place appointed, thou damned fiend.*
> Wo: *Oh, hee is in my great toe.*
> Pri: *Goe to the place appointed, thou damned fiend.*
> Wo: *Oh, he is in my toe next to my little toe.*
> Pri: *Goe to the place appointed, thou damned fiend.*
> Wo: *Oh fie upon him, he is in the toe next the great toe.*
> Pri: *I commaund thee to goe into the dead of her nayle.*

With that the devil gave a rush up into the womans body as though hee would have torne her in peeces; then the priest commaunded him to *goe downe damned fiend as he was, otherwise his Judge would damne him into the bottomlesse pit of hell;* and with that the woman confessed that *the devill was in the place appointed.* Then the priest charged him that he should lie there *till the next exorcisme to be holden by him or some of his brethren.*

[1]The wench was Jane Ashton, a girl dispossessed by John Darrell in 1597 at the house of Mr. Starkey in Lancashire: "which Jane is since fallen into the hands of certain Seminarie priests, and hath beene caried by them up and downe that countrey, to sundry recusants houses . . . and by her cunning counterfaiting of certaine fits, & staying of herselfe by the secret directions of the said Priestes, she hath gotten God knoweth what: they by such lewdnes have wonne great credit, but her Majesties subjectes, have in the meane time beene shamefully abused" *(DFP,* sig. B1v–B2). Jane Ashton may also be the heroine of the anecdote above, 223. See also *The Triall of Maist. Dorrell,* sig. A8v: *"Jane Ashton* . . . is repossessed, & by Popish Priestes made a spectacle to Papistes."

[2]See the record. [H].

I doe verily suspect this wonder was acted somehat neere *Gotham,*[1] and that the spectators were the posteritie of them that drowned the Eele: that never an unhappy fellow in the company shewed so much unhappie wit as to offer to take a knife and pare away the devil lying in the dead of the nayle, and throw him into the fire for acting his part so baldly; but I nothing doubt, but the devil-maister priest would have had an eye to this least he or some of his brethren at the next exorcisme holden should for want of a devil have spoiled a good play. And would not this have spighted any devil, to be thus hardly handled by a priest, to be turned out of his warme nest where hee cabined in the wench, and to be lodged at little ease in the edge of her nayle next to wind and weather, where hee must lye for a skout like the Sentinel in a watch, and suffer every boy to play bo-peepe with his devilship, and he not able to stirre eyther out or in? O that *Will Sommer* had come to this pleasant bargaine betweene the Exorcist and the devil;[2] how handsomly would he have belaboured them both with his bable for playing theyr parts so handsomlie.

But this was but a pedling Exorcist of the rascal crue, who wandered like a chapman of smal wares with a wench and a trusse, beeing never free of his companie. Our wardens of the science had a little more art to lodge theyr devils. Such an art of lodging they had, and some of theyr lodges so obscure and retrayte, as none but a priest or a devil could ever have sented it out. Some of these devil-lodges in *Sara* and *Fid,* without a praeface of deprecation to your modesty, I must not once name for feare of [a] check from your chast eares, and a change of colour in mine inke and paper at such uncouth termes. I will onely leape over this kennell of turpitude with a note of unsavorie smels, and remit you to that clause of *Sara Williams* relation, who as a woman hath touched it as modestly as she can, giving us to understand by her timorous declaration that our holy order have a ticket from his *Holines* of Rome to harrow hell it selfe, and be never the worse.

It was wisely cauteled by the penner of these savory miracles in the end of his booke, why *Sara* being a seely young innocent wench of sixteen yeeres should be more devil-haunted then any of the possessed men; there was a pad in the straw[3] the poore man would faine have out. But a Sceptike will make an other *Quaere* to

---

[1]A village in Nottinghamshire proverbial for the stupidity of its inhabitants.

[2]A musician's apprentice of Nottingham, supposed to be possessed; the chief subject of the Puritan dispossesser John Darrell. Murphy, *Darkness and Devils,* 175, points out that the name can also refer to Henry VIII's fool, Will Summers, the presenter of Nashe's play *Summer's Last Will and Testament.*

[3]Proverbial: "more than meets the eye." See Tilley, P9. A pad is a toad.

our holy order to soile, how it comes to passe that wee reade in auncient possessions of old, of moore men to be possessed then women, and now in these novell upstart miracles from Rome still it is the ill hap of more women to be haunted then men? This sore being salved with a little blessed oyle from Rome, an other doubt wil arise, what the cause is why our holy order having under their holy hands not onely *Fid, Sara,* and *Anne Smith,* women, but *Trayford, Marwood,* and Ma: *Maynie* that were men, there is no mention at all of common lodging and couching the devil in a peculiar part of the body, but onely in the wenches?

Let us goe to old *Lockwood, Mengus* their maister, and loke upon his Canon for couching and lodging of the devil, and happily we may thence pick out some English to this purpose. In the seaventh formidable exorcisme of his devil-whip, his Canon lyes thus: *Si energumenus non fuerit liberatus, et tamen urgente neces-sitate dimittenda sit conjuratio, tunc praecipe omnibus spiritibus remanentibus in corpore, eos cogendo ut recedant a capite, et corde, et stomacho, et descendant ad partes inferiores corporis.*[1] Heere you have the Canon for lodging the devil, that you be sure to lodge him not in the head nor stomack, but in the inferiour parts: an excellent proviso, teaching us that the devil is of the nature of a cup of new strong Sack, that cannot hurt a man if it be kept out of his stomack and head. But old *Lockwood* knew what he did in assigning the inferiour parts for a peculiar lodge for the devil. This was the traynd sent; he knew his dogges were old sures-by at this; this was the haunt they would not be halowed off. Let *Sara Williams* be my Interpreter for the rest.[2] *Sometime* (she saith) *they lodged the devill in her toe, sometime in her legge, sometime in her knee. Sometime, &c.* Let the devil and his holy charmers make up the rest.

Fie holy Fathers fie, is this the trailed sent you so greedily pursue with full crie and open mouth? Is this the game you hunt called gayning of soules? Is this the haunt you quest on in Italy, Spain, and England? Is this the foile you sent so hotely that neither Sea nor Land will make you at a fault, but that you call upon it still over hill and dale, through thick and thin, and make good the chase through Colledges, Cloysters, Palaces, houses, yea, even into hell it selfe; and thence start the devil, and hunt him a fresh, and lodge him with *Sara Williams* in such muses, conny-beries, and holes as the poore devil but for your hote pursuite would never have come in? It is wel that you quit the devil with gaining of some store of

[1]Mengus, Flag. Daem: [H]. The passage is from Exorcismus 7.

[2]See her examin: [H].

soules for hell, else can I not easily see how you could readily make him amends. It is high time to call off from this unsavory trayle. Alack poore honest devil, in this case farre more honest then the priest, that would not downe into his lodge without much adjuration, toyling, and sweat. Was it any mervaile, considering he was to be commaunded into so unseemely a lodge?

## CHAP. 13.

*Of dislodging, rouzing, and hunting the devill by the dreadfull power of the presence, approach, and bodily touch of a Priest.*

They that delight in hunting, being men of quality and sort, when they would entertaine their friends with that pleasing sport, doe use to have an Hare-finder, who setting the Hare before, doth bring them speedily to their game.[1] The company was many times great, and the strangers of note, that resorted to see and wonder at this coursing of the devill; and it was accordingly provided by the Hunt-maisters of the game that they had a devil ready lodged against any solemne hunting day, that the spectators might not be delayed with tediousnes before they came to their pastime. Thus all being seated, and standing at gaze for the game, the next office was to stirre and rouze the devill that the people might behold how he would bestirre himselfe. Unto this they have many potent Engines and meanes, some whereof had the ability both to course and expell the devill: but of the fearefull act of expelling I meane not heere to speake but onely of their various powerfull vertues of rouzing, chasing, and chafing the devill.

These dreadfull super-infernall powers doe flow either from the priests owne person or his adjuncts. In his person we consider his bodily presence and approach towards the possessed, his breath, his touch, his parts. His adjuncts are either belonging to his person, as his hose, his gloves, his girdle, his coyfe, his rags; or common to his office, as holy water, holy oyle, the holy candell, hallowed brimstone, the holy potion, *Avemaries,* invocation of Saints, the holy Crosse, the stole, the amice, the blessed Sacrament, and the corporall presence of our blessed Lady. Of these infernall whips according to their severall dignities and worth.

For the first, we are to understand that it is otherwise betweene a Priest and a devill then it is betweene an Hound and an Hare: for

---

[1]Harsnett's imagery from hunting reflects his love of the sport. In 1627 Sir Gawen Harvey bequeathed to Harsnett his entire kennel of beagles, "all but Nancy, which I give to Henry Mildmaie, of Wanstead" (William Addison, *Epping Forest,* 62).

an Hare, if she be formed, will sit sure, though the Hound doe trayle neere her and call hotly on the sent; but the devil stands in such bodily feare of the presence of a Catholique priest, that as soone as he comes in to the roome where the possessed is, he begins sometime to startle; and if hee approach neere, he rages as he were mad. Nay, many times hee will not endure his presence at all (notwithstanding we reade that the devill is so bold, as he dares to come into the presence of Almighty God), but he skuds out of the possessed as soone as ever he heares but tydings of the priests comming.

*Gordianus* the Emperour had a daughter possessed with a devill: and hearing that they had sent for *Tryphon* to come and exorcise the mayd, the devill did not endure forsooth to looke him in the face, but trusses up and away ere the holy man could come.[1] Some stay till the Exorcist be come within view, fearing (as seemes) cosenage, least for one an other should come; and as soone as he sees by his nose that it is his good Maister in deede, he slips closely away without taking any leave. Thus did a whole legion in a young man serve Bishop *Arnolphus: Quae mox viso* Arnolpho *episcopo discessit,* saith *Thyraeus:* no sooner had the devil descried his good face, but he was gone.[2]

Some punie rash devil doth stay till the holy priest be come some-what neere, as into the chamber where the demoniack doth abide, purposing, as seemes, to try a pluck with the priest: and then his hart sodainly failing him (as *Demas* when hee saw his enemie *Clinias* approach), cries out, he is tormented with the presence of the priest, and so is fierd out of his hold, to his greater disgrace.

This is an huge vertue in a priest, that casts so farre off. We doe not reade that the demoniacks in the Gospel did ever thus skud from our Saviour Christ; but that is to little purpose. God needed not so much to grace his sonne, who by the power of his Divinity was able to manifest himselfe to be the power of God; but our Exorcists being deemed in most places of the world for no better then jugling mates, there is great reason, pardy, they should be graced with more gracefull miracles then ever were accomplished by our Saviour Christ.

This frighting and tormenting power in presence of a priest is not given equally to al a-like, as the devils themselves are not all of a pitch. If he be an old sturdy devill, and stand out the priests presence, then as the priest hath this tormenting power in more especiall measure, and approaches in person neerer to the pos-

---

[1] Thyrae: 181. [H].

[2] Thyraeus, p. 181. [H].

sessed, the more is the devil in the party afflicted and tormented. *Marwoods* devil, being a tough weather-beaten spirit, was not much moved at the presence of *Stamp* the priest, who had this tormenting power as seemes but *remissis gradibus*. But when *Edmunds* came, and had invested himselfe in his holy roabes, heare how the devil fared, in *Edmunds* owne termes: *Jubet sacerdos ita ubi erat sacris indutus vestibus, ante se infirmum constitui,* *Edmunds* commanding in his sacred geare to bring in the demoniack and set him in his presence. And marke what followed: *Hic ille toto corpore contremiscere, et horrere, et aestuare caepit.* Instantly began the possessed to tremble, to have horrour, and rage thorough out his whole body. This the devil suffered at the meere presence of *Edmunds,* not onely before any dreadfull Exorcisme were thundred against him, but before any word was spoken by the Jesuit.

*Dibdale* the priest removes from *Hackney* to *Fulmer* in the night, and caries his trincket *Sara* behind him on a horse; shee felt her selfe so tormented with heate, sitting behind him, as she had much adoe to be kept from falling from her seate.

Heere the object was neere, the power wrought the stronger, but you shall see this power extended it selfe much farther then thus. *Trayford* comes behind plodding upon a Jade, and this tormenting heate from the person of the priest reaches unto him: hee felt such an exceeding burning in his head (saith the Authour of the miracles), as he cryed all the way as he rode, *water, water,* and yet we find this remove was the 8 or 9 of *November,* when men doe not commonly surfet of heat. This sprite-tormenting vertue is so top ful in the body of a priest, and of so potent an activity, as many times it runnes over, and many times issues from his person (as beames doe from the sunne) without his owne privitie or sence. And it hath not the qualities of *Stygian* fire alone, to scorch, burne, torment, and fugate the devil, but it hath a power Antiperistian besides, to repel and bandie backe the devil into his kenel againe, and this without any action, motion, or intendement of the priest; so as a priest may baffle a devil standing stone stil without stirring hand or mooving a foote. This befel to *Hilcho, Trayfords* sneaking devil: who, finding his corner grew too hote by the bodily approch of the Exorcist, would faine to refresh himselfe have come out at *Trayfords* mouth; but peeping out and finding the priests mouth approching somewhat neere, suddainly bolted backe againe as a cony from a net, and was faine to slip out closely at his right eare in the fashion of a Mouse. This *Dibdale* the priest neither knew nor dreamed, that he had reverberated the devil with the direful power of his holy hellish mouth; but *Sara, Trayfords* devil-felow, saw the attempt of the devil to come forth, saw his bandie backe againe, and saw his going out at *Trayfords* eare in the shape of a Mouse, and discovered the true cause why hee came not foorth: for the *neerenesse of the priests mouth to the mouth of the possessed.*

Now if any man wil aske me how it comes to passe that any devil could stay in the body of any party possessed whom the priests did visit, considering the frightful scorching heate, that issuing out of the bodie of the priest, did scald and torment the devil when the priest drew neere, and did make him to tremble, quake, and rage as you heard in *Marwoods* devil: I aunswer that the devils, as you have heard out of *Thyraeus,* were not all of a temper and constitution alike, but some could endure these scorching flames of the priests better then some. Next, the priests had not this hel fire all in a degree, but some burned the devil neere at hand, some a farre off, according to the proportion of hell fire that was in the priest; and thirdly, the priests did many times by their soveraigne power of priesthood hold the devil in by force for his greater torment, and manifestation of the power of the Romish Catholique Church; and first did toast and broyle him wel with theyr owne hel fire within the body of the possessed, and then did lay cart-loades of fire and Brimstone uppon his backe, and sent him to be broyled [a] thousand yeeres in the pit of hell.

The *Lancashire* devil in the wandering wench of whom you heard afore, cries out that hee was scalded and tormented by the priest, and desires hee might be gone. The priest tells him he shal not, but that he would torment him stil; and when he had so done, lodged him (as you have heard) in a most dangerous desperat place. Now it may be wondered by some plaine witted folkes, how the body of an holy priest doth catch such a fire that all the parties possessed did stil complaine they burned; and this burning was so sore in *Fid.* and *Sara* as the marks thereof are at this day to be seene.

These questionists must be sent to the Catholique Church to schoole, to learne to beleeve and to make no curious speculations. And sure it is without doubt, that a fell-burning heate they had in theyr bodies indeede; and the neerer they did approch to *Fid.* and *Sara* the more they felt theyr heate. Yet not to let any reasonable man goe away unsatisfied, wee wil take a little paines to open the case. True it is, that this devil-burning heat in the priests could not be any elementary fire, for that no element can effectuate beyond his owne Sphaere, and a devill having in his nature no elementarie combination, it is not possible hee should receive from any element any sensible impression. Much lesse can it be in the power of any naturall innate heate to torment a devil, for it fits not to *calor nativus* to scald or broyle at all. A caelestial heate least of all can it be conceited, for that his influence is sweet and helpful, tending to generation. There is but a fourth fire left, and that is the fire of hel, which beeing disputed and resolved by deepe Divines to be neither natural nor mixt of elementary condition, but the coales of Gods wrath and feareful indignation: if they cary in theyr bodies an heate that doth vex and torment a devil wheresoever they finde him, it can be no other then the heat of hel. For what other fire can vexe and torment the devil? I would be sorie they should be concluded of so hellish a disposition; it is far better to take it as *Sara* and all the rest of her fellow Comedians doe contest, that all was a *Stygian* comedy to make silly people afraid. A fier indeede she felt from the spritly power of the Priest, but it was of a more gentle and pleasing impression. And for that other part that she played, feigning that she was burned and tormented at the presence of a Catholique priest: that had she learned from the wise prompting of her skilful maisters the priests, who did stil harpe of that string in their ordinary narrations of strange possessions beyond seas, that *the possessed could not endure the presence of a Catholique priest.* Which she as an apt scholler observed for her cue, and acted it as comly and gracefully as you have heard. Thus much of the power of theyr bodily presence.

## CHAP. 14.

*Of the strange power of a Catholique Priests breath, and of the admirable fier that is in a Priests hands to burne the devill.*

*Plinie* in his naturall storie tells us of certaine people that doe *anhelitu oris enecare homines*, kill men with the breath that comes from their mouthes.[1] *Scaliger* recounts a whole linage of men that could *oculis fascinare*, bewitch with their eyes though they did not touch. The *Leno* in the Comedy is noted to be of so strong a breath that hee had almost blowne downe the young gallant that stoode in his way;[2] but the Poets tell us that hell hath a more deadly breathing then all, so as if a bird doe by chaunce flie over the Stygian flood she is quelled with the smell, and falls downe stark dead. We have heere to acquaint you with a breathing company of priests that for potency of breath doe put downe *Plinie,*

[1]Untraced. Perhaps Harsnett has reversed his references; Pliny (7.2.16–17) describes people who bewitch with their eyes.

[2]Perhaps a confused memory of Plautus, *Pseudolus* 1295–1301, where the slave Pseudolus belches in the face of the old man, Simo.

*Scaliger,* the bawde, hell, the devill and all; for the devill, who can wel enough endure the loathsome odours and evaporations of hell, is not able to endure the vapour issuing from the mouth of a priest, but had rather goe to hell then abide his smell.

Now what a monstrous coyle would sixe or seaven *ignivomous* priests keepe in hell if they should let loose the full fury of their blasts as *Aeolus* did upon the Sea, and distend their holy bellowes in consort amongst the poore ghosts? Were it not a plaine danger that they were likely to puffe all the devils out of hell? *Mengus* the Canonist for hel gives us a rule that if the devil be stubburne and wil not obey the formidable exorcisme of the priest, then that the priest shal *os suum quam-proxime ad energumenum admovere,* bring his mouth as neer to the possesseds mouth as he can; and by that time the devil hath tasted on his breath, if there be any life in him, hee wil be glad to stirre.

Heere now you see the reason why *Trayfords* devil rebounded at the dint of the Priests breath and was so glad to get him out at *Trayfords* right eare like a Mouse, rather then he would come out jump against the priests mouth. The little children were never so afrayd of hell mouth in the old plaies, painted with great gang teeth, staring eyes, and a foule bottle nose, as the poore devils are skared with the hel mouth of a priest.

Take an example from *Sara Williams* of the vigorousnesse of their breath. *Shee lay* (saith the penner of their miracles) *past all sence in a traunce, beeing utterly bereaved of all her sences at once. The priest no sooner came neere her, but she discerned him by the smell.* Was not this (trow you) a jolly ranke smel that was able to awake a poore wench out of a traunce? Verily these doe out-smel the devil by farre. For though the devil hath (as is commonly reputed) a fel ranke smel, yet I never heard of any that could discerne a devil by his smel.

The like soveraigne smel is in the sacrament of theyr Masse, for *Sara could alwaies* (saith our Authour) *verie exactly reckon up how many had communicated by discerning them by theyr smell.* But for this they may have an easie evasion: happily they had beene so deepe in the Challice, as a quick-sented man might have savoured them a far off without helpe of the devil. Their breath, which is nothing but ayre exhaled from theyr lunges, beeing (as you see) of this affrighting power over the devil: what may wee deeme of the power of theyr holie hands if they come once to be applyed to the devil?

First, theyr holy fingers had in them the same divine power, if not in an higher measure, that wee read to have beene in our Saviour Christ: with a bare touch of theyr finger, without any other ceremonie used by our blessed Saviour in like case, they restored hearing and sight to theyr patients beeing blind and deafe. So hath the *Miracle-Maister* cleerely set downe that *Sara* being bereaved of all her sences as in a traunce, the Exorcist toucheth her eares and eyes with his finger, and she sees and heares.

This is but a flea-biting to that which *Ignatius* his great grand-childe *Edmunds* exploited with his holy hand. *Jupiter* armed with his dreadful thunder never made hel so to crack. Heare it thorough the Jesuits own trumpet as himselfe hath proclaimed it to the world. *Vix dum exorcismos inchoare manusque imponere capiti, cum ille statim furere, in altum erigi, manibus pedibusque elaborare, sacerdotis manum depellere, omnia complere vocibus, juramentis, maledictis blasphemis.* Edmunds *had scarcely begun his adjuration, and layd his hand on* Marwoods *head, but he presently falls into a furie, stretches out his body, beats with his feete and hands, snatches at the priests hand, makes all to ring with crying, swearing, and blaspheming.* This was wel roared of a young devil for a *praeludium* to the play, uppon the bare touch of *Edmunds* hand. But marke when the devil grew hote with the continuing of this holy tricke and of hell (*Edmunds* hand) on his head still. *Sacerdos officium reparat, manum in capite tenens,* the priest falls a fresh to his worke, holding stil his hand on the possesseds head. Now begins hel to worke. *Hic novae tragoediae inusitatae voces et verba in omnium auribus insonant. Quid non venitis daemones (inquit) et tu* Pippine *(quod nomen erat infestantis daemonis) non vindicas? nihil opus, nihil auxilii in inferno reliqui est? auferte cito miserum, flammis tradite; sin minus communem hanc contumeliam vos non vultis aut non potestis vindicare, tum jacula, gladii, cultri, confodite me, ignis, pestis, canes, malum consumite. Domus non corruis? neque dehiscens me vult terra absorbere nec de caelo fulmen aliquod pessundare? Quis hoc tolerare, quis tantum incendium pati, quis ita (uti mille unguibus) discerpi unquam visus est?* that is: *Heere strange tragicall exclamations filled all our eares. Devils why come yee not? and thou* Pippin *(which was the name of the tormenting devill) doost thou not revenge my quarrell? is there no ayde, no succour left in hel? Take mee miserable caytife and hurle mee into the infernall flames: but if eyther you will not or cannot right this disgrace, then you launces, swords, and knives dash thorough me: fire, dogs, plague, mischiefe consume me, house fall upon me, earth swallow mee, lightning from heaven devoure mee: who can beare my burden? who can endure my heate? who can be thus torne in peeces, beeing rent with a thousand nayles?* Who would not think that hee heard *Hercules furens* or *Ajax flagellifer* newly come from hell?

Was ever *Prometheus* with his Vulture, *Sisyphus* with his stone, *Ixion* with his wheele in such a case? Did ever the God-gastring Giants whom *Jupiter* overwhelmed with *Pelion* and *Ossa* so complaine of theyr loade? Or *Phaeton* so bellow when he was burned with *Jupiters* flames, as poore *Marwood* heere bellowes and roares under *Edmunds* fierie flames, and all with the onely touch of his head with his *Ignatian* hand? Was it not by divine Oracle that his maisters name should be *Ignatius* when his disciple caried such an unsupportable waight of hel fier in his hand? Will not his hand be an excellent instrument for *Lucifer* in hel to plague, broile, and torment his infernall fiends, that hath such a fiend-tormenting power heere on earth? Now here pittifull *Marwood* goe on in his direfull notes.

*Apage (inquit) manum illam cum omnibus daemoniis. Take away that dreadfull hand, in the name of all the devils in hell. Ut me vexas et torques, nunquam sine cruciatibus sine incendio esse patiens? How doost thou vexe, how doost thou wring me? Thou art never but plaguing me with torment and fire.* Then cries he out of his head, his heart, his bowels, his bones. *Manum tamen non dimittit sacerdos.* Yet Edmunds *would not be moved to remit his hand,* but begins a new chase. *In sequitur manu per tergum, et cet. He pursues the devill downe along his backe, his reines, his close parts, his thighes, his legges,* usque ad talos, *downe to his ankle-bone:* Thence he fetches him backe againe with a *Susurrare,* downe his knee, his belly, his breast, his neck, and there graspes him round about the neck with both his holy hands, which cast the devil into so strange an agonie and passion, as *Edmunds* himselfe breakes forth into an exclamation: *Deus immortalis quanta tum ille passeus fuit? nec mille hominum linguas explicare posse existimo. Good God! into what a passion was he then cast? not the tongues of a thousand men (I imagine) can expresse it.*

A little tast of the inexplicable agony he gives us by this, that the sweat that flowed from *Marwoods* face was in such current streames as it was the office of one man to stand and dry them up. *Digitus* Ignatii *est hic:* this was the finger of *Ignatius* devil indeede, to teach a yong Popish Rakehell so cunningly to act and feigne the passions and agonies of the devil that the whole companie of spectators shal by his false illusions be brought into such commiseration and compassion as they shal all weepe, crie, and exclaime as loude as the counterfet devil; and the end and *plaudite* of the act must be this: *O Catholicam fidem! O fidem Catholicam, vere fidem, sanctam, castam, operatricem fidem: tu daemonibus terribilis, inferno formidabilis, tibi cedunt catervae, legiones daemonum contremiscunt ad tuas voces, tuas voces insuperabiles fugiunt, horrent, et te audire nolunt.* That is: *O the Catholique faith, O the faith Catholique, truly faith, holy, pure, powerfull faith: Thou art terrible to devils, formidable to hell, troupes submit to thee, legions of devils doe tremble at thy voyce, they flie from thy unresistable commaund, they quake, and dare not abide thy sound.* Now by that time *Sara* and her play- fellowes be come upon the stage, and have told you how they were burned and handled likewise, I doubt not but you will helpe their *plaudite* with an *O* too: *O diabolicam fraudem! O fraudem diabolicam! O diros actores! O ineptos spectatores!*

*Sara* was content to play the she-devil touching your presence and approach, and to grace you with an *Oh I burne, oh I cannot abide the presence of a Catholique.* Mary, when you came neerer then in manhood you should offer or she in modesty suffer, as to hunt her with your holy hote hands, she could in her woman-hood have beene content you would have forborne; but that way lay your game, and therefore there was no remedy but you would have your hunting sport. Your game being by hote chase embossed did commonly take soyle, and there you let him lodge, and hunted him a fresh upon the old foyle, and counter too, which none but Curres of an impure sent wil doe.

*Sara* saith you began with your fiery hands at her foot, and so up all along her leg, to her knee, her thigh, and so along all parts of her body, and that you followed the chase so close that it could neither double nor squat, but you were ready to pinch.

Was this a fayre chase for holy anointed priests to make, especially with those holy hands that had instantlie before celebrated the Holy Masse, blessed the chalice, made (as they suppose) a new God, elevated the Hoast, handled and devided the very body of Christ? to bring the same holy hands piping hote from the Altar to the chayre where *Sara* sate at Masse, to seize with the same hands upon her toe, slip them up along her legge, her knee, her thigh, and so along all parts of her body till you came neere her neck, and by the way with the same holy hands to handle, pinch, and gripe where the devil in his blacke modesty did forbeare, till you made her crie *oh?* And then you to crie *O, that* oh *is the devill?* Now the great devil pinch you all for me; and that I may say without malignity, for I wel know he dares not. You are so devil-holy all over, head, hart, and hands, that the devil dares not come neere you; and therefore you neede not to care a rush for either devil or hell, for you wil either with your holines make holy both the devil and hell, or make him crie *oh!* when you come there with your holy pinch.

*Fid. Williams* doth complaine (looke in their owne confessions) that with your holy hote burning hands you did hunt the devil counter in her too, and did toe-burne, shin-burne, knee-burne her, and so forth, till you made her crie *oh:* for they were the sweet paire of your holy devils that were alwayes in chase.

And heere we see the cause why *Trayford* was soone dispatched of his devil after a bout or two, and was never devil hunted from toe to top with your holy hote hands; nor Ma: *Maynie* was never troubled with this pinching sport, but *Sara* and *Fid.* stuck long in your fingers, or your fingers about them, and ever and anone they were at the holy chayre, and this dislodging, coursing, and pinching; the devil was still in their Parkes. Alack, the poore soules had no worse devils then *Trayford* and *Maynie* had, for *Maynie* had the soveraigne *Dictator* of hell in him; but their walke was faire for your course, their game pleasing, their sute hote, your sent fuller. And therefore no mervaile though your dogges, being curres, did hunt ryot so often after this fallow Deare.

And heere I must remember you that you were so fierie hote and so sharpe set upon this game that you forgat your Maisters *Mengus, Thyraeus, Sprenger, Nider,* and all; and did as schooleboyes doe when they have an *otium* to play, give a showt, and for hast of their sport cast satchel, bookes, and paper behind at their heeles. For in your graund *probato,* when *Sara* at my Lord *Vaux* his house was to receave her solemne graund exorcisme and so be quit the Court, this high day being held for her finall *quietus est;* where you should have had speciall regard to have dignified and graced every holy Engine in his due order and place serviceable to this great worke (as the Amice, the Albe, holy water, holy candell, the Crosse, *Brians* bones, and your Ma: *Mengus* his formidable devil-whip above the rest): you having *Sara* your game set faire in her forme, for joy and showt of your sport could not abstaine, but like *Lycurgus* his Hound that having an Hare and a kitchin pot set both before him, left the Hare and ranne to the pot and thrust in his head up to the eares, so you having in your hand your Ma: *Mengus* his dreadfull booke of Exorcisme entituled worthily *Fustis, fuga, flagellum daemonum,* the cudgel, the whip, and the flight of the devil (loe the furious force of your fierie heate), threw *Mengus* your devil-whipper away and ranne unto *Sara,* and with your burning hands catched *Sara* by the foot, and so fired the devill along till you made him slip out where no man must name.

Now a few questions I must soyle, and then I wil proceede to your holy geare. *1.* It may be asked how your hands came so holy as to shine at the top of your fingers like unto the sunne? Wherin you shal heare a peece of a Dialogue betweene *Fid.* and Ma: *Maynie* theyr Captaine scholler, who sitting by *Fid.* his pue-fellow, and a priest hard by them, did affirme that *unto his sight the priests finger and thumb did shine with brightnes, especially on the inner sides;* where-unto the priest aunswered that *it might well be so, because* (quoth he) *they were anointed with holy oyle when I was made priest.* At which words *Fid.* laughing and calling Ma: *Maynie* dissembling hypocrit, the priest said *It was not* Fid. *but the devill that did so laugh and rayle.* Heere you see a plaine reason how the priests hand comes shining and holy, and hath this pinching holy quality in it to cause a wench cry *oh;* and hee that wil laugh at this reason may hap to catch a devil. 2. If any curious merry head wil demaund what needs the Amice, the Albe, holy candle, holy crosse, holy brimstone, *Brians* bones, the sacrament, *Salve Regina, S. Barbara, Mengus* his devil-whip, his devil-club, his fray-devil, and the rest of that infernal rable, since the onely holy hands of *Edmunds* the Jesuit hath power alone to rouse, hunt, chase, baffle, broyle, and toste the devil, and to make him to roare that hel it selfe did quake and tremble, skudde and flye from his holy hand alone more fearefully and ghastfully then ever poore Mouse did tremble and flie from the sight of a glaring Cat?

To this I aunswer that as all starres doe not participate alike the light of the sunne, so all holy priests doe not receive alike the influence of this hel-tormenting fire; but as they come neerer to that *Fons caloris, Origo luminis, Oculus caeli, Ignatius* the fountaine of this holie-devil-driving heate as his name dooth import (as *Edmunds* his grand-child did), so are there more potent and abundant beames of that miraculous fire communicated unto them, able to fry and broyle all the devils in hell; and as they stand farther off from the pure raies of his hell-fiering face, so they are as the Moone, but spotted and sprinckled with this satanicall flame. *3,* If this wil not content you, but you wil pursue me with questions stil, and know why *Edmunds, Dibdale,* and some other who had the devils plenty of this devil-frying heat in theyr holy hands did not dispatch the devil quite, and fire him out of his denne at once with theyr holy hands alone, but elongated their worke, and tooke in the Albe, the amice, holy candle, holy host, and all the lousie holy wardrop to assist in the holy worke? I aunswer: this was theyr good nature, to take in those petty implements and to doe them some grace, that theyr mother holy Church, whose hangings they are, may thanke them for theyr labour, especially considering they grow now adaies somewhat fusty for want of cleane use. And lastly, if they should have dispatched hastily, much good hunting sport had been lost, the pleasure had been short, the action by facility would not have been so admirably esteemed, the holy Church had lost theyr applause; and the grace of the action, by sodaine quick passage, would have received much eclipse and diminution. And so I proceed to view their holy implements.

## CHAP. 15.

*Of the admirable power in a Priests gloves, his hose, his girdle, his shirt, to scorch the devill.*

Gentle Reader, thou must not mervaile to heare those supernaturall powers, spoken of before, to have beene lodged in the bodies of holy priests: considering that as the plague doth infect and hang in the implements and garments, and the leprosie upon walls and beames of houses, so wee finde those powerful vertues, which shewed themselves apparantly in the constitution of the Priests, to transfuse themselves, and inhaere as effectually in the priests gloves, theyr hose, theyr girdle, their shirts, their ragges, their patches, yea in the water that some of their powerful hands had been washed withall. So as these holy companions, if they had beene metamorphosed into Fishes, as *Ulysses* folowers were turned into swine, they would have proved notable good Cod-fish, of whom the Fishermen report there is no part within them nor without that is bad.

A little I doubt mee old *Thyraeus* is to blame, who painting a whole chapter with the glorious parts and qualities of an Exorcist, intituling his discourse *De Conditionibus Exorcistarum,* hee is silent in this Maister-qualitie, infixed in the temper and mould of a Priest,[1] or received from his splendent unction, that he should have this dreadful fire to burne out a devil; and so by convivencie doth smother it in his garments and implements too. *Thyraeus* was of some watry and earthy constitution, and likely dooth cantle all Exorcists by himselfe. Sure I am, we finde them as lively, quick, and mightie in operation in theyr exteriour ornaments as in theyr interiour complexion, and therefore we must not do them that wrong to bury them in oblivion.

*Maho, Saras* chiefe devil, with much adoe was compelled to tel his name, and the first word hee spake was out of *Saras* hand. Then was one of the priests gloves taken, and put uppon her hand; *Maho* durst not abide it, but went his way straight, and hee was so skared as we do not finde that ever he came there after. It seemes he had stepped thether only to grace the priests gloves; for you have observed that her hand was none of his ordinary haunt, or els, if he could not endure the glove by reason of some senting quality

---

[1] *De Daemoniacis,* Cap xxxviii. [H].

the priests hand had left behind him, wee may imagine the priest had beene using his hand holily and well when it savoured so strongly that the devil could not abide it. And now it is not without great cause, as you may see, that our Catholique Gentlewomen heere in England doe hold in such deere esteeme our wandring Catholique priests, enriching them with guilt rapiers, hangings, girdles, Jerkins, and coyfes more beseeming a noble man then a jugling Impostor to weare: if they receive no other possessive kindnesse (whereof wee all see they be no niggards of theyr store), yet this recompence at their pleasure they may entertaine, to have a precious payre of priested gloves so sprightly perfumed with the pure odour-spicing from the hands of a hote ghostly father, as they may use for a sure preservative against any sparrow-blasting or sprite-blasting of the devil. This precious odour against a devil, that dooth continually issue from their annointed complexion, dooth not onely ascend into theyr upper, and extend it selfe into theyr utter ornaments, as into their gloves; but it descends also, and distils into theyr inferiour habit, and for want of a fit receptacle is readie many times to drop out at their heeles. *Dibdale, Saras* ghostly Father, had of his fatherly kindnesse lent his ghostly child a payre of his old stockins that happilie had seene *Venice* and *Rome;* she as a spiritual token of his carnall kindnes doth weare them on her legs. See thys odoriferous vertue, in what exceeding measure it had discended downe and filled the very seames of *Dibdales* hose. *Saras* devil had been very turbulent and stirring in her body, and was to be delivered downe to his baser lodge; he passed quietly downe til he came at her knee, and comming downe hil too fast, slipt ere he was aware into *Saras* legge, where finding himselfe caught within the priests hose beeing on her legge, he plunges and tumbles like a Salmon taken in a net, and cries harro ho, out alas, pul off, pul off, off in all hast with the priests hose, or els he must marre all, for there he could not stay: and all hast was made accordingly to ease the poore devil of his paine, and let him lie at his repose; and was not this a goodly ginne to catch a Woodcocke withall, and cause him to shoote out his long bil and cry *O the vertue of the priesthood, ô the power of the Catholique Church,* when they saw with their owne eyes the hose hastily snatched off, heard with their owne long eares *Saras* devil cry *oh,* beheld her legge quiet when it was bare without the hose, and observed how reverently the priests touched, handled, and bestowed the hose when it was off, and with what elevation of their eyes to heaven they finished the wonder.

I cannot but wonder that in the heate of theyr zeale, love, and admiration of the holinesse of the priests, the spectators did not runne uppon them at once, as the daughters of *Scaeva* the Jew did upon the Exorcists;[1] and of pure holy zeale rend, snatch, and teare off all their holy apparel from off their backs, even unto their bare, and catch and carrie away, some a peece of the Priests coate, some a ragge of the amice, some a patch of his breeches, some a corner of his shirt, and lay them up in an holy casket for reliques against a raynie day. The priests themselves doe full devoutly casket up as homelie and brayed wares as these, God wote. Heere make you no doubt, but all more then comely hast was made to pull off *Dibdales* hose, that the devil might quickly cabin in his lodge; for there was the devils covert where they were said to rouze him, when they came to the next hunt, with their fiery holy hands: which was not long intermitted (as the wenches doe wofully complaine), the priests having a ranke itch in their fingers to be fidling at that sport.

You are next to be informed that this devil-killing vertue did not lye in the priests head onely, as the poyson of an Adder doth, nor yet in his taile alone, as the light of a Glow-worme, but was universally diffused over all and every part of his body, and so transfused into all and every part of the apparel that came neere his body. *Campians* girdle that he wore (as seemes) at *Tiburne*[2] (and I wonder how they missed the roape that embraced his holy necke), being enritched with an outlandish grace that it came from *Jerusalem* (as Fa: *Edmunds* tells us), and had there girded about the sepulcher of our Saviour Christ, shal tell you stranger newes then *Dibdales* stockins did.

*Marwoods* devil being a stiffe resty spirit, of kin (as seemes) to a malt-horse of *Ware*[3] that wil not out of his way, had beene conjured at *Hackney* by *Stemp* and other priests by the space of a moneth. *Mengus* his club, his whip, his scare-devil, had beene many and sundry times assayed, the invocation of the blessed Trinity many times used, *Missa de spiritu sancto (Edmunds* owne words) *celebrata: A choise Masse of the holy Ghost had beene celebrated,* dreadfull infernall Exorcismes had been thundered abroad, *Hic tamen nihil quicquam sentire visus est:* The sullen spirit seemed not to care for it a rush. But when *Edmunds* came in

---

[1] Acts 19:13–20. Harsnett's memory of the text is confused. The exorcists were the seven sons of Scaeva, who "took upon them to call over them which had evil spirits the name of the Lord Jesus." The spirit answered, "Jesus I know, and Paul I know, but who are ye?" He then "leaped upon them, and overcame them, and prevailed against them, so that they fled out of that house naked and wounded."

[2] See Edmunds tract: [H].

[3] Hertfordshire was famous for its horses. "Their teams of horses oft-times deservedly advanced from the cart to the coach, are kept in excellent equipage, much alike in colour and stature, fat and fair" (Fuller, *Worthies,* 229).

*accepto bissino*[1] *quodam funiculo, quem ipse* Edmundus Campianus *semper secum gestabat, et in sacrificiis utebatur (quem Salvatoris sepulchrum vinxisse* Hierosolymis *solebat dicere), hunc Sacerdos ad latus applicuit: Ad cuius contactum hic statim trepidare et conturbari coepit, doloremque eius presentia in aliam corporis partem concessisse, qua ille re perspecta energumenum esse manifesto deprehendit.* Taking in his hand a certaine silken twist which Fa: *Campion* did alwayes cary about with him, and used it at the celebration of the Masse, and which he often said had beene at Jerusalem, and girded our Saviours tombe: applied the same gently to *Marwoods* side, at the touch whereof he presently began to tremble and turmoile, and the paine of his side shifted into a new place, whereby *Edmunds* discerned that *Marwood* was a Demoniack in deede.

What a wonderfull Saint-maker is *Tyburne* by this, that in a quarter of an houre shall miscreate a Saint, whose girdle or twist (provided it be worne by the old Saint at the gallowes) shal put downe at scaring of a devil *Mengus* his club-devil, whip-devil, scare-devil, the Masse, the invocation of God, our Saviour Christ, the holy Ghost, and all? I doe very much mervaile there were never strange miracles performed by the wood of those trees, considering it hath beene blessed by some of their sacred bodies, and bedewed with their last spritefull breath, which have power to infuse their soveraigne vertue into more remote objects, and into things of as hard and repugnant a consistence. It seemes they have changed courses with the transfusion of miraculous vertue imagined by their idle braines to issue from our blessed Saviour at time of his death: whose coates that he wore at his blessed passion they leave as bare and naked, without any powerfull miraculous vertue at all, and bestow all his divine influences upon the holy Crosse. Contrariwise, these communicate all the riches of their miraculous graces upon their girdles and cloutes, and leave nothing for the poore gallowes to grace them withall.

But this holy potent girdle is not thus barely left. You shal heare *Edmunds* gracing it in an higher straine. *Patris etiam* Campiani *sacrum illum funiculum ad latus, et os unus ex circumstantibus admovit: quin ille iterum vehementer execratur et detestatur omnes eiusmodi res, ore discerpit, mandit dentibus, conspuit, daemoni commendat illam rem, quae tantam ei molestiam faceret, tantum excruciaret, corpori et animae ad omnia extrema perpetienda causa esset.* One of the by-standers takes father *Campian* his

---

[1]Harsnett translates *bissino* as "silken," but Du Cange glosses *bissinica* as *vestio candida,* and in medieval Italian *bissinica* meant "fine linen." I have not traced Weston's form. Campion's *bissinus funiculus* or "linen cord" will have been his priest's cincture.

sacred girdle, and with it touches the mouth and side of the possessed; he againe curses and detests all manner such geare, he
teares it with his mouth, bites it with his teeth, spits upon it amaine,
wishes the devil take that ill-favored thing that troubled him so
much, vexed him so sore, and was the cause of his extreame torments, both in body and minde.

Now take with you, I entreate you, a short and sweet Dialogue
betweene the Jesuit and the devil. *Sed quid nam (inquit Sacerdos)
pessime daemon, fatere veritate (non quod ego abs te, qui mendax
ab initio fuisti, veritatem volo discere) quid isto funiculo ita
torqueris, qui vel fortissima quaeque mundi tam facile contemnis?
unde ergo venit?* Wicked fiend (saith *Edmunds*) come on, goe to
now, and tell true (not that I desire to learne truth of thee, that hast
beene a lyer from the beginning), what is the cause thou art so cruelly tormented with this girdle, who doost not care for the potentest
thinges that are in the world? Whence then proceedeth this? Thus
farre *Edmunds* the devil *senior*. Now heare *Edmunds* devil *Junior*,
or *Marwood*, *Edmunds* ghost. *Hierosolyma (inquit) bene novit, ad
quem pertinuit;* Tiburnus *non ignorat (qui locus erat, ubi pater
ipse* Campianus *martyrio coronatus erat). Tum Sacerdos
assistantes compellat: testes inquit estote, patris* Campiani
*clarissimi martyrii, cuius hic vel minutissimus funiculus, quem ipsi
prius in vita nunquam viderant, tantas illi faces miserat. Jerusalem*
(quoth the devil) knowes whose girdle it is. *Tiburne* (the place
where Fa: *Campian* received his crowne of martyrdome) is wel
acquainted with it. Heere *Edmunds* calls aloude to all the standers
by: beare witnes my maisters of Fa: *Campians* most glorious martyrdom, whose smallest cord, which before that time they had
never seene with their eyes, hath cast the devil into such an heate.

See heere three most grave and authentike witnesses of a
Romish Saint: *Jerusalem, Tyburne,* and the devil. And the poore
gulls that held the candell to the devil called in for the fourth, to
make up a messe. *Campians* Saintship had been in a faire taking
but for the gallows and the devil; and would it not doe any man
good to be thus Sainted from hel?

And now the devil was a Sainting, and that his hand was in, it
was much over-seene of *Edmunds* the Presenter that he did not
name him *Story, Felton, Sommervile, Arden, Parrie,* and *Lopez*,[1]

---

[1]Six famous Elizabethan treason cases. John Story (1510–71) was the first professor
of civil law at Oxford. He left England under Edward VI, returned under Mary, and took
part in the suppression of heresy, serving as Queen's proctor at the trial of Cranmer. At
Elizabeth's accession he again left England and settled in Flanders as a Spanish subject.
In 1570 the English kidnapped him and took him into England, where he was tried for
treason, found guilty, and executed 1 July 1571. He was beatified by papal decree, 1886.
John Felton was a Catholic layman who published the papal bull *Regnans in Excelsis*
deposing Elizabeth by fixing it to the gate of the bishop of London's palace, 15 May

and the rest of that Saint-traytorly crue whom Tiburne and the devil were as familiar with-all as with S. *Campian,* I wis; and knew as wel the causes, motives, and end of their Saint-ships alike, the devil himselfe having beene the Author and inspirer to them all, and therefore no doubt but he would have beene as kinde to them as to S. *Campian;* and the more the merier, and the greater shout and applause would have beene of the holy Traytorly rout that were lookers on, and the *Echo* the shriller when they cried: *O Catholicam fidem! O fidem Catholicam!* And if they be not already sainted with the devil (as I trust if they be dead, God gave them better grace), but if they be living, and stand as lewdly affected to these diabolical cosenages as heere they did when they held the devil, alias *Edmunds,* the candel, it is to be hartily wished they were sent to the Creator of the Romish Saints, *Tiburne* their *Coronator,* by him to be convayed where Gods mercy shal designe.

But the close of this Dialogue betweene *Edmunds* and the devil, or the devil *Edmunds* and *Edmunds* the devil (for he played both parts himselfe), is the pretiest of all. *Campians* dreadful girdle had so heat the devil and intoxicated his braine as it made the devil to cry out, as you have heard: *O me stultum et infelicem, qui ista dicerem!* O foole and wretch that I am for saying thus much! Heere you see the devil was cleane gone, and confesseth himselfe to be out of his wits. And this was but an admotion, or touch, of the gir-

---

1570. Convicted of treason, he was hanged in front of the palace 8 August 1570. He too is now beatified. John Somerville was a young Catholic gentleman of Warwickshire, married to Margaret, daughter of Edward Arden of Park Hall. In midsummer 1583 he became affected with "a frantic humour" that to free his religion from persecution he must "die for the commonwealth." On 24 October said he would go to court and shoot the Queen with his "dag." He made no secret of his intention, and assaulted several people on the way to London. He was arrested, confessed, and implicated his father-in-law, his wife, and a priest, Hugh Hall, living at Park Hall as a gardener. At his trial, 16 December 1583, he pleaded guilty. The others pleaded not guilty, but his father-in-law was condemned with him. The women and the priest were pardoned. Somerville was later found strangled in his cell at Newgate. Edward Arden was executed 20 December. His and Somerville's heads were exhibited at London Bridge. Edward Arden (1542–83), head of an ancient and illustrious family of pre-Conquest descent, and William Shakespeare were kinsmen by common descent from Walter Arden of Park Hall, Shakespeare's great-great-grandfather. The facts and arguments relating to this genealogy are set out elegantly and concisely by Smart, *Shakespeare,* 59–65. For William Parry, arrested 1585 for plotting to assassinate the Queen, see Read, *Walsingham,* 2:399–405. Roderigo Lopez was a Portuguese Jew who professed Christianity, settled in England in 1559, and became chief physician to the Queen in 1586. When a claimant to the Portuguese throne came to England in 1592, Lopez involved himself in intrigue on his behalf. The earl of Essex denounced him as a traitor and accused him of plotting to poison the Queen and the pretender, Don Antonio. Although the Queen consistently supported him, he was tried and convicted, 28 February 1594. His execution was delayed until June, and after his death the Queen, by exercise of the prerogative, allowed his family to inherit his goods (*DNB;* Roth, *History of the Jews,* 140–43).

dle; what would this sacred twist have done if it had girt the devil about as it girt our Saviours Tomb at Jerusalem? Verily it cannot be imagined what hel-work it wold have wrought: the devil had certainly become a bedlamit at the least, and then his keeper would have had some-what adoe; the club and the whip and all must have walked.

Meane while *Campians* Saint-ship comes of a faire house, and hangs by a goodly three-fold threed. For the devil heere now, when he dubbed him and proclaimed him a Saint, is in *Edmunds* censure a lier, in his own confession a foole, and by imputation a devil; and so he was created by a devil, a foole, and a liar. And these three in one was none but *Edmunds* alone, the Author, Actor, and penner of this play, who deserves as worthily to be crowned at *Tiburne* for this foolish, fond, impious diabolical fascination, and to be proclaimed from hell for an infernal Saint, as ever *Campian* and his complices did.

I have their shirt behind, as the last service to the devils nunchion. Which because it is not so cleanly as I could wish, *Fid.* (the Laundresse to these devils incarnat) shal serve in this dish. *Fid.* was washing in mistris *Peckhams* kitchin a bucke of foule cloathes, amongst the which was one of the priest-Exorcists shirts.[1] The devil comes sneaking behind her, trips up her heeles, and pitches her on her hip; and upon that advantage takes possession of her (as it seemes by the story), for from that fall she grew to be possessed. And wote you why the devil playd her this unmannerly sneaking tricke? The *Miracle-maker* tels us it was because shee was washing out a foule shirt of one of the priests, and what further matter, their examinations may with lesse offence to your modesty report then my selfe. I proceede to their priestly attire.

## CHAP. 16.

*Of the wonderfull power in a Priests Albe, his amice, his maniple, his stole, to whip and plague the devill.*

The Heathen who saw not God and things intelligible with a cleere eye, but with the owle-light of nature and glimse of theyr owne discourse, did deeme of spirits and devils that they were *aëreae substantiae,* of an ayrie patible substance, or els that they were the spirits of naughty men departed this life. According to theyr dimme conceit they had superstitious devises, by sacrifices and charmes, *placandi manes* and *imperandi* both, sometime to

[1]See her examin: [H].

please them, somtime to commaund them, as you may see by *Virgil* and other Poets, in *Aeneas* and *Theseus* descensions into hel. Their pleasing and soothing their angry *daemones* was by sacrifice; their controling, checking, and commaunding them was by charmes, fumigations, execrations, lights, sacred vestments, and scepters of their consecrated priests.

Our Papisme, the corruption of the sincere worship of Christ, beeing naught els but a perfect apisme and imitation of Gentilisme and Hethenish superstition, doth naught els but play over all the toyes, tricks, and trumperies of Ethnick superstition againe, especially in this matter of scaring, tormenting, and afflicting of the devil, not only with the body, breath, smel, touch, but with the ordinary apparel, as hose, gloves, girdle, shirt, and as you shal now hear, with the exterior ornaments of a sacred priest, as his amice, his albe, his stole, and the like.[1]

The difference betweene a Pagan and a Popish priest, as I take it, is this, that the one doth seriously and in good sadnesse perswade himselfe that his halowed person, charmes, and consecrate attire, as his scepter, his crowne, and Albe, doth awe, terrifie, and depel the devil indeed; the other doth not in earnest so thinke or dreame, but doth know the cleane contrary, that there is neither vertue, ability, nor proportion in any of these gewgawes to move or stil the devil, no more then there is in a white sheet to scare a sober man; but dooth onely of impious policie act, fashion, and play them, *ad terrorem incutiendum, et fucum faciendum populo,* to gull, terrifie, and amaze the simple ignorant people, and by bringing them into an admiration of the power of their priest-hood, the sanctitie of theyr attire, and the divine potencie of theyr Romish Catholique church, by this meanes to enchaunt and bewitch their innocent simple soules, and so to offer them up for a pray to their great Idole at *Rome.*

[1] Alb, from late Latin *alba,* as in *vestis alba,* a white tunic or shirt; in ecclesiastical use a white linen vestment reaching to the ankles, a kind of long surplice with close sleeves, bound at the waist with a girdle or cincture. The amice, from Latin *amictus,* a cloak, has two forms: 1) a cap or hood, later the academic hood, made of or lined with fur, worn by prebendaries, canons, and singing men in pre-Reformation times, and still correct dress (as the academic hood) for the officiant at the Church of England choir offices; and 2) a eucharistic vestment, a white linen neckpiece, put on before the alb, and sometimes worn with an apparel or decorative panel surrounding the neck. This latter is probably the vestment used by the exorcists. The maniple, from Latin *manipulus,* "a handful," is a strip of material two to four feet long, attached to the left arm near the wrist of the celebrant, deacon, or subdeacon at mass. It derives from the napkin used by Roman officials at court and symbolizes Jesus' washing of his disciples' feet. It is now abolished in the Roman church. The stole is a narrow strip of silk or linen, worn over the shoulders, often elaborately decorated. It is a sign of priestly authority, worn at the administration of the sacraments and, with the surplice, at exorcisms. Hence its association with exorcism, as by Greene, *Friar Bacon and Friar Bungay,* 4.3: "Conjuring and adjuring divels and fiends, / With stole and albe and strange Pentagoron."

See *Tirrell, Stemp,* and *Thomson,*[1] three Rectors of this devil-tragaedie, doe put off theyr Romane visards and tel us jumpe as much. It was theyr good nature, or rather Gods good grace, they should deale so plainly with us; but we need not be beholden to them for this necessarie kindnesse one jote: for by that time all the parts of this tragedie have been acted on the stage, you have never a child of tenne yeeres that is a looker on, but will see and discerne their grosse packing, rude bungling, and palpable jugling so apparantlie, as hee wil dare to take the devil by the visard, and play with the fooles nose, and cry, away with the priest and the devil, they have marred a good play.

We are now come to their hunting and chasing the devil with their holy attire. In a wel sorted cry of hounds the dogs are not all of a qualitie and sise: some be great, some of a midle, some of a low pitch; some good at a hote chase, some at a cold sent; some swift and shalow, some slow and sure; some deepe and hollow-mouthed, some verie pleasant, and merrie at traile. So is it in this consorted kennel of hell, and in these direful engines and Machines of the Romish Church to rouse, chase, and torment the devil. The bodie and hand of a sacred priest (yee see) are greater torments to the devil then hel. His girdle, gloves, and hose, they are the devils scorpions and whyps (as neerest unto the origen and fountaine it selfe); but his exterior ornaments, though ornaments of his office (as his Amice, his Albe, his stole), yet beeing more remote, and so participating the vertue of the priest but in weake degrees, be in this devil-hunting sport in stead of little beagles to fill up the cry: and yet by your leave sometime they give the devil a shrewd pinch, and therfore they be worth the whistling out, and not to be left in the Popes kennel at home.

It is not a light argument of the sacred power of an *Amice* against a spirit, that the reporter of the Miracles tells us that a priest layd it uppon *Saras* face to prevent illusions, and that a spirit puffed at it and could not endure to let it alone. It had as seemes a choaking quality to suffocat a devil. And indeede *Lustie Dicke,* that devil, for all his lustier parts, had endured a shrewd chase by a long exorcisme a little afore, and shewed himselfe a lustie stout devil of a large winde and lasting breath, that hee sunke no sooner; and nowe beeing cleane spent and lying at bay, it was but an hard part of the priest, when he found him panting and gasping for ayre after so hote and sore a chase, not to breathe the devil a little, but to come upon him with a suffocating *Amice* to quel him out-right.

Now *Sara* tels us that it was she her selfe that puffed at the holy *Amice,* as beeing none of the sweetest. But who was likest to know

---

[1] See Tirrels exam: and Fids. [H]. The reference to Fid is mistaken.

best whether shee or the devil puffed? I hope the priest, who knew the devil as readily by his puffe as the devil did him by his smel. The priest shewed a good wit in taking the devil so soone. This holy relique lay pent for want of a grace from the devil, and the devil beeing brought so low had nothing but a puffe, or a worse ayre, to vent upon it.

The holy *Stole* was brought three or foure times uppon the stage, and shewed it selfe an *Antidaemoniack* of special account, manifesting it selfe to be a true implement and hanging of the devil-quelling church. First it served in the nature of a stop-devil in Fa: *Edmunds* own hand,[1] who after he had belabored the devil with his holy hands into *Marwoods* head, and finding his hands heavy with the massie waight of vertue that was compacted in them: he took the sacred *Stole,* and wound it about *Marwoods* neck, and so begirt the devil in *Marwoods* head, where the devil lay so pent by the vertue issuing out of the blessed *Stole,* as he stared, fumed, and fomed as he had beene starke mad, and in the end was squeased out with pure violence, as water out of a squirt.

The *Miracle-master* tels us of an heroical combat performed betweene *Maho* and the priest, during seaven houres long, when *Maho* the devil, standing uppon his guard, would not come in. He was summoned by the priest first with *Mengus* club, then with his whip, with holy water, *Salve regina, Ave maria,* the great Heralds for hell. *Maho* stoode out till the priest prepared him selfe (saith the Author) to afflict him with the *Stole,* and then he came in and yeelded to parly or dialogue with the priest, in a milde and temperate voyce. See the power of the Catholique Romish church, whose seeliest ragge hath power to change the devils roaring note, and to cause him to speake in a milde moderate key.

This blessed implement hath in it, as you see, a stinging cord for a devil more then *Mengus* whip; and how was the poore devil then rent, battered, and torne, may we deeme, when for not telling his name he was enjoyned untrusse, and to take quietly five lashes with the *Stole,* and (that which was worst of al, and I am sure went most against his stomacke, being an haughty spirit) was commaunded to kisse the rod, and to say over, with a lamentable trembling voyce fifteen *Ave maries,* five for our Ladies five sorrowes, five for her five joyes, and five for her five glories.[2]

---

[1]See Edmunds tract: [H].

[2]These are the fifteen mysteries of the rosary: the five joyful mysteries (the annunciation, visitation, nativity, presentation, and finding in the temple); the five sorrowful mysteries (the agony in the garden, the scourging, the crowning with thorns, the carrying of the cross, the crucifixion and death of Jesus); the five glorious mysteries (the resurrection, the ascension, the descent of the Holy Ghost, the assumption, and the coronation of the blessed Virgin Mary).

And all this the devil most dutifully performed, like a dutiful obedient sonne to his curst holie Mother, the holy church of Rome. But heare you, fellow Comedians: heere you had like to have spoiled the play, for you belaboured your *Fid,* your fellow she-devil, with your *Stole* so hard, as she whined indeed, and in choler had like to have pulled off her devils vizard, and shewed her owne face, and to have told the Spectators that she was *Fid.* your kinde fidler in deed, and no he-devil, God wote, and that she knew the time when you would have laboured her more kindly; for she felt this stole-whipping three or foure dayes after, and had the marks of it uppon her armes longer to be seene.[1] But she remembred you would finde time and place with kinder usage to make her amends, therefore she was content for once to beare it.

*Latet anguis in herba:*[2] a man would little suspect, when he meetes with the *Amice,* the *Stole,* and the *Maniple,* wound up in a little casket, that there were such blacke hel-mettal within them to excoriat and lancinate a devil; and it grieves me, I confesse, when I see our little children, when they have them, how they in a natural childish instinct doe take them for fit gawdes to trick up their babies with-all, and themselves doe put them for sport, some upon their owne fingers, some upon their breasts, some upon their foreheads; and a little I muse when I see it (considering the infused divine vertue, inherent in this sacred geare, to discover, manifest, and torment the devil), how it commeth to passe that we and our children being in *Edmunds* and the Catholiques opinions all of us possessed, that these potent Engines doe not shew forth their manifesting, tormenting vertue in none of our little children, and cause them to tumble, foame, and speake fustian, as they doe in theyr owne.

To this may be aunswered that we and our children be out of their church, and so out of the sphere of the activitie of these holy Jewels, and then that this is not a seated fixed vertue in these novels,[3] but a moving transitive grace that goes out and in in them like a shittle in a Weavers loome. But *Sara* and *Fid* doe furnish us with an apter and fuller aunswer then both; that is, that we are not *idonea subjecta,* not fit matter for these devil-powers to work

---

[1] See her exam: [H].

[2] Virgil, *Eclogues* 3.93. Proverbial: "There's a snake in the grass."

[3] The vestments are novelties because they are not scriptural. For this reason the more extreme Protestants argued against their use in the Church of England. Harsnett's own strongly Protestant origins show in this and similar passages, but by 1603 when he was archdeacon, canon, rector, and vicar, he disliked antivestiarian Protestantism. His funeral brass shows him fully vested as a bishop with mitre and crozier. His appeal to strong Protestant feeling in passages like this is calculated and insincere.

upon, till we have been at their schoole, and have learned to spel our horne-booke and the Crosse rowe with them. For they themselves at first were no more moved with an *Amice* and a *Stole* then they were with a dish-clout and a malkin, til they had taken out an holy lesson out of the priests play bookes, and then they felt an heate that they wist not of before.

It is a currant tale of *Achilles,* that his mother *Thetis* dipped him in the Sea all but his heele, and so made him impenetrable against the point of any weapon. Our holie Exorcists have surely beene plunged in the River *Styx* in their holy attire, for they have neither speck of their body nor ragge belonging unto them, but it is helproofe and devil-proofe altogether; and that which *Achilles* had not, it hath besides a power destructive and triumphant over hel and the devil. The Priests poore *Maniple* that an ignorant Landresse would scarce have bestowed the wrincing upon, put about *Trayfords* neck (saith the *miracle-founder*), baricadoed up the devil in *Trayfords* head that he durst not stirre, and there he stoode so distressed for want of provant that with a penny Mousetrap you might have caught him without a bayt at *Trayfords* right eare.

These priests ditements being severally so many infernal serpents and Scorpions to sting and bite the devil, what would you say if you see the poore devil ensnared in them altogether, and entangled in this sacred geare as *Mars* was in *Vulcans* net? How pittifully, imagine you, would he look, to see himselfe so priestbitten as *Aesops* Foxe was flie-bitten; and how would hee winch, skip, and curvet, having so many fiery needles in his skin at once? In this woful plight the wonder-writer presents him to your view, telling you that for encrease of his torment they stripped *Sara* of her garments, and put uppon her body all the priests implements at once; and then how they tricked *Saraes* devil, being adorned with their priestly robes, let the devil or *Sara* tell:[1] I have other Cod fish in water that must not be forgotten.

# CHAP. 17.

*Certaine questions aunswered, concerning the Church of Rome her making and accumulating yet more dreadfull tooles and engines for the devill.*

There is no good natured man (as I thinke) that should heare of these various and dreadfull whyps spoken of before to be inflicted

[1] See her exam: [H].

upon the devils backe in a fierie consort at once, but would have some feeling remorse of the paines of the devil, and say with the wofull man, *nunc non est novae plagae locus:* there is no free place left uppon the devils skinne for any new lash. But when this good natured man shal heare of the more various and more direful not whips but scorpions, stings, and fiery serpents of the holy Church; the blacke gloomie armour, embellished with the thicke smoake and vapour of hell; the swords, darts, and speares of fire, pointed with grisly death, that the Church doth arme her infernall souldiers (the Exorcists) withall against the princedome and power of hell, hee will cry out with *Marwoods* tormented devil, *terra dehisce, ne sentiam illas plagas,* earth swallow mee up before I come neere the scorch of those flames.

And these are in a blacke row, as they stand in the blacke Miracle booke, holy water, holy candle, halowed frankensence, halowed brimstone, the potion, the crosse, the sacrament, *Tiburne* reliques: the picture of an Asse burnt in fire, nick-names to the devil, the picture of our Lady, *Ave Maries, salve Reginaes,* the presence of S. *Barbara,* and the presence of our Lady: which you must read over very silently, least the devil hearing the names, you heare him presently roare uppon you for feare.

The Poets, to strike us with a terror of the torments of *Styx,* doe present before our eyes the three *Eumenides* sisters, the Furies and tormentors of hell, with black ugly visages grisly with smoake, with whips of blood and fire in theyr hands, theyr armes gored with blood, and a huge bunch of a thousand snakes crawling down theyr haire. Let me present you an Exorcist armed by the Church at all poynts to encounter hell and the devil, you wil laugh the *Eumenides* from off the stage. First I must set him before your view (as hee is in shew) a thumbe-annointed priest accomplished in his holy geare, in his albe, his amice, his maniple, and his stole; now imagine him as he is indeed, and as you have heard of him for hel, his body a piller of burning brasse, his hands flames of fire; his gloves, his girdle, his hose, his shirt, lumps of sea-coales of hell; his amice, his maniple, and his stole, streamers of scorching smoake; the sacrament of gore-blood in one hand, the crosse of tormenting coales in the other; sprouting out holy-water with his mouth, breathing out fire and brimstone at his nostrils, evaporating frankinsence at his eyes, the picture of an asse burning brimly at his eares, his head crawling with dead-mens bones, the picture of our Lady flashing at his breast, nicknames of fire and blood running upon his backe, *ave-maries* and *salve Reginaes* sparkling downe to his heeles: what a little hel doe you imagine walking uppon the earth? And ere you stirre your imagination, doe but imagine him a little further, walking in our London streets a little before day light, what time the Chimny-sweepers use to make theyr walke, and crying in his hellish hollow voyce, *hay ye ere a devil to drive? hay yee ere a wench to fire? hay yee ere a boy to dispossesse?* What a feare trow yee would the spirit be in to heare young hell thus roare, and how would he labour to get out at the parties breech, as *Hiaclito* did at *Trayfords,* before hee would dare to looke this hell-mouth on the face?

Heere now comes in a bundle of *Quaeres* that steppe over our way, and will needes have parlie with us ere we go any further. First, whence derive these fierie weapons theyr vigor and strength of goring the devil, which you call the publique armes and ensignes of the Church? To this I aunswer that these publique weapons of holy Church, that you have heard, some have their strength and power of themselves, as the sacrament and the Crosse; some of the institution of holy Church, as exorcismes, *ave-maries, salve Reginaes, et caet;* some from the consecration and halowing of the Church to these potent ends and effects, as holy water, holy candle, holy brimstone, holy Frankensence, and the holy potion, nick-names, and the Asses eares.

And if heereuppon a *Quaerist* wil demaund, *ad quid perditio haec?*[1] what needes the holy Church to open her Armorie for hel, and muster out her fiery weapons in such troupes and throngs, considering that every one of theyr thumb-annointed priests (as yee have heard) doth at his holy unction receive this heate and fire into his hand and his body by the oyle of his thumbe: wherby he is able with all his holy implements that hang uppon his backe to fire out the strongest devil in hel with his owne proper hands and his hote holy geare; as *Edmunds* did *Marwoods* devil, and *Dibdale* did fire *Maho* out of *Sara* with his fiery engines: this *Quaerist* I see doth not wel observe.

I have touched before, that though every priest be indeed annoynted with holy oyle on his thumbe, and by that oyle doth receive in that devil-burning heate that doth dilate it selfe through his body, garments, and all; yet, because every priest doth not bring his thumb prepared and qualified alike, but some have a Millers, some a souters, some a Coliers thumb, that wil not take in oyle wel;[2] and then some stand remote and asquint from the

---

[1]Matthew 26:8: "To what purpose is this waste?"

[2]A sensitive thumb was necessary in taking toll of flour, and millers were proverbially dishonest. Cf. the proverb "An honest miller hath a golden thumb" (Tilley, M953). A *souter* is still a cobbler in Scotland, but in England the word came to mean a workman of little or no education. A souter's thumb, unlike a miller's, is hardened and dirtied by his work, and so is a collier's.

sunne of light, and miraculous heate of Fa: *Ignatius*, the Miracle-maister; it falls out that theyr burning glasses doe not so readilie take fire, and their devil-worke by their holy hands and holy geare doth not alwaies fortunatly succeed. Yea, it falls out many times, by your leave, that the subject where-uppon they should worke being indisposed, as not well managed and prepared by the priest (as what fire can burne where the matter is not combustible and of touch), the priests fire is striken, and no great combustion dooth ensue; and this seemes the cause there was so little fire-worke between *Anne Smith* and them; and sometime the priests powder it selfe, for want of good looking to, is danke, and then though the stroke be good, no great sparkles doe arise.

It was therefore wisely foreseene by the providence and deepe insight of theyr kinde Mother theyr holy Church to provide them *copias succedaneas,* seconding and fresh supplies of fire-workes, that if their owne fire doe faile, they may light and fire it againe at the Churches holy candle. Yea sometimes they light uppon such a laxe, watry, and reumaticke devil that hee squirts out the priests fire, the holy brimstone, holy candle, and all, and goes laughing away. This is when they are too busie, and imprudently apply theyr fire-worke too oppositely and directly against the devils spouting place; and then there is no way but to winde up all their holy trinkets in a capcase, and to ayre them handsomly againe at the next pitch for a devil.

If the Sceptick wil pry higher, and demaund whence the Pope and his consistory doe borrow that divine power to consecrate water, candle, brimstone, Frankinsence, potions, Exorcismes, nick-names, and asses eares, and to sublimate theyr nature, and put into them such a fïery scorching flame as shal turne them into serpents and scorpions to bite and sting the devil and to fire him out of his hold, as men smoke out a Foxe out of his burrow: these beeing of theyr owne nature and in shew silly poore stuffe to hold such divine facultie in them? This is a saucie question and deserves to be aunswered with scorne. But because wee wil give reason of all that proceeds from that sacred head, wel may his *holines* and his Chapter doe as much as S. *Peter* did: for as for our Saviour and his holy Apostles, wee never read that they halowed candle, nor dealt with nick-names and Asses eares in casting out devils; but of Peter, by your leave, there lies a tale, and that is this, as *Thyraeus* doth tel it out of one *Martinus* a Saint.

*Simon Magus* the Sorcerer sent unto *Peter* the Apostle certaine devils in the likenes of dogges to devoure the blessed Apostle. S. *Peter* being taken on a suddaine, not looking for such currish guests (as beeing belike at dinner), consecrates on a suddaine certaine morsels of bread and throwes them to the dogge-devils, and by the power of that bread they were all put to flight. And is not this a faire tale of *Simon* and his hel-dogges that would have snapt up S. *Peter* but onely for a soppe of bread? and is it not a faire strong thred to hang a whole castle of fire-works upon? *Martin* hath a black braine, conceiting bul-beares and black band dogges of Saint *Peter*. *Ergo* the Pope and his Church have authority and power to consecrate and hallow water, oyle, salt, wax, brimstone, frankensence, potions, Exorcismes, nicknames, and asses eares, and to put in them a scorching fire to sindge the devils beard. Because the consequence is so validous, we wil looke a little into these holy fire-works, but very sparingly and cursorily, for holding you too long in these unsavory perfumes.

## CHAP. 18.

*Of the dreadfull power of holy water, halowed candell, Frankincense, Brimstone, the booke of Exorcismes,and the* holy potion, *to scald, broyle, and to sizle the devill.*

If you look upon the bare face of these holy Engines, you wil take them for very trifles and toyes: but I must say unto you in good sadnes, as the wise Orator of Rome said of omission of like trifles in another sence: *Istis minutiis concidit respublica Romana,* the common-weale of Rome fell by omitting and neglecting those pettie thinges; so *istis minutiis constitit Ecclesia Romana,* the Church of Rome hath beene founded, pillard, and propped up onely by these gawdes, trifles, and toyes. So as *Anthony* told *Crassus* when hee had caried a cause by affecting the people with his gesture and teares, *nisi pueris et lachrymis usus esset, poenas dedisset,* but for little boyes and the Orators fained teares, his Client had lost the day: wee may truly and plainly tell the Church of Rome, *nisi naeniis, tricis, et puppis usa esset, poenas iam diu dedisset,* if it were not for puppets, apes-faces, and gaudes with which she allures, maskes, and disguises the poore seely people, she had long since sung the doleful song mentioned in holy writ: *Desolatione magna desolata est, et turpitudo eius gentibus revelata,* that is, *she had lien cleane desolate, and her turpitude had beene opened to the eyes of all the world.*[1]

It is a point of high sapience in the Church of Rome to choose and select out these poore, base, and impotent Elements, as water,

[1]Not a scriptural quotation, but a compilation of scriptural phrases such as Jeremiah 12:11, Leviticus 18:7.

oyle, candel, and the rest, for her champions, tormenters, and monster-beaters of devils. First, for that these elements be obvious, easie, and common, so as a devil-Comedy may be plaid in a chimnies end with an halfe peny worth of cost. Next, for that every kitchin-maide, Hob, and John, doth wel see and know that a spoonful of water, a cursie of oyle, and a candels end can have of themselves no power and strength to scald, broyle, or torture a devil: now, when this good Hob, John, or Sisse shal bring a spoonful of water, a cursie of oyle, or a candels end to the priest, and he shal crosse, blesse, and chaunt over it a few broken words: and then presently after, Hob, John, and Sisse shal see the very same water and candels end applied towards the nose of a supposed Demoniack wench, and then shal thinke they heare the devil to roare, fume, and tremble: is it any mervaile that the poore Conies doe wonder and crie out, *O Catholicam fidem! O fidem Catholicam! O the Catholique faith! O the power of the faith Catholique!* Many devises they have to grace these puppets and toyes for the gayning and winning this applause and acclamation of the people, which is one of the chiefe ends where-unto the actors and Comedians ayme. First, it must be so acted and handsomly conveyed that it may seeme and appeare that as the devil cannot abide the name, the approach, the sight, the smel, the breath, the touch, the apparel, or the ornament of a Catholique priest (which is one of the demonstrative signes of a devil in the party), no more must the devill abide the sprinkling of holy water, nor the approch of an halowed candle. This *Saras* she-devil acted wel in the beginning of her part, crying *Away with holy water, holy candle, and the Crosse, they make mine eyes sore.*

The next grace we find of this holy element is to allay and mitigate the force of the devil, and to bring the partie out of an extasie to her selfe. This *Sara* performed very laudably too, being in a very strange fit, past hearing, seeing, smelling, and all: after three draughts of holy-water she came unto her selfe, and therefore the Author tels us that the ordinary remedies to be applied in a fit were holy water, reliques, and the Crosse.

And see the wonderous Antipathie betweene this sacred element and the devil. If it come neere the devils nose, he findeth it straight. First, by the smel: for you must remember that all this consecrate holy geare have one and the selfe same smel, as the church, the priests body, his neather-stocks, and all; that is, such a ranke senting savour that as soone as they come neere, the devil sents them straight and cries out *Oh.* So saith the miracle-blazer, that there being so smal a drop of holy water put into *Saras* drinke as no mortal man could discerne the tast, as soone as it came neere

*Sara* she writhed her face and bad, *Have it away*. And two glasses being brought her, one of consecrate, the other common water, this ranke savour was so validous and strong that it sented through the glasse and stroke her on the nose, so as she pointed directly to the halowed glasse. *2,* whereas water of it owne nature is refreshing and comfortable to the eyes, your holy water hath a piercing pernicious quality, so as the devil complaines at first sight, as you heare, that it makes his eyes sore; and indeede you watered him so much that you made him starke blind, so as hee could not finde the way out of *Sara,* but foyled himselfe like a beetle[1] where he should not have come. And the noter of these gay miracles saith that *Sara,* or her devil, became a sprinkler too (she had been so long amongst priests, as she was entered into their holy orders), and that she, or her devil, by the pure vertue of holy water made a devil let goe his hold upon *Trayfords* lege, where he was fast seased in the likenes of a Toade; and that shee, or her devil likewise, with a few sprinckles of the same, made the devil that came to *Trayford* into his chamber in the likenes of an English Minister, and was disswading him from the Catholique Romish church, to betake him to his heeles, and for hast to leap out at the window without taking his leave. I see your church wil entertaine he-Exorcists and she-Exorcists both, and *Saras* devil, for a neede, for an exorcist too: and yet the poore wench, or the devil, that by the vertue of holy water could scare away two devils from *Trayford* (one in the likenes of a Minister, the other of a Toad), had not the grace to besprinckle her selfe, but kept her devils stil. Marie this was of no ill meaning, be sure; they were reserved for your owne fingring, kinde indigiting holy priests.

And is it not great pitty that all this faire water should be spoild and tainted with one crap of a word dropt out *Sara* since: that all this holy water grace was (as all the rest) bare coggery, and devised *ad ornandam scenam,* to furnish out the play, and to bring into request againe these old water glasses of the church, that for want of sale had stoode so long on their shelves as they grew fusty and naught.

Let not good father *Edmunds* be discouraged for all this, for he shal be beleeved never the worse: who in his learned treatise prefixed to this Diarie of miracles (touching the power and custome of the Romish Church for dispossessing of devils), in enucleating the divine vertues, powers, and dignities of things consecrated by holy Church for commaund over devils, sets out holy water for his

---

[1]On beetles landing in dung ("foyle"), see the proverb "The beetle flies over many a sweet flower and lights in a cowshard" (Tilley, B221).

graund champion to encounter all commers, telling us that worthy memorable story of Saint *Macarius* for demonstration of all: who by the onely sprinckling of holy water did remorphize an olde woman that had been turned into a Mare.[1] The miracle had beene stronger if she had been turned into a horse.

And yet I trust you wil not say but that this holy water was strong enough thus; for *Circes* drench could doe little more, that turned *Ulysses* men into Swine: and yet that was faine to be taken downe ere it could doe the feate; this, onely besprincked, did turne a Mare into a woman againe.

*Lucians* oyntment,[2] I confesse (that he got a little of by peeping in at a crevise and spying the Witch annoynt her body withall), came neere the force of this forcible water of Rome. For *Lucian* tels us himselfe that by that time hee had annointed himselfe all over with that enchaunted oyle, he was turned into an Asse, and that hee so lived by the space of six or seaven yeeres in the shape of an Asse, under very cruell maisters that whipped him sore, as under a Gardiner, a tyle man, a Corier, and such like, and that at last hee was metamorphosed into the shape of a man by eating of Roses. What would a little of that Asse-making oyle doe if it had the good hap to be blessed and super-charmed by his Blessednesse at Rome?

Well, this holy water of Rome had as fayre a discent as that *Lucian* oyle; for that did come from a Witch of *Thessalia,* and this holy water doth come from the witch of *Delphos,* of whom the Roman Poet saith thus, *Spargit aqua captos lustrali Graia sacerdos:*[3] whence *Numa Pompilius*[4] the grand sorcerer and the Popes grand founder of holy trinckets tooke it; and of him the Romane Wisard Pope *Sixtus* or Pope *Alexander* begged it, and hath left it for an holy devil-whippe to his deere mother Church.

And heere I must needes confesse a slippe of my memory (as who can beare all this dreadful hel-geare in his head without a surcharge), that before I had recounted you the wonderful powers of this *Aqua fortis* to scald out a devil and make a woman of a mare, I should have acquainted you how the Miracle-minter in his miracle booke doth solemnly tell us that the devil himselfe did solemnly proclaime from hel that there were foure dreadful devil-scourges in

[1] A frequently cited story, e.g. Kittredge, *Witchcraft,* 184.

[2] The name should be Lucius. See Lucius Apuleius, *Metamorphoses* 3.21.

[3] Ovid, *Ex Ponto* 3.2.73.

[4] Second king of Rome, said to have reigned from 715 B.C. to 673 B.C. The magical documents for which he was later notorious were supposed to have been books of Roman religious practice, buried with him, and recovered, 183 B.C. They were forgeries meant to give authority to custom.

the priests holy budget: holy water, halowed candle, frankensence, and the booke of Exorcismes: whereby you may plainly see that with theyr intoxicating potions they had confounded the devils wits, and made him as wise as goodman *Buttons* boy of *Waltham,* who having beene used to be beaten, sometime with birch, sometime with apple-tree twiggs, sometime with Willow, tells his Maister wisely that of all three apple-tree was the worst, whereby his Maister knew how to sting him the more soundly. And what needs now any more wier-drawing and prophaning of holy scripture for the founding and crediting of your enchaunted water? It hath the same warrant of his soveraigntie as *Campian* had of his martyrdome: hel and the devil, *ipse dixit,* who (you know) doth not use to faile.

But *Sara Williams* tels us that she said no such thing, and that the priests themselves, for the better gracing of those foure holy scourges, were the devils Heralds, and did proclaime them in her name or the name of the devil, and so put it downe in theyr Miracle-booke as the devils owne words: as they were faine at every turne, in her fits, pageants, and traunces, to help out the devil in her part, beeing oft *non plus,* and many things falling in better *extempore* to grace the play withall, then that which was meditated and set downe in her part. And therefore they would often say and write downe that *Saraes* devil said thus and so, where none but the priest-devil himselfe, who played three parts in one, somtime the priest, sometimes the devil, sometimes the devils prompter or Interpreter (as the puppets have alwaies a mimicall prolocutor to tel what they meane), said one word.

And why might not they, to keepe the stage ful, cog in a devil when they listed, as gamesters cogge in a Die? when *Agazarius* the Jesuit[1] tels us that hee having brought from Rome certaine halowed holy graines, and having given them to his holy children for their severall necessities and wants, they by misfortune lost the said graines; and he comforts his holy shrivelings, his ghostly good children, telling them in honest termes that a little pretty peble stone taken up out of a gutter would serve the turne even as well, so it were received and kept with humility and devotion. But our holy tragedians were, as seemes, afraid that these old brayed geare (holy water, halowed candle, and frankensence) would not hold out and play their parts wel, and therefore they thought good to cry them

---

[1]Alphonsus Agazarius, first rector of the English College, Rome, "a very industrious person, and very fond of the English nation. During the seven years of his government of the College he not only brought the administration into order, but added to the buildings, and increased the revenues, and left the place in good order" (Pollen, *Memoirs of Father Robert Parsons,* 100).

out of hand, as they use to cry Mackerels when they are afraide of smelling. This feare was very needlesse, for as you see holy water in this devil-pageant hath acquit it selfe wel, especially in the miracle of the Mare: so you shal see holy candle, frankincense, and the rest, play theyr parts no worse; for they were all devil-whippes of the maker, of a straight stocke, cleane corde, and sure twist, as true and wel-knotted stuffe as ever *Wades myll* did afford.[1]

You shal have holy candle play his part, in the Authour his owne phrase and penning, for his better grace. The whole house at *Denham,* saith the Miracle-maker, was so haunted with spirits that a mayde could not carie a candle lighted in her hand *except it were halowed.* No mervaile though the candles went out so thicke at *Denham:* for there the devils kept theyr acts *in tenebris* so thicke with the poore maids, as *Sara* confesseth she durst not goe to *Dibdales* chamber alone, for feare of devil-puffing; as little gessing, by his unholy handling, he had beene an holy priest. Yet the baudy Poet tells them that somtime a little candle-light doth not amisse at that devil-worke;[2] and therfore not amisse inserted by the Author, that an halowed candel should sometime burne before the devil.

But in an other passage, the miracle-noter tels us that the devil puffed at the holy candel as hard as he could, and could not get it out; this, *Sara* saith, was puffed in by the penner to puffe up a part for the holy candel to play. But I am verily of opinion that the devil puffed indeede, and that the priests had a just scantling and size of the devils breath, to know how strong and deepe the devil was able to puffe, and when he puffed his best, themselves having often out-breathed and out-puffed him, as you have formerly heard; and therefore they knew how to hallow a candle so high, and to such a pitch, as the devil with all the breath in his belly should not be able to puffe it out. And why not as easily, and with as good a grace, as to hallow a candel to such a sublimitie, abstract and quintessential nature, as doth this day burne before the blessed shrine of our Lady at *Arras* without wasting or diminution, without receaving any adition of matter to feede and preserve the light, except nutriment onely. It was no great disgrace to the devils puffe that could not blow out the holy candel, being happily supported by the holy candlestick of the priest.

But you must be enformed of a farre greater foyle sustained by the devil at the hands of a young child by the vertue of this holy

---

[1] Wade is a village in Hertfordshire. The mill there manufactured very good whips.

[2] This could be Ovid, *Ars Amatoria* 2.619–20, 3.807–808, or *Amores* 1.5.3–8, or Martial, 11.104 or 14.39.

candel holden in his hand. Heare the Miraclist report it in his owne gracious Idiome. Sara *being set in a chaire, shee raged more then ere shee did before, especially at the presence of an infant holding a holy candell, crying oft with terrible voyce and countenance, I will eate thee; but the child nothing abashed thereat, was brought to hold the candell to her nose, and to put him to silence. O Catholicam fidem! O fidem Catholicam!* that hast such a check and soveraignty over all the power of hell as that thy priests leade about devils after them as men leade Beares by the nose or Jack an Apes in a string, and enduest thy young Infants with such heroicall magnanimitie as they dare play with the devils nose, and crie *Jack devill, ho devill, blow out the candell, devill:* and the poore devil stands like a mute in a blacke sanctus, with a bone in his mouth, and dares not speake one word.[1]

The two next devil-scourges proclaimed from hel were Frankincense and the booke of Exorcismes: the former whereof though it pleased you not to grace with any special miracle accomplished alone, having many new initiats to advaunce that stood you in more stead: yet to shew that your deere Mother-church did not bestow her blessing uppon such a jewel for naught, you gave him his due time, order, and place, and marshalled him very honourably according to his discent, somtime with the powerful potion, sometime with brimstone, sometime with holy water, sometime with holy candle, shewing us by the worthines of his companion that hee was none of the rascal crue.

Indeede you needed be the lesse careful for this by reason it is alwaies of worth very sufficient to grace and advaunce it selfe, both in regard of the antiquity as also of the honourable discent thereof, as springing from no meaner stemme then the three Kings of *Cullen* that brought it with gold and Mirrhe for a present unto our Saviour Christ.[2] And therefore it hath beene worth the keeping and esteeme in your Mother-church ever since, and hath received her deere motherly blessing by consecration and benediction.

And so wee find that your holy Mother hath layd her holy hands uppon gold likewise, and consecrated and blessed that amiable mettall too, whereby it hath had and shewed as much power over

---

[1]Cf. *Merchant of Venice,* 1.2.50–52: "I had rather be married to a death's head with a bone in his mouth," and the proverb "He has a bone in his mouth" (Tilley, B517), meaning "He is slow to talk." A black sanctus is either a burlesque hymn or, the more likely meaning here, a funeral lament.

[2]I.e., Kings of Cologne. The supposed bodies of the three wise men, having been discovered in 1158 in the church of San Eustorgio, Milan, were taken to Cologne by Rainald of Dassel in 1164. At that time they were incorrupt, "integra exterius quantum ad cutem et capillos" (*The Three Kings of Cologne,* ed. Horstmann, xvii–xviii).

devils haunting houses, walking in Churchyeards, and speaking out of images, as Frankincense, holy candle, and holy water have. But little did those three good Kings of *Cullen* know what a powerful rich present they had brought unto our Saviour when they presented him with Frankincense, as little deeming of fuming any devil in theyr way, or profugating a devil from the body of our blessed Saviour. But your eyes pierced farther then these three Kings could (notwithstanding it is generally accounted they had eye-sight enough, as comming from the head and fountaine of wisedome, understanding, and wit), and you cleerely saw that the Egyptian priests, perfuming theyr two grand Idols, *Isis* and *Osiris,* with this holy smoake, and hearing *Tully* proclaime of theyr Images at Rome, *in omnibus vicis, statuae factae, ad eas thus et cerei,*[1] that they halowed them and theyr Altars with frankinsence and candle: you have very wisely, devoutly, and hea-thenishly smoaked your Altars, your images, your Churches, your vestments, your reliques, your beades, your bookes, your breeches with this perfume, for feare of devil-blasting; and therefore you needed not uppon our devil Theater to grace it with any new won-der.

The fourth fearefull whip halowed out of hel was the booke of Exorcismes,[2] which though *Stemp* the priest shewed *Sara* a little corner of out of his pocket when he was new come from London to *Denham,* telling her he had brought her Maister a whip, and that *Sara* knew it as wel by the crosses and figures as a begger knew his dish, or an old curre a kitchin whippe by a corner of the steale, it had beene so often thundred upon; yet we find in our tragedie that this plaid not the most tragicall monster-part, nor did not the greatest wonders, and that uppon very wise and important consid-erations. First this booke was *sicut fortis equus, spatio qui saepe supremo vicit Olympia.*[3] It had playd so many worthy parts, and caried away the garland so oft in all the Lists, Turnaments, and Justs with the devil that it needed no new *Io paean*[4] to be honoured with-all.

Secondly, it hath hanging on it all the seales and stamps of holy popes for many hundred yeeres, with all their potent benedictions; and it hath had the deere and loving mothers blessing, with

---

[1]Cicero, *De Officiis* 3.20.80.

[2]Although Devlin, "Anthony Tyrrell," 346, says that "some quite unauthorised French ritual" was used for the exorcisms, this passage makes it almost certain that the rites used were from Girolamo Menghi, *Flagellum daemonum,* first published at Bologna, 1578. Law, "Devil-Hunting," 404, made the same deduction.

[3]Ennius, *Annales* 15, fragment 4, quoted by Cicero, *De Senectute* 5.14.

[4]A common cry of rejoicing, e.g. Ovid, *Ars* 2.1.

priviledge of birth-right and priority of honour besides, and there-fore it might wel stand and breath a while without any new addition or title of advauncement. Thirdly, it served wonderous aptly *ad terrorem et stuporem incutiendum populo:* in steede of thunder and lightning to bring *Jupiter* upon the stage, by these dreadful frightful Exorcismes, thundring, clapping and flashing out the astonishing of Gods names, *Jehovah, Tetragrammaton, Adonai,* and the rest, to amaze and terrifie the poore people, and to possesse them with an expectation of some huge monster-devil to appeare. Who standing at gaze with trembling and feare, hearing the huge thunder-cracke of adjuration flie abroad, and no devils to roare; and then seeing the Exorcist in a rage to throw away his thunder booke behind him, and hunt the devil with his owne holy hands; and instantly hearing the devil rouze out of his cabin as a Lyon out of his denn, and bellow out with his roaring voyce, *Oh, oh, oh, I burne, I burne, I scald, I broyle, I am tormented:* this must needes make the poore Madge Owlets cry out in admiration of the power of the potent priesthood, *O Catholicam fidem! O fidem Catholicam. O the Catholique faith! O the power of the faith Catholique.*

Brimstone and the *holy potion* needed no Herrauld from hell to proclaime their potency and might; for where so ever they went, they caried hel before them, both for ugly blacknes, smoake, scorching, broyling, and heate, as you may see in the poore she-devil *Sara,* that bore in her face the very *Idaea* of hell imprinted and branded in her by these dreadful fumigations. For the force, use, and application of this Engine, I referre you to the tenth chap-ter: not that you must think that the loathsome hellish potion of Sacke, Sallet-oyle, and Rue mashed together, and by force poured downe into her stomacke a full pint at a time, did of their owne natural qualities fume up and intoxicate her braine, as *Tobacco,* Giniper, and Henbane mingled together would doe: or that the owne unkind fulsomnes of Sack, Oyle, and Rue did distemper her stomacke, and enforced her to straine, vomite, and crie: or the pes-tilent, choaking, stuffing, pernicious fume of Brimstone, filling her eyes, mouth, nose, and scorching her with the coales and fire til she looked as blacke as hel mouth, did of their owne proper force cause her to crie, scritch, and howle: for what hellish Butchers would ever put a poore wench to such paine: but you are to imag-ine that these loathing, intoxicating, piercing, broyling, choaking qualities were suspended in their proper subjects by the soveraigne consecrating power of the kinde mother church of Rome: that these consecrate Engines made the poore devil in *Sara* to tremble, fume, vomit, straine, scritch, and roare, by the pure vertue of the kind churches sweet benediction. And hoping you wil be thus kindly affected for their sakes, who wish you as wel as they did *Sara,* and would use you as kindly if they had you in their fingrings, as being perswaded that you are all and every each one possessed with devils: I wil spend no time to entreate you, but proceede to my farther taske.

## CHAP. 19.

*Of the astonishable power of Nicknames, Reliques, and Asses eares in afflicting and tormenting the devill.*

When a lyon, a Fox, and an Asse were met together in pilgrimage, it was much wondered at by the common-wealth of beasts what that consociation meant, considering the dissimilitude and disparitie of the beasts. So when a man shal meete with these three in a ranke, Reliques, Nicknames, and Asses eares, hee may perhaps muse at this unequall combination; but when hee shall understand *quo iter una capiunt,* whether they bend theyr course so lovingly together, and shal be advertised that they march hand in hand in an equipage to set upon a devil, to afflict, torment, and cast him out of his hold, he wil muse much more. This gentle muser must be put out of his dumpes by taking out his first primer lesson, *Ignorantia causarum genuit admirationem,* it is nothing but ignorance of causes that is the mother of admiration; and therefore when we have instructed this admirator in the secret causes and principles of this unseemely connexion, we shal ease him of his labour and cause his wonderment to cease.

The maine ground, pillar, and principle of all is the bottomlesse deitie of the holy Church of Rome, who as she is able to make Gods of bread, Saints of devils, and to place them in heaven, so is she as able to change flies into Serpents, fleas into Scorpions, Nicknames into whips, Asses eares into scourges to chastise and chase away all the devils in hel. So as that these two, Nicknames and Asses eares, are indeede but two crystal looking glasses wherein you may behold lively represented unto you the authority and divine prudence of the holy Romish Church: Authority, in choosing out such shadowes and Nihilëities to controll the principalities and powers of darknes; prudence, in selecting the base and ridiculous things of the world to confound all the wisedome and policy of the devil.

I am therefore in gentle and kind wise to advise and entreate you that you use these looking glasses carefullie and aright thorough-out the whole course of this our admirable blacke Arte, and that you measure not our proceedings heerein by the scale of sence, understanding, or wit, judging of things according to their owne nature, qualities, and formes; for so wee may be thought to have dealt not onely childishly and ridiculously, but many times impiously and blasphemously too: but to esteeme of things used and imployed in this admirable science according as they are improved, sublimate and advaunced by the authority of holy church of Rome, and according to the secrets and mysteries of the Arte.

As for example, what man judging according to wit, understanding or sence can imagine that a Witch can transforme her selfe into the likenes of a Cat, a Mouse, or an Hare: and that shee being hunted with Hounds in the forme of an Hare, and pinched by the breech, or whipped with scourges in the similitude of a Cat, the same pinch or marke shal be found in the breech of the Witch that was before made by the Hounds in the breech of an Hare? And yet shal you see this sencelesse, witlesse, and brainlesse conceite verified and made sooth in the practise of our holy conjuring crue, the thing being really acted and performed indeed.

Looke in *Fid. Williams* Deposition, and there you shal finde that the whole Quier of our twelve holy priests had a solemne assembly at the whipping of a Cat, and did whip the Cat so long in a Parlor at *Denham* til shee vanished out of their sight: and sending next day to *Bushie* to see in what case the Witch was whose spirit they had Cat-hunted over night, the Witch was found in child-bed, and her childe newly dead. Whereby it plainly appeares that the whipping of the Cat, so it be done by Catholique priests, is no jest, nor the hunting of the Witch heere no fabulous apprehension, but a good Catholique sooth agreeable to the majestie, gravitie, and wisedome of that venerable holy Church.

And so wil you judge likewise of nicknames and Asses eares by that time I have shewed how gravely and reverendly the holy Church hath set them upon the devils head; and how by her soveraigne authority and commaund she hath made him to weare and beare them in spite of his fuming nose. First, you shal have the Canon and constitution as I finde it set out in *Mengus,* the Licentiate and authorized Maister for Hel, and next the practise of the Canon by our twelve holy legates, according to the constitution of their deere mother Church.

The Canon for nick-naming and rayling on the devil runnes thus in *Mengus* his fourth Exorcisme of his dreadful devil club. *If after the Masse celebrated of the holy Ghost, signing the possessed with five signes of the Crosse, sprinkling him with holy water, invocating over him the name of the Father, Sonne, and holy*

*Ghost, with* Ave Maria, *and thundering out the potent Exorcisme armed with all the dreadfull and astonishable tytles of God, the devill shew him selfe refractarie, and will not depart nor expresse his name,* tum sunt in eum dicenda improperia, *then you must come upon him with as many nick-names as you can possibilie devise.*[1] Now, if you wil learne to nick-name the devil in print and *cum privilegio* under the signet and seale of the holy Church at Rome, take heere a messe of nick-names as they are dressed and served in from the Popes Maister-Cooke and scalder for hel; and let hel it selfe be raked, you shal never finde the like: *Audi igitur insensate, false, reprobe: daemonum magister, miserrima creatura, tentator hominum, deceptor malorum angelorum, fallax animarum, dux haereticorum, pater mendacii: fatue, bestialis, insipiens, ebriose: praedo infernalis, serpens iniquissime, lupe rapacissime, sus macra, famelica, immundissima: bestia Scabiosa, bestia truculentissima, bestia crudelis, bestia cruenta, bestia omnium bestiarum bestialissima: spiritus Acherontine, spiritus fuliginose, spiritus Tartaree:* That is, *Heare therfore thou sencelesse false lewd spirit: maister of devils, miserable creature, tempter of men, deceaver of bad Angels, defrauder of soules, Captaine of Heretiques, father of lyes: fatuous, bestial, Ninnie, drunkard: infernall theefe, wicked serpent, ravening Wolfe, leane hunger-bitten impure Sow: seely beast, truculent beast, cruell beast, bloody beast, beast of all beasts the most bestiall: Acherontall spirit, smoakie spirit, Tartareous spirit.* Is not this pretily wel rayled of an olde Mother Church that hath nere a tooth for age in her head, but hath lived these seaven hundred yeeres and more of pure milke of our Lady? Clap on heere the Canon for the long Asses eares, and seare them to the devils head with a little holie fire and brimstone, and let us see how the seely *hunger-bitten Sowe-devill* wil looke. *Hic exorcista projiciat imaginem pictam in ignem: Heere take the picture of the devill, that you have drawne in paper, and cast it into the fire.* And what turmoyle these wrought in hel, our holy Exorcists by their practise are prest to tel you.

Heare the Miraclist report it, who himselfe was an Actor. *The Priest having placed* Sara *in a chayre, he commaundeth the devill to tell his name. The devill aunswered* Bon-jour, *and began to make a shew of speaking French. The Exorcist then reviling the devil and calling him Asse in the French tongue, he sayd, I am no Asse, I will not be mocked.* This was a sober reply to the Asse,

---

[1]Mengus fust. Daemon: exorcis: [H]. The reference is to Menghi, *Fustis daemonum,* ed., Bologna, 1586, 244–47. Harsnett quotes most of the nicknames in the fourth exorcism.

without much adoe. But when *Maho* trifled, and mocked the priest in *Sara,* and would by no dint of adjuration be brought to tel his name, heare the Miracle-teller againe: *The Exorcist seeing the devill thus to trifle, and that hee would not tell his name, for abating his pride caused to be drawne uppon a peece of paper the picture of a vice in a play, and the same to be burned with halowed brimstone, whereat the devil cryed out as beeing grievously tormented.* No mervaile, when hee had a paire of vices eares clapt red hote to his head with the soader of holy brimstone.

Heere have you both rule and practise of this tormenting the devil with nicknames and glowing eares. Now we must a little for our benefit observe the sweet documents that doe flow out of this nicknaming vaine. First we see by *Mengus* her proloquutor that our holy mother church beeing in her last breath hath not lost her lungs, but hath both breath and stomacke at will, and dares speake more lustily and swaggering-like to the devil then ever *Michaell* the Archangel durst. For hee having an opposition and contention with the devil, and the devil playing (as seemes) the part of our swaggering old Mother with rayling and reviling termes, durst not revile againe, but onely prayed GOD to rebuke the foule-mouthed fiend.

Secondly wee see that our Catholique priests devils stood in more awe of Nicknames and the paper-vice then they did of the dreadful names of our blessed Saviour or the high and astonishable titles of almightie God: whereby it is apparant that the old and auncient way of calling uppon the Name of Jesus over the possessed, at whose blessed Name wee read the devils in the possessed did tremble and quake, is an obsolete, antiquated way with our holy Mother-church, and not woorth the naming; and that her devils be new upstart spirits of the queynt cut, that stand upon theyr reputation for feare least theyr fellow devils in a quarrell should take them by theyr long eares in hel.

It was a pretty part in the old Church-playes when the nimble Vice would skip up nimbly like a Jacke an Apes into the devils necke, and ride the devil a course, and belabour him with his woodden dagger til he made him roare, wherat the people would laugh to see the devil so vice-haunted. This action and passion had som semblance by reason the devil looked like a patible old *Coridon* with a payre of hornes on his head, and a Cowes tayle at his breech; but for a devil to be so vice-haunted as that he should roare at the picture of a vice burnt in a pece of paper, especially beeing without his hornes and tayle, is a passion exceeding al apprehension but that our old deere mother the Romish church doth warrant it by Canon. Her devils be surely some of those old vice-haunted cassiered woodden-beaten devils that were wont to frequent the stages, and have had theyr hornes beaten off with *Mengus* his clubbe, and theyr tayles cut off with a smart lash of his stinging whip: who are so skared with the *Idaea* of a vice and a dagger, as they durst never since looke a paper-vice in the face.

Or if you wil needes hunt us into a demonstration to let you plainly see how a morsel of paper burnt, with a vices long eares, should enforce a devil to roare: remember I beseech you *Aesops* couragious Lyon, lying in the Hunters nets after his fresh wounds, how he roared at the nipping of silly ants, biting him on the bare. Was there ever Lion in our devils case, before he comes to be vice-bitten with a peece of burnt paper, scalded all over with holy water, burnt with the crosse, seared with *Ave maries,* rent with reliques, torne with the stole, battered with the amice, stung with the maniple, whipped from top to toe with exorcismes? And beeing thus excoriated and all over raw, a burning vice, with the least drop of brimstone falling upon his bare, would make a stout Lionly devil (I weene) for to roare.

For his ill bearing of Nicknames I must needs take the devils part. For though that I could have wished he had borne those contumelies and indignities with a better aequanimity and grace, for that none but children and fooles are distempered with nicknames and taunts: yet considering the devil looked into *Denham* house as *Prestons* dogge looked into his neighbours doore, of no malicious intent to eate any *Christmas-pie,* but to see how *Christmas* went: and seeing a play towards, and that they wanted a devil, was content to make one in the play, and to curvet, foame, and tumble with a very good devils grace: now, when he was surbatted, or weary, and could no more *woe penny ho,* to be come uppon with such strange nicknames for his good-wil as *Bedlam* could never spit out worse, and be called *Ninny, drunkard, scabby beast, beast of all beastes,* and *hungerbitten sow* (especially the Exorcists beeing pleased for want of better recreation to play all *Christmas* games with those sowes, as *laugh and lye downe,* and *my sow hath pigd:*[1] and the devil beeing but a prompter and candle-holder to that sport), would have mooved impatience in a right well-stayed devil.

And withall to deale plainly with the devils too, and to tell them of theyr over-sight with their devilships good leave: it is a folly to be laughed at by some, and to be wondered at by many, that any

---

[1]"Laugh and lie down" is a card game in which the player who holds a certain combination of cards lays them down on the table and is supposed to laugh at his success in winning the stakes (E.C. Gordon, ed., *County Folklore (Suffolk),* 59). The phrase is also a proverb (Tilley, L92), as is "My sow hath pigd" (Tilley, P305).

devils in hel should be so starke mad as to come in the Exorcists way, to appeare within his circuit, or to crosse his walke, considering that *Aeacus, Minos,* and *Radamanthus,* the three Judges of hel, be nothing so inexorable, nor in any part so cruell, tyrannicall, and tormenting over the devils as our Exorcists are, who carry about upon theyr backs the whole Panoplie of hel, Styx, Phlegeton, Cocytus: clubs, bats, whips, scourges, serpents, scorpions, brimstone, coales, flames, besides the bottomlesse power that every Exorcist hath (every one having, as seemes, a privie key to the bottomlesse burning pit, to let out and in according to theyr liking) to multiply the torments of hel-fire upon any devil, unto immensity of weight and infinity in perduration. Take but a little say of this from the parlie betweene *Dibdale* and the devil.

The devil was a little *Colli-mollie,* and would not come off.[1] *Dibdale* laies upon him by his soveraigne commaund and his privie key to hell, twenty thousand yeeres torment in the deepest pit of hel, with fire and brimstone on his back; and for the multiplication of his paine and torment which hee had in hel before, hee tels the devil it shal be fifteene hundred times as much. Now then let us make up our audite but at gesse, and cast in a grosse sum, how many legions of devils have been thus served by all the Exorcists in the Romane Church since theyr first creation and commission for hel; and what an huge heape of millions wil this make of poore tormented devils stacked up top-ful in hel with twenty thousand yeeres torment, and that fifteene hundred times doubled uppon them; and all these lye yelling and grinding theyr teeth in hel under this immensity of weight of torments, and these innumerable chaines of darknes, that the Exorcists have layd upon them.

And these theyr fellow devils, friends, and companions, our Christmas devils heere in *Sara, Fid,* and *Anne Smith,* must needes know, and daily see and behold with theyr eyes, and heare with theyr eares, their most lamentable estate: and for them, for all this, to come out of hel, where they were fifteene hundred and twentie thousand times in better case, and to stand in our Exorcists walke, and meete them at *Fulmer, Hackney,* or *Denham:* are they not

---

[1]Cf. Nashe, *Works* 3:53: "I would you might be cole-carriers or pioners in a colepit, whiles colliers ride upon collimol cuts." McKerrow suggests that "collimol" is "a humorous perversion of 'melancholy.'" Since Harsnett's "colli-mollie" describes a devil, and since Nashe is quibbling on "coal," the joke probably lies in a combination of meanings: (1) "black," because of the coal/collier pun; (2) "melancholy," because of the echoic relationship between the words, and (3) "little devil," because the word is a diminutive, and the devil/collier joke is very common, as in *Twelfth Night,* 3.4.117, "Hang him, foul Collier!" Harsnett means that the devil was a black, melancholy, and hence obstinate little spirit. (The "cuts" of Nashe's passage are horses. The melancholy of colliers' horses was proverbial; see *The Return from Parnassus,* 1472, in Leishman, *The Three Parnassus Plays.)*

justly served, to have a volley of nicknames discharged uppon them, and to be tricked up in the vices coate with long eares, and so to be sent backe into hel to theyr fellowes to be tormented equally with them: and this torment of advantage above all the rest, to be mocked, flouted, and jeared at by theyr fellowes, and to be taken by the coat and eares for not having thus much wit, as by other devils harmes to learne to beware?

I come now to the third champion mustered in this worthy ranke with nicknames and Asses eares, and that is holy reliques, which march last of the three, not in regard of theyr unworthinesse, but in respect of theyr worth. For these three woorthies in this blacke field against hel, nicknames &c., are the last and final ranke of our infernal campe, excepting the two maine Standards for all, the holy Crosse and the blessed sacrament, which are yet to display, and then you have your Army royall for hel. And the order of our infernall battaile is the old auncient order observed by the Romans, who placed their *Triarios* last, unto whose lot it never came to fight till the day grew dangerous and the victorie very doubtful. Semblably the worthiest and most approved ranke of our *Triarii* against hel are nicknames, asses eares, and holy reliques, which are drawne up into the vant-gard and front of the battaile at a dreadfull pinch, when holy water, holy candle, the amice, the maniple, the stole, exorcismes, *Avemaries* and all, have retired and in some sort have abandoned the field, and devil stands strong at shock, and gives not an inch of ground.

These dreadful tormenters for hel we have heere in hand are not the auncient, famous, renowmed, glorious reliques jewelled up in the Popes Propitiatorie at Rome (as the sacred violl of our Ladies milke, a peece of S. Paules breeches and chaire, the tayle of the Asse whereon our Saviour rode to Jerusalem, and the rest); but our reliques heere used for the most dreadful and tyrannical tormenters of the devil were native home-bred reliques sprung out of our soyle, and so most likelie to be of greatest force and commaund against the devils of our owne *Horizon*. Which (as wee finde them recorded and advaunced in the golden legend booke) are the thumbs, bones, and joynts of the three worthy Champions sent from his *Holinesse* and from Hel for fire-worke heere in England about *anno 82, Cottam, Brian,* and *Campian:* who for haynous and unnatural treasons against our Soveraigne and the state were executed at *Tiburne,* canonized at Rome, and Sainted by the devils owne mouth from Hel, as you have formerly heard of *Campian,* and now shal heare of *Brian* in the devils owne voyce as the Miracle-father hath recorded it.

*Exor: I charge thee to tell me whose bone this is.* Devil: *It is* Brians *bone. Hee is a Saint indeede; hee never came in Purgatorie.* Loe heere *Brian* as fully sainted from hel by the devil as S. *Campian* was: and what timorous, scrupulous Catholique can now make any doubt but these be infernal Saints, considering *Maho* the Prince of hel hath heere dubbed them with his owne mouth? Now for the grace that the devil shewed unto these new Hel-created Saints of the devils owne making and to their hellish reliques, you may be sure it was not meane. Let the Recorder of hel report you, who was both mouth and Notarie for the priests and the devils.

*By often invocation of the blessed Trinitie, of our Saviour there present in the blessed Sacrament: by often calling upon the blessed virgin, with* salve Regina: *and by calling on all holy Martyrs, especially blessed Fa:* Campian, *with the rest of the Martyrs that had suffered at* Tiburne: *and by applying of their holy reliques unto the afflicted body:* Frateretto, Fliberdigibet, Hoberdicut, Cocabatto, *with fourtie assistants, were expelled.* Heere you see our blessed Saviour and the Trinitie are winged out afore in the forelorne Hope as of little value and account. And the dreadful kilcowes[1] come behinde, with *especially Tiburne* and *reliques* blased in their banner, and these doe the dreadful feate upon the devils of the round. We never read in all the Miracle-booke that the devil trembled at the name of our blessed Saviour; *but* Brians *bone being applied* (saith the Author) *and S.* Cottam *being called upon, the devil aunswered in a trembling, quivering voyce, thou shalt not have thy prayer.* And he was scarcely to be understoode, the poore devil chattered his teeth so sore. What then should I tel you of *Campians* thumbe[2] put into *Fids* mouth, *Brians* bone pinched hard to *Saras* bare legge, as hard as a priest could hold it, the great old rusty nayle crammed into *Fids* mouth amongst an handful of other choaking reliques, what wonders they wrought with these poore she-devils: how these made them to vomite, scritch, and quackle like Geese that had swalowed downe a gagge?

Heare Fa: *Edmunds* for all, like *Julius Caesar* the commenter of his owne worthy exploites, in his monster-miracle acted upon *Marwood*.

*Hic patris etiam Campiani corporis quaedam reliquiae mirifice usserunt, ut omnia omnium sensuum organa dissolui sibi et*

---

[1]Cf. Nashe, *Works* 1:261: "I come to *The kilcow champion of the three brethren.*" "Killing a calf" seems to have been an extempore bragging performance. John Aubrey repeats without understanding it a Stratford tradition that young Shakespeare was good at "killing a calf" (Dick, *Aubrey's Brief Lives*, 334). See also *Hamlet*, 3.2.105–6.

[2]This relic was still at St. John's, Roehampton, earlier in this century. See Camm, *Forgotten Shrines*, 363, 377–78.

*dissipari viderentur; modo enim oculos, modo aures, tum linguam sibi divelli et abripi exclamat, inter quos etiam cruciatus insolito vomitu, ita ut etiam viscera de ore ejicere putaretur, vexatus est.* That is: *Heere certaine peeces of father* Campians *body did wonderfully burne the devill, all the organs of all his sences seeming to be broken and rent asunder, crying out one while his eyes, one while his eares, one while his tongue was rent out and rent in peeces; and besides other excruciations, hee was tormented with such a strange vomite as though he would have spued out his very entralls and guts.*

Heere the devil was on the racke by the vertue of *Campians* relique. Now heare his comming downe. *Extrema tamen omnium (quae laus deo sit) omnibus miserantibus et prae misericordia lachrymatibus, ipso etiam* Edmunde, Edmunde *clamante, liberatus est.* That is: *Last of all (thanks be to God), all of us pittying and weeping for remorse,* Marwood *crying out* Edmunds, Edmunds, *he was quit of the devill.*

The sound had beene harsh, and the period not worth a point, if it had runne thus, *O Christe, Christe, O Salvator, Salvator,* O Christ, ô Saviour; but ô *Edmund,* ô *Edmund* falls with a goodlyer grace. Very wisely sure: as who would say that our Exorcists ever meant to doe God, our Saviour Christ, or the holy Ghost so much honour as to cause any one devil amongst all the devils in hel that they had in hammering once to name eyther God the Father, the Sonne, or the holy Ghost? These (I trust) neede no grace nor honour from the devil; but these *Tiburne* semidevils sainted from hel (*Brian, Cottam,* and *Campian*) were the Gods that stood in need of their holy helping hand.

And heerein I commend their wisedome in choyse of their reliques very much. First, in that they took fresh greene new reliques that were not antiquated and out of date. For reliques (for oft wee see) worke like an Apothecaries potion or new Ale: they have best strength and verd at the first, and therefore *Campians* girdle, now like old Rubarb, begins to allay. Secondly, for that if they had brought of the olde renowmed reliques from Rome, som unstayed body would have made question whether they had beene Saints bones indeed or rather the bones of dogges, Cats, or Rats, or else of an old Sow: especially now we have learned *Agazarius* holesome rule. Thirdly, our devils being home-devils, and our Saints sainted heere from hel, it was no reason that forraine reliques should obtrude themselves into others possessions, and rob them of the honour that they worthily deserved. But the last and best point of their wisedom is this: that we should have had some scruple of the Saintship of *Brian, Cottam,* and *Campian* if wee had not heard them thus solemnly, lowdly, and ceremoniously sainted from *Tiburne,* hel, and the devil.

Heere I had concluded this part of the Pageant, but that *Sara* nips me by the eare, and tells me that I have forgotten a special point of relique-service, and points me to her deposition, which when I had turned my booke and reade over, I pointed at her againe, and willed her to pen that point her selfe; and therefore thus she tels her owne tale.

*At one time* (saith she) *when it began to be with me after the manner of women, the Priests did pretend that the devill did rest in the most secret part of my body, whereuppon they devised to apply the reliques unto that place.*[1] Good God, what doe we heare? Or is it but a dreame? Or have we eares to heare such impious unnatural villanie?

S. *Campian,* S. *Brian,* S. devil or sainting devil helpe out with this, for I am at a stand. Reliques to that place? It is able to possesse a man with *Marwoods* fury to crie out *terra dehisce, infernum absorbe. Earth gape, and hell swallow* such devil-saints, such devil-reliques, such devil priests and all. Was it ever heard that any heathen durst ever abuse the vilest thing consecrated to their Idol-devils in such execrable manner? Holy Saints, holie reliques, holy priests, holy devil that made them and moved them to this! It was no mervaile they made so much hast with the devil to Saint their Champions, *Campian* and his crue from hell, and to deifie or hellifie their reliques, since they were to be applied to such a diabolical service as the devil himselfe without such a relique could never have accomplished. Nay, wee never reade that the devil durst abuse any thing consecrated but in shew, to any so despicable imployment. *Tiburne* doth blush that bare them, the devil doth shame that made such devil-saints and hellish reliques; and yet the priests, the consecrators, devisers, and appliers, doe shew their bare hel-burnt faces without blushing at all. *Diris devoveo et actores et spectatores.* So I proceede.

# CHAP. 20

*Of the dreadfull power of the Crosse and Sacrament of the Altar, to torment the devill, and to make him roare.*

As farre as the holy Fathers doe deeme of the Crosse, so farre doe we affectionatly embrace and esteeme of the same as an honourable and reverend monument in our Christian profession.

[1] See her exam: [H].

But the common enemy of mankind, not brooking any moderation, taking advantage of the proclivity of our nature unto superstition, hath so farre bewitched the minds of some, as they have brought into the Christian Church that which *Tertullian* dooth so much protest against in the name of all Christians, *staurolatrian,* a performing of divine honor before a peece of wood, then which the Heathen never did performe more before the statue of *Jupiter:* and another branch likewise springing from the same roote, that is *stauropoïsan,* a feigning, counterfeiting, and stamping of signes, miracles, and wonders to be done not onely by the Crosse, but by the expression and signification of the same, after the very same fashion that the Heathen did fabulously imagine and devise strange fountaines of delicacies to flow from the horne of *Jupiters* Goat.

These two superstitious delirations have made us partly odious, partly ridiculous to the prophane Heathen people. *Lucian* found this doting humor betimes in some Christians of his time, and makes himselfe and the world sport with it, as he did at the fancies and exorbitancies of all other religions: telling us a tale of one *Eucrates,* who had a ring made of a peece of old Iron which had sometime beene a peece of an Iron crosse, and that ring was an amulet against all malignant spirits.[1] And blind *Thyraeus* the Jesuit repeats the same rustie tale of the ring as if scoffing *Lucian* had meant nothing but sooth. But hee may as good cheape affoord us the tale of *Eucrates* as hee dooth the story of S. *Margaret:* who with the bare signe of the Crosse afrighted a devil that was comming unto her in the forme of a great Dragon.[2] Or that of *Martian* and *Julian* who with the signe of the Crosse went up and downe killing of serpents, as *Hercules* did Monsters: or that of the old man who spying an Aspe in the bottom of a fountaine did front the entrance to the fountaine with so many signes of the Crosse, as hee went downe to the bottom, filled his pot with water, and returned from the Aspe without any harme: or that of Bishop *Sabin* who having poyson mingled in his cup by an Archdeacon, who meant to make him away, signed himselfe with the Crosse, drunk off the poysond cup, and felt not the least grudging or distemper after the same. I doubt the Pope his Maister would hardly believe him in this, who would give some good store of crownes to be secured by crosses from the danger of poyson. I doe not see poysoning any where so rife as in Italy, and especially at Rome, where Crosses are not dainty.

[1]Lucian, *The Lover of Lies* 17.

[2]Thyraeus tells this and the following stories, *De daemoniacis,* chap. 44, par. 599–603.

And what becomes of that goodly auncient Poem made and sung in honour of the Crosse?

> *Ista suos fortiores*
> *Semper facit et victores:*
> *Morbos sanat et languores:*
> *Reprimit daemonia.*[1]

That is,

> *The crosse in battaile is a shield,*
> *Which who so beares still winnes the field;*
> *Against diseases tis a spell,*
> *A charme against the power of hell.*

It is very great reason they should doe it divine honour called *Latria,* and sweat, and spit, and clamor in theyr *Sorbone* for the same, since they give it the divine supreame power of our blessed Saviour. For what did our Saviour heere on earth, or what could he do more, or what did he adorne his owne style withall to S. *John,* sending his disciples unto him to know whether hee were Christ? He said no more then this: *Goe backe unto* John, *and tell him what you have seene and heard: how that the blind see, the lame go, the deafe heare, and unto the simple is the gospell preached.* And dooth not this bring us plainly within compasse of the heathen challenge, that we be *lignei dei cultores,* worshippers and servaunts to a woodden god?

Our devill-comedians, whose ayme was (as you see) by playing over all the trinkets, toyes, and pedlars ware of the Popes holy budget, and by gracing them with some seeming quality against the devil to advaunce the credit of the Catholique church, and to bring into admiration theyr owne persons and priestly power, that so they might catch the poore Gudgins they fished so industriously for: left out no old ceremonie nor Engine of the Romane Church that had any name or reputed faculty that way. And therefore they mustered the Church standard amongst theyr fierie troupes, but they did advaunce and adorne with moe miracles their new reliques and theyr owne proper persons, theyr hands, theyr gloves, theyr stokings, theyr priestly ornaments, as theyr amice, stole, maniple, and albe, then they did the old approoved coate-armour of the Church; and that upon a right wise ground, in regard that these did more properly, neerely, and effectually worke for the magnifying of themselves and theyr priestly authority.

---

[1]From a sequence for the Exaltation of the Holy Cross, readily available in *The Oxford Book of Medieval Latin Verse,* 204–8, and probably taken by Harsnett from Scot, *Discoverie,* Bk. 12, chap. 9. Harsnett's translation, probably his own, is much superior to that in Scot, which is by Abraham Fleming.

Therefore the holy Crosse was often presented on the stage, but never with that acclamation and *plaudite* that their other forenamed holy implements were. The first honour the Miraclist doth bestow uppon it is this: that it served to discover *Sara* to have a devil, in that shee could hardly be brought to signe herselfe with the signe of the Crosse. Next it, holy water at a pinch, when it would not goe downe past *Saras* mouth into her throat, but stucke in the way, her throat was signed with the crosse, and then it slipped down as easily as a draught of Ale. It seemes that holy water was old, for you see when it was fresh the devil himselfe was not able to come within the smell, but leapt out at a window for hast to be gone. Thirdly, it restored speech to *Sarah* when it was lost. *Sara could not speake* (saies the Recorder) *till the priest had signed her throat with the crosse*. *Sara* was now a scholler of some standing (as shee saith) and knew when her cue came to say over her geare.

Fourthly, *Sara* knew a peece of the crosse by the smell, and that might she doe right wel; for they kept it so sweet in a boxe (saith *Sara*)[1] that she must have had a shrewd pose that should not have found it. Fiftly, it brought *Sara* to her selfe when shee was in a traunce, or opened her eyes when shee was broade awake. Yet old *Edmunds* bestowes more grace uppon it alone then all these; for when he had hunted up the devil into *Marwoods* head with his holy hands, meaning to barricado him there that the people might see him looke out at *Marwoods* eyes, eares, and nose as a prisoner doth use to looke out at an yron grate: hee signes *Marwoods* throat with the signe of the Crosse with this holy adjuration, *hic Christi limen est, hos limites ne transcende, this is Christes owne limit, see that yee step not over this line;* and yet (as seemes) for feare the devil should have adventured to put his foote over the line, hee claps on the sacred maniple too, and winds it about his neck, that if there were neede the Crosse might call to his good neighbour to helpe stop the thiefe. For these holy hunting Engines were better managed then our ordinary cry of hounds that wil flie out, every one striving to leade away the chase and leave his fellowes behind: our hunting dogges had beene managed to stay for each other that the cry might be ful, and that one might help out another at a dead fault. And thus they dismissed the holy Crosse the stage without any great alarum or sound of the common drum. Enters the holy Sacrament uppon their stage, deformed by these hell-monsters into a most detestable Idoll of the masse, with a farre more solemne grace (worthy of a far better place, if these miscreants had not playd so long with hel-smoake that it had put out theyr eyes

[1] See her examina: [H].

cleane), but they that have playd with God, Christ, and the holy Ghost, the devill must give them leave to play with Christes blessed institution too. I say they present it with great pompe in regard of the thrise glorious state impiously, blasphemously, and chimerically conceited by them to be in royall person within, such a monstrous metamorphosis as *Homer, Pindarus, Hesiode,* nor all the fabulous Grecian wits put in a mash durst never faine, forge, or dreame of any their despicable gods: that any God should be made of a morsell of bread.

This new-molded masse-Idoll, laughed at by some, loathed by many, detested of all pious and ingenuous spirits that have not intoxicated their wits with that enchaunted Babylonian chalice; wanting witnesse in heaven, and beeing hissed at on earth, must be brought uppon our devil-stage to be graced, honoured, and confirmed from hell. And the same devil that sainted *Campian* and *Brian* must with the same blacke breath and foule mouth deïfie this bread-Idoll, and make it a God. And that it may be a perfect *Chimaera,* compounded all of fiction and fantasticall imagination, the smoake, the fire, the stench, the roare, hell and the devill must be cogged, feigned, and playd to help out with this infernall and diabolicall fascination.

Would it not cause men and Angels to wonder at the desperate boldnes of the Ethnick Romish Church, that should dare so impiously and blasphemously to prophane the most sacred reverend Supper of our blessed Saviour: whose end and Essence is to be taken, receaved, and eaten as the bread of life, the strength, health, and sweete comfort of our soule: all whose divine energie, power, and vertue is to the receaver onely, the promise of life to the worthy receaver, the menace of death to the unworthy receaver: all matter, forme, effect, and end directed to the receaver. To disguise, difforme, and monster-like to mishape the nature of this thrice blessed communion as to make it a Monster-Engine of all prodigious signes, cogged miracles, and grosse Heathenish conceited wonders, and to blaze this their hellish impiety before the eyes of all the world, they have compiled a booke containing no lesse then foure and fortie several chapters treating onely *De miraculis veri Sacramenti Sancti Eucharistiae,* that is, *Of the Miracles that the venerable Sacrament of the sacred Eucharist hath performed,* transforming the nature of the blessed supper into a prodigious monster of wonders.[1] Some of the heads of which *Chimaera,* for a sample of the rest, I wil point out unto you. *Cap. 1. De Praedio*

---

[1]Tilman: De Mirac: Eucharist: [H]. This is Franciscus Tittelmans (Tilmanus), *Tractatus de expositione mysteriorum missae* (Antwerp, 1530, and Louvain, 1549).

*ab infestatione malignorum spirituum liberato, per oblationem sacrificii corporis Christi.* Of a Farme house freed from the haunting of bad spirits by celebrating the Masse. *Cap. 2. De* Saxoniae *Duce, qui sub sacrificio Missae vidit speciem elegantis pueruli in Eucharistia.* Of a Duke of *Saxonie,* who at the time of the celebration of the Masse, saw the forme of an elegant young child in the Eucharist. *Cap. 5. De quodam cuius vincula solvebantur tempore quo pro illo offerebatur sacrificium missae.* Of one whose shackles fel off at the time when a masse was said for him. *Cap. 6. De* Baraca *Nauta per salutarem hostiam Eucharistiae a naufragio liberato.* Of one *Baraca* a Mariner that by the Eucharist escaped a tempest. *Cap. 20. Quomodo* Satyrus *divi* Ambrosii *frater, Eucharistiam collo appensam habens, in naufragio incolumis servatur.* How one *Satyrus,* S. *Ambrose* his brother, was saved in a ship-wrack by having the Eucharist hanging about his necke. *Cap. 29. De Eucharistia quae a terra suapte virtute sublimata per aera ferebatur ad altare, ibidemque in specie venustissimi pueri apparuit.* Of the Eucharist flying in the ayre unto the Altar, and there appearing in the forme of a most beautiful child. *Cap. 36. De hostia tertio ab altari divinitus projecta, eo quod cimice esset contaminata.* Of an Oast thrice skipping from off the Altar, *by reason it was defiled by a little flie.* Enough for a tast, the whole tunne is of the same liquor, colour, and tang. And who would after this deeme *Mahomet* an Impostor for carying the Moone in his pocket, and mounting up, when he was dead, thorough the ayre unto the roofe of a Chappell?

Heare our owne Miracle-monger and his crue, how handsomly they act this masse-monster from hel. First, *Saras* devil findes the Communicants that had beene at Masse by the smel. The Romaine Church and her implements are of one and the same perfume, that doe out-smel the fuming lake spoken of in the *Apocalips,*[1] nay hel, the devil and all. Next the blessed Sacrament was presented in a Pix; heere *Saras devill roared like a Bull.* It should have beene: *bellowed like a Cow,* for hers was a she-devil. Heere the real presence is roared out by *Saras* devil. Then *Saras* devil was brought unto the Altar at the time of elevation, and could not behold the Sacrament for the brightnes that shined about it. Heere the glorious presence of our Saviour in the Sacrament is spied out by the devil. At an other elevation *Saras* devil could not abide to looke upon the Sacrament, and when shee looked up shee could see nothing but the priests fingers. Heere is an evident demonstration that our Saviour was there present, in that he made the hoast to vanish out of *Saras* devils sight.

[1]Revelation 19:20.

When nothing would doe, the presence of the Sacrament made *Maho* tel his name, controlled him, calmed him, couched him as quiet and gentle as a dogge under a bench. *Maho, Saras* devil, being commaunded to kisse the blessed Sacrament, durst not disobey, but kissed it very reverently, as children kisse the rod. The devil being commaunded to take his oath uppon the blessed Sacrament, he durst not refuse, but swore very devoutly that he would tel his name and be gone; and yet like a false rake-hel perjured himselfe, and stayed stil. And when hee should be brought to his booke againe, he swore he would breake his owne necke ere he would sweare the second time; and for feare (as seemes) that the devil should make away himselfe, and so the play be mard afore the *plaudite,* they let him alone.

These are demonstrations, by deduction from the devil, of our Saviour his real presence; but wil you heare the devil put you out of doubt by his owne authentical asseveration? *Dibdale* the priest put his finger into *Saras* mouth, and bid the devil bite it if he durst. The devil aunswered, saith the Miraclist, that *it had touched the Lord.* But *Sara* tels us, now she hath put off her devils vizard, that had she not stoode more in feare of a boxe on the eare then of any Lord there, shee would have made so bold as to have had a snap at the priests finger.[1] *Saras* devil was brought by a new commaund to kisse the Sacrament more sure: And being asked what he had kissed, he aunswered, *The body of Christ, and that it had eyes in it.* Heere you have the devils owne testimonie; what needes any more witnes? And yet if you wil have it fuller, heare *Saras* devil againe, when the priest holding him the blessed Sacrament and bidding him to adore his Lord and God, the devil aunswered maleapartly, *He is thy God indeede; and if thou doe not beleeve, cut it with a knife, and thou shalt see it bleede.* Was not this part wel played, to prove the *eyes,* the *body,* the *blood* of our Saviour in the Sacrament from out of hell? Were it not great pitty this devil, hel, and oath should be cogged, and not a true devil indeede? For what a great deale of labour, expence of candel, beating of braines, forging of fathers, counsels and authorities, wresting of Scripture, falsifying of Authors, coyning of wonders would this one Comedy spare? If you wil not beleeve that our Saviour is in the Sacrament, goe to Sir *George Peckhams* house at *Denham,* or my Lord *Vaux* his house at *Hackney,* and aske the devil, who saw our Saviours eyes (as hee sayes) with his owne eyes, touched him with his finger, kissed him with his mouth; and to make it past doubt, tooke his oath upon the Sacrament that it was true. Or else trie if the argument wil not run

[1] See her exam: [H].

in better moode and figure thus. The very same devil that Sainted *Brian* and *Campian* at *Tiburne,* that proclaimed himselfe a Dotrel, a Ninnie, and a mad foole at *Hackney,* that had the Asses eares clapt close to his head at *Denham,* hath said, roared, and sworne so; therefore it is true. Or else thus. The same *Edmunds* and his twelve holy disciples that have feigned a devil Tragedie, sorted it into actes and scenes, furnished it with hangings, set up a stage of forgerie, replenished it with personated actors, adorned it with fictious devises, dreames, imaginations, and ridiculous wonders, have cogged a new hel, new devils, new roarings, new oathes, new kisses to cogge our Saviour into the Sacrament: therfore you may be cock-sure to finde him there.

# CHAP. 21.
## *Of the strange formes, shapes, and apparitions of the devills.*

It is a question moved by *Scaliger: Why men of a melancholick constitution be more subject to feares, fancies, and imagination of devils and witches then other tempers be?* His aunswer is, *quia ab atra bile atri et fuliginosi generantur spiritus, qui cerebrum pingunt turbulentis phantasmatibus,* because from their blacke and sooty blood gloomie fuliginous spirits do fume into their braine, which bring blacke, gloomy, and frightful images, representations, and similitudes in them, wherwith the understanding is troubled and opprest.[1] Men of this duskie, turbulent, and fantasticall disposition, as they are very stiffe in their conceit, absolute in their owne apprehension, extreame violent and peremptory in their resolution (which al grow from the earthy dry stiffenesse of the discursive melancholicke spirits that doe possesse theyr braine), so are they so full of speculations, fansies, and imaginations of spirits and devils, and those so Chimericall and strange, as the Philosophers old *aphorisme* is, *cerebrum Melancholicum est sedes daemonum,* a melancholicke braine is the chaire of estate for the devil. And an other *aphorisme* they have founded on experience, *nullum magnum ingenium sine dementia,* there is no great wit without some mixture

---

[1] I have not traced this question nor the source of the "Philosophers old *aphorisme*" below, but the ideas are common. See Burton, *Anatomy,* 1.2.1.2 (ed. Dell and Smith, 174–75): "This humour of Melancholy is called the Devil's Bath. . . . Agrippa and Lavater are persuaded, that this humour invites the Devil to it, wheresoever it is in extremity, and, of all other, melancholy persons are most subject to diabolical temptations and illusions, and most apt to entertain them, and the Devil best able to work upon them."

of madnesse.[1] *John Bodin* the Frenchman[2] is a perfect *Idaea* of both these, who beeing in his younger yeeres of a most piercing, quicke, speculative wit, which grew of a light, stirring, and discursive melancholie in him, fell (as *Hermogenes* the mirror of wit did) in the midle of his age to be a pure sot. The cause whereof is the cooling and thickning of his melancholicke blood, and the spending or going out of that lightsome, active, and stirring spirit which the heat of blood in his youth did better maintaine.

This man, though during the prime of his wit he was of a most pregnant, ripe, and subtile discourse, yet his wit beeing deepe woaded with that melancholick blacke dye, had his braine *veram sedem daemonum*, the theater and sporting house for devils to daunce in: for he hath in his braine such strange speculations, fantasmes, and theoremes for devils, as a man may see a great deale of madnes mixed with his great wit. For he holds that devils may transforme themselves into any shape of beasts or similitude of men, and may eate, drinke, and converse familiarly with them, and may have the act of generation with women, as they please. And not that onely, but that a Witch by oyntments and charmes may transforme herselfe into the shape of any beast, bird, or fish; that she may flie in the ayre, that she may deprive men of their generative power, that she may transferre corne out of one field into another, and may cause haile, thunder, and winde at her pleasure. And hee defends *lycanthropia* and the change of *Ulysses* men into swine by the Witch *Circe* to be reall and true; and above all tels that unsavory, melancholicke, ridiculous tale of an Egge, which a Witch sold to an Englishman,[3] and by the same transformed him into an Asse, and made him her Market-mule three yeeeres, to ride on to buy butter; and how that at last shee remorphized him into the native shape of a man againe.

This mans *cerebrum melancholicum* is a notable forge for our popish Ethnicks to hammer a motly devil out of. But they have more auncient and authenticke records for their Night-owles then this: as namely, that canonicall story in *Virgill*, of *Creüsa*, *Aeneas* his wife: how *Aeneas*, flying with *Anchises* his father and *Creüsa* his wife thorough the streets of Troy, being all on a light flame, lost his wife *Creüsa* in a crowde as he posted thorough the Citty, and how that *Creüsa* appeared to him in her ghost as *Aeneas* went

[1] Seneca, *De tranquillitate animi* 17.10: "Nullum magnum ingenium sine mixtura dementiae fuit." Seneca says that Aristotle is his source for this commonplace. See *Problemata* 30.1, and cf. Plato, *Phaedrus* 245A.

[2] French jurist, author of *Démonomanie des sorciers* (1580), the book from which Harsnett inferred his decline.

[3] Also told by Scot from Bodin, *Discoverie*, bk. 5, chap. 3.

out at the gate, and told him that she was dead, and was become one of the walking night-ghosts, bidding him to take his father *Anchises,* and shift for himselfe.[1] This is a most redoubted record of the walking of womens ghosts. And for the appearing of bad and hurtful spirits in ugly and monstrous formes, they have their president and originall in the history of *Marcus Brutus,* who having put all his Army in a readines for the last fatall fielde to be fought betwixt him and *Augustus,* and beeing alone at his booke in the deepe and silent night, suddainly he heares a great rushing in the roome where hee sate, and casting up his head sees a foule, ougly, monstrous shaped ghost standing afore him: and asking it angerly, *quis tu? Deus aut daemon?* what art thou? a God or a devil? the ghost answers, *sum malus tuus genius,* I am thine evil angel. The captaine askes fiercely again, *et quid me vis?* amd what doost thou heere? The ghost sayes, *cras Philippis me videbis,* to morrow I wil meet thee at the fields of *Philippi.* The captaine aunswers resolutely, *videbo,* Ile meet thee, and so falls constantly to his booke againe, not bidding it God night. *Brutus* recounts this *spectrum* to *Cassius,* his fellow in Armes, and *Cassius* perswades him that it was but a dreame.[2] But out of this and such like Heathenish dreames, what a world of hel-worke, devil-worke, and Elve-worke had we walking amongst us heere in England, what time that popish mist had befogged the eyes of our poore people? How were our children, old women, and maides afraid to crosse a Churchyeard or a three-way leet, or to goe for spoones into the Kitchin without a candle? And no marveile. First, because the devil comes from a smoakie blacke house, he, or a lewd frier[3] was still at hand with ougly hornes on his head, fire in his mouth, a cowes tayle in his breech, eyes like a bason, fangs like a dogge, clawes like a Beare, a skinne like a Neger, and a voyce roaring like a Lyon; then *boh* or *oh* in the dark was enough to make their haire stand upright. And if that the bowle of curds and creame were not duly set out for *Robin good-fellow* the Frier and *Sisse* the dairymaide to meete at *hinch pinch and laugh not* when the good wife was a bed, why then, either the pottage was burnt to next day in the pot, or the cheese would not curdle, or the butter would not come, or the ale in the fat would never have good head. But if a *Peeterpenny* or an houzle-egge were behind, or a patch of tyth unpaid to

---

[1]*Aeneid* 2.778ff.

[2]Plutarch, *Life of Brutus* 36.

[3]This passage from "a lewd frier" to "stand upright" is plagiarized from Scot, *Discoverie,* bk. 7, chap. 15.

the Church (*Jesu Maria*),[1] then ware where you walke for feare of *bull-beggers, spirits, witches, urchins, Elves, hags, fairies, Satyrs, Pans, Faunes, Sylvans, Kit with the candlesticke, Tritons, Centaurs, Dwarffs, Giants, impes, Calcars, conjurers, Nymphes, changlings, scritchowles, Incubus, the spurne, the mare, the man in the oake, helwayne, the fire-drake, the puckle, Tom thumbe, hobgoblin, Tom-tumbler, Boneles, and the rest;*[2] and what girle, boy, or old wisard would be so hardy to step over the threshold in the night for an half-penny worth of mustard amongst this frightfull crue, without a dosen *avemaries,* two dosen of crosses surely signed, and halfe a dosen *Pater nosters,* and the commending himselfe to the tuition of S. *Uncumber*[3] or els our blessed Lady?

These be the Popes, and his holy Legats, and those of his holy mission and commission from hell their frightful crue, theyr blackguard with which they work wonders amongst a faithlesse, sencelesse generation: these shoute about them, attend them, and are of theyr guard and trayne wheresoever they goe or walke, as *Styx, Phlegeton,* and the *Eumenides* doe guard *Aeacus* in hell; with these they worke their wonders, making Images to speake, vautes to sound, trunks to carry tales, Churchyeards to swarme, houses to rush, rumble, and clatter with chaynes, high-waies, old graves, pittes, and woods ends to be haunted with lights, owles, and poakers; with these they adrad and gaster sencelesse old women, witlesse children, and melancholike dottrels out of their wits.

These Monster-swarmes his *Holinesse* and his helly crue have scraped and raked together out of old doating heathen Historiographers, wisardizing Augurs, imposturizing South-sayers, dreaming Poets, Chimerial conceiters, and coyners of fables, such as puffe up our young gallants with bigge lookes and bombast phrases, as the booke of *Lancelot du Lake, Guy of Warwicke, The Mirrour of Knighthoode, Amadis de Gaule,* and such like their Legends; out of these they conceit their monstrous shapes, ugly bug-beares,

[1]Another insincere passage. Harsnett the churchman objected strongly to unpaid tithes.

[2]See Scots book of Witches. [H]. The italicized passage is quoted from bk. 7, chap. 15.

[3]According to legend, Maid Uncumber was originally Liberata, Christian daughter of a pagan king of Portugal. About to be married to the king of Sicily, she prayed to be saved from that fate, and in answer to her prayer received a flowing beard. She was later crucified. In France she was called St. Wilgeforte, in Germany and the Netherlands St. Onkommer. Her cult was widespread in England in the later Middle Ages. Women believed that for an offering of oats Uncumber would relieve them of unwanted husbands. There was an image said to be hers in old St. Paul's (Coulton, *Five Centuries of Religion* 1:546–51). She appears in the Sarum calendar on 7 July under the name Sancta Liberata.

hydeous apparitions of ghosts; out of these they conforme their charmes, enchauntments, periapts, amulets, characters, wast-coates and smockes of proofe against hayle, thunder, lightning, biting of mad dogges, gnawing of Rats, against botches, biles, crosbiting, sparrow-blasting, Owle-hunting, and the like.[1]

Out of these is shaped us the true *Idaea* of a Witch, an olde weather-beaten Croane, having her chinne and her knees meeting for age, walking like a bow leaning on a shaft, hollow eyed, untoothed, furrowed on her face, having her lips trembling with the palsie, going mumbling in the streetes, one that hath forgotten her *pater noster,* and hath yet a shrewd tongue in her head to call a drab a drab. If shee have learned of an olde wife in a chimnies end, *Pax, max, fax* for a spel, or can say Sir *John of Grantams* curse for the Millers Eeles that were stolne, *All you that have stolne the Millers Eeles,* Laudate dominum de caelis; *And all they that have consented thereto,* benedicamus domino:[2] why then ho, beware, looke about you my neighbours; if any of you have a sheepe sicke of the giddies, or an hogge of the mumps, or an horse of the staggers, or a knavish boy of the schoole, or an idle girle of the wheele, or a young drab of the sullens, and hath not fat enough for her porredge, nor her father and mother butter enough for their bread, and she have a little helpe of the *Mother, Epilepsie,* or *Cramp* to teach her role her eyes, wrie her mouth, gnash her teeth, startle with her body, hold her armes and hands stiffe, make anticke faces, girne, mow, and mop like an Ape, tumble like a Hedgehogge, and can mutter out two or three words of gibridg, as *obus, bobus,* and

---

[1]This list is from Scot, *Discoverie,* who discusses "Popish periapts, amulets and charmes, agnus Dei, a wastcote of proofe" in bk. 12, chap. 9, and gives instructions for making "a holie garment called a wastcote for necessitie . . . much used of our forefathers, as a holy relike," which would protect the male wearer from "shot or other violence," and ensure "quicke deliverance" to a woman. Scot also uses "character" to mean a written charm.

[2]This story was originally one of *A C Mery Tales,* but it is missing from the imperfect surviving copy. Hazlitt, *A Hundred Mery Tales,* 106, 129, reproduced it from Scot, *Discoverie,* bk. 12, chap. 17, where no doubt Harsnett found it, too:

So it was, that a certeine sir *John,* with some of his companie, once went abroad a jetting, and in a moone light evening robbed a millers weire, and stole all his eeles. The poore miller made his mone to sir *John* himselfe, who willed him to be quiet; for he would so cursse the theefe, and all his confederates, with bell, booke, and candell, that they should have small joy of their fish. And therefore the next sundaie, sir *John* got him to the pulpit, with his surplisse on his backe, and his stole about his necke, and pronounced these words following in the audience of the people.
*All you that have stolne the millers eeles,*
*Laudate Dominum de coelis,*
*And all they that have consented thereto.*
*Benedicamus Domino.*
Lo (saith he) there is sauce for your eeles my maisters."

then with-all old mother *Nobs* hath called her by chaunce idle young huswife, or bid the devil scratch her: then no doubt but mother *Nobs* is the Witch; the young girle is Owle-blasted and possessed; and it goes hard, but ye shal have some idle, adle, giddie, lymphaticall, illuminate dotrel, who being out of credite, learning, sobriety, honesty, and wit, wil take this holy advantage to raise the ruines of his desperate decayed name, and for his better glory wil be-pray the jugling drab, and cast out *Mopp* the devil.[1] They that have their braines baited and their fancies distempered with the imaginations and apprehensions of Witches, Conjurers, and Fayries, and all that Lymphatical *Chimaera,* I finde to be marshalled in one of these five rankes: children, fooles, women, cowards, sick or blacke, melancholicke, discomposed wits. The Scythians being a warlike Nation (as *Plutarch* reports) never saw any visions.[2]

The frightful fancies and fond gastful opinions of all the other dotrels arise out of one of these two rootes: weakenes of wit or unstayednes in religion. *Horace* the Heathen spied long agoe that a Witch, a Wizard, and a Conjurer were but bul-beggers to scare fooles, writing thus to one that had so much wit as to discerne a poled sheepe from a parlous beast:[3]

> *Somnia, terrores Magicos, miracula, sagas,*
> *Nocturnos Lemures, portentaque Thessala rides.*[4]

That is,

> *Dreames and Magicall affrights,*
> *Wonders, Witches, walking sprights,*
> *What Thessalian Hags can doe,*
> *All this seemes a jest to you.*

And *Geoffry Chaucer,* who had his two eyes, wit, and learning in his head, spying that all these brainlesse imaginations of witchings, possessings, house-hanting, and the rest, were the forgeries, cosenages, Imposturs, and legerdemaine of craftie priests and leacherous Friers, either to maske their venerie, or to enritch their

---

[1]The passage refers to John Darrell.

[2]Another borrowing from Scot, *Discoverie,* bk. 7, chap. 15: "The *Scythians,* being a stout and warlike nation (as divers writers report) never see anie vaine sights or spirits." Harsnett supplies the reference to Plutarch. Scot in turn probably took the sentence from Lavater, *Of Ghostes and Spirites Walking by Nyght* (1572), sig. B2v: "It is reported of the Scythians, a warlike nation dwelling in mountaynes (from whom it is thought the Turkes take their originall) that they never see any vayne sightes of spirits."

[3]From Scot, *Discoverie,* bk. 7, chap. 15: "A polled sheepe is a parlous beast." Cf. Tilley, S296: "A black sheep is a perilous beast." "Polled" means "shorn."

[4]Horace, *Epistles* 2.2.208, but taken from Scot, *Discoverie,* bk. 6, chap. 3. Harsnett's translation is much superior to Scot's.

purses by selling their Pope-trumpery (as *Medals, agnus dei, Blessed beades, holy water, halowed Crosses, periapts, amulets, smocks of proofe,* and such) at a good rate: as who would not give soundly for a Medal defensive against the devil? writes in good plaine termes of the holy Covent of Friers thus:

> *For there as wont to walken was an* Elfe,
> *There walketh now the* Limitor *himselfe:*
> *In every bush and under every tree,*
> *There nis none other* Incubus *but hee.*[1]

Now see our holy Comedians, if they have not dressed their *Denham* devils, after the old Romaine fashion, fit to amaze *Will Sommers* with-all. Heare the grave Miraclist, how aunciently hee attires the devil for *Sara. Shee had beene divers times affrighted with uglie visions.* You shal never heare a prologue to a Popish possession, but it begins with that style. *As she sate by the fire somewhat late with an other mayde of the same house, being both in a readines to goe to bed, they fell into a slumber, and drousing thus by the fire, there approached neere unto them three Cats making a terrible noyse, and sprawling about this young mayde, one of them leapt over her head, and an other crept betwixt her legges* (By *Malleus* and *Mengus* his rules, this might be a priest in the likenes of a Cat: their hunt was all that way): *whereat shee sodainly looking behind her* (as having beene used to such creeping Cats), *she beheld a strange huge Cat of the bignes of a Mastiffe-dogge, staring in her face with eyes very great and bright, to the bignes of a sawcer.*[2] Heere is a right priests Hobgoblin or *Tom Spanner* in the darke. And wil you heare *Sara* her selfe uncase you this bugge? Looke in her deposition. *Shee was looking for egges in a bush by her Maisters house, and sodainly a Cat leapt out, whereat she gave a startle.* And this Cat, by this priestly power (*O Catholicam fidem*) is sodainlie Hobgoblinizd, and hath gotten a shape *as bigge as a Mastiffe,* and *eyes as bigge as a sawcer:* O monstrous Catholique faith, that canst turne ordinarie Cats in a moment into Mastiffes! You shal have them rancked together, as they came from the Popes tyring-house, that ye may see which devil you like best to set the Asses eares upon. *At supper the Cat afore-said was turned into a dogge of two colours, blacke and greene; and therewith-all a Spaniel bayed* (and therefore *Maho* was certainly come). *At another time the devill came downe*

---

[1] "The Wife of Bath's Tale" (Chaucer, *Works,* ed. Robinson, *Canterbury Tales,* frag. 3, 873–4, 879–80). Taken from Scot, *Discoverie,* bk. 4, chap. 12.

[2] See the beginning of her examin: [H].

*the chimney in a* Winde, *and blew the ashes about the chamber. Sometime he appeared in the likenes of a* Man, *sometime of a* Bright thing *that sate upon our Ladies image, sometime in the likenes of an* Irish boy *with a blacke curled head, sometime of a great* Black dogge. *Sometime he came flying like a* Sparrowe *with a Woodcocks bill, sometime like a* Toade *with a nose like a* Moale, *sometime like a* Mouse, *sometime like a* Minister, *sometime like an* Ey *without a head, sometimes like a* Ruffian *with curled haire, somtimes like an* Old man *with a long beard; and above all, he came in with a drumme and seaven motly vizards, daunceing about the chamber.* This was at the Lord *Vaux* his house at *Hackney,* to conclude their holy Christmasse with the devils motly mummerie.

And which of all these shal we choose to weare *Mengus* his Asses eares? The *Hedge-sparrow* is furnished already with the *Woodcocks bill;* the *Toade* is preferd to weare the *Moales nose;* the *Ruffian* with the curled haire would swagger; the *Irish curled pated boy* would likely runne away with them. Wee had best reserve them for *Edmunds* the Miraclists owne wearing, for fancying, cogging, and faigning such comly cases and faces for the devil; wherof *Sara* saw neither hide nor haire, top, taile, nor shadow, except the *motly vizards,* which happily she dreamed of in a Christmasse night, having seene Maskers in the day, and feasted the priests highly next day with this faigned relation. The rest are all of the devil-priests owne devising, and therefore he may take his Maister *Mengus* long eares, to make up a ful suit.

## CHAP. 22.

*Of the admirable finall act of expelling the devils, and of their formes in theyr departing.*

It is a rule in *Mengus* the *devill-mastix,*[1] and *Thyraeus* the *devill-varnisher,* that the devill which is to be dispossessed must be commaunded to goe out in a visible forme, and for the evidence of his departing be enjoynd to cracke a quarrie in the glasse window, or to blow out a candle: which beeing two such supernaturall actions as by a consorted conspirator with the Exorcist, without the

[1]E.g., Menghi, *Flagellum Daemonum,* Exorcismus 1, which instructs the exorcist to ask the devil his name, the names of his companions, the name of his master, his rank, his reason for being in the possessed, whether his presence is due to sorcery, and if so, how the spell is to be undone, how long he has been present, by what holy thing he can be made to leave, by which person, and what sign he will give in his leaving. The rubric ends by reminding the exorcist that his object is to "deliver a creature of God," not "to talk with demons."

helpe of a cherry-stone, or the suddaine puffe of a wenches breath, or the swinge of her sleeve, cannot cleanly be conveied, it is no marvell though they be a made a demonstration that the devil is surely gone. The penner of our devil-tragaedy hath not forgotten to keepe good *decorum* in this, for hee hath fancied and feigned divers well seeming formes and similitudes for his stage devils to weare at their taking their leave.

The first devill that was disseised was *Smolkin, Trayfords* spirit, whom *Sara* espied (saith the Miraclist) to goe out at *Trayfords* right eare in the forme of a *Mouse,* and it made the poor wench at the sight of the *Mouse* almost out of her wits. The next devil dsispossessed was *Hilcho* at *Uxbridge,* who appeared (saith our Authour) to the possessed parties at his going out, like *a flame of fire,* and lay glowing in the fire in *Trayfords* sight till he had a new charge. The third was *Haberdidance, Saras* dauncing devil, who appeared to the patient like a *whirlwind,* turning round like a flame of fire; and his voyce was heard by a Cooke, as hee flew over the Larder. Captaine *Filpot* went his way in the likenes of a *smoke,* turning round, and so tooke his way up into the chimney. *Lusty Dicke* (as seemes) did slippe a button in one of his turnes above ground; for he went out in a foule unsavory *stench. Delicate* and *Lusty Jolly Jenkin* went out, one whirling like a *snake,* the other in a *vapor* not verie sweet. *Lusty Huffcappe* went out in the likenes of a *Cat. Killico, Hob,* and the third *Anonymos,* all Captaines, went out in a *wind. Purre* went out in a *little whirlewind, Frateretto* in a *smoke.*

*Maister Maynie* had in him (as you have heard) the Maister-devils of the seaven deadly sinnes, and therefore his devils went out in the forme of those creatures that have neerest resemblance unto those sinnes: as for example, the spirit of *Pride* went out in the forme of a *Peacocke* (forsooth), the spirit of *Sloth* in the likenesse of an *Asse,* the spirit of *Envy* in the similitude of a *Dog,* the spirit of *Gluttony* in the forme of a *Woolfe.* But it is to be wondered at that Generall *Maho,* at the last and most dreadfull exorcisme of all, when hee was expelled with twenty-two thousand yeeres torment layd uppon his backe, hee slunke out without any similitude at all. And more, an ordinary Reader will wonder that *Maho,* beeing *Dictator* of hell, is said in the Legend of Miracles, and so noted by *Sara,* to have chosen such a strange part in *Sara* for his passage out as I dare not name: and yet devils, comedians, and their reporters may have licence in all Courts to call all things by their name. And indeede heere lyes the wonder of all, considering that that namelesse part, the devils port-gate in *Sara,* was the priests quest and haunt which they had hunted sore, had crossed,

recrossed, and surcrossed with their holy hands, had sacred or
seared with application of their reverend strong reliques and other
their potent holy parts (as you have heard poore *Sara* herselfe
confesse): [that] the devill should once dare to come neere that part
that had been harowed (I would say halowed) and enriched with so
many precious Jewels from Rome. But you shall finde the Authour
noted that part, and assigned it for *Maho* the devils passage uppon
very sage and prudent consideration. For they had kept such revel
rout thereabouts as they themselves gave out to such as were suters
to *Sara* (as you reade in her deposition) that they and the devil (*O
fidem Catholicam!*) had taken such order *as marry her who would,
she should never have child.*

But to returne to our similitudes and devil visages againe, the
Miracle-minter deales heere with these formes and faces of devils
as *Sosia* in *Amphitryo* dealt with the battaile at *Teliboiis,* who
ranges two maine Armies, devides them into squadrons, wings, and
flanks, and makes them meete and encounter, and none but
himselfe alone is upon the stage. And indeed it is good *decorum* in
a Comedie to give us emptie names for things, and to tell us of
strange Monsters within, where there be none. When a man heares
of these frightful similitudes wherein the devils are conceited to
depart, as *flames, whirlewinds, snakes, cats, fire,* and *smoake,* hee
would imagine the spectators should be much gastred and skared at
the going out of the devils in these feareful formes, and that the
chambers and roomes where the demoniacks and the company are,
should be shaken with the whirlewind, scorched with the flames,
and soiled with brimstone and smoake; and that the assembly
should tremble to see the devill whirle about in the similitude of a
*snake,* as a fire-dragon spoutes and whirles in the ayre; but at our
gentle devils departure there was neither shape seene nor wind
heard, nor motion felt, nor flames, nor smoake, nor whirling fire-
snake perceived at all; and therefore you must heedfullie observe
the Authours clause alwaies annexed (As *Amen* to a masse) unto
the end of the sentence: *As seemed, or appeared to the possessed.*

So as the out-casting of these ugly devils visards lyes thus. The
priests doe report often in their patients hearing the dreadful
formes, similitudes, and shapes that the devils use to depart in out
of those possessed bodies which they have dealt with-all beyond
Seas. And this they tell with so grave a countenance, pathetical
termes, and accommodate action, as it leaves a very deepe impression in the memory and fancie of their actors. So as when it comes
to their cue to play the same part over (as namely, when after
dreadful adjuration the devil is said to goe out), then doth the Exorcist very soberly aske the party in what forme or similitude the

devil appeared unto him at his departing; and he having conned his lesson of formes and shapes before from the priest, lights upon some such forme and shape as he hath receaved from the priest. And then the *Echo* is: *Thanks to the blessed virgin and the whole Quier of heaven.* And if the Exorcist doe suspect the wit or memory of his scholler, as being nothing perfect in his Kalender of formes, he wil not stick to prompt him by his question (being afore an Auditory of Romish guls, whose braines swarme with bulbeggers), as to aske him if the devil did not depart in such or such a forme; and then the actor either for feare or flatterie of his good maister dares not but say yea.

Another rule you must learne in a Comedie wel acted and convaied for the devil: that the demoniacks be so neerely placed (yet in several roomes) each to other, that one may heare without benefit of *Midas* long eares what is said unto or by the other; and so the second may be yare and ready to take his cue and turne of the former, and put to a little of his owne wit for the better gracing the wonder. Or else if propinquitie and fitnes of the roomes wil not serve for one to be the others Parrat and *Echo* touching the shape, let the shape be handsomly agreed of by the devil-actors before, or else provide a mistris *Plater* for an intelligencer or intercursitor betweene them, that may in a trice relate to one what the other hath done and said.[1]

*Lusty Jolly Jenkin* was conceited and given out by the Exorcist to goe out of *Sara* in the similitude of a *whirling snake*. *Trayford* was in another roome, yet so neere as he caught the snake by the tayle, and cryes out where he lay at the dreadful sight, adding that hee saw it come whirling by his window with a wind in most terrible wise. Heare Maister *Maynie* for all report you this devise, the daintiest actor that ever came uppon devil-stage. *And as I aunswer to this point, so doe I unto that other, as touching the devils supposed similitudes in theyr pretended departing out of me. Eyther it is altogether false and devised by themselves, or else they led me to say so by theyr questions: as, if they asked mee whether* Pride *did not depart from me in the likenes of a* Peacock, *it is very probable that I sayd he did; and so of all the rest. Or otherwise they tolde some in my hearing that such devils did use to depart from such as they possessed in such kind of formes. I pray GOD forgive them for all theyr bad dealing with me.*

Thus you have these Romish devil-vizards of formes, similitudes, and shapes of the devils departing layd open unto you by

---

[1]Alice Plater was Anne Smith's sister, a servant in Lord Stafford's household (*DEP,* 381).

their owne schollers and actors to be naught els save squibs, crackers, and fire-works forged out of the priests owne fancie; and that there was no devil but *Edmunds* or *Dibdale* the Priest. Now let us a little looke upon the last and most artificial act of this infernal Tragedie (namely, the final dispossessing and extruding the devils), by which of their ghastly dreadful Engines this conclusion was best and most cunningly performed.

The first honour of this great and admirable act of finall dispossessing the devil did by great providence fall upon a little casket of reliques, wherein there falls out wonder upon wonder. For *Trayford,* the possessed party, espying a casket of reliques in *Saras* hand, snatches them sodainly from her, and applying the casket to his mouth, did expel *Smolkin* his owne Mouse-devil. Where the super wonder is that a man should without Exorcist, Albe, *Ave marie* or *Salve Regina* dispossesse himselfe of a devil as wee finde *Trayford* did, or rather the devil dispossesse himselfe. For *Trayford* the possessed was moved, ruled, and caried by the devil as a wheele is by a turnspit curre that is put into it; so as it was not *Trayford* that snatched the casket, but the devil: nor *Trayford* that applied them to his mouth and expelled the devil at his right eare in the likenes of a *Mouse,* but the devil.

This doth plainly instruct you in these two excellent points: first, the dreadful power of reliques when they lie pent and packed close together in a little roome: that they worke like bottle-ale that is close kept from vent, ready as soone as they be stirred to spout devils, dragons, and all in a mans face. Next, it reades you a plaine Lecture of the bodily feare of the devil at the approach of an holy priest, who chooses rather to make his owne squib, fill it with Gunne-powder, and setting it on fire, to burne and blowe up himselfe as *Sardanapalus* did, then to attend the comming of a scalding Catholique priest.

The next expulsion of the devil was by holy water alone, wherein the power of the holy relique is the more advaunced in that it came not from the hand of any anointed priest, but was taken by *Sara* and sprinckled upon the devil in the likenes of a *Toad,* and towards the *devil-minister* that came into *Trayfords* chamber, and they both vanished away. So as by these powerful instruments a devil may not onely dispossesse himselfe (which a man must imagine he had neede of great help to doe), but also put to flight any other devil that stands in his way or wil presume to come within his walke without his good leave. For else what reason had *Saras* devil to be displeased at his fellow devils comming into *Trayfords* chamber, and to sprinckle him away, but that it seemes he came rudely in, without *by your leave.*

The holy Crosse put to flight a whole Quier of *Puppets* that appeare dauncing the Morrice at the end of a gallerie; and dissolved them so cleane as there appeared neither *flame, smoake,* nor *ill odor* from them. And this wonder was accomplished by *Sara;* for *Sara* (saith the Miraclist) *signing her selfe with many signes of the Crosse, the devils in the likenes of* Puppets *vanished out of sight.*

Heere our wonder like *Amphitryos* goblet begets an other wonder stil. *Sara* by Crosses puts to flight a whole troupe of *Puppet*-devils, and yet the devil within *Sara* cared not for the Crosses one jote. These (as seemes) were but punie urchin spirits that for want of good cheere at *Denham* house were pined and made feeble before the Exorcists came thither. But *Purre* was a spirit of a tough mold and in reasonable good plight: hee held the Exorcist good tacke til at length (saith the Reporter) by often invocation of our blessed Lady and the whole company of heaven, with *Ave maries* and other *Anthemes* of our blessed Lady, especially *Salve Regina, Purre* was cast out. Here Church *Anthemes,* as you see, caried away the bucklers in expelling the devil. *Sara,* the devils sweet dauncing schoole, had chosen amongst all the heavenly Quier S. *Barbara* for her patronesse and Saint: who pittying her poor Client, seeing all the devils of hel in the poore wench, and *Maho* theyr commaunder, came downe her selfe from heaven to shew her grace she had there, and that Saints may come from heaven a devil-hunting if it stand with their good pleasure; and assuming the office of an Exorcist into her owne hands, casts out *Maho* the black Prince.

*Maho* takes this as no faire play, and therefore himselfe complaines of it in his Dialogue with *Dibdale: that a woman had cast him out before, upon her owne feastivall day*

This is no meane office, you may be sure, nor of little moment and waight, when the glorious Saints of heaven come downe to discharge it. Nay, you shal see that for the dignifying of this conjuring profession, and to stop the mouthes of all carping obloquutors, our blessed Lady her selfe vouchsafed to grace it with her presence in her owne proper person, and to come in state with a princely trayne of celestial virgins attending uppon her: whom the devil in scorne calls by a by-name, *Saffron-bagge.*[1] *Loe yonder* (cries the devil to the Exorcist) *comes* Saffron-bagge *with her com-*

[1] The Protestant Robert Barnes was accused of calling the Blessed Virgin "a saffron bag" (*Remains of Myles Coverdale,* 147). Skelton's *Elynour Romyng* explains the insult: "Some wenches come unlased, / Some huswyves come unbrased, / Wyth theyr naked pappes, / That flyppes and flappes; / It wygges and it wagges, / Lyke tawny saffron bagges . . . " *(Works* 1:99).

*pany of tripping mayds. Thou canst doe nothing without her.* And the Miracle-maister sticks not to tell us that shee played the Exorcists part too in helping of *Sara. After a long and painfull combat* (saith he), *Sara sayd somewhat cheerefully: now our blessed Lady hath knowne my neede, and hath holpen me.* For the devil was gone out. And it shal I trust be no disparagement to our Lady in this case to have a simple word in shew matched unto her highnesse, which with the very sound, pronunciation, and name had the same vertue in expelling a devil that her owne gracious presence in proper person had. And that is in the Creede, neither the name of God the Father, God the Sonne, nor God the holy Ghost, nor the name of the virgin *Mary* (which as you see is notwithstanding dreadful to the devil), but the bare naming and pronouncing of this word *Catholique* alone: with the sounding of which sillables onely, *Sara* (sayth our Author) *did put to flight all her pernicious devils.* So as this word *Catholique* in the Creede is as deepe a devil-conjurer as ever *Mengus* was.

These several Champions (as you see) doe severally triumph and erect their severall Trophies with spoiles of several devils. But it falls out sometimes that the graund Prince of darknes doth combine and unite his forces, calling to his ayde his Leaders, Colonels, and Captaines for hel, as *Hiaclito, Helcmodian,* and the rest, and pitches a maine field, so as his forces stand strong against any one of these alone. Then heare the General of our ghostly Camp, how he marshals his bands and troupes against the front of hel. *But the blessed Sacrament being brought, invocation made to our blessed Lady and all the Quier of heaven by the helpe of* Ave maries, Salve Reginaes, *and calling upon the blessed Martyrs, and applying their holy reliques,* especially *of Fa:* Campian, *Fa:* Brian, *and the rest that had beene martyred at* Tiburne, *hell it selfe quailes, the devils roare, and the Prince with all his assistants and commaunders are finally cast out.* These are the troupes that prevaile against principalities, powers, dominions, and all the kingdome of darknes: these larded *Maho* and *Modu* (the two Generals of the infernal furies) with fire and brimstone, and banished them, for a final doome, to be tormented in the bottomlesse pit of hell.

And thus closed up our worthy Author his woorthy tragedie with the confusion of the great Maister-devils and the consolation of his pittiful possessed captives, and that loude famous acclamation of the spectators, *O Catholicam fidem! O fidem Catholicam!* But the lamentable *Chorus* and *Nuntios* of this tragedie (Maister *Maynie,* gentleman, *Fid. Williams, Sara Williams, Anne Smith,* and Maister *Tirrell*) doe tell us another tale, ending this devill tragedie with their own teares, sighes, exclamations, and hideous out-cries against the devill-priests, the coggers, coyners, mynters, and actors of this wicked lewd play. Who were not content to play *Maho* and *Modu* the grand devils themselves, to play at *bo-peepe* with Almighty God, our blessed Saviour, his holy Angels and blessed Saints in heaven, presenting them on this feigned Theater, and making them to squeale, pype, and tumble like puppits in a pageant after their owne impious fashion, and to prophane and prostitute the blessed Sacrament, making it a Pandar to their foule and monstrous lust; but partly by flattery, partly by feare, partly by the bond of violated chastitie, partly by their lothsome potions and unnaturall fumigations, brought them into the same dissimulation with themselves, and to act the chiefe and principall parts in their diabolicall legerdemaine. And when they had once masked them in theyr popish nets, and gotten them into theyr holy ginnes, they did so unmanly, so unpriestly, and so unnaturally use them, as the devil himselfe if he had beene indeed in presence, could not have used them worse.

And these misguided bewitched creatures, now of better remorse, doe tell us that the trussing up of theyr jugling sticks, winding up theyr Pope-budget, and packing up their Romane pedlarie grew from another cause: which was because they understood by some of their Sentinels that their jugling, packing, and legerdemaine did peepe out abroade in the Country, and occasioned divers opinions and constructions of the same, whereby present danger to theyr persons and stage-robes was like to ensue. This mooved them to let *Maho* the devil slinke out of *Sara* in that homly manner as you have heard, that they might (though uncleanlie) ridde theyr hands of him. And now I pray you observe how sutably to theyr former affaires they sorted themselves thence.

It is the fashion of vagabond players that coast from Towne to Towne with a trusse and a cast of fiddles to carry in theyr consort broken queanes and *Ganimedes,* as well for their night pleasance as their dayes pastime. Our devil-holy consort at theyr breaking up house at *Denham* departed every priest suted with his wench after the same good custome. *Edmunds* the Jesuit (saith one of their owne covey[1]) had for his darling Mistris *Cressy; Anne Smith* was at the disposition of Ma: *Dryland; Sara Williams* of Ma: *Dibdale;* Mistrisse *Altham* of *Cornelius;* and *Fid. Williams* of Ma: *Leigh.* And was not this a very seemely Catholicke complement trow you, to see a Fidler and his case, a Tinker and his bitch, a Priest and his Leman, a devil and his damme, combined sweetly together? I trust our devils would never make sute to goe into any

---

[1] See the last end of Fid: examin: [H].

herd of swine, so long as they had such kinde tender cattell to possesse, dispossesse, repossesse, and surpossesse at theyr pleasure. And this in the holy dialect is called *gaining of soules: scilicet* for the devill.

## CHAP. 23.
*Of the ayme, end, and marke of all this pestilent tragaedy.*

The end of a Comedie is a *plaudite* to the Authour and Actors, the one for his invention, the other for his good action; of a Tragaedie the end is moving of affection and passion in the spectators. Our *Daemono-poiia,* or devil-fiction, is *Tragico-comaedia,* a mixture of both, as *Amphitryo* in *Plautus* is; and did by the good invention and cariage obtaine both these ends. First, it had a *plaudite* often: *O Catholicam fidem!* and *O that all the Protestants in England did see the power of the Catholick Church.* And it mooved affection with expression of teares: *Marwood* did tumble, foame, and rage so lively when hee was touched with *Campians* girdle, as the gulld spectators did weepe to see the jugling knave in such a supposed plight.[1] But our Romane Authors, *Edmunds* and his holy crue (his twelve holy disciples), the plotters of this devil-play, had a farther and deeper end, which by this impious devise they had atchieved pretie well; and that was (after the Popes dialect) *the gaining of soules* for his Holines and for Hell, the bewitching of the poore people with an admiration of the power of theyr Romish Church and priesthood by these cogd miracles and wonders, and thereby robbing them of theyr fayth towards God and theyr loyaltie to theyr Prince, and reconciling them to the Pope, the Monster of Christianitie. And for the obtayning of this maine marke and end, they used two chiefe subordinate ends. The one was to bring in the devill on the stage (thorough the whole course of theyr tragedie) as the father of us all, and as the founder, protector, and favourer of us and of our most Christian profession, the other, by causing theyr devils to speake, act, and behave themselves as an hostile and sworne enemy to them and to theyr

---

[1]On this passage as dramatic criticism, see Herbert Berry, "Italian Definitions of Comedy Arrive in England" (*SEL* 14:179–87), who argues that by omitting content and the instruction of the audience from his definition, Harsnett anticipates later, nonrhetorical and affective theories of tragedy in England. Professor Berry does not comment upon Harsnett's next sentence, which in fact says that Weston as author did indeed have an instructional purpose as his "deeper end," i.e. the inculcation of treason. This passage strengthens Professor Berry's case by showing how strongly Harsnett felt that actors had no business presenting themselves as teachers. This is one of many passages in the book reflecting Harsnett's contempt for actors and the theater.

Romish superstition. Which the besotted people conceiving as the very true voyce of the devill indeede, were brought to phancie and imagine of us all as of the grand children and heires of Satan and of hell, and to esteeme of them as of the children of light and the undoubted heires apparant to the celestiall kingdome of heaven. In this theyr bewitched conceit, they were brought to renounce theyr duty, love, and allegeance to theyr naturall Soveraigne, and to sweare theyr fealty and obedience to the unnaturall monster of hell.

Unto the atchieving of this impious and trecherous designe (namely the revolt of the besotted people from their Prince and the most Christian Religion, by the pure profession and swearing theyr obedience unto the Pope of Rome) they spared no person, no condition, no calling, no profession in either our Church or common weale, but abandoned them all in theyr devil-comedie to the bottomlesse pit of hell. And that the seven horned *Babylonian* beast might appeare in his lively orient colours to be he that durst open his blasphemous mouth against the Almightie and his Saints, his accursed brood heere doe that in the assumed feigned person of the devil which the devil himselfe (though a spirit of blasphemie) never dared to doe: that is, to curse and blaspheme (ô hellish impietie, my hart doth tremble at the sound) the most beloved, thrice-blessed annointed of the Lord, the sacred person of our dread Soveraigne, making her no other in this devillish tragedie then the devils principal darling. Heare the devil or *Edmunds* in the devils person (who yet draweth his breath from the beames of her princely mercy, whom himselfe accursed to the pit of hel) in his owne dialect, if your Christian eares dare to heare that which those Popish miscreants dare proclaime upon their stage.

*Oh* (cries *Maho* the devil in *Sara*) *yonder commeth Saffron-bagge* (meaning our blessed Lady), *shee is come to helpe thee; but shee cannot away with a principall person in this Realme, and therefore I cannot away with her.*[1] Heere the play-devil is conceited so to love the Queene as he must needes hate our Lady for not loving her Majestie. And to expresse his devilships good wil (forsooth) unto her Majestie, on S. *Hughes* day[2] hee threatens the Exorcist that he would goe ring for the Queene; and in another fit tels *Dibdale* in a rage that he would goe to the Court, and complaine of him to the Queene, and cause his head to be set upon *London bridge.* In another fit hee cryes out of *Sara* in a loude voyce, *God save the Queene and her Ministers,* expressing his

---

[1]Beholde your loyall Priests. [H].

[2]See Saras examin: [H]. The Queen's accession day, 17 November 1559. For an account of the development of these festivities, see Strong, *Cult of Elizabeth,* 117ff.

devilships not onely good affection, but zealous devotion to her Majestie and her Clergie. But that which shewes their diaboticall impietie, and opens the treasury of their hearts fraught with treachery and treason, they solemnly present the devil in *Sara* upon theyr stage, roaring out an oath touching her Majestie in this wise: *By my troth she is mine.* And the Queene of heaven beeing called uppon, hee sayde aloude: *Another Queene is my Queene.* O detestable Romish villany! *et tamen vivunt,* and are at this day plotting a new invasion to set up a new Queene, who have and doe thus desperatly blaspheme God and the King.[1]

And is her Majesties Court more beholden to this Romish hellish Consort then her Majesties sacred person? Heare *Modu, Maynies* devil, vaunting in his devils voyce upon S. *Georges* day that *he would goe brave it out at the Court, for they were all his friends.* This is the gentle quittance your holy renegadoes doe returne you for the favour or convivencie which they finde, in that her Majesties Lawes are no more severely executed against them. They bring you home a placard from his hellishnes at Rome to assure you that you are all in league and amity with the devil. For so the devil, or *Edmunds,* doth proclaime you from hel, or Rome.

Those famous renowmed Worthies of her Majesties privie Counsel whose bodies sleepe in peace, and their soules (as I trust) repose in *Abrahams* blessed bosome, how our infernal tragedians have disturbed their rest, prophaned their happy memory, violated their tombs, and called forth their spirits like the Witch of *Endor,* making them tennis-bals for their devils to bandy on their stage: take a true view of in the passage of a Dialogue betweene the Exorcist and the devil.

*Yonder* (cries the devil in *Sara* nodding her head towards one part of the chamber) *stands such a one* (whom he had named before) *full of devils; and* Leicester *at this present houre even now, now, under the right arme of that one* (before mentioned), *and all the Court are my friends.* Then went he forward with his speech, naming certaine persons, and said that they are now gone to the devil; and amongst the rest named *Bedford* already departed, and that *his soule is even now with me in this chamber, and so passed*

---

[1]The reference must be to James I, Lady Arbella Stuart, and the Bye and Main plots, which became public knowledge in July 1603. The earliest mention of a plot of the kind appears in an anonymous letter of April 1603 *(CSP Dom., James I,* vol. 1, no. 63). On 12 July, Bishop Bancroft interviewed Anthony Copley, one of the accused, and on 13 July the Privy council issued arrest warrants *(CSP Dom., James I,* vol. 2, no. 43; *APC,* 32:500). As Bancroft's senior chaplain, Harsnett would have early knowledge of this affair, although he would not have mentioned it publicly while it was still secret. Hence, although *A Declaration* was registered 16 March 1602/3, Harsnett was still tinkering with the book in June-July, perhaps while earlier parts were already at press.

*on in his talke, and passed on to matters of treason, and therefore they are not to be mentioned.* Thus farre theyr owne Recorder in his owne sweet termes. And were not those matters of treason uttered by the devil strange matters from hel, trow ye, that the penner durst not commit them to writing, having written so much touching our most sacred Prince, her Court, and Counsel before as the devil himselfe durst not inspire more into his pen? And who doth not feele this palpable legerdemaine at his fingers ends? The devil speakes treason against the Prince and state for the winning and gaining of Subjects from her Majestie to the Pope, and making them become traytors by his treasonable perswasions; and this stands for good Romish Rhetorick and popish Divinitie whilest it was spoken and acted by the Popes Orator the devil; and the devil shewed himselfe an absolute powerful speaker for his graund maister the Pope, enchaunting by his sweet eloquence five hundred, or as their owne disciples confesse upon record,[1] foure or five thousand soules in a short time, whom hee wonne from the Queene, and reconciled them to the Pope by this wel acted tragedie. And might the devil speake treason so aptly, distinctly, and elegantly on the stage that it enchaunted the harts and affections of the poore bewitched people, and chained them to the Pope? And is not this sweet, enchaunting treason to be mentioned in wryting? *Quis causam nescit?* You were afraid, good devil-tragedians, to be sainted at *Tiburne* for this sweet enchaunting treason uttered by your proloquutor the devill; and it must be committed to none but your sworne new proselytes that knew how to keepe it from stragling abroad: whom you have by this one sentence of your wise Orator the devil manteled in the same degree of horrible unspeakable treasons with your selves, not onely for concealing and entertaining treason not to be mentioned or spoken for the abhomination of it, but for yeelding themselves, their faith and fealty, to the Pope, the true end and ayme of all those unspeakable treasons. *Et quis hic daemon?* And who was the devil, the brocher, herald, and perswader of these unutterable treasons, but *Weston* the Jesuit, the chiefe plotter and the arch-impostor, *Dibdale* the priest, or *Stemp,* or all the holy Covey of the twelve devilish comedians in their several turnes? For there was neither devil nor urchin nor Elfe but themselves, who did metamorphoze themselves in every scene into the person eyther of the devil himselfe or of his Interpreter; and made the devils names their Puppet, to squeake, pipe, and fume out what they pleased to inspire. And thus, as the devil would have it by a devilish inconsiderate clause inserted, *that the devill*

[1] See Fids & Maynies exam: [H].

*spoke treasons not once to be mentioned,* have you proclaimed your selves and your five thousand new adhaerents for unspeakable, unutterable, detestable Traytors.

The estate of our Cleargie they have adorned with a special grace, *the devill appearing unto Trayford* (sayth the Miraclist) *in the likenes of an* English Minister, *and disswading him to leave the Catholique Romish Church, &c.* This was a signe (say they) of our especial favour with the devil, in that he pleased rather to put on our habite then the vestments of a Catholique Romish Priest: and yet all circumstances considered, this was no great favor done unto our profession, in regard their holy geare was too hote for the devils wearing. A sute of purgatorie fire had beene much easier for the devil then an Albe or vestment of that consecrate attire. But a greater argument of love and mutual good affection is the liberal commendation which *Saras* devil doth very frankly bestow upon our *Ministers,* affirming by his devils honestie that *hee likes them well, and that they be much better then the Catholique Romish priests.* Which the poore Ideot spectators tooke to be sooth indeede, and deemed us to be too great in the devils bookes ever to be good. And above all, General *Maho* being straightlie charged by the Exorcist to tel his name, he standing upon his dictatorship tels the Exorcist plainly that *hee cannot commaund him, but that the* English Ministers *may. What, and their wives too?* quoth the Exorcist. *Marry thou a wife too,* quoth the devil. Loe here (good gentle Conies that come to weare the Woodcocks bil) you heare the devil alias *Dibdale* plainly tel you that the *English Ministers* and *their marrying of wives* come both out of hel, and are the devils alias *Dibdales* owne counsel to the priest, and so cannot be good. But hunting, nipping, and cros-biting a prety wench on the bare: crossing, recrossing, sucrossing her with priestly hote holy hands *per honesta et inhonesta:* giving her such a Catholique close pinch that you make her crie *oh,* and possessing her with a shee devil uppon the same: afterwards dispossessing, repossessing, and superpossessing her againe til the poore wench is so handled amongst you, as the devil and you give out, *Marrie her who will, she can never have child:*[1] This is but his *Holines* owne hunt and chase for his holy hellish disciples, in which Catholique sport the devil himselfe making one, he can take no just exception there-unto.

After the devils gracing our several callings by his devilish commendation, he must needes of his good nature speake something in favour of our religion too, especially in behalfe of those points wherein we have opposition with the Church of Rome.

---

[1]See Saras examina: [H].

First therefore, for his and our better credit the devil tels the priest that *himselfe is an heretique,* and that *heresie came first into England in the raigne of King* Henry the eight, that *he teaches the Protestants to call themselves Catholiques.* His good devilship *caused* Sara *to weepe for her father and mother because they went to the English Churches,* and tels the Exorcist very kindly that *young children, though they want understanding, must be kept from the Church, because they may be plagued for so going for their parents faults that suffer them to goe.* Heere we must suppose that the devil had taken so much of the priests blessed potion (Sacke, *Galbanum,* and Rue), that he was *Maudelen-drunke,* and in his kinde drunkennes, of pure compassion and good nature, doth reveale thus much against himselfe, to have children and good folkes saved. For being sober and in his right wits, you shal by and by finde him in another key.

*Sara* was tempted (forsooth) to say first that *there was no Purgatory.* This was a sore temptation indeede, to wish *Sara* to say that fire was not, whereof there is not one sparkle to be seene in all the booke of God: which fire the pillers of Gods Church have alwaies held for an Heathenish dreame and a Platonick fiction: whose coles, brands, and skorching flames have beene purgatives for mens purses, houses, and lands, and have annihilated more mettall, and evaporated it into smoake, then all the conceited fireworkes of our Chymicall Impostors have done. And here I feare the devils braine was a little too much heated with the smoke of holy brimston, and grew somewhat adle, in advising *Sara* to goe about to put this enchaunted fire out of peoples heads; for that the conceited opinion of this imaginarie fire hath brought more sootysoiled soules into hell in a fancied hope of a purge after this life, which they can never meete withall, then any one cheating devise besides in all the Popes budget.

*Saras* second temptation was to say, *the priest saide naught in saying of Masse,* a Christmas temptation after the devil was wel whitled. This was a pretty gul of your merry Christmas devil, as your selves had gulled and impostured the world. For what can be greater glee and pleasance to the devil then to behold you the Archjuglers and Impostors of the world to put downe in this craft the Sorcerers of *Aegypt,* the Heathen, *Mahomet* and all. To see you first jugle with Almighty God and our blessed Saviour, and then with all his saints, turning his most blessed institution into a massemonster, a *Chimera* of puppets and gaudes: approching unto the holy celebration like *Bacchanall* priests with a stole, an albe, maniple, an amice, a tunicle, and such phantasticall attire: putting uppon the blessed institution of our Saviour a forraine *Babylonian* name of a masse: making it a night catch or round to be chopped up betweene a boy and a priest: perverting the nature of the holy communion to a private nunchion for a priest alone: severing those two maine pillers of our soules comfort, the body and blood of our Saviour, and renting them in sunder which God had so neerely conjoyned: making the reverend celebration a pageant of moppes, mowes, elevations, crouches, and ridiculous gesticulations: evacuating the power of that perfect and absolute oblation of the body and blood of our Saviour by a quotidian imaginarie oblation of a sacrifice without blood: offering up in a blasphemous conceit the body of our Saviour which sitteth for ever at the right hand of GOD:[1] giving it for the dead, which our Saviour did to and for the living receivers onely: and above all sacriledge and heathenish blasphemie, offering up our Saviour unto God his father thus, *beseeching him that he with a mercifull pleasant countenaunce will behold the offering up of his onely begotten and living sonne Christ Jesus, and that he will accept the same, even as hee accepted* Abels *offering and the sacrifice of* Abraham *and of* Melchisedech *the high priest:*[2] heereby sacrilegiously making your selves not onelie the true *Melchisedech* (an honour appropriat unto our Saviour by the saying of the holy Ghost), but most blasphemously intruding your selves as Mediators not onely betweene God and man, but also betweene Almightie God and his Sonne: beseeching him to accept of *the oblation of his sonne with a pleasant countenaunce* (O hellish blasphemy) *at your intercession!*

[1]See the missall. [H].

[2]A misrepresentation of the prayer at the oblation, *Supra quae propitio* as it appears in either the Sarum or Tridentine canons: "Vouchsafe to look upon them [i.e., the consecrated gifts] with a countenance merciful and kind, and to receive them, as thou wast pleased to receive the gifts of thy just servant Abel, and the sacrifice of our father Abraham, and that which Melchisedech thy high-priest offered up to thee, a holy sacrifice and spotless victim." The words to which Harsnett objected are probably those at the end of the prayer *Unde et memores:* "Wherefore, O Lord, we thy servants . . . do offer unto thy most excellent majesty of thine own gifts bestowed upon us, a clean victim, a holy victim, a spotless victim, the holy bread of life everlasting, and the chalice of eternal salvation." In the Church of England canon of 1559 that Harsnett used, there is no oblation of the gifts. Instead, at the thanksgiving after the communion, there is a self-oblation of the communicants. Catholically minded Church of England priests have always variously modified the authorized rite to supply what they consider a deficiency. Lancelot Andrewes, after receiving the elements from a server, would offer them in the name of the whole congregation "upon the altar," indicating by his use of "altar" instead of "table" that he believed the communion to be a service of sacrifice and thanksgiving. He also used "wafer-bread," performed the washing of the hands, and the fraction, or breaking of the wafer after consecration ("Notes on the Book of Common Prayer," *Works* 11:152–56). Whatever their later personal and political differences, Harsnett agreed with Andrewes upon theological and ecclesiastical matters, and his own ceremonial must have been similar. Like his mockery of vestments (e.g., in chap. 16) and tithes (306), this attack on the Roman mass is not entirely sincere.

Thirdly, *Sara* was tempted by the devil to say *the blessed sacrament was bread, and not to be adored.* This was an old potent temptation indeed. The blessed Apostle was thus tempted fifteen hundred yeeres agoe to call it expreslie by the name of *bread,* and to wil us to remember by the breaking of it that it was none other but bread. *Platoes Idaea* of an essence subsisting in nature without existence in individuall substances (long since hissed out of the schooles for a fantasticall fiction) is nothing unto this Popish brainsick imagination: that the colour, forme, tast, savour, and dimensions of bread should subsist and exist reall objects to our sences, without the substance and nature of bread: that all these sensible accidents should be made pendulous in the ayre like *Archimedes* Dome,[1] or els stript from their proper substance, and adhaere to an indeterminate, vagrant, unbounded beeing: which all the subtile wits of all the Eagle-eyed Schoolemen in the world could yet never christen with a name. These are the Italian Monsters hatched of the egges of schoole Crocodiles, the winding serpentine wits of prophane uncircumcised spirits that take libertie to themselves to descant upon Almightie God, upon his beloved sonne, and his blessed institution, as they descant upon *haecceïtie, nihileïtie,* and all those conceited schoole-tricks.

Our Saviour Christ I suppose would have had somewhat adoe to have instructed his twelve holy disciples, at the first celebration of the supper, in this Lecture of flying formes and vagrant substances; and if our Saviour had told S. *Peter* that the bread which he brake and gave him was no true bread indeed, but the accidents of bread (who could not conceive of leven that our Saviour mentioned, but he thought of houshold bread), it would have caused him to moove many odde questions, and have troubled his braines, and hindered his devotion much in that reverend and sacred action. But our Saviours blessed disciples were but *gross capita* to our subtiliated, sublimated new spirits of the *Sorbon.* The blessed Apostle Saint *John* did thinke hee had brought an argument of good assurance to the Jewes when he beganne his Epistle thus: *That which wee have seene with our eyes, handled with our hands, and beene conversant withall, the Lord of life:* which if he had written to a quirking Sorbonist, or a scoffing Lucianist, that had his braine puffed up with this theorie of formes, hee would say the Apostle wrote like a good plaine John a nods; for those accidents of speech, favour, proportion, and feeling might be *in individuo vago,* in a wandering Hobgoblin that had no similitude of nature with the Lord of life. Verily, neither this new coyne of conceited formes, nor the imagi-

---

[1] A kind of orrery showing the motions of the heavenly bodies.

nation of any Idolatrous adoration was once in theyr understanding who received the blessed sacrament leaning one uppon anothers breast, and therefore this temptation was as auncient as the originall institution, *that the sacrament was bread, and not to be adored.*

Fourthly, *Sara* was tempted by the devill to thinke that *our English Ministers were as good as the priests.* If the devil had not tempted *Sara* to this, hee had beene much to blame; for he beeing one of their *chorus* and a principal actor in their play, and so familiar with all their legerdemaine, did well see that if hell it selfe had beene raked (as they say), and thirteen of the devils most devilish Ministers fetched from thence, they could not have passed *Weston* and his twelve devilish tragedians in any degree. Dissemblers, juglers, impostors, players with God, his Sonne, his angels, his saints: devisers of new devils, feigned tormentors of spirits, usurpers of the key of the bottomlessse pit, whippers, scourgers, batfoulers of fiends, Pandars, Ganimedeans, enhaunsers of lust, deflowrers of virgins, defilers of houses, uncivil, unmanlie, unnaturall venereans, offerers of theyr owne masse to supposed devils, depravers of theyr owne reliques, applying them to unspeakable, detestable, monstrous deformities: prostituters of all the rites, ornaments, and ceremonies of theyr Church to impure villanies: prophaners of all parts of the service, worship, and honour of God: violators of tombes, sacrilegious blasphemers of God, the blessed Trinitie, and the virgin *Marie,* in the person of a counterfet devill: seducers of subjects, plotters, conspirators, contrivers of bloody and detestable treasons against their annointed Soveraigne: it would pose all hell to sample them with such another dosen.

Fiftly, *Sara* was tempted by the devil *not to say her prayers in Latine because God had not so commaunded; but in English, as she had learned of the Minister in her mothers house: Deerely beloved brethren, the Scripture moveth us in sundry places, humbly to acknowledge and confesse our manifold sinnes and wickednes:*[1] *God save the Queene and her Ministers.*

Are not these mens faces sorely scorched with the flames of hel fire, and their consciences seared with those hote burning coales, that dare publish this desperate impietie to the world, that the confession of our sinnes according to Gods holy wil and fatherly admonitions in the Scripture (which is the first beginning of our worship and service of almighty God, appointed and established in

---

[1]The opening sentence of the exhortation to the General Confession at Matins and Evensong in the Church of England's Book of Common Prayer, appearing in all rescensions since 1552.

our publique forme of prayer in the Church) is the devils temptation? Was it ever heard of before, from eyther Heathenist or divine, that the devil did tempt any, *humbly to acknowledge and confesse his sinnes before almighty God:* which are the expresse words of our service booke, derided by these hellish Impostors and fathered uppon the devil? What are our faith, our hope, our charity, our zeale, our worship of almightie God, but Pharisaical cloudes and wandring starres, accursed of God, without true and unfaigned humiliation going afore? And what shal become of their much-commended mortification, penance, affliction, and taming of the body to bring it into due obedience under the government of Gods holy spirit, or in what order and ranke shal wee place these, if dejection of minde and humiliation of spirit, the acceptable sacrifices unto God, be the cognisances of the devil? Blinde and desperate malice cares not what it speakes, so it may speak. For that addition, in scorne and superbious contempt annexed by you unto our publique prayer, *God save the Queene,* wee doe glory in it, and pray unto God from the bottome of our harts that wee long so pray. It demonstrateth plainly to the world with what spirit you are led, namely by the spirit of Satanical pride and desperate disobedience, that dare referre that pious loyal prayer to the devil.

Thus hath the devil (forsooth) spoken in favor of our Prince, her worthy Counsailors, her renowmed Courtiers, her learned Ministers: in favor of the Sacraments and publique service of almighty God established in our Church: now let us heare the same devil, as you have presented him on the stage, pleading for your Church, and patronizing your heathenish superstition and diabolical inventions in the same. *Dibdale* to the devil. *What sayest thou to the Virgin Mary?* Devil. *Oh, shee had no originall sinne, I had not a bit of her, neither within nor without.* Heere you see a plaine blasphemy of the Church of Rome, that could never before be warranted by Scripture, reason, nor auncient Father, that any (except the unspotted sonne of God) should be borne without original sinne, now warranted and stamped with the signet of the devil for good, namely that *the virgin Mary was borne without sinne.*

Dibdale. *What sayest thou to* Gregory *the thirteenth?* Devil. *Oh, he is a Saint in heaven, he never came in Purgatorie.* This favour the devil bestowes on that Pope because he had beene a bountiful founder and benefactor to the English renegadoes, and a most pestilent deviser against the life of our Soveraigne: who for this good service was caried on the devils backe, as seemes, over Purgatorie into heaven. Dibdale. *What sayest thou to* Brian? *Came he into Purgatorie?* Devil. *Oh no, he is a Saint in deede, he is in heaven.* This man was one of the arch-traytors that came over with *Parsons* and *Campian* with special designes of treason from the Pope, and therefore the devil ought him a special good turne, and could not requite him better then to enroll him amongst his Saints.

Dibdale. *What sayest thou to the blessed Sacramant of the Altar?* Devil. *It is the very body of Christ: cut it, and thou shalt see it bleede.* It had beene an easie experiment to have tried whether that the devil would have beene true of his word; but *Dibdale* had an evasion readie twined for this, and that was: *Hee would not cut it, for tempting his Creator.* It was no tempting of God to aske counsel of the devil touching the Sacrament; but it had beene a sore temptation to have made proofe of the bleeding. And yet there was no man of good sence but would rather have given credit to his eyes, if he had seene it to bleede, then to the devils bare affirmation in so waighty a case. But whom should the children of lyes, coggeries, and Impostures beleeve, if they should not beleeve their father, the graund father of lyes?

Weston. *What sayest thou to* Campians *girdle? Whence hath it this vertue, being a seely twist, to afflict, intoxicate, and amaze thee?* Devil. *Jerusalem novit, Tiburnus novit. Jerusalem and Tiburne can tell you.*[1]

Thus farre the worthie dialogue betweene *Dibdale* and the devill wherein are many points of high and prudent consideration. If we may be so bold with his devilships good leave, wee would gladly aske a question or two. First, why cutting should make the sacrament to bleed, and not breaking doe the same, if the body of our Saviour be really there? For veines beeing the vessels of blood, there is fluxe of blood caused as well by rupture of a veine caused by violence (and for the most part in greater aboundance) as by dissection of the same. And againe I imagine that (according to theyr most monstrous opinion) our Saviour had been in the Sacrament, as the soule is said to be in the body, that is, *totus Christus in toto sacramento, et totus in qualibet parte sacramenti.* So as whether you cut or breake the sacrament after consecration, the part that you distribute doth containe whole Christ and every part of him; then can no incision devide our Saviours body and cause it to bleed, no more then cutting off an arme can devide the soule. I feare his devilship was too suddaine in this resolution of bleeding, or els that his wits were troubled with smoake.

Secondly I wonder (considering the deepe wit and policy of the devil) how it standeth with his wisedome to resolve so cleare and easily on the Romish Catholicks side all the deepest matters depending betweene us and them, considering (as *Edmunds* the

---

[1] Westons Tractat of Marwood. [H].

devils *privado* affirmeth) that Protestants be all friend to the devil, and Catholicks his sworne enemies. This is to weaken himselfe and his forces, and to cause his friends to forsake his colours, and flie unto his enemies; as wee find, by these his temerarious resolutions hee lost four or five thousand long-bild birds at a clap. Either all is not well with the devill in his wits, or els the priests had so scalded him in the breech as he durst doe no other. And what a strange advantage have the Romists of us Protestants, that have gotten them two heads whereof neither can erre, a Pope and a devill?

The devils aunswers and resolutions here to cases propounded by the priests are divine Oracles farre passing the old Oracles hee was wont to make in *Apollos* Temple at *Delphos* or the *Trophonian* denne; for they were mixed with aequivocation (the new Jesuitical and old diabolicall tricke), but these are cleere, direct, and plaine. Dibdale. *What sayest thou to the Sacrament of the Altar?* Devil. *It is the very body of Christ, cut it and thou shalt see it bleede.* And heerein the devils headship surpasseth the Popes headship by farre; for the Popes head-peece may ake with strong wine, stirring choller, or strong poyson; and his Holines must have a counsel called, and he must be placed in his Consistorian chaire (as *Caiphas* in the seate of the High priest) ere hee can prophecie certaine and right: and it must be *in causis fundamentalibus fidei* too, and then he shal speake truth whether he wil or no, like *Balams* Asse; but the devils headship needes none of these molestations, solemnities, nor exceptions. His censure is *in actu ultimo,* ready, quick, certaine, sound, infallible, cleere, admitting no interpretation: who being alwaies ready at hand to commaund by *Mengus* his whip, his club, or his devil-bugge, or an Exorcists holy hands, more potent then all these, and having his taile wel sizled with brimstone or scalded soundly with holy water afore, what a good-yeere needs all this level coyle and stirre for determinations of counsels, resolutions of Popes, allegations of Fathers, disputations of *subtilissimus, angelicis, Seraphicus doctor ex ordine minorum,* that doe cramp mens wits and turne them out of their sockets? *Ecce* your *subtilissimus, angelicissimus, Seraphicissimus Doctor* the devil, and tis no more then thus. Exorcist. *Devill, what sayest thou to the Pope? Is hee Antichrist or head of the Church, yea or no?* Devil. *Oh no, he is the head of the* Church. Exorcist. *May hee excommunicate Princes and divest them from theyr crownes?* Devil. *Oh he may, he may.* Exorcist. *Hath hee the temporall sword directly or no? and is hee* Rex regum *of the world, and all the Emperors, Kings, and Princes his Lieutenants, to place and displace at his pleasure?* Devil. *Oh they be all his vassals.* Exorcist. *May the Jesuits (his spirits)* in ordine ad Deum *cog, lye, aequivocate, adulterate, murther, stab, poyson Christian Princes, for advauncing the Popes Monarchie and the King of Spaine, or no?* Devil. *Oh they may doe what they list* in ordine ad deum. This is a short cut, tis but an *Oh* for a preface, and the rest is an Oracle; and so all the grand cases for either Church or Common-wealth are dispatched.

And if they want devils in Italy to exorcise and aske Oracles of, let them come but over into London in England, and wee have ready for them *Darrells wife, Moores Minion, Sharpe, Skelton, Evans, Swan,* and *Lewis,*[1] the devil-finders and devil-puffers, or devil-prayers; and they shal start them a devil in a lane as soone as an Hare in *Waltham* forrest, that shal nick it with aunswers as dead as *Westons* and *Dibdales* devils did. And wee shal as easily finde them a route, rable, and swarme of giddy, adle, lunaticke, illumi-nate holy spectators of both sexes, but especially a Sisternity of mimpes, mops, and idle holy women that shal grace *Modu* the devil with their idle holy presence, and be as ready to cry out at the mowing of an apish wench and the lowing or bellowing of a brainlesse empty fellow, *O the glory of God: O the power of prayer,* as the Romish guls did troupe abour *Sara, Fid,* and *Anne Smith,* and cry out at the conjuration of the Exorcist, *O the Catholique fayth! O the power of the fayth Catholique. Haec tempora, hi mores.* These are the times wherein we are sicke and mad of *Robin good fellow* and the devil to walke againe amongst

[1]Darrell's and More's wives were active in their husbands' defense. Skelton, Evans, Swan, and Lewis were four of the six preachers who dispossessed Mary Glover. The others were Barber and Bridges. John Swan wrote his *A True and Breife Report, of Mary Glovers Vexation* (1603) in reply to this passage, as he tells King James I in the epistle dedicatory: "The cause hath bin blasphemed, our persons pursued, and our names traduced, and that openly in print by one S.H, a Chaplain (as I take it) to the Bishopp of London, whose evill dealinge I thinke not fit, to lay open to your Princely selfe. . . . I could not in silence let pass his speach, wherein he termeth the holy practice of prayer (used on the behalfe of poore distressed Creatures) Devill-puffinge, and Devil-praying: as also that, wherin he compts Witches to be but *Bul-beggers,* and the opinion of Witcherie, to be *brainles imaginations*" (sig. A2v). An interesting feature of this case is that Mary Glover was the grand-daughter of the famous Marian martyr Robert Glover, burnt at Lichfield, 20 September 1555. As she felt herself about to be cured by the preachers' praying and preaching, she cried out "The comforter is come, O Lord thou hast delivered me," and her father shouted out, through his tears, "This was the crye of her grandfather goeing to be burned" (sig. G1). For the account of her grandfather's words, "He is come, He is come," see Foxe, *Actes and Monuments* 2:1713, col. 2). Swan believes such posses-sions and dispossessions to be "the strange works of God in these our dayes . . . the prints of his presence," and implies that Bancroft and Harsnett, if not exactly atheists, favor atheists, and are in some danger of divine visitation themselves. It emerges from this pamphlet that the dispossessing was carefully prepared, and that like Darrell's cases, it was a rallying point for the more extreme Protestants in London. The phenomena, which are curious, are carefully described; Mary had her fits every two days, and the disposses-sion was accomplished by a marathon session of extempore prayer and preaching, lasting twelve hours. When it was over, all concerned broke their fast with a hearty meal.

us; and (I feare) the latter times, wherein lying signes, faigned wonders, cogged miracles, the companions of Antichrist, shal prevaile with the children of pride, giddines, and misbeleefe.

We doe not assever that the devil cannot say a troth, or that he hath not some-time proclaimed the truth; we know he cried and said to our Saviour Christ, *We know thee, who thou art, the holy one of God:* wherein he sayd and cried truly; but this was upon coaction from the mighty hand of God, and not uppon questioning and dialoguizing with the devil; which we never read that eyther our Saviour or his holy disciples did. Nay, wee see that our Saviour checked the devil so saying truly of him, and commaunded him to hold his peace, as not accepting of any witnes or testimony from the devils. If *Edmunds* and his twelve devilish tragedians could in deede have conjured a devil (as the devil of a devil there was but the cogging, conjuring knaves themselves) that would have given testimonie to the prayers, Sacraments, and service of God established in our Church (as they faigned *Modu* their devil to doe), we would have disdained and rejected his testimonie as our Saviour Christ did.

But see *Westons* great wit, the Author and contriver of this devill-sport. When the cogge-devill speakes of us, O that is our disgrace and confusion; when he speakes of the Romish church and the bleeding of the Sacrament, O that is Gods oracle and their triumphant exaltation. O despicable heathenish beggerie, to goe a begging good wordes and credit from the devil! And loe heere (good Christian Reader) plaine Gentilisme,[1] without welt or cover. The Gentiles beeing forsaken of God and given up into a reprobate minde, did resort unto theyr Oracles to aske other counsels and resolutions from the devil; and what doe our Romish Impostors lesse, or in other sort, then *Croesus, Alexander, Pyrrhus,* and the rest of the heathen Captaines did? Let some subtile Sorbonist give mee an essential difference betweene them. They asked the devil questions; so doe our priests. They asked about matters of their commonweale; our priests doe more, they aske about matters of God and the Church. They tooke the devils word for a graceful divine favour unto them; so doe our priests. They accounted the devils answer as the oracles of God; so doe our priests. *It is the body of Christ* (cries the devill), *cut it, and thou shalt see it bleede.* Why now tis cock or devil-sure against all the Protestants in the world, except the difference be this: the devill

---

[1]Paganism. Harsnett's thesis throughout is that Roman Catholic ritual and ceremonial is pagan, not Christian, a survival from Roman and Greek practices. This was a popular hypothesis among the learned in Protestant England; it is the basis of John Aubrey's *Remaines of Gentilisme and Judaisme.*

never aunswered the heathen Captaines, in any matter of import, but in *amphibologies* and clowdes for feare of beeing taken tripping in a lye. Our Romish devils doe give their answers bare-faced without any circuition or aequivocation at all; and therefore our Romish devils are sure the sonnes of theyr sweet Sire the Pope, and the darlings of theyr deere mother the holy Church of Rome. But ô lamentable desperation of the church of Rome! When King *Saule* for his disobedience was deprived of the good spirit of God, and had a bad spirit sent from God to haunt and afflict him, and that Almighty God in his heavy displeasure would neither aunswer him by *Urim, Thummim,* nor revelation from heaven, he then in a desperate mood goes to the Witch at *Endor* to aske counsel of her. *Quid dicis? What sayest thou to my state?* The loathsome abhominations and Ethnike Impostures of the Church of Rome where-with they have gulled and made drunken the Kings of the Nations, being by the piercing glorious light of the Gospel displayed and uncovered to the open view of the world: and that church for her whoredome being deprived of the holy spirit of Almighty God, and given over to the spirit of darknes, giddines, and jugling deceite, having now neyther testimonie from Gods divine Oracles, nor breathings from that heavenly cleare fountaine, nor presence of holy Fathers to countenance their monstrous deformations: doe in a desperate fury and hellish resolution resort unto the Oracles of the devil, and would conjure up from hel the Prince and power of darknes to be their proloquutor, and to grace them with a wonder.

Heare their lamentable voyce, fraught with despaire, *quid dicis?* Prince of darknes, what sayest thou for our Masse? What sayest thou for our Sacrament of the Altar? And now (good Reader) observe the top of hellish resolution and the gulfe of dispaire wherein the Romish church is plunged, when neither God, Angel, nor devil can be gotten to speake for them, for heere was neither Angel, S. *Mary,* S. *Barbara,* nor devil, nor spirit, in all this faigned tragedie, as we have let you to see thorough the whole course of the same. O lamentable desolation! *Weston* and his twelve Priests doe play the devils themselves, and all to grace from hel (being now forsaken of heaven) their pope, their Masse, their Sacraments, their Medalls, their *agnus Dei,* their charmes, their enchauntments, their conjurations, their reliques, their hellish sorceries. *Et praevaluit haec potestas tenebrarum.*[1] This power of darknes,

[1]Not a quotation, but a compilation of biblical words and phrases, as in Luke 22:53: "Haec est hora vestra et potestas tenebrarum" ("This is your hour and the power of darknes"), and Psalm 52:7 (Vulgate 51:9): "Et praevaluit in vanitate sua" ("And he strengthened himself in his wickedness").

played by the children of darknes, prevailed to the gayning unto his holines and to hel foure or five thousand soules, and that in a very little and short time. Whose heart wil not bleede for pitty, and his eyes gush out with teares, for compassion of our blinded, besotted, bewitched poore Nation? The rather when he shal cast his eye upon the maine worke, shape, and end of all this devillish devise, which was this. One of the chiefe impediments that have hindered from time to time the designements of the Pope, the King of Spaine, and their agents, against her Majestie and this Kingdome, hath beene the want of a sufficient number of Catholiques heere in England to assist them; for the supplying whereof, his *Holines* hath from time to time set on worke all his instruments of hell.

When the Lords in the *North* were to take up armes against her Majestie and the state, the Pope denounced his Excommunication against her and against all that should take her part; and sent his Priests hither, not onelie to intimate unto them what the Pope had done therein, but likewise to sollicite as many Catholiques as they could to unite themselves in strengthening that rebellion: assuring them that they were absolved from their duty and allegeance, and that they were bound under paine of the Popes displeasure, and of incurring the like censure, if they should refuse so to doe. And *Saunders* is confident that if there had beene sufficient notice in time of the said excommunication, the number of the Catholiques that would have taken part with the said Earles would have beene so great as that her Majestie with all the forces she could make could not have been able to have withstoode them.

At what time the second attempt (as I have touched in the beginning) by force was in plotting betwixt the Pope and the King of Spaine for the sending over into England of the Duke of *Guise* (*Saunders* being gone about that time into Ireland to animate and assist the Traytor *Desmond,* and likewise to incite and allure her Majesties subjects there to take his part), the feare of want of sufficient assistance heere at home did greatly perplex them: whereupon, about the yeere 1580 and a little after, many more priests (and some Jesuits also) were sent into this Realme then at any time before to labour by all meanes possible for the with-drawing of her Majesties subjects from their duty and allegeance, by reconciling and uniting their harts to her mortal enemie the Pope. To which purpose, it were hard to recount their false and alluring enticements, by exclaiming without all civil modesty and truth against the doctrine of the Church of England now established, by depraving her Majesties government and the whole estate of the Realme in most barbarous and outragious invectives and libels, and by terrifying of some, and perverting of others, with strange reports of the strength and preparation of the King of Spaine and the Pope, ready to invade this Land. About this time also their traffique and merchandizing, by pardons, medals, graines, Crosses, *Agnus deies,* was exceeding all measure, where-with they deluded and inveigled many of the simpler sort. But all these devises notwithstanding, either for that the number they laboured for did not so encrease as they desired, or that the Jesuits had an ambitious desire to carie away the garland from the rest of their brethren and companions in this service: Fa: *Weston,* then the *Provinciall* of all the Jesuits in England, devised this hellish trick of casting out devils: by the which they so prevailed as they gayned in a very short space foure of five thousand to be reconciled to the Pope. And such was at that time the zeale or rather fury of these new gayned Proselytes and the elder sort of Pharisaical hypocrites, so kindled and enflamed with the admiration of the divine power which they supposed to be in these priests, as (besides the large contributions which they gave them) no mervaile if they would have followed them through thick and thin, fire and water, purgatorie and hel, to assist any forraine or domestical power against her Majestie and her Kingdome. I wish and earnestly pray for these gulled, deluded, bewitched poore soules, that they may now at last lay their hand on their harts, or that God would open their harts, to loath those despicable Impostures, and returne unto the truth: assuring themselves that never any true religion did assist and credite it selfe by such diabolical dissimulation.

---

*FINIS.*

---

# THE
# Copies of the severall
## Examinations, and confes-
sions of the parties pretended to be possessed, and dispossessed by *Weston* the Jesuit, and his adherents: set downe word for word as they were taken upon oath before her Majesties Commissioners for causes Ecclesiasticall,[1] and are

*extant uppon Record in the same*
*Court*

---

[1]The ecclesiastical court of high commission evolved after Henry VIII's schism with Rome out of the need for an institutional form through which to exercise the ecclesiastical authority now vested in the Crown. By the last years of Elizabeth's reign, the ecclesiastical commission for the province of Canterbury had become a busy administrative court, staffed mostly with senior clerics and civil lawyers. Parliament abolished the court in 1641, seizing and destroying its records. Like the court of Star Chamber, which was the Privy Council in judicial session, the High Commission was a prerogative court. The common lawyers were hostile to it, but in its later years it was efficient, careful, and scrupulous. See Usher, *The Rise and Fall of the High Commission.*

# The examination of

*Sara Williams,* taken upon her oath, *the 24 of Aprill 1602, before the Lord* Bishop of *London,* Ma: Doctor Andrewes, *Deane of Westminster,* Ma: Doctor *Stanhop,* and Ma: Doctor *Mountford.*[1]

THE beginning of the *history* taken with *Barnes* beeing read unto this examinate, how she began first to be possessed, beeing about the age of fifteen or sixteen yeeres, viz: *how shee had beene divers times scared with ugly visions: how sitting one night late by the fire, three terrible Cats sprauled about this examinate: how one leapt over her head, another crept betweene her legs: how a strange huge Cat as big as a Mastiffe stared uppon her with eyes as big as a saucer: and how afterward the same wicked spirit met her in the likenes of a Cat, comming out of a hollow tree as she was seeking for eggs:*[2] she saith that all these things thus written of her are most false, and that shee greatly wondreth that any man would so write: onely she sayth that from a child she could never endure the sight of a Cat. And that when shee dwelt with Maister *Maynie* at *Denham*[3] (which was about a yere before she went to Mistris *Peckham*[4]), shee walking one day in a wood by the house, and

---

[1]Besides Bishop Bancroft and Dean Andrewes, the presiding commissioners were Thomas Mountford, D.D., prebendary of St. Pauls and a canon of Westminster, and Edward Stanhope, chancellor of the diocese of London, a successful civil lawyer, knighted in 1603.

[2]"An interesting feature in Sarah's sayings is the large part played in them by small animals: the red-breast, the wren, the mouse, the toad, the cat with burning eyes, and the dog which changed its colour" (Pollen, "Supposed Cases of Possession," 455.

[3]John, older brother of Richard. They were the sons of Sir Walter Mainy of the manor of Spilshill, Staplehurst, Kent. Sir Walter was the younger son of John Mainy of Biddenden, Kent. The Mainies claimed descent from a companion of the Conqueror, Walter de Mainy, and their most famous ancestor was Sir Walter de Mainy, a soldier under Edward III, and a founder of the London Charterhouse. The Spilshill Mainies lost their property in the reign of James I, when John Mainy sold it to a wealthy clothier. The senior branch of the family were keen royalists in the civil wars, and as a result of their losses sold their property after the Restoration (Hasted, *History . . . of the County of Kent* 4:367–69, 7:123–24). Richard's brother John had married Sir George Peckham's daughter. Like others in his family and circle, he was arrested in the wake of the Babington Plot, but the authorities found nothing against him except obstinate recusancy, and released him. Since he was a major organizer of the exorcisms, the implication is that the government made no significant connection between the exorcisms and the plot (*CRS* 2 [1906]: 257, 259).

[4]Dorothy, wife of Edmund Peckham, daughter of Sir Thomas Gerard of Bryn, Lancashire. Her brother Thomas was married to John Mainy's sister, Cecily (Pollen, "Supposed Cases," 458).

looking for some Hennes (as shee remembreth) shee espyed a Cat comming out of a hedge, which did feare her greatly, and made her to tremble and shake (as shee often doth when shee is afraid), but she sayeth that she was the more scared then because she was alone. This tale, she thinketh, shee told first to her Mistris, and afterwards to certaine Priests, and further saith that if any Priest or other Catholick hath beene the author of those words before read unto her, they have falsly contrived them, as she thinketh, upon the occasion of the said Cat. For she denieth that ever she had been used, before she fell into the priests hands, to be affrighted with any ugly visions, or that ever any Cat (to her knowledge) did either leape over her head or runne betwixt her legges, or that she heard any such terrible noyse, or that shee ever saw any Cat as bigge as a mastiffe, with eyes as broad as a saucer.

Shee saith that when shee came to *Fulmer* to dwell with Mistris *Peckham*, which was about *Michaelmas* (as she remembreth), shee had not beene there long before she heard that the house was troubled with spirits, so as every noyse and thing that shee heard or saw did feare her.

Shee further saith that the tale read unto her out of the said booke concerning her leaving of her supper beeing greatly afraid, the 12 of October, Anno 1585, is most false: as that *she perceived beeing at supper a puffe of wind comming in at the doore, that shee saw a dog of two cullours, blacke and greene: that therewith a spaniell of the house bayed once: that shee this examinate was then pulled by the eyes, that the thing that pulled her by the eyes went into her mouth, and resting at her hart, burnt her intolerably: and that thereuppon she cast away her knife, and would eate no more meate for that time.* At the hearing of these things read unto her, she used these words: *O Jesus that any body should report so of me.* That which happened at that time was as followeth.

She saith that beeing at supper, there was great thunder and lightning, and that there hapning one great flash of lightning and a great clap of thunder, the dogges therewith ran out of the hall barking. And herewith she confesseth that she was greatly afraid, left off her supper, and grew to be sickly after it. And more then this shee denyeth to be true, and marvaileth that any should be so wicked as to write in that sort of her.

She further saith that after her comming to Mistris *Peckham* (GOD having done his part for her) diverse men did attempt to offer her some injury; and that amongst the rest she was very loth to goe into any place where Ma: *Dibdale* the priest was, not knowing him then to be a priest. Insomuch as when her Mistris would send her with water to his chamber, or uppon any other busines, and she shewing herselfe unwilling thereunto, they told her afterward that out of doubt it did proceed from a wicked spirit that was then in her that she could not at such former times well indure to be in Ma: *Dibdales* company or to goe into his chamber, he beeing a priest as afterwards she perceived.

Concerning her Mistris moving of her to blesse herselfe with the signe of the crosse, shee saith, that when she came to dwell with her she taught her to blesse her selfe in Latine, and at some words to make a crosse on her forhead, at others on her belly, at others, first on one shoulder, and then on the other shoulder, and with the last words upon her breast. This prayer and manner of blessing herselfe she saith that beeing dull to learne, it was a good time before shee could doe it rightly. So as when her Mistris and Ma: *Dibdale* willed her to blesse herselfe and to use the signes of the crosse, shee beeing very evil at ease that night after the lightning, she could not easily hit upon the words. Also she wel remembreth that in saying the Creede, she stumbled at the word *Catholicke Church.* Otherwise she saith that all these particulers are most false, as that *she could not abide M.* Dibdales *presence for burning, especially when he laid his hand upon her diseased place:* that she should say, *her Master had commaunded her that she should not blesse herselfe with the signe of the crosse,* or that *she could not indure a casket of reliques,* or that shee ever so much as dreamed at that time that *she was possessed,* or that *the devill was her Maister,* or that shee ever said, *our Lady did not love her,* or that *our Lady was with her, and chid her, and said shee loved her not.* These things she saith she verily believeth to be false, and that it was very evil done of them, whosoever they were that writ them.

She also saith that those things are most false which are written to have beene uttered by her upon the 17. of October, as that *she should say that her father, mother, and friends were in a damnable case by going to the Church.* For at that time she this examinate was not a recusant, nor disliked going to the Church: or that shee affirmed that *it was dangerous for little children to goe to the Church.* Shee further saith that about this time they began to give her things to drinke which she could not endure, for that she perceived they made her sicke, as holy water offended her because it was salt: and at such times she sayth that they (Ma: *Dibdale,* and such others as were present) would say, *it was not she that disliked them, but the devil in her.*

Further she saith that within about a fortnight (as she remembreth) they prevailed with her to make her a Romish Catholick, and then notwithstanding the devil was in her, as they said, yet they caused her to receive the blessed sacrament, as farre as shee remembreth.

Shee further saith that in the booke concerning the sights which are pretended that she should see at masse, all that therein is set downe is most false, as that *she should see a blacke man standing at the doore and beckning at her to come away:* that *she could hardly looke up in the elevation time:* or that *shee saw nothing then but the priests fingers.* But she saith that she doth not certainly know whether she told them any such thing or no: confessing that she did very often tell them those things which were untrue, after she perceived how she could please them.

Also she saith that it is likewise very false that is written of her, as that she should uppon the 30 of October *see the likenes of a Wrenne upon the top of the priests fingers.* This examinat further hearing the report out of the booke how it is said that *she was troubled upon* All Saints day, she saith she doth not remember the particuler times when they bound her in the chayre, and applyed theyr reliques unto her. But addeth that they troubled her very often, praying God to forgive them, and saying that when she came to the chayre, she was so used as that every time (if she might have had her choice) she would rather have chosen to have ended her life then to have gone into it.

And concerning her dumbnes and coldnes, that *shee could not speake till they had signed her throat with the signe of the crosse, and applyed holy reliques unto it:* she saith that she doth not remember any such thing, but thinketh it is altogether untrue. At the least, if at any time she were past the use of her sences, it was by reason of such waters and drinks as they compelled her to take: and that if she were at any time silent, and did afterwards speake, it was not because they had signed her throat with the signe of the crosse, or applyed holy reliques unto it; albeit she confesseth that whatsoever shee did or spake, they would ever expound it as they list themselves, and say it was done or spoken by vertue of holy water and other consecrated things.

Further, touching the report of that which is pretended to have beene seene and spoken of by this examinate upon *All Soules* day after dinner, she saith shee is ashamed to heare such things to be written, God almighty knowing that they are very false. And this shee affirmeth (she saith) as in the sight of Almighty God, and would so say if all the priests that were there were here present. And she further affirmeth that shee is well advised that shee never saw any devill in the forme of a man that should depart from her when shee used these words (as is pretended), *Credo sanctam ecclesiam Catholicam,* Almighty God forgive them.

She further saith as concerning the *byrd* mentioned in the booke: she confesseth that a bird came suddainly flying in, whereby she was scared, and strooke it with her beades, and that the bird did afterwards (beeing a Robin red-breast) escape out, beeing on the floore at a hole in the boords, there beeing light to be seene and wide lathes underneath unmorterd, so as the bird might easily escape. But for the rest shee saith that it is most false, as that *a blacke man should perswade her to breake her necke downe a paire of staires,* and another time *to cut her owne throat with a knife,* and that *she saw the forme of a rough dog uppon the communion table,* or that *there was any grunting in her like swyne, or croaking like a toade,* or that *she ever received her sight by the priests fingers or by theyr breathing upon her.* It pittieth (she saith) her hart that any that pretend to have any conscience should so write of her.

Touching the report that *she should affirme that one of the servaunts in the house was sore haunted by the enemie* (meaning as shee thinketh Ma: *Trayford) and that shee could never abide the sight of him, because of a thing that followed him,* she saith it is utterly untrue, adding that shee was so farre from disliking the sight of him as that shee rather thinketh she loved him too well.

Concerning the *ceremonies of baptisme* mentioned, she saith that the priests did perswade her that her baptisme could not availe her except she also were partaker of their ceremonies, which were holy oyle, holy salt, and holy spittle, as she remembreth. The salt they put into her mouth, and with their fingers, wet eyther with spittle or oyle, did touch her lips, her nose, her eyes, and her eares, as she thinketh, and in the meane time she had a Chrisome cast over her head, being of halfe an ell of holland with a crosse in the midst of it. At that time they changed her name from *Sara* to *Mary,* where-unto she was the more willing because they told her there was never any Saint was called *Sara,* and the name of *Marie* pleased her better.

She also saith that neyther *by the feeling or smelling of a Priest she eyther receaved at any time her hearing or sight,* never having beene hetherto blinde or deafe (she thanketh God): onely she saith that through their evil usage of her she grew to be troubled with the passion of the hart because she conceaved very great griefe by theyr bad using of her, and that through the said passion she hath divers times swounded. At which times upon her recoverie they would usually say that she receaved her sight and hearing and other sences againe by the vertue of their reliques and touching of her. And at that time she partly beleeved them: but since having beene divers times troubled in that sort since she was married (as her husband knoweth), for the which she may thank the said priests, she hath by Gods goodnes recovered her health againe without any of the priests helps, wherby she now perswadeth her selfe in her hart that she was then greatly deluded by them. She further saith that she wel remembreth that Ma: *Trayford* one night did seeme to be greatly troubled, and afterwards did pretend to be sodainly wel, Ma: *Dibdale* the priest having catched him in his armes: but she utterly denieth that she ever saw any *Mouse offering to come out of his mouth, or after going out at his eare,* or that *the Priests mouth did hinder the devill from comming out at Ma:* Trayfords *mouth.* These things, she saith, are all fained and false, and farther addeth that she wel remembreth, when she was with them they would tel many things of her which she knew to be false, but durst not say any thing against them, for offending of them.

Where it is said that *one devill perswaded Ma:* Trayford *to have hanged himselfe,* and that *another moved this examinat to goe out at Masse time,* and that *she thereby hindered Ma:* Trayfords *ungracious purpose:* Jesus have mercy upon me (quoth this examinat), what wickednes is this? God is my Judge that it is most false.

Also she saith that it is a shameful untruth where it is reported of her that *she by crying upon God and her blessed Lady, and by casting holy water upon Ma:* Trayford, *made the devill to leave his hold, having* (as the book saith) *in the likenes of a* Toad *catched him by the leg.*

Touching the child *George Peckham,*[1] she confesseth that one time, the priests holding of her hands, he did beate this Examinate with one of their *Stoles* pittifully about the face in such sort as she did not love him ever since. For though the *Stole* could give no great blow, yet it made her face to smart exceedingly. But this, she saith, was at *Denham,* and denieth that for ought shee knoweth or remembreth *he ever kept the devill from her at* Uxbridge, *eyther with holy water or holy candell.*

Thus much also of *Hobberdidaunce* (as it is in the booke) she wel remembreth, and saith that her Mistres as they were at worke had told them a merry tale of *Hobberdidaunce* that used his cunning to make a Lady laugh: which tale she this examinate doth very wel yet remember, and therfore is fully perswaded that when the priests did pretend that the

[1] Son of Edmund, and heir to the Peckham estates after his father's death in 1586.

spirit was gone out of her, and urged her to tel what name it had, she affirmed it to be called *Hobberdidaunce*.

There being reade to this examinate out of the same booke the pretended names of divers spirits which the priests gave out that they cast out of her, and that the said priests delivered whilst they were in her, as *Lustie Dick, Killico, Hob, Cornercap, Puffe, Purre, Frateretto, Fliberdigibet, Haberdicut, Cocobatto, Maho, Kellicocam, Wilkin, Smolkin, Nur, Lustie Jolly Jenkin, Portericho, Pudding of Thame, Pourdieu, Bonjour, Motubizanto, Bernon, Delicate,* this examinate sayth that there were very strange names written upon the wals at Sir *George Peckhams* house under the hangings, which they said were names of spirits. And addeth that she perceaving stil that when they said it was the devil that spake in her, and that they would needes have her from time to time to give it some name, she to content them did alwayes devise one name or other, and verily thinketh that shee came neere some-times to some of the names which were written upon the wall, because she had often heard them, and saith that they runne then in her head. And she further thinketh that the priests themselves did set them downe in better order then she did utter them. But amongst the rest, she saith that the name of *Maho* came into her minde for that she had heard before her uncle reade the same out of a booke, there being a tale therein of *Maho*.

The tale of *Lusty Dick* mentioned in the said book, shee saith, is set downe falsly, even as he that made the book list. The Amice therin mentioned was a cloath that the priest had put over his head when he went to Masse, which did signifie the cloath where-with the Jewes did blindfold Christ, and saith it is likely that if they did lay it over her mouth, she might blow it up least it should stop her wind. And for the other speeches, she saith it may be that when they urged her to aunswer those questions, she aunswered as it came in her minde accordingly. And for the stinke of brimstone, she verily thinketh it may be true, for that the chamber did stil stinke of it, they used it so much. That which is reported of her in the said booke of *three Captaine devils that should goe out of her eares, having every one of them three hundred with them, which this examinate should have felt in divers parts of her body:* she saith it is an abhominable untruth, and that she mervaileth what they that so have reported of her should meane, in that manner to abuse her a poore wretch that never meant them any harme. Touching that which is written of the pretended spirit named *Puffe,* as that *he should say upon S. Hughs day he would goe ring for the Queene,* she verily beleeveth that eyther those words have beene devised by the writer of the booke, or else that if shee this examinate uttered them, it was because she heard them speaking of ringing that day in honour of the Queene, and knew that thereby she should please them. For (as partly before hath beene touched) she alwayes framed her selfe to use such words as she thought would content the Priests. And where there is mention made that *she should say that spirits have beene raysed up by a Conjurer to keepe money,* she confesseth it may be she might use such speeches, because she had heard talke that there had beene conjuring about the house for money. As touching that tale of the xviii. of November, *how* Purre *was cast out of*

*her, how she was bound fast in a chayre, and how the Crosse being layd*
*upon her head did so burne the devill, as that shee thought it would have*
*burnt out that part of her head which it touched:* she aunswereth that all
of it almost is eyther falsly devised (as she perceaveth a number of things
are in the said booke) or else that it may be that she her selfe did then
pretend something of it to be true. But shee doth not now remember it.
For she saith there were so many things done, and so long since, as she
thinketh she cannot remember a great part of them: onely she addeth that
she cannot forget her binding in a chayre manie times. The manner
whereof was as followeth.

When the priests were purposed to make the wicked spirit to shew
himselfe in this examinate, and to expel him (as they said), they would
cause her to be bound fast in a chayre, and then give unto her a certaine
drinke, which as she remembreth was a hallowed drinke consisting of
Oyle, Sack, Rue, and some other things which are now out of her minde.
But this she wel remembreth, that looke what she most disliked and
hated they would stil compel her to take, pretending that it was not she
but the devil, that disliked it. And although she knew that therein they
did abuse her, and that few women there are that would not indeede
abhorre such a drinke, yet she durst not but seeme to yeeld unto them:
but indeed they did compel her stil, alledging that whatsoever she said or
did against it, it was the devil that did it and not she: whereas in very
deede she tooke such a dislike at that time of those things as yet to this
day she cannot endure them. In so much as about three yeeres since, this
examinate having a pangue of sicknes in the Market at *Oxford,* some of
her neighbours gave her Sack at unawares unto her, which as soone as
she perceaved, she fel to be very sore sicke upon it, and was constrayned
to lye there all night, the offence of the Sacke being the onelie griefe she
had after shee was recovered of her sayd pangue.

At some times also they would burne brimstone under her nose, at
another time feathers and divers such loathsome smels which they said
were hallowed: and then they would with very maine strength, though
she strugled very much, bend her face just over the smoke which was by
the burning of the said brimstone and other things in a chafing-dish:
which they would hold so neer her nose as sometimes, besides the smell,
the very heate would trouble her. When she was thus holden, she saith
that the very paine she felt caused her to cry and scrich very loude, and to
struggle as much as possibly she could till her strength failed her. At one
time shee was so extreamely afflicted with the said drinks and smoke as
that her sences went from her, and she remained in a swoune as afterward it was told her: upon her recovery, she remembreth that the priest
said that the devil did then goe downe into the lower part of her body:
and that commonly when her strength failed her so, that shee could struggle no longer, they would say that then the devill grew quiet. At such
times when she cried, they would say *it was the devill and not shee, that*
*so cryed.* When she was in this taking and so bound in the chayre, her
head beeing giddy with the said drinke, and her sences troubled with the
smoake, she doubteth not but she spake many idle and foolish words
which the priests would expound as they thought good: which shee doth

now perceive especially by hearing those things which are written of her in the same booke.

As touching the fit that it is said shee had upon the 15 *November,* she saith that it may well be that shee used hard speeches against the priests in the heate of her griefe. And she wel remembreth that divers times, though she was loath to displease them, yet when they handled her so extreamely shee did sometimes use some hard words towards them, and threatned to complaine of them. And then their common saying was *that it was the devill and not she that spake* because he could not indure any Catholick priest. Her sister *Frauncis* beeing then in the house, and seeing how badly shee was used, did divers times perswade this examinate to steale away, and goe home, and complaine how she had beene handled by the said priests.

At one time shee was so vexed as indeede shee ranne away towards a little brooke that was not past halfe a yard deepe, meaning to have runne through it and so to have escaped from them, thinking that they would not have followed her through the water. But they catched her before shee came to the brooke, for they watched her so diligently at all times as they would not suffer her to goe out of their sights. And their pretence was for so dooing, least she should have made away her selfe: which she saith (she thanketh God) shee never intended, but onely to have beene delivered out of theyr hands: whereas she saith, it is very likely that they had such a watchful eye over her least she should escape, as fearing she would complaine of them. At the same time she ranne away as before is expressed, one of them that ranne after her, which was her Maister Ma: *Peckham* (as she remembreth), gave it out that she was carried above ground; and the priests affirmed that the devil did meane at that time to have drowned her. And it is not unlikely, this examinate saith, but that shee herselfe to please them did confesse asmuch. Her pretended carying in the ayre was made amongst them a kinde of miracle, whereas this examinate doth know it to be a lye, and dooth perfectly remember that she ranne indeede, as fast as she could, but for any flying, it is a meer fable, although at that time she was content to sooth them in it.

Concerning the casting out of her of Captaine *Frateretto* with all his company of evil spirits (as is pretended in the booke) upon the 21 of November, she saith that it was the ordinary custome of the priests to be talking of such as had beene possessed beyond the seas, and to tell the manner of theyr fits, and what they spake in them: also what ugly sights they saw somtimes, and at other times what joyfull sights, and how when reliques were applied unto them the parties would roare: how they could not abide holy water nor the sight of the sacrament, nor the annointed priests of the Catholique Church, nor any good thing, but how they would greatly commend such as were hereticks: and many such things besides she hath heard them report, as how the devils would complaine that when the priests touched the parties that they burnt them, and put them into an extreame heate, and how somtimes they could smel the priest. These things (she saith) she now remembreth by hearing those things which are written in the booke of her selfe, and confesseth that by the said tales shee well perceived how shee might please them, and did frame herselfe accordingly at such times as she well perceived it was their intent she should so doe.

Also shee well remembreth that at one time they thrust into her mouth a relique, beeing a peece of one of *Campions* bones, which they did by force, shee herselfe loathing the same, it beeing as she thinketh against nature to have a bone of a man put into ones mouth.

As touching the pretended trouble that shee should have upon the 25 of November, shee saith that there were so many such speeches amongst them as she doth not herselfe remember whether any such things were at that time otherwise then as before shee hath confessed. Also she saith that it was no mervaile though they made her talke, after they had given her the *blessed potion* they speake of. And touching her *smiling*, shee confesseth that when she was well, if shee did either smile to herselfe or upon occasion of some speech that shee had heard, or at other times if for griefe to consider how she was dealt withall she sometimes wept, as oft she did, they would ordinarily (when they thought good) say it was the devil that did so smile or weepe: which put this examinate almost to her wits end, desiring nothing more then to be rid from them. Shee also further saith that she well remembreth how one time walking in the garden with one of the priests, who led her by the arme because she was weake, she beganne to complaine unto him of her hard usage, and told him that shee verilie thought they did her injury, and that she was not troubled with any wicked spirits in her more then they were. Whereupon he cast his head aside, and looking fullie upon her face under her hat, *What, (quoth he) is this* Sara *or the devill that speaketh these words? No, no, it is not* Sara *but the devil.* And then this examinate perceiving she could have no other reliefe at his hands, fell a weeping: which weeping also he said was the weeping of the evill spirit. By hearing of that which is written of her, shee saith she remembreth these stories, which shee thinketh she should not otherwise have thought of.

As touching the report *that* Maho *should bid her pray unto him as to a Saint, and tell her that it was but madnes to become religious or to use penance towards her body: also that the priest said nought in Masse: and that shee this examinate must pray as the Parson taught her at her mothers,* Deerely beloved brethren, the scripture mooveth us in sundry places, God save the Queene and her Ministers: *that shee must not pray in Latine because God had not commaunded her so to pray:* she this examinate saith that shee doth not remember that ever she used those words, but rather thinketh they are devised by him that writ the booke. Howbeit, she confesseth it may well be that she did use them uppon such occasions as they gave her by theyr owne speeches, shee beeing alwaies ready (as shee hath said before) to speake and doe as she thought might please them.

Furthermore, concerning the pretended *vision of things like puppets at the end of a gallery,* she saith that she verily believeth it is all fained by the writer of the booke or by some that gave him directions so to write. For she saith she dooth not remember any one part of it, but yet dare not uppon her oath affirme that shee told the priest no such thing: for it might be that shee dreamed of such a matter, and that she told the priests of the said dreame, who have made such a matter of it.

Againe, that which is written to have been spoken by her upon the *Thursday* as though she understood some *Latine* words: shee well remembreth that at one time the priests were talking of some such things to those that were present, as though this examinate understood *Latine,* which they said was the evill spirit in her: but she then knew that therein they said untruly, and saith that shee perceived they made what they list of any thing. For the word *Saffron-bag,* it may be (she confesseth) that shee used it, but she doth not remember it.

Likewise, where it is said that *she oft threatned to raise the towne and country against the priests, and to cause theyr heads to be set on London bridge, and threatned the Exorcist to complaine on him to the Queene:* shee saith that they who have so written of her may say what they list. She doth not thinke, although she was oft angry with the priests, that she durst use so hard words of them as to threaten them with hanging. And touching her *roaring,* it may be, if they meane that she cryed when they had her in a chayre, or gave her the *holy potion,* and burnt brimstone under her nose, that they say truly: but for *roaring like a Bull,* she saith it is false.

As concerning that which is pretended to have hapned unto her upon S. *Barbaraes*[1] day, she verily believeth that the Priests might wish that all the Protestants in England did know *the power of the Catholicke Church:* but she doth not remember that she said so herselfe.

And touching her coate that was pulled off, she well remembreth that it was a new gowne which her mother had given her, being laced upon the sleeves: which being a good pretty faire gowne, the Priests did pretend that she was proud of it, and therefore took it from her; and putting upon her an old gowne (she knoweth not where they had it), bestowed hers shee knoweth not where, but she could never see it after. But that *she should say her gowne was naught, and full of spirits:* she beleeveth it is untrue: or that *if they put any of their consecrated attire upon her, that she should crie, I burne, I burne:* shee beleeveth that she did it onely to please them, knowing that she felt no more burning by any of their consecrated things then she did by the rest of her owne apparell.

Likewise as touching those things which are reported to have beene uttered and done by this examinate upon the xviii. of November: she saith that she doth not remember any one part of the pretended *vision of a Ladie accompanied with Gentlemen all booted that should offer her to be a Lady if she would goe with them, nor of the dogge of two colours that should terrifie this examinate from yeelding to her motion:* but she remembreth that they would oftentimes bring the *Pix* with the sacrament in it for her to kisse, which she did alwayes very willingly, and confesseth that she beleeved the Host in the *Pix* to be the body of Christ, and that it is therefore very likely if any of the priests did aske her what she did kisse, that she aunswered *it was the body of Christ.* But she mervaileth why they write that *the devill should say it was the body of*

---

[1] 4 December.

*Christ:* and thinketh that the priests would never have caused her to kisse it if they had thought that it had been the devil that then had kissed it, and not this examinate.

She remembreth that she did feare the corne-chamber (that the booke speaketh of) in Sir *George Peckhams* house, because the report amongst them was that there had beene conjuring there for money. And as touching the rest of that long discourse which was read unto her, how *she should say that all the Court were her friends, that the Earle of* Bedfords *soule was in hell, that the English Ministers had power to cast out devils:* she saith she doth not remember any part of it. But acknowledgeth that for as much as it is said in the said booke that she was constrained to take the *holy potion* which shee so much detested, and other their slibber-sawces, and that they burnt brimstone under her nose, she verily thinketh she might utter much tittle-tattle that now she cannot call to minde. And amongst the rest mervaileth that any priest would write or say that ever *he caused the devill to take an oath upon the blessed Sacrament.* And whereas it is reported that now this spirit, and now that spirit went out of her: she saith it might be that they then said so, and that she this examinate was contented they should say what they list, as now she perceaveth (as she saith) that they have written.

She further saith that whilst she was at *Denham* one *Richard Maynie* being there also, pretended himselfe to be possessed, and the Priests had dealings with him. This *Maynie* did behave himselfe in the presence of the priests as though he had beene a Saint. It was mervailous to consider what devotion he did pretend. One time being at Masse, this examinate doth wel remember that at the elevation time he fel downe secretly backwards, and lay a while as though he had beene in a traunce. And when he came unto himselfe againe, he said that the glory which he saw about the Altar did strike him into that traunce. But for all his pretences, this examinate saith that he was but a dissembler and a man but of a lewd disposition. He would needes have perswaded this examinates sister to have gone thence with him in the apparel of a youth, to have beene his boy, and to have wayted uppon him. Hee dealt with this examinate to have confessed her selfe unto him, saying that he had as good authority to heare confessions as any of the priests had. Also he urged this examinate divers times to have yeelded to his carnal desires, using very unfit tricks with her. There was also a very proper woman, one Mistres *Plater,* with whom this examinate perceaved he had many allurements, shewing great tokens of extraordinarie affection towards her. By which his courses she perceaved that he was very wickedly bent. Of all these things concerning the said *Maynie* this examinate enformed Ma: *Dibdale,* and told him that out of doubt he did but counterfet all his holines, and that except he and the rest of the priests tooke heede to themselves, he would in the end bring them to some trouble: where-upon Ma: *Dibdale* was very sorrie that ever he had had any dealing with him.

She further saith that at such times as they pretended that she had fits, which was eyther when she had any fit of the mother (where-with she was then troubled), or when she had beene constrained to drinke their *holy potion:* or when she was otherwise evil at ease by reason of their bad usage of her, they would in the end (when they were weary with dealing with her) say that the wicked spirits were gone downe into her legge, and sometimes into her foote, and that they should rest there for that time. And againe, when they tooke her in hand the next time, they would begin to hunt the devil from the foote to bring him upwards, of purpose as they said to cause him, when they had him in her head, to goe out of her mouth, eares, eyes, or nose. And the manner of their hunting of him was to folow him with their hands (as they did pretend) along all the parts of her body. At one time, when it began to be with this examinate according to the manner of women (as since she hath perceaved), whereby she was much troubled, the priests did pretend that the devil did rest in the most secret part of her body. Where-upon they devised to apply the reliques unto it, and gave her such sliber-sawces as made her (as she was perswaded) much worse then otherwise she thinketh she should have beene. At some times they would cause a maid that served the Lord *Vaux* to apply the reliques unto the place: the which their dealing with her (she saith) she doth now loath the memory of it.

Furthermore, this examinate saith that after she was delivered out of the priests hands, and that they had no further dealing with her upon pretence that she was possessed, she hath divers times, being in speech with Ma: *Yaxly*[1] a priest, but her especial friend, said unto him to this effect: Jesus Ma: *Yaxly,* I mervaile what Ma: *Dibdale* and the other priests meant to deale with me as they did: I am fully perswaded that I was never at any time more possessed then they themselves were, and yet you have heard how they have used me. And he shaking his head would wil me to be contented, seeing the matter was past, and that I should trouble my head no more about it, and saying that he was very sorrie for it, and that he hoped they had repented themselves for dealing so with her. Why but, would this examinate say, tel me I pray you Sir, what you thinke of it, whether was I possessed or no, in your opinion. And stil he would give her no other aunswer, but shaking his head, wil her to be contented, seeing all was now past.

She further saith that the first time that the priests began to have dealing with her, one day they had given her certaine things to drinke that had made her verie sick, and being in that respect troubled, Ma: *Stamp* comming from London viewed with a flearing countenance this examinate in the face, and said unto her, as though he had spoken unto a spirit within her: *Ah Sirra, I have brought a thing for you: I have a whip in my pocket that will bridle thee.* At that present she understoode him not, what he meant, but within a while after, hee pulled a booke out of his pocket, which was of Exorcismes, which was the whip he meant. She also wel remembreth that the rest in the house told Ma: *Stamp* how

[1]Richard Yaxley was a seminary priest, born at Boston, Lincolnshire; he arrived at Rheims in May 1582, received minor orders in 1583 in a group that included Richard Mainy, was ordained 21 September 1585, and sent into England, 28 January 1586. He worked mostly at Oxford, where he was arrested, sent up to London, and imprisoned in Bridewell, where he was cruelly treated. After trial and condemnation, he was sent back to Oxford for execution, 5 July 1589 (*CRS* 5 [1908]: 168; Knox, *Douay Diaries* 2:198; Anstruther, *Seminary Priests* 1:250–52, 389–90).

greatly shee had beene vexed all that day, and that they said it was because the spirit was afraid of that booke which hee brought with him, and the devil knew that it was comming.

Whilst she was in the priests hands at *Denham,* one *Haines* was a suter unto her, and although Ma: *Dibdale* commaunded her in no sort to entertaine him, yet her sister bringing unto her a blacke Jet ring from him as a token, she put the same upon her little finger, which being somewhat too little caused her finger to swel, as now she beleeveth: and thereupon this examinate in her confession acknowledging that shee had received that ring from *Haines* contrary to Ma: *Dibdales* commaundement, they said it was the devill under the ring that caused her finger to swell: and wetting her finger, and making crosses upon it, they pulled off the ring by little and little, and said that it came off by vertue of those crosses, the devill having no longer power to keepe it on.

This examinate also further remembreth that comming towards London from *Hackney* in a Coach with Ma: *Dibdale,* shee espied in the way a ragged Colt,[1] and being the first that shee had ever seene so ragged, shee asked Ma: *Dibdale,* what it was? And he said it was the devill: which put this examinate into a great feare, whereas since she hath seene twenty such ragged Colts, and is therefore fully perswaded that Ma: *Dibdale* did abuse her in saying the Colt she then saw was the devill.

She also saith that one *Sherwood* a priest, while shee was at *Denham,* and tyed in her chaire, would usuallie pinch her by the armes and necke and hands, and the places thereupon remaining blew, he and the rest would say that it was the devil that had so pinched her. At such times as this examinate when he so pinched her did complaine of it, and reproved him for it, they would say it was the devill, and not this examinate, that so reprooved him. Of this injury she hath complayned to Ma: *Dibdale,* being well, and hee would say unto her that hee was sure Ma: *Sherwood* would not use her so, and that she was deceived in that she thought so of him.

She also further saith that shee well remembreth that she could neither doe nor say any thing, but when they list, they would say, *it was the devill.* At some times when she was well, if companie came in to whom they meant to shew any thing, they would take occasion to peepe in her face, and use such foolish words unto her as might make her to laugh. And if she did but so much as laugh uppon that occasion, or looke away, turning her head from them, they had then enough, *it was the devil* (they would say) *that laughed in her;* and then sometimes shee must to the chayre, and at some other times they would conjure the spirit, as they did pretend, commaunding him to goe downe into her body, and be quiet. And when this examinate held her peace, which was when they spake no more to her, then they would say the spirit was gone downe. At these and such like times, when they gave her nothing to make her sicke, she found her selfe no worse then shee was before, but was content to sooth all what they said.

[1]Usually defined as a rough-haired colt, but the real meaning of "ragged" seems to be "sexually excited."

Shee further sayth that a maide that came from the Lord *Vaux* was appointed at *Denham* to keepe this examinate, who did alwaies tell the priests what shee this examinate either did or spake, and of herselfe would alwaies tell this examinate that it was the devill that so did or spake: when this examinate did very well know that shee did and spake at such times according as she was wont to doe before she came to the priests hands. By reason of such her bad dealing with this examinate, shee this examinate did not love her, and talking of her hard dealing with her, shee this examinate said she had thought one day to have thrust her downe the stayres. And heereof the priests made a great matter, but did not blame this examinate for it, because (as they said) *it was not she, but the devil* that meant to have thrust her downe the stayres.

Also she saith that if at any time she did belch, as oftentimes she did by reason that shee was troubled with a wind in her stomacke, the priests would say at such times that then the spirit began to rise in her. Whereas divers times since she hath beene likewise troubled with such wind in her stomack and rifting, and thereby perceiveth that they said untruly when they said that that wind was the devil. But as shee saith, if they heard any croaking in her belly (a thing whereunto many women are subject, especially when they are fasting), then they would make a wonderful matter of that. One time shee remembreth that shee having the said croaking in her belly, or making of herselfe some such noyse in her bed, they said it was the devill that was about the bedde that spake with the voyce of a Toade, and there-with they seemed as though they were greatly afraid. But this examinate, though shee knew there was no such cause of theyr feare, if they were indeed at all afraid as they did pretend, yet did shee let them alone, and said nothing unto them.

She further saith that one night whilst this examinate was in bedde, there was a scraping in the corner of the chamber about the seeling, as if it had been the scraping of a rat, whereupon some that were in the chamber ran forth, saying it was an evill spirit that made that noyse. And Ma: *Cornelius*, a priest, beeing in the next chamber came presently foorth in his gowne, with his booke of Exorcismes in his hand, and went into the corner where the noise was. There he began to charge the devil upon paine of many torments that he should depart. Hee flung holy water upon the walls, and used such earnest speeches as this examinate was very much afraid. Howbeit, she saith she well observed that for all his speakings, and sprinckling of holy water, the noise did not cease till he had knockt with some thing uppon the seeling, whereby she since hath verily thought, and still dooth, that it was either a rat or some such thing that made the noise, and not the devil.

She further saith that she never dreamed in the night but she did tel the priests of it in the morning, for it was their commandement that she should so doe. And such her dreames she hath learned by their speeches to call them visions. Of these visions they would make of them what they thought good. Whereas this examinate confesseth that divers of them were such toyes as came into her head, being woken, and that she mervailed how they could make such matters of them. This examinate further saith that oftentimes when she was wel, and that the priests upon

her laughing, or words, would say, *It was not she, but the devill,* she did
verily suspect that they did not say truly therein, and that she was not at
all possessed: marrie, she confesseth that being young and unexperi-
enced, when they came unto her in so devoute a manner with their holy
vestures uppon them, with holy water, holy candels, and with the *Pix*
having the sacrament in it, and prayed, as it seemed, so earnestly, she did
then alwayes suspect that there was something amisse in her, as supposing that otherwise they would never have dealt in that sort. But afterwards when she was wel againe, she had ever a great desire to be gone
from them, being verily perswaded that then she should be wel.

She further saith that except it were at such times as by giving her the
holy potion, and burning brimstone under her nose, she knew not often-
times what either she did or spake. The greatest feare which she had at
other times, when they used their Exorcisme, was least they meant
thereby to conjure up some spirit, they kept such a stirre, and made mention of so many names, which they said were names of so many spirits.

Whereas in the afore-said booke there are a number of things reported
of this examinate, what she should doe, see, and speake in her fits: she
verily thinketh that (some foolish things of her owne devise excepted)
she neither did speake nor pretended to see any thing but in such sort as
she had heard the priests report that other women beyond the Seas had
done, seene, and spoken: According to which reports, she this examinate
being in the priests hands did frame her selfe to doe and speake and
report she saw this and that, as she had heard of them, that those parties
did, that thereby shee might please them.

Concerning the reports in the said booke that this examinate *should
see upon Christmas even at night, after twelve of the clocke, when
Masses doe begin, viz: great beames of lightning to proceede from the
Sacrament, as it had beene sonne beames shining out of a cloude: that
upon Newyeares day she should see fire to flash in at the window, and a
browne dogge as big as a Bullock: that the Sonday after, the sacrament
being reserved, and lying upon the patten, she could not see it for a great
brightnes: and that at the same time, the Priest seemed to be cloathed in
silver, that stoode by the patten:* She this examinate aunswereth that she
is perswaded in her conscience they be all untrue reports of her. For she
saith she doubteth not but that otherwise she should have remembred
some of them as wel as she hath done other things in the said booke.
Onely she confesseth that she hath heard such things reported of *Richard
Maynie,* that he should have such sights: but sure she is, she never saw
them.

Concerning the report of her that *she should say that the blessed Sacrament was but bread: that there was no Purgatorie: that the service in
England, being in English, was as good as the other in Latine: and that
she should commend some Ministers:* She saith that it may wel be that
she hath asked some questions touching the Sacrament, Purgatorie, and
the English service, and that she hath spoken wel of some Ministers: but
she is fully perswaded that when she demaunded such questions, she did
it of her selfe to be instructed, and that it was not the devil that spake so
in her. Also she saith that when she commended some Ministers, she said

therein truly, and that she thinketh there are of them, as there are of the priests, some good, and some bad.

Where it is reported of this examinate that *upon the third day of Januarie she should see Christ in proper forme when she receaved the Sacrament: that she found ease of the paine in her stomack by the application of a holy relique: and that she flung away her beades, saying to the Priests, fie on you:* She saith that she wel remembreth, that one offending her, she threw her beades at the party, but she denieth that ever she receaved any ease by applying of any holy reliques unto her for ought that she perceaved, how so ever the priests have reported: or that she ever saw any such thing when she receaved the Sacrament: but thinketh that the Author of the booke hath devised it of himselfe. Marrie, she saith, it is not unlike that she might wel enough say Fie upon some of the priests, both because there were of them that used her hardly, and for that she knew wel that they disliked not such words, because they would take occasion therby to shew to those that were present that the devil could not endure a Catholique priest.

That which is reported of her of the fourth of Januarie as touching the booke of Exorcisme, she saith that she knew that booke very wel from any other, both by the Letter it selfe (because she can reade), and by the great number of crosses which are in many places, a great number of them together. And no other knowledge she had of any such booke, although it be given out that she knew the booke of Exorcisme, being lapt up in a paper, before otherwise she saw it.

Where it is said that *this examinate should affirme there were foure scourges of devils, viz: the booke of Exorcismes, holy water, the holy candell, and hallowed Frankinsence,* she doth not remember that she termed them scourges, but saith it is like enough that she said that the devil could abide none of them, because the priests had told her so.

As touching that which is written of this examinate of the fifth of January, that *being exorcised, shee used many idle words: that she prated and scoffed, cursed and sung, called for a piper: when the Priest bad the devill tell him his name, he should make aunswer in her, Pudding of Thame:* all which is said to have beene spoken by the spirit in her: she saith that she might speake such words when her head was so troubled, but she doth not remember them. And for the *Pudding of Thame,* she saith she hath oft heard it spoken of jestingly when she was a child. And where it is said that she should affirme that the devil could not tarry in her legge or foote as he was commaunded because of her hose which had beene worne by a vertuous and godly priest: she confesseth that indeede she ware a payre of Ma: *Dibdales* netherstocks, and thinketh it not to be unlikely that upon occasion she said that the hose she ware had beene Ma: *Dibdales:* but that further hearing some of the priests say that was the cause that the devil would not remaine in her legge or foote, she did say as much her selfe.

Concerning that which is written of this examinate of the 6. of January, that *after consecration shee saw in the Challice a little head, as it were of a child: that shee should call for dyce to play with: that shee should see two at either corner of the Altar, glistering like silver: that she should tell a tale of a Mummery that came into the chamber where shee lay: that shee scoffed at the Sacrament: that a propper man in a short blacke garment girt about him, having the rest of his apparrell also blacke, and long haire turned up, also great ruffes starched with blew starch: that shee complained that the priests hand burned her, and that his breath tormented her:* shee saith shee remembreth no part of all these. What she might speake when her head was troubled with their drinks, she knoweth not, but she dooth not remember that ever she said that she saw such a little head in a chalice, or that if she had seene it she should ever have forgot it.

Whereas also it is said of her that *there appeared unto her in a fit the said 6. of January a Mummery comming in at the doore with a bright eye before them, a drumme sounding, and sixe in number with motly vizards, which daunced once about her, and so departed:* she aunswereth that she believeth that it is but a made tale by some of the priests, or that if she told any such her selfe, it was but a dreame or some such thing as shee had before heard of amongst them, it beeing Christmas.

Also as touching the report of her, that *shee knew a peece of the holy Crosse by the smell: that a priest put his finger into her mouth and bad the devill bite it if hee durst, and that the devill in this examinate should aunswer, hee durst not bite it because it had touched the Lord:* shee saith shee well remembreth that she heard them talke that they had a peece of the holy Crosse, but shee dooth not believe that shee knew it by the smell, unlesse it had beene sweetly kept, and that she might smell the savour thereof when it came neere her. And further saith that it is not unlike but that she refused to bite the priests finger, for if it had beene Maister *Dibdales* finger she knew he was very likely to have given her a box on the eare if shee had bitten it. And it might be also that shee said *she would not bite it because it had touched the Lord,* shee being then wel acquainted with those things: but whether she did so or no, she doth not now remember.

Whereas it is said that *in one of her fits she was sencelesse the same day untill the blessed Sacrament was applyed unto one of her eares, and that then she felt a cold wind to come in at one, and a hote ayre to goe out at the other:* shee answereth that she remembreth no such thing, as neither another report of a vision she should have that night of a whole bench of devils. Although she confesseth, that as her manner was, the most mornings shee would tell them one tale or other, or els (as she saith) how should they have had writing worke: but she remembreth not whether she told them this tale or no.

That which is reported to have been done by her the seaventh of January, as that *she should (as she thought) let her beades fall downe to the ground because they seemed to burne her hand, whereas the devill threw them directly upon the Altar, and strooke downe the corner of the Chalice:* this examinate remembreth no such thing, but mervaileth that the devil durst meddle with her beades, because they were hallowed.

Where it is said that the same day *this examinate or* (as they pretended) *the devill in her was unwilling to adore the blessed sacrament because of the brightnes of it: that at the second elevation she should say, I will not be blessed: At* Pax domini sit semper vobiscum,[1] *I will none of that: At* Agnus Dei qui tollis peccata mundi, miserere nobis,[2] *upon thee and not uppon mee: At the offering of the* Pax *to kisse,*[3] it stinketh: *when the priest said,* Domine non sum dignus,[4] *and betweene the receiving of both kinds:*[5] I will not receive: this examinate saith that the priests had taught her the English of the Latine words before mentioned, so as she verily thinketh that shee was not unlike to say as it is reported of her when she heard those Latine words. But she thinketh those things false that are reported of her to have beene done by her the 8 of January, as that *shee should talke to the Exorcist in French,* whereas shee knoweth very few words in French, but such as shee heard amongst them as, *Bonjour,* or two or three more.

As touching the long reports of this examinate, how *she was handled the ninth and tenth dayes of January,* viz: amongst many other things, how *the devill was remooved out of her hands by the putting on of the Exorcists gloves: how* Maho *the chiefe devill* (that was pretended to be in her) *who had two thousand devils at his commaundement, had beene in England ever since king* Henry *the eyghts time: how the said* Maho *should tell the Exorcist that if he would cut the sacrament with his knife hee should see it bleed: and that he the sayd* Maho *could not choose but be tormented at the offering of it: how* Maho *did first sweare upon the blessed sacrament, and kissed it, and then uppon the booke of exorcismes, and then kist that likewise: how this examinate was vexed when the priests laboured with theyr holy hands and by touching of her with sacred reliques, till they had brought* Maho *into her belly:* she aunswereth with many teares, God forgive them that thus did abuse me, there was never I thinke poore soule so dealt with. And afterwards for further aunswer she saith that it appeareth by the booke that the said tenth day of January they gave her the holy potion, and burnt brimstone and Frankinsence under her nose, which did so trouble her as shee thinketh that she might speake she knew not what, and they likewise write and report of her as they thought good, and as shee perceived they had done by the rest she had heard read unto her out of that booke.

[1]"The peace of the Lord be always with you," the salutation spoken at Mass by the celebrant after the fracture or breaking of the consecrated host, and before the Agnus Dei.

[2]"O Lamb of God, that takest away the sins of the world, have mercy upon us," sometimes called the anthem of sacrifice, spoken three times by the celebrant before the administration of communion.

[3]In the Tridentine canon of the Mass, the prayer for the peace of the Church followed the Agnus Dei; then the celebrant offered the kiss of peace with "Pax tecum," "Peace be with you." The pax was a tablet bearing a depiction of a pious image, often of the crucifixion, kissed by celebrant and worshipers.

[4]Spoken three times by the celebrant before he receives communion: from the words of the centurion (Matthew 8:8): "Lord, I am not worthy that thou shouldest come under my roof, but speak the word only and my soul shall be healed."

[5]I.e., the receiving of the bread and the wine by the priest. By behaving irreverently at this part of the Mass, which prepares priest and people to receive communion, Sara was refusing to take her part as a lay person in the service.

She further saith that beeing at the Lord *Vaux* his house at *Hackney,* the priests a little before (as she remembreth) that shee was exorcised in the chayre, caused a woman to squirt somthing by her privie parts into her body, which made her very sick. She was so used once or twice more at *Hackney,* and once at *Denham,* whereby she knoweth as she saith that she sustained very great hurt.

Furthermore she saith that the last time that shee was exorcised at *Hackney,* the priests gave it out that the devill departed out of her by her priviest part. And upon her marriage some of them told her husband that shee would never bring him any children because as they affirmed, the devill had torne those parts in such sort as that she could not conceive, which shee thanketh God proveth to be false, for shee hath had (as shee saith) five children. But shee saith by hearing the booke read that is written of her, shee hath called many things to mind, and doth perceive that shee hath beene very badly dealt with. And further shee saith that after shee once came to be under their hands, they used the matter so with her as that she never durst doe any thing but what she thought did please them: so as the longer she continued with them, the more they wrought upon her, because she had learned what words did best like them, as her rayling against priests, and commending of Protestants, and speaking of many vaine and foolish words whereof they would make what they list. Likewise she could tel how to feed them with visions, saying she had seene this and that when she had seene no such matter, but onely spake to content them.

Besides, in Christmas time there was gaming and mumming at the Lord *Vaux* his house, and (as she saith) she saw the mummers dressed with their vizards: whereby she learned to talke of such things, when they said, the spirit began to ascend out of her foote: that is, when he began from time to time (as they say) to trouble her.

Againe, as before, she saith that whilst she was at *Denham* she told Ma: *Dibdale* that she verily thought she was no more possessed then any of them were (meaning the rest of the priests). And likewise as she perceaved three or foure yeeres after by Ma: *Yaxleyes* words, and shaking of his head, when she complained unto him how she had been dealt with, that he himselfe did think no otherwise of her: so she this examinate, as wel at other times whilst she was at *Denham* as afterwards manie times, stil thought; but now (as she saith) by hearing of the booke they have written of her read, she is not onlie fully perswaded that she was never at all possessed, but seeth that they have written of her most abhominablie and villanously, and she prayeth God to forgive them, saying that she needeth not to wish them worse hurt then hath, or wil, come to them for their false and dissembling dealing with her.

Whilst this examinate was in the priests hands at *Denham,* she wel remembreth (as she saith) that one Ma: *Babington* and divers other Gentlemen were there. Also Ma: *Edmunds* the Jesuit was there, or at the least, such a man as they called Fa: *Edmunds,* who was a chiefe man amongst them and over the rest (as she hath heard). Likewise, she saith that there were many, both men and women, that came thither to see miracles (as it was given out) who were daily reconciled. She also remembreth that the priests would say that those who came thither and would not be reconciled were in great danger, whereas if they would submit themselves and reconcile themselves, then the devil should have no power of them. The number, she saith, that upon these occasions were reconciled, was very great. It was an usual saying with the priests that many Protestants were possessed, and that if they were once reconciled the devil would shew himselfe in them; and they brought her this examinate for an instance, saying that til she was reconciled the devil was quiet in her. Whereas, she saith, she wel knoweth that she was (she thanketh God) as free from the devil possessing of her til she fel into their hands, as any of the priests were.

After the priests gave over the exorcising of this examinate, she was at their direction convayed from place to place for almost foure yeeres, and maintained for the most part at their charges, saving so much as she had for her paines in those places where she remained.

When this examinate should be married, Ma: *Yaxly* the priest told her a story of *Tobias* sonne, and wished her that in any wise she should refraine from the company of her husband for the first three nights, which counsel (she saith) she followed, being wholy at that time ruled by him.[1]

She further saith that if Ma: *Dibdale* had lived but a moneth longer, she this examinate had not beene heere to have beene now examined of this matter. For he was purposed (as he said) to have sent her beyond the Seas that she might have beene a Nun. And to that end he had provided fourty pound, part whereof was in Ma: *Yaxlyes* hands, and part in her owne. But after Ma: *Dibdales* death, that which this examinate had Ma: *Yaxley* tooke from her, and promised her husband when she was to be married fourty pound, whereof notwithstanding he never receaved above five pounds, as she thinketh.

Againe, she saith that whilst she was in their hands, she had silver and gold given her of those that came to see her, which she stil gave to Ma: *Dibdale,* because he perswaded her that she might not have it her selfe for that the devil thereby would tempt her, and doe her hurt. When he the said *Dibdale* was afterwards executed, this examinate had of his a purse full of gold, which he left with her: where-with Ma: *Alexander* a priest being acquainted, she this examinate by his commaundement deivered it unto him.

She also saith that by one *Hodgskins* meanes, a Pursuivant, she was a little after Ma: *Dibdales* death committed to prison at *Oxford* for recusancie, where she remained about fourteen weekes. At what time Ma: *Yaxley* caused divers to make earnest sute for her: much venison (as

---

[1]The story, from the apocryphal Book of Tobit, of Tobias, son of Tobit, tells how he married Sarah, daughter of Raguel, whose first seven husbands had been killed on the wedding night by the demon Asmodeus. On the advice of the angel Raphael, Tobias drove out the demon with the smoke of the heart and liver of a fish, burned on a fire of incense. Did Sara's possession lead Fr. Yaxley to fear for Sara's husband, or did he merely want her to imitate the piety of the scriptural characters? Presumably this story authorized the exorcists' fumigation of their patients.

she hath heard) was bestowed upon the Schollers, and at the last she was called before a Doctor, and after some fewe speeches delivered.

About nine or tenne yeares since, this examinate was sent for by two Justices of the peace, Sir *Anthony Cope*, and Ma: *Doily*, to be examined, partly about these matters of possession.[1] But she never did confesse a word unto them of it. At other times also she hath beene examined, but disclosed nothing. When upon these occasions she was at any time in trouble, she was stil maintayned and her costs borne by the priests meanes. She also saith that because she would confesse nothing, she was very much made of. It was ordinarie with the priests to charge her in any wise that if she happened at any time to be examined, she should never take any oath, for that was verie dangerous, and told her that then she might say any thing, though it were untrue, to excuse her selfe. They also warned her to be very careful what she said, and in no wise to confesse any thing that might touch any priest and doe them any harme, saying that if she did, the devil would surely possesse her againe, because thereby she should dishonour God and his Priests, and be a slander to the Catholique Church. And they told her an example of a woman that after a priest had dispossessed her, she dealt amisse, and there-upon the devil came into her againe, and continued in her so long as she lived. And so, they said, he would deale with her this examinate if she did or confessed any thing against them. But notwithstanding she now saith that shee is very glad she hath discharged her conscience and unburdened her minde of these things, by telling the truth. Nothing doubting but that Almighty God wil pardon her, in that she yeelded so farre to be in such sort abused by them: and that heereafter the devil shal never have power, by the perswasion of any priests or other persons what so ever, to draw her to such wicked courses heereafter.

---

[1]Cope was high sheriff of Oxfordshire in 1580, 1591, and 1603, and M.P. for Banbury. He was a Puritan, imprisoned in 1587 for presenting to the speaker of the House of Commons a Puritan revision of The Book of Common Prayer, and a bill abrogating ecclesiastical law *(DNB)*. Thomas D'Oyly was a physician and scholar of Spanish. He practiced in London, where he was physician to St. Bartholomew's Hospital, but he also maintained connections with Oxford *(DNB)*.

# The examination of *Friswood*
## alias *Frauncis Williams,* taken upon oath the second of March 1598, but augmented and repeated the 17. of May 1602. before the Lord *Bishop of London,* Master Doctor *Andrewes* Deane of Westminster, Ma: Doctor *Stanhop,* and Ma: Doctor *Swale.*[1]

SHEE saith that about seventeen yeeres since, shee beeing then about seventeen yeeres of age served on Mistrisse *Peckham* the wife of Ma: *Edmund Peckham* dwelling then at *Denham* in *Buckingham-shire.* This Mistris *Peckham* was the daughter of Sir *Thomas Jarret* in *Lancashire.*

The cause of this examinats serving the said Mistrisse *Peckham* was for that this examinates sister *Sara Williams* (that likewise served her) was then in the hands of certaine Priests, who said she was possessed. At that time also, one *Trayford* Maister *Peckhams* man was there likewise in the same case with this examinats sister. By meanes of these troubles there, this examinats father being Sir *George Peckhams* man, father to the said Ma: *Edmund,* shee this examinate, as now shee verilie believeth, was thought a meet person to be entertained in the house as one who they thought would keepe all theyr counsels, howsoever they should deale and practise with her or any other in that place.

This examinate further saith that as she remembreth, the distinct time of her comming to serve Mistris *Peckham* was about three or four daies after that shee the said Mistrisse *Peckham* came from *Fulmer* to *Denham* with all her houshold, bringing with her the said two possessed parties, as it was then pretended. Upon this examinats first entertainement, many priests resorted to *Denham* under pretence to cast the devils out of those persons. Amongst them all one Ma: *Edmunds* a Jesuit was the chiefe that bare the sway, and gave directions in those matters, and Ma: *Dibdale* was the next, who tooke especiall paines in their exorcisings. The names of other priests that resorted thether, as farre as shee remembreth, were these: Ma: *Driland,* Ma: *Midleton,* Ma: *Yaxley,* Ma: *Sherwood,* Ma: *Stampe,* Ma: *Tirrell,* Ma: *Thomson,* Ma: *Thulice,* Ma: *Cornelius,* Ma: *Browne,* Ma: *Ballard,* Ma: *Blackman,* Ma: *Greene,* Ma: *Bruerton.*[2] There were besides these a great number whose names she hath forgot-

---

[1]Swale (1545–1608) was a civil lawyer who like Bancroft had been a fellow of Jesus College, Cambridge, and a protégé of Sir Christopher Hatton. Besides being chancellor and vicar-general of the diocese of Ely, he held the prebend of Newbald, York, and the rectory of Emneth. At Cambridge in the 1580s he was accused of popery. Like his colleague Stanhope, he was knighted in 1603 *(DNB).*

[2]On Fid Williams's list of priests, see Appendix A.

ten, that resorted thether. And many, especially of the younger priests that were lately come over, did not tell theyr names, at the least this examinate did not know them.

Uppon her first comming to *Denham*, and so for five or sixe weekes, this examinate heard much in the house of her sister and Ma: *Trayfords* fits: and it was not long after her Mistris comming from *Fulmer* before one *Marwood* was brought to *Denham*, and then shortly one Ma: *Richard Mainy*, who both of them did pretend themselves to be likewise possessed. Ma: *Ballard* the Priest brought the said *Marwood* thether, and in his companie there came twelve or thirteene as shee remembreth, viz. Ma: *Babington*, Ma: *Tichburne*, Ma: *Dun*, Ma: *Gage*, Ma: *Tilny*, and the most of the rest that were executed with Ma: *Babington*: they came thether in foure or five Coaches.

When this examinate first came to Mistris *Peckham*, shee had before ever used to goe to the Church, but then the priests laboured to perswade her to the contrary. The parties that dealt with her to that purpose in the beginning were Ma: *Edmund Peckham* and one *Alexander* an Apothecarie, but since a priest.[1]

About the end of the said five or sixe weekes, the priests beganne to practise with this examinate to make her believe also that she was possessed. The manner whereof was in this sort. Shee beeing washing of clothes in the Kitchen at *Denham*, maister *Dibdale* the priest came in, and clapping her upon the shoulder, told her that her mistrisse looked for her. To whom this examinate answered that she had almost done, and then she would come unto her. Presently after, this examinate and one of her fellowes having filled a tub of water to rince theyr clothes, this examinate lifting up the tub, her feete slipped from under her, the kitchen beeing paved, and having a shrewd fall, did hurt her hip, with the griefe whereof she was compelled to keepe her bed for two or three dayes.

Heereupon maister *Dibdale* comming to this examinate told her that it was a wicked spirit that gave her that fal, and said that the cause that moved the spirit so to doe was for that shee had washed his the said maister *Dibdales* shirt, which the wicked spirit tooke in evill part because he was a Catholique priest, to whom the devill could not endure that any kindnes should be shewed: and for that also the same his shirt was fouled

---

[1]There is no record of a missionary priest, regular or secular, called Alexander, although "Willm Alexonder an old priest," i.e., a Marian priest, was in the Gatehouse "lately committed," 25 September 1586 (*CRS* 2 [1906]: 258). If Alexander was the apothecary's first name, then—as Pollen suggested—he will have been Alexander Rawlins, committed to Newgate by Justice Young in June, discharged by him 15 July, and recommitted 8 September (*CRS* 2 [1906]: 267; Pollen, "Supposed Cases," 461). He was born at Oxford, 1560, and educated at Winchester and Oxford. After his second imprisonment in 1586, he was banished as "an obstinate papist and a follower of Semynaries" (*CRS* 2 [1906]: 264), and arrived at Rheims 23 December 1587. He was ordained at Soissons, 18 March 1590, and sent to England 9 April. He worked in York and Durham. On Christmas Day, 1594, he was arrested at Winston, Durham. He was condemned at York, 4 April 1595, and martyred at Knavesmeer with Henry Walpole, 7 April (Anstruther, *Seminary Priests* 1:285–86). Anstruther follows Pollen in identifying him with the apothecary. Fid calls the apothecary "Master Alexander" (226–27), and this suggests that Alexander was his surname—but Fid is not to be relied on.

with the sweat which came from him in taking paines to exorcise the parties supposed to be possessed. He did also at the same time and afterwards likewise deale earnestlie with this examinate to perswade her to be a Catholick, and from the time of her said fall ceased not to tell her that she was possessed: and so did the rest of the priests that then were there. The said maister *Dibdale* did urge her to be advised by him, promising that if so she would, she should receive great ease and comfort therein.

She also saith that upon occasion of speech with maister *Dibdale* of the ache of her hip, he entred into a further examination of her, if she had not before that time felt some paine in her body. And shee confessing that somtimes she had a paine in one of her sides: Ah quoth he, I thought even so; out of question, you are possessed, and so have beene for a good while, the paine you speake of proceeding from the said spirit.

Thus labouring with this examinate to make her to believe that shee was possessed, they told her that before they could doe her any good, she must needs become a Catholique: and at the length, by telling her that shee was in state of damnation and out of the Church, and that she must believe the articles of the Creede, whereof one was that shee ought to believe the *Catholique Church* which was (as they said) the Church of *Rome,* shee did yeeld unto them to be reconciled, as she thinketh they terme it.

At the time that this examinate was thus become a Catholique, the priests told her that her baptisme received in the protestants Church must be amended, because it wanted many ceremonies of the Catholique Church. And thereuppon they used such things as they thought good to make her baptisme perfect. They cast a white cloth over her head with a crosse upon it, and using certaine words, they put salt into her mouth, and did annoint her lippes, her nose, her eyes, and her eares. At that time also, they caused her to change her name, so as she being when she was christned, called *Friswood,* from that time forward shee hath been called *Frauncis.* They told her divers tales of S. *Frauncis,* that he was so holy a man that he might commaund the birds of the ayre to come unto him, and that therefore his name was made common both for men and women.

Shee further saith that after shee had kept her bedde two or three daies (as before is mentioned), she did (notwithstanding her said hurt) follow her busines as wel as shee could, though she halted. This her so halting, the priests still said that the devil caused it, and after omitted no occasion to tell her of the paine in her side, and annointing her hip, did alwaies say that it was the devill that lay there; till at last this examinate began (especially after she was a Catholique) to thinke they said truly, and that she was indeed possessed. Although (as now shee saith) shee afterwards perceived that shee had never any other trouble after her hip was well, but now and then a paine as she was wont to have in her side, which paine doth still continue, beeing a griefe of the spleene, as the Physicians tell her, for ease whereof shee is commonlie let blood once a yeere. And for any other vexation or griefe whilst she was under the priests hands, shee sayth shee had none but such as they procured by theyr drinks and perfumes and other bad usage of her.

Furthermore shee saith that within a while after that she was a Catholique, the priests told her that according to their promise they would now try to make her well, and to rid her from the wicked spirit. The manner whereof was as followeth. At the end of the first Masse that ever she saw, which was said by maister *Dibdale*, he told her that now they would make triall what was in her; and thereupon shee beeing perfectly well, and telling maister *Dibdale* and the rest as much, yet they would needs have her to sit downe in a chayre, which shee did. Then they began to binde her with towels, whereat she greatly mervailed, and was there-with cast into a great feare, as not knowing what they meant to doe with her. Beeing in this case, maister *Dibdale* began to read upon his booke of Exorcismes, and after a good while, seeing no other alteration in her then the tokens of feare (for she confesseth the same increased by reason of his words and other his dealings with her), then they urged her to drinke above a pint of Sack and Sallet-oyle, being hallowed, and mingled with some kind of spices. When she tasted this drinke, which they termed a *holy potion*, it did so much dislike her that shee could drinke but a little of it at once (her stomacke greatly loathing of it). And then the priests said all that came from the devill, who hated nothing worse then that holy drinke. So as she was held, and by very force caused to drinke it up at divers draughts. Heere-upon (as she saith) she grew to be very sicke and giddie in her head, and began to fal into a cold sweate, verily then beleeving that as the priests said it was a wicked spirit that caused her to be in such case. Whereas afterwards when shee better had considered of their dealings with her, she easily perceaved that the drinke they gave her was such as might have made a horse sicke.

Againe she saith that being thus in the priests hands from a little before Christmas til two or three dayes before Whitsonday following, she was often abused in this manner: and at some times when she was bound (as is before said), and had drunk the holy potion ful sore against her wil, they would burne brimstone in a chafing-dish, and hold her nose by force over it: by which meanes she nothing doubteth but that she did commonly grow into some great outrages, and spake she can not tel now what.

There was (as she thinketh) a discourse made of her fits by some of the priests, the which if she could heare, she supposeth she should remember many more things then now she doth. But shee cannot forget (she saith) that many times she did complaine of hard dealing used towards her in her pretended fits, and how injuriously they dealt with her by giving her that loathsome drink, and burning brimstone under her nose. Where-unto the priests would commonly give this aunswer, eyther *it was not she that spake, but the devill,* or otherwise when she was so wel that they could have no pretence so to say, then they would bid her be contented, and tel her that she should by that meanes merit heaven, and gaine a crowne of glory. And they would stand much upon this last reason in shewing how much this examinate had merited at Gods hands when any by seeing of her in her fits, and the Priests dealings with her, were reconciled.

She further saith that the priests would be often talking in this examinates hearing of certaine women that were possessed beyond the Seas: how the devils in them could not abide the *holy potion,* nor the burning of hallowed brimstone, nor the applying unto them of holy reliques, nor the presence or touching of Catholique priests, nor holy water, nor the holy candel, nor the blessed sacrament: but would start, say they burned, rage and raile against the priests, and commend upon every occasion those that were the soundest Protestants.

By this meanes, this examinate saith for her selfe (and she thinketh she may safely so say for her sister and the rest) that she learned what to say and doe when the priests had her in hand: that is, to start some times when they brought reliques unto her, to pretend that shee could not endure the presence of the Sacrament, and many things besides: as, if the treatise of her may be gotten, wil appeare. Howbeit, she saith that after some sixe or seaven weekes, although at the first she did not marke the priests doings, nor greatly observe her own, yet then she began to finde their juglings, and how she her selfe, in saying this or that, spake nothing but what she had learned of the priests.

The chiefe reason that (she thinketh) moved her not to mark them at the first was the good opinion she had conceaved of them, being newly reconciled: and yet as shee saith, when shee saw before that time into what case they had brought her sister, she thought that they used her not wel, and perswaded her to runne away from them.

This examinate further saith that shee wel remembreth how one time Ma: *Sherwood* told her that one Ma: *Bridges* had gotten one of his mothers mayds with child, and bad her tel him of it when he should come next thither, and that this examinate was troubled. Where-upon she saith, that accordingly, as soone as she saw the said Ma: *Bridges,* being her selfe in health and no way troubled, and in the presence of Ma: *Sherwood,* Goe to, quoth she, Ma: *Bridges,* you have gotten your Mothers chambermayde with child, and make no conscience of it. Which words were no sooner uttered by her, but Ma: *Sherwood* tooke hold of them, saying, Yea sirra, canst thou tel that? Thou shalt be constrained to tel more anone! And thus he said, pretending it was not this examinate but the devil that uttered those words. Heere-with Ma: *Bridges* was greatly amazed and afraid, and much speech was of it, as if it had been some great miracle.

The said Ma: *Sherwood,* as this examinate saith, at one time, as she was tyed in the chayre, did thrust a pinne into her shoulder, and she there-with crying, and saying, what doe you? O, saith he, heare you not the devil, what hee saith? No, quoth this examinate, it is not the devil, but my selfe, that spake unto you. But he stil affirming that it was the devil, this examinate could not be beleeved, and so it was reckoned amongst them.

Againe, she saith that in one of the fits where-into they cast her by their holy potion and brimstone, there were two needles thrust into her legge by some of the priests (as she is now perswaded in her conscience), and uppon her comming to her sences, finding a paine in the place where the needles were, she complained of it, and would have put down her hose to have seene what her legge ayled; but the priests would in no wise suffer that, but presently they got holy reliques, and tyed them about her legge, affirming that the paine was procured by the wicked spirit, and could not be eased but by those reliques. When they had so tyed them about her legge, they charged her in any wise not to touch them; but yet notwithstanding, this examinate saith that being greatly troubled with paine, and desirous to ease her selfe, she did now and then attempt to slacken the reliques, being tyed too hard (as she thought). At what time the priests stil watching of her, as that she could do nothing but they would see her, they did blame her for touching of the reliques, bad her let them alone, and said it was the devil that tempted her to touch them.

The custom of the priests was, as this examinate saith, to appoint a set time when they meant to have any solemne Exorcismes, and then this examinate was one, when she was in their hands, that for the most part must goe to the chayre. After that the said needles had beene in this examinates legge from the fore-noone the one day until eleven of the clocke the next day, she was brought up into a gallerie, the Sermon being finished, and a great number there present. At her comming in and complaining of the sorenes of her legge, the priests bad her be of good cheere, and said they would see if they could helpe her. Where-upon Ma: *Dibdale* (as she remembreth) said unto her, Goe *Frauncis*, sit downe, and put downe thy hose: which she did: and then Ma: *Stamp,* another priest, when her hose was put downe, came unto her very reverently, and with divers ceremonies untyed the reliques which were about her legge; which being taken away, he looked upon the sore place, and handled it gently, and in the end thrusting downe with his fingers the skin and flesh where one needle stuck so as the same appeared, he called unto him those that were present, and said unto them: See what the devil had done, and so pulled it out. Then feeling her legge a little while longer, and using his fingers as is before mentioned, he also disclosed the second needle: which the people that were present beholding, were in a great maze, especially to heare what Ma: *Dibdale* and Ma: *Stamp* made of the matter: how they said it was the devils doing, and much other speech to that effect. As soone as the needles were taken forth, this examinate was caried downe againe out of the gallerie, and feeling her leg very wel eased, it began to amend every day more and more, which they said was by reason of the holy water where-with they washed her legge when they pulled out the needles.

She further saith that the priests had a custome to thrust certaine things into the mouthes of such as they said were possessed, under pretence of reliques. And she wel remembreth that at one time when she began to be troubled with her drink and brimstone, they thrust into her mouth some of the said reliques: whereof this examinate complained, and said, Why doe you put these filthy things in my mouth? Ah, quoth they: hark how the devil cannot endure these holy things. Afterwards when this examinate put them out of her mouth, then they asked her what reliques they were? And she told them, This is a peece of such a man, and this of another. And at one time they put into her mouth a peece of *Campions* thumbe or his finger, she remembreth not whether. When this examinate at this time, and so likewise, both she and others, at other times, did name these reliques, and shewed their dislike to have them put into their mouthes, the priests would bidde the people that were present marke how the devil knew all holy reliques, of what Martyrs they were, and how hee could not abide them: whereas this deponent saith that both she and the rest that were dealt with as shee was did know all these reliques that the priests had there, having the sight of them almost everie day, and hearing the priests tell of whom they were. So that as soone as this examinate saw any of them, she could name them very readily, and say: This is such a peece of Father *Campian,* this of Ma: *Sherwin,* this of maister *Brian,* this of maister *Cottam,* this of mistris *Clithero:*[1] and so of a great number more which she hath now forgotten.

At another time also, this examinate wel remembreth that the priests filling her mouth with reliques, they conveyed in with them a big rustie naile,[2] as she is verily perswaded in her conscience, so as when they pulled out the reliques, she was almost choked with the nayle, and much ado they had to get it out. They made her mouth there-with to bleed, and affirmed to the people that it came out of her stomacke by vertue of the said reliques.

Againe, she saith that beeing in speech once with maister *Dibdale* concerning maister *Richard Mainy,* he told her divers things of him, what wonderful sights he saw about the Altar and the sacrament at Masse time. And further said unto her that if shee would say, when shee was to be exorcised in the chaire, at the bringing of the *Pix* unto her (as the manner was), that shee saw the bodie of Christ there in a great brightnesse, shee should by that meanes greatly glorifie God. And thereuppon, as she confesseth, she said as he advised her at her next exorcising, and a great wonder was made of it.

Shee further saith that beeing brought up with her mother, shee had learned to sing by hart certaine *Geneva* Psalmes, and that being under the priests hands, when now and then forgetting her selfe, she sung any of them as she sate at work, the priests, and so others in the house, when they heard her, would earnestly blame her for it, and say one to another, Doe you not heare how sweetly the devil singeth these *Geneva* psalmes?

Also she saith that when the priests had drawne her to be of their Church, as is before mentioned, and that shee should come to receave the Sacrament, they told her she must first vow, and promise, by the vertue of that holy Sacrament, that shee would ever afterwards hold the Religion of the Church of Rome, and never goe againe to any of the Protestants Churches, nor ever reade the English Service, or the English Byble, or any other English books written by the Protestants in matters of Reli-

[1]Blessed Margaret Clitherow, wife of a tradesman of York, was indicted in March 1586 for harboring and relieving seminary priests, and for hearing Mass. She refused to plead, and was in consequence sentenced to be pressed to death. When the sentence was carried out, she was a quarter of an hour dying. No relic of her would have been used in the exorcisms ("Mr. John Mush's Life of Margaret Clitherow" in Morris, *Troubles* 3:333–440).

[2]According to Richard Davis's eyewitness account of the exorcisms of Anne Smith and Fid Williams, sent over to Douai in 1626, the nail and other objects came out of Anne Smith (Challoner, *Memoirs,* 117).

gion. And this vow, she saith, is ordinarily made by all that are reconciled.

She also saith that she hath often times heard some of the priests
affirme that it was an ordinary thing with the devil which was in Ma:
*Maynie,* that when they the said priests have demaunded of the devil
(pretended to be in him) why he troubled the Catholiques with imprisonment and many daungers, whilest the Protestants lived in pleasure, his
aunswer was that the Protestants were his already, and that he troubled
the Catholiques because he would draw them to himselfe, and make them
Protestants if he could, adding that he would never have troubled *Job* as
he did, if he had thought he could not have him made to curse God. This
examinate also saith that she her selfe hath heard som of the priests and
(as she thinketh) Ma: *Edmunds* aske *Mainy* that question, and he the said
*Mainy* so to have aunswered them. Also she saith that the priests in talking of Protestants, have affirmed of them in her hearing that the greatest
share of them were possessed, and that when England should be againe
as it had beene, the devils would then shew themselves in them, and they
should have theyr hands ful of chaire-worke, meaning their exorcisings,
to cast them out.

At one time, she saith, she wel remembreth, that Ma: *Greene,*
comming from beyond the Seas, brought with him certaine graines, medals, and *Agnus dei;* and that seeing the priests and others make so great
account of them, shee said to Ma: *Greene,* Good Lord, what meane you
to make so great a-doe about these things? What is that waxe better then
other waxe? or that bugle better then another, whereof you may buy a
great number for a penny? Where-upon Ma: *Greene* said *it was the
devill, and not she* that spake those words. But this examinate told him
againe that shee spake those words her selfe, and that she mervailed why
they laboured so earnestly to make both her and all others beleeve that
whatsoever she or they did or spake, it was not she, nor they, but the
devil; but he persisted, and said it was the devil indeede, and not she,
whatsoever shee thought to the contrarie.

This examinate further saith that one *Alexander* an Apothecarie, having brought with him from London to *Denham* on a time a new halter
and two blades of knives, did leave the same upon the gallerie floare in
her Maisters house. The next morning he tooke occasion to goe with this
examinate into the said gallerie, where she espying the said halter and
blades, asked Ma: *Alexander* what they did there. Hee making the matter
strange, aunswered that he saw them not, though hee looked fully upon
them, she her selfe pointing to them with her finger, where they lay
within a yard of them, where they stoode both together. No (quoth this
examinate), doe you not see them? and so taking them up, said, looke
you heere. Ah (quoth he), now I see them indeed, but before I could not
see them; and therefore, saith he, I perceave that the devil hath layd them
heere to worke some mischiefe upon you that are possessed.

Heereuppon maister *Alexander* told the priests what a strange thing
had happened, and a great search was made in the house to know how
the said halter and knife blades came thether; but it could not in any wise
be found out, as it was pretended, till Ma: *Mainy* in his next fit said, as it

was reported, that the devil layd them in the Gallery, that some of those that were possessed might either hang themselves with the halter, or kil themselves with the blades.

Now this examinate further saith that shee herselfe did espy the end of the halter in maister *Alexanders* pocket the night before shee saw it and the blades in the Gallery, at such time as he drew out of his pocket a certaine boxe of Wafer-cakes for Masses. Whereby shee is fully perswaded, as she saith, that he the said *Alexander* was himselfe the devil that layde the halter and knife-blades in the said Gallerie, and as she saith, she told maister *Dibdale* as much, when the search was, how they should come thether. Whereat maister *Dibdale,* beeing much mooved, said *it was not she but the devill* that spake so unto him of maister *Alexander.* And for this her report and speeches, she felt, as shee saith, some smart afterwards. For within a day or two after, they had her againe to the chayre, and did use theyr exorcismes with her, the manner whereof was something strange unto her.

They had in a readines the picture of an Asse, and of the devil, and of Ma: *Fox,* as if hee were writing the booke of Martyrs. The Asse (they said) resembled this examinate, and the devill within her (being a malicious lying spirit that sought to slaunder the dooings of the Catholique priests) betokened Ma: *Fox,* who (as they said) had beene a malicious lyer. They had there also a long girdle made of whipcord (as shee remembreth); it was full of knots, and termed S. *Peters girdle.* This girdle was hallowed, and being lapped into foure doubles, was like a whip.

These things beeing thus readily prepared, this examinate was bound full sore against her will in a chayre. They compelled her to drinke the *holy potion,* whereof shee made five or sixe draughts. They burnt brimstone under her nose, and withall the said three pictures one after another. They pulled off her gowne, and whipped her uppon the armes with the holy girdle, pretending that they meant thereby to hunt the devill out of her. They gave her five blowes in remembrance of the five wounds of Christ, and seaven in honour of the seaven Sacraments, and three in memory of the blessed Trinitie, and she knoweth not now how many more. With these blowes shee beeing constrained to cry out, they said *it was not shee but the devill* within her that so cryed, because he was not able to endure the vertue of that holy girdle. But this examinate saith that howsoever the devill fared, she well knoweth that shee bare away the smart, and that her armes were blacke almost a moneth after with the blowes.

The priests also (shee saith) had another custome. At the end of every exorcisme, they would say that the spirit was gone downe, sometimes into the foote, and sometimes into the great toe of the partie exorcised. And when strangers came, before whom they intended to worke some great matters, they would bring the partie againe to the chayre, and beeing bound therein, they would begin (as they said) to make the devil shew himselfe, which they did with this examinate in this sort. The Exorcist having a relique in his hand, as a bone, or some such hard thing, would graspe her by the legge, and aske her if she felt any paine that seemed to prick her; and this examinate confessing (as the truth was) that she felt a paine (the said bone or hard thing in his hand hurting her shrewdly), Ah (would the Exorcist say), now he beginneth to stirre. Thus would the Exorcist goe pinching of her legge twice or thrice before they came to her knee, and then they would wring her indeed so hard, as that she should sometimes screech, and sometimes start. And then the Exorcist and the rest of the priests that were present would say, now the spirit will up into her body; you shal heare more of him anon. And hast was commonly made at such times to give us the holy potion, which beeing so lothsome a drinke, divers Gentlewomen, seeing it given unto us, have wept for pitty to see us compelled to take it. But the priests would tell them that there was no remedy; for otherwise, except the strength and force of the wicked spirit were thereby abated, there was great danger that hee would teare theyr guts and inward parts in peeces as hee was ascending upwards to goe out of them.

This examinate saith that when shee had wel considered of the priests dealing with her, and how all the troubles she had was by reason of their intollerable drinks, perfumings, and practises with her, where-with her body was brought to great weakenes, she grew to some more boldnes, and did now and then speake her minde somwhat plainly, though it booted not; for they would say it was the devil that uttered it, whatsoever it was that this examinate spake, if they disliked it. She wel remembreth, that sitting at her worke one time, and Ma: *Sherwood* sitting also by her looking on a booke, she this examinate being very angry in her minde to consider how she was used, and with him in particuler, for thrusting a pin into her shoulder, and for divers other his hard usages towards her, said unto him that shee very greatly mervailed how he and the rest durst deale with her and the rest as they did, adding that if she this examinate or any other should complaine of them, they would certainly all of them be hanged. For (quoth she) how many of the Queenes subjects have you drawne from her by these your practises heere? Heere-with Ma: *Sherwood* was much moved, and went to the priests to acquaint them with her words. Some of them (as she hath heard) were of opinion that it were best to put her away from her Mistres; but Ma: *Dibdale* liked not that counsel, fearing (as she beleeveth) that shee should have disclosed theyr dealings. For these her said speeches, shee was within three or foure houres very hardly entreated. Ma: *Sherwood* and the other priests, returning unto her, put her in minde what she had said, and told her, *That it was not she, but the devill* that uttered those words, and thereupon had her to the chayre, and with their holy potion and brimstone so plagued her, as being there-with wonderful sick, shee fel (as she thinketh) into a swound.

Shee further saith that whilest these matters were in hand at *Denham,* there came very many thither from time to time. The Catholiques would bring with them such of their friends as they durst trust, being Protestants, of purpose to draw them to the Romish Religion. And she certainly knoweth that there was a very great number upon those occasions reconciled, sometimes an hundred a weeke, at the least. Marrie at one time, she remembreth that one Ma: *Hampden* of *Hampden* (as she thinketh) being brought thither by Ma: *Edward Ashefield*,[1] now in prison as shee hath heard, did greatly deceave the priests expectations, and put them into a great feare. The manner was, she saith, of those who were pretended to be possessed, when any Protestants came in, to commend them greatly, and to raile upon the priests, in so much as Ma: *Mainy*, when he saw Ma: *Hampden*, did presently salute him by the name of his fellow Justice, and use such other words unto him, as when he heard how they were expounded, hee was greatly discontented with them; and there-upon speaking aloude, said thus in effect unto him that brought him thither (as farre as she remembreth), being her selfe then present, *Coosen* Ned, *I had thought you would have brought me where I should have seene some godlines, and not to have heard the devill; but this dealing I see is abhominable, and I mervaile that the house sinketh not for such wickednes committed in it.* And so he departed. With these his speeches the priests were greatly amazed, and fearing the worst, got them away for that night.

Furthermore, she saith, that perceaving many things were false that the priests told to those that came unto them, for the better confirming of her judgement therein she devised (of her selfe) this tale: she told them that being in bed, there came a morrice-daunce into her chamber, having these persons in it, a man with a Taber and a Pipe, the Earle of *Bedford* that was dead before (but one that the priests did greatly hate), and some other noble men also she named who are now out of her memory. All these, she told them, after they had daunced about the table in the chamber, went out againe as they came in. When the priests had this by the end, they made great matters of it, termed it a vision, and told it the Catholiques for a very truth; whereat this examinate laughed in her minde, but durst not gaine-say it, and so it went amongst them for a currant vision. And shee thinketh in her conscience it was even as true as the rest of their reports, both of this examinate and of the others there that were pretended to be possessed.

Also she saith that there was a notable devise amongst the Priests to have it thought that the wicked spirits came into this examinate and her sister by witcherie.[2] Ma: *Richard Mainy* before mentioned, being the notablest counterfeit (as she thinketh) that ever the priests had in their fingers, said in one of his fits, or rather the devil in him (as it was pretended), that one good-wife *White* of *Bushie* had bewitched this examinate and her saide sister. This good-wife *White* was commonly talked of in the Country to be a Witch. The said *Mainy* also told the occasion how they were bewitched. There were (as it was pretended that the devil said in *Mainy*) certaine cattel bewitched in *Denham* some two or three yeeres before, which could not be eased, except the two spirits which troubled them were sent into two Christian bodies; and there-

---

[1]The family was recusant; a Humphrey Ashfield was committed to the Poultry prison for recusancy, 19 November 1577 (*CRS* 1:63).

[2]The following stories of the supposed witch, the cat, and the nightingale, all center on Mainy. As Pollen says, "Another disagreeable feature about Mainey is that he is connected with acts of cruelty" ("Supposed Cases," 459).

upon, quoth hee, to deliver the cattel she sent those two spirits into this examinates sister and her selfe. When the priests heard these words, they seemed to conjure the devil in Ma: *Mainy* to bring the witches spirit (whereby she wrought) thither to *Denham.* And the night folowing, this prank was played by the priests. They had gotten in the night a Cat amongst them in the Parlor, which they said was the witches spirit. About the whipping of this Cat they pretended great paines, and that they whipped her so long, til at the last she vanished away out of their sight. Afterwards they gave it out that out of all question the Witch, whilest they were whipping of the Cat, was greatly vexed, and there-uppon they sent a messenger to *Bushie* to see in what estate the Witch was; who at his returne reported that when hee came to *Bushie,* hee found the Witch in child-bed, and that her child was dead. When the priests heard this report, see (quoth the priests to those that were present), how it falleth out to be true that we told you. The whipping of her spirit in the likenes of a Cat was the cause that her child died. Yea (quoth this examinate), is that true? Why then you are murderers. Whereat the priests were moved, but they knew how to aunswer that, as they did, in saying that *it was not she, but the devill* in her that uttered those words. Of this whipping of the Cat there was great speeches, and many that beleeved them wondred at it. The messenger that was sent to *Bushie,* hearing what a mervaile they made heereof, became a recusant, being at that time a Protestant.

There was also another strange thing that happened at *Denham,* about a bird. Mistris *Peckham* had a Nightingale which she kept in a Cage, wherein Ma: *Dibdale* tooke great delight, and would often be playing with it. This Nightingale was one night convayed out of the Cage, and being the next morning diligently sought for, could not be heard of, til Ma: *Mainies* devil in one of his fits (as it was pretended) affirmed that the wicked spirit which was in this examinates sister had taken the bird out of the Cage, and killed it in despite of Ma: *Dibdale.* And further, he told them that the birds necke was broken, and did lie under a Rosemarie bush in the Garden. Where-upon three or foure going downe and finding the bird there, they made a great wonderment of it, whereat this examinate doth verily beleeve that eyther *Mainy* had killed the bird, and laid it there himselfe, or else that this examinates sister did it, and had told *Mainy* of it. For she saith that her sister and *Mainy* were very great.

Also this examinate saith that if the story she had heard hath beene written of *Mainyes* fits could be got, there would appeare very many notable practises. Ma: *Edmunds* the Jesuit was the chiefe man that dealt with *Mainy,* and hath written (as she hath heard) a great booke of them. This *Edmunds,* as hath beene said before, was a chiefe man, and therfore whereas the rest had but their Albes on when they exorcised any, he commonly had upon him either a vestment or a cope. She wel remembreth that the said *Mainy,* sitting upon a time by one of the priests, affirmed that unto his sight the priests finger and thumbe did shine with brightnes, especially on the inner sides;[1] where-unto the Priest aunswered that it might wel so be because (quoth he) they were anointed

---

[1]Cf. Mainy's Confession, 406.

with holy oyle when I was made Priest. At which words this examinate laughing, and calling Ma: *Mainy* a dissembling hypocrite, the priest said that *it was not she, but the devill* that did so laugh and raile.

Furthermore, this examinate well remembreth that Ma: *Richard Mainy* being exorcised in the presence of a hundred people at the least on S. *Georges* day in the morning, the priests affirmed that seaven devils did then shew themselves in him by such gestures and signes as declared them to be the Authors of the seaven deadlie sinnes.[1] This examinate saith that she hath almost forgotten the gestures, but she will set them down as neere as her memory will serve her. The said maister *Mainy* beeing bound in the chayre, did lift up his head, looking highly, and made gestures with his hand as though hee were tricking up himselfe; whereupon the priests said that the spirit that was comming up then was *Pride,* as it appeared by the said gestures. Afterwards the said *Mainy* beginning to gape and snort, the priests said that the spirit that then rose up in him was *Sloth.* Then hee fell to vomiting, and the priests said that the spirit that then rose was *Gluttony* and drunkennes. Againe, he the said *Mainy* talking of purses, and thus much in the hundred, and of the forfeyting of this or that lease, the devil that then was risen the priests called *Covetousnesse.* And thus the priests and hee went through all the deadly sinnes, the said *Mainy,* or the devill in him (as was pretended), commending the Protestants for his good friends because they had all the said seven deadly sinnes in them, but railing at Catholiques for that they could not endure them, but did ever and anon cut them off by confession.

The same day also shee well remembreth two things that Ma: *Mainy* spake of betwixt his descriptions of the said seaven deadly sinnes. *Oh* (quoth hee), *this is a great day of pompe at the Court; I will stay no longer amongst you raskall priests, but will go thether amongst my fellowes; they all love me there, I am theirs, and they are all mine,* or to this effect. Also one *Robert Bedell* of *Denham,* beeing a very zealous Protestant, was buried the same day; in that forenoone there happened a storme, whereuppon *Mainy* pretended that the devil spake to this purpose in him, viz., *Now they are about to bury* Bedell, *and because he served mee all his life time, I am sending of him into hell.* At which words many that were present wept, and prayed that if it were possible he might be saved. This matter was so urged and talked of as afterwards they drew his wife to become a Romish Catholique, and so she died.

This examinate further saith that one *Anne Smith,* about the Christmas the same yeere, came to *Denham* where shee had remained but a little while before the priests had got her into their hands, and said shee was possessed. Touching this woman, a number of things hath

beene written of her, as this examinate hath heard, all which this examinate saith she verily believeth in her conscience (as also of all the practises and tales of the priests touching both this examinate and all the

---

[1]Cf. Mainy's Confession, 409ff., and especially 410: "Sloth was described *by gaping and snorting as if hee had been a sleepe.*" These and other close correspondences between Fid's statement and Mainy's suggest that she had recently read either *The Book of Miracles* or Mainy's statement. Her sister was literate; no doubt she was, too.

rest with whom they dealt) that they were altogether knaveries and meer
inventions, to deceive the people by procuring an admiration of theyr
priesthood, and thereby to withdraw her Majesties subjects to their religion.

Shee well remembreth (as she saith) that at one time Ma: *Dibdale*
charged the devill in *Anne Smith* (as it was pretended) to speake unto
him, and aunswer him to that which he demaunded; but notwithstanding
she held her peace. Then he commaunded her to speak in the name of the
Father, the sonne, and the holy Ghost, and by the vertue of the holy Sacrament; but yet she was silent. Heerewith Ma: *Dibdale* growing to be
more earnest, charged her (or the devil that was pretended to be in her) to
speake to him by the power and vertue of his holy priesthood; and then
she aunswered him. Where-upon this examinate being present said to
maister *Dibdale, Why Ma:* Dibdale, *is there more vertue in your priesthood then in the blessed Trinity and the holy Sacrament?* And hee
aunswered that though hee were but a simple man, yet it pleased God for
the honour of his Church to shew by this meanes the power of the priesthood.

Againe this examinate saith that after she perceived the deceit which
the priests used, she would rather then her life have gotten from them;
but she was so watched, and so were the rest (she meaneth the other
women), as they could by no meanes escape out of their fingers. Theyr
pretence was least the devil should cause them to drowne or kill themselves. But this examinate is perswaded in her conscience that the truth
was, why they kept them so straightly, least going home to their friends,
they should have disclosed theyr dissimulation and false pretenses of
casting devils out of those who were as free from them as themselves.
This examinate and her sister did not see either Father or mother, beeing
in the same towne, all the while that they were in theyr hands; neither
would they suffer either their father or mother to speake with them,
though they desired it many times.

At one time this examinate remembreth that beeing in the Kitchen garden at *Denham,* shee heard a noyse in her unckles garden on the other
side of the wall, and supposing that her unckle might be there, she cryed
out as loude as shee could, *unckle, unckle,* who beeing there by chaunce,
and hearing of her, knew her voyce, and asked her what shee would
have. *Oh* (quoth shee), *good unckle helpe me from hence, for I am almost
killed already amongst them heere, and shall not live if I continue heere
long.* Upon this occasion, this examinats mother came to have spoken
with her, but she could not be suffered. The priests told her that her
daughters were bewitched, and possessed with wicked spirits, and that
they were thereby cast away if they did not helpe them by their authority,
saying that therfore she theyr mother might by no meanes speake with
them untill they had delivered them from the said wicked spirits. With
this and such like aunswers they sent away theyr mother divers times
weeping. Howbeit she saith that at sometimes her mother, not contented
with those aunswers, would grow to some earnestnesse and hard speech,
because shee could not be permitted to see her daughters. And then the
Priests would shake her off with angry words, and tell her that shee

herselfe had asmuch neede to be exorcised as her daughters. And at one time Mistris *Katherine* that served Mistris *Peckham,* beeing present when the priests and her mother had such speeches, told her that if the priests did well they should deale with her as they did with her daughters.

After this examinate had beene in the priests hands for a fortnight or three weekes before Christmas (as shee remembreth) untill after the Ascension day next ensuing, and had long perceived their coosening practises with her, and thereupon being growne to great weakenesse, and almost desperate, shee told the priests plainly at the end of one of her fits whereinto they had cast her by their drinks, slibber-sawces, and brim-stone, that if shee had a devill in her, they were best cast him out. *For (quoth shee) if ever you torment mee so againe, dispatch mee if you list; otherwise I will certainly by one meanes or other get away from you, and tell my friends of all your proceedings and dealings here both with me and others.* Heere-upon Ma: *Dibdale* willed her to be content, and said that the next time they hoped to dispossesse her altogether. And accord-ingly, within three or foure dayes after, they had her to the chaire, and there using her as they had done many times before, when shee came to her selfe againe they told her that now the devil was gone, and she was delivered.

This examinate further saith that the maner of the priests was to say often-times that they had cast out this or that devil out of the parties; but stil when they list they would take a smal occasion to say that yet there were some other devils remaining within them. And this examinate saith that she doubteth they would have dealt so with her at that time too, but that there began to be great speeches in the Country about the priests doings at *Denham;* in so much as divers auncient Catholiques themselves did utterly dislike them, and the priests them selves grew to be afraid. Howbeit, when this examinate was thus at some quiet, yet they would not suffer her to goe home to her father and mother, but carried her up to London, and placed her there with a sure friend of theirs, one Mistres *White;*[1] and so they dealt with this examinats sister, not suffering her to see her parents almost for foure yeeres after, as this examinate remembreth.

Also she saith that when the priests thought good to meddle no more with her, they caried her to London, and placed her with one Mistres *Dorothie White* as hath beene said, a recusant, who then and since hath

[1]Dorothy White was a helper and concealer of hunted Catholics. When John Greene was betrayed by his fellow-priest Anthony Tyrrell, he was hiding with Mrs. White. She was herself arrested, September 1586. It was intended to proceed against her as an "obsti-nate recusant and receiver of seminary priests," but Justice Young released her, 22 Octo-ber (*CRS* 2 [1906]: 258, 264, 269; Anstruther, *Seminary Priests* 1:136–37). Fid says that she stayed with Mrs. White for several years. A badly faded document among the state papers, endorsed by a later hand 30 August 1586, says that "a mayde which was pos-sessed in the howse of one Whyte dwelling in the olde Pallace at Westminster . . . is nowe repossessed with a good spiryte and prophesies and telleth wonders that must come to passe about Michellmas next. The maydens name is [Frauncis]" (SP 12/192, no. 57). The name is almost completely illegible but Pollen thinks this is Fid, and he is probably right ("Supposed Cases," 463, n. 2). Fid's later account of her state of mind after the flight from Denham is therefore false.

beene so beneficiall unto them as that shee hath cleane overthrowne her state, and undone her children. The cause why they placed her there was (as she verily thinketh) least beeing amongst her owne friends, shee might disclose theyr bad dealings with her.

It was not long after this examinate came to mistrisse *White,* but that one *Harrington* growing into acquaintance with her did afterwards marry her, as shee believeth.[1] The marriage was in the Marshalsea, where after a Masse one *Lister*[2] a priest (as shee remembreth), then prisoner there, used certaine Latine words,[3] whereby they said she and the same *Harrington* were married together. There were present there five or sixe. After which time the said *Harrington* lived with this examinate at times for the space of about four or five yeeres, shee notwithstanding continuing her service with Mistrisse *White.*

After this examinate had kept company with the said *Harrington* for about four yeres, she grew to be with child, and thereupon went first to her sisters in *Oxfordshire,* and then to her parents at *Denham.* Being at *Denham,* she was presented for a recusant, and thereupon committed to the gayle at *Alesbury.* At her beeing there in prison, Ma: *Harrington* wrote a Letter unto her within three or foure daies (as she remembreth) after her commitment, the effect whereof was that if shee were examined who was the father of her child, she should lay it upon some that was gone beyond the seas for a souldier, but in no wise to say it was his; and the rather to perswade her, he signified unto her that it was not onelie his advise, but likewise the counsaile of Mistris *White* her Mistris, and Maister *Blackman* a priest.[4]

---

[1]This is William Harrington, a seminary priest, born 1566 at Mount St. John, Felixkirk, Yorkshire. He entered the Rheims seminary 25 September 1582, aged sixteen, and left in September 1584 to enter the Society of Jesus. His health forced him to return to England; he was betrayed upon landing, arrested, and sent to his father in Yorkshire, where he apparently stayed for the next seven years. In 1591 he left England again, reentering the college at Rheims, 28 February 1591. He was ordained 14 March 1592 and returned to England, where he was arrested, May 1593, in the chamber of Henry Dunne. After imprisonment in Bridewell, he was moved to Newgate, where he was tried and condemned, June 1593. A letter to Lord Keeper Puckering in which he refuses to give information suggests that an attempt was made to "turn" him: this would explain the long delay in his execution, which was carried out, very cruelly, on 18 February 1594 (Challoner, *Memoirs,* 197; Anstruther, *Seminary Priests* 1:149–50; *CSP Dom., Elizabeth* vol. 245, no. 66; Morris, *Troubles* 2:105–7). There is no evidence that Harrington was in London in 1586. Fid's story is incredible, but peculiarly detailed. On her own admission she was a government spy by about 1590/91; she may have been involved in a failed attempt to blackmail Harrington into collaboration.

[2]There was a priest called Lister in the Marshalsea in July 1586, and he was still there in December. He was a seminary priest, born in Lancashire, ordained at Soissons, 13 June 1584, and sent to England 2 October 1584. He was arrested at Prescot, Lancashire, and sent to London, where he was committed to the Marshalsea 15 March 1585. In January 1588 he was moved to Wisbech Castle, in a group that included Weston, Dryland, Green, Stamp, and Thules, and no more is heard of him (*CRS* 2 [1906]: 254, 273, 279; Anstruther, *Seminary Priests* 1:210–11).

[3]The words of a marriage ceremony would have been English, a point made by Morris, *Troubles* 2:105.

[4]Although Fid includes this name in her list of exorcists, no priest of the name is known. She may be making the name up, or she may mean mean George Blackwell, born 1547, educated at Trinity College, Oxford, where he became a fellow in 1564. He

With this Letter this examinate was greatly mooved, and then calling to mind how shee had beene used at *Denham*, and afterwards kept at Mistris *Whites* from her friends; and remembring also how the priests were ever wont to perswade her that she should never speake any thing as touching her possessing or dispossessing that might turne to theyr discredite and to the dishonor of the Church of Rome, she this examinate beganne to suspect that the religion that the priests professed was like unto themselves. But the most principall thing with the rest that made her so to thinke was another poynt in Ma: *Harringtons* Letter, wherein hee perswaded her that *if shee were examined upon her oath, it forced not, the Church did dispence with her so as shee might aunswer what shee thought good notwithstanding; because an oath did not bind her to confesse any thing that might tend to the dishonor of theyr priesthood or of the Catholique Church.*

When this examinate was first brought before the Justices at *Alesbury*, she confessed that she was reconciled; and shee is verily perswaded that if the said Letter had not come unto her afterwards, and mooved her as is aforesaid, notwithstanding all the abuses offred her at *Denham*, she had continued still a wilfull recusant though it had cost her her life. Marry, upon the occasions before mentioned, this examinate having bethought herselfe better, desired to speake with old Ma: *Pigot* of *Dodersall*,[1] a Justice of peace in *Buckinghamshire*, unto whom she signified who was the father of her child, and that she could be contented to alter her course of life, and goe to the Church againe as before she had done. Hereuppon Ma: *Pigot* tooke this examinate in his Coach with him to Sir *John Goodwins*,[2] where she found the Lord *Grey*[3] and divers others, before whom, after shee had submitted herselfe, as she had done to Ma: *Pigot*, shee was sent to the Court by the Lord *Grey* with two of his servaunts to the Lord *Treasurer*.[4] At her comming to the Court she saith shee was examined of divers matters before the Lords of the Counsell concerning her knowledge of sundry priests and Jesuits, and as touching one *Stoughton*,[5] who was a notable spy that carried over young maids and

resigned his fellowship and entered the seminary at Douai, 1574. In 1575 he was ordained and in 1576 went to England. In 1586 and 1588 he was reported to be in Lancashire with "widow Mayney," Miles Gerard of Ince, and Thomas Gerard, Edmund Peckham's father-in-law. In 1598 he was appointed "archpriest" or superior of the secular clergy in England, an appointment that precipitated the Appellant controversy and divided the English Catholics (Anstruther, *Seminary Priests* 1:39–41).

[1]The manor of Doddeshall passed to the Pigots in 1495; Fid's Mr. Thomas Pigot died in 1606 (*VCH, Buckinghamshire* 4:96).

[2]Goodwin was head of an old Buckinghamshire family with extensive properties in the county. He was knighted and appointed sheriff of Buckinghamshire in 1587. He died in 1597 and is buried in Woburn parish church (*VCH, Buckinghamshire* 3:109–10).

[3]Arthur Grey, Baron Grey de Wilton (1536–93), Lord Deputy of Ireland, 1580, retired to Whaddon, Buckinghamshire, where he spent the rest of his life (*DNB*).

[4]William Cecil, Lord Burghley.

[5]Probably "John Stoughton, gent, prisonner vij monethes" in the Tower, July 1588 (*CRS* 2 [1906]: 281).

boyes to be Nunnes and priests, and brought over Letters as occasion served, and continueth (as shee thinketh) the same trade still.

After that this examinate had beene at the Court above a weeke, and examined in that space three or foure times, the servaunts of the said Lord *Grey* remaining there still, it pleased the Lords of her Majesties Counsell to send her backe with them to the Lord *Anderson,*[1] and to write theyr letter to his Lordship that he should send for this examinates father, and not onely to deale with him to see that this examinate went to the Church, according as she had promised, but also that there might be no further proceeding in law against her, in respect that she had beene reconciled; the which direction the Lord *Anderson* did accomplish, so as this examinate continued at her fathers untill the yeere 1594.

After this examinate had remained thus with her father about three or foure moneths, the said Ma: *Harrington* came unto her, and told her he had beene all that while beyond the seas; and keeping company with her againe as a man ought to doe with his wife, sometimes at *Denham,* and sometimes this examinate comming to him to London, hee allowed her after the rate of about twenty marks by the yeere. She likewise saith that when maister *Harrington* suspected this examinate to be with child, he put an hundred pounds into one Ma: *Fits* his hand to the use of her and her child if she had any.

This examinate further saith that within about a yeere after that the said maister *Harrington* had come from beyond the seas (as hee pretended) and kept companie with her as his lawfull wife, hee was apprehended for a priest, and first committed to the Towre, and then to the Marshalsea. Beeing in prison, this examinate had a warrant from Ma: *Young*[2] to goe unto him; and at her comming unto him he wept, and said that if hee might for shame, hee would take another course then hee did. He cryed her mercy for the abuse offred unto her, and promised that if she would be content she should never want. Howbeit (as she was enformed) he told such Catholiques as came unto him (who had understanding that this examinate did challenge him for her husband), that shee this examinate did greatly slaunder him; and utterly denied that ever hee was married unto her, or ever kept company with her as men doe with theyr wives. Whereupon all such Catholiques as heard thereof did greatly rate this examinate for challenging of him to be her husband, and said shee did belie him, and that *it was the devill* that caused her to raise that slaunder of him, being a Catholique priest.

She further saith that the said *Harrington* being condemned, and executed the 18 of February 1593 (as she remembreth), she married againe with *Ralfe Dallidowne* a Smith in Holborne, the 20 of January 1594 as shee thinketh. And having received herselfe the said hundred pound from Ma: *Fits,* her husband *Dallidowne* had it all, except it were some six or seven pound which she had spent before.

---

[1]Edmund Anderson, Lord Chief Justice of the Court of Common Pleas; a keen supporter of the Crown against Catholics and Puritans; a bully.

[2]Richard Young, justice of the Middlesex Court of Sessions, bully, torturer and associate of Richard Topcliffe (Meyer, *England and the Catholic Church,* 182, n. 4).

This examinate further saith that many times since shee hath conformed her selfe, many priests have greatly blamed her, using words to this effect unto her, viz., they have tolde her that they wondred how shee could be brought to goe to the English Church, considering the great power of the priesthood and of the holy reliques of the Church of Rome. To whom this examinate hath sometimes aunswered that she was well before she came into theyr hands, and still so continueth shee thanked God, and thereupon hath desired them that they would deale no more with her, but let her alone.

When shee hath thus aunswered them, they have often said to her that it was the devill for a certaintie, that still hunting of her, did perswade her to goe to the Heretiques Church; and that if they had thought she would have taken this course, they would never have dispossessed her. To whom this examinate by way of aunswer hath replied, A murren take you: I was well enough before you dealt with mee, and so have beene ever since you left me.

Shee further saith that since shee was first examined before the Lord Bishop of London in March 1598, divers priests have urged her greatly that shee should say nothing against the possessing or dispossessing used at *Denham*, either concerning her selfe or any other, bidding her aunswer that beeing then young, she had forgotten all those things; and threatning of her, that if she confessed any thing against the holy priesthood or power of the Church in casting out devils, she should be burnt for an Heretique if ever the world changed. The names of the priests that have thus dealt with her, both before shee was called for to be examined before the Lord Bishop of London, and since (at the least some of them) are Ma: *Sherwood*, Ma: *Gerrard*, Ma: *Blackman*, Ma: *John Greene*, and Ma: *William Bruerton*.[1]

This examinate also saith that about foure yeeres since it happened that her husband in a fray killed a man, whereupon she was compelled to borrow ten pound of mistris *White* to be used in her husbands businesse. Certaine priests thought then that they might peradventure have drawne this examinate unto them againe, and so resorting unto her, namely (as she remembreth) maister *Blackman*, maister *Greene*, Maister *Wells*,[2]

---

[1] At the period of these alleged threats, c. 1599, nearly all the exorcists were dead or imprisoned. The exceptions were Stamp, released from Wisbech in 1594 (after which no more is heard of him), and Tyrrell, who had apostasized. Fid mentions neither of them, nor another elusive figure, Dakins, who may have been still alive and active, but who may not have been an exorcist. Of the names she gives, Sherwood had died in Dorsetshire in 1593, Greene was in Wisbech, and Bruerton alias Yardley was not a priest. No Blackman is known, but Fid may mean George Blackwell, appointed archpriest in 1598. Since she does not know his name properly, it is unlikely that he spoke to her. John Gerard, S.J., had been imprisoned in the Tower from spring 1594 to October 1597, when he escaped. In 1598 he made visits to London, but in his own narrative of his experiences he mentions no conversation or encounter remotely like this.

[2] Blessed Swithin Wells, layman and martyr, was arrested at Denham, June 1586 (*DEP*, 383), committed to prison by Justice Young, but then released by him, 4 July. A few years later, after Edmund Geninges had been captured saying Mass in Mr. Wells's house, both he and his wife were condemned to death. Mrs. Wells was pardoned on the day that her husband, "a man of good birth and ancient years, his head almost as white as snow," was hanged with Fr. Geninges before his own house in Holborn, 10 December

with two or three other priests whom she knew not, they told her that her falling from the Catholique Church was the cause that the devill had made her husband to kill the said man.

Of late also, she saith that one *Perry* servaunt to maister *Roper* that lieth in Southampton-house, challenging her for that she had revealed where her sister *Sara* dwelt, said that she played the Ferret, and sought many mens lives, that it was pittie she lived, and that it were a good deede to shoote her through with a pistoll as she goeth in the streets. Howbeit this examinate saith that shee never meant any Catholique in England hurt (some priests excepted who have dealt hardly with her). But beeing now upon her oath to speake the truth, shee hopeth that no honest man or woman will be angry with her for discharging her conscience; adding, that if it had not been so long ago since she was in the priests hands, she could have delivered many moe things as touching their bad proceedings.

Shee further saith that the priests at theyr departure from *Denham* tooke every one thence his woman with him: Ma: *Edmunds* the Jesuit had for his darling mistris *Cressy,* then a widdow, who was a daily guest there, and one that did contribute very much both to him and the rest of the priests; *Anne Smith* was at the disposition of Ma: *Driland; Sara Williams* of maister *Dibdale;* mistris *Altham* of *Cornelius,* and this examinate of Ma: *Leigh,* a priest likewise.[1]

---

1591. Obviously, Master Wells had no conversations with Fid "about foure yeeres" before 1598, nor was he a priest. Swithin Wells, who had been a schoolmaster, was a poet. For an example of his verse and an account of his life, see Guiney, *Recusant Poets,* 171–74.

[1] A final example of Fid's reckless lying. There were two Leighs. Edward Leigh, of the old Cheshire family of Leigh, born 1553, was not a priest in 1586. He entered the English College, Rome, 23 May 1592, and was ordained subdeacon January 1595. There is no record of his ordination, but he was sent to England as a priest. Nothing else is known of him. Richard Leigh, born in London, 1561, was not in England in time for the exorcisms. He was ordained 11 February 1586 in the Lateran, Rome, and left Rheims for England, 16 June 1586. He was martyred at Tyburn, 30 August 1588. There was also Richard Sergeant, who used the alias Lea, but he was dead when the priests and their patients left Denham, executed with the exorcising priest William Thomson, 20 April 1586. Of these men Fid, lying sixteen years later, probably intended to slander the best-known, the martyr Richard (Anstruther, *Seminary Priests* 1:208, 305).

# The examination of *Anne Smith,* alias *Atkinson,* taken by vertue of her oath, the 12 of March, 1598.

SHE saith that dwelling with one Ma: *Bold* at *Bold-hall* in *Lancashire*,[1] the yeere that the Earle of *Leicester* went into the Low-Countries,[2] she was sicke of a disease called the Mother; that she then having a sister, one *Alice Plater,* that boorded at the Lady *Staffords,* was sent by her Mistres to her said sister at London, the said Lady *Stafford* then lying at *Ivie bridge;* where she remained (as she saith) about a yeere, using the help of *Phisicke* for the said disease. She saith that Ma: *Edmund Peckham* did boord at the said Lady *Staffords* from about the Christmas that this examinate came to London till about Easter following.

Shee saith further that about three weekes before Christmas next ensuing, her sister being advertised by the said Ma: *Peckham* that *Sara* and *William Trayford* were possessed at his house, she (her said sister) went thither, where finding the manner of their troubles, she conceaved that this examinate was likewise possessed as they were.

There-upon she saith that upon the Christmas even she went to *Denham* unto her sister, where shee found *Trayford,* but he did not make any shew as though hee were possessed, but did waite orderly upon Ma: *Peckham* his Maister; and *Sara* was then gone to the Lord *Vaux* his house, being caried thither by one *Dibdale* a priest.

After she had beene at *Denham* about a moneth, she attended upon Mistres *Peckham* to a churching in *Denham* Towne, where she saith her fore-said disease did trouble her; and likewise being then recovered, it tooke her againe as she was going homewards, where-upon one *White,*[3] a priest that used much that house, was sent to London for *Cornelius* another priest (who kept at Sir *John Arundells* in *Clarkenwell*) by the meanes of her said sister, who told this examinate that she was surely possessed. When her sister said she was possessed, she this examinate

---

[1]Richard Bold, a notable Catholic gentleman. Besides his property in Lancashire, he had a house in Berkshire, where Tyrrell and William Weston visited him, and where he maintained an elaborate musical establishment with an organ and instruments in his chapel. Weston and Tyrrell met William Byrd there, and it was for just such a household that Byrd composed his Latin motets and masses (Morris, *Troubles* 2:140, 145). Caraman suggests that after the raids on Denham house, Robert Dibdale was briefly a chaplain with Mr. Bold (Caraman, *An Autobiography,* 72).

[2]Leicester landed at Flushing on 10 December 1585.

[3]This can only be Richard White, of whom almost nothing is known. He was sent to England 31 May 1582, and was still alive in Oxfordshire in 1610 (Anstruther, *Seminary Priests* 1:378).

denied it, and so she did when the said *Cornelius* came unto her. She saith that the said *Cornelius* comming to *Denham* the same day at night that hee was sent for, brought in his company one *Stamp* a priest, *Thomson* a priest (as she thinketh), and one *Christopher Tulice* a priest, with Mistres *Cressey,* Ma: *Gardner* and his wife.[1]

The day after the priests came unto her, they tooke upon them to exorcise her from morning till towards night, and then left her.

She saith that besides the disease of the Mother, shee grew to be sicke, and receaved Physick by Doctor *Griffithes* prescription at *Alexander* the Apothecaries hands; but not recovering her health thereby, after about two moneths her said sister procured her to be sent to Mistris *Mainy* in *Channon Row,* with whom shee was to dwell about the beginning of Lent.

She continued with Ma: *Mainy* in the Earle of *Lincolnes* house in *Channon Row* til after Easter weeke. In which time she saith onely *Elizabeth Calthrope* (as this examinate remembreth), dwelling likewise with Mistres *Mainy,* was supposed by the priests to be possessed, and being there-upon removed to Ma: *Mainyes* owne house in *Greenes Alley,* there she was exorcised, until she died there.

She further saith she was present when *Mainy* did counterfeit himselfe that he should die upon the *Good Friday,* he the said *Mainy* then lying at the Earle of *Lincolnes* house, against which time a great number came thither to see him depart.

The said *Mainy* came to her Mistres house (she being his sister[2]) about a moneth or five weekes before Easter, and every *Friday* the said *Mainy* did pretend himselfe to be wonderfully tormented; and when he was recovered out of his traunce, he would use to say he had beene in Purgatorie; and there-upon gave it out that he should die on *Good Friday,* and goe immediatly to heaven, having beene already in Purgatorie.

She saith that all the said Lent she continued with Mistres *Mainy,* she was stil evill at ease, and that the priests that came thither did stil endevour to perswade her that she was possessed, saying that she must beleeve them therein, that she was possessed, and that they could help her, and not otherwise.

The priests names, as she remembreth, were Ma: *Cornelius,* Ma: *Dryland,* Ma: *Tirrell,* Ma: *Stamp,* Ma: *Tulice,* Ma: *Ballard.*

She further saith that about three weekes after Easter, the said priests stil continuing to perswade her that she was possessed, and that if shee beleeved so, then they would helpe her; she this examinate continuing to be evill at ease, and hoping by their meanes to be helped, yeelded to say that she thought she was possessed, therby to see if she might be helped, although all the while she had a conceite in her selfe that she was not possessed.

She further saith that whilest she did withstand the priests said perswasions, affirming that shee knew shee was not possessed, they told her, *it was the devill within her* that caused her so to say.

---

[1]For the priests Anne names as exorcists here and further on in her statement, see Appendix A.

[2]I.e., his sister-in-law.

When shee had thus yeelded unto them, Ma: *Stamp* caried her to *Denham,* accompanied with one *Harris,* Ma: *Mainyes* man.

She saith that about sixteene days after the said Easter, this examinate and *Elizabeth Calthrope,* being both sicke, and supposed by the priests to be possessed, her Maister left them both in the Earle of *Lincolnes* house, and went to *Babingtons* house the traytor in *Barbican;* and the third or fourth day after, this examinate was caried to *Denham* (as afore-said) where shee and all the house were maintayned at the common charge of the priests that resorted thither.

At her comming to *Denham,* they tooke in hand to exorcise her, and continued that course with her til Whitsontide. About a fortnight after Whitsontide (as she remembreth) certaine Pursuivants came, and searched the house, and finding there Ma: *Dryland* the priest and other men, viz., *Alexander* the Apothecarie, *Swythen Wells* (after executed in *Holborne*), and *James Stanborow,* Ma: *Peckhams* man, they caried them to prison, leaving this examinate and two other women in the house.[1]

She saith that the rest of the priests, when the Pursuivants came, were gone with *Fid,* and *Sara Owen,* alias *Frauncis* and *Sara Williams,* as this examinate hath been enformed.

It was Sonday when the Pursuivants caried the said parties to prison; and upon the Monday after the said *Drylands* man caried this examinate to London, where shee was placed that night by Ma: *Maryne* at one *Alexanders* house in a little Lane going out of *Thames streete,* and is (as now she is enformed) betwixt *Lyons key* and *Billingsgate.*

Shee continued at the said *Alexanders* house about seaven weekes, her charges being first defrayed by the said Ma: *Maryne,* and afterwards by Ma: *Pownd,* late prisoner at *Wisbitch.*[2] Her acquaintance with Ma: *Maryne* grew at *Denham,* and with Ma: *Pownd* at the said *Alexanders* house.

Ma: *Pownd,* in respect of the charge hee was at with her at *Alexanders,* paying ten shillings a weeke for her boord, removed her thence to mistris *Lowes* to *Newington* in *Surrey;* where remayning not past three or foure dayes, the said *Pownd* carried her to his Mothers house, one mistris *Pownd,* dwelling in the same Towne, where she remained til Ma: *Pownd*

---

[1] Anne's date for these arrests, a fortnight after Whitsuntide, would be 5 June, a Sunday, as she says. Dryland, however, was committed on 20 June, the servant James Stanborough on 19 June (*CSP Dom., Elizabeth,* vol. 194, no. 34). A prison list of 18 June has Dryland's name in an added note with the comment, "newly taken" (*CSP Dom., Elizabeth,* vol. 190, no. 42).

[2] Like Swithin Wells a native of Hampshire, Thomas Pound was first a courtier, an esquire of the body to Elizabeth I. He then became seriously Catholic, and from 1574–1604, when James I liberated him on bail, he was continuously imprisoned. On 1 September 1586, after a brief interval of liberty, the High Commission committed him to the White Lyon prison, from which he was later moved to Wisbech. Anne's reference to him as "late prisoner at *Wisbitch*" must relate to the time of her examination, not of her story. Pound is an attractive figure, generous, courageous, and a writer of poetry and prose as well as a voluminous correspondence. In 1578, while in prison, he applied for admission to the Society of Jesus, and was accepted as a brother, 1 December 1578. He died in 1614 (*CRS* 2 [1906]: 267, 278–79; Guiney, *Recusant Poets,* 182–86).

was taken, which was upon the day when bon fires were made for *Babingtons* apprehension, viz. the 15 of July.

The said mistris *Pownd* was of her sonnes Religion, where-upon after he was apprehended she had no joy to stay there, but was caried thence by one Ma: *Goodmans* direction unto mistris *Leicester,* dwelling in *Fleet-streete* at the signe of the dogges head in the pot; where shee had not remained above two dayes, but uppon a search was taken and committed to prison for recusancie, where she remained about a moneth, and then escaped thence.

In this meane while, viz. from Whitsontide before specified, *Dibdale, Lowe,* and *Adams* were apprehended, and being arraigned, this examinate was brought by maister *Youngs* meanes, whilest she was prisoner, to give in evidence against them at their arraignment. The cause why she was brought to give in evidence against them was for that maister *Young* hearing her name, did examine her, whether she was not one that did pretend her selfe to be possessed at *Denham,* with whom *Dibdale* and the rest of the priests had dealt; and there-upon examined her touching her possession and the devils dealing with her, and particulerly of a peece of a knife which the priests said came out of her body.

This examinate was prisoner in *Bridewell,* where the said *Fid.* was likewise prisoner with her; where this examinate found such favour as, having the liberty of the prison by maister *Youngs* appointment, and thereby being trusted with some keyes, she and *Fid.* by her meanes escaped thence, taking with them the *Matrones* girle; which girle by the said maister *Pownds* direction was sent into *Hampshire,* and placed with his Mother, who had a house in the said County, and did then lie there.

After she was escaped, shee was placed by Ma: *Pownds* direction first in *Cow-lane,* then by her mothers meanes with the French Embassadors wife,[1] where disliking, she was by maister *Pownds* meanes placed in a poore womans house by the *Marshalsea,* and then againe with his mother; and then going to the *White-Lyon* to see maister *Pownd,* with her mistris, she this examinate (whilst they two were talking together) going to maister *Simpsons* chamber a priest,[2] was againe there apprehended and committed by maister *Young* againe to *Bridewell,* where shee

---

[1] Anthony Tyrrell confirms Anne's story of her escape from prison with Fid, but in his version both girls were concealed with the French ambassador. Since it was Tyrrell who betrayed them, his version can be relied upon (Morris, *Troubles* 2:421–24).

[2] This will have been Thomas Simpson, ordained at Rheims, April 1585, sent to England three days later and captured on landing, 3 May. He was imprisoned, then banished. He returned, June 1586, was captured again and imprisoned in the White Lion, where Anne went to visit him. By July 1587 he had been moved to the Marshalsea, and in March 1588 he was in Wisbech Castle. In 1589 he escaped, was captured, and imprisoned again. Although Justice Young, March 1587, described him as "a most perilous person and the most obstinate gainesayer of her majesties lawes, denienge that wee have the churche or any lawfull Bishops or mynisters" (*CRS* 2 [1906]: 276), he seems to have been completely ineffective as an underground priest, and in 1593 he apostasized. In 1604 he received the Church of England living of Kelvedon, Essex, but lost it in 1609 for preaching Catholic doctrine (*CRS* 2 [1906]: 272, 273, 277–79; Anstruther, *Seminary Priests* 1:317–18).

remained about twenty-one weekes, in which time the Queene of Scots was beheaded.

Shee was discharged out of *Bridewell* by maister *Secretary Walsinghams* meanes at the sute of maister *Dale*, a Merchant in *Gracious-street*, and then remaining with her mother a while, was placed with the said Lady *Stafford*, with whom shee dwelt about two yeeres, viz., till she was married.

She saith that when first she fell into the priests hands, shee was about eighteen yeeres of age, and that shee is verily perswaded she never was possessed with a wicked spirit (for the which shee thanketh Almighty God from the bottom of her hart), but verily thinketh that she was verie much abused by the said priests, in that they did perswade her (as is before expressed) that shee was possessed.

Besides, shee saith that where it was given out by the priests that a peece of a knife came out of her mouth when she was in one of her fits, she then was fully perswaded that they said untruly therein, although at that time, being wholely addicted to Poperie, she did reverence them very much, and durst not contradict them.

She further saith that when *Cornelius* did first begin to exorcise her, the manner thereof was this: She being wel and in perfect memory, and at that time not troubled with her former disease called the mother, *Cornelius* and the rest set her in a chayre, and bound her fast with towells; then *Cornelius* having ended a short speech or Sermon (the effect whereof she doth not now remember) which was made before shee was bound in the chayre, and being in his Albe, and having a stole about his neck, began to reade his Exorcismes, whereat this examinate doth now remember that shee began greatlie to shiver and quake, being then strooke with a great feare, as though the devill would greatlie torment and teare her because they had so bound her.

Besides shee saith (which did encrease her feare) she had beene told by divers how others had beene troubled, viz., how in their fits they were greatly tormented; how they could not endure the Priests to come neere them; how when a priest did lay his hand uppon any part of them, the said part would be so hote as though it would burne them to the bone; how the devil in them would raile upon the Catholiques, and greatly commend the Protestants, and many other such things they reported, which this examinate hath forgotten.

She further saith that she was then so zealous in Poperie, and had such an opinion of the said priests, that if shee could have gotten under the Altar-cloath with a crosse in her mouth and a candel in her hand, she thought her selfe safe from the devil. When shee was exorcised the first time, and so afterwards being bound in the chayre, where shee seemed still to be wel notwithstanding their Exorcismes, then they would pretend to give her somewhat, either to comfort her stomacke (she seeming to faint through feare), or to disclose the devil, which was hallowed, and was very loathsome to her to take. This hallowed medicine, as she remembreth, had Rue and oyle in it, and was ugly to behold, such as she thinketh they could not have taken themselves. Also she saith they would burne brimstone under her nose, which shee saith would greatly trouble her, and as shee supposeth, did take away her sences from her. Thus she saith they dealt with her, as she supposeth, some five or sixe times.

She further saith that they did bind her so fast at those times in a chayre, as they almost lamed her armes, and so brused all the parts of her body with holding, tying, and turmoyling of her, that she was so sore, she was compelled afterwards by the space of three yeeres to swathe her body.

She further saith that now she prayeth God for the priests that be alive, that God would forgive them for dealing so with her, and is very hartily sorie that ever she came into their company.

She further saith that upon Wednesday in Whitson-weeke, whilst shee was at *Denham,* there came thether maister *Salisbury* that was executed, Ma: *John Gerrard,*[1] and Ma: *George Peckham.*

She also saith that she thanketh God shee never saw any thing that might terrifie her, but onely the priests when they were exorcising; that she never saw any visions; and whatsoever they write or affirme of her touching any such matter, shee affirmeth that they are all fained and untrue. And she addeth that she mervaileth that they should set downe any thing of her that shee should speake in her fits, considering that it was given out, the spirit that was in her was a sullen and dumbe spirit, and would not therefore be brought to aunswer the priests; and that the said spirit that was supposed to be in her was such a one, the devil that was in *Mainy* (who was named *Modion*) did affirme, as many reported.

This examinate further saith that shee being present by *Mainy* when he was in exorcising, after that shee the first time had been exorcised by *Cornelius,* Ma: *Edmunds* the Jesuit did aske the devil in *Mainy* whether she this examinate was possessed or not; and the devil aunswered that she was. Then quoth Ma: *Edmunds,* how chaunce he could not be brought to speake this other day when she was exorcised? He the said devil, as she then supposed, aunswered that the reason was because the spirit that was in her was sullen and dumbe. Then they demaunding of his devil what was the name of the spirit that was in this examinate, he aunswered *Soforce.* And this was betwixt Christmas and Shrovetide.

She further saith that it was a common thing amongst them to give out words as though Protestants were all possessed, and there-upon the priests would aske some that were pretended to be possessed, or the devil in them (as it was supposed), whilest they were exorcising them, why they did not trouble them before whilest they were Protestants. And the devil would aunswer that there was no reason for them so to doe because the Protestants were theirs already.

She further saith that after the time she was out of the priests hands, her former disease of the Mother did divers times take her, and continued with her as before it had done, untill being married she had children. Since which time she hath beene rid of that disease, she thanketh God.

---

[1]John Gerard was not yet a priest, being ordained and admitted to the Society of Jesus in 1588. Having been arrested and imprisoned upon his return from Europe, he was lately free on bail, put up by his friend Anthony Babington. Dorothy Peckham was his sister.

She further saith that shee wel remembreth the morning when *Alexander* the Apothecarie was to goe to London to fetch more priests, the day before this examinate was first exorcised, his horse prauncing and flinging of him downe, he returned backe againe, and constantly affirmed that the wicked spirit that was in this examinate had caused his horse to fling him: whereat when this examinate laughed, he the said *Alexander* affirmed that *it was the devill* that laughed at him.

# The confession of Ma. *Anthonie Tyrrell* Clerke,[1] written with his owne hand, and avouched upon his oath the 15 of June 1602.

Divers interrogatories beeing propounded to this examinate concerning the pretended casting out of devils by maister *Edmunds*, alias *Weston*, a Jesuit, and certaine other Seminary priests in the yeeres 1585 and 1586 at *Hackney, Denham,* and other places; and as touching likewise the occasions or inducements that mooved them at that time to take such matters upon them, hee hath set downe his aunswer as followeth.

I will first answer to the circumstance of time which is heere propounded unto me. In the yeere 1584 I and *John Ballard* priest (since executed with Ma: *Babington* and the rest), comming together from Rome through *Burgundy,* found there a great presse of souldiours, and were advertised that they were to serve under the *Duke of Guise.* When wee came to *Roane,* wee heard then directly that the said preparations were against England. The same yeere (as I remember), Ma: *Crighton* a Scottish Jesuit[2] was taken at the sea, and after brought into England, who by occasion of certaine writings which he had, was driven to confesse at large (as I have beene informed) what the whole plot was; and how far both the Pope and the King of Spaine had ingaged themselves in it. Hereof I doubt not but that sundry Catholiques in England had sufficient notice from beyond the seas, and especially Ma: *Edmunds,* alias *Weston,* the Jesuit, who was then the chiefe, as maister *Garnet* (as I take it) is at this present, and therefore could not be ignorant of such important matters wherein principall men of his owne societie were engaged.

Not long after my comming into England in the yeere 1585, maister *Martin Aray* a priest, meeting with me at the end of *Cheapside* as I was turning to enter into *Paules* Churchyard, tooke mee by the hand, and whispering me in the eare, bad me *be of good cheere, for that all things went now very well forward. The king of Spayne* (quoth he) *is now almost ready with his forces to come into England, and we shall be sure to heare some good newes therof very shortly; wherefore it standeth us now in hand that be priests to further the Catholique cause as much as possibly in us lyeth,* or to this effect. And this was the state of that time, nourished (I well perceived) with great hope of some great alteration by the meanes before expressed.

About the time of maister *Arayes* aforesaid communication with me, maister *Edmunds,* alias *Weston,* had lately (as it was reported) cast a devill out of one *Marwood;* whereupon he the said maister *Aray,* at the

---

[1]For Tyrrell, see Appendix A.

[2]On Fr. Crichton and his role in these affairs, see Pollen, *Mary Queen of Scots,* xv–xvi, 151–68.

time before mentioned, did highly commend unto mee the exorcismes of Fa: *Edmunds,* saying that *hee* (the said *Edmunds*) *would make the devils themselves now confesse that theyr kingdome was neere at an end.* Upon the pretended dispossession of the said *Marwood,* sundry other priests mooved thereunto (I am perswaded) by the instigation of maister *Edmunds,* or for that they meant to shew theyr zeale in imitating of him, did take upon them to exorcise and cast devils out of divers persons, viz., *Sara* and *Friswood Williams, William Trayford, Anne Smith, Richard Mainy,* and *Elizabeth Calthrop,* whose necke was found broken at the bottome of a payre of stayres (as the brute went then amongst us). When I saw this course, I liked it well, and was my selfe an Actor in it, and did well perceive that it was the matter whereat Ma: *Aray* had aymed when he told me that *it stoode us Priests in hand to further the Catholique cause as much as possibly wee could.* And indeed our proceedings therein had for a time wonderfull successe. I cannot in my conscience esteeme the number fewer that in the compasse of halfe a yeere were by that meanes reconciled to the Church of Rome then five hundred persons; some have said three or foure thousand. As touching the severall manners of dispossessing the said parties, and of theyr fits, traunces, and visions, divers discourses were penned, amongst the which I my selfe did penne one. Ma: *Edmunds* likewise writ (I am perswaded) a quire of paper of Ma: *Mainyes* pretended visions. For he thought, as it seemed, to have wrought some great matter by him, but was disappointed very ridiculously, so as I thinke the said visions will hardly come to light. There was also a Treatise framed to proved first, *that in former times divers had been possessed.* Secondly, *that Christ hath left to his Church certaine remedies for the dispossessing of such parties.* Thirdly, *that in the casting out of devils there hath beene great use of application to the Daemoniacks of holy reliques.* In prosecution of the first part, amongst other points the Author sheweth that *GOD permitteth some to be possessed that thereby the faithlesse Atheists may learne that there is both a God and a devill; and that the faith of the Catholique Church may also be confirmed by the power left unto her in casting out of devils.* In the handling of the second point, *hee tryumpheth against the Protestants, saying that for all theyr reformation which they talke of to be so neere the order of the Primitive Church, yet they are not able either to discerne who are possessed amongst them, nor how to give them remedy.* The third part is handled more largely, to the great advauncement and power of Reliques. As *for holy water: that S.* Macarius *thereby cured a woman who by Magicall enchauntment seemed to be turned into a Mare.* Likewise, how S. *Peter hallowed bread against the assault of certaine devils which were sent by* Simon Magus *in the likenes of dogges to devoure him.* For the power of priesthood, there is an example alledged of S. *Martin, how he putting his fingers into the mouth of a Daemoniacke, the devill durst not bite him, though he bad him to bite him if he had any power so to doe.* There is also mention made of the vertue of the blessed sacrament, of holy oyle, and of the bones of Saints. The use of all those things was very frequent in the exorcising of the parties possessed. Insomuch as wee omitted not the reliques and bones of Ma: *Campian,* Ma:

*Sherwin,* Ma: *Brian,* and Ma: *Cottam,* to have some little testimonie by implication from the devill, to proove them holy Martyrs.

If I be not deceived, Ma: *Edmunds* alias *Weston* was the Author of this booke, and the examples by him alledged were brought of purpose to give the more credit to his and our proceedings with the said parties before mentioned. And indeed he was not therein deceived, for wee that were priests were thereby greatlie magnified by Catholiques, schismaticks, and weak protestants; the two former beeing confirmed in the Romane Catholicke faith, and the third sort thereunto reconciled, as hath beene before mentioned. And that cannot be denied, but that in the course which wee held with the said pretended Demoniacks, many occasions were given and aptly taken to scorne and deride the orders and service now established by her Majesties lawes in the Church of England.

Likewise I must confesse that the course we held was so pleasing to such as saw it or were informed of it by those that they trusted, as it prooved very gainfull unto us all that were priests; wee had out of question procured unto our selves very great favour, credit, and reputation, so as it was no mervaile if some young Gentlemen, as Ma: *Babington* and the rest, were allured to those strange attempts which they tooke in hand by maister *Ballard,* who was an Agent amongst us. They saw, as they supposed (for both maister *Babington* and divers of his company were oftentimes at the exorcisings), that we had a great commandement over devils, which prevailed greatly with them, as I think. It would have been a very strange thing (I am perswaded) that wee could not have wrought men at that time to attempt: which was prudently foreseene by Fa: *Edmunds* of purpose (as I am resolved in my conscience) to prepare the harts and minds of Catholiques by those practises, that when such forces as were intended should have come into England, they might have been more readily drawn by him and us to have joyned theyr forces with them. And this is that I can say concerning the occasions, or inducements, that such matters were taken in hand at the time articulated.

Now as touching the substance of the generall interrogatory it selfe, I have perused the severall examinations and confessions of *Sara Williams* and *Friswood* her sister, of *Anne Smith,* and of *Richard Mainy* gentleman, and am fully perswaded that they have deposed the truth in such poynts whereof they were examined belonging to theyr pretended possession and dispossession. The effect wherof is, that they were drawn by our cunning carriage of matters to seeme as though they had beene possessed when as in truth they were not; neither were there any of the priests ignorant in my conscience of their dissimulation, nor the parties themselves (as now it appeareth) of our dissembled proceeding with them.

After I had beene my selfe first at one of theyr exorcisings, it was my chaunce to lie that night with maister *Thomson,* a priest and a great Actor in those matters,[1] at his chamber by the *Spittle;* and falling into some conference about it, I used some such words as though I doubted whether the party were actually and really possessed. For I my selfe being not

[1]See Appendix A.

acquainted with anie plot devised by Fa: *Edmunds* or any other, spake my minde some-what more plainely then I perceaved Ma: *Thomson* wel liked of. His aunswer unto me was in effect that *he being my friend did earnestly wish me to cast forth no such speeches, whatsoever I did thinke. For* (quoth he) *the matter is judged to be so by Fa:* Edmunds *and some others that are Priests. Besides such Catholiques as have beene present at such fits have received it for a truth that the parties are possessed. And although I for my part will not make it an article of my Creede, yet I thinke that godlie credulitie doth much good for the furthering of the Catholique cause, and for the defacing of our common enemies and their proceedings,* or to this effect. Not long after, also talking with Ma: *Stamp*[1] at the Lord *Vaux* his house in *Hackney* concerning these matters, and demaunding of him seriously his opinion, what he thought of them, his aunswer was that *they were things of such importance as would further the Catholique cause more then all the bookes that had beene written of late yeeres about the controversies in Religion with the Protestants;* with which aunswer I seemed to rest contented, because I saw thereby he was not willing to enter into any playner course with me.

I would not have this my confession further extended then my meaning is; I doe not take upon me either directly or indirectly to oppose my selfe to the three poynts of the Treatise before mentioned, which are strengthened with some authorities both of the Scriptures and of the auncient Fathers and Writers. How be it, as I account it presumption to denie all those Histories, as touching the casting out of devils in the Primitive Church since the Apostles times; so to beleeve all that is written thereof, I hold it a point of great madnes, and I doubt not but the soundest Catholiques in *Europe* are of my opinion. For be it true that is alledged in the said treatise of S. *Ambrose,* that he never heard of any that could counterfeit himselfe to be a Demoniack, yet later experience hath taught us the contrary. And indeede, the artificiall skil considered where-unto priests have attained, it is a very easie matter to bring a young girle or a youth to doe and speake those things which the Exorcists can readily colour and interpret as if it were both done and spoken by devils that did possesse them. But yet this I wil say, and give it for a rule to all Catholiques heereafter that wil not purposely suffer themselves to be deluded: let them but mark diligently when they are present at any such actions, what the parties pretended to be possessed doe eyther act or speak; and then they shal perceave nothing but may very well be dissembled or otherwise uttered in great distemper procured by loathsome potions and violent fumigations. And they shal be very wel armed against all such deceites if ever it be their haps to heare or read the confessions and examinations of the parties before mentioned. Marrie, they must keepe their owne counsel; for I am perswaded that if any shall seeme to be a curious beholder at such times, and a mover of questions, he shal not be any welcome guest unto them. Heereof any may be further advertised that wil take the paines to reade a little French Treatise of a

[1] See Appendix A.

counterfeit Demoniack at *Paris*,[1] and how the Exorcists could in no sort endure the questions and doubts that were propounded unto them when they were at their work, but pretended that such curiosity and want of faith did greatly hinder them in their proceedings.

There will be many exceptions taken to that which heere I have delivered upon my conscience, to prove that the said parties pretended to be possessed were not counterfeits, as that some things fell out which were not possible to be dissembled. The chiefe objection wil be as touching a peece of a knife, in length about two inches and a halfe, which was said to come out of the bodie of *Anne Smith,* having beene convaied into her before, as it was pretended, by the devil. And to cleare the matter, the devil was made (forsooth) to shew by Philosophie that he was able to doe such a thing; for to this effect it was given out, that the devil should reade us (as I may terme it) a Lecture: *I am as you know by creation a spirit, and have lost no part of my knowledge and cunning in the secrets of nature, and that I can dissolve any Iron or hard matter at my pleasure into a liquid substance; and so I did, and poured it into her porredge, which she eating, swallowed up the knife in that liquid substance, and the same being so in her body, I reduced it into the artificiall forme which before it had. And thus much you may beleeve* (quoth the devil) *if you be but Philosophers,* or to this effect. Whereunto for aunswer as the truth is, so farre forth as I know or beleeve. First as the peece of the knife came out of her mouth without hurting of her (if it came out of her mouth at all, and that there were not a shift of legerdemaine used to make it seeme indeede to those that were present that it came out of her mouth), so might it be taken forth againe, having beene put into her mouth by the Exorcist himselfe for ought I know; as some of the said parties have acknowledged that the Exorcists somtimes would thrust bigge bones and peeces of reliques into their mouthes. Amongst the which *Friswood Williams* deposeth that as she verily beleeveth they thrust a rustie naile into her mouth, and afterwards pretended that it came out of her body. 2, *Anne Smith* hath deposed that she is fully perswaded that they have reported untruly of the taking of a peece of a knife out of her mouth. Howbeit, shee saith shee durst not at that time contradict them. But it is needelesse for mee to aunswer this or any such like objection. For the things are in themselves so ridiculous as I think no man will be so mad as to take uppon him to defend them. And when wee our selves that were actors in those matters thought wee had wonne our spurres, yet divers auncient priests, as Maister *Heywood,* Maister *Dolman,* Maister *Redman,* and some others hearing of the course we held, did shake their heads at it, and shewed their great dislike of it.[2] Likewise the graver sort that

---

[1]Martha Brossier [H].

[2]These were three priests. Oliver Heywood was committed by Justice Young in summer 1586, dying in Newgate 15 July (*CRS* 2 [1906]: 267). Dolman was "an ancient missioner;" according to Gillow (*A Literary and Biographical History* 2:85), this means that he was ordained before the accession of Elizabeth I. He was committed to prison February 1585, and described in December 1586 as "at libertye, but fitt for Wisbich & to be restrayned" (*CRS* 2 [1906]: 273). He was much respected, and made collections for the prisoners in Wisbech, whom he visited. When the notorious "stirs" began there, he attempted to reconcile the parties. His only serious embarrassment occurred when Robert

were then imprisoned at *Wisbich* were greatly offended there-with (as I have beene credibly informed), and said that howsoever for a time wee might be admired, yet in the end wee would thereby marre all, and utterly discredit both our selves and our calling. Where-upon wee the younger sort of the Seminarie priests that were then dealers herein thought our selves hardly dealt with by them, and that they did but envie at the commendation which they saw wee daily gayned, themselves being no actors amongst us. But now I see that the said aunctient Fathers had beene acquainted of likelihood with such devises beyond the Seas, and were greatly greeved to have them brought into England. Notwith-standing, Ma: *Edmunds* and the rest would needes proceede (as is before in part expressed), and have thereby to their perpetual shame made them true Prophets.

I have my selfe before confessed that my pen is in the booke that was taken with Ma: *Barnes,* wherein I layd together those things that *Sara Williams* was pretended to have done and said in one of her fits at *Hack-ney,* the 10 of Januarie, some things whereof I saw and heard my selfe, others I receaved by peece-meale of Maister *Thomson,* Ma: *Thulice,* and others, and layd them altogether with the best skill I had to make them seeme strange and wonderfull. For although both my selfe (as I said before), and so I thinke of the rest, did know that all was but counterfeite, yet for as much as we perceaved that thereby great credit did grow to the Catholique cause, and great discredit to the Protestants, wee held it lawfull to doe as we did.

Shortly after I had first conformed my selfe to the state of the Church established heere in England, and there-upon disclosed many things to the late Lord *Treasurer* concerning sundry very pernicious designments against her Majestie and this state, I fell againe to my old course by the perswasion of some of my auncient acquaintance that were priests, hav-ing had small time to ground my selfe by study, thereby to defend my said conformitie. I was no sooner come to my old byace but they soone drew mee for the good of the Catholique cause to say that all in effect was false that I had before confessed. Although not long after, the treasons did so breake forth, and were so fully confessed by *Babington* himselfe, that not onely that which I had reported was justified by them to be true, but a great deale more then ever I knew or dreamed of. Like-wise I having detected in some part the folly of the said exorcisings, it is scarce credible how earnest the said priests were with me to avow them againe for matters of veritie. Whereunto for the reason before mentioned, I did willingly yeeld, nothing doubting but that if God should once againe so draw his grace from mee as that I should become to be as then I was (that is, wholy addicted to popery, as I trust in his mercy hee will never doe), I should be as ready againe to deny all that now I have affirmed upon my oath as I was before. For the generall conceit amongst

---

Parson published his *Conference about the Next Succession* (1595) under the pseudonym R. Doleman, a name Parsons chose to signify "sorrowful man." See Gillow 2:85–87. Redman was "an aged man, made priest in Queen Mary's time" (Pollen, "Supposed Cases," 117:460).

all the priests of that order is that they may deny any thing which beeing confessed doth turne to the dishonour of the Catholique Church of Rome. Besides, they have other objections that serve theyr turnes, as that the Magistrates in England are no competent Judges, the Queene herselfe standing excommunicate, and that therefore the examinations taken before them are of no validitie to bind the examinats, but that all that they doe confesse is *tanquam coram non Judice.* A number of other shifts they have, which I doe not now remember.

The Apostolicall rule is that *evill shall not be doone that good may come of it;* but they doe not account it evill (as I verily thinke) to calumniate the Protestants by any devise whatsoever that may carry any probabilitie with it, nor make any conscience to tell and publish any untruthes which they thinke, beeing believed, may advaunce and promote such poynts and matters as they take upon them to defend for the honour of the church of Rome and dignitie of their priesthood.

*Anth: Tyrrell*

# The confession of *Richard Mainy* Gentleman, written by himselfe, and avouched uppon his oath the sixt of June. 1602.

THE said *Richard Mainy* had read unto him some parts of a discourse or two written by certaine Seminary priests of a pretended possession and dispossession both of himselfe and of certaine others, viz. one *Marwood, Trayford, Sara* and *Francis Williams,* two sisters, and *Anne Smith.* These parties were said to be possessed and dispossessed of many wicked spirits. The priests that dealt with them were divers, but the especiall men that had *Richard Mainy* in hand were Ma: *Edmunds* the Jesuit, alias *Weston, Cornelius,* and one *Dibdale,* men wholy at the devotion and direction of the said *Edmunds.* It was in the yeeres 1585 and 1586 when these stratagems were executed. Such dealings as they had with the said *Mainy* were at *Denham,* at one Ma: *Fittons* two miles from *Windsore,*[1] and at the Earle of *Lincolnes* house in *Channon-row,* where *John Mainy* his brother did then remaine.

[1] The Fittons were a Berkshire family, living at a house called Bailes near Windsor. According to the spy, Berden, Richard Davis alias Winkfield alias Foster alias Cook reconciled them to the Church. Davis, described by Challoner as "an ancient missioner," was a remarkable man who worked for the Catholic cause as a lay volunteer, like Barnes and Pound. He accompanied Campion and Parsons, and in 1582, Dorothy White was presented for harboring him. He then crossed to the college at Rheims where, in September 1583, he was admitted to minor orders in a group that included Richard Mainy. Davis, therefore, provides the link between Richard Mainy, Denham, and the Fittons. It is characteristic of Mainy's account that he should keep Davis out of it, a small but important sign that his confession is not to be taken entirely at face value (Challoner, *Memoirs,* 118; Morris, *Troubles* 2:155; *CRS* 2 [1906]: 255; Knox, *Douay Diaries* 2:198; Anstruther, *Seminary Priests* 1:97–98). Davis attended the exorcisms, being arrested 12 May after leaving Denham and imprisoned in the Woodstreet Counter. He was identified as a layman ("a great guide unto the Jesuitts, but not knowen but for Davis a gentilman and no Priest"), yet although the government knew what he had done, they remained uncertain about what he was: "This Companyon was shyfted oute for a laye man by the name of Davys" is Berden's ambiguous note about him (*CRS* 2 [1906]: 275). Anstruther reads this to mean that Davis passed for a layman, and lists him as a priest because he was indicted as a priest at the Middlesex Sessions (Jeaffreson, *Middlesex County Records* 2:196). "Shyfted oute for a laye man," however, more probably means "was finally discovered, or decided, to be a layman." If he was a priest, ordained after September 1583, it is peculiar, though not unprecedented, that there seems to be no record of the ordination; what is truly remarkable is that with his record he escaped execution or banishment. He is last mentioned in English records as a prisoner in Newgate in 1615 under the name Hill. According to Challoner he was still alive in 1626, when he sent an account of his experiences over to Douai, in which he says that his arrest in 1586 occurred while he was "saying my prime," but this need not mean that he was a priest. He also says that he was with Anthony Babington the night before Babington's arrest (although the prison records show Davis to have been in prison himself at that time) and he gives a description of Dibdale's exorcisms, including the rumor that Fid later became Bancroft's mistress and had a child by him.

Of these matters the said *Mainy* beeing demaunded divers questions desired that hee might have leave to aunswer them after his owne fashion, and not to be tied to the order of the said demaunds, for that hee thought he could set downe those things which hee remembred more plainly to his owne understanding then otherwise he should be able, if he were bound to follow the order propounded unto him by the said demaunds. And that which he hath set downe is the discourse following, not much disagreeing from the order of the interrogatories ministred unto him.

And hath Ma: *Edmunds* and the rest of the priests thus dealt with mee? I am very sorry for it. It might have beene sufficient for them to have practised theyr purposes upon me and the rest, youthes and almost girles, although they had not published the same to the world. But of likelihood theyr glory and our discredit were so joyned together as the one could not stand without the other. This course whereunto they have therby drawne me wil procure me great displeasure (I know) amongst my friends, and worke me much hinderance in my private estate. But what remedie? Beeing called by publique authoritie, and enforced by vertue of mine oath to deliver the truth, I cannot see how with any conscience I can deny those things which I find to be truly layd to my charge, and could never have beene thought of if their writings had never come to the Magistrats hands. The particulers which now of necessity I must deliver I was purposed to have concealed from all men living, although heeretofore in generall termes I have beene driven to say somewhat of these matters.

About fourteen yeeres since, the Lords of her Majesties most honourable privie Counsell (*Henry, Earle* of *Darby* being one), having gotten some notice of the pretended possessions and dispossessions at the places before mentioned, and that I was one of the parties that had beene dealt with, did write their letter unto *Ferdinando,* then Lord *Strange,* to examine me.[1] It seemeth they had beene informed that I should publish how I was possessed with certaine wicked spirits, and of them dispossessed by some priests of the Catholique Romane Church, and that I should take upon mee in companie where I came to justifie the same. So as being called before the said Lord *Strange,* he demaunded of me whether I had given out such speeches. Hee examined mee upon my oath, and my aunswer was according to the truth, as I was perswaded in mine owne conscience, and as farre as my memory did serve me: viz., that I was never possessed with any wicked spirit, nor had reported any such thing; and that I was so farre from justifying of it that I was fully perswaded that in all the courses which the priests tooke with me when they pretended that I was possessed, there was nothing but deceit, falshood, illusions, and juglings. This was the effect of my aunswer at that time if my memory doe not much faile me, and thereupon I was by his Lordship dismissed.

[1]Ferdinando Stanley, fifth earl of Derby, 1559–1594, who succeeded on the death of his father, Henry, 25 September 1593.

With this aunswer (I suppose) the Jesuits were long since acquainted, which hath greatly already hindered me, and alienated the harts of some of my deerest friends from mee. And the same aunswer that I made then before his Lordship I must now make againe to the substance of all those questions which have been demaunded of mee, viz., that I was never possessed with any wicked spirit otherwise then all other sinners are, but ever as free (I thank GOD) from having any devils in me, as either Ma: *Edmunds* himselfe or any other of the Priests that had to deale with me, for ought I know.

This aunswer I thought would have beene sufficient to have satisfied all those things which are objected against me, but I am urged with sundry particulers, and therefore I must of necessity yeeld to the cleering of my selfe in them, and yet no otherwise then the truth requireth. When I was about thirteen yeeres old, I was sent by my mothers direction to *Rhemes* in Fraunce, where there was then an English Seminary. The intent of my mother and other of my friends was ( as I thinke) to have had mee to have been a priest. I remained in *Rhemes* about two yeres, and was there maintained with my mothers exhibition and allowance. Towards the end of the said two yeeres, of a childish curiositie, I entred into the observances of certaine religious men, termed in that country *Bonhommes* or *fratres minimi,* and became a young probationer amongst them. This order was devised by *Fraunces de Paula,* who is canonized for a saint, of whom there is mention made in the *Romane breviary* as having his place appointed in the Kalender on the second of Aprill. There his office and course of life is set downe and briefly described.

After I had remained about a quarter of a yeere or somewhat more in this probation, I was sent by the *Rector* of the house with some other of my fellowes to the house of the *Bonhommes* at *Paris,* where I had scarcely remained a quarter of a yeere but I grew weary of that profession. Their rules seemed unto me to be too strict for me, and their diet beeing nothing but fish I began to dislike it. Besides, I had a disease wherewith I had been troubled before I went out of England, that tooke me there againe; and thereupon I gave over that order altogether.

About that time, there was a proclamation published heere in England (as I was told) that *all English gentlemen and others should repaire home into theyr Country within a certaine time, upon danger of her Majesties displeasure, and losse of theyr goods and lands,* or to that effect. Whereuppon I was perswaded by some of my friends that saw my course of life there, having given over my studie, to returne home againe, and the rather for that I had some land left unto mee by my father. Leaving therefore *Paris,* I tooke my journy homeward by *Roane* towards *Diepe* where I tooke shipping, and landed at *Rie.* At my arrivall, the Maior offering unto mee the oath of her Majesties supremacy, I willinglie tooke it, and afterwards repayred of mine owne accord diligently to the Church and service of God established in England by her Majesties lawes. I continued in Sussex, Kent, and other places from *Good friday* (the time of my arrivall) untill it was towards *Alhallontide* following, which time I spent as other young Gentlemen did with whom I fell acquainted, untill through meere necessity, having then no part of my living in my hands, I was constrained through want to repaire to my brother *John Mainy* at London, upon whom I did for a while especially relye.

I had not beene long in London before it was my hap to dine at the Lord *Vaux* his house with my said brother, eyther at *Hackney* or *Hogsdon* (I doe not wel remember whether). His Lordship was not then at home, but the table was kept, and entertainment given by his sonne and daughter. In that dinner-while there was much communication of the late possession and dispossession of one *Marwood* by certaine priests, and chiefely (if I doe not forget my selfe) by Ma: *Edmunds*. The tales which were told of that matter seemed strange unto me, as what extraordinarie strength he had in his fits, how he roared like a Bull; and many other things were then mentioned, which now I have forgotten. While my chiefe continuance was in London, I rode sometimes with my brother to *Denham,* the house of Sir *George Peckham,* and in the parish of *Denham* (he having married Sir *George Peckhams* daughter, and the whole furniture of the house appertayning unto him as part of his dowrie with his wife). At that time also he kept servants there. I went likewise sometimes to *Denham* of mine owne accord, and remained there some two or three dayes at a time. It fell out hardly with me (as now I perceave) that I came to London about Alhallontide before mentioned, for then there was nothing in effect in the mouthes of Catholiques but of the casting out of devils. A little before there was much to doe with the said *Marwood,* as I finde by the story that is written of him, beginning *Erat quidam invenis,* &c.[1] Immediatly after (as also it is plaine by an other story which I am enformed was taken with one Ma: *Barnes*), there was at Hollantide great busines at *Fulmer* with *Trayford* and *Sara Williams.* And such were then those times, as now I understand and did then partly finde by experience, that a small occasion was matter sufficient for the priests to worke uppon to charge any one that they liked to deale with, that he was possessed.

It seemeth also by that which is written in the sayd booke taken with Ma: *Barnes,* and by some other tales which I have heard, that the priests, or some for them, understanding that I tooke no course to be a priest, and how I had left the *Bonhommes,* and how I had been troubled with my former disease at *Paris,* and how after my returne I had behaved my selfe youthfully amongst other Gentlemen, gave it out that I was surely possessed; and afterwards, to make the same good, have published in the same booke the testimonie of the devil himselfe, as it is pretended. Whereof anon.

Upon this report I could doe nothing (as I am enformed), but it was said that the devil did direct me in it. In so much as when I rode to *Denham* my selfe (as is before expressed), it was given forth, as I perceave, that the horse I rid upon was a devil, and that I had devils attending upon me in liverie coates, by that which I find written and reported of me. There was never young Gentleman (I think) more abused then I have been.

[1]By Edmunds in Latine, extant upon record. [H].

After some time spent at *Fulmer* by the priests with the said *Trayford* and *Sara Williams,* they came all of them with Ma: *Edmond Peckham* and his wife to *Denham* (as it is mentioned in the said booke), and I not knowing at that time what reports were bruted abroad of me, resorting thither (as I was wont) fell into their snares, which I would surely have avoyded if possibly I could have suspected that they would ever have dealt with me as afterwards they did.

At my comming thither amongst them, I was kindly used, and lodged in the furthest part of the house. The other chambers were then supplied with other guests that I knew not of untill a mayde in the house, who had beene my brothers Cooke, did tell me of them. Upon the comming of Ma: *Edmond Peckham* to *Denham,* my brothers servants departed, and left the house to him (as I thinke), except it were this mayd, to whom I was much beholding for her kindnes towards me. Within a day or two after this my comming to *Denham,* the said maid-Cooke signified unto me that there was great walking of spirits about the house, and that divers had been greatlie affrighted by them. The first night that I came thither (as I remember), I was some-what evill at ease, and whether this report that did some-thing astonish me did make me worse or no, I cannot tell; but I grew worse and worse, in so much as my old disease at a very wicked time did there take hold of me.

The disease I spake of was a spice of the *Mother,* where-with I had beene troubled (as is before mentioned) before my going into Fraunce. Whether I doe rightly terme it the *Mother* or no, I know not; but it is wel knowne to the Physicians in London that be alive and were then of any name, that my eldest brother *Thomas Mainy* had the same disease, and that he died of it; and Ma: *Edmond Peckham* (as I have beene credibly enformed) was likewise troubled with it. When I was sick of this disease in Fraunce, a Scottish Doctor of Physick then in *Paris* called it, as I remember, *Vertiginem capitis.* It riseth (as he said, and I have often felt) of a wind in the bottome of the belly, and proceeding with a great swelling, causeth a very painfull collicke in the stomack, and an extraordinary giddines in the head. With this disease I am still once in foure or five yeeres troubled, and I doe greatly suspect that it wil end me, as it did my brother.

I began no sooner to be troubled at *Denham* (as is before said) but, as now I perceave, the priests had that which they looked for. The women of the house (whose names I doe not now remember) that came to help and attend me, told me first, as my brothers maid had done before, how greatly the house was troubled with spirits, and afterwards that there were two possessed in the house with devils, the manner of whose fits they described unto me in such sort as I was much amazed therewith. Whether these women were required by the Priests to tell me these things or no, I know not; but shortly after Ma: *Dibdale* and Ma: *Cornelius,* two priests, comming unto me, after sundry questions and speeches used with me, they fell to be of opinion (as it seemed, and so told me) that I was possessed with a wicked spirit. I say *as it seemed,* for I am fully perswaded in my conscience that they knew wel enough that neither I nor any of the rest before mentioned were indeede possessed; but that they did pretend so, to worke thereby such matters as they had propounded unto themselves, whereof for my part I wil no further judge. Of this my perswasion I have some reasons by that which I finde written and deposed by others to that purpose.

When I first heard them say that I was possessed, I told them that I doubted not but that they were deceaved therein. I acquainted them with the nature of my disease, and how long I had beene troubled with it; but they persisted in their opinion. For that time leaving me, they came shortly unto me againe, and began where before they had left. Then they told me what extraordinarie strength I shewed in one of my pangues, which moved me litle. For the nature of that disease is to cause ones belly to swel in such sort as two or three are not able (using any good discretion) to keepe downe the wind that seeketh to ascend, as it is very wel knowne to those that have seene eyther a man or woman in that fit, and as it is likely the priests themselves knew by their experience in Ma: *Edmond Peckham,* who was verie oft troubled with it (as is before expressed).

Divers other reasons they used unto me to cause me to suspect the worst of my selfe, and these as I think were some of them: they put me in minde of giving over my study beyond the Seas, of leaving the course I had begun with the *Bonhommes,* and of my more youthfull conversation since my returne. These and such like poynts they used as arguments to convince me that I was possessed. But I replying for my selfe as I could, and telling them what a discredit it would be unto me to have it reported of me that I was possessed with a devil, and how it would be a blemish and a disgrace unto me whilest I lived: they made little account thereof, saying that *it was a lesse discredit, and not so hurtfull for a man to have ten thousand devils in him, then to have committed one deadly sinne;* and to this purpose they alledged a place out of Saint *Augustine* (as farre as I remember). Besides, they reasoned with me, to prove it the safest way for me, to submit my selfe to their triall, whether I were possessed or no; for that (as they said) if the devill were not in mee, I could take no hurt by theyr triall, whereas if I were possessed, it could not but be very dangerous unto mee that the devill should still continue in me. By these and such like meanes they perswaded mee to yeeld my selfe to be directed by them for the triall of my estate. When they had me at this point, then they permitted mee to have accesse unto *Sara Williams* when she was in her fits, and informed me likewise of the manner, how shee and others had beene troubled.

This course held with me, they drew me to confession, and to promise that I would goe no more to the Protestants Churches, affirming that they could doe me no good untill I was become againe a member of the Catholique Romaine Church. After I had beene at one or two of *Saras* fits, and submitted my selfe (as is before expressed), a pangue of my olde disease taking hold on me, Ma: *Dibdale* affirmed publiquely to the company that then it was apparant that I was possessed. Upon my recoverie he told me that by applying of holy reliques unto my belly, hee had compelled the wicked spirit to give me ease; whereas I never found benefit by any such things, but was eased (as I had been at other times before when the fit of the Mother left me) by bending of my body forward, which is a cause of breaking of wind, and consequently of apparant ease. And heereby (as I am perswaded) I was at that time eased, and not by any reliques. Within a day or two after (as I remember), they told me that it was necessary for me to be exorcised; where unto although I was loath to yeeld because I had seene their manner of dealing therein eyther with *Sara* or *Frauncis Williams,* who by this time was said to be also possessed, yet I had submitted my selfe so farre that now it was too late for me to draw backe. All things therefore being in a readines, and I in good health, and no wayes troubled with my disease, they bound me fast in a chayre, and fell to their Exorcismes with much solemnity and shew of great devotion. Then they urged me to drink a very unpleasant potion, which troubled me greatly, in so much as I desired them to untye me, and give me leave to lye downe uppon my bed; but they regarded not my words or earnest entreaty, saying, *It was the devill,* and not my selfe, that desired such rest that so he might not be disturbed in me. At other times when they had me bound in such like manner, besides the said drinke they used to burne brimstone under my nose, and some other things else, which vexed me exceedingly. What I did and spake at those times I doe not now remember. By that which I see they have written of *Marwood, Trayford,* of *Sara* and *Frauncis Williams,* I doubt not but many things have beene reported of me which are untrue. It is not unlike but that when I found my selfe so entangled with them as that I could not rid my selfe from them, I did and spake many things which were inconvenient, and whereof I think I should be ashamed if I did remember them. For after I had learned their humour, and perceaved as wel by the rest as by mine own experience what would content them, I framed my selfe accordingly.

Whilest I was thus at *Denham* with them, I was never almost suffered to be quiet, but eyther I was to be exorcised my selfe, or urged to be with *Sara* or her sister *Frauncis,* or kept privately in my chamber, and one way or other tossed and turmoyled by them till at the last after sundry Exorcismes and much further trouble procured by their drinkes and violent fumigations, they gave it forth that they had cast one devil out of me, but with such intimation as might breede a suspition that there were some other left in me. By this time Christmas drew neere, and whether it was for that they meant to deale with *Sara* at *Hackney,* or for what other cause they knew best, they gave me over for a while, and sent me to Ma: *Fittons* by *Windsor,* where I suppose they thought I should be wel looked unto, and ready afterwards when they should send for me.

I remayned at Ma: *Fittons* till after the end of the holy dayes (as I remember), and being free from their vexations, did solace my selfe with merrie company as the time and occasion served. In so much as some gave it out, peradventure by the priests procurement, that I was still possessed with a merry devil; and others said that if I were possessed indeede, it could not otherwise choose but that he was a devil that was not much troubled with melancholly, or to that effect. Of these reports I heard nothing my selfe whilest I was at Ma: *Fittons,* for if I had they would much have abated the edge of my mirth which they spake of. But now it is meete to be considered how notably they joyned their matters together. It greeveth me much that I am constrained to deale in these matters thus farre; but yet I see that if this occasion had not fallen out, I should never have so well discerned their dealing with me.

Although they gave it out that they had cast a devil out of me (as is before mentioned), and amongst many other reasons had alledged that the devill entred into me because I gave over the order of the *Bonhommes,* and further, because some might peradventure suspect that notwithstanding all that they had either done or said of me, yet all the disease that I had was but onely the Mother, now they have a devise to cleere all these poynts, as it is apparant in the saide booke so often before mentioned. On Monday the tenth of *January, Sara Williams* is pretended to have a mervailous great fit at *Hackney,* and amongst many other speeches which the priest that exorcised her then used, hee commeth at last to these: *There is one* (saith hee to the devill as it was pretended) *that hath the* Mother, *what sayest thou to him?* The devill aunswereth, *that is a* Mother *indeed.* So heereby they would make it plaine that it was not the *Mother* that I was troubled with. But the priest goeth forward, saying, *was there any spirit cast out of him?* and the devill aunswered, *yea, a little one, but to no purpose.* So as now they have a sufficient testimonie that I was dispossessed of one devill whilst I was at *Denham.*

Furthermore, it is pretended by *Saras* devill that there remaineth still in mee the Prince of all other devils, whose name should be *Modu,* which gave them matter enough to worke upon againe with me. But yet all doubts were not cleered, and therefore the said priest demanded this question of *Saras* devill: *Came the prince* Modu (saith he) *into him to bring him from the house of S.* Frauncis de Paula *his order? Yea in troth,* quoth the devill. And thus they thought they had sufficiently justified all that they had reported of him, as appeareth by the said booke. But all this notwithstanding, I am more and more confirmed heereby in my former opinion of their bad proceeding with mee, and the rather because (as I am informed) *Sara Williams* uppon her oath hath denied that ever shee used any such speeches of mee, as farre as she remembreth.

When the said priests had dispatched their busines at *Hackney,* they then returned towards mee, uppon pretence to cast the great Prince *Modu* (as I suppose) out of mee. I beeing at Ma: *Fittons* (as is before said), it fell out that by reason of good company I daunced that night so long that I cast my selfe into a very great sweat, and was weary. Afterward, whether before I went to bed, or when I was in bed, I doe not well remember, I had a fit of the *Mother* as I have had before and often times since upon such violent exercises. It happened that this night som of the said priests that were at *Hackney* (as I thinke) came to Ma: *Fittons,* who hearing of my fit, said it was no mervaile, for it was confessed by the devill in *Sara* that I had the Prince of many devils in me, or words to that effect. Heereuppon in the morning one Mistris *Anne More,* an gentlewoman waiting upon Mistris *Fitton,* came unto me, and told mee with weeping eyes which of the priests were come that night to the house, and what they had reported of mee, and how much I was deceived in that I thought my selfe to be troubled with nothing but the *Mother.* I aunswered her (as if she be alive she can well beare me witnes) that I knew very well, whatsoever they said, that the *Mother* was the onely disease wherewith I was vexed, and that I was free (I thanked GOD) from the possession of anie wicked spirit.

All the while they wrought upon me before, I had found no other trouble in mee but of mine old griefe when I had it, saving such paine as they cast mee into by theyr drinkes and perfumes. And when they said that the devill was cast out of mee, yet I found my selfe neither better nor worse, which caused me to thinke that those things were most untrue which they reported of me.

I was so confident heerein, that the better to colour (as I thinke) their future proceedings with me, they sent to a Physician, one Doctor *Griffith*,[1] who gave me, as it is said, some Physicke. But through their information (as I am perswaded) the conclusion amongst them was that there was no naturall cause of my disease, and so there was no remedy but I must needes be possessed. Then it was thought meete that I should be caried backe againe, whether to *Denham* or to *Channon-row,* I doe not wel remember, but rather (as I conjecture) it was to *Denham.* And for as much as the report was that the spirit supposed to be in me was the Prince of all the devils which were in the parties possessed, Ma: *Edmunds* the Jesuit, and chiefe of all the priests that had to deale then in these actions, was thought the meetest man (as I suppose) to encounter with him. After that time, so far as I remember, none of the priests had to deale with me but himselfe. He was my ghostly Father, and to him (as it is given out) I revealed many things.

When he had the managing of these matters with me, there was very great resort to the place where we were, and a very extraordinarie expectation (as I have heard) of some strange event to fall out.

The course which he held with me was much more rigorous then at any time before. When hee had me bound, if I did not frame my selfe in every thing to his contentment (as sometimes being angry with his usage of me I thinke I did not), then he would say the devil was obstinate in me. In which case sometimes I was constrained by him to drinke most loathsome draughts of such confections as he had ready for me; and sometimes they burnt such abhominable stinking and violent things, holding my nose by force over the smoake, as (I think) would make a horse mad. No man (I suppose) is able to endure such a perfume without extreame torment. He dealt thus hardly with me, as I thinke, upon pretence that the great Prince of devils that was in me would not otherwise be tamed. I have seene them sometimes so perfume *Sara Williams* with such lyke smoakes as her face hath looked blacker then ever I saw a chimney sweepers. Which heates and smels together with their potions did make her to talke and rage as if she had beene mad. And the priests would make some use of every thing she said. And so I thinke I may by her esteeme of mine owne case; when they had made me in effect mad, no mervaile though I spake and fared like a mad man.

[1]Pollen, very reasonably, explains the presence of a physician and an apothecary at Denham by Edmund Peckham's ill-health ("Supposed Cases," 456).

Being thus dealt with, I became very weake and sicklie. Little meate that I tooke would endure with me above an houre or two, and I was at my wits end what I should doe. The best meanes that I could thinke of for mine owne ease was to frame my selfe in such sort as might be most agreeable to Ma: *Edmunds* liking: which then I began to doe with some extraordinarie care. I omitted no occasion to goe to confession. None shewed more zeale at Masse time then my selfe. At the elevation I pretended to see extraordinarie lights as if they had beene the Sunne beames, and that the same did so astonish me as sometimes I would fall backwards when I was kneeling, as though I could not endure the glittering of so glorious a sight; whereas I protest before God I never saw indeede any such light, or was astonished, but therein I did as I had heard the priests report that both *Frauncis* and *Sara Williams* had done before me. And I doe verily thinke they told me the same to no other end but that I my selfe should put the same in practise. For I found my selfe very apt to follow such examples, and doe suppose that any, being in that case that I and the rest were, would assay to speak and doe as they should be enformed that others in their estate had done or spoken.

Of my said pretended astonishments, Ma: *Edmunds* would make large discourses concerning the presence of Christ in the Sacrament. And where it is reported of me in writing, as these things last mentioned are likewise, that I did pretend to see a glittering light come from the thumbs and fore-fingers of the priests at sundry times, I confesse it may be that I have so affirmed, eyther for that they themselves have asked me if I did see no such thing, or else have told me that the rest in my case had seene such lights, whereby I was induced to say as much of my selfe; whereas indeede whatsoever I said thereof was altogether untrue. For I never saw other lights about their thumbs or fingers then such as is ordinarie to all other mens hands or fingers. The colour of the pretence of such lights (as I remember) was for that the priests thumbs and fore-fingers are anointed with holy oyle (as I have heard) when they are made priests, and because they doe with them at Masse time handle the body of Christ.

Furthermore, I found it did well content Ma: *Edmunds* and the rest of the priests that I should sometimes rayle very earnestly both against him and the rest of his fellowes then present, and generally against all priests, and that I should on the contrary commend as earnestly the service of the protestants, the Magistrates, the Ministers, and the chiefest in authoritie. So I knew that *Sara Williams* and the rest had done, and so I did my selfe, no doubt as artificially as any of them, if not in better sort. For wee all knew how they would expound them for theyr owne glory, in that the devils (as they pretended) could not endure them, and to the great discredite of the other side because the devils extolled them as theyr loving friends. And certaine it is that the Catholiques that were present to my understanding did take great contentment by such our speeches and their expositions of them. By this my readines to doe and speake whatsoever I found that Ma: *Edmunds* liked, I escaped sometimes (as I thinke) theyr lothsome drinks and intolerable fumigations.

After some time thus spent with mee at *Denham* (as I suppose), I was carried to the Earle of *Lincolnes* house in *Channon-row,* where my

brother and his wife were, as I remember. I was then not past sixteen or
seventeen yeeres old as farre as I can gesse, and therefore (to speake a
little in mine owne excuse) no mervaile, all circumstances dulie considered, that I was drawne by the cunning practises of the said priests into
these dissembling courses which now I utterly dislike and detest. I am
fully perswaded that there is never a youth in England, were he of never
so ripe and pregnant a wit, but if he should fall into the hands of such
priests he would in a short time be so bewitched by them as that hee
would be soone drawne to stoope to their lure, and doe as I did.

When I was going, and come to *Channon-row,* I was very much
grieved and in feare (as far as I remember) of theyr further proceedings
with mee. For I was then brought to such weakenes as I was scarce able
to goe alone unlesse I were upheld. We were no sooner come thether but
that there was great concourse of many Catholiques to see (as I thinke)
the event of things, especially because Ma: *Edmunds,* a man of great
account amongst them, was the onely dealer in effect with me. By those
things which I find written and reported of mee, and which I had otherwise forgotten of my selfe, at my comming to *Channon-row* I did pretend some traunces, and in them to have sundry visions, into which
course I was led (as I am fully perswaded) by some speeches of the
priests, whom I had oft heard talke how *Sara Williams* and divers others
had many times certaine traunces wherein they lay as if they had beene
sencelesse, and in them had sundry visions, which uppon theyr recoverie
they did usually tell unto the priests and divers others; whereupon I verily thinke that the first Sunday after I came to *Channon-row* (as afore-
said), I fained my selfe to be in a traunce, and afterwards told Ma:
*Edmunds* many tales of my beeing all that time in Purgatory, and what
I had seene and indured there. I also told him at that time (as farre as I
remember) that I perceived by one of the visions which I then had, how
I was every Sunday to have the like traunces and visions about the same
houres untill *Good-friday* next ensuing, and that then I should depart in a
traunce out of this life, and goe immediatly into heaven.

There are divers things further reported of mee as touching these my
pretended traunces and visions (as that after I shewed my selfe to be
recovered I did foretell of great afflictions and persecutions which should
happen to the Catholiques in England, and of sundry such matters), but
whether they be true or not I doe not remember. If I used any such
words, either Ma: *Edmunds* or some of the rest induced mee thereunto by
some of their *leading questions,* or I had heard them before speake themselves to that effect, or else the report is altogether false, and devised by
themselves to serve theyr owne turnes; for of my selfe I doe not believe
that I had any apprehension of any such matters.

It is written also of mee how after some other of my pretended
traunces and visions, I used divers times to fall into strange exclamations, making the company to believe that I saw Christ himselfe, accompanied with a number of Angels in such a corner of the chamber, and at
other times the virgin *Mary,* attended with a trayne of blessed virgins;
and that thereupon my manner was to urge them that were present to fall
downe upon their knees to worship them, and to pray unto them. These

things I doe in some sort remember, and doe partly believe them to be true, because I well remember that uppon my said motions and urging of them, both Ma: *Edmunds* and the rest did usually lift up their hands, now in this corner, now in that corner, and prayed uppon theyr knees with theyr hands holden up as though Christ and the virgine *Mary* had beene there indeed. Whereas I doe faithfully avow it that I never saw any such sights, but did therein *frame my selfe* to doe as I had heard by the priests and others that *Sara Williams* and the rest had done before mee. And I doe believe that Ma: *Edmunds* himselfe knew as much, and that hee did but seeme to worship (as is before expressed), thereby to induce the rest of the company so to doe.

It seemeth that Ma: *Edmunds* hath written a long discourse of about a quire of paper of all my said pretended traunces and visions, and (it may be) likewise of all the rest of the proceedings held with me eyther by him selfe or the rest of the priests. If ever that booke come to further light, so as any in authority doe take notice of it, I will be ready (if I be called thereunto) to give my aunswere truly to all the particulers so farre foorth as I shall remember. In the meane time, as touching all my pretended visions in generall (of my sufferings in Purgatory and the rest), they were all feigned by mee to please Fa: *Edmunds* and, it may be, to gaine to my selfe a little foolish commendation or admiration, because I saw how the Catholiques that heard of them, and were present at many of my fond speeches, did seeme to wonder at me.

When *Good-friday* came, there was great resort to the said house where I was, and of my behaviour that day a priest (I perceive) hath written at large. Of my selfe I should have remembred little that did happen at that time, but beeing urged to aunswer something to that which is written of me, I will first set downe the authors owne words.

*Lying* (saith he) *that day upon his bed, he made (as it were) a solemne exhortation, and telling the Catholiques present that his houre was now come, hee willed them to continue constant in their profession, saying that they were yet to indure the brunt of many persecutions, howbeit, they that persevered unto the end should be saved; and so falling from his exhortations unto prayer, he desired all the company to pray with him, whereupon hee began to recite the* Letanie, *and they that were present followed in aunswering of him, every person present beeing mooved to great devotion. Thus continuing for a while, he then seemed to fall into a slumber, and after that into a traunce which indured above two houres, so as many that were present did verily believe he would never have awaked againe, but in the same have given up the ghost. At the last, of himselfe hee did awake, fetching a great sigh and a groane, and then used these words:* My time is not yet come; our blessed Lady hath appeared unto me and told mee that I must live longer yet, for that God hath reserved me for a further purpose to doe more good, and to tell of strange wonders. *With that there began t? be a great muttering among the company, many greatly mervailing what this should meane. Whereuppon Fa:* Edmunds *made an exhortation to those that were present, and told them that he thought it convenient to prolong the time no longer, but to fall to exorcising of him, whereby they should perceive*

*whether all were true that hee had reported unto them, or whether it had*
*beene the enemy that sought to delude them.*

Thus farre the priest, whose report (I thinke) is true in substance, though peradventure he may erre in some circumstance; but my memory is not so good as that I am able to controull him in any particuler, and therefore I wil let it passe as it goeth. The fault is not mine that these things are thus published. What moved me to pretend that I should die upon *Good Friday*, I cannot set downe directly; but sure I am the devise was boyish and foolish, and very sutable (as I think) to the rest of my proceedings, being greatly besotted by them, as may appeare by my whole course, and by their dealings with me. As farre as I can gesse my simple drift therein was that when it should be apparant that I had lyed unto them, they would for shame have then dismissed me from them. For there was nothing in the world that I desired more. But I found I was deceaved in my simple plot, and doe now perceave by the said priests words that Ma: *Edmunds* was provided how to salve the matter if the worst fell out. God knoweth whether he supposed that I would have taken some course to have shortned mine owne time against that day, as constrained in some sort there-unto by the great weakenes and indeede wearines of my life, where-unto he and the rest had brought me; but I wil judge the best. This onely I perceave, that when he found my simple plot, he was ready to insinuate to the Catholiques present that out of doubt the report that I made of my death was but an illusion of Sathan, and this must be made manifest out of hand by an Exorcisme; for as the said priest hath in writing reported (although I my selfe had forgotten it), being againe exorcised in the presence of all the company before they departed, I shewed no signes of any distemper, but rather of great devotion and piety, whereby Ma: *Edmunds* collected that out of all question it was Sathan in me that said I should die upon *Good Friday*. And so the company departed very well satisfied. If he had given me at that time his holy potion, and perfumed my nose with brimstone, *Assa faetida,* and I know not what other vile smell (as before he had done) I should not surely have beene so quiet; but he had another drift, as wel it appeareth.

From the said *Good-friday,* for ought I remember, untill the three and twentith of April (which was then S. *Georges* day), Ma: *Edmunds* suffered me to be quiet, I thinke now to gather some strength, and imagined then that he would never have troubled me further. But it fell out that a day or two before Saint *Georges* day (as it should seeme) that I had againe a fit of the *Mother*, where-upon they tooke occasion to have me in handling againe, for (as they said) *Modu* the Prince of devils was yet in me; and now they pretended (as I remember) to do the best they could to cast him out of me that so I might be rid for altogether.

Ma: *Edmunds* and the rest dealt with me at this time very extreamely, and I must confesse that in hope to be now dispatched I bent my selfe (as farre as possibly I could) to faine and affirme every thing that I perceaved they expected at my hands. But what I then did or said, if I should have beene tortured upon the rack (had I not seene what was published in writing of me at that time) I could not now have remembred so many particulers. After that Ma: *Edmunds* had exorcised and perfumed me (as often-times he had done before), the devil that had lyen secret long in me (as the writing saith) began to appeare. But I wil set downe the effect of the said priests reports as touching this matter.

*By commaundement of the Exorcist* (which was Ma: *Edmunds), the devill in Ma:* Mainy *confessed his name to be* Modu, *and that he had besides himselfe seaven other spirits, all of them Captaines, and of great fame. There-upon Ma:* Edmunds *commaunded that every one of the seaven should come up in their degrees one after another, and to declare his name by his principall quality. Then Ma:* Mainy *by the instigation of the first of the seaven began to set his hands unto his side, curled his haire, and used such gestures as Ma:* Edmunds *presently affirmed that that spirit was* Pride. *Heere-with he began to curse and banne, saying,* What a poxe doe I heere? I wil stay no longer amongst a company of rascall Priests, but goe to the Court, and brave it amongst my fellowes, the noble men there assembled. *And then after Ma:* Edmunds *had said that hee shewed himselfe thereby to be the spirit of* Pride, *he went downe againe, and Ma:* Mainy *became very quiet, and fell to his prayers. But Ma:* Mainy *could not tell one word (as he reported) of any thing that had beene then said, onely he affirmed that he had all the while felt a great paine in his body. Then Ma:* Edmunds *did proceede againe with his Exorcismes, and suddainly the sences of* Mainy *were taken from him, his belly began to swell, and his eyes to stare, and suddainly cryed out,* ten pounds in the hundred; *he called for a Scrivener to make a bond, swearing* that hee would not lend his money without a pawne. *Ma:* Edmunds *demaunding of that devill whether he were the same that had spoken before, he said no; but yet affirmed that hee was a good fellow, and a companion of his, and one that bare as great rule in England as any other devill. There could be no other talke had of this spirit but of mony, bargaining, and usury, so as all the company deemed this devill to be the author of* Covetousnesse, *not expecting any instruction therein from Fa:* Edmunds. *After a while this devill goeth downe as the other did. Ma:* Mainy *recovereth his sences, falleth to his prayers, and ere long Ma:* Edmunds *beginneth againe his Exorcismes, wherein hee had not proceeded farre but up commeth another spirit, singing most filthy and baudy songs. Every word almost that hee spake was nothing but ribaldry. They that were present with one voyce affirmed that devill to be the author of* Luxury. *And Ma:* Edmunds *beeing not able to endure such lewd speeches, commaunded him to be silent, and to get him downe forthwith againe. The devill obeyed, Ma:* Mainy *recovereth, falleth to his prayers, and afterwards Ma:* Edmunds *goeth forward with the rest. And thus he did proceed, till he had raised up all the seaven Captaines, and compelled them to shew themselves as the other had doone. Envy was described by disdainfull lookes, and contemptuous speeches;* Wrath *by furious gestures, and talke as though hee would have fought;* Gluttony *by vomiting, and* Sloth *by gaping and snorting as if hee had been a sleepe, Ma:* Mainy *at every time recovering his sences and falling to prayer as he had done before. After these seaven devils had thus shewed themselves and were againe at rest in Ma:* Mainy, *it seemed good to Ma:* Edmunds *to try what he could doe with* Modu *their prince and Captaine.*

*He beginneth againe his exorcismes, and continued the same till after a while the said* Modu *rose up againe, and asked Ma:* Edmunds *how hee liked his seaven Brethren before mentioned, who had appeared one after another? And furthermore hee fell a cursing, and said,* A pox on you all for popish priests. My fellowes the protestants can make very much of my said Brethren, and give them good entertainment, bidding them welcome whensoever they come; but you scurvy priests can neither abide them your selves, nor suffer them to be quiet whensoever you are conversant. *Heereunto Ma:* Edmunds *aunswered that they would be enemies both to him and them all during their lives, and commaunded both him and the rest of his companions for to depart out of Ma:* Mainy, *urging them with such severall adjurations as are set downe to that purpose in the booke of Exorcismes. Whilst he was thus proceeding with him, he required* Modu *by the authority of his Priesthood, and power left by Christ in the Catholique Romane church, to tell him truly concerning these visions that appeared unto* Mainy. *With that the devill in* Mainy *fell out into a great laughter, saying that* it had doone him very much good that he had coosened so many priests, and made all the company for to worship him. For (saith hee) all that time that you and the rest seemed to pray unto Christ and unto *Saffronbag*, it was I and all my company that you worshipped. *Heerewith Ma:* Edmunds *beeing greatly mooved, defied him, and said that they had no intention of worshipping him, and that if any were so deceived, it was of ignorance, and that his torments should be the greater for so intolerable an illusion. Then Ma:* Edmunds *began againe his exorcismes with great earnestnes, and all the company cried out upon God, the blessed virgin, S.* George, *and all the company of heaven to helpe and succour them in that holy action, so as both that wicked Prince* Modu *and all his company might be cast out of Ma:* Mainy. *And accordingly God heard their prayers, for shortly after they were all cast forth, and that in such sort as Ma:* Edmunds *directed them; which was that every devill should depart in some certaine forme, representing either a beast or some other creature that had resemblance of that sinne whereof he was the chiefe Author. Where-upon the spirit of* Pride *departed in the forme of a* Peacock, *the spirit of* Sloth *in the likenes of an* Asse, *the spirit of* Envie *in the similitude of a* Dog, *the spirit of* Gluttony *in the forme of a* Wolfe. *And the other devills had also in their departure their particuler likenesses agreeable to their natures.*

Hetherto the Author of the said Treatise, though in some more words, yet to this effect. Concerning the which report, the world must needes beare me witnes, if ever it come to their publique view, that I have great cause to blame them for making of these things common, which were wrought by themselves in private, so much to my discredite. My charity shall deserve very great commendations, as I thinke, if I doe not hereafter seeke to be revenged both upon Ma: *Edmunds* and the rest that have thus dealt with me. But to the matter it selfe as I am required. It is very likely that upon Saint *Georges* day here mentioned I railed against the priests and spake of the Court, as that time gave occasion. But I doe verily thinke that I used the said speeches as being led unto them by some words uttered eyther by the priests or by some in the company, and that they had some farther drift then I doe know of in appoynting that day for their dealings with me.

And touching my describing of the said seaven devils by signes and gestures signifying the seaven deadly sinnes, I doe wel remember that I used some such like gestures to that end, but I am perswaded that they are heere set downe in farre better sort then I did act them, as their usuall manner was in reporting of any thing that was done eyther by me or any of the rest. They would make a faire tale of any thing, though it were never so simple, that any of us did or said. But for mine owne part, how I should be able to describe the said sinnes, though it were never so simple, I cannot directly aunswer. This onely I think, and am perswaded in my conscience, that what I did therein, I was eyther led unto it by some of the Priests *instructing questions,* or else I had beene told before that others in my case had described such devils by such gestures that did signifie such and such sinnes. For being not then fully seventeen yeeres of age, as I take it, I doe not thinke that any such things would ever have come into my head if I had not beene cunningly instructed.

It seemeth strange unto me when I remember divers things concerning these matters; as I may say of my self, so I have beene informed concerning the rest that eyther had beene or were then in my case. Wee were never suffered to be quiet; few nights escaped, but either Mistris *Peckham* when she was present, or Mistris *Plater,* or some other of the women where we remained, would be with us, eyther to bring us newes severally what each of us had done or said apart, when we were exorcised the day before, or else to tell us strange tales which they said they had heard of some of the priests, concerning divers things which had beene done and spoken by such as had beene possessed in other Countries. Whether they did thus by the direction of the priests or no, I cannot tell; but I verily beleeve that wee all of us learned thereby to doe many things which otherwise we should never have thought of. And whether I learned from them the skill I had to doe the gestures before mentioned, I know not. It may be I did.

And as I aunswer to this point, so doe I unto that other as touching the devils supposed similitudes in their pretended departing out of me. Eyther it is altogether false, and devised by themselves, or else they led me to say so by their questions. As if they asked me, whether *Pride* did not depart from me in the likenesse of a *Peacock,* it is very probable that I said he did. And so of all the rest. Or otherwise they told some in my hearing that such devils did use to depart from such as they possessed in such kinde of formes: I pray God forgive them for all their bad dealings with me. My chiefe comfort is that as I said in the beginning, I am fully perswaded that I was never possessed, and that all I did or spake, I did it and spake it my selfe, being sometimes enforced, and sometimes induced so to doe, as before I have mentioned. And also that the most of those things which are written of me are eyther utterly false or greatly altered in the telling. And that the priests themselves that dealt with me are of right to beare the blame for that which eyther I or any of the rest said or did that might give any just cause of offence, eyther to her Majestie or the state heere in England.

Upon my speeches before mentioned to the Lord *Strange*, the priests and others, especially those that favour Ma: *Edmunds*, as I thinke, did give it out that I was still possessed. And I doubt not but if at any time they understand of this my confession, it wil be said that now I have many devils in me. I had forgotten to set downe how I have had a long time an ache in one of my knees, which I thinke I got when I was a child by a cold; and how when I told the priests of it first, they used that for one argument to prove that I was possessed, saying that it was very likely that the devil kept about that place. Also I feare I shall be troubled with my old disease, as I have before said. So as if they shall determine to hold on so wicked a course, they are like to have the same causes to say that I am still possessed, that they had before. But I hope they wil not dare to presume to have any further dealing with me, and that God will deliver me from them. And this is all I can say to all such points and matters as have beene propounded unto me.

*Richard Mainy.*

*FINIS*

# Textual Notes

195.25 *ingenuous*] *ingenious*   196.21 *ingenuous*] *ingenious*   198.22 *amongst*] *amougst*   198.23 *demonstration*] *demonstation*   198.33 *especially*] *especally*   201.16 *Richard*] *Robert*   204.17 *Ridolphi*] *Godolphi*   206.5 contrive] continue [from Errata list]   215.25 Cat] Rat [from errata list]   219.20 two] hope [from errata list]   227.36 became] becam   229.1 *Parsons*] *Parson*   231.6 their] there   232.2 distortions] discortions   238.9–10 *in some*] *by some*   239.28 *profundo*] *profoundo*   241.27 *Maho*] *Modu*   244.1 into] in   247.33 of an hundred] of 100   251.25 devil-lodges] devil-lodgers   252.25 sures-by] suers-by   253.6 commaunded] commannded   255.2 *Marwoods*] *Trayfords*   261.23 to her] so her   262.38 no] on   263.11 sacrament, *Salve*] sacrament the crosse, *Salve*   263.14 Jesuit hath] Jesuit alone, hath   265.39 hose,] house,   267.28 they] thy   268.21 *assistantes*] *astantes*   277.17 consecration] conservation [from errata list]   277.36 qualified] qualfied   284.6 straight] staight   290.1 *with*] *which*   301.11 ingenuous] ingenious   301.3 *Sancti Eucharistiae*] Rom. in *Q.*   305.36 of] on   310.9 Incubus] Iucubus   310.21 *Malleus*] *Melleus*   314.25 *Trayford*] *Marwood*   315.13 mouth] owne [An error of anticipation caused by "owne Mouse-" in the next line]   319.11 *Protestants*] *Protestans*   326.13 Dome] Dove   332.14 of a devil] of devil   334.24 Earles] Earle   353.29 *sonne*] *some*   354.42 that upon] that when upon   356.2 peccata] peccati   364.19 priests] prests   378.76 write] writ   384.8 recusancie] reeusancie   384.29 maister] maisters   385.10 wicked] wieked   397.12 *Lincolnes*] *Loncolnes*   400.7 dinner-while] dinner while   400.15 daughter] daughters   403.7 also] all so   403.40 afterwards] afterwads

415

# Glossary

| | |
|---|---|
| *adj.* | adjective |
| *adv.* | adverb |
| *ger.* | gerund |
| *n.* | noun |
| *n.pl.* | noun plural |
| *phr.* | phrase |
| *pp.* | past participle |
| *prp.* | present participle |
| *v.* | verb |

*allectives, n.pl.* Enticements.

*amphibologies, n.pl.* A corruption of *amphiboly,* "ambiguity."

*anticke-sute, n.* Grotesque succession.

*antiperistian, adj.* A variant of *antiperistatic,* meaning "able to repel or push back." A learned scatologism, probably Harsnett's invention.

*assistants, n.pl.* Those present.

*badger, n.* Itinerant dealer, cadger, or huckster.

*band dogges, n.pl.* Dogs that are tied up, either for fierceness or because they are guard dogs.

*batfoulers, n.pl.* Swindlers, victimizers. "Bat-fowlers" are people who catch sleeping birds, hence make easy prey of something.

*bench-hole, n.* Privy-hole, latrine seat.

*besprincked, pp.* The only part of the verb *bespreng* to survive after c. 1600. *Besprinkle* replaced it.

*black-guard, n.* A body of menials, villainous or criminal.

*brayed wares.* "Braided" or damaged goods.

*brimly, adv.* "Bremely," i.e. hotly or fiercely: an unusually late use.

*budget, n.* Bag.

*bug-beares, n.pl.* "Bogies," supposed to frighten children.

*bugge, n.* An object of terror to simple and superstitious people.

*bugle, n.* A tube-shaped glass bead, used as an ornament on clothes.

*bugs words.* Words intended to frighten.

*cantle, v.* Measure.

*capcase, n.* A kind of valise.

*cassier, v.* Get rid of.

*cast of fiddles, phr.* Consort or set of fiddles.

*cauteled, pp.* Devised. Nashe, *Works* 1:316, describes the word as a Harveyism in its n. and adj. forms "cauteles" and "cautelous."

*chimerial, adj.* Visionary, absurd.

*chrisme, n.* Consecrated oil used in sacramental anointing.

*chrisome, n.* A white christening robe, often considered an heirloom.

*coife, n.* Ecclesiastical headgear; a close-fitting cap covering the top, back, and sides of the head.

*conceited, adj.* Whimsical.

*conies, n.pl.* Dupes. Pronounced to rhyme with "money."

*conny-beries, n.pl.* rabbit holes.

*contested, pp.* Corroborated, borne witness to.

*convivencie, n.* This word may be a misprint for *connivencie,* mentioned by Nashe as a Harveyism (*Works* 3:15). If the word is Harsnett's own, and not a misprint, it should mean "by closeness of contact."

*Coridon, n.* A rustic, pastoral name used to mean a bumpkin.

*corier, n.* Currier.

*coseners, n.pl.* Cheats. Probably a cant, underworld word.

*counter, to hunt, phr.* To follow the scent to its place of origin instead of following the game.

*crap, n.* Chaff, or the residue of rendered fat; fig., worthless scrap.

*crosbiting, n.* Deception or blighting.

*cursie, n.* A variant of "crusie," from French *croiseul.* "The crusie proper is now out of date. It was a spoon-shaped vessel filled with oil, in which was adjusted the pith of rushes so as to burn and give light. It was common in country districts in farm kitchens before the introduction of mineral oil lamps" (Wright).

*cut, n.* Style. "Queynt cut" means "curious, newfangled style."

*deliration, n.* Delirium, madness; here mental aberration. From Latin *delirare.*

*devill-mastix, n.* Scourge of the devil.

*discomposed, adj.* Disordered.

*ditements, n.pl.* Garments, i.e., things in which one is "dight" or arrayed.

*dotrel, n.* A kind of plover, now rare in Britain, thought to be rather stupid; hence, fig., an idiot.

*double, v.* To turn, used of hunted game.

*embossed, adj.* Foaming at the mouth from excitement and exhaustion: a hunting term.

*enucleating, prp.* Extracting the nucleus or essence.

*errand, adj.* A form of "errant," meaning astray, often confused with "arrant," meaning unmitigated.

*ethnick, adj.* A term of abuse, meaning a heathen or pagan.

*excoriat, v.* To strip off the hide, to flay. From *excoriare.*

*exorbitant, adj.* Lit., wandering out of one's due course; fig., forgetting one's place.

*exploded, pp.* Rejected with contempt. From *explaudere,* to drive out by clapping, to send off the stage.

*facile, adv.* Smoothly.

*fascination, n.* Enchantment, from *fascinare,* to bewitch.

*fleere, v.* To pull a face, laugh coarsely.

*flight, v.* To rout, put to flight.

*foile, n.* Track or spoor of a hunted animal.

*forbid, n.* Prohibition. Nashe, *Works* 3:68, has a similar use: "He is, beyond all reason or Gods forbod, distractedly enamourd of his own beautie."

*forelorne Hope, phr.* A vanguard or storming party sent on ahead to begin an attack. From sixteenth-century Dutch *verloren hoop,* "lost band."

*formed, pp.* Hidden.

*formes, n.pl.* Hiding places; lit., hares' nests.

*foyle, n.* Dung; track or scent.

*foyle, v.* To dirty.

*fugate, v.* To put to flight.

*Ganimedes, n.pl.* Catamites.

*gawdes, n.pl.* Baubles; originally the large paternoster beads in a rosary, one for each mystery. From *gaudia,* meaning "joys."

*giddies, n.* A sheep's brain disease.

*ginnes, n.pl.* Snares.

*gippe, v.* To clean a fish for curing.

*girne, v.* To bare the teeth in rage. Cf. Spenser, *Faerie Queene,* 5.12.15: "His face was ugly and his countenance sterne . . . / And gaped like a gulfe, when he did gerne." Still in dialect use to mean pulling a face, and girning contests are still held at country fetes.

*God-gastring, adj.* God-frightening, a Harsnettian compound.

*gore-blood, n.* Clotted blood. "Gore" can mean filth, dung, or putrefied matter of any kind.

*guegawes, n.pl.* Trifles, baubles.

*gull, n.* Imposture.

*haecceïtie, n.* Latin *haecceitas,* "thisness."

*hobgoblins, n.pl.* Terrifying apparitions.

*horizon, n.* Sphere of experience.

*hote-house, n.* A bathhouse with hot baths. Although they were used for hygienic and medical purposes, association of bathhouses with hanky-panky made the word into slang for a brothel.

*houzle-egge, n.* Some kind of church-dues, with a pun on "houzle" ("houzle" is the consecrated bread of the sacrament, as in "houzle-bread") and "ouzle," a blackbird.

*ignivomous, adj.* Fire-vomiting, from *ignem vomere.*

*illuminate, adj.* Inspired by the inner light.

*indigiting, prp.* Putting the finger in.

*intelligences, n.pl.* Planetary spirits supposed to guide the spheres of the Ptolemaic cosmos.

*John a nods, n.* A sleepyhead.

*journalls, n.pl.* Days' journeys.

*just tale.* Full count.

*kiddier, n.* Synonymous with *badger.*

*kilcowes, n.pl.* Braggarts, bullies.

*lancinate, v.* To rend in pieces, to pierce. From *lancinare,*

*leet, n.* A crossroads.

*Lucianist, n.* A disciple of Lucian; a satirist.

*lymphaticall, adj.* Frenzied.

*madge-Owlets, n.pl.* Barn owls: silly-billies.

*malkin, n.* A kind of mop.

*mammaday, n.* Of obscure origin, its literal meaning seems to be "nurse's milk." Cf. Gabriel Harvey, *Pierces Supererogation* (1593), sig. K2v: "nothing, but pure Mammaday, and a fewe morsels of fly-blowne Euphuisme, somewhat nicely minced for puling stomackes."

*many, n.* Multitude, troop, or crowd of common soldiers.

*mate, v.* Render helpless.

*mattachina, n.* A variant of *Matachin,* originally an Arabic word describing a kind of sword-dancer in a fantastic costume. A grotesque performer.

*Maudelen-drunke, adj.* Cf. Nashe, *Works* 1:207: " . . . the fifth [kind of drunkenness] is Mawdlen drunke when a fellowe will weepe for kindnes in the midst of his Ale."

*months minde.* Literally, a commemoration of the dead by a mass one month after death, but used popularly to mean a fancy or a liking for something.

*mops, n.pl.* Grimaces, often used of apes. Cf. Nashe, *Works* 1:306: "no bodie at home but an ape that sate in the Porch and made mops and mows at him."

*muses, n.pl.* Hiding places.

*nihileïtie, n.* Latin *nihileitas,* "nullity."

*novels, n.pl.* Novelties.

*nunchion, n.* Light afternoon meal.

*obloquutors, n.pl.* Detractors, gainsayers.

*otium, n.* Playtime or break.

*owle-blasted, adj.* Bewitched.

*owle-hunting, n.* Probably means the same as "Owle-blasted," i.e., possessed or bewitched.

*parkes, n.pl.* Besides its literal meaning, this word also meant the private part of a woman's body.

*patible, adj.* Long suffering.

*periapt, n.* A charm or amulet, from Greek *periapton,* "to fasten about."

*pix, n.* Vessel in which the consecrated host is reserved.

*placard, n.* A formal document.

*plaudite, n.* "Applaud ye!"--the customary appeal at the end of a play.

*poakers, n.pl.* Goblins.

*point, n.* A period.

*polypragmon, n.* A meddler, a busybody.

*pose, n.* Catarrh.

*preoccupate, v.* To influence, predispose.

*privada, n.* An intimate or favorite, from the Spanish for "close friend."

*profugating, ger.* Driving away.

*propitiatorie, n.* Strictly speaking, God's mercy seat or throne.

*provant, n.* Provision.

*puntilios, n.pl.* Punctilious people.

*quarrie, n.* A "quarrel" or square, cognate with French *carré.*

*questionist, n.* At Cambridge University, an undergraduate in his last term before proceeding, hence an enthusiastic debater.

*runnagate, n.* A form of "renegate," i.e., "renegado," in common use c. 1550-1700, meaning "apostate," with the abusive connotations of "fugitive" and "vagabond."

*sacrist, n.* Someone in charge of sacred objects, such as vessels, vestments, and relics.

*say, n.* A sample. An aphetic form of "assay."

*scantling, n.* A carpenter's measuring stick. Fig., an estimate.

*secluse, adj.* A Latinism, from *seclusus,* meaning "remote," "secluded."

*setter, n.* A cony-catcher's expression, as in Nashe, *Works* 1:257: "Connicatching is divided into three parts, the *verser,* the *Setter,* and the *Barnacle."*

*skar-buggs, n.pl.* Frightening creatures. Harsnett uses the word to mean those able to terrify and drive off monsters.

*societies, n.pl.* Colleges.

*soile, v.* To resolve or expound, from Latin *solvere,* "to release or loosen."

*soyle, n.* Dirt, turpitude.

*soyle, take, phr.* Seek out a hiding place, from French *prendre souille, souille* being a wild pig's wallowing place.

*soyles, v.* The primary meaning is "tarnishes" or "dirties;" there is a secondary meaning, "to expound."

*sparrow-blasting, n.phr.* The state of being stricken or blighted by an unseen power.

*spice of the gowt.* A touch of the gout.

*squat, v.* "To squat" was used of a hare crouching on its haunches.

*stagers, n.pl.* Veterans.

*staggers, n.* A catchall word for various diseases in domestic animals.

*steale, n.* Handle.

*stigmaticall, adj.* Infamous, deserving to be branded.

*stocke, n.* A ledge or brick at the back or side of a fireplace.

*stond horse.* A "Stand horse," "stand" being dialect for a stall or stable (Wright, *English Dialect Dictionary*), and "to stand" used of a horse meaning "to be kept in a stable or stall" *(OED).*

*subtiliated, adj.* Rarified.

*surbatted, pp.* Footsore. Used of dogs in hunting.

*sures-by, old.* One who can be depended upon.

*suspendite, n.* Either a nonce usage analogous to *plaudite*, or a customary usage describing an interruption for applause or an encore.

*susurrare, n.* A murmuring or whispering.

*tew, n.pl.* Tools; a collective noun analogous to German *zeug*.

*thrumming, prp.* Crowding or cramming.

*tinckling, n.* A tingling, from Old English *tinclian*.

*triarios, n.pl.* A class of Roman soldiers who formed the third rank from the front.

*trusse, n.* A pack of small wares.

*untrusse, at, phr.* With his breeches unbuttoned.

*untrusse, v.* To unfasten the breeches. Cf. Nashe, *Works* 1:196: "Off with thy gowne and untrusse, for I meane to lash thee mightily."

*untrusses, v.* Unfastens his breeches.

*ure, n.* Practice.

*verd, n.* Freshness.

*vicenarie, n.* One with command over twenty.

*welt, n.* A strip of leather or material used as a border or fringe; hence, fig., ornament. Nashe also uses the word figuratively: " . . . for he kept a plaine alehouse without welt or gard of anie ivybush" *(Works* 2:210).

*whitled, adj.* Plied with drink.

*wier-drawing, n.* Fig., drawing out too fine and too long as in the process of manufacturing wire.

*woaded, pp.* Saturated or dyed.

# Manuscripts and Books Cited

## *Manuscripts*

BODLEIAN LIBRARY
   Rawlinson MS D 1349
   Tanner MSS 114, 137, 177, 138, 228
BORTHWICK INSTITUTE YORK
   MS R. Bp. 8/4a–c
BRITISH LIBRARY:
   Additional MSS 4122, 5845, 5860, 5873, 29372–7, 39948
   Egerton MS 2650
   Harleian MSS 703, 3142, 7029–34, 7038
   Royal MS 17C xxv
   Sloane MS 4122
CAMBRIDGE UNIVERSITY LIBRARY
   MS Ff. 5. 25
   MS Mm. I. 44
   MSS. Additional 4021, 3126
CHICHESTER DIOCESAN RECORD OFFICE
   Bishop Harsnett's Register
   MS EP 1/75/1
   Statute Book B
DR. WILLIAMS'S LIBRARY
   Morrice MSS
ESSEX RECORD OFFICE
   Wills
LAMBETH PALACE
   MS 660
   Archbishop Bancroft's Register
   Archbishop Whitgift's Register
ARBERRY HALL
   Newdigate MSS
NORWICH DIOCESAN REGISTRY
   MS HAR/3
   Bishop Harsnett's Register
PEMBROKE COLLEGE
   College MSS 1–23
   MS A.γ
   MS C.θ
   LC. II. 230
   Treasury Accounts
PUBLIC RECORD OFFICE
   State Papers, Domestic, Elizabeth I, James I, Charles I

## *Books, Articles, and Published Archival Material*

Addison, William. *Epping Forest*. London: J. M. Dent, 1945.

Andrewes, Lancelot. *Works*. Edited by J. P. Wilson and James Bliss. 11 vols. Oxford, 1841–54.

Anstruther, Godfrey. *The Seminary Priests: A Dictionary of the Secular Clergy of England and Wales, 1558–1850*. 4 vols. Ware: St. Edmund's College, and Durham: Ushaw College, 1968.

———. *Vaux of Harrowden: A Recusant Family*. Newport, Monmouthshire: R. H. Johns, 1953.

Arber, Edward, ed. *A Transcript of the Registers of the Company of Stationers of London, 1554–1640 A.D.* 5 vols. London, 1876–77 (vols. 1–4); Birmingham, 1894 (vol. 5). Reprint. New York: Peter Smith, 1950.

Attwater, Aubrey. *Pembroke College*. Cambridge: Cambridge University Press, 1936.

Aubrey, John. *Remaines of Gentilisme and Judaisme*. In *Three Prose Works*, edited by John Buchanan Brown. Fontewell, Sussex: Centaur Press, 1972.

Babbage, Stuart. *Puritanism and Richard Bancroft*. London: SPCK Press for the Church Historical Society, 1962.

Bakeless, John. *The Tragical History of Christopher Marlowe*. 2 vols. Cambridge: Harvard University Press, 1942.

*Balaam the Devil*. London, 1636.

Bancroft, Richard. *Daungerous Positions and Proceedings, Published and Practised within this Iland of Brytaine*. London, 1593.

———. *A Survey of the Pretended Holy Discipline*. London, 1593.

Bee, Jesse. *The Most Wonderfull and True Storie of a Certain Witch named Alse Gooderige of Stapen Hill . . . As also a True Report of the Strange Torments of Thomas Darling, a Boy of Thirteene Yeres of Age, that was Possessed by the Devill*. London, 1597.

Benham, W. Gurney. *Archbishop Samuel Harsnett*. Colchester: Benham & Co., 1932.

———. "Pedigree of Archbishop Samuel Harsnett." *Essex Review* 40 (1931): 105.

Berry, Herbert. "Italian Definitions of Tragedy and Comedy Arrive in England." *Studies in English Literature* 14 (1974): 179–87.

———. *Shakespeare's Playhouses*. New York: AMS Press, 1987.

*Biographia Britannica*. 6 vols. London, 1746–66.

Bishop, J. G. *Lancelot Andrewes, Bishop of Chichester, 1605–1609*. The Chichester Papers, No. 33. Chichester: Chichester City Council, 1963.

Blomefield, Francis. *An Essay Towards a Topographical History of the County of Norfolk*. 11 vols. London, 1805–10.

Bradbrook, M. C. *Shakespeare: The Poet in His World*. London: Weidenfeld and Nicolson, 1978.

Brownlow, F. W. "John Shakespeare's Recusancy: New Light on an Old Document." *Shakespeare Quarterly* 40 (1989): 186–91.

———. "Samuel Harsnett and the Meaning of Othello's 'Suffocating Streams.'" *Philological Quarterly* 58 (1979): 107–15.

————. "Shakespeare and Southwell" in *KM 80: A Birthday Album for Kenneth Muir*. Liverpool: Printed for private circulation by Liverpool University Press, 1987), 27.

Burton, Robert. *The Anatomy of Melancholy*. Edited by Floyd Dell and Paul Jordan-Smith. New York: Tudor Publishing Co., 1955.

Calamy, Edmund. *The Nonconformist's Memorial*. "The Second Edition." 3 vols. London, 1802–3.

Camm, Bede. *Forgotten Shrines*. London: MacDonald and Evans, 1910.

Caraman, Philip, ed. and trans. *An Autobiography from the Jesuit Underground*. New York: Farrar, Strauss and Cudahy, 1955.

Carlisle, Nicholas. *A Concise Description of the Endowed Grammar Schools in England and Wales*. 2 vols. London, 1818.

Cauthen, I. B. "Another Chaucer Allusion in Harsnet." *Notes and Queries*, n.s., 5 (1958): 248.

————. "The Foule Flibbertigibbet." *Notes and Queries*, n.s., 5 (1958): 98.

Challoner, Richard. *Memoirs of Missionary Priests*. Edited by John Hungerford Pollen. London: Burns, Oates and Co., 1923.

Chamberlain, John. *The Letters of John Chamberlain*. Edited by N. E. McClure. 2 vols. Philadelphia: American Philosophical Society, 1939.

Child, Francis James, ed. *The English and Scottish Popular Ballads*. 5 vols. 1884–98. Reprint. New York: Dover Publications, 1965.

Clancy, Thomas H. *Papist Pamphleteers: The Allen-Persons Party and the Political Thought of the Counter-Reformation in England, 1572–1615*. Chicago: Loyola University Press, 1964.

Collier, Jeremy. *An Ecclesiastical History of Great Britain, Chiefly of England*. 9 vols. London, 1840.

Collinson, Patrick. *The Elizabethan Puritan Movement*. Berkeley and Los Angeles: University of California Press, 1967.

*Constitutiones sive canones ecclesiastici*. London, 1604.

Cooper, C. H., and Thompson Cooper, eds. *Athenae Cantabrigienses*. 3 vols. Cambridge, 1858–1913.

Corbet, Richard. *Poems*. Edited by J. A. W. Bennet and H. R. Trevor-Roper. Oxford: Clarendon Press, 1956.

Coulton, George Gordon. *Five Centuries of Religion*. 4 vols. Cambridge: Cambridge University Press, 1923–50.

Coverdale, Myles. *Remains of Myles Coverdale*. Edited by George Pearson. London, 1846.

Dahlberg, Charles. *The Literature of Unlikeness*. Hanover, N.H.: University Presses of New England, 1988.

Darrell, John. *An Apologie, or Defence of the Possession of William Sommers, a Young Man of Nottingham*. [Amsterdam?], 1599?

————. *A Breife Narration of the Possession, Dispossession, and, Repossession of William Somers*. [Middelburg], 1598.

————. *A Brief Apologie Proving the Possession of William Sommers*. [Middelburg], 1599.

————. *A Detection of that Sinnful Shamful, Lying, and Ridiculous Discours of Samuel Harshnet*. [English secret press?], 1600.

————. *The Replie of John Darrell to the Answer of John Deacon, and John Walker*. [English secret press?], 1602.

————. *A Survey of Certaine Dialogical Discourses . . . Concerning the Doctrine of Possession and Dispossession of Divels.* [English secret press?], 1601.

————. *A True Narration of the Strange and Grevous Vexation by the Devil, of 7. Persons in Lancashire, and William Somers of Nottingham.* [English secret press?], 1600.

Dart, Thurston. "Music and Musicians at Chichester Cathedral, 1545–1642." *Music and Letters* 42 (1961): 221–26.

Dawley, P. M. *John Whitgift and the Reformation.* London: A. & C. Black, 1955.

De Groot, John Henry. *The Shakespeares and "The Old Faith."* New York: Columbia University Press, 1946.

Deacon, John, and John Walker. *Dialogicall Discourses of Spirits and Divels.* London, 1601.

————. *A Summarie Answere to al the Material Points in Any of Master Darel his Bookes.* London, 1601.

Devlin, Christopher. "The Case of Anthony Tyrrell." *The Month* 192 (1951): 346–58.

————. *Hamlet's Divinity and Other Essays.* 1963. Reprint. Freeport, N.Y.: Books for Libraries Press, 1970.

————. *The Life of Robert Southwell, Poet and Martyr.* London: Longmans, 1956.

Dick, Oliver Lawson, ed. *Aubrey's Brief Lives.* London: Secker & Warburg, 1949.

Dowling, Margaret. "John Hayward's Troubles over His *Life of Henry IV.*" *The Library,* 4th ser., 11 (1930): 212–24.

Eccles, Mark. *Shakespeare in Warwickshire.* Madison: University of Wisconsin Press, 1961.

Elton, William. *King Lear and the Gods.* San Marino, Calif.: Huntington Library, 1966.

Erasmus, Desiderius, *Adagia.* In *D. Erasmi Roterodami opera omnia emendatiora et auctiora.* 10 vols. 1703–6. Reprint. London: Gregg Press, [1961].

————. *Colloquies.* Translated by Craig R. Thompson. Chicago: Chicago University Press, 1965.

Field, Richard. *Of the Church, Five Books. Vol. I: Containing the First Three Books.* Cambridge, 1847.

Foley, Henry, ed. *Records of the English Province of the Society of Jesus.* 7 vols. London, 1877–84.

Fortescue, Adrian, and J. B. O'Connell. *The Ceremonies of the Roman Rite Described.* London: Burns, Oates, 1937.

Foster, Joseph, ed. *Alumni Oxonienses, 1500–1714.* 4 vols. Oxford, 1891–92.

Foxe, John. *Actes and Monuments of Matters Most Speciall and Memorable, Happening in the Church.* 2 vols. London, 1583.

Fripp, Edgar I. *Shakespeare's Haunts Near Stratford.* Oxford: Oxford University Press, 1929.

Fuller, Thomas. *Abel Redivivus.* London, 1651.

————. *The Church History of Britain.* London, 1655.

————. *The History of the University of Cambridge.* Edited by John Nichols. London, 1840.

————. *The Worthies of England.* Edited by John Nichols. London, 1811.

————. *The Worthies of England* [abridged]. Edited by John Freeman. Allen & Unwin, 1952.

Furness, H. H., ed. *The Variorum "King Lear."* Philadelphia, c. 1880.

Gardiner, S. R. *The History of England from the Accession of James I to the Outbreak of the Civil War, 1603–1642.* 10 vols. London and New York, 1894–96.

————, ed. *Notes of Debates in the House of Lords, officially taken by Henry Elsing, Clerk of the Parliaments.* The Camden Society, n.s., no. 24. London: Royal Historical Society, 1879.

Gaskell, Lady Catherine Milnes. "Old Wenlock and its Folklore." *Nineteenth Century* 35 (1894): 259–67.

Gee, John. *The Foot out of the Snare.* London, 1624.

Gillow, Joseph. *A Literary and Biographical History, or Biographical Dictionary of the English Catholics; from the Breach with Rome in 1574 to the Present Time.* 5 vols. 1885–92. Reprint. New York: Burt Franklin, n.d.

Goodwin, Gordon. *A Catalogue of the Harsnett Library.* London, 1888.

————. "The Harsnett Family." *Notes and Queries,* 8th ser., 11: 166, 225.

Great Britain. Historical Manuscripts Commission.

————. *Calendar of the Manuscripts of the Most Honourable the Marquess of Salisbury.* 24 vols. London, 1883–1976.

————. *Fifth Report.* London, 1876.

————. *Report on Manuscripts in Various Collections.* Vol. 1. London, 1901.

————. *Seventh Report.* London, 1879.

————. *Twelfth Report.* London, 1890.

Great Britain. The Privy Council. *Acts of the Privy Council of England. New Series, 1547–1631.* Edited by J. R. Dasent (vols. 1–32), H. C. Maxwell (vols. 33–34), J. V. Lyle (vols. 35–46). 46 vols. London, 1890–1964.

Great Britain. The Public Record Office. *Calendar of State Papers, Domestic Series, of the Reigns of Edward VI, Mary, Elizabeth, and James I.* Edited by Robert Lemon (vols. 1–2), Mary Anne Everett Green (vols. 3–12). 12 vols. London, 1856–1872.

————. *Calendar of State Papers, Domestic Series, of the Reign of Charles I.* Edited by John Bruce (vols. 1–12), J. Bruce and W. D. Hamilton (vol. 13), W. D. Hamilton (vols. 14–22), W. D. Hamilton and S. C. Thomas (vol. 23). 23 vols. London, 1858–97.

Greenblatt, Stephen. "*King Lear* and Harsnett's 'Devil-fiction.'" *Genre* 15 (1982): 239–42. Reprinted in *The Power of Forms in the English Renaissance,* edited by Stephen Greenblatt. Norman, Okla.: Pilgrim Books, 1982.

————. "Shakespeare and the Exorcists." In *After Strange Texts: The Role of Theory in the Study of Literature.* Edited by Gregory S. Jay and David L. Miller. Tuscaloosa: University of Alabama Press, 1984.

————. "Shakespeare and the Exorcists." In *Shakespeare and the Question of Theory.* Edited by Patricia Parker and Geoffrey Hartman. New ork and London: Methuen, 1985.

————. "Shakespeare and the Exorcists." In *Shakespearean Negotiations: The Circulation of Social Energy in Renaissance England.* Berkeley and Los Angeles: University of California Press, 1988.

Greg, W. W. "Samuel Harsnett and Hayward's *Henry IV.*" *The Library,* 5th ser., 11 (1956): 1—10.

————. *Some Aspects and Problems of London Publishing Between 1550* and *1650.* Oxford: Clarendon Press, 1956.

Greg, W. W., and E. Boswell, eds. *Records of the Court of the Stationers' Company, 1576–1602, from Register B.* London: Bibliographical Society, 1930.

Guiney, Louise Imogen, ed. *Recusant Poets: Vol. I. Saint Thomas More to Ben Jonson.* New York: Sheed & Ward, 1939. (Vol. II was never issued.)

Hacket, John. *Scrinia Reserata: A Memorial Offer'd to the Great Deservings of John Williams, D.D.* London, 1693.

Harington, Sir John. *Nugae Antiquae.* 3 vols. London, 1779.

Harsnett, Samuel. *A Discovery of the Fraudulent Practises of One John* Darrel Bachelor of *Arts.* London, 1599.

Harmsen, T. H. B. M., ed. *John Gee's 'Foot Out Of The Snare.'* Nijmegen: The Cicero Press, 1992.

Hartwell, Abraham, trans. *A True Discourse, upon the Matter of Martha Brossier of Romorantin, Pretended to be Possessed by a Devill.* London, 1599.

Harvey, Gabriel. *Works.* Edited by A. B. Grosart. 3 vols. London and Aylesbury, 1884–85.

Hasted, Edward. *The History and Topographical Survey of the County of Kent.* 12 vols. Canterbury, 1797–1801.

Hazlitt, W. C., ed. *English Drama and Stage.* London, 1869.

————. *Tales and Legends of National Origin.* London, 1892.

Hennessy, George. *Novum repertorium ecclesiasticum parochiale Londinense.* London, 1898.

Hervey, Mary F. S. *The Life, Correspondence and Collections of Thomas Howard Earl of Arundel.* Cambridge: Cambridge University Press, 1921.

Heylyn, Peter. *Cyprianus Anglicus.* London, 1668.

Hill, Christopher. *Society and Puritanism.* New York: Schocken Books, 1964.

Hill, Geoffrey. *The Lords of Limit.* London: André Deutsch, 1984.

Honigmann, Ernst. *Shakespeare: The 'Lost Years.'* Totowa, N.J.: Barnes and Noble, 1985.

Hooker, Richard. *The Folger Library Edition of the Works of Richard Hooker,* general ed., W. Speed Hill. 4 vols. Cambridge: Belknap Press of Harvard University Press, 1977–82.

Horstmann, Carl, ed. *The Three Kings of Cologne.* London, 1886.

Hughes, Philip. *The Reformation in England.* 3 vols. New York: Macmillan Co., 1954.

Hyde, Edward, Earl of Clarendon. *History of the Great Rebellion.* 8 vols. Oxford, 1826.

Isaacson, Henry. *An Exact Narration of the Life and Death of . . Lancelot Andrewes.* Newcastle-upon-Tyne, 1817.

James I. *Daemonologie, in Forme of a Dialogue.* Edinburgh, 1597.

Jeaffreson, John Cordy, ed. *Middlesex County Records.* 4 vols. London, 1886–92.

Jordan, Edward. *A Briefe Discourse of a Disease Called the Suffocation of the Mother.* London, 1603.

Kaula, David. *Shakespeare and the Archpriest Controversy.* The Hague: Mouton, 1975.

Kittredge, George Lyman. *Witchcraft in Old and New England.* New York: Athenaeum, 1957.

Knox, T. F., ed. *The First and Second Douay Diaries.* 2 vols. London, 1878.

———. *Letters and Papers of Cardinal William Allen.* 1882. Reprint. Ridgewood, N.J.: Gregg Press, 1965.

Laud, William. *Works.* 7 vols. Oxford, 1847–60.

Lavater, Lewis. *Of Ghostes and Spirites Walking by Nyght.* Trans. R. H. London, 1572.

Law, T. G. "Devil-Hunting in Elizabethan England." *The Nineteenth Century* 35 (1894): 397–411.

———. *A Historical Sketch of the Conflicts between Jesuits and Seculars in the Reign of Queen Elizabeth.* London, 1889.

———, ed. *The Archpriest Controversy. Documents Relating to the Dissensions of the Roman Catholic Clergy, 1597–1602.* 2 vols. London: The Camden Society, 1896, 1898 (n.s. 56, 58).

Le Neve, John. *Fasti ecclesiae anglicanae.* Corrected and continued by T. Duffus Hardy. 3 vols. Oxford, 1854.

Leishman, J. B., ed. *The Three Parnassus Plays, 1598–1601.* London: Ivor Nicholson and Watson, 1949.

Lysons, Daniel. *The Environs of London.* 4 vols. London, 1796.

Maclure, Millar. *The Paul's Cross Sermons, 1534–1642.* Toronto: University of Toronto Press, 1958.

Marchant, Ronald A. *The Puritans and the Church Courts in the Diocese of York, 1560–1642.* London: Longmans, 1960.

Martin, Malachi. *Hostage to the Devil.* 1976. Reprint. New York: Bantam Books, 1977.

Martz, Louis. L. *The Poetry of Meditation.* New Haven: Yale University Press, rev. ed. 1962.

Menghi, Girolamo. *Flagellum daemonum. Exorcismos terribiles, potentissimos, et efficaces, remediaque probatissima ac doctrinam singularem in malignos spiritus expellendos.* Bologna, 1586.

———. *Fuga daemonum. Adjurationes potentissimas et exorcismos formidabiles, atque efficaces in malignos spiritus propulsandos et maleficia ab energumenis pellenda.* Venice, 1596.

———. *Fustis daemonum. Adjurationes formidabiles, potentissimas, et efficaces in malignos spiritus fugandos de oppressis corporibus humanis.* Bologna, 1586.

Metcalfe, W. C., ed. *Visitations of Norfolk.* 2 vols. London, 1875.

Meyer, Arnold Oskar. *England and the Catholic Church under Queen Elizabeth.* Translated by J. R. McKee. London: Kegan Paul, 1916.

Milward, Peter. *Biblical Inluences in Shakespeare's Great Tragedies.* Bloomington: University of Indiana Press, 1987.

————. *Shakespeare's Other Dimension.* Renaissance Monographs no. 15. Tokyo: The Renaissance Institute, Sophia University, 1987.

————. *Shakespeare's Religious Background.* Bloomington: Indiana University Press, 1973.

Morant, Philip. *The History and Antiquities of the County of Essex.* 2 vols. Chelmsford, 1816.

————. *The History and Antiquities of the Most Ancient Town and Borough of Colchester.* 2 vols. Chelmsford, 1815.

More, George. *A True Discourse Concerning the Certaine Possession and Dispossession of 7 Persons in One Familie in Lancashire.* Middelburg, 1600.

Morris, John. *Troubles of Our Catholic Forefathers.* 3 vols. 1872–77. Reprint. Farnborough, U.K.: Gregg International, 1970.

Muir, Kenneth. "Samuel Harsnett and *King Lear.*" *Review of English Studies,* n.s., 2 (1951): 11–21.

————. *Shakespeare's Sources.* London: Methuen, 1957. Rev. ed. New Haven: Yale University Press, 1977.

Murphy, John L. *Darkness and Devils: Exorcism and 'King Lear.'* Athens: Ohio University Press, 1984.

Nashe, Thomas. *Works.* Edited by Ronald B. McKerrow. 5 vols. London: A. H. Bullen, 1908. Revised and reprinted with supplement by F. P. Wilson. Oxford: Basil Blackwell, 1958.

Newcourt, Richard. *Repertorium ecclesiasticum parochiale Londinense.* 2 vols. London, 1778.

Nichols, John. *The Progresses, Processions, and Magnificent Festivities of King James I.* 4 vols. London, 1828.

Opie, Iona, and Peter Opie. *The Lore and Language of Schoolchildren.* Oxford: Clarendon Press, 1959.

Partridge, Eric. *Origins: A Short Etymological Dictionary of Modern English.* 2d ed. New York: Macmillan Co, 1959.

Paul, H. N. *The Royal Play of Macbeth.* New York: Macmillan Co., 1950.

Peckham, W. D., ed. *Acts of the Dean and Chapter of the Cathedral Church of Chichester, 1545–1642.* Lewes: Publications of the Sussex Record Society, Vol. 58, 1959.

Peel, Albert, ed. *The Seconde Part of a Register.* 2 vols. Cambridge: Cambridge University Press, 1915.

Pollen, John Hungerford. *Mary Queen of Scots and The Babington Plot.* Edinburgh: Edinburgh University Press for the Scottish History Society, 1922.

————. "The Politics of the English Catholics during the Reign of Queen Elizabeth." *The Month* 108 (July 1902): 71–85.

————. "Supposed Cases of Diabolical Possession in 1585–6." *The Month* 117 (May 1911): 449–64.

————, ed. *The Memoirs of Father Robert Persons.* CRS 2 (1906), 4 (1907).

————, ed. "Official Lists of Prisoners for Religion, 1562–1602." *CRS* 1 (1905): 45–71; 2 (1906): 219–88.

————, ed. "Unpublished Documents Relating to the English Martyrs. I: 1584–1603." *CRS* 5 (1908).

Porter, H. C. *Reformation and Reaction in Tudor Cambridge.* Cambridge: Cambridge University Press, 1958.

Prynne, William. *The Antipathie of the English Lordly Prelacie.* London, 1641.

――――. *A Breviate of the Prelates Intollerable Usurpations.* Amsterdam, 1637.

Read, Conyers. *Lord Burghley and Queen Elizabeth.* New York: Alfred Knopf, 1960.

――――. *Mr. Secretary Cecil and Queen Elizabeth.* New York: Alfred Knopf, 1955.

――――. *Sir Francis Walsingham.* 3 vols. Oxford: Clarendon Press, 1925.

Relf, F. H., ed. *Notes of Debates in the House of Lords, 1621, 1625, 1628.* London: Offices of the Royal Historical Society (Camden Series, 3d ser., 42), 1929.

Renold, P., ed. *The Wisbech Stirs, 1595–1598. CRS* 51 (1958).

Rickert, C. H. *The Case of John Darrell, Minister and Exorcist.* Gainsville: University of Florida Press, 1962.

Ridge, C. Harold, ed. *Prerogative Court of Canterbury, Administrations, 1581–1595.* London: British Record Society, 1954.

Roth, Cecil. *History of the Jews in England.* Oxford: Clarendon Press, 1941.

Round, J. H. "The Harsnett Library." *The Athenaeum,* no. 2909 (28 July 1883).

Salingar, Leo. "*King Lear,* Montaigne, and Harsnett." *Aligarh Journal of English Studies* 8 (1983): 124–66.

Schell, Edgar. *Strangers and Pilgrims: From* The Castle of Perseverance *to* King Lear. Chicago: University of Chicago Press, 1983.

Schoenbaum, S. *Shakespeare: A Documentary Life.* Oxford: Clarendon Press, 1975.

Scot, Reginald. *The Discoverie of Witchcraft.* London, 1584.

Shakespeare, William. *The Works of Shakespeare.* Edited by Lewis Theobald. 7 vols. London, 1733.

Sharpe, Kevin, ed. *Faction and Parliament: Essays on Early Stuart History.* Oxford: Clarendon Press, 1978.

Sisson, C. J. "Shakespeare's Quartos as Prompt-Copies." *Review of English Studies* 18 (1942): 134–40.

Smart, John Semple. *Shakespeare: Truth and Tradition.* London: Edward Arnold, 1928.

Southwell, Robert. *An Epistle of Comfort, to the Reverend Priestes, & to the Honorable, Worshipfull, & Other of the Laye Sort Restrayned in Durance for the Catholicke Fayth.* Paris, 1604 [English secret press? 1605?].

Spurgeon, Caroline. *Shakespeare's Imagery and What It Tells Us.* Cambridge: Cambridge University Press, 1935.

Stephens, W. R. W. *The South Saxon Diocese, Selsey-Chichester.* London, 1881.

Stevenson, Robert. *Shakespeare's Religious Frontier.* The Hague: Martinus Nijhoff, 1958.

Strong, Roy. *The Cult of Elizabeth.* London: Thames and Hudson, 1977.

Strype, John. *Annals of the Reformation.* 3 vols. Oxford, 1824.

――――. *The Life and Acts of John Whitgift.* 3 vols. Oxford, 1822.

Stuart, Dr. Richard. *Three Sermons.* London, 1656.

Suckling, Alfred Inigo. *The History and Antiquities of the County of Suffolk.* 2 vols. London, 1846–48.

Summers, Montague, ed. *The Discoverie of Witchcraft by Reginald Scot.* 1930. Reprint. New York: Dover Press, 1972.

Swan, John. *A True and Breife Report, of Mary Glovers Vexation, and of Her Deliverance by the Meanes of Fastinge and Prayer.* [London], 1603.

Swinden, Henry. *The History and Antiquities of the Ancient Burgh of Great Yarmouth.* Norwich, 1772.

Thayer, Calvin. *Shakespearean Politics.* Athens: Ohio University Press, 1983.

*The Boy of Bilson.* London, 1622

*The Greate Herball.* London, 1561.

The New Oxford History of Music. Volume 4: *The Age of Humanism, 1540–1630,* compiled by Gerald Abrahams. London & New York: Oxford University Press, 1968.

*The Triall of Maist. Dorrell.* [Middelburg], 1599.

Thomas, Keith. *Religion and the Decline of Magic.* London: Weidenfeld and Nicolson, 1971.

Thyraeus, Petrus. *De daemoniacis liber unus.* Cologne, 1594.

Tierney, Mark Aloysius. *The History and Antiquities of the Castle and the Town of Arundel.* London, 1834.

Tilley, Morris Palmer, ed. *A Dictionary of the Proverbs in England in the Sixteenth and Seventeenth Centuries.* Ann Arbor: University of Michigan Press, 1950.

Usher, Ronald G. *The Reconstruction of the English Church.* 2 vols. New York and London: Appleton & Co., 1910.

―――. *The Rise and Fall of the High Commission.* Oxford: Oxford University Press, 1913.

―――, ed. *The Presbyterian Movement in the Reign of Queen Elizabeth as Illustrated by the Minute Book of the Dedham Classis.* Royal Historical Society Publications. Camden series, 3d ser., vol. 8. London, 1905.

Venn, John, ed. *Grace Book Δ.* Cambridge: Cambridge University Press, 1910.

Venn, John, and J. A. Venn, eds. *Alumni Cantabrigienses, Part 1: From the Earliest Times to 1751.* 4 vols. Cambridge: Cambridge University Press, 1922–27.

―――. *University of Cambridge: Matriculations and Degrees . . . from 1544 to 1659.* Cambridge: Cambridge University Press, 1913.

Walker, D. P. *Unclean Spirits: Possession and Exorcism in France and England in the Late Sixteenth and Early Seventeenth Centuries.* London: Scolar Press, 1981.

Waterworth, J. *Canons and Decrees of the Sacred and Oecumenical Council of Trent.* London, 1848.

Waugh, Evelyn. *The Letters of Evelyn Waugh.* Edited by Mark Amory. New York: Ticknor and Fields, 1980.

Weber, H. "L'exorcisme à la fin du XVIe siècle, instrument de la Contre Réforme et spectacle baroque." *Nouvelle Revue du Seizième Siècle* 1 (1983): 79–101.

Welch, C. E. *Two Cathedral Organists: Thomas Weelkes (1601–1623) and Thomas Kelway (1720–1744).* The Chichester Papers, No. 8. Chichester: Chichester City Council, 1957.

Welsby, Paul. *George Abbot: The Unwanted Archbishop, 1562–1633.* London: SPCK Press, 1962.

―――. *Lancelot Andrewes, 1555–1626.* London: SPCK Press, 1958.

White, Helen C. *Tudor Books of Private Devotion.* Madison: University of Wisconsin Press, 1951.

Willett, Pamela J. "The Identity of Thomas Myriell." *Music and Letters* 53 (1972): 431–33.

————. "Musical Connections of Thomas Myriell." *Music and Letters* 49 (1968): 36–42.

Williams, J. F., and B. Cozens-Hardy, eds. *Extracts from the Two Earliest Minute Books of the Dean and Chapter of Norwich Cathedral, 1566–1649.* Publications of the Norfolk Record Society, vol. 24. Norwich: Norfolk Record Society, 1953.

Williams, Robert Folkstone, ed. *The Court and Times of Charles I.* 2 vols. London, 1848.

Willis, Browne. *An History of the Mitred Parliamentary Abbies, and Conventual Cathedral Churches.* 2 vols. London, 1718–19.

Wood, Anthony à. *Athenae Oxonienses.* Edited by Philip Bliss. 2 vols. London, 1813–20.

Wright, Joseph. *The English Dialect Dictionary.* London: Henry Frowde, 1898–1905.

# Index of Names

Abbot, George, 37n, 89n, 104, 137n, 138, 144n, 153, 155, 157, 162
Abbot, Robert, 45
Agazarius, Alphonsus, 167, 283
Alexander the apothecary. See Rawlins, Alexander.
Allen, William, 59, 205n, 228
Anderson, Edmund, 57, 61, 64–65, 89, 167, 378
Andrewes, Lancelot, 37n, 39, 42, 45, 47, 51n, 91, 92, 134, 138, 148n, 162, 196n, 339, 361; as bishop of Chichester, 135; intrigues against Harsnett, 139–41
Anstruther, Godfrey, 165n, 166, 208n, 362n, 380n, 384n, 397n
Arden, Edward, 109, 269n
Arden, Walter, 109
Array, Martin, 207–8, 389
Arundel, Sir John, 167, 169
Ashfield, Mr., 26, 371
Ashton, Jane, 55n, 250
Attwater, Aubrey, 91n, 138n, 140, 141n
Aubrey, John, 332n
Augustine, St., 120
Aylmer, John, 37, 174

Babbage, Stuart, 35n
Babington, Anthony, 24, 27, 165, 386n, 389; and the exorcisms, 30ff., 79–80, 80n, 208
Bacon, Lady Anne, 40n
Bacon, Sir Francis, 45–46, 175
Ballard, John, 31, 79, 80n, 165, 170, 208, 389
Bancroft, Richard, 22, 26, 53, 104, 133–34, 162, 186, 339, 361; early career, 35–37; employs and promotes Harsnett, 46–47; acquires *Miracle Book*, 67; inquires into Catholic exorcisms, 67; conducts case against John Darrell, 57–58;

foments archpriest controversy, 68–70; links Catholic and Puritan exorcists, 74–75; thought to have written the *Declaration*, 187–88; promulgates canon against exorcising, 64
Barlow, Randolph, 91n, 139
Barlow, William, 64n, 137n, 148n
Barnes, Robert, Protestant, 316n
Barnes, Robert, recusant, 21–22, 67, 166
Baro, Peter, 42, 46
Beale, Jerome, 141
Beaton, James, archbishop of Glasgow, 206n
Bee, Jesse, 53n, 54
Bellamy, Anne, 21
Bellamy, Robert, 170
Benham, W. G., 38n
Bentley, William, 41–42
Berden, Nicholas, 166, 168, 169
Bernard, Richard, 63
Berry, Herbert, 319n
Betjeman, John, 51n
Blackwell, George, 69, 165, 376n
Bold, Richard, 381
Bodin, Jean, 305
Bosgrave, James, 167
Bowden, H. S., 110n
Bowes, Lady, 54
Bradbrook, M. C., 94n, 99, 102, 104, 108n, 110
Bridges, Mr., 23
Bridgewater, Richard, 38
Briggs, Agnes, 73n
Brinsley, John, the elder, 63
Brinsley, John, the younger, 151–52
Bristol, earl of. See Digby, John.
Brooke, Henry, baron Cobham, 186
Brooke, Lord. See Greville, Robert.
Brossier, Martha, 30n, 63n, 210
Brownrigg, Ralph, 141
Bruerton. See Yardley, Roger.